Between Empire and Continent

Studies in British and Imperial History
Published for the German Historical Institute, London
Editor: Andreas Gestrich, Director of the German Historical Institute, London

Volume 1
The Rise of Market Society in England, 1066–1800
Christiane Eisenberg
Translated by Deborah Cohen

Volume 2
Sacral Kingship between Disenchantment and Re-enchantment:
The French and English Monarchies 1587–1688
Ronald G. Asch

Volume 3
The Forgotten Majority:
German Merchants in London, Naturalization and Global Trade, 1660–1815
Margit Schulte Beerbühl
Translated by Cynthia Klohr

Volume 4
Crown, Church and Constitution
Popular Conservatism in England, 1815–1867
Jörg Neuheiser
Translated by Jennifer Walcoff Neuheiser

Volume 5
Between Empire and Continent
British Foreign Policy before the First World War
Andreas Rose
Translated by Rona Johnston

BETWEEN EMPIRE AND CONTINENT

British Foreign Policy before the First World War

Andreas Rose

Translated by Rona Johnston

berghahn
NEW YORK • OXFORD
www.berghahnbooks.com

Published in 2017 by
Berghahn Books
www.berghahnbooks.com

English-language edition © 2017, 2019 Berghahn Books
First paperback edition published in 2019

Originally published in German as *Zwischen Empire und Kontinent,*
© 2011 Oldenbourg Wissenschaftsverlag GmbH München. All rights reserved.

The translation of this work was funded by Geisteswissenschaften International –
Translation Funding for Humanities and Social Sciences from Germany,
a joint initiative of the Fritz Thyssen Foundation, the German Federal
Foreign Office, the collecting society VG WORT and the Börsenverein des
Deutschen Buchhandels (German Publishers & Booksellers Association).

All rights reserved. Except for the quotation of short passages
for the purposes of criticism and review, no part of this book
may be reproduced in any form or by any means, electronic or
mechanical, including photocopying, recording, or any information
storage and retrieval system now known or to be invented,
without written permission of the publisher.

Library of Congress Cataloging-in-Publication Data
A C.I.P. cataloging record is available from the Library of Congress

British Library Cataloguing in Publication Data
A catalogue record for this book is available from the British Library

ISBN 978-1-78533-578-5 hardback
ISBN 978-1-78920-507-7 paperback
ISBN 978-1-78533-579-2 ebook

Contents

List of Illustrations	vi
List of Abbreviations	vii
Acknowledgements	x
Foreword by Sir Christopher Clark	xiii
Introduction	1
1 The Public Sphere in Edwardian London	11
2 The Policy of Drift? Balance of Power, Concert of Europe, or Political Power Blocs?	72
3 Safety First: The Politics of Defence and the Realities behind Diplomacy	129
4 Imperial Defence or Continental Commitment?	182
5 Foreign Policy under Lansdowne and Balfour	216
6 The Myth of Continuity: Foreign Policy under Edward Grey	273
7 The Committee of Four: The German Peril Revisited	306
8 At the Cost of Stability: The Anglo-Russian Convention and its European Implications	344
9 'More Russian than the Russians'? British Balkan Diplomacy and the Annexation of Bosnia 1908/9	401
Conclusion and Perspectives: The Triad of British Foreign Politics	462
Bibliography	483
Index	521

Illustrations

Tables
3.1 Naval planning for the period 1900 to 1920   136
3.2 Fleet strength (September 1903)   152
7.1 'Effective Fighting Fleets of the Nations' (31 March 1906)   309
7.2 'British Fighting Fleet Compared' (31 March 1909)   325

Figure
1.1 The invasion of 1910   53

Abbreviations

AA	Auswärtiges Amt (German Foreign Office)
ADM	Admiralty
AP	Accounts and Papers
APS	Die Auswärtige Politik Serbiens, 1903–1914
BA-MA	Bundesarchiv-Militärarchiv, Freiburg
BD	British Documents on the Origins of the War, 1898–1914
BDFA	British Documents on Foreign Affairs
BDS	Graf Benckendorffs Diplomatischer Schriftwechsel, ed. by Benno von Siebert, Leipzig 1921.
BelD	Die Belgischen Dokumente zur Vorgeschichte des Weltkrieges, 1905–1914
BelZ	Die Belgischen Zirkulare
BL	British Library, London
BLPES	British Library of Political and Economic Science, London
BMH	Berliner Monatshefte
BOD	Bodleian Library, Oxford
BUL	Birmingham University Library, Birmingham
CC	Churchill College Archive Centre, Cambridge
Cd.	Command Papers (HCPP)
CO	Colonial Office
CR	*Contemporary Review*
CUL	Cambridge University Library, Cambridge
DA	Diplomatische Aktenstücke zur Geschichte der Ententepolitik
DDF	Documents Diplomatiques Français, $2^{\text{ième}}$ Series, 1871–1914
DDS	Diplomatische Dokumente der Schweiz, 1848–1945
DNB	Oxford Dictionary of National Biography, 2nd Edition, London 1908-9.
DNI	Director of Naval Intelligence
EHR	*English Historical Review*
ER	*Edinburgh Review*
FDSF	*From Dreadnought to Scapa Flow*, Ed. Arthur Marder, London 1961
FGDN	*Fear God and Dread Nought*, Ed. Arthur Marder, London 1952–1959
FO	Foreign Office
FR	*Fortnightly Review*

FRUS	Papers Relating to the Foreign Relations of the United States
GL	Guildhall Library, London
GP	*Die Große Politik der Europäischen Kabinette, 1871–1914*
GStA	Geheimes Staatsarchiv Preußischer Kulturbesitz
HCPP	House of Commons Parliamentary Papers
HH	Hatfield House, Hertfordshire
HHStA	Haus-, Hof- und Staatsarchiv, Vienna
HJ	*Historical Journal*
HLRO	House of Lords Record Office, London
HMM	*Harper's Monthly Magazine*
HoT III	History of *The Times*, Vol. III, London 1947
IHR	*International History Review*
IOL	India Office Library, London
IWM	Imperial War Museum, London
JBS	*Journal of British Studies*
JCH	*Journal of Contemporary History*
JICH	*Journal of Imperial and Commonwealth History*
JL	Brett, Maurice V., and Viscount Esher (Eds.), *Journals and Letters of Reginald Viscount Esher*, 4 Vols., London 1938.
JMH	*Journal of Modern History*
JRSA	*Journal of the Royal Society of Arts*
JRUSI	*Journal of the Royal United Services Institute*
JSS	*Journal of Strategic Studies*
KA	Krasnyiarchiv, Moskau, Bde. 69–70
LHCMA	Liddell Hart Centre for Military Archives, King's College London
LoC	Library of Congress, Washington
MÖSTA	Mitteilungen des Österreichischen Staatsarchivs
MR	*Monthly Review*
NA	National Archives, Kew
NAM	National Army Museum, London
NAR	*North American Review*
NAS	National Archives of Scotland, Edinburgh
NC	*Nineteenth Century and After*
NIA	News International Archives (Times Archive), London
NLS	National Library of Scotland, Edinburgh
NMM	National Maritime Museum, London
NR	*National Review*
NRAS	National Register of Archives of Scotland, Edinburgh
NRO	Norfolk Record Office
NRS	Naval Records Society
ÖUA	Österreich-Ungarns Außenpolitik von der Bosnischen Krise 1908 bis zum Kriegsausbruch 1914

PA	Parliamentary Archives, London
PA-AA	Politisches Archiv des Auswärtigen Amtes, Berlin
PD	Hansard's Parliamentary Debates
QR	*Quarterly Review*
RL	The Letters of Lieutenant Colonel Charles à Court Repington
RR	*The Review of Reviews*
USL	University of Southampton, Hartley Library, Southampton
USM	*United Service Magazine*
WO	War Office
WSRO	West Sussex Record Office, Chichester

Acknowledgements

At the end of a long project, it is time to take a deep breath, to pause for a moment and to remember all those without whom this project never would have been completed. A book is always a product of many people's inspiration, assistance, collegiality and support. I am especially grateful to my doctoral supervisor Professor Guenther Kronenbitter who has been a role model of support, inspiration, and encouragement. I can never thank Guenther enough for all his support and open ears over the last decade. Very special thanks are also due to my co-supervisor Professor Andreas Wirsching. Moreover I am especially grateful to Professor Dominik Geppert, who has given me a new academic home at the University of Bonn, for his keen interest in the project, his judgment and experience but even more for his friendship over the years that have past.

My special thanks also go to Dr Ulrich Janiesch without whom I never would have studied Modern History at all and onto whose advice I can built on now for nearly 30 years and Dr Jürgen Luh who has always been not only an inspiration for me as a historian but also the best friend one could imagine during a lengthy research project with all its ups and downs and the uncertainties of todays academic careers in Germany. Many thanks also go to Professor Juergen Angelow and Professor Konrad Canis for numerous thought-provoking seminars at the University of Potsdam and the Humboldt-University at Berlin. Both have set me on the path of Anglo-German relations when I was an undergraduate.

For inspiration, assistance, collegiality and enduring support, I have been privileged to have met many outstanding scholars who have fostered my interests not only in Anglo-German relations but especially into the backgrounds of British politics, diplomacy, military and naval policies and the British Empire as a whole. I am therefore indebted to Professor Andrew N. Porter, my supervisor at King's College London, who was the first who has greatly enhanced my continental perspective by the imperial mindset of the Victorian age; to Professor Miles Taylor who has ignited my interest in British party politics and to Professor Michael L. Dockrill for his great knowledge of the sources. I have greatly benefited from innumerable discussions over the years and my special thanks go to John T. Sumida, Andrew Lambert, Nicholas A. Lambert, Katherine Epstein and Patrick Kelly whom I met at the "Woodstock for Naval Historians" at the United States Naval Academy in Annapolis; Professor Hagen Schulze (†), Professor Andreas Gestrich, Professor Lothar Kettenacker,

Dr Markus Mößlang, Dr Karsten Plöger at the German Historical Institute London; and Dr Tanja Bührer, Professor Magnus Brechtken, Professor John Charmley, Professor Sir Christopher Clark, Professor Niall Ferguson, Professor Stig Förster, Professor Lothar Höbelt, Professor Peter Hoeres, Dr Christian Hoyer, Professor Friedrich Kießling, Professor Hans-Christof Kraus, Professor Heinz-Joachim Müllenbrock, Professor Frank Müller, Dr William Mulligan, Professor Keith Neilson (†), Professor Sönke Neitzel, Professor Thomas Otte, Professor Matthew Seligmann, Dr Markus Pöhlmann, Professor Rainer F. Schmidt, Professor Zara Steiner, Professor Hew Strachan, Professor Karina Urbach, and Professor Thomas Weber. I particularly thankful to my colleagues at the University of Bonn: Juliane Clegg, Ben Behschnitt, Peter Beule, Dr Thomas Freiberger, Jonas Klein, Dr Kristof Niese, Dr Philip Rosin, Dr Jürgen P. Schmied, Dr Christoph Studt and last but by no means least Gaby Nohr, the invaluable kind soul of the Chair for Modern History at Bonn.

I am also extremely grateful to Marion Berghahn for giving my book a home at Berghahn books, as well as Chris Chappell and Caroline Kuhtz for so ably seeing my book through the publication process and Anke Simon from the Börsenverein especially for her patience during the long process of translation.

I have also incurred debts to audiences who listened patiently to me and generously offered constructive criticism at seminars and conferences at Augsburg University, Bern University, Bonn University, Glasgow University, Mainz University, Oxford University, Potsdam University, Würzburg University as well as at conferences of the US Naval Academy Annapolis, the German Historical Institute London, the German Historical Institute Paris, the Friedrich Naumann Foundation, the International Graduate Centre for the Study of Culture at Gießen or the Southern History Association at Baltimore.

In the course of my work I was greatly assisted by innumerous archivists and librarians without whom historians would be helpless. In place of so many helping hands I would like to thank particularly the staff of the National Archives at Kew Gardens, of the Churchill College Archive Center in Cambridge, Colin Harris and the whole staff of the Bodleian Library, Dr William Frame of the British Library, Frances Lansley from the West Sussex Record Office, Mike Bevan from the National Maritime Museum, and Eamon Dyas from the News International Archive of The Times.

International research would be impossible without financial support and therefore I would like to thank especially the German Scholarship Foundation, the German Historical Institute London, and last but not least the Börsenverein des Deutschen Buchhandels and the German Foreign Office for awarding me the price 'Geisteswissenschaften International' for the translation into English. I am deeply grateful to Rona Johnston who ventures on such an onerous task of a translation from my lengthy German sentences into readable English.

Finally, my biggest thank goes to my family, to my parents and my sister Carina, my wife Anne-Katrin for their continuous and loving support and to our son Felix who enriches our lives every day and who constantly reminds me what really is of importance in life. It is to him this book is dedicated.

Foreword

by Sir Christopher Clark

'If you get an exam question on the origins of the First World War', our history teacher told us on a hot Sydney afternoon in 1977, 'just remember the five German provocations!' Raising his right hand with the thumb and fingers splayed, he counted off the German transgressions: First, German naval expansion unsettled the British. Then, in 1905, Berlin challenged France in Africa, provoking the Moroccan Crisis. Three years later, the Germans backed Austria against Russia in the Bosnian Annexation Crisis of 1908. In 1911 they provoked France again in Morocco. Finally, as if all this were not bad enough, Germany's leaders decided, in the midst of the crisis triggered by the assassinations at Sarajevo in June 1914, to supply Austria with the unconditional assurance of military support that came to be known as the 'blank cheque'.

This memorable five-point analysis, simplified for pedagogical effect, conveyed the essence of the consensus that emerged in the aftermath of the Fischer controversy of the 1960s and 1970s. The case for German culpability in the outbreak of war advanced by the Hamburg historian Fritz Fischer, his collaborator Imanuel Geiss and a growing band of historiographical disciples and allies triggered bitter contention in Germany. But Fischer's view soon established itself as the new orthodoxy in Anglophone academia. The disruptive presence in the pre-war European system of states, so the argument ran, was Germany. From this it followed that the foreign ministries of the other European states were preoccupied with the task of containing Germany and countering German provocations. Upon Britain above all fell the task of balancing the system to ensure that German misbehaviour did not endanger the general peace. The picture that resulted was strikingly unipolar: prior to 1914, Germany was the sun in the European solar system, in whose gravitational field the other powers were trapped like helpless planets.

Andreas Rose's powerfully argued book presents a very different view. In *Between Empire and Continent*, Britain emerges not as the peacekeeper and umpire reacting to German initiatives, but as a shrewd and powerful player in its own right. British naval expansion in the pre-war years was not a panicked reaction to the noxious designs of Admiral Tirpitz, but a complex and self-assured programme drawn up by strategists confident of their superiority and determined to defend Britain's global power share against a plurality of potential threats. The British decision to seek closer relations with Russia and France was not driven by fear of Germany, but by the conviction that Germany was too weak to offer meaningful help against the global heft of the Franco-Russian alliance. The German war-scares that periodically crackled across the British press had less to do with objective dangers than with inter-service rivalries and the battle for resources between the Army and the Navy. Foreign Secretary Sir Edward Grey was not the neutral observer of European affairs depicted in many accounts, but a partisan participant in continental geopolitics who, having decided early on to throw in his lot with Paris and St. Petersburg, soon lost control of these unpredictable partners. Far from keeping the peace, Grey's increasingly pro-Russian and anti-Austrian management of the pre-war Balkan crises amplified existing risks.

In developing these arguments, Rose builds in part, as all historians must, on recent trends in the historiography. He expands the arguments of the 'naval revisionists' Jon T. Sumida and Nicholas Lambert, and of Keith Wilson and Keith Neilson, who have stressed the continuing importance of Britain's rivalry with Russia as a factor driving Foreign Office thinking. Rose counters those who have seen introversion and inertia as core features of the British foreign policy establishment. But he also advances new and original lines of argument about the impact of British policy on Balkan geopolitics, the relationship between the global and the imperial, and the continental imperatives in British strategy and the internal structural tensions that shaped the formulation of British policy in an era when issues arising from external relations tended to generate division rather than consensus. The book's power derives not just from the way in which these arguments have been woven together to produce a new picture of Britain's place in the events that brought war to Europe, but also from the fact that it draws on a wide range of sources culled from 28 archives, a source base that allows Rose to set his account of decision-making in a deep political, cultural and institutional context.

Yet this is not a crude work of 'revisionism' – a point worth emphasising in light of the politicised climate of the current 1914 debate. Rose makes no attempt to rehabilitate German policy before 1914. Nor does he attempt to shift culpability for the outbreak of war from Berlin to London. On the other hand, this book does break with what Samuel Williamson has called the 'German paradigm'. It places to one side the question of culpability in order to examine the actions and processes that generated risk within the system. It insists on the proactive agency of all state actors and the complexity of the threats perceived by all decision-makers. The Britain depicted in this book is not the lonely voice for peace depicted in many older accounts, but a great power among great powers. British policy-makers were focused, as they had to be, on securing strategic and tactical advantages, and in pursuing what they took to be Britain's best interests, they fuelled the volatility of the international system in the last pre-war years, just as their continental partners and opponents did.

Introduction

This book investigates international failures that were instrumental for the 'great seminal catastrophe' of the First World War.[1] But it does not examine the July Crisis, or talk of immediate causes and short fuses. It is founded on the awareness that while the outbreak of war in 1914 was neither irresistible nor improbable, many contemporaries always reckoned it possible. Its principal characters are gamblers rather than 'sleepwalkers'.[2] It investigates the return of imperial tensions, diverted to the periphery during the Bismarckian era, to the European centre and explores the growing fragility of the international states system. And Great Britain, traditionally deemed a 'spectator of events' forced to respond to external aggression, now takes up its rightful place centre stage in this story. The book attacks a long-held orthodoxy that has seen the Central Powers as the gravitational centre, whose pull meant all other powers, and Great Britain in particular, were forced to act to safeguard international stability by means of balance of power politics and a general realignment. Instead, this study argues, the British Empire – part of the traditional Vienna settlement and the largest empire the world had ever seen, credited with the greatest bargaining power but preoccupied with its countless interests beyond the continent – failed to act on its responsibilities for that balance of power and thus fuelled the volatility and instability of the international system.

The story begins at the end of the nineteenth century. Great Power relations were undergoing a fundamental reworking of which the most visible expression was the Franco-Russian Dual Alliance of 1892/94, which posed a challenge to both the European Central Powers and the global possessions of Great Britain.[3] Yet rather than respond with immediate countermeasures and above all with closer Anglo-German relations,[4] London and Berlin even loosened their indirect ties generated by the Mediterranean Agreements, designed to safeguard the status

---

Notes for this chapter begin on page 7.

quo in south-eastern Europe. 'Isolation', wrote Lord Salisbury confidently to a noticeably troubled Queen Victoria, 'is a much less danger than the danger of being dragged into wars which do not concern us'.[5] By avoiding alliances, and the entanglements that they signified, the prime minister explicitly conveyed to Germany and Austria-Hungary alike that he wished 'to lean to the Triple Alliance without belonging to it'.[6] At the same time, he rebuffed Russia by informing the tsar that Britain would 'not abandon the allies by whom we stayed so long'.[7] However much Salisbury hoped for better relations with the Russian Empire, he was evidently too well acquainted with the mechanisms of the Great Power system to ignore the potential repercussions. In 1901, towards the end of his term, he warned against the systemic consequences of an alignment between the two least vulnerable powers when he explained to Malcolm MacColl, publicist and his intellectual correspondent, 'Other statesmen are acutely watching the Chess-Board of Europe, and they perfectly know that a real sympathy between Russia and England would place the other Great Powers in a very inferior position'.[8]

Only four years later, liberal Foreign Secretary Edward Grey declared real sympathies with France and Russia to be the 'cardinal points' of his foreign policy.[9] Leap forward another four years and we find Great Britain behaving 'more Russian than the Russians' in supporting Serbia against Austria-Hungary during the annexation of Bosnia.[10] And in October 1912, at the start of the Balkan Wars, not only did Great Britain accept responsibility for the French Atlantic coast,[11] but Grey also insisted on informing Russian Foreign Minister Sergei Sazonov of an Anglo-French agreement to send British expeditionary forces to the continent in case of an attack by the Central Powers.[12]

Historians have proposed that responsibility for what they have identified as the end of Britain's isolation, its new alignments with revisionist France and Russia, which had been its arch-rivals, and the general transformation of Great Power relations before the Great War be ascribed principally to the Kaiserreich.[13] The established interpretation runs thus: by the end of the 1890s, Germany had embarked on the construction of a battle fleet, as a result of which Great Britain had no choice but to react to this 'unique German threat' found 'at her own front door' by regrouping the fleets of the Royal Navy and starting an unprecedented ship-building programme.[14] The narrative continues: the German peril at sea made clear to London's political and diplomatic elites that the policy of avoiding entanglements altogether must be abandoned. One eminent political historian has summarized the causal nexus of naval race and pre-war diplomacy: 'The fundamental change in the states system originated from the German Reich and depended on the British reaction. In other words: It was without doubt the construction of the German battle fleet' that forced Britain's hand and 'contributed significantly to the revolution of the states system before 1914'.[15]

In countering this widely held paradigm of German action and British reaction by placing Britain at the heart of the international process of change, this study reveals a much more complex truth. It turns its gaze on the role generally attributed to Britain as an arbitrator and mediator within the states system and on London's contribution to the consolidation of alliance structures before 1914, focusing not only on the still-controversial question of the continuity of Lansdowne's and Grey's diplomacy,[16] but also on the interaction of imperial and continental interests, and especially on the hitherto much-neglected interaction on the domestic side of London's foreign policy of party politics, press politics and public debate, defence politics that involved home and imperial defence, and inter-departmental conflict.

Against the background of shifting risk assessment and developing self-perception after the mid 1890s and the emergence of a new generation of decision makers,[17] the study looks specifically at the complex connections between threat perception and self-assertion. Noting critical and alternative responses to foreign policy along with the growing influence of the public on parliament and press, as well as public debate on security and armament policy, the book describes a public arena that determined the atmosphere in which foreign policy was intensely debated, and in which decisions were taken.[18] Its aim is to unpick the interweaving of foreign policy and security policy for a Britain that was both a 'world power in Europe' and supposedly the epitome of a parliamentary state.[19] Unlike the majority of previous studies, its focus is not on the remaining years of peace after the second Moroccan Crisis (1911) but on the frequently neglected yet widely identified 'crucial' formative years between the South African War and the first test of Anglo-Russian cooperation on the continent, with the Bosnian Annexation Crisis of 1908/9.[20]

The starting point for this study is a historiographical observation. The implications of decades of searching for a guilty party and disputing the theses of the Fritz Fischer school and Germany's major share in European developments before 1914[21] have meant, but not been limited to, the significant relativization of German foreign policy as an embodiment of permanent failure. Historians are now more likely to emphasize the constraints the Central Powers faced, rather than their possible options, and are also more likely to bring other players onto the field.[22] Additionally, the notion that British diplomacy was overwhelmingly reactive has been one casualty in this new game. Most notably, historical examination of the continuity of Edwardian diplomacy and the continental bias of existing interpretation has been promoted not only by the debates surrounding Niall Ferguson's intriguing if controversial *The Pity of War* but also by John Charmley's less promoted but by no means less brilliant *Splendid Isolation?*[23] Both Ferguson and Charmley follow Keith Wilson's earlier, often neglected but always inspirational essays on British entente diplomacy after 1904[24] and Keith Neilson's brilliant study of Britain's policy towards Russia.[25] Wilson and Neilson challenge the Eurocentric and Germany-focused perspective on the pre-war years and convincingly contend that London's alignments first with

France and later with Russia were conceived as a stratagem that would secure the Empire and not primarily as a balancing act intended to contain Germany.[26] All of these works share an imperial perspective on British foreign policy and thus shed new light on the string of established milestones that led up to the July Crisis.[27] Too often, as Neilson pointed out at the outset of his outstanding study *Britain and the Last Tsar*, pre-war history was interpreted in reverse, and thus teleologically, while the Russian threat on India's north-western frontier was neglected.[28] For Wilson and Neilson, London had no choice but to seek an Anglo-Russian agreement.[29]

Although the global perspective adds a long-overdue approach to interpretation of British foreign policy and British overall strategy, global thinking only formed one of the numerous parameters of decision making at Whitehall. As Zara Steiner has pointed out, the focus on London and St Petersburg's bilateral relations, which has joined Eurocentric and Germany-focused perspectives, is too one-dimensional for a fundamental re-evaluation of London's pre-war policy.[30] And indeed, isolated analysis of London's policy towards Berlin and towards St Petersburg distorts the contemporary picture, which was shaped, as the journalist Emile Dillon noted, by viewing Germany and Russia as 'two seeming bits of threats wholly disconnected in appearance but one and the same threat, not cut at all'.[31]

Dillon thus describes a fundamental premise of this book – Edwardian decision makers saw imperial challenges and continental challenges as two sides of the same medal; imperial or continental interests were only ever given additional weight temporarily. That judgement makes the search for alternative opportunities, examination of public controversies surrounding the rapprochement with St Petersburg, and analysis of the rising antagonism towards Germany all the more stimulating. Although deeply concerned with the British perception of Russia, Neilson misses the connection with the simultaneously evolving Germanophobia, while his general assumptions about continuity seem to work in reverse, with 1907 as their starting point – Salisbury and Lansdowne had already sought agreement with Russia, with Grey following the guidelines set by his predecessors. Differences between the approaches and goals of unionist foreign policy and liberal imperialist foreign policy – whether the traditional anti-Russian bias of radical liberals influenced the overall course, for example – remained blurred, while systemic repercussions in the Balkans were overlooked or even deliberately ignored. The Anglo-Russian convention put the south-eastern European periphery, a safety valve for pan-Slav expansionism and where Russia and Austria-Hungary gambled for the highest stakes, back on the agenda, yet London's Balkan diplomacy has certainly not been given the attention it merits,[32] which is all the more surprising as Lord Salisbury had understood the Central Asian and the Near Eastern question as 'two halves of one problem'.[33] A serious re-evaluation of London's pre-war diplomacy, especially with regards to its old Austrian and new Russian friends, must explore whether ultimately Whitehall used Anglo-Russian rapprochement as a 'tool' to manage international tensions or as a 'weapon of power'.[34]

The second historiographical observation on which the book is based concerns naval history, which still has a surprisingly long way to go if it is to move beyond bibliographies and take up the analytical reflection found in modern diplomatic histories. In recent years, however, naval historians have challenged the commonly held notion of German *action* and inevitable British *reaction*.[35] Instead of focusing on Germany and extrapolating Great Britain's naval policy from German aims,[36] they have highlighted the complex British context formed by financial pressure after the Boer War, naval thinking, technological innovation and grand strategy. Thus, their results have proven in more than one way Paul W. Schroeder, that it is still 'one thing to show that Germany blundered and had dangerous aims; quite another to prove that these really caused the outcome, or that, had Germany not made them, the overall outcome would have been drastically changed'.[37] Yet political and particularly diplomatic historians have largely turned a deaf ear to the four driving forces behind British naval policy that have been identified by revisionist historians such as Jon Sumida and Nicholas Lambert: first, the heavy financial burden of naval armament at the beginning of the twentieth century, which drove home a need to cut costs and improve efficiency;[38] secondly, the technological revolution marked by telegraphic communication, greater speed, and inventions such as the torpedo, submarine and battle-cruiser;[39] thirdly, a grand strategy that did not focus only on Germany or on the over-rated two-power standard – an instrument used to placate parliament – but was aimed at sustaining overall supremacy over all modern fleets, especially over the French and US navies, not through numbers but through quality and mobility (the designation of Gibraltar as a new major station, thirty hours' steaming from the North Sea, must, for example, be seen in light of this global strategy);[40] and fourthly, a more nuanced vision of sea power that – unlike the approach of new and less experienced naval powers such as Japan, the United States or Germany – was profoundly different from the concepts found in the popular writings of Alfred Thayer Mahan,[41] whose emphasis on capital ships, tonnage, command of the sea and decisive battles was criticized by First Sealord John Fisher, Lord Selborne, Julian Corbett and others.[42]

However persuasive the case made by the revisionists, we are still left with the question of why pre-war British public opinion was so emotionally charged when it came to the German navy, far more so than for any other foreign navy. Jan Rüger's study of naval celebrations – his innovative integration of naval and cultural history allowed Rüger to demonstrate how sea power was constructed – shows us how we might account for the public's obsession with German power at sea. He defines the cult of the naval race as part of what can be called the theatre of diplomatic relations before the First World War, where demonstration of power and deterrence counted for more than the facts themselves.[43] By combining naval history with modern media history, the study of party and propaganda politics and consideration of departmental rivalries, we can also investigate the growing public hysteria's associations with political decision making.

This leads to the third observation and premise this book is built on. It refers to the still neglected public dimension of foreign and defence politics. Shortly before Salisbury handed over to his nephew Arthur J. Balfour he not only warned against the repercussions of an Anglo-Russian rapprochement but he also emphasized structural changes within the public sphere of policy making: 'Another insuperable difficulty lies in the attitude of what is called public opinion here. The diplomacy of nations is now conducted quite as much in the letters of special correspondents as in the despatches of the Foreign Office'.[44] The book takes up this insight and conceives political journalists, special correspondents and certain publishers as influential political actors of their own right within the policy process in London.

Traditionally, the emotional build-up among the British and German publics has been interpreted in contrasting ways: while German public opinion has always been explained by cynical manipulation of the press bureau or a dangerous self-mobilization,[45] the influence of public opinion in Britain has usually been interpreted as something positive and useful.[46] However, recent research on the press as a rising political actor in both Germany and Britain has stressed that the 'similarities between the two countries' are more striking than the differences and that 'the political and cultural liberalism' in pre-war Britain has often been 'overestimated'.[47] The press should not be used as an expression of unfiltered perception. Moreover it should be understood that it followed its own rules and political agendas.[48] Analytically satisfying conclusions require a combination of approaches and the identification of links between the cultural sphere and decision making. That method is applied, for example, when the emotional public debate on science-fiction stories, invasion and spy stories, theatre plays and press campaigns is contrasted with naval and military experts' viewpoints – revealing surprising differences between the latter's risk assessment of the German battle fleet and the public scares.[49]

This study tries to combine Eurocentric as well as global and domestic approaches to British foreign policy and builds on Sumida's and Lambert's research, broadening their arguments along such lines. Its central cause is that we have to take the complex domestic realities behind British foreign politics more seriously than has hitherto been the case.[50] The most striking paradox of the general consensus on British policy before 1914 is that while all major studies agree that Great Britain represented the epitome of a parliamentarian system before the Great War, it has been taken for granted that its diplomacy was directed somewhat autocratically by a caste of diplomats and a few politicians and was conducted in a strange vacuum, independent of influences beyond the corridors of Whitehall.⁵¹ A modern analysis of foreign politics in the late Victorian and Edwardian era must question this contradiction. It must scrutinize assumptions about above-party continuity in British foreign policy and about an official thinking that was untouched by public interests, influences and pressures. It must consider interest groups, financial and trade concerns, tradition, ad hoc contingencies, imperial issues alongside continental or British issues, personal and institutional interests, institutional frameworks, the public and party dimensions manifest in foreign policy debates, military issues, risk assessments and so on and so forth. In short, it must bear in mind that Great Britain was not only an empire or a continental Great Power, it was also a very modern state, with all that comes with that designation.

Notes

1. Kennan, *The Decline of Bismarck's European Order*, 12.
2. For Wilfrid Scawen Blunt especially Edward Grey ventured a gambler's game. Blunt, *Diaries*, Vol. 2, 420; See Clark, *Sleepwalkers*.
3. Beaumont (DNI), 'Memorandum on Naval Policy Viewed under the Existing Conditions', 28 Oct. 1896, NA, ADM 116/866B; see also Marder, *Anatomy*, 578–80.
4. Salisbury, Memorandum, 29 May 1901, NA, CAB 37/57/52.
5. Salisbury to Victoria, 12 Jan. 1896, cited in Buckle, *Letters of Queen Victoria*, Vol. 3, 21; see Howard, *Splendid Isolation*. For the label 'splendid isolation', see *The Times*, 22 Jan. 1896; Howard, *Splendid Isolation*, 14–15. For Salisbury's alleged isolationism, see Roberts, *Salisbury – Victorian Titan*, 628–31.
6. Salisbury to Lascelles, 10 March 1896, NA, FO 800/9; Salisbury to Rumbold, 20 Jan. 1897, NA, FO 120/730; compare this with Salisbury's convictions about Britain's European responsibility. Salisbury to Rosebery, 18 Aug. 1892, cited in Bourne, *Foreign Policy*, No. 119, 432–33.
7. Salisbury, Report on his audience with the Tsar at Balmoral, 27 and 29 Sept. 1896, NA, CAB 37/42/35.
8. Salisbury to MacColl, 6 Sept. 1901, cited in Russell, *Malcolm MacColl*, 282–83.
9. Grey (City), *The Times*, 21 Oct. 1905.
10. Dillon to Spring Rice, 28 Aug. 1909, CC, CASR 1/33.
11. Grey to Cambon, 22 Nov. 1912, BD X/2, No. 416, 614–15.
12. Sazonov to Nicholas II, Oct. 1912, cited in Stieve, *Schriftwechsel Iswolskis*, Vol. 2, No. 508, 291; see Wilson, Memorandum, 'The Necessity for Co-operation with France in the Event of War between It and Germany', 11 Aug. 1911, NA, WO 106/47/23. On the impact of such open-heartedness by Grey on Franco-Russian decision making in July 1914, see Schmidt, 'Révanche pour Sedan', in *Historische Zeitschrift* 381 (2016), 393–425.
13. See Kennedy, *Rise of Anglo-German Antagonism*, esp. 223–90; Steiner and Neilson, *Britain and the Origins*, 264; Mombauer, *Origins*, 223–24; Hewitson, *Germany*, passim.
14. Marder, *Anatomy*, 489–93, 496; Fischer, *Krieg der Illusionen*, 102–3; Seligmann, *Royal Navy and the German Threat*; Seligmann and Epkenhans, *Abyss*.
15. Hildebrand, 'Staatskunst und Kriegshandwerk', 28. 'It was the foreign policy of Germany that caused the Anglo-Russian rapprochement' [trans. A.R.], Hildebrand, *Das vergangene*

Reich, 203; see also Brechtken, *Scharnierzeit*, 58; Ivo N. Lambi, *The Navy and German Power Politics*, 290; as concerns the inevitability of the Dreadnought, see Marder, *Anatomy*, 457–67; more doubtful, especially on Marder's sources, is Fairbanks, 'The Dreadnought Revolution'; Mackay, *Fisher*, 273–349; Sumida, *In Defence*, passim; Lambert, *Sir John Fisher's Naval Revolution*, passim.

16. See Monger, *End of Isolation*; Grenville, *Lord Salisbury*; Nish, *Anglo-Japanese Alliance*; Rolo, *Entente*; Williamson, *Politics of Grand Strategy*.
17. See the definition of the 'Edwardian generation' by Keith Neilson, *Britain and the Last Tsar*, 3–50; Wohl, *Generation of 1914*, 1–4; Rose, *Zwischen Empire und Kontinent*, 27–40.
18. See Rose, 'Der politische Raum Londons', 95–121 (chaps. 1 and 2).
19. See Low, *Governance of England*.
20. See Adams, *Brothers*; Schroeder, 'Embedded Counterfactuals', 170. For Charmley, Lansdowne is the least studied of British twentieth-century foreign secretaries. Charmley, *Splendid Isolation*, 279; see Newton, *Lord Lansdowne*; Monger, *End of Isolation*.
21. Fischer, *Griff nach der Weltmacht*; Ritter, 'Kriegsschuldthese', 646–48; Schöllgen, 'Griff nach der Weltmacht'.
22. On Germany, see Canis, *Weg in den Abgrund*; on France, see Schmidt, *Frankreichs Außenpolitik*; on Russia, see McMeekin, *Russian Origins* and Lieven, *Towards the Flame*; on Austria, see Kronenbitter, *Krieg im Frieden* and Canis, *Die bedrängte Großmacht*.
23. Ferguson, *Pity of War*; see also Winkler, 'Der falsche Krieg'; Michalka, 'Blick voraus'; Mommsen, *Weltkrieg*; Charmley, *Splendid Isolation*; Kennedy, 'Why Britain Went to War'; Harris, *Britain*, 298.
24. Wilson, *Policy of the Entente*.
25. Neilson, *Britain and the Last Tsar*, passim; Neilson, 'My Beloved Russians', 551–54; Neilson, 'Greatly Exaggerated'.
26. Wilson, *Policy of the Entente*, passim; idem., Limits of Eurocentricity, esp. 7–21; Neilson, *Britain and the Last Tsar*, passim.
27. See also Otte, *China Question*, esp. 4–5.
28. Neilson, *Britain and the Last Tsar*, xi–xv.
29. Ibid., esp. 110–47; Wilson, 'Anglo-Japanese Alliance'; Ferguson, *Pity of War*, 39–45; see Steiner and Neilson, *Britain and the Origins*, 84–99.
30. Steiner, 'Review of Keith Neilson, *Britain and the Last Tsar*' 223–25.
31. Dillon to Spring Rice, 9 Oct. 1909, CC, CASR.
32. Neilson does not pay much attention to the Balkans. See Neilson, *Britain and the Last Tsar*.
33. Cited in Hoyer, *Salisbury und Deutschland*, 318.
34. Schroeder, 'Alliances, 1815–1945', 195–223.
35. Mackay, *Fisher*; Sumida, *In Defence*; Sumida, 'Sir John Fisher and the Dreadnought'; Fairbanks, 'The Dreadnought Revolution', 263; Lambert, *Sir John Fisher's Naval Revolution*. On the historiographical debate in the wake of the Fischer controversy, see Rose, *Zwischen Empire und Kontinent*, 171–76. For a plea to combine naval history with political and diplomatic history, see Rose and Geppert, 'Machtpolitik und Flottenbau'. Most recently, Christopher Clark has seized on these ideas. Clark, *Sleepwalkers*, 148–50.
36. A typical example of a study that merely extrapolates Britain's naval policy from German sources is Brechtken, *Scharnierzeit*.
37. Schroeder, 'International Politics', 196.

38. An example is the harbour at Rosyth: Maconochie (M.P.) to Selborne, 30 Dec. 1904; Reply, 31 Dec. 1904, *The Times*, 3 Jan. 1905; Kerr to Selborne, 11 March 1902, cited in Lambert, *Sir John Fisher's Naval Revolution*, 34; Archibald S. Hurd, 'The Navy First', in *United Service Magazine* 148 (1903), 117–26; Mackay, *Fisher*, 337–38.
39. Sumida, *In Defence*; Sumida, 'British Naval Administration'; Sumida, 'Sir John Fisher and the Dreadnought'.
40. Lambert, *Sir John Fisher's Naval Revolution*; Lambert, 'Admiral Sir John Fisher'.
41. Ropp, *Development of a Modern Navy*; Hobson, *Maritimer Imperialismus*. Older studies, but also recent works, largely extrapolate the British way of thinking from the Kaiser's belief in Mahan: Kennedy, 'Mahan vs. Mackinder', 39; Kennedy, *Rise of Anglo-German Antagonism*, 237, 420–21; Marder, *From Dreadnought to Scapa Flow*, Vol. I, 344, 364–68; Langer, *Diplomacy of Imperialism*, 423; Steiner and Neilson, *Britain and the Origins*, 52; Steinberg, 'The German Background to Anglo-German Relations', 193–215. For Japan, see Asada, *From Mahan to Pearl Harbor*, and Schencking, *Making Waves*, 128–29. For the United States, see Proksch, *Alfred Thayer Mahan*.
42. Tonnage was viewed as a 'worthless' measure: Selborne to Lansdowne, 7 Dec. 1901, BL, MSS Lansdowne, LANS/PL 1; Balfour to Lansdowne, 1904, BL, MSS Balfour, Add. 49698; Lambert, *Sir John Fisher's Naval Revolution*, 17–21; Herbert W. Wilson, 'The New German Navy', in *Harper's Monthly Magazine* 103/2 (1901), 529–37, 534; Excubitor (Archibald S. Hurd), 'Our Position of Naval Peril', in *Fortnightly Review* 82 (1907), 241–52, 247; Bellairs, 6 Dec. 1906, cited in 'The Standard of Naval Strength', in *The Journal of the Royal United Service Institution* 51/1 (1907), 123–83, 128; White, 6 Dec. 1906, cited in ibid., 168. Far more important than tonnage or the concentration on capital ships seemed to be the modern mix of ships and their technology: White, *The Times*, 22 Jan. 1903; White, 19 Feb. 1906, Cantor Lectures, 'Modern Warships', in *Journal of the Society of Arts* 54 (1905/1906), 866–71, 868; Fisher to Tweedmouth, 5 Oct. 1906, cited in Marder, FGDN, Vol. 2, No. 51, 95–97; Balfour to Mahan, 20 Dec. 1899, BL, MSS Balfour, Add. 49742; Thursfield to Sydenham, 11 Aug. 1898, NIA, MSS Thursfield, TT/NAVAL/JRT/2/190; Lambert, 'Admiral Sir John Fisher', 646; Hobson, 'Maritimer Imperialismus', 170–71. Mahan's seminal work was *The Influence of Sea-Power upon History 1660–1783*, published in 1890.
43. Rüger, *The Great Naval Game*.
44. Salisbury to MacColl, 6 Sept. 1901, cited in Russell, *Malcolm MacColl*, 282–83.
45. Eley, *Reshaping the Right*, 27–54; Eley, 'Sammlungspolitik', 110–53.
46. Marder, *Anatomy*, 465; Kennedy, *Rise of Anglo-German Antagonism*, 251.
47. Bösch, Öffentliche *Geheimnisse*, 470; Geppert, Pressekriege, 1–27, 421–438
48. Niedhart, 'Selektive Wahrnehmung und politisches Handeln', 141–58. For a plea for a multidimensional approach, see Rose and Geppert, 'Machtpolitik und Flottenbau'.
49. See Geppert, *Pressekriege*.
50. For Fischer's thesis about the primacy of domestic affairs, see Fischer, *Krieg der Illusionen*. For comparison, see Kennedy, *The Realities behind Diplomacy*, which, despite its promising title, due to its scope of 135 years can provide nothing more than a start. A closer comparison with Fritz Fischer's primacy of the domestic is provided by Keith Wilson's stimulating essays, which unfortunately so far have not led to a comprehensive analysis of Edwardian diplomacy. Wilson, *Policy of the Entente*.
51. Steiner, *The Foreign Office*.

Chapter 1

THE PUBLIC SPHERE IN EDWARDIAN LONDON

Much can be learned from British public opinion in the years after the mid 1890s. We hear about British preoccupation with the country's future role as a world power operating within international power structures, about political options and the principal issues involved, about depictions of the enemy and possible responses to that enemy, and we also see how growing insecurity in the face of the Dual Alliance developed into a downright pathological fear of Germany. Both the principal decision makers and those lower down the chain of government found themselves confronted by an increasingly politicized public, its ability to influence events dramatically extended by the communications revolution of the late nineteenth century.

But we also see that contemporaries were divided on how to respond to this newfound influence. For example, while the Conservative leadership looked on with much scepticism at the London media and its regular campaigns,[1] and to some extent sought to sidestep, ignore or counter its influence, younger liberal forces were far less inhibited in their dealings with the various organs of the press.[2] Richard Haldane or David Lloyd George were very open about their contacts with journalists such as William Thomas Stead.[3] Herbert Asquith even considered bringing on board someone such as Leopold Maxse with whom he would work exclusively.[4] While a young opposition politician, Edward Grey developed a close relationship with John Spender of the *Westminster Gazette*,[5] and later, as foreign secretary, he repeatedly stressed the importance of public opinion.[6] As numerous of his statements make evident, from the very start he sought to ensure that his politics were expressly in tune with public opinion.[7]

As a young man, Lord Robert Salisbury had written regularly for the *Quarterly Review*, but as prime minister and foreign secretary he, unlike Grey, distanced

---

Notes for this chapter begin on page 58.

himself from that world, in effect deliberately maintaining an aura of detachment. Contact with important organs such as the *Times* or the *Daily Mail* was the responsibility of his private secretary, Sir Schomberg Kerr McDonnell. Salisbury expressly warned his longstanding friend Thomas Sanderson not to have dealings with Valentine Chirol or George Buckle.[8] Although Arthur Balfour, his nephew and successor, boasted of never reading the papers, he was certainly aware of their increased relevance. Balfour similarly delegated his contact with the press, and in particular with Ernest Bruce Iwan-Müller of the *Daily Telegraph*, to his private secretary, in his case to John S. Sandars.[9] By contrast, Lord Lansdowne felt himself permanently patronized by the press and at times complained very greatly about their unqualified meddling in his politics.[10] We know of no regular direct or indirect contact by Lansdowne with the press, and such an association cannot be reconstructed from his papers. The situation was very different for Joseph Chamberlain, Admiral John Fisher and his rival Admiral Charles Beresford. All three men were in frequent and direct contact with journalists, who included Arnold White, Archibald Hurd, John Spender and Richard Thursfield; they also proposed articles or more substantial press campaigns, and even took up the pen themselves on occasion.[11] Other contemporaries confirmed that the growing relevance of the press would be a seminal trait of their age. Wilhelm II, also known as the 'media kaiser', was far from indifferent to the views of the fourth estate.[12] And his cousin in St Petersburg, Tsar Nicholas II, raised the issue of the negative impact of the press on foreign relations with British military attaché Herbert Napier.[13] Investigation of public opinion and its political ramifications, as Zara Steiner and Keith Neilson in their brilliant analysis of the British origins of the war state, remains without question 'one of the richest veins in current historiography'.[14]

Given the profound political impact of English publishing and its close links to political developments, a study of the influences on and by Fleet Street[15] therefore would seem well worth the effort. Also productive, however, is consideration of a far less known phenomenon of political publishing: novels about invasion and espionage, which found a very substantial readership.[16] There was good reason for British decision makers to be well-nigh 'obsessed with the idea of public opinion'.[17] But this study is very specifically *not* another impressionistic attempt to understand political events through the lens of the press,[18] nor does it seek to revisit the theoretical concept of *public opinion*, a term that was certainly much used by contemporaries but does not lend itself methodologically to empirical definition.

The intention here is to raise the profile of journalism and publishing as political protagonists. The presentation and discussion of political options by journalists enabled decision makers to determine how those options might be received within the public sphere. And the role of journalists as political actors was not limited to conveying what was possible, for they also commented on political decisions and actions, providing a first source of interpretation. Journalists thereby exerted considerable influence, and their writings provide historians with much more than simply a mirror of events. Furthermore, this study also looks behind the scenes by drawing on the correspondence and contacts of leading journalists and commentators. The goal, then, is to map the flow of information and gain a sense of the very possibilities inherent in contemporary forms of international politics, with that information and those politics then examined together as historical phenomena.[19]

Political journalism and political fiction highlight particular themes, but their contribution to historical understanding goes further, for they allow us to explore the atmosphere within the London political scene, a space inhabited by the political elite of government officials and by politicians, writers and journalists in the City, in which daily discussions of political matters took place and from which political action emanated. The established concept of the *official mind*[20] is deliberately expanded in this study to become the *public mind*, a term that has already been deployed by Norman Angell and here encompasses journalists who wrote about foreign policy, commentators and communicators such as Valentine Chirol (*Times*), Henry Spenser Wilkinson (*Morning Post*), Emile J. Dillon (*Daily Telegraph/Contemporary Review*) and James L. Garvin (*Observer*), figures who exercised a great influence on decision making in Whitehall.[21] Contemporaries were themselves increasingly likely to note the connections between the media and diplomacy and to talk of two established forms of diplomacy, with correspondents recognized as unofficial 'ambassadors'[22] or 'amateur diplomatists'.[23]

The breadth of this perspective holds out the possibility of revealing additional fundamental structures within which British foreign policy was formulated and possible influences on that policy, including its immediate circumstances.[24] Representatives of the media knew that they were now held in greater esteem. In light of his ability to make sound political judgements, John Spender was expressly valued as a 'colleague' by Grey,[25] and had good reason to record that 'it is impossible to write a chapter upon any aspect of public life without at some point having to consider the activities of the newspapers'.[26] Further, Spender continued, it would be 'scarcely an exaggeration to say that about six proprietors and a score of writers and editors between them make the entire opinion of the Metropolitan Press that counts'.[27]

William T. Stead, publisher of the *Review of Reviews* and the pacifist 'enfant terrible'[28] of writers in London, ruminated more deeply on the blessings of modern journalism. In April 1898, he commented with largely positive intent that the newspaper correspondent was the 'ambassador of democracy', noting that 'he manufactures the opinion to which it is the function of the regular ambassador to give effect. It is difficult to overestimate his importance or to measure his influence for weal or for woe'.[29] Elsewhere that same year, however, he criticized the press's potential impact on international relations:

> The fact is that the intervention of the Press in international disputes tends daily to become more and more hostile to peace and civilization. ... [M]uch of our modern journalism is the most potent weapon yet invented by the devil for banishing peace and goodwill from the earth. Sooner or later the nations will in self-defence have to provide some means of silencing newspaper comment when international questions are in debate...[30]

When it came to the development and consolidation of democratic structures, the press seems to have been identified as a valuable tool, yet it could be also unpredictable and hard to control. Stead knew only too well what he was talking about. During the Boer War, he had organized an invasion hysteria in the press, the effect of which lingered through the whole pre-war period. The rumour he had planted in the *Review of Reviews* about anti-British collaboration instigated by Berlin and an imminent invasion of the British Isles proved long-lived.[31] As one of the most vehement critics of the war, Stead had sought to dramatize its consequences in order to win over as many readers as possible for an anti-war campaign. Instead, however, his actions only ensured that whenever rumours of a Napoleon-like threat again raised their head, the focus was increasingly likely to be on Germany, even though during the Boer War Germany had successfully opposed the creation of the continental alliance desired by France and Russia.[32] Stead's use of the threat of invasion for impact had a profound effect when that possibility was picked up by political decision makers. Despite the Foreign Office's better knowledge, this supposed danger was still deployed to counter a possible Anglo-German rapprochement, while also cited in the War Office and the Admiralty as grounds for additional reforms and investment in armaments.[33]

A further frame of reference is provided by the focus on the English capital. Without doubt, public life was concentrated on London. The political and the intellectual had a closely interwoven existence on the banks of the Thames. This centralization meant that almost every professional journalist felt compelled to be based in the capital, unlike in Germany, for example,[34] a reality that corresponded fully with a contemporary self-perception that placed the writer in the midst of the political process. In 1899, Fleet Street, set between the Strand and Ludgate Hill and barely 500 metres long, was home to the editorial offices of over thirty-four of the most important daily newspapers and magazines in the Empire.[35] The political sphere in the capital encompassed not only visible institutions such as parliament, Downing Street, the Cabinet Office and the individual ministries, but also places where the groundwork was laid for subsequent political positions and decisions: the political parties, gentlemen's clubs, the lobby, and debating institutions such as the royal societies, the Commission on Oriental Studies at the University of London, and the Royal United Service Institute (RUSI), and other associations where people who came together might exchange political ideas. Unsurprisingly, the most significant clubs were to be found in London's exclusive West End, in Pall Mall, St James's Street, Piccadilly and Whitehall, hence in close proximity not only to the government quarter but also to the press district.[36]

As loci for informal discussions and the free-and-easy exchange of often momentous ideas, these clubs were essential to the very nature of the British political press, and indeed indispensable for politics as a whole. Here politicians, diplomats and journalists met to lunch or dine together, discussed the problems of the day, and reached agreement on political strategies and possibilities and on the ground rules for the discussion of disputed issues.[37] Tories liked to meet in the Carlton Club and Liberals at the Reform Club, while army and navy officers preferred the Army and Navy Club. And here too were found the launching pads for various journalistic alliances and campaigns – the editors associated with the Northcliffe Press met the editors of the *Daily Telegraph*, the *Spectator* and the *National Review* at the Garrick Club in Covent Garden, for example.[38]

Not only were leading authors and journalists known to one another, but as they participated in the obligatory social life, they also inevitably intersected with the circles that set the political tone, especially since the publishing elite self-recruited for the most part from the political ruling class and were likewise the product of renowned public schools and universities. The constant contact between these two worlds proved an ideal scenario for the exchange of ideas, for long-term mutual assistance and for the exertion of influence. That interaction suggests that political processes did not develop within a vacuum,[39] but were rather a concrete component of contemporary realities. The intensive exchange of information and ideas between political writings and public life in England principally concerned issues that were essentially either, on one hand, social or religious or cultural in character or, on the other, concerned with political or economic problems. A picture emerges of a debating elite and a practice whereby such ongoing political debate produced shared positions that then became recommendations.

At a time when international relations was not part of the canon studied at Oxbridge or other universities, and when ideas were not yet being forged at the Royal Institute of International Affairs, the forum created by such elite political debate, and above all by the London press in all its forms, had a particular status. That prominence was all the greater because the first decades of the twentieth century would prove to be a golden age of the English popular press. In no other country had the professionalization and spatial concentration of the media already advanced so far. And technological developments such as the rotary printing press, the telegraph and, later, the telephone intensified and accelerated the press's international links. Between 1888 and 1906, the telegraph network grew by almost 60 per cent. In 1906, 93.8 million messages were transmitted through 56,600 miles of cable in Great Britain. The expansion of the telephone network was even more breathtaking. In Germany in only five years, from 1901 to 1906, the length of the telephone cable increased by 54 per cent, from 59,000 miles to 91,300 miles, with the number of messages sent in the same period increasing from 766 million to 1,352 million, while in Great Britain more than 550 million messages were transmitted in 1905 alone.[40] The rise of press agencies such as Reuters, Havas, and Wolffs Telegraphisches Büro (WTB) would have been unthinkable without these developments. In 1894, Reuters, the largest British press agency, had thirty-four offices spread throughout the world; by 1906, that number had grown to forty-seven.[41] Viewed in comparison with Great Britain's forty-eight official diplomatic missions, with four alone in the German Reich, this information network was impressive. And it would prove invaluable to the Foreign Office.[42]

Against the background of such speedy developments, Alfred Harmsworth was already dreaming of a 'simultaneous press', that is to say, a coordinated press whose political power would lie, he proposed, in bringing about 'unity of thought and action'. For this press baron, the influence of the media lay not necessarily in the plausibility of its arguments but came from its 'literation of an idea until it becomes familiar, by the reading matter selected and by the quotation of opinions as news'. He continued: 'And this influence is all the more potent because it is indirect, and not perceived by the reader'.[43] While there was no question of the political elite losing control over military and diplomatic relations, international relations could not remain unaffected. The downside of this influence was noted by John Hobson for one, who recorded that 'the popularization of the power to read has made the Press the chief instrument of brutality', a development that, he noted, could be felt especially in foreign affairs.[44]

By the turn of the century, publishers and journalists alike were enjoying previously unknown political influence and were now considered 'His Majesty's Public Councillors'. Whereas Victorian attitudes had identified a clear distinction between politicians and journalists according to which 'the politician did things, and the journalist commented on them',[45] at the beginning of the twentieth century that gulf was gradually disappearing. Politicians increasingly wooed publishers and journalists, enticing them with the bait of social advancement and entry into exclusive gentlemen's clubs in the City, some of which were centuries old. The London communication space was becoming increasingly dense. Suddenly, publishers such as the Harmsworth brothers or Owen Seaman of *Punch* had access to exclusive circles, were knighted, and might themselves strive to go into politics – although in the case of Harmsworth, alias Lord Northcliffe, with only modest success. Shortly after the Boer War, the membership of the House of Commons included no fewer than thirty newspaper owners and journalists, and the journalist's profession was being held in ever-higher esteem.[46] In 1906, journalists formed the third largest professional grouping in the Commons, after officers and lawyers.[47] Oxbridge colleges were now producing not only politicians, diplomats and professors, but also the leader writers of the major daily and weekly papers. These men organized political campaigns, as we see in the press wars and the battles over protective tariffs and military reforms; they were also increasingly likely to appear in person as speakers at political events.[48]

Unlike the continental Great Powers, the British government had no official press office, but the London press was hardly independent and often had distinct party loyalties.[49] Unofficial personal contacts were very much part and parcel of England's parliamentary system, and both politics and press were covered by the highly productive old boys' network. Since Gladstone's two Midlothian campaigns (1879/80) at the latest, politicians had made use of friends in publishing to help spread their ideas and programmes to a wider audience, and capable and ambitious journalists were in turn able to use that service to their own advantage, requiring compensation in the form of political influence. Charismatic and ambitious journalists who were intellectually engaged used such relationships as sources of first-hand information and for the targeted dissemination of information that enabled their own voices to be heard in the government's political planning; here the reference is to figures such as Valentine Chirol, Henry Wickham Steed, George Saunders, Charles Repington (all from the *Times*), Emile J. Dillon (*Daily Telegraph/Contemporary Review*), Henry Spenser Wilkinson (*Morning Post*), John A. Spender (*Westminster Gazette*), Charles P. Scott (*Manchester Guardian*), Leopold J. Maxse (*National Review*), John St. Loe Strachey (*Spectator*) and James L. Garvin (*Observer/Fortnightly Review*).[50]

Unofficial connections were cultivated, the diplomatic mail was sometimes used as a matter of course,[51] and the two parties regularly met over dinner, at the club or as they gathered for hunting parties held at country estates.[52] A contemporary observer's description provided of the political manoeuvring at the heart of government was well observed, and it also usefully identifies the stage occupied by our actors in the next part of this study:

> The Governing Cliques can govern because they see one another daily; they are always calling on each other, or lunching or dining, or attending receptions together; they have been at the same schools and colleges; they have shot together, hunted together, yachted together, they stay at the same country houses, when they leave the dozen or so of the streets and squares in London where they all live; and good half of them are connected by the ties of blood or marriage.[53]

Facing the additional challenge of the 'new journalism' that could be found in the so-called 'tabloids' – the sensation-seeking press intended for the masses – which had been launched with the first issue of the *Daily Mail* on 4 May 1896, the established quality press sought to strengthen its position in the battle for advertising revenue and readers. In 1900, the publisher Henry Massingham[54] recognized an essential equation: 'Since the modern newspapers depend heavily upon their advertisements it is in the interests of the advertisers to please the mass of readers, and the proprietors' interest to please the advertisers'.[55] Both in Fleet Street and in Printing House Square, where the office of the renowned *Times* was located, the daily press increasingly struggled to attract readers and increase revenue. The soberly analytical style that had determined the choice of topic and the content of reports fell victim to these pressures. It soon became evident that the traditional papers had little to throw against the halfpenny press, at only a sixth of its cost. Harmsworth's *Daily Mail* and Pearson's *Daily Express* dominated the mass market, with some 1.5 million daily readers between them. Their new concept, which prioritized sensationalism, the Empire and patriotism,[56] proved very successful and for the first time broke with customary party affiliations. With their party links, traditional papers such as the *Daily Telegraph*, which lost some 60,000 readers,[57] found themselves fearing for their survival. In 1908, when press baron Northcliffe decided to buy the *Times*, that great institution among newspapers had a daily run of only 38,000. The owner of the *Daily Mail* and the *Evening News* had already rescued the *Observer*, a Sunday paper, when the once-so-respected weekly's readership dropped to only 3,000. The Harmsworths' press empire now dominated the major part of the English market. In the provinces, only the *Manchester Guardian* could hold its own against the London papers.

While foreign affairs reporting in the daily press was primarily concerned with describing crises, commentary could be found in reports by experts that appeared in weekly and monthly publications. These specialists understood their principal task as providing their already informed readers with additional explanation and discussion. Here the tone was sharper. Using pseudonyms such as Calchas (Garvin), Zeta, Diplomaticus (Lucien Wolf), Excubitor (Hurd), Ignotus (Wesselitzki), Navalis (Thursfield), Pollex, or simply *X* (Garvin), well-known journalists published pamphlets that were usually conspicuously one-sided and increasingly polemical in their stance against Germany, and at an early date called for the isolation of the Central Powers by means of a new triple alliance comprising England, France and Russia. But politicians such as Charles Dilke, Henry Norman and Lord Brassey were also very ready to provide their own commentary, to put the record straight or to give political advice. The Boer War years had marked a turning point, for from then on, and right up until 1914, periodicals contained much greater public discussion of foreign affairs.[58]

The periodicals' relatively small print runs should not be allowed to disguise the extent of their influence. These publications were aimed very firmly at the politically engaged London elite, and they would have been readily available for perusing in the reading rooms of London clubs and libraries. With its unusually large print run of some 22,000 copies, John Strachey's *Spectator* – Strachey was a close acquaintance of Grey – was the most influential of the political papers. But Courtney's *Fortnightly Review*, in which foreign policy expert James Garvin published, the *Contemporary Review*, which provided a second income for the *Daily Telegraph*'s St Petersburg correspondent, Emile Dillon, Leo Maxse's *National*

Review and, from 1907, the *Nation*, which was owned by the renowned Henry Massingham, a critic of Grey and a radical liberal, were, despite their relatively sparse print runs of some 5,000 to 10,000 copies,[59] among the most influential papers precisely because their readership included leading decision makers.

Newspaper alliances were also formed, as for instance between the *Times*, the *Spectator* and the *National Review*. The *Times*, for example, repeatedly made reference to especially noteworthy articles elsewhere,[60] while the *Outlook* wrote of Maxse's magazine that its pages 'are packed with vital writing ... foreign and domestic affairs are discussed with masculine ability and vigour'. The *Spectator* described the columns entitled 'Episodes of the Month', written by Maxse, to be the 'most brilliant contributions to modern political journalism' and deemed them distinguished above all by their powerful and unconventional style.[61] The *National Review* was the only political journal to advertise in the *Times*, on a whole or half-page spread. In addition, every subscriber to the *Times* received an exclusive 50 per cent discount on that monthly publication, which set about attracting readers by publishing lists of its expert contributors. Editorial opinion at the *Times* held that the *National Review* was performing not only the tasks of the press but also the 'tasks of the government', not least because the writers who provided material for that magazine included the most senior political decision makers of the Empire.[62] If we think only in terms of numbers, then we must acknowledge that in these years the quality press certainly saw fewer copies sold. Nevertheless, the praise by the *Times* was certainly well founded, for among politically relevant circles, the *National Review* continued to be considered as in a class of its own in light of its numerous insights and links to high politics.[63]

The first high point for the political influence of the press occurred during Balfour's term in office, when with the support of the *Spectator*, the *National Review* and the *Times*, some members of the House of Commons were able to bring to bear such massive public pressure on Lansdowne, the foreign secretary, that he ended Anglo-German cooperation in Venezuela and broke off promising discussions with Germany about the Baghdad railway. Subsequently, Fleet Street drummed up massive opposition to the Central Powers, while less and less was written about the anti-Semitic pogroms in Russia, or about Russia's repeated violations of treaties in the Middle East, Far East and Baltic, or about Russia's threatening behaviour towards Finland, an ally of Britain. The *Times* was in no doubt that Germany was behind not only the two Moroccan crises but also the Aland Question and the tensions in the Balkans.[64] Similarly, the *Observer*, now headed by Maxse's protégée Garvin, held that in view of the permanent threat from Berlin in the Baltic and the Balkans, England's best response was to enter into close and lasting alliances with Russia and France, ensuring that Germany was hemmed in.[65] The *Morning Post*, the *Daily Telegraph* and the *Daily Mirror* all agreed and, additionally, regularly described Austria-Hungary as Berlin's 'cat's paw'.[66] The *Morning Post* believed that it was vital that the Dual Alliance 'keep its powder dry' during the tensions surrounding Austria-Hungary's Sanjak railway project, to which we will return.[67]

Where political campaigning ended and the internal workings of the new media market began is hard to determine. That distinction can often only be revealed through investigation of unpublished material concerning those involved. While not everything was a product of political conviction or political discussion, the business interests of the respective publishers and journalists also often cannot stand as sole explanation. Yet such commercial interests were certainly relevant. With its sensational revelations about Germany's alleged intentions, Northcliffe's press empire stood out from the rest. The press baron stated the guiding principle for his paper when he acknowledged that 'the average Briton liked a good hate'.[68] First and foremost, Northcliffe was the head of a business enterprise. When he took over the *Times*, he was concerned to make clear that he would not interfere with the journalistic freedom of his editors for economic reasons provided that they repeatedly warned of the ultimate danger posed by Germany. In an interview with the Paris *Matin*, he went even further: 'Yes, we detest the Germans and cordially. I will not allow any newspaper to be printed, which might injure France, although it might be agreeable to Germany'.[69]

By contrast, Leo Maxse and John Strachey were driven by their political convictions and a missionary zeal. Tellingly, Maxse's *National Review* long operated in the red, and both men used their private fortunes to travel throughout Great Britain to announce their views from the rostrum. A similar zeal could be found in journalists for whom writing was not just a means to earn a living but also a political mission.[70] The group of young liberal imperialists that gathered around Edward Grey, for example, was much applauded by these journalists for taking a courageous course that led towards France and Russia. At times, Grey's foreign policy was judged too hesitant, but for the most part it received high marks, whereas both his predecessors were reproached for their lack of planning and purpose. In general, the right-wing liberals in the cabinet, unlike their radical liberal colleagues, could rely on the support of the predominantly conservative press.[71] The latter's only dependable liberally minded ally was John Spender, who was considered the mouthpiece of Edward Grey,[72] for the *Manchester Guardian* and the *Daily News*, both radical liberal papers, criticized Grey for his distinctly biased attitude against Germany and in favour of Russia.[73] However, of all the papers, the *Times* had the hotline to the cabinet and to individual departments, and for this reason will be the focus of our attention here.

The *Times* had the densest network of foreign representatives and funnelled all foreign news to the provincial press.[74] The political influence of these foreign correspondents, exercised through their direct contacts with individual diplomats and politicians and their links with foreign governments, can hardly be overestimated. As a rule, these men were extremely well-informed members of a network, able to provide Whitehall with additional and often secret information to which the chargés d'affaires had no access. For example, Mackenzie Wallace, a close friend of Arthur Nicolson's, supported Nicolson directly at the Algeciras Conference, and as an expert on Russia and having been based in St Petersburg as a correspondent, he could later provide Nicolson with better information than could the ambassador to that city.[75] Henry W. Steed not only gained the trust of George Goschen but also exerted such great influence that even the Foreign Office soon put more faith in his reports than in the ambassador's. George Ernest Morrison was known for providing information on Russian activities in the Far East before the dispatches of the British diplomats had even reached London. George W. Smalley, the *Times'* agent in the United States, had a decisive influence on the Hay-Pauncefote negotiations.[76] Among the most important correspondents were William Lavino, who was stationed first in Vienna and from 1903 in Paris (Lavino played a significant mediating role in the establishment of the Entente Cordiale), Henry W. Steed, who was first in Berlin, then in Rome, and from 1902 to 1913 in Vienna, before succeeding Valentine Chirol as foreign editor in London, and, without doubt, George Saunders, who from 1897 to 1908 was in Berlin.

As the Russian office of the *Times* was unoccupied for many years after the expulsion of Dudley Disraeli Braham, in 1903, reports on Russia were written in London, which no doubt explains why in these years the *Times'* reporting on Russia largely addressed the government's policy towards Russia. As long as the Tories were in power, that reporting tended to be critical; under the Liberals, and especially with Charles Hardinge, who had excellent contact with Valentine Chirol, heading up policy on Russia, the *Times'* attitude towards relations with Russia changed.

George Saunders was certainly behind the *Times'* notorious Germanophobia at the turn of the century. As Berlin correspondent for the *Morning Post*, he had never really given Germany a chance. A close friend of Sir Morell Mackenzie, the emperor's personal physician, Saunders arrived in Berlin during the short 99-day reign of Frederick III, and was immediately embittered by seeing the Empress Victoria so unpopular among the German people.[77] He would never revisit the judgement he passed three months later: he hated the Prussians and he hated Berlin. In numerous private letters to members of his family, he explained that only two races had a great future before them: the Slavs, headed by Russia, and the Anglo-Saxons, headed by England and the United States. In his opinion, the Germans were 'too besotted and dull and lazy' to see that their empire per se was a nonsense. By contrast, all paths lay open to the Russians, of whom he wrote: 'They might be our allies. If they were, the alliance would carry all before it'.[78] Berlin would remain for him the 'city of the plain'; German women were 'ugly squaws' and Prussian men mere 'cannon fodder'. He considered the German Reich a gigantic fraud and German politics thoroughly perfidious and despicable.[79] His contempt for everything German did not prevent him from marrying the daughter of a Jewish-German banker, thereby nurturing the best of contacts in Berlin. It speaks volumes of his fundamental political position in these years that he was the only Briton of his generation to rejoice, almost euphorically, at the news of the Dual Alliance between France and Russia.[80] Since the late 1880s, he had preached untiringly in his correspondence of the need for a bridge between Russia and England, not as a necessary counterbalance to the ambitions of the German Reich, but in order to control the world.[81] Doubtlessly, the extreme nature of his views brought Saunders to the notice of Mackenzie Wallace, the Russophile department head at the *Times*.[82] Valentine Chirol at first found nothing appealing in his younger colleague, who was so animated by his prejudices, but when Chirol no longer wanted to remain in Berlin after the Krüger telegram, he had no say in the selection of his successor.[83]

Saunders was never content with the role of detached observer. His goal was not to ensure the British public was objectively informed but rather, and first and foremost, to convince London's political class of the necessity of an alliance with Russia and France that would isolate the German Reich.[84] He extracted from German papers every passage that was antagonistic towards England and did not shrink from intensifying their impact by deliberate omissions or reworkings of the text.[85] Nothing was left untried when it came to publicizing his political views on Germany and his commitment to an Anglo-Russian agreement. He fostered contacts with other publishers in order to find additional outlets for his views, corresponded with liberal politicians and especially with liberal imperialists such as Rosebery, and was finally rewarded when on assuming office Edward Grey requested that as an established expert on Germany, he provide an analysis of the German press.[86] He was seen as a 'sound man on Germany',[87] and in the years before 1908, when he was moved to Paris, his colourful reports and numerous personal and professional contacts allowed him to exert an influence on publishers, diplomats and politicians that should not be underestimated.[88] Eyre Crowe usually deemed Saunders' reports significant and frequently derived conclusions from them that then made their way into his analysis of Germany.[89]

News received from the various offices abroad was coordinated by the *Times'* 'foreign minister', as Valentine Chirol was termed by his colleagues. Trained at the Foreign Office and a close friend of diplomats such as Charles Hardinge and Cecil Spring Rice, Chirol was practically part of the furniture at Whitehall and could be found almost every day at the Foreign Office, much like Charles Repington, a former soldier and diplomat[90] who had spied for the Foreign Office during the Fashoda crisis[91] and who, together with Major Philippe Huguet, the French military attaché in London, initiated the secret discussions of the general staff at the beginning of 1906. Henry Spenser Wilkinson, military expert for the *Morning Post* and Eyre Crowe's brother-in-law, also knew his way around the corridors of the Foreign Office.[92] As chief editor for international affairs, Chirol undertook innumerable journeys abroad and had personal contacts throughout the world. While his competence in foreign policy was without doubt enormous, objectivity and detachment were not always in evidence. During his early tenure, as an expert on the Middle East who was highly critical of Russia, he had frequently faulted Saunders for supporting an Anglo-Russian alliance and for making unproven assertions, which, in Chirol's opinion, were a product of Saunders' willingness to be led by feelings rather than by fact.[93] A crisis of self-confidence and the Boer War brought about a radical U-turn for many in their estimation of the overall political picture, and Chirol had been typical of those who came to support vehemently Joseph Chamberlain's idea of an alliance between England and Germany. But with the collapse of Anglo-German negotiations, and in light of the open Anglophobia of the German public during the Boer War, he gradually developed into a passionate opponent of the German Reich.[94] As his disillusionment grew, the final straw for Chirol was the rumour that Germany sought a new Napoleonic bloc.[95] Against the background of George Saunders' reports and with his own problematic experience of the German telegram to Ohm Krüger in mind, Chirol's opinion now matched that of Saunders:[96]

> The British Public never expected very much from France and Russia, but, after the Imperial visit and the warm-hearted reception of the Kaiser, we expected better things of Germany. It is a question whether it would not be preferable to join with open enemies like France and Russia, even at the greatest sacrifice, than with a double faced friend like Germany.[97]

As early as 1904, Chirol had been instructed by Hardinge himself to canvas in the *Times* for an alliance with Russia.[98] Saunders' reports provided support for Chirol and Moberly Bell at the *Times* and for Strachey at the *Spectator*; Maxse's anti-German campaigns in the *National Review* would have been unimaginable without Saunders' contributions to the cause.[99]

Leopold Maxse's campaign for an Anglo-Russian alliance

At the heart of the London-centred network of politicians and journalists was Leopold James Maxse, the publisher and owner of the *National Review* – a seismograph of the Edwardian public sphere and politics. Hardly had the first battles of the First World War been fought than he was pointing out to his readers that he had long foreseen that war. His propagandistic assemblage of earlier writings, *Germany on the Brain: The Obsession of a Crank*, published in 1915, provided just the evidence needed to establish a paradigm for Anglo-German antagonism. Although undoubtedly an extremist, he would in the end be proved all too right, and Maxse has therefore served as a prime witness for those who seek to claim that the English had no other option when they responded to the danger posed by Germany. So why look at someone who seems to tell us only the known story? Maxse himself has been identified as a 'right-wing' journalist who always dismissed radical liberals as 'radical, flatulent fools forever on the peace path'.[100] However this implies a proximity to conservatism which in reality only partially existed. On closer scrutiny, his political recommendations seemed by and large far more drastic than those of Lord Salisbury, Arthur Balfour or Lord Lansdowne. Indeed, his observations and his political network show that on some points he was in much greater agreement with the liberal imperialists who gathered around Herbert Asquith and Edward Grey. The microscope has been turned on Maxse's Germanophobia, but that attitude has to be understood in light of the causal links between Anglo-German alienation and Anglo-Russian rapprochement. Certainly his articles, like those of many like-minded writers for the *National Review*, warned unceasingly of the German Empire's aggressive intentions, but that estimation was always inseparable from evaluation of the positioning of the Empire and also with an increasingly strong plea for a comprehensive partnership not only with France but also with Russia.[101] The potential risks of that plan, the intermediate stages or alternatives that their observations on international politics identified, and the background, political goals and impact of their views all reveal much about the possibilities open to British foreign policy before the First World War, and tell us also of the debates that accompanied such decision making.

Maxse has been judged 'one of the few men of his day who exercised any real influence upon public opinion', with that influence evident from the mid 1890s on.[102] Educated at Harrow and King's College Cambridge, he benefitted from an elite upbringing that gave him access to the politically influential circles in London.[103] In 1895, he would record that as owner of the *National Review* he considered it his 'fate' to belong to the 'so-called governing class'.[104] In 1893, his father, Admiral Frederick Maxse, had bought that ailing but renowned paper from Alfred Austin for £1,500.[105] After a rather undistinguished military career, Frederick Maxse had failed as a politician and then tried his hand at journalism, and along with the newspaper itself, he brought his son indispensable contacts to the Cecil family, the Chamberlains[106] and numerous other political and military figures,[107] without which his inexperienced son would have found the early years of his career far harder.

Having inherited his father's ability to nurture contacts, Leo Maxse went on to build a dense network of acquaintances that he used as a route to both information and influence. He soon found himself involved in a long-lasting association with the foreign affairs staff of the *Times*, and he had a direct line, based on friendship, to Valentine Chirol, Charles Repington, Henry Wickham Steed and George Saunders. By the turn of the century, his London house in Montpelier Square had become a popular meeting place, where 'men of all types and opinions met, and he [L.J. Maxse] played no small part in forming the views and characters of some of the political leaders of the nation'.[108] Among his regular visitors were publishers and journalists such as Lord Northcliffe and John St. Loe Strachey of the *Spectator*, men with whom he frequently arranged press campaigns; diplomats and politicians such as Eyre Crowe, Charles Hardinge, Cecil Spring Rice, John Sanders or Edward Grey, and George Lloyd; and military men such as Alan Percy, the Duke of Northumberland, Lord Roberts, and Charles Repington. Strachey described his friend, not without reason, as the *watchdog* for the foreign-policy decision makers.[109] Among Maxse's closest comrades-in-arms were without doubt Rowland Blennerhasset, the untiring political commentator on the *National Review*, and the young James Garvin, who had begun his career in the capital city as Maxse's assistant and whom Northcliffe would later select as editor of the *Observer*.[110]

In his father's friend Georges Clemenceau, the young Maxse had a man who could open doors for him on the international scene, and he had Clemenceau to thank not least for his close contact with Théophile Delcassé, the foreign minister of France.[111] Since boyhood, Maxse had spent a considerable amount of time in France, and he therefore always felt a particular empathy with that country and its people. That attachment did not mean, however, that he was at all willing to gloss over French pressure on the Empire. At the very beginning of his career, he was extremely aggravated by England's constant problems with France and openly sought alternative courses for his country's foreign relations.[112] As patterns of power began to shift, he believed that England was playing with fire when as a result of pressure from France and Russia, the government regularly rebuffed all Germany's attempts at rapprochement. In Maxse's eyes, the time had come to declare to Berlin 'that we are ready to join her'.[113] A month later, in January 1894, he recorded, 'If the report of the Franco-Russian alliance will be confirmed, England has no alternative but to join the Triple Alliance'.[114]

As is immediately clear from these early essays, Maxse believed that sooner or later Great Britain would have to take up a place within the system of continental alliances. That he raised the possibility of Britain's joining the Central Powers seems surprising, above all when that recommendation is set against the background of his later Germanophobia. But recognition of these earlier positions helps us to detect how Maxse's thinking developed, a process that was definitely shaped by the events of the 1890s. We can see that recognition of Germany as the principal threat to Britain's empire was not the impetus for the fundamental reorientation that would be characteristic of the later Edwardian generation. More decisive, as Maxse's early writings reflect, was a noticeably Social Darwinian expectancy about the coming century, in which Great Britain would certainly not be able to defend its imperial existence on its own. Even Maxse saw behind Germany's repeated attempts at rapprochement in the 1890s the geopolitical predicament of the German Empire in the face of Russia and

France.¹¹⁵ The apparent shared interests of Great Britain and Germany would soon develop, however, in a new direction.

For the first half of the 1890s, Maxse was highly critical of the liberal leadership in Whitehall, in particular when it came to the repeated rejection of overtures from Berlin. His judgement on Lord Rosebery's short intermezzo at the Foreign Office was suitably withering: 'No Foreign Minister for many years exhibited such singular incompetence'. For Maxse, the German Empire was blameless in this instance, and its actions completely legitimate: 'Her [Germany's] only failure was to take advantage of the blunders and weaknesses of British Ministers and secure substantial advantages for herself'.¹¹⁶ The *Times* also described Germany's behaviour as 'a signal proof of the firm foundations upon which Anglo-German relations now rest',¹¹⁷ and that paper even praised the Wilhelmstrasse for resisting pressure within Germany from extremists who were insistent that it was high time Germany receive colonial compensation for her repeated support of Britain in the Far East, Samoa and Egypt.¹¹⁸ This praise was of little use in Berlin, however, given that the London press did not yet have the influence it would acquire in later years. England's repeated rebuttal of Germany's overtures of friendship increasingly seemed to suggest that Germany was being used and would have to withstand the pressure from the Dual Alliance alone.¹¹⁹

While Maxse did indeed regret Rosebery's attitude, rather than opt for a proven method in the form of a closer relationship between Britain and the Central Powers to balance the Franco-Russian alliance, he soon recognized an additional option that was much more favourable for the Empire. In the accession of Tsar Nicholas II in autumn 1894, he saw the possibility of a revolutionary combination in international affairs. First, he hoped that the Franco-Russian alliance would be broken, 'which is nothing if it be not anti-German and anti-British'.¹²⁰ Rumours suggested that settlement of the Straits dispute in favour of Russia would enable the creation of a new triple alliance involving Great Britain, Russia and Germany, thereby forging an agreement that would lead to lasting peace in Europe.¹²¹ Unlike the Tory leadership, Maxse paid little attention England's partners, Italy or Austria-Hungary. For Maxse, only British interests mattered, and therefore also the possibility of closer ties with Paris achieved on the back of Anglo-Russian rapprochement. The great obstacle to Anglo-Russian rapprochement, he was clear, was the Near Eastern Question.¹²² In any case, that arrangement would inevitably have increased pressure on south-east Europe, and as Germany evidently wanted to bring her ally Austria-Hungary into this new constellation, significant hurdles laid before this plan from the start. Soon even Maxse preferred an Anglo-Russian entente without Berlin.

Maxse's changing views are indicative of a distinct development in his thinking. Commitment to the Triple Alliance was, in effect, a traditional solution, one that sought to maintain a balance of power, with Russia and France on the opposite side of the scales. If an Anglo-Russian rapprochement seemed possible, however, then that option would be more attractive, for it would bring the greatest possible security for Britain's position globally and the minimal security necessary for Britain on the continent, since, if it came to the worst, the geopolitical dependency of the Central Powers on Russia would draw them in and hold them in check, with France included via Russia. Austria-Hungary never appeared in Maxse's calculations. In his opinion, the multinational state on the Danube was already doomed and in its moribund state could at most be deployed to meet unfulfilled pan-Slavonic interests. But at this point he still recommended against an open alliance directed against Germany, warning that Berlin might then panic and withdraw its indispensable support in Egypt.[123]

Hence, in January 1895, a year before the crisis occasioned by the Krüger telegram, an event that is frequently cited as the spark that ignited anti-German sentiment,[124] Maxse was already reflecting openly on whether rapprochement with France and Russia, the arch-enemies of the British Empire, might be an advantageous course to follow. This possibility, we must note, emerged in its own right out of the contemporary international situation, and without Germany's having been identified as a full-blown enemy of Britain. And we should note in particular that in Maxse's eyes, if the situation became urgent, Germany and Austria-Hungary would be too weak to escape the gravitational pull of Russia. In order that the German Empire not feel encircled, he held, any agreement with Paris and St Petersburg should at least appear limited to imperial interests. For Maxse, the contours of possible rapprochement at this point were determined by a distinction between continental and imperial interests, even if that division meant a solution for Britain that was less than ideal in light of the country's role as both an imperial power and a continental power.[125] In any case, Maxse thought it was time for England finally to cease 'drifting' and to get on board with Great Power alliance politics. The possibility of an Anglo-Russian agreement still remained on the distant horizon though. In light of the situation in Egypt, the Triple Alliance of Germany, Austria and Italy remained a preferable partner. The change in government brought with it the opportunity for a change in course towards the Triple Alliance, a new direction warmly anticipated in Berlin, where Rosebery's purely Empire-oriented policy had been judged fatal to bilateral relations.[126]

In August 1895, Maxse still seemed confident that Salisbury would change course and quickly enter an entente with Germany. The fluid game that the powers had been playing was to be replaced by a predictable system, and ideally by a quadruple global alliance involving England, Germany, France and Russia, with Russia even granted access to an ice-free port.[127] A permanent global system covering the four dominant Great Powers of Europe and codified by treaty would have been a complete break with the traditional flexible balancing of power, and the time was far from ripe for such a system of collective security. On taking up the reins of government, Salisbury followed standard practice by speaking of continuity in foreign policy, even though he was himself anything but agreeable to Rosebery's course. There followed an autumn and winter full of misunderstandings that left wounded feelings on both sides of the English Channel. Under Salisbury, London continued to keep Berlin at arm's length. The Kaiser insulted his uncle Prince Albert, later Edward VII; Salisbury and Wilhelm II talked past each other on the Near Eastern Question; and in January 1896, the Kaiser felt obliged to send his famous but incredibly clumsy telegram to South Africa, leaving a bad taste with the British public, who now saw an excellent opportunity to vent on Germany the injury to their national pride that had come with the fall of their hero Leander Starr Jameson.[128]

For Maxse, as for many of his colleagues and contemporaries, the Krüger telegram marked a visible break.[129] In his initial reaction, he evidently remembered his own criticism of Rosebery's policy towards Germany and understood the telegram as a logical tit-for-tat response to the many rebuffs received from London,[130] but within a month Berlin's behaviour had become an act of 'fratricide'.[131] Enraged by the Jameson raid, France, too, had been the scene of anti-English demonstrations, but Maxse joined with Strachey in reassurance that nothing else should be expected of an arch-enemy.[132] But the disloyal Kaiser was not to be allowed to get away with this affront. Wilhelm II was declared a public threat 'which can only be rendered harmless by isolation'.[133] The Reich could not now be viewed with any dispassion. As retaliation for Germany's disloyalty, Maxse called for a new bloc to be created by an alliance with Russia and France against Germany. His harsh criticism of Rosebery for repeatedly leaving the Triple Alliance in the lurch was forgotten. Suddenly, he seemed to have discovered that since the Congress of Berlin in 1878, London's primary concern had been for the well-being of Germany, ahead even of England's own interests, yet Berlin had never repaid Britain for this selflessness. Worse still, ungrateful Berlin had now even dared to stab its loyal friend in the back.[134]

Published commentaries make evident that until this point, Germany had been thought of as the junior partner, ready to act at England's command. Where Germany's rapprochement with Russia had previously been seen as all too sensible, now it was judged a perfect example of German perfidy.[135] The whole summer long, the *National Review* was preoccupied with German treachery, and in October came to the conclusion that the Central Powers had acted above all out of their weakness in the face of Russia. Soon, Maxse insisted, the continent would be completely controlled by the Dual Alliance.[136] In this case, as an 'official' wrote, the law of the jungle prevailed, and sooner or later Germany would be forced to submit.[137] This official continued by insisting that Germany be prevented from forming an alliance with Russia out of weakness. English rapprochement with Russia could ensure that the tension between the powers continued.[138]

According to his biographer, Leo Maxse knew neither moderation nor discrimination; once he was on a mission, full steam ahead was the only option.[139] Now he was as convinced of Germany's hostility as of his own duty to enlighten his countrymen, or, seen from another angle, of the role and lasting impact of the political media: 'As the British Foreign Office ultimately conforms to public opinion, of which it stands in exaggerated awe, the opinion of the ordinary Englishman on matters of foreign policy is of no little importance'.[140] Both his personality and his journalistic style, developed just as the popular press was taking shape, enabled him to draw his readers down a predetermined path with boundless energy, leaving uncomfortable facts by the wayside and assisted by untiring repetition. Thus, he hit the nerve of his time. Lord Northcliffe, too, was convinced that unceasing repetition was required to keep his readership on course: 'The British public never understand a point until it has been put before them ad nauseam, and it is absolutely essential to go on saying things month after month, two or three times every month, and I must do it, even at the risk of my reputation'.[141]

And so Maxse also blamed Germany for the Fashoda crisis,[142] and half a year later wrote of the utterly perfidious plans of Kaiser Wilhelm II, who, in Maxse's opinion, had filled his head with intrigue, believing that only thus could the survival of Germany be ensured.[143] As far as Maxse was concerned, the incident had demonstrated yet again that Germany lacked any sympathy for the Empire's global ambitions. The agitation orchestrated by the *National Review* entered a new phase, with heightened fear of a new Napoleonic bloc led by Germany at the forefront.[144] From January 1900, the *National Review* spoke out vehemently against Joseph Chamberlain's ideas of Anglo-German rapprochement, not least because in a pinch Germany could not be trusted to resist the pressure of France and Russia.[145] Not only was Berlin's refusal to join Paris and St Petersburg in an anti-English bloc during the Boer War left entirely out of the picture, but the massive French protests against British plans in South Africa were likewise ignored,[146] with only the pro-English views of a few friends, such as Georges Clemenceau, printed.[147] Rowland Blennerhasset even managed to present the widespread Anglophobia in Europe, not apparent in Austria-Hungary of all countries, as largely a product of the machinations of German agents.[148] Berlin's diplomacy he believed to be motivated entirely by a desire to attack England as long as she remained involved in South Africa.[149]

In order to counter Germany's bid for hegemony by means of shady political tricks, the *National Review* adopted a position in the reform debate in favour of general conscription and a military build-up.[150] Germany was deployed by the paper as a problem in English political discourse about reform, but a problem that various interests could rally together to tackle. During this phase, Maxse repeatedly cited the Krüger episode as completely characteristic of German behaviour,[151] and repeatedly regretted that London had not used the telegram as grounds for a pre-emptive war.[152] Maxse knew no mercy. While the British public's reaction to the Kaiser's visit to Victoria's deathbed was both positive and conciliatory, Maxse dismissed Wilhelm II's action as sheer hypocrisy,[153] believing, as like-minded Garvin wrote, that 'England should be deceived until she can be defied'.[154] Henceforth, every act by Germany, whether passive, friendly or hostile, was read in the same way by being interpreted to Germany's disadvantage. A perfidious plan could be found at every turn. The Yangtze agreement, for example, appeared as a 'grand design' by the Kaiser to lull Britain into a false sense of security. And Maxse warned that if Great Britain did not see what was really happening, its demise was inevitable.[155]

Dedicated to his mission to his countrymen, Maxse even turned down the lucrative position of editor of the *Cape Times*.[156] During the Boer War, together with George Saunders, whom he had come to know and respect in November 1899 in Berlin,[157] and his comrades-in-arms Garvin, Strachey and Blennerhasset, Maxse developed his own theory about German behaviour and set the future course of his paper accordingly.[158] Their starting point was not, however, the strength of the German Reich so frequently cited by later historians, with the breathtaking rise of the German Reich and its *Weltpolitik*,[159] an expression that entered the English language partly thanks to Maxse. For Maxse and his fellow thinkers, the issue was rather the German Reich's geopolitical weakness. The group was united in believing that that weakness, and the terrifying strength of unassailable Russia, would lead the German Reich always to err on the side of subordination. While Salisbury too had his doubts concerning German backing against its powerful eastern neighbour,[160] Maxse and his companions went way further. They believed that in Berlin's eyes, the torpedoing of any British rapprochement with France of Russia, whatever the cost, had become the only course that could ensure Germany's survival. They would unceasingly promote this view of the notorious German mischief-maker in newspapers and journals and in public appearances right up until 1914. Maxse even took to the rostrum at public events, dispensing his insight in lectures for the Tariff Reform League and, in particular, for the National Service League. Every opportunity was a chance to plead for increased military power and the introduction of universal conscription.[161]

Maxse was supported in his campaign by Lord Roberts, Spenser Wilkinson and Charles Repington, all of whom had recognized that his arguments bolstered their own plans for conscription.[162] In Eyre Crowe, Francis Bertie, Charles Hardinge, Cecil Spring Rice and Arthur Nicolson, and not least in Edward Grey and Henry Norman, he also found a ready audience for his assertions.[163] But no echoes of those ideas could be heard among the old guard at the Foreign Office, Frank Lascelles, Edmund Monson or Thomas Sanderson. Indeed, Lord Selbourne believed that Maxse was mentally unbalanced and had completely lost his judgement skills.[164] John Sandars, Balfour's secretary, who was in regular contact with Maxse, considered any response to the articles that appeared in the *National Review* to be a complete waste of time.[165]

Yet the image of Germany held by those journalists who, like Maxse, belonged to a rather loose grouping made up of the so-called radical right was not exclusively negative.[166] Garvin, whose bookshelves at his own admission overflowed with first editions of the works of Immanuel Kant, Carl von Clausewitz, Wilhelm Treitschke, Heinrich von Sybel and Theodor Mommsen, maintained that few non-Germans respected the German people as much as he did. Spenser Wilkinson and Rowland Blennerhasset also thought very highly of German efficiency. But such respect made Germany seem all the more dangerous, as we will see when we come to look at the Coefficients and liberal imperialists. In the eyes of these younger Edwardians, what distinguished Germany was precisely what they most missed in England. Garvin himself wrote, 'They have every qualification for taking our place and are bound to aspire to it more ardently as time goes on'.[167] Yet, as the journalists were well aware, that was a long-term prognosis; they diagnosed Germany as at present too weak to be able to stand with England against the Dual Alliance but able to generate a serious threat if she joined with Russia. Maxse would write in 1902, 'The conclusion is irresistible that the Kaiser is either the powerless friend or the secret enemy of England. In either event our only policy is to remain *toujours en vendette*'.[168]

The writings of the radical right at this time revolved essentially around four central themes: (1) an enduring reorientation towards France, the United States and Russia; (2) reform of British policies on armaments and security, with a demand for either universal conscription or adoption of Strachey's massive expansion of volunteer forces; (3) reform of the government's social and taxation policies; and (4) a wake-up call that would prepare the minds of the public for the fight to the death against Britain's global rivals that they believed imminent. Maxse, Garvin and Blennerhasset were not alone in their uncertainty about whether England could survive the twentieth century.[169] All these themes spoke to the pervasive idea of efficiency. And as a unique model of efficiency, the German Reich found itself at the heart of a debate that fundamentally determined London political discourse across all political parties.[170]

'A.B.C. etc.': Political Journals and the Reorientation of Foreign Policy

These four central themes addressed Britain's potential over-extension and provided a possible formula for the self-assertion of the Empire in the twentieth century. At the beginning of that century, analysis of foreign policy and debates over the strategic implications of these themes were ubiquitous in the London political press and even beyond. Tradition and experience were pushed to one side, to be replaced increasingly by expectations for the future, which increasingly also determined the paths that decision makers might follow. These paths were much discussed by influential journals, among them the *Nineteenth Century* and the *Contemporary Review*, and by the *Review of Reviews*, the *Fortnightly Review*, the *Spectator* or *Saturday Review*, the *Outlook* and a number of other daily papers.

The dominance of the Social Darwinian premise that international affairs were primarily about a struggle that only the fittest of global empires would survive[171] led Salisbury's traditional English foreign policy to be criticized as aimless 'muddling through', as piecemeal work that lacked any 'grand design'.[172] Domestic policy and foreign policy were to be considered together and a comprehensive solution was required. The Social and Political Education League was not alone in seeing in the backlog of domestic reforms parallels with the decline and fall of Rome. While demands were heard for a long-overdue constructive reordering of internal affairs,[173] plans were drafted for a new phase in foreign policy that would see a globally construed alliance with Russia and the United States. Racial Anglo-Saxon thinking had its part to play here, as did the firm conviction that with the establishment of the Dual Alliance, Russia was now in a position to become the hegemon of Europe. Although a number of authors were clearly aware of the potential negative repercussions[174] – on the Central Powers, for example – remarkably not only was there little talk of a classical response that would have seen the creation of a counterweight, but when that possibility was raised, it was rejected as all too unpredictable.

In the *Contemporary Review*, Fred T. Jane for example painted a picture of how he believed the future might look. Although a dominant Anglo-Russian alliance remained, he proposed, 'a canvas too daring to be yet painted', such imaginings were not utterly utopian. Such an arrangement, with all its advantages, was not to be rejected out of hand. Germany, France, Austria and Italy could not be relied upon to play a role on the world stage in the approaching century, and therefore the tasks of the future would not be tackled with their assistance. Jane believed, however, that as the interests of England and Russia were so very different and ran in parallel, with no risk of collision, the long-sought millennium of eternal peace could be launched by these two powers together. He recognized that the greatest obstacle to this plan was the existing widespread scepticism about Russia, and therefore proposed that a new emphasis be brought to bear, turning away from experiences that were predominantly negative and looking instead to future possibilities. An Anglo-Russian alliance would surely lead to the exclusion of Japan and Germany and the collapse of the Great Power system in Europe, suggested Jane, but even if every moral code and all of tradition spoke against such a relationship, it remained without doubt in the imperial interests of Great Britain. To tread the path towards a lasting global system, England would have to free herself of her European traditions.[175] As referee of the balance of power in Europe, Britain ran the risk that her global empire would be torn apart when she decided in favour of one or other of the parties on the continent.

Ever since the creation of the alliance between France and Russia, the situation in Europe had been extremely precarious. Jane proceeded with his diagnosis: France was the richest nation, but her population was too small; Germany's population was certainly greater, but economically dependent, and if its population continued to grow at the same rate, then Germany would soon be in need of greater elbow room; Italy was bankrupt; Austria-Hungary lived from hand to mouth and hovered on the brink of the abyss; Turkey could not be tolerated as an independent state; and the United States had many irons in the fire of international relations. While Great Britain, Jane wrote, 'drifts about like the rest in this sea of trouble', only Russia needed not fear even a single external enemy. For these reasons, he advised, 'Let us leave out the consideration of the past. ... There is absolutely no point in which we cannot treat, independently of all other nations direct with Russia upon matters concerning our joint interests with her'.[176] The Habsburg Empire would sooner or later have to fall into the Slav orbit and there was no reason 'why England should attempt to thwart Russia's policy in Turkey'.[177] Russia, Jane suggested, had behaved in a gentlemanly manner for years, a remarkable conclusion that despite so much evidence to the contrary now gained a life of its own.

Why Jane sought to curry favour with Russia, which had behaved with neither restraint nor courtesy in Alaska, Egypt, Abyssinia, Siam and Persia, was stated openly: the Franco-Russian alliance could help itself at any time to the global empire and England would only be able to look on helplessly. In Jane's opinion, 'It is in our own interest to make advances, and give her [Russia] what she wants of our own accord'.[178] Jane acknowledged that

> peace would probably not be preserved in this way; the formal adhesion of England to the Franco-Russian alliance would mean such a preponderance of naval and military power that the Triple Alliance would be reduced to such intolerable insignificance that she could not afford to keep the peace.[179]

Yet while London would run the risk of conflict with the Central Powers, she would at least have bought some time when it came to Russia, the most dangerous opponent. A number of commentators found in an alliance with France a possibility of averting a war that seemed unavoidable, for France might exert a moderating influence on its Russian partner.[180]

Numerous critics spoke out against this somewhat gloomy prognosis and against Anglo-Russian rapprochement, which might have global implications but would simultaneously neglect the stability of the continent, and their concerns did not go unheard. Lucien Wolf, alias Diplomaticus, the foreign editor of the *Daily Graphic*, Frederick Greenwood, a well-known philosopher, and Emile

Joseph Dillon, Russian correspondent of the *Daily Telegraph*, commentator on foreign affairs for the *Contemporary Review* and an intimate of Count Witte, the Russian minister of finance, all repeatedly warned of the rise of Russia and of the systemic consequences of bridge building across the width of the continent. Greenwood advised remaining calm in the face of Germany's ambitions, whereas until the outbreak of the Russo-Japanese war, Dillon canvassed alternately for membership of the Triple Alliance and for a policy that would maintain the balance of power against the weight of Russia and bring a colonial settlement.[181] Greenwood, by contrast, called vehemently for Britain's entry into the Triple Alliance, since, in his view, despite all the difficulties generated by the Krüger telegram, international stability remained the priority. He saw Britain as dutybound to stand by its allies of many years, even resisting when necessary the pressure of the new Dual Alliance. Greenwood believed Germany's annoyance at English egoism to be completely understandable, reminding his readership that the Triple Alliance was a stabilizing influence and a guarantor of peace, 'maintained at the cost and risk of Germany, Austria and Italy'.[182] For decades, he believed, England had been the greatest beneficiary of this alliance. The anger at England and the new demonstrative policy adopted by the Central Powers were absolutely logical and consistent. The Central Powers saw therein their only chance of maintaining the status quo as long as Great Britain insisted on remaining *tertius gaudens* in *European* questions, making no contribution of its own. In an alliance with Russia, London would be no more than a junior partner, with that alliance nothing more than 'a purchase of a promise for peace'. The decision to enter such an alliance could be based only on such a promise and certainly not on experience, as throughout its long history Russia had shown itself to be anything but trustworthy.[183] A.J. Wilson, the historian John Mahaffy and John Morley, a well-known politician, emphasized in their contributions that Great Britain had only herself to blame for the current international predicament, which they believed to be the result of years of arrogant behaviour.[184]

After the Boer War, however, such statements, in all their variety, were increasingly few and far between. Louder and much more prominent were the voices of the group around Maxse, Garvin and Strachey, which month after month in various publications demanded once-and-for-all solutions for the coming century, warned of the tremendous size of the Russian nation and of its invulnerability, and insisted that the fate of the Empire depended on rapprochement. If England did not wish to have sunk to the level of a third-class power by the year 2001, wrote Garvin in January 1901, then England must at last wake up and begin a thoroughgoing reform; he continued: 'The real task and best chance of success will be the struggle with Germany for the second place behind the US and Russia'.[185] Although there was still time in hand, he believed, preparations must be launched with all haste, beginning, he proposed, with a new prime minister, the implementation of a three-power standard, the introduction of universal conscription, and a firm alliance with Russia, which would then dominate the world.[186]

Soon after, an essay in Strachey's *Spectator* proved so sensational that Thomas Sanderson brought it to the attention of the foreign secretary. The analysis of the situation was all the more surprising because it appeared in a journal that was not thought particularly pro-German. Sanderson's accompanying note suggests that the permanent under-secretary shared the author's assessment of the situation.[187] The essay that appeared in this influential weekly publication spoke of a German nightmare:

> We English constantly forget it, because we at once admire and slightly dread the action of the German Emperor, but no people are anything like so dangerously situated as the Germans, who at three days' notice may all be fighting for their lives. ... We English get panics occasionally, but we have always a secret confidence in the sea.

Situated at the heart of the continent, not only did Germany not enjoy the same sense of security as Britain, but in comparison with other powers, too, Germany came off more poorly. Although the Austrians certainly had many internal problems in their multinational state to bemoan, the text continued, unlike the Germans, they had only one real enemy, and one whom at present they could even call a friend. The over-anxious French were vulnerable only on one side and not only did their long history suggest that they were well able to defeat their arch-enemy, but they were also allied to an invincible power that at any time could fall upon and destroy their only enemy. The Germans, however, could be attacked at any time on two sides, and by the strongest and largest armies in Europe at that.[188] Britain faced nothing like such a threat. And indeed, the article added, the latest information indicated that thanks to a new deployment of troops, the tsar was now even in a position to send several armies across the eastern frontier of Germany simultaneously within just twenty-four hours. 'Just think', the author enjoined his readers, 'what that means':

> It means not that 'Russia would be opposed to Germany', which is the way Diplomatists and Journalists put it, but that the most numerous Army in the world, drawn from a population three times that of Germany, would be on German soil ravaging, shooting, burning, levying contributions, and to give it its full credit, fighting desperately hard. Victory might remain with German science, but the loss of life in a succession of Zorndorffs[189] would be something appalling.

Britain must always remember that this 'Russian terror' necessarily dictated German policy. It was understandable that Germany would hope for tension between England and Russia, for such circumstances would at least divert some of the pressure from Russia. For the very sake of its country's self-preservation, the German government could not join in an alliance against Russia. For all these reasons, the *Spectator* held that Germany's militarism, much criticized in Britain, and her universal conscription should be understood not as evidence of that country's aggressive intentions but as existential necessities: Germany's three million soldiers found themselves wedged between nine and a half million Russian and French soldiers hungry for revenge. The *Spectator* brought its message home: 'We say our free system is better, and it is under our circumstances; but if five millions of our strongest enemies could enter Lincolnshire at will, while another two millions were divided from Hampshire by no sea, we take it that the young man who resisted conscription would be deemed a traitor'.[190]

But what did this assessment mean for Britain's policy with regard to Germany? With such analysis of the situation in mind, some prominent voices certainly continued to speak of support for the German Empire or the Triple Alliance. Balfour, Sanderson and Lansdowne were among this grouping, at least on occasion, as was Russophobe George Curzon, who was primarily motivated, however, by imperial concerns. Pro-German Frank Lascelles, for many years ambassador to Berlin, and Lansdowne's brother, Edmond Fitzmaurice, who was critical of Russia, also favoured the traditional course.[191] The *Spectator*'s view was shared by Jean de Bloch, a well-known military theoretician. He, too, was certain that Germany was the most vulnerable nation on the continent and in the long run would be unable to counter the Dual Alliance. He held Italy to be a complete loss and believed that partnership with Austria-Hungary would be pointless as that country would not be able to withstand Russia and France. Moreover, in the years since 1870, the military strength of Germany in relation to its neighbours had fallen by some 70 per cent and the supposed prosperity of the Reich was simply a delusion, since it was entirely based on debt.[192]

For future *Weltpolitik*, the continental situation seems to have appeared increasingly less important, since Germany apparently had no inclination to act as a junior partner, which might have meant, for example, that Germany could be encouraged to push against Russia in the Far East and Middle East. Lurking behind the position adopted in the *Spectator* and the *National Review* and in many other pieces with a similar assessment of the situation was the conclusion that Germany would sooner or later join the Dual Alliance. At the very point when Germany was still seeking rapprochement with London, supposedly weak Germany's dependence on Russia was being declared inevitable. Six months later, the *National Review* renewed its demand that in its own interests Britain move closer to the stronger Franco-Russian bloc and look to raise tension between Germany and Russia. Not only was the potential material gain for Britain's own security noted, but a number of individuals, including Rowland Blennerhasset, also insisted that its current situation would naturally soon force Germany to become an ally of Russia and hence an enemy of Britain. London's only possible move, Blennerhasset proposed, was to pre-empt this development by enticing Russia away with concessions. Austria-Hungary could not survive in any case – sooner or later it would be divided up in the Darwinian race involving Russia, the Balkan states and Germany.[193]

What, we might well wonder, did the decision makers think when they read such proposals and prognoses? Balfour and Sanderson undoubtedly rejected any such course. They looked for guidance to experience rather than expectation and were therefore extremely sceptical of Russia. And Balfour even stressed England's continental obligations.[194]

Edward Grey, the later foreign secretary, was of a different opinion. Prime evidence comes from, of all places, Maxse's most spectacular new venture, which garnered both national and international attention. In November and December 1901, Maxse started his anti-German and pro-Russian 'A.B.C. etc.' campaign. The first articles to appear under this pseudonym were entitled 'British Foreign Policy' and 'Some Thoughts of an Anglo-Russian Understanding'. These writings were expressly labelled the 'handiwork of several patriotic writers',[195] with the authors seemingly united in their eagerness to promote a reorientation of British foreign policy towards France and Russia and against the Central Powers.[196] A series of articles thus initiated would run irregularly from 1901 to 1914 and had enormous impact.[197] Moreover, each was delivered as an offprint in advance and free of charge to every significant editor and government department.[198] Paul Wolff-Metternich zur Gracht, the popular and interconnected German ambassador to London,[199] claimed that even the Russian government received advance copies.[200] Maxse's aim was to 'educate' the broadest and most influential readership possible,[201] and the time could hardly have been better, for at this very moment the German and English media were feuding over Joseph Chamberlain's disputed comments on the Prussian army and the Wars of Unification.

In concrete terms, the articles were concerned with propagating a comprehensive alliance with Russia and France against Germany. In addition to recognition of Russian ambitions in the Far East, St Petersburg was to be allowed a free hand for its historical mission in the Balkans; in return, Russia would guarantee the status quo in Egypt.[202] The sensation caused by the A.B.C. etc. articles can be explained not only by their highly explosive content, but also by the careful planning that was invested in them and by the mystery of their origins and authorship. While Paul Cambon, the French ambassador to London, suspected Blennerhasset was behind them[203] and the Paris *Matin* claimed to have recognized Lord Lansdowne as their author,[204] German investigations had reached the conclusion that the authors concealed behind the pseudonym 'A.B.C.' were probably Maxse, Blennerhasset and Sergei Tatistchev, a Russian financial agent in London.[205] For the influential *Times* at any rate the articles were proof enough 'that many persons, thoroughly informed about our external policies, have been arriving slowly, and, perhaps reluctantly, at the same conclusions'.[206] As was to be expected, the *Spectator* also judged the content of the articles positively.[207]

The first two articles were without doubt a joint production of several authors. No conservative politicians were among those authors, however, contrary to a recent suggestion.[208] Lord Salisbury certainly received a first draft, although he made no comment on it.[209] Rosebery, too, expressed no opinion.[210] All the more intense, then, were the exchanges with Tatistchev, who not only received a draft but also promised to see that it was passed on via Sergei Witte,[211] and with Rowland Blennerhasset,[212] Edward Cook, editor of the *Daily News*,[213] George Saunders,[214] Arthur Ponsonby,[215] William Tyrrell[216] and with Charles Hardinge and Edward Grey. The exchange with the last two named, who would later be responsible for England's foreign policy and in particular for the Anglo-Russian convention, is of particular interest. Hardinge was the first to congratulate Maxse on his initial version, which still had the title 'The Future British Policy' when he received it. Hardinge wished the article every possible success. With his many years as ambassador to Teheran, he wrote, he believed Russia's desire to reach an agreement to be sincere. However, Maxse was right, he continued, that generous concessions would be necessary, for Russian ambitions would never be satisfied if Russia did not receive a port on the Gulf as well as the prospect of a railway to Bandar Abbas. He was therefore less inclined to be concerned about the Afghanistan question and with regard to the Near East and the Balkans considered a demonstrative policy of 'désintéressement' on England's part to be the best solution.[217]

Edward Grey's comments and corrections are also very telling. The then liberal speaker on foreign policy and later foreign minister found the article altogether 'most valuable' and hoped it would have a wide impact, shaking the people out of their current lethargy. He commented, 'My notes will not repay you in kind for the interest I have had in reading the article'.[218] He continued:

> It ought to stir the people to think. We have lost the habit of thinking to any purpose about foreign affairs. ... It seems to me that Lord Salisbury, who thinks deeply, does so without purpose, and Chamberlain, who is full of purpose, doesn't think deep. They would be a formidable combination, but they don't combine, and so we suffer from the defects of both; .... The opposition is of course still impossible and my only hope for the immediate future is to see the present Government resign and an entirely new one formed out of the best elements to be found on the present treasury benches and behind them.[219]

Grey also saw no reason why the anti-German statements of the second article, which he likewise amended, 'should not find expression in organs of public opinion here'. He considered it far more important to avoid annoying Russia, and indeed felt drawing closer to that country was the way forward. Germany could only be a hindrance to such rapprochement and therefore it was important 'to eliminate in that quarter the German broker, who keeps England and Russia apart and levies a constant communication upon us while preventing us from doing any business with Russia'. But, he continued, 'this will have to be done quietly and cautiously'. This precise wording was adopted into the final version of the article as it appeared in the *National Review*.

Grey's indirect involvement is even clearer from a comparison of the amendments suggested and the final text, from which the first draft can be reconstructed in part. Maxse's rough draft contained ten separate points explaining the benefits of an Anglo-Russian alliance; Grey condensed this list to cover the four vital regions: the Far East, Persia, Central Asia and the Near East. He expressed his particular pleasure at and approval of Maxse's inclusion of France:

> The French are one of the very few nations, if not the only one, which will make sacrifices and run risks for the sake of a friend and which is capable of sentimental attachment; it is a pity that the suspicion of instability always attaches to them.[220]

This passage appeared word for word in the published version in the *National Review*.[221] And Grey considered it extremely important for these arguments to be read by both Russia and France:[222]

> By all means have the article published; it is most interesting and must do good. I long to see an Anglo-Russian understanding to defeat the German policy of keeping her [Russia] opposed to us. ... The idea, in face of the Franco-Russian alliance, of supporting ourselves against either Russia or France by an alliance with Germany is rotten. ... Your article will do something to remove Russian suspicion.[223]

George Saunders and Arthur Ponsonby were among those who ensured the article reached a wide audience.[224] They were eager that it should gain the attention of influential Russians above all. Tatistchev promised to send the article on to Count Witte; Ponsonby passed it on to Benckendorff; John Dalton, an intimate of Edward VII's, promised to have a copy sent to the tsar.[225] One month later, Maxse followed up with an article entitled 'Consequences of an Anglo-Russian Understanding', which also passed through the hands of members of the most important circles.[226]

Subsequent articles discussed in some detail the aims and consequences of such a policy. Taking up the opportunity afforded by the second A.B.C. article, Garvin supported its arguments in the liberal *Fortnightly Review*, where he wrote that Russia's failure to react was an obvious sign that England had to offer more; London must be willing to proffer up Persia and the Near East.[227] The practical import of Grey's words was always present: Germany should be eliminated as broker between the powers to her east and west and direct negotiations with St Petersburg and Paris should be launched.[228] The isolation of Berlin quickly became part of public discourse about future foreign policy.[229] The wording used by Eyre Crowe in his well-known memorandum of New Year's Day 1907 repeated almost verbatim argumentation that had appeared in the *National*

Review six years earlier.²³⁰ Repeatedly we see stated, even if between the lines, that the threat from Germany lay not in her strength but, indirectly, in her potential role as a partner for a Franco-Russian grouping. Germany may have been too weak to merit her receiving any concessions in a global context, but the Reich could make all the difference to a continental alliance. Germany's current position suggested two conflicting possibilities for English policy: London could maintain its links to Berlin and support Germany, or London could seek the systematic isolation of the Reich. Whichever course was adopted, Germany's relations with its neighbours to the west and the east would remain strained. Even if a product of weakness, rather than strength, a continental alliance must be prevented at all costs. After the Krüger telegram incident, Maxse had opted for the isolation variant, a view that was evidently becoming increasingly popular among potential decision makers at a time when a lack of nuance in German diplomacy, which would be evident during the two Moroccan crises and the naval armament race, was not yet apparent.

In January 1902, another article with which Grey had been involved also caused a sensation.²³¹ When his party colleague Joseph Walton consequently moved in the House of Commons that this 'succession of articles of a most astonishing character' be discussed, Grey feigned a lack of prior knowledge but expressed his agreement with the tenor of the articles. Speaking from the opposition benches, he criticized the government's policy, which he believed irresponsible, as the 'policy of drift'.²³² Salisbury's cabinet was attacked in this new article, with a particular focus on Lansdowne, the foreign secretary, and was warned in no uncertain terms against pursuing a friendly policy towards Berlin.

> The British foreign policy of the future must work for the isolation of Germany. Then, co-operation from the continental powers would be assured, not against, but for Great Britain. It must always be remembered that German policy is menacing the whole world.²³³

That German menace was to be found not in specific aggressive undertakings but in Treitschke's notoriously anti-British view of history and the world. The very laws of nature, readers were informed, made Prussia-Germany per se synonymous with enmity towards the Empire and the British nation.²³⁴ Like Edward Grey at the Coefficients and later as foreign secretary, the *National Review* argued that the 'ABC' and the 'XYZ' of British policy on Europe must be to add Russia to the Entente Cordiale, turning that alliance into an effective power bloc. The only alternative, at the other extreme, was held to be the creation of an anti-British continental power bloc.²³⁵

Opposition from among those to whom Maxse had sent the articles came in particular from Gertrude Bell, Valentine Chirol and, rather surprisingly, Eyre Crowe, for whom the evidence presented was far too one-sided and anti-German.

Eyre Crowe, of all people, commented that such constant ingratiation with Russia would have serious implications for England's ability to negotiate, and that Maxse was greatly mistaken if he thought that the difficulties between Russia and England could be resolved simply with a little good will and common sense; for years, Eyre Crowe insisted, England had been trying to reach an agreement with Russia and had reached the bounds of what could be deemed reasonable.

> The answers are always in the nature of studied insults, and the most transparent lies and frauds are palmed off on us .... There is not the slightest indication that there is on the part of any Russian party or authority the slightest desire for a good understanding with us. And you do not realize how very seriously our position is weakened by the constant overtures made to Russia by our press, begging for a good understanding.[236]

The weight that Maxse's commentary carried is evident in the roll call of those involved with the A.B.C. texts.[237] After its successful campaigns against Anglo-German cooperation in the Venezuela crisis and in the matter of the Baghdad railway, the *National Review*, also called 'NAT'[238] soon became one of the most influential of political papers. In early 1905, Sidney Low was already singing its praises: 'I think without doubt it is more read and more quoted than any other Review, … it exercises a more important influence on public opinion than any other similar publication'.[239] The *National Review* owed its influence above all to Maxse's political contacts and its presentation of its material. Politicians such as Viscount Esher used the journal as a platform 'because people read it and they don't read the others'.[240] The young cohort of liberal imperialists in particular had quickly recognized and increasingly deployed that potential. Shortly before taking up the reins of government, Asquith had even promised Maxse that he would make Maxse's paper a mouthpiece of the new government.[241] In addition, Maxse maintained his close contact with Charles Hardinge, Eyre Crowe, Cecil Spring Rice, William Tyrrell and others. He had long been part of a regular exchange of views on foreign policy with Edward Grey at the Coefficients, and now experts such as Spenser Wilkinson and Alfred Thayer Mahan were very ready to fall into line with Maxse's editorial requirements; in place of objective analysis, they now wrote to order.[242] Other periodicals adopted the tenor of the articles and painted Germany in an ever more threatening light. And the frequent anti-Jewish pogroms in Russia passed by without comment, while reports on developments in Russia more generally were very rosy.[243]

Not until 1907, with the foundation of the radical liberal *Nation*, was there any push back among political publications against the opinions promulgated in the *National Review*,[244] and to date studies of foreign policy have paid very little attention to this particular journal.[245] In marked contrast to the general tenor of the English press, the *Nation* advised caution in dealings with Russia and wrote of a loose concert solution as far preferable to any system based on the formation of political power blocs. Above all, as we will see in the analysis of Edward Grey's foreign policy, the *Nation* was critical of Grey's repeated indulgence of Russia. The paper also campaigned against the absurd suggestions that accompanied the hysteria about invasion and spying, and against the associated exaggerations about the German fleet,[246] which it unmasked as pure propaganda in favour of building up Britain's military capability.[247] In February 1908, in the midst of a renewed Committee of Imperial Defence (CID) investigation, the *Nation* pronounced its unambiguous verdict: 'It is the writers, not the sailors, who have largely poisoned the Anglo-German situation'.[248] No less a figure than Garvin himself confirmed that judgement when he wrote, 'If the German scare helps us to get an extra Dreadnought, as seems most likely, then the work of the last four months will have done the best it could',[249] identifying in turn the motivation behind the argumentation found in the *National Review* and other papers. Rather than return repeatedly to the complicated dialectic of a policy purportedly aimed at a balance of power, journals of the radical right preferred sensationalist announcements of the German threat, which must be countered. But it was not left to journalists alone to mould political opinion in London through enemy stereotypes. While the *National Review* reported without a hint of misgiving sensational stories about German spies who cycled along the south coast of England inspecting every railway line and every possible landing place,[250] here was the stuff of another genre – literature of invasion and espionage.

The Power of Fiction: Invasion and Espionage Fever

For Walter Bagehot, Victorian theoretician of the state and editor of the *Economist*, ages, like nations, had their own unmistakable character. That Zeitgeist, he believed, was clearly expressed by particular writers of the age, but his reference was not necessary to the literary geniuses. The credo of an epoch was more likely to be found in works that were less original in character, and also less polished, whose authors were principally concerned with the number of copies sold and with communicating particular ideas. According to Bagehot, 'They seize on the public mind, and ... catch the words that are in the air and the rhythm which comes to them they do not know from whence'.[251]

The rhythm of England at the turn of the century can without doubt be found most readily in the innumerable adventure stories that as a so-called 'literature of action' created a new genre at the end of the nineteenth century, with its titles appearing frequently on the bestseller lists. England, and especially the younger generation, had become much concerned with the maintenance of the Empire and the security of the Mother Country,[252] and one product of that preoccupation was found in innumerable, predominantly politically motivated tales of espionage and invasion. Reflected in these works were both a strong push for self-assertion and an insecurity and scepticism about the future. Like the journalists who wrote for the daily, weekly and monthly press, politicizing novelists were not simply compliant participants; they forced their own wake-up call on Britain.[253]

While there was undoubtedly no systematic pressure, either private or public, English literature provided a useful malleability as far as choice of theme and content was concerned.[254] The majority of these authors were inspired by the daily exchanges of social and political life in London. In turn, the myths and legends that they peddled not only conveyed a growing self-doubt but also increasingly provided the motive for political decisions. National images and stereotypes were common themes, and especially when it came to Germany such representations often replaced the facts of foreign or security policy to provide vehicles for reinterpreting the evidence and spreading rumours. Thus, while Germany feared encirclement and an attack under the command of Fisher, the fiery First Sea Lord,[255] England trembled at least until around 1910 almost daily at warnings of an imminent invasion, presented all too credibly. Even ten years before the July Crisis, British readers of newspapers or novels believed that thousands of German spies, disguised as waiters, hairdressers and salesmen, had taken their measure of the island, down to the last inch, in preparation for an invasion.

In 1870, historian Frederick William Maitland reported that Germans were still customarily characterized in English literature as an impractical, somewhat dreamy and sentimental folk, 'looking out with mild blue eyes into a cloud of music, metaphysics and tobacco smoke'.[256] By the time Maitland's letters were published, in 1911, short story writer Katherine Mansfield was painting a very different picture. In her first collection of essays, *In a German Pension*, she returned in a short story entitled 'Germans at Meat' to the blue-eye image, but now these eyes were anything but mild and good-natured; they were cold and dangerous, 'with an expression which suggested a thousand premeditated invasions'.[257] In the same year, popular patriotic poet Rudyard Kipling[258] took up the allegory of the blue eyes and depicted how the 'Teutons' were only waiting to attack England at the first possible opportunity.[259] The spiked helmet had replaced the good-natured *Michel* to become the symbol of German power to strike. The transformation of the image of Germany can be traced dramatically in the development from Maitland's good-natured Germans to the cold and aggressive Germans of Mansfield and Kipling. Whereas Maitland had had an apolitical romantic land of poets and thinkers in his mind's eye, the two younger authors emphasized the unambiguously aggressive aspirations of the young Reich.

But if that was not already enough, Mansfield blatantly imputed to Wilhelmine Germany the intention to invade. That possibility had shaken society back to life after the Boer War, but it had also led to a stubborn and irrational Germanophobia, an attitude based on stereotypes. The English image of Germany had much to do with the circumstances of English society and politics and had a complex effect on bilateral relations. In light of such internal circumstances, the view, still dominant today, that proposes that England was forced to react in response to the threat from Germany must be reconsidered,[260] and public perceptions of danger compared with the views of experts, based on fact.

Symptomatic of the instability at the beginning of the new century, Germany began to morph from rival into enemy. Gradually, and not only in the sensational press but also in political writings, Germany would take the role previously held by the Franco-Russian alliance.[261] Until the first two years of the new century, concerns about France's naval manoeuvres or the threat posed by Russia in Central Asia still dominated the political as well as the public scenery.[262] William Thomas Stead thought he could see England punished for the war against the Boers when he prophesied that the French Tricolour would soon be flying over the Palace of Westminster.[263] Depictions of the tsardom remained dark and barbaric. William Le Queux's first bestseller of 1894, published as the Franco-Russian alliance was made public, dealt with an invasion by Britain's two arch-enemies, with a gigantic army marauding through the cities of England. Here, still, was the traditional nineteenth-century English image of Russia, as barbaric, uncivilized and Asiatic.[264] Some influential editors and journalists, among them Leo Maxse, Donald Mackenzie Wallace and Emile Dillon, were already endeavouring to throw a more positive light on this picture of the tsardom and to relativize it by pointing to Germany.[265] Spying Russians were still the protagonists in Rudyard Kipling's 1901 novel *Kim*, but soon German spies would suddenly appear in a multitude of adventure stories.[266] Established authors proved extremely skilled at intensifying the insecurity generated by the Boer War by shifting their focus from threats to the Empire to write instead of a more original fear, its origins reaching back to Napoleon, of a possible invasion of the Mother Country itself. Just as Germany feared encirclement, Britain talked of home defence, looking to her continental neighbours as the real threat to her security. At the same time, however, such thoughts conjured up memories of England's greatest victories, and the possibility that they could be repeated. Imminent danger and confident self-assertion repeatedly appeared as two sides of the same coin. Negative intentions and plans for an invasion were read from Germany's strength, economic power, methodical efficiency and impetuous actions. While tabloids such as the *Daily Mail* and socialist papers such as the *Clarion* first focused on the economic competition presented by Germany, in an attempt to win over workers who might fear unemployment,[267] liberal and conservative papers explored the political and military threat posed by the Reich with a newfound intensity, greater even than that present in the anti-Russian or anti-French writings of the 1890s. Although war-like intentions were to be expected of one's arch-rivals, it was especially shocking that a traditionally friendly nation, a nation viewed in some respects as a kindred spirit and much admired, might turn against Britain.

The age of Germanophobic invasion and espionage literature was launched in 1899 with the publication of Headon Hill's *The Spies of the Wight*.[268] Hill presented an account of the underhand betrayal of a friendly nation. German spies had wormed their way into the lives of the unsuspecting and peace-loving English and were awaiting their chance to attack. This particular form of treachery would become a regular stylistic feature when Germany was involved. Many authors, among them notable writers such as H(erbert) G(eorge) Wells, Joseph Conrad, Arthur Conan Doyle and the aforementioned Katherine Mansfield, fell into line in with similar scenarios, creating a new genre that centred on the theme of invasion.[269] In Albert Curtis's fictive work *A New Trafalgar* – the allusion to the great fear of Napoleonic invasion, around for a century, could hardly have been clearer – Great Britain was saved only by a wondrous new ship.[270]

Barely a year later, the most famous of all espionage and invasion stories, *The Riddle of the Sands*, became the first real bestseller of this new genre. The author, Erskine Childers, worked as a parliamentary clerk from 1895 until 1910, served during the Boer War, made his mark with repeated proposals for military reform, and also wrote the fifth volume of the well-known *Times* series on war, initiated by his friend, politician and journalist Leo Amery.[271] Later, such was the grotesque and tragic irony of his life, he was revealed during the war to be a double agent who among various activities as a fervid Irish Nationalist had smuggled German weapons into Ireland. In 1922, he was arrested on a charge of high treason and summarily shot. His work was a typical espionage story of the age, symptomatic of growing mistrust of Germany, enthusiastically endorsed by the popular press, and had clear pedagogic purpose. The enthusiastic reader found an imagined account of German preparations for an invasion of England, with a narrative based on precise, official-sounding, topographical knowledge.[272] Like Childers himself, his two heroes, Carruthers and Davies, are amateur yachtsmen. During a sailing trip and almost by accident, they uncover German plans for an invasion, which are discussed in the novel in detail, providing a genuine sense of the military possibilities.[273] Childers had published his work in the style of a serious and fact-based account, and the result, unlike earlier novels, was able to fool some readers; it not only brought about a veritable storm of protest among the public and innumerable letters to the editor, but it also prompted an official investigation. The first discussion of the book in the *Times Literary Supplement* commented on the usefulness of its observations for the Admiralty and War Office. Childers gave his story a veneer of truth by adding a preface and epilogue and by naming himself only the editor of the work.[274] He maintained that he had endeavoured to conceal the identity of the English characters but called on the reader to remember 'that these persons are now living in the midst of us'. His epilogue ends with an exhortation: 'The time has come for training all Englishmen systematically either for the sea or for the rifle'.[275]

That Childers' story sparked a process that saw fiction become a presence in the political sphere and stir up political passions is evident from the example of Lord Selborne, the then First Lord of the Admiralty. Selborne was essentially down to earth and restrained, and not at all given to panic, but even he was initially unsettled by the enormous success of *The Riddle of the Sands*. Even though German naval build-up was hardly a blip on the horizon, he felt compelled to have a copy of Childers' work sent to Admiral Louis Battenberg (DNI), the head of naval defence, for careful examination.

> I have several times spoken to you about a book called 'The Riddle of the Sands', and I think you told me that ... it had been examined in your Department. ... It is very remarkable how many people have been struck by it and who constantly come to me about it. The last who did so was Sir William White,[276] who was immensely impressed by it. ... Unless the book was examined by an officer in whom you have complete confidence ..., I shall be greatly obliged if you will again have it examined thoroughly.[277]

Journalism took an easier route. John St. Loe Strachey of the *Spectator* had warmly recommended the story of Carruthers and Davies to his fellow countrymen. For Strachey, closer examination was not necessary before he pronounced, without any sign of doubt, that the work was clearly not fictional, but 'based on a solid groundwork of facts'. In any case, vitally, it was a book with a mission: 'we are so persuaded by Mr Childers' cunning to take it seriously'.[278] While the paper *To-Day* remained somewhat uncertain whether it was 'fiction in the guise of reality, or reality in the guise of fiction', the *Birmingham Post* stepped forward to proclaim Childers' work the book of the year.[279] Backed by such hymns of praise, copies sold out very quickly and even a third edition could not long assuage the thirst in London. For experts, however, the proposal fell flat. Battenberg could hardly have been clearer: 'As a novel, it is excellent, but as a war plan it is rubbish. It suggests a scheme of invasion, to be put into execution that instant war breaks out, and without reference to the Royal Navy. Apart from the unsoundness of the principle, the details are absurd'.[280]

Battenberg knew what he was talking about. Since the 1880s, he had been intensively involved with naval operations. Moreover, thanks to regular visits to the continent, he was well informed about the German navy, both its capabilities and its limitations.[281] Yet despite Battenberg's negative verdict, a discussion had now been launched that would be continued first in the CID and then in the Naval Intelligence Division (NID) and the Military Intelligence Division (MID) in the War Office. With the press setting the terms of that discussion, it continued without interruption until the end of the war and even beyond.

After the success of Childers' novel, the appearance of scare stories gained pace, right up until 1910. The frequency with which such works appeared, portraying events with apparent objectivity and in detail, along with the political seal of approval they were given by the military and politicians and by the National Service League in particular, helped ensure that no other country was under such intense scrutiny as Germany. Aggression by Germany, designed to ensure that country's dominance, gradually became part of everyday rhetoric among decision-making elites, as apparently long-established fact.[282]

Yet when Germany was considered objectively and German activities were compared to the actions of the United States, France or Russia, the Reich was hardly exceptional. Certainly, following détente with Paris and Washington, the alliance with Japan and the destruction of the Russian fleet, Germany remained the only threat, although an improbable threat at that.[283] All the more fortuitously, the German navy came nowhere near to rivalling the Franco-Russian threat of the 1890s.[284] On 20 October 1905, shortly before the change of government, even the Admiralty came to the optimistic conclusion that the Royal Navy dominated the world much as it had after its victory at Trafalgar, one hundred years earlier.[285] And yet, at the time of the change of government in 1906, longstanding and persistent rumours had ensured that the 'German peril'[286] had taken on a life of its own, interpreted, spread publicly and exploited in ways never experienced by the threat posed by Britain's traditional rivals, France and Russia.[287]

Alongside the influence exercised by the media, both socially and politically, England's security had ceased to be only a relative aim and had become instead an absolute goal. No longer was it sufficient for the existence of the English navy to make invasion seem improbable, or, as the investigations carried out by the CID suggested, even impossible. Invasion might be highly unlikely, but it was still necessary to be prepared.[288] Brodrick, the secretary of state for war, had declared that the possibility of invasion was 'an off-chance', but, he continued, 'you cannot run an Empire of this size on off-chances'.[289] Whether Britain could survive a maritime Colenso was a question frequently posed in the wake of the Boer War.[290] 'They told us that our navy was our all in all', as Charles Repington noted to Leo Maxse, 'but we thought differently when we got to the Drakensberg'.[291] Security experts such as George Sydenham Clarke, Admiral Louis Battenberg and Prime Minister Arthur Balfour considered absolute security to be a utopian dream and believed acceptance of a certain risk unavoidable; for Balfour, 'off-chances' were part and parcel of maintaining an empire.[292] These two points of view – relaxed Victorian acceptance of probabilities and Edwardian desire for predictability – embodied the poles of English security policy at the beginning of the twentieth century, with these political concerns taking their place alongside traditional inter-ministerial tensions.

The threat was no longer to Britain's imperial window dressing, in other words to colonial possessions or trade rights for which compensation could be sought; now the Mother Country itself was at risk. Caricatures in *Punch* had changed easy-going *Michel*'s expression of earlier days into a hideous grimace, and this fearful representation gradually acquired cult status, becoming an omnipresent polar opposite of that original image. By autumn 1905, the public's attitude to Germany had reached such a low point that a number of prominent figures, often with family ties to Germany, resolved to establish a fraternal Anglo-German friendship society.[293] Such efforts proved relatively ineffectual. Germany was all too useful for both the press and the new policy of entente. Its performance as enemy par excellence was too good for a short run. Fabian Ware, head editor of the *Morning Post*, was pointed and succinct: 'To allay fears of Germany is to throw away our only chance of getting the people here to bestir themselves.'[294] The Coefficients club saw a great need to 'aim at such supremacy upon the sea as would remove the possibility of invasion, holding that there was a moral value in the liability to such invasion'. Its members held up the example of Switzerland as evidence of the importance for the national character 'that every man is prepared to defend his home'.[295]

The German threat had thus become a stimulus for integration that would foster the sense of togetherness that all parties believed necessary. Certainly, sales figures played their part, but in addition to such practical concerns, many notable writers considered themselves on a mission. They made use of established stereotypes and negative images of Germany either to arouse awareness in Great Britain of an imminent danger in which they themselves only partly believed or to spur on long-demanded reforms. Whatever their cause, they were poisoning the political atmosphere of the pre-war period, and in so doing on occasion they considerably narrowed the options available to decision makers.

The literati, always happy to respond to the patriotic call, frequently allowed themselves be harnessed to the propaganda wagon, especially that driven by the National Service League (NSL). Their writings were designed to win over the public to the need for investment in armaments, particularly in the face of radical-liberal ideas of disarmament. The activities of Lord Frederick Sleigh Roberts, the popular war hero of Kandahar, were especially successful in this regard. At the end of 1905, outraged by Balfour's public equanimity, he resigned from the CID and as chairman of the NSL agitated throughout the country for universal conscription, frequently arguing his case on the grounds of an imminent invasion by Germany.[296] Instead of focusing his efforts on the reform of conscription, which was both complicated and unpopular, as he had done previously, Roberts, advised by Repington, adopted the 'German peril' as his simple and catchy propagandistic slogan. The NSL now concentrated on the rivalry between the German and English fleets, which the general public found somewhat abstract but for that very reason all the more exciting. Its membership suddenly soared, from 2,000 at the end of 1905 to more than 200,000 by 1914, including more than a hundred members of parliament. To those numbers we can add the 150,000 members of the Boy Scout movement.[297] By comparison, in the years up to 1914, the Navy League, which advocated for the retention of existing security-related measures, never had a membership greater than around 100,000.[298] And while the NSL, the War Office and the General Staff were in close cahoots, the Navy League had no direct access to the Admiralty and those at its head.[299]

At the heart of the movement formed around Roberts and the NSL was the assumption that Britain was suffering from a moral decline that could only be halted by an iron medieval discipline. This view was voiced during innumerable public appearances and could be read both in their own publications, such as the *National Defence*, and in Charles Repington's contributions in the *Times*, Strachey's *Spectator* and Maxse's *National Review*. Like Roberts, Maxse insisted on travelling the length and breadth of the country to give speeches, always of the same tenor, demanding discipline, a readiness for sacrifice, staunch character and patriotism and castigating the supposed decadence of urban life. Unlike Le Queux, Northcliffe and to some extent Repington, neither Maxse nor Roberts had personal profit in mind, although personal respect played its part. Their motivation came unambiguously from their militaristic and patriotic zeal. At the time of the Boer War, James Bryce had already considered Britain 'intoxicated with militarism, blinded by arrogance and indifferent to truth and justice',[300] and now that attitude gained a new dynamic. By 1910, more than 150 schools and universities had founded Officer Training Corps (OTCs) to compensate for the lack of conscription; a number are still existence today. While these novels had no original or valuable cultural contribution to make, just as British foreign relations adopted a specific character and orientation, they hammered home to the population and the next generation of military officers an enemy stereotype that was summed up simply as 'the Hun'.

One of the most talented, most famous and perhaps most influential visionaries among the politically active literati of London in those days was without doubt H.G. Wells.[301] As a co-founder and active member of the Coefficients, he had at his disposal excellent political contacts, and in his dystopias and his contemporary criticisms he kept pace with international politics like no other. On several occasions, Wells had already indirectly presented Germany as a threat for England, and years before the Entente Cordiale he was already calling for a close alliance with Paris and Rome. Nonetheless, unlike many of his fellow writers, he did not overlook Germany's geopolitical weakness. In his work *Anticipations*, published in 1901, he drew a sharp-sighted conclusion: 'Before Germany can unify to the East she must fight the Russians and to unify to the West she must fight the French and perhaps the English and she may have to fight a combination of these powers'.[302] In his works, Wells recorded the political reverberations of his time accurately, and his network of contacts ensured that his interpretation contained something of the political reality.[303] His observations, woven into his literary works, reflected the political trends of the moment and are therefore of considerable historiographical value, although their significance awaits a full investigation.

Wells' autobiography is very revealing of the thoughts and motives of the new London political elite as they passed their verdict on Germany and of the dichotomy they faced. The liberal imperialists, his principal source, were obsessed with a future major war for two reasons, he believed: first, Germany was a model of 'a bolder intellectual training and a harsher spirit'; and secondly, repeated scenarios full of foreboding seemed to be 'the only thing capable of bracing English minds to education, sustained constructive effort and research'. But, he conceded, a price would have to be paid for creating an atmosphere of panic, with over-hasty preparation, emotional impatience and an immediacy that was both extravagant and pointless. Yet, like Fabian Ware, Wells believed that the welfare of Britain required the guarantee of war, which alone could rouse England from its lethargy.[304] He was well aware of the impact on the public of narratives of invasion. He described George Meredith's *One of Our Conquerors*, published in 1898, as one of the most moving works ever and as a book that had left a lasting impact on his contemporaries, especially fellow members of the Coefficients and liberal imperialists, whom it had roused out of their stupor.[305] Convinced that Germany and England stood on the brink of war,[306] in *In the Days of the Comet*, Wells described the dangers of a German attack and called for an all-out alliance with France. The level of detail he included in his depictions of an Anglo-French agreement gives us cause to suspect that he had inside information on secret bilateral military talks of which even the radical members of the cabinet knew nothing; Colonel Repington, an acquaintance from the Coefficients would seem a possible source.[307]

While in 1906 Wells had been somewhat alarmed at the rapid alienation of Germany and England and had even been (self-)critical of the irresponsible agitation and polemics of the English press, by the time his next depiction of war appeared, in his 1908 work *The War in the Air*, any scruples on that front had vanished. Ten years earlier, in 1898, in his most famous work, *The War of the Worlds*, more indirectly the extra-terrestrial invaders had been endowed with an efficiency that evoked Germany. Now, however, the enemy was clearly and unmistakably Germany. One of the principal figures in the novel is Prince Karl Albert, whose character is modelled on the heroic ideals of Friedrich Nietzsche. Their prejudices already awakened, Wells' contemporaries would not have missed the significance of Wells' numerous allusions to 'Teutons'. Germany is depicted as a military state, armed to the teeth, and has acquired yet another terrible weapon in the form of an immense fleet of Zeppelins. Using this air power for an underhand attack on fraternal America, Germany triggers a world war.

In the public debate that followed, the politicization of the negative image of Germany knew no bounds. With the latest developments of the Zeppelin in mind, the Northcliffe press gratefully seized on Wells' depictions and posed their readership an existential question: could England still be counted an island? A discussion had been launched that would dominate the London gazettes throughout the summer of 1908 and refused to die down entirely in the years before the outbreak of the First World War. Again, the *Daily Mail* was the catalyst, but the quality press readily adopted its arguments and in part even its style.[308]

That novels and newspaper and journal articles had not only entertainment value, but also a part to play in economic and political calculations is made evident above all by two bestsellers by William Le Queux, *The Invasion of 1910* and *Spies for the Kaiser*. If the seal of approval from the military for *The Invasion of 1910* is insufficient to uphold that case, we can also note the book's proven political repercussions. Field-Marshall Lord Roberts, in part responsible, via the NSL, for the writing of the book, provided the preface, while H.W. Wilson, a well-known reporter on naval affairs,[309] provided chapters on the navy that gave the book an authority that enabled Le Queux's fiction to make the transition into the realm of the factual. These factors played a significant role in the book's success, with over a million copies sold. 'Though written in the form of fiction', the *Publisher's Circular* commented, 'the book is based on serious facts'.[310] Le Queux, who had previously written only penny dreadful of dubious quality,[311] now became the most-read author of those years, with his works translated into twenty-seven languages. His personal friendship with Northcliffe proved its worth when it came to both the writing and marketing of the book.[312] The press baron and owner of the *Daily Mail* had encouraged Le Queux to write on this topic and financed his months of research on the east coast. Northcliffe also introduced Le Queux to Roberts, who helped him greatly with his description of the German invasion:

> As a direct outcome of your Lordship's recent speech regarding our unpreparedness for war, I am about to write in the *Daily Mail* a dramatic forecast of what must happen in the case of an invasion, and it will no doubt have the effect of awakening the public to a sense of their insecurity. Instead of being a fantastic novel as was 'The Great War' this will be a *serious* [emphasis in original] description of an invasion in 1910, and in the writing of it I shall be assisted by several well-known naval and military experts. In addition I am about to visit the various districts where the supposed battles are to take place in order that the description shall be perfect in every detail.[313]

Roberts' passionate and meticulous work was scarcely reflected, however, in the final version of the novel itself. Le Queux and Roberts' military designs had a fatal flaw: none of the larger cities in which the *Daily Mail* was sold were affected by their plans. The German strategy they had so cleverly designed had to yield to Northcliffe's circulation figures.[314] Roberts, with his overcooked popularity as a national hero and bearer of the Victoria Cross, the highest military decoration in England, could bear the blow; what really mattered to him was that the book was read. Readers of the newspaper were confronted with a full-page advertisement with the title, 'What Lord Roberts says to you'. All advertisements for the book and all copies of the book itself bore a warning from Roberts: 'The catastrophe that may happen if we still remain in our present state of unpreparedness is vividly and forcibly illustrated in Mr Le Queux's new book which I recommend to the perusal of everyone who has the welfare of the British at heart'.[315] Months after the first edition of the book had appeared, the *Times* was still advertising on its front page the work's extraordinary prognosis of an invasion by Germany, while a lower-priced special edition of the work was available in the renowned *Times* Book Club.[316]

With his eye on future editions and a rich variety of advertising strategies, when it came to marketing the book Northcliffe's enthusiasm knew no bounds. First, he shrewdly advertised the text as a serial in three parts – *The Invasion of 1910*, *The Siege of London* and *The Revenge*. Its subsequent publication as a novel was announced to a curious and eager public by means of a full-page advertisement in all the major daily papers in the form of an invasion map, which every reader was encouraged to retain for his or her personal use should the worst happen. And in a sensational advertising coup, the map was also distributed in Piccadilly to passers-by, handed to them by sandwich board-wearing men decked out in spiked helmets and German uniforms.[317]

The difference between Le Queux's *The Invasion* and Childers' *Riddle of the Sands* lay not just in the remarkable marketing of the former. Le Queux wrote some two hundred books in the course of his career, but his style remained consistently that of pulp fiction; by contrast, Childers, a literary novice, demonstrated distinct talent in his sole novel. A comparison of the two texts reveals an evident intensification in subject matter. Fictitious planning in Childers' work had become a feasible reality for Le Queux, who carried his reader into a world in which a German invasion actually took place. His picture of the German Hun, for which he used the most brutal tones, was far more melodramatic and imposed on Germans the worst of enemy stereotypes, anticipating wartime propaganda.[318] Germans burnt and pillaged; they massacred women and children; and they forced their victims to dig their own graves,[319] the very picture drawn by artists during the war years. But Northcliffe was little interested in that form of impact by the book. With Le Queux and Roberts he had scored a remarkable success, both financial and with the public; asked in May 1909 by Sir Edward Grey for his opinion on the danger from Germany, he responded, 'I do not believe the Germans seriously contemplate invasion at all'.[320]

Attack by Germany was likewise the theme of a play that proved a box office hit and by far the greatest theatrical success of the pre-war period. *An Englishman's Home*, 'which floated to notoriety on a wave of politics',[321] was the work of Guy du Maurier, the son of an officer, actor and writer. In February 1909, the play became the talk of the town and gave cause for both diplomatic and political reconsideration.[322] The title *An Englishman's Home* – 'a phrase

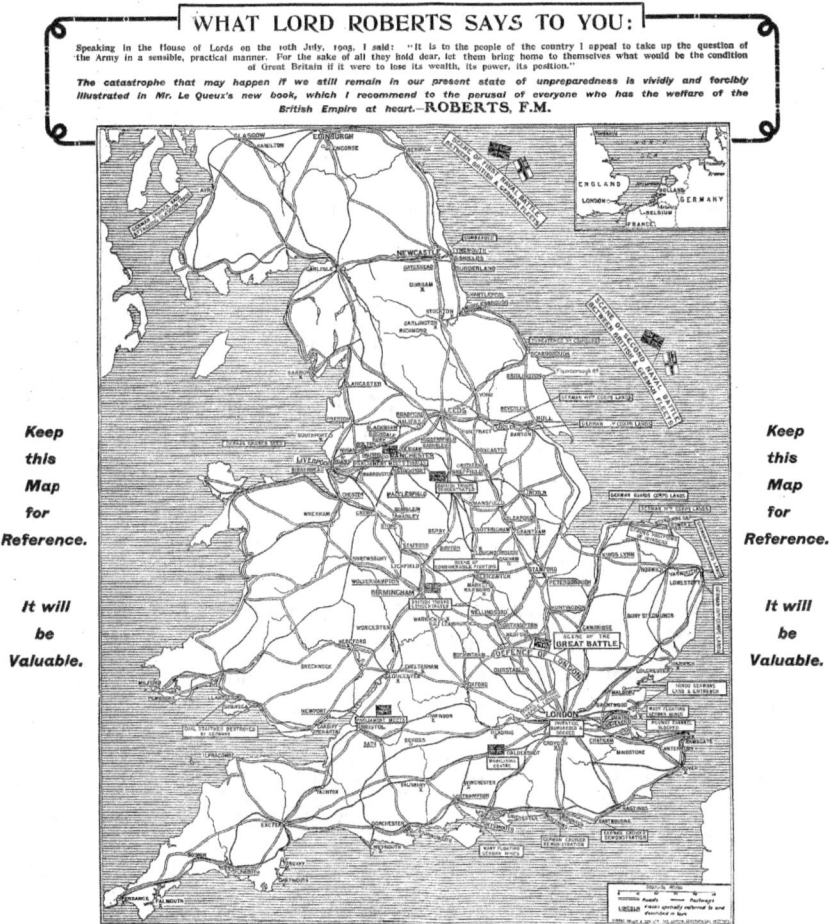

Figure 1.1. The invasion of 1910.

very much in people's mouths just now', according to Member of Parliament John Albert Bright – subsequently became a widely known and well-established synonym for homeland defence.[323] Even more significant than the title were the play's royal patronage, the official ban on its parodying and, above all, the work's resounding success, the very reason for its being copied. Six months later, Officer Townroe organized a successful tour of his play, *A Nation in Arms*, on which the *Times* reported as enthusiastically as on du Maurier's production, writing, 'The scenes are by no means an exaggerated picture of what would occur were an invading army to effect a landing on our shores'. The paper commented that the play served the nation rather than profit,[324] and, indeed, the government seriously considered having the work performed throughout the country at public expense.[325] The appeal for the audience, and what led people to flock to performances, was certainly not the undistinguished content, for the script of *An Englishman's Home* could hardly have been more trite. The attraction lay rather in the popular message the play proclaimed. As so often, Germany was presented as a bloodthirsty enemy with concrete plans for invasion, and only an England well armed on land would be in a position to defend itself. The impetuous Reich, its monarchs equally admired and despised, served as an almost ideal integration tool, not only for Britain but also for the Empire. As expected, *An Englishman's Home* flopped when it was performed in Berlin in April 1909, but in Sydney spontaneous ovation broke out, and the audience sprang to their feet at the end of the last act and sang the British national anthem.[326]

The *Times* pointed emphatically to the close analogies between Repington's lectures in Aldershot, Roberts' speeches on overdue reform of the army given throughout Britain, and du Maurier's play.[327] The play's success seemed to bear out the correctness of the case for conscription: volunteers for military service increased tenfold. Resonances of scare stories such as *An Englishman's Home*, *The Riddle of the Sands* or *The Invasion of 1910* can be found not just in newspaper commentaries and articles, but also in the readers' letters to the editor, which clearly indicate that readers were increasingly likely to take the fictional world as real. On 6 May 1907, the *Morning Post* published a letter whose author maintained that some 90,000 German spies were active in Great Britain, with their arsenals hidden in every city of reasonable size.[328] The War Office was far from immune to such outlandish suggestions. 'There is much truth in some of this as you know',[329] was the official response when Colonel Edward Gleichen sent this letter to his superior, Lieutenant-Colonel James Edmonds, the head of the Directorate of Military Operations (DMO). Having translated the memoirs of a French agent, Edmonds was convinced 'that every German living in a foreign country is a spy',[330] a claim that the *Daily Mail* had been making for a decade, largely without contradiction. Even a fleeting glance through a number of issues of that tabloid delivers a run of references to German intentions to invade and examples of German espionage.[331] The paper warned its readership repeatedly about so-called 'spy pigeons',[332] and demanded a parliamentary hearing on the subject and a law that would forbid the flight of pigeons in specific areas, over military installations in particular. The origins of this cause lay in the annual competitions held by pigeon breeders from Germany and England, with the pigeon-racing competitions run between Dover and Düsseldorf rumoured to be used for espionage purposes. The *Daily Mail* believed such activity was a monstrous breach of international etiquette, and suggested, 'It is useless for Government to control the telegraphs and cables in the event of war if spies can send intelligence by means of pigeon post'.[333]

Where such alarm might lead as it grew, even in government circles, can be seen from the example of the Tweedmouth affair of spring 1908, to which we will return, when the bilateral damage was out of all proportion to the events themselves. By late 1908 and early 1909, espionage and invasion fever had reached a critical point, intensified by the Casablanca crisis, continuing tensions in the Balkans and rumours about the intentions of the German fleet. From his reading of Le Queux's just-published *Spies for the Kaiser*[334] and the subsequent flood of letters from enraged readers sent to the *Daily Mail* and the War Office, Edmonds constructed a close-knit system of German informers composed of hairdressers, waiters and tourists.[335] He concluded his report with the observation that Great Britain now found itself in the situation France had faced in 1870.[336]

Le Queux's literary outpourings about his character Hermann Hartmann, top German spy, made a lasting impression on Prime Minister Asquith. Asquith had been talking of the imminent naval superiority of Germany[337] even before parliament debated the claims of a provincial paper that a quarter of a mile from Charing Cross, 50,000 Mauser rifles and 7.5 million rounds of ammunition were being held in readiness for some 60,000 German reservists who had gone to ground in London.[338] Both claims were no more than products of the wild imaginings rife at the time, but the political reaction to these nightmarish depictions cannot be overlooked. While the Conservatives had repeatedly endeavoured to bring a more moderate and better-informed tone to the debate,[339] and Campbell-Bannerman had tried to prevent Anglo-German discord, Asquith seemed to be far more interested in the political capital that could be acquired from all the commotion. On good grounds, the liberal *Nation* exposed Asquith's deliberate exaggerations and termed him one of the greatest 'scaremongers' of all, a man all too happy to condone tensions in foreign policy for the sake of domestic policy and internal party politics.[340]

A year earlier, a cache of weapons had indeed been found, but this arsenal turned out to belong to Russian revolutionaries and agents and was not even mentioned in the popular press.[341] Now, however, Asquith was eager to convene a subcommittee of the CID to examine books that discussed invasion and espionage and letters submitted by newspaper readers and to establish whether the plans they contained were feasible and credible. The members of this committee, all persons of significant standing, were certainly not paranoid dreamers; they included Asquith himself, Edward Grey, Richard Haldane, Reginald McKenna, Herbert Gladstone, Lord Esher and a number of military men. And yet, to a man, they seem to have been convinced by the scenarios Le Queux had described. They expressed no doubts about Edmonds' system for gathering information, and they raised no questions about the credibility of his informants. At the end of the proceedings, they all approved without comment Haldane's conclusion that a great number of Germans were currently spying in Britain in preparation for an invasion, and that England housed an extensive network of German spies.[342]

Senior officials at the Foreign Office shared and spread this assessment. The rather reassuring report by Philip Dumas, the naval attaché, of a discussion with Tirpitz met with the following comment from Charles Hardinge, the permanent under-secretary, Eyre Crowe, the senior clerk, and Edward Grey, the minister: 'There is no doubt whatever that the Germans have studied and are studying the question [of invasion]. It is a danger to us to be borne in mind in all contingencies'.[343] Hardinge was so convinced that decades later he was still talking of a German spy network that covered Britain, although its existence had long since been disproved.[344] At the diplomatic and political level, the existence of a German threat appears not even to have been a matter for debate. In February 1908, Grey had emphatically declared to his pro-German ambassador in Berlin that he was convinced that Germans who holidayed in England were there for the sole purpose of measuring up the English coast in preparation for an invasion.[345] Even Grey's one-time mentor Rosebery was resigned to the extreme campaign against Germany, and in a conversation with the Austro-Hungarian ambassador, Count Mensdorff, he deemed the campaign simply a domestic matter and proposed that the Reich not take it too seriously and see it only as a sign of esteem for Germany.[346] Mensdorff, however, was shocked that the public should be treated so recklessly.[347] Much influenced by Hardinge, the concluding CID report was the impetus for the foundation of a military and coordinated secret service, MO5. This newly formed British espionage institution was to be concerned solely with Germany.[348]

As a consequence of the rumours and the increased attention paid to the continent, from January 1909 until the end of the war the CID was entirely preoccupied with the possibility of a German invasion; the defence of the Empire, the task for which it was intended, was of only distant, secondary interest.[349] The legal system could not remain unaffected, as made evident by the Official Secrets Act of 1911, which for the first time placed the burden of proof on the accused. A flood of spying ensued, accompanied by a spate of indiscriminate accusations, but few actual spies were uncovered. At the beginning of the war, more than 10,500 Germans and alleged sympathizers were interned as a precautionary measure, a step that was undoubtedly a product of the long-standing fear of sabotage.[350] On the other side of the Channel, the new British overseas secret service intensified its activities even before the war, heightening tension between the two countries. Childers' novel had again proved its worth: Captain Trench and Lieutenant Brandon, the two British naval officers tried in

Leipzig as spies, had used the chart Childers had included in his book as they sailed the German coast spying on harbour installations and taking soundings in coastal waters.[351]

While Le Queux had his novel end with a costly victory over the invaders, Alec Dawson's *The Message*, which followed a year later, depicted the dreaded defeat and occupation of England. Once again, as so often before, an invasion had been planned over years and down to the smallest detail by German spies disguised as waiters, bellhops and servants.[352] The book was distributed via the National Service League as a political tract 'addressed to Little Englanders',[353] with its primary message 'the ideal of duty and self-sacrifice'.[354] Espionage and invasion fever hit a high between 1906 and 1909 with earlier suspicions apparently confirmed, bolstering a fresh hysteria. Up and down the country, thanks to rumourmongers, the Reich had become the enemy par excellence, a role no state had held before. By contrast, Russia made only fleeting appearances on the pages of the daily press. The comprehensive press coverage meant that even readers little interested in politics would have found it hard to escape the threat of invasion or the hostility of Germany. Novelist Henry James sat increasingly uneasily in his house in Rye, on the East Sussex coast, fearing in all seriousness 'that when the German Emperor carries the next war into this country, my chimney-pots, visible to a certain distance out at sea, may be his first objective'.[355]

The state of alarm that preoccupied the English public throughout the first decade of the twentieth century had significant implications. It hung over the reformulation of international relations, poisoning Anglo-German relations in the long term. In the 1890s, Germany was seen as only one of many potential threats to Britain.[356] With the new century, however, Germany's rivals for the position of arch-enemy were on the retreat, falling away in both quantity and quality, until only Germany remained. While the threat from France and Russia in the 1890s had been cited as grounds for rapprochement with these two countries, the German threat was packaged as an opportunity to unite England, both domestically and in relation to its foreign interests. Two visions of Germany – exemplary Germany and Germany the monster under the bed – were fused to form a single political tool.

The Reich served in many regards as a model: here was what could happen in a modern industrial nation when professionalism and efficiency won out over British 'muddling through'. But Germany was also the enemy and in effect a rallying call for Britain. Some journalists certainly had a personal motive for keeping alive mythical and legendary tales of German attack. But a number of the most prominent writers were determined above all to shake their compatriots out of the lethargy that typified fin-de-siècle England after the Boer War. As a result of their efforts, the public grew increasingly certain that England was under siege by Germany and became more receptive to the propaganda of the navy and army leagues. In 1907, Lord Esher explained to Fisher the motives behind the politically fostered hysteria in simple terms: 'A nation that believes itself secure all history teaches is doomed. Anxiety, not a sense of security, lies at the root of readiness for war. An invasion scare is the mill of God which grinds you a Navy of Dreadnoughts, and keeps the British people warlike in spirit'.[357]

The German threat was kept in circulation to encourage the English to spring to their own defence and as part of the debate over universal conscription and the increase in Britain's naval capacity.[358] Even at an early stage, the German threat also played into British diplomacy and continental strategy. Against the background of the 'German peril', an alliance with despotic Russia, the former arch-enemy, seemed not only justified but also advisable, for the sake of English self-preservation; it was all the more necessary when the only and risky alternative to adopting the alliance policy of the continental powers was to remain a free agent and try to preserve the balance of powers. In addressing foreign policy, leader writers were often prepared to go much further than politicians, who could be held to account. The greater the apparent danger of invasion, the greater the willingness of the radical-liberal majority[359] to make concessions and break with traditional foreign policy or with the traditionally tight military budget. With English self-confidence dented and so much talk of national decline, by painting Germany as an overwhelming threat, one could, as Spring Rice openly admitted,[360] ensure one's own relevance. Thus, fiction became fact because that fictional reality was useful, be it in making one's case or making political decisions.[361] Grey was all too aware of the impact of invasion fever on the man in the street. According to the foreign secretary, the image of twenty one German battleships gathered at Wilhelmshaven left an indelible impression of imminent invasion on every Englishman.[362] His principal concern was to make clear to his party and his fellow countrymen why a new approach to continental politics was necessary.[363] In recognizing this reality, we will also recognize that our frame of reference for the revered argument about German naval armament as a leitmotif of British policy has also shifted.[364]

Notes

1. Langer, *Diplomacy of Imperialism*, 85. For Lansdowne and the press, see Grenville, *Lord Salisbury*, 437; Monger, *End of Isolation*, 122–23; Salisbury, Memorandum, 29 May 1901, BD II, No. 86, 68–69.
2. Wilson, 'The Making and Putative Implementation'.
3. Correspondence in MSS Stead, CC, STED 1.
4. Asquith to Maxse, 8 Oct. 1905, WSRO, MAXSE/453.
5. See Spender, *Life, Journalism and Politics*.
6. Robbins, 'Public Opinion', 70–88, 70; Steiner, *Foreign Office*, 186–92. For the methodological challenges of the category 'public opinion', see Lippmann, *Öffentliche Meinung*; Luhmann, 'Öffentliche Meinung'.

7. Grey to Mallet, 25 Feb. 1906, NA, FO 800/35. *The Nation* quoted Edward Grey as saying 'public opinion must in the end dictate the degree of intimacy to which this new friendship [with Russia] attains'. 'The Foreign Policy of Sir Edward Grey', *The Nation*, 3 Aug. 1907, 822–23. For contemporary understanding of public opinion, see further Fisher to Amery, 16 Dec. 1903, CC, AMEL 1/1/14.
8. Salisbury to Lascelles, 3 Dec. 1896, NA, FO 800/23; Sanderson to Lascelles, 23 Aug. 1900, NA, FO 800/9.
9. Iwan-Müller to Sandars, Feb. 1906, BOD, MSS Sandars, MS Eng. hist. 751.
10. Grenville, *Lord Salisbury*, 437.
11. Jones, *Fleet Street*, 94. For Fisher, see FGDN II, passim. For Beresford, see Massie, *Dreadnought*, 509.
12. Glaab, 'Wilhelm II. und die Presse', 205; Wilhelm II to Nicholas II, 8 May 1909, GP XXVI/2, No. 9533, 786–88.
13. Napier to Nicolson, 25 April 1907, No. 266, BD IV, 288–89; see also Fay, 'Influence of the Pre-war Press', 8; Taylor, *Struggle for Mastery*, 569.
14. Steiner and Neilson, *Britain and the Origins*, vii; see also Fritzinger, *Diplomat without Portfolio*.
15. The term 'Fleet Street' is used here as a synonym for all the London press.
16. The 'main purpose' of the political novel 'is party propaganda, public reform or exposition of the lives of the personages who maintain government'. Janiesch, *Satire und politischer Roman*, 15; see also Müllenbrock, *Literatur*, 216–18.
17. Hill, 'Public Opinion', 73–74.
18. E.g. Schramm, *Deutschlandbild*.
19. Oron J. Hale differentiated between 'public opinion' and 'publicity'. Hale, *Publicity*, 3–12.
20. On this official mind, see the recent brilliant account by Thomas Otte, *Foreign Office Mind*.
21. Angell, *Public Mind*.
22. Hale, *Publicity*, vi–vii, 3–12; Anon., 'Diplomacy as a Profession', *Current Literature* 28, 6/1900, 242–43; Anon., 'Journalists and Diplomatists', *Living Age* 226, 9/1900, 123–25; 'New Diplomacy', *The Outlook*, 22 July 1900, 202–3; 'Diplomacy and Journalism', *The Spectator*, 15 Oct. 1898, 513–14. Saunders called Chirol the 'Ambassador' of *The Times*. Saunders, 12 March 1912, CC, SAUN 3/GS/10/15.
23. Scott to Salisbury, 12 Jan. 1899, BL, Add. 52303. Buckle called Chirol the 'Foreign Secretary of *The Times*'. Buckle to Curzon, 25 July 1903, IOL, EUR. F. 111/182.
24. The intention here is to look within what is in effect a synopsis for additional influences and outcomes that, by complementing, hastening or exacerbating existing trends, helped generate the established British model of security, stability and influence; in so doing, the study will throw light on the turn towards alliance-based political thinking within English diplomacy.
25. Grey to Spender, 23 Aug. 1908, BL, MSS Spender, Add. 46389.
26. Spender, *Public Life*, Vol. 2, 95.
27. Ibid., 115. Those 'six proprietors' could have covered the Harmsworth brothers, Cyril Pearson, Leonard Courtney, John St. Loe Strachey and Leopold J. Maxse.
28. Lavino to Bell, 31 May 1899, NIA, MSS Bell; Chirol to Spring Rice, 3 Oct. 1905, CC, CASR 1/11.
29. Stead, 'The Foreign Press Association', RR, 4/1898, 429.

30. Cited in Langer, *Diplomacy of Imperialism*, 85.
31. RR, 15 Jan. 1899, 32–34; 15 Feb. 1899, 123–25; 15 April 1899, 315; Maxse, Episodes of the Month [hereafter, Episodes], NR, 1/1900, 3–4. As a consequence, Rosebery warned in the House of Lords against the threat from invasion. See Langer, *Diplomacy of Imperialism*, 663.
32. Ibid., 669; Anon., 'Delcassé and the Entente cordiale', NR 7/1908, 712–19; Lee, *Edward VII*, Vol. 1, 765–67; Eckardstein, *Lebenserinnerungen*, Vol. 2, 167–69; Buckle, *Letters of Queen Victoria*, Vol. 3, 499–500, 503, 507–8. Victoria, Salisbury and the Prince of Wales thanked the Kaiser. Bülow, 12 Jan. 1900, GP XV, No. 4463, 506–8.
33. Mallet, 25 Feb. 1907, BD III, Appendix B, 431–32; Hardinge to Nicolson, 30 Oct. 1907, NA, FO 800/341.
34. Ayerst, *Garvin*, 35–41.
35. Whitaker, *Whitaker's Almanack* 1900, 695.
36. See the list of club addresses in ibid., 277–85 and 696.
37. Lejeune, *Gentlemen's Clubs*, passim; see also the description of the exchanges that took place in the St. James's Club, the Foreign Office, the editorial offices of the *Spectator* or at the Commission on Oriental Studies at the University of London, in Graves, *Storm Centres*, 231–32.
38. Geppert, *Pressekriege*, 64–65.
39. See Courtney, *Making of an Editor*, 231.
40. All figures taken from Webb, *Statistics* (1911).
41. Ibid.; Read, *Power*, 108; Harmsworth, 'Simultaneous Newspapers', NAR 1/1901, 72–90, 72.
42. Whitaker, *Whitaker's Almanack* 1900, 84; Steiner, 'Last Years of the Old Foreign Office', 66.
43. Harmsworth, 'Simultaneous Newspapers', NAR 1/1901, 72–90, 87.
44. Hobson, *Psychology of Jingoism*, 29.
45. Spender, *Public Life*, Vol. 2, 116.
46. See Griffiths, *Encyclopedia*, 34. Among the most prominent commentators were Henry Norman, Thomas Barclay, William Blunt, Thomas A. Brassey, Charles Dilke and Herbert Samuel.
47. Ibid., 40. For the National Union of Journalists, see Tracey, *Press*, 75.
48. See Geppert, *Pressekriege*, passim.
49. See Wilson, 'The Foreign Office and the Education; Steiner, *Foreign Office*, 186–92.
50. Courtney, *Making of an Editor*, 161–76; Gollin, *Observer*, 191.
51. Chirol to an unknown informant, 4 May 1905, NIA, FELB 4/60.
52. Kennedy, *Rise of Anglo-German Antagonism*, 366; Courtney, *Making of an Editor*, 231.
53. Low, *Governance of England*, 187.
54. Henry W. Massingham was one of the most important liberal journalists of the prewar era. As parliamentary special correspondent and lead editor of the *Daily Chronicle*, in 1894 he played a part in building Lord Rosebery's liberal cabinet. In 1899, his pro-Boer sympathies led to his departure from the *Chronicle*. In 1907, he founded *The Nation*, which under his leadership very quickly became a leading liberal publication, giving voice to a liberalism of a Gladstonian type. Massingham himself often provided lead articles on foreign policy. Escott, *Masters of English Journalism*, 281.
55. Massingham, cited in Griffiths, *Encyclopedia*, 41.
56. Hale, *Publicity*, 16.

57. On the declining importance of the *Daily Telegraph*, see Courtney, *Making of an Editor*, 38.
58. 'From that year [1902] onwards anonymous articles increase, largely on foreign policy and not infrequently from people too highly, or too specially placed to wish to disclose their identity. M. Iswolsky wrote frequently, sometimes signing, sometimes not.' Courtney, *Making of an Editor*, 176.
59. Sales figures for the *National Review* grew by around 50 per cent at the beginning of the century. *The Times*, 6 Feb. 1900, 12. In the first half of 1905, around 7,000 copies of each issue were sold on average. See Auditors' Certificate, 23 June 1905.
60. Admiral Penrose, for example, made reference to the well-known Edelsheim article that appeared in the *National Review* on the danger of a German invasion. *The Times*, 13 May 1905.
61. *The Times*, advertisement, 15 Nov. 1905.
62. *The Times*, 30 July 1904.
63. Robbins, 'Public Opinion', 82.
64. *The Times*, 2 March 1906; 1 Aug. 1908; 28 Sept. 1908; 6 Oct. 1908.
65. *Observer*, 1 Sept. 1907; 16 Feb. 1908. The poetry of a certain Adrian Ross appeared regularly in that same paper; Ross repeatedly made a case for a massive investment in armaments in light of the threat from the Central Powers. *The Observer*, 9 Feb. 1908; 16 Feb. 1908; 14 June 1908.
66. *Morning Post*, 24 Feb. 1908; *Daily Telegraph*, 1 March 1908; *Daily Mirror*, 26 Feb. 1908.
67. *Morning Post*, 24 Feb. 1908.
68. Cited in Kennedy, *Rise of Anglo-German Antagonism*, 362; see also Langer, *Diplomacy of Imperialism*, 81.
69. 'Oui, nous détestons les Allemands et cordialement. … Je ne permettrai pas qu'on imprime dans mon journal la moindre chose qui pût blesser la France, mais je ne voudrais pas qu'on y insérât quoique ce fût qui pût être agréable à l'Allemagne', cited in Morris, *Scaremongers*, 6.
70. Lalaing to Davignon, 24 May 1907, BelD, No. 30, 81–83, 81.
71. Shaw to Haldane, 6 Nov. 1907, NLS, MSS Haldane 5907.
72. Spender vehemently rejected this characterization. Spender, *Life, Journalism and Politics*, Vol. 1, 170; see also Harris, *Spender*, 30.
73. Trevelyan, *Grey of Fallodon*, 227.
74. Hale, *Publicity*, 30. For a list of the Metropolitan Press, see Anon., *History of The Times*, Vol. 4, App. 11, 1130–36.
75. Anon., *History of The Times*, Vol. 3, 480.
76. Adams, *Brothers across the Ocean*, 42, 60.
77. Saunders to his father David Saunders, 24 Feb. 1888, CC, SAUN 2/GS/1/37. The author is currently working on an edition of the Saunders papers.
78. Saunders to David Saunders, 26 May 1888, CC, SAUN 2/GS/1/40.
79. Saunders to David Saunders, 3 August 1888, CC, SAUN 3/GS/2/11; 7 Jan. 1889, SAUN 2/GS/1/51.
80. Saunders to David Saunders, 27 Nov. 1893, CC, SAUN 2/GS/1/79.
81. Saunders to David Saunders, 28 Sept. 1896, CC, SAUN 2/GS/1/111.
82. Anon., *History of The Times*, Vol. 3, 300.
83. Chirol to Bell, 28 Dec. 1896, NIA, MSS Bell.

84. See Geppert, *Pressekriege*, 162–66.
85. According to an obituary, most likely by Hale, written during the 1920s. NIA, MSS Saunders.
86. On his manifold contacts, see his papers in Cambridge: e.g. Saunders to Sinclair, 23 March 1898, CC, SAUN 3/GS/6/1/1; Rosebery to Saunders, 21 Jan. 1900, CC, SAUN DHS/215; to David Saunders, 29 Jan. 1900, CC, SAUN 2/GS/1/142. On his expertise on the press: Saunders, Memorandum, o. D., BDFA XIX/F, No. 228, 296–303.
87. Cited in Hale, *Publicity*, 369.
88. Chirol to Lascelles, 18 April 1902, CC, CASR 1/14; 16 June 1902; 2 Oct. 1906, CASR 1/11; 14 June 1903, CUL, MSS Hardinge, Vol. 7; Saunders to Maxse, 11 Feb. 1906, WSRO, MAXSE/455.
89. Crowe, Grey, Notes, BD III, No. 418, 358–59.
90. Spring Rice to Th. Roosevelt, 9 Nov. 1904, CC, CASR 9/2.
91. Morris, *Letters of Lieutenant-Colonel Charles à Court*, 5; 280, n. 19.
92. Crowe to Asta, 2 July 1895, BOD, MS Eng. d. 2897; to Clema, 1 Aug. 1911, BOD, MS Eng. d. 2902.
93. Chirol to Saunders, 4 Sept. 1899, NIA, FELB IV/428; Anon., *History of The Times*, Vol. 3, 300–302.
94. Chirol to Lavino, 3 Nov. 1899, NIA, FELB IV/477.
95. Monson to Salisbury, 19 Jan. 1900, BD II, 247.
96. *The Times*, 5 Feb. 1900; Chirol to Saunders, 5 March 1900, NIA, FELB IV/515.
97. Chirol, cited in Eckardstein, *Ten Years*, 140–41; Anon., *History of The Times*, Vol. 3, 316.
98. '*The Times* is a power for good and evil as a political weapon. You know our policy is to maintain friendly relations with Russia … it is necessary to lose no time in preparing public opinion for it'. Hardinge to Chirol, 3 June 1904, cited in Morris, *Scaremongers*, 60.
99. Richthofen refused to shake his hand, stating: 'No one has contributed more to the poisoning of public opinion in England against Germany than you'. Cited in Hale, *Publicity*, 16.
100. Cited in Morris, *Scaremongers*, 37–46, 39.
101. Works on Maxse generally address his attitude towards Germany. See ibid., 37–46.
102. Newton, 'Maxse', NR 2/1933, 187.
103. See Spring Rice to Luxmore, 15 Nov. 1898, GL I, 17–20.
104. Maxse, 'Episodes', NR, 6/1895, 451.
105. Morris, *Maxse*, 8.
106. Spring Rice to Lady Helen, 16 Jan. 1902, GL I, n. 1; 350; Christian, *Maxse*, 2; F.I. Maxse to Mahan, 7 April 1894, Library of Congress, Mahan Papers, Reel 6.
107. Among his closest contacts were Alfred Lyttelton, Lord Milner, Lord Newton, Lord Acton, Lord Selborne, Leo S. Amery, George Wyndham and Charles Repington. His correspondence and papers stored at West Sussex Record Office read like the who's who of Edwardian politics and cover all Edwardian policy issues.
108. *Daily Mail*, 23 Jan. 1932; Grigg, 'Leo Maxse', NR 2/1932, 151; Christian, *Maxse*, 344–45.
109. Strachey, *Adventure of Living*, 297.
110. Newton, 'Maxse', NR 2/1933, 186. For Blennerhasset, see Morris, *Scaremongers*, 40.
111. Garvin, *Chamberlain*, Vol. I, 156.

112. Maxse, 'Episodes', NR, 10/1893, 155–57.
113. Maxse, 'Episodes', NR, 12/1893, 434.
114. Maxse, 'Episodes', NR, 1/1894, 731.
115. Maxse, 'Episodes', NR, 7/1895, 592; 11/1895, 286.
116. Maxse, 'Episodes', NR 9/1894, 17.
117. *The Times*, 23 June 1894, cited in Carroll, *Germany*, 328.
118. Ibid.
119. Marschall to Hatzfeldt, 18 April 1894, GP VIII, No. 2024, 416–19.
120. Maxse, 'Episodes', NR 9/1894, 15.
121. Maxse, 'Episodes', NR 1/1895, 585–86; on the British retreat, see Wilson, 'Constantinople or Cairo'.
122. Maxse, 'Episodes', NR, 9/1894, 15.
123. Maxse, 'Episodes', NR, 1/1895, 585.
124. Morris, *Scaremongers*, 46; Geppert, *Pressekriege*, 91–122, 180.
125. Maxse, 'Episodes', NR, 1/1895, 586; 7/1895, 592; Hutcheson, *Leopold Maxse*, 113.
126. Maxse, 'Episodes', NR, 7/1895, 577–79; 8/1895, 739; 10/95, 150.
127. Maxse, 'Episodes', NR, 8/1895, 739; 10/1895, 150.
128. Hatzfeldt to AA, 7 Aug. 1895, GP X, No. 2385, 25–27; Langer, *Diplomacy of Imperialism*, 240.
129. Maxse, 'Episodes', NR, 2/1896, 720.
130. Ibid., 721.
131. 'Et tu Brute', cited in Christian, *Maxse*, 73.
132. Maxse, 'Episodes', NR, 2/1896, 717–23; Strachey, 'Our Foreign Policy', NR, 2/1896, 741–57.
133. Maxse, 'Episodes', NR, 3/1896, 5.
134. Ibid.
135. Maxse, 'Episodes', NR, 12/1893, 434; 8/1895, 739; Anon., 'The Strength of Russia', NR, 10/1896, 227; Maxse, 'Episodes', NR, 7/1897, 640.
136. Maxse, 'Episodes', NR, 7/1897, 655.
137. (An Official), 'An Understanding between Russia and Great Britain', NR, 8/1897, 836.
138. A view that at precisely the same time and in almost identical form was also voiced by Spring Rice, which might lead us to conclude that Spring Rice himself was hiding behind the pseudonym 'An Official'. Spring Rice to Villiers, 24 July 1897, GL I, 224–26.
139. Christian, *Maxse*, 17.
140. Maxse, 'Episodes', NR, 8/1900, 879.
141. Cited in Christian, *Maxse*, 20.
142. Anon., 'Britain vs. France and Russia', NR 6/1898, 502–22; Maxse, 'Episodes', NR, 2/1898, 812.
143. Maxse, 'Episodes', NR, 12/1898, 466–68; 1/1900, 651–58.
144. Maxse, 'Episodes', NR, 12/1899, 319.
145. Maxse, 'Episodes', NR, 1/1900, 654–58
146. Maxse, 'Episodes', NR, 12/1899, 476–679.
147. Maxse, 'Episodes', NR, 1/1900, 649–50.
148. Blennerhasset, 'Great Britain and the European Powers', NR, 3/1900, 28–39.
149. Maxse, 'Episodes', NR, 2/1900, 809–10; 3/1900, 16–21; 4/1900, 189–90; 5/1900, 361; Blennerhasset, 'The Man in the Street', NR, 3/1900, 61–74.

150. Maxse, 'Episodes', NR, 1/1900, 646–50; 3/1900, 1–4; 5/1900, 373; 6/1900, 525; Anon., 'The Causes of Reverse', NR, 2/1900, 830–42; Spenser Wilkinson, 'War and Government', NR, 2/1900, 843–51; Arnold-Forster, 'The War Office and the War', NR, 3/1900, 40–60; Colomb, 'War and Confusion in the Navy', NR, 3/1900, 128–48; Anon., 'The Man in the Cabinet', NR, 3/1900, 61–74; Whitmore, 'Where Is the Incapacity?', NR, 5/1900, 389–99; Blennerhasset, 'Great Britain and the Dual Monarchy', NR, 6/1900, 550–59; Coulton, 'The Swiss Army', NR, 7/1900, 839–49.
151. Maxse, 'Episodes', NR, 2/1900, 807–8.
152. Maxse, 'Episodes', NR, 5/1902, 355; 4/1900, 195; *The Spectator*, 3 April 1903, cited in Carroll, *Germany*, 475.
153. Maxse, 'Episodes', NR, 2/1901, 783.
154. X. (Garvin), 'The German Danger in the Far East', NR, 10/1900, 178–95.
155. (An Englishman), 'Reconstruction of Catastrophe', NR, 11/1900, 330–40.
156. Hutcheson, *Leopold Maxse*, 127.
157. Maxse, 'Episodes', NR, 11/1899, 326.
158. Saunders to Maxse, 15 July 1900, WSRO, MAXSE/447/746–47; Garvin to Maxse, 4 Sept. 1900, WSRO, MAXSE/447/777; Maxse to Mahan, 15 March 1902 and 2 May 1902, Library of Congress, Mahan Papers, Reel 6.
159. Canis, *Von Bismarck zur Weltpolitik*, 397.
160. Roberts, *Salisbury*, 234.
161. Maxse's public speeches were announced in *The Times*: 11 Jan. 1907 (Bromley); 2 Feb. 1907 (Hitchin); 9 March 1909 (with Milner, Kensington Hall); 31 Oct. 1908; 6 Nov. 1908 (Oxford); 10 Feb. 1909 (Winchester).
162. Roberts to Maxse, 6 May 1909; Repington to Maxse, 15 May 1909; Wilkinson to Maxse, 6 May 1909, WSRO, MAXSE/459; for Maxse and Spenser Wilkinson, see Coerper to Tirpitz, 2 April 1902, PA AA 5959.
163. Hardinge to Maxse, 2 July 1900, WSRO, MAXSE/447; Crowe to Maxse, 29 Sept. 1902, WSRO, MAXSE/447; Grey to Maxse, 12 Oct. 1902, 15 Oct. 1902, MAXSE/450; Spring Rice to Mrs Maxse, 9 July 1903, WSRO, MAXSE/427; Nicolson to Maxse, 4 Jan. 1909, MAXSE/459.
164. Monger, *End of Isolation*, 110.
165. 'Mr Maxse *is* the *NR*'. Sandars, cited in Hutcheson, *Leopold Maxse*, 36.
166. Bauerkämper, *Die 'radikale Rechte' in Großbritannien*, passim.
167. Garvin to Northcliffe, 20 Aug. 1909, cited in Morris, *Scaremongers*, 8.
168. Maxse, *Germany*, 67.
169. Calchas (Garvin), 'Will England Last the Century', FR, 1/1901, 20–35.
170. Geppert, *Pressekriege*, 182.
171. Adams, 'Civilization and Decay', *Edinburgh Review*, 1/1896, 237–66; Mitchell, 'A Biological View of Our Foreign Policy', *Saturday Review*, 1 Feb. 1896, 118–20; Browne, 'Is Great Britain Falling into Economic Decay?', CR, 10/1901, 492–502; Stead, 'Mr Chamberlain's Long Spoon', CR, 6/1898, 761–77.
172. Anon., 'Lord Salisbury and the Eastern Question', FR, 3/1897, 456–66; Anon., 'Where Lord Salisbury Has Failed', FR, 4/1898, 513–23.
173. Hodgkin, 'The Fall of the Roman Empire and Its Lessons for Us', CR, 1/1898, 51–70.
174. Anon., 'The Kaiser's Foreign Policy', RR, 9/1897, 258.
175. Jane, 'The Problem in the Far East', CR, 3/1898, 387–93.
176. Ibid., 392.

177. Ibid.
178. Ibid.
179. Ibid.
180. (Quorum Paris Fui), 'The Balance of Power', CR 4/1898, 593–608; Pressensé, 'France, Russia, and the England of the Jubilee', *Nineteenth Century*, 7/1897, 173–84.
181. Greenwood, 'The Law of the Wild Beast', *Nineteenth Century*, 10/1897, cited in RR, 10/1897, 377; Greenwood, 'Europe at War with England', RR, 2/1898, 152; Dillon, 'Russia and Europe', CR, 11/1896, 609–22; Dillon, 'Foreign Affairs', CR, 8/1902, 583–95; Diplomaticus (Lucien Wolf), 'Count Mouravieff's Indiscretion', FR, 12/1899, 1036–45; Blennerhasset, 'England and Russia', NR, 2/1909, 209–16.
182. Greenwood, RR, 2/1896, 151.
183. Ibid.; Edward Dicey, RR, 2/1896, 158.
184. Wilson, RR, 3/1896, 227; Mahaffy, RR, 5/1896, 343. An opinion shared by some Americans; see Hazletine, 'Why Some Americans Hate England', RR, 8/1897, 143.
185. Calchas (Garvin), 'Will England Last the Century', FR, 1/1901, 20–35.
186. Ibid.
187. Sanderson to Lansdowne, 18 May 1901, NA, FO 800/115.
188. *The Spectator*, 18 May 1901.
189. Battle of Zorndorff (1758) stands for the Russian invasion deep into the Prussian heartland.
190. *The Spectator*, 18 May 1901.
191. Lascelles to Fitzmaurice, 2 June 1906 and 28 Sept. 1906; Fitzmaurice to Lascelles, 21 Sept. 1906, NA, FO 800/13.
192. De Bloch, *Revue des Deux Mondes*, cited in RR 1/1901, 56.
193. Blennerhasset, 'The Austrian Problem', FR, 4/1905, 589–609; Blennerhasset, 'England and Russia', NR, 2/1908, 209–16.
194. Balfour, Memorandum, 12 Dec. 1901, cited in Bourne, *Foreign Policy*, No. 139, 471–74.
195. Maxse, 'Episodes', NR, 11/1901, 317; 343–58; Morris, *Scaremongers*, 37–46.
196. Maxse, *Germany*, 47.
197. Metternich to Bülow, 14 Nov. 1901, GP XVII, No. 5345, 535; 14 March 1902, ibid., No. 5351, 542–44.
198. Letters to Balfour, Brodrick, Spring Rice, Crowe, Hardinge, Grey, Cartwright, Lascelles, Chirol, Strachey, Salisbury, Bell, Ponsonby et al. See WSRO, MAXSE/448; Metternich to Bülow, 3 Dec. 1901, GP XVII, No. 5346, 535–36.
199. For Wolff-Metternich, see Chamberlain, *Sir Austen Chamberlain. Englische Politik*, 574.
200. Metternich to Bülow, 14 Nov. 1901, GP XVII, No. 5345, 535–36; 14 March 1902, ibid., No. 5351, 542–44.
201. Maxse, 'Episodes', NR, 11/1901, 317–22.
202. A.B.C. etc., 'British Foreign Policy', NR, 11/1901, 343–58; Younghusband, *The Times*, 2 Dec. 1901; Maxse to Mahan, 6 Dec. 1901, Library of Congress, Mahan Papers, Reel 6.
203. DDF, 2nd. Ser., Vol. II, 601.
204. *The Times*, 18 Nov. and 21 Nov. 1901.
205. Metternich to Bülow, 14 Nov. 1901, GP XVII, No. 5345, 535–36.
206. *The Times*, 29 Oct. 1901.
207. *The Spectator*, 2 Nov. 1901, 98.

208. Geppert, *Pressekriege*, 193.
209. Salisbury to Maxse, 20 Oct. 1901, WSRO, MAXSE/448.
210. Rosebery to Maxse, 13 Oct. 1901, WSRO, MAXSE/448.
211. Tastistchev to Maxse, 29 Oct. 1901, WSRO, MAXSE/448; Maxse to Hardinge, 31 Oct. 1901, CUL, MSS Hardinge, Vol. 3.
212. Blennerhasset to Maxse, 10 Oct. 1901, 13 Oct. 1901, WSRO, MAXSE/448.
213. Cook to Maxse, 8 Oct. 1901, WSRO, MAXSE/448.
214. Ibid.
215. Ponsonby to Maxse, 19 Oct. 1901, WSRO, MAXSE/448.
216. Tyrrell to Maxse, 16 Oct. 1901, WSRO, MAXSE/448.
217. Hardinge to Maxse, 16 Oct. 1901, WSRO, MAXSE/448; Maxse to Hardinge, 31 Oct. 1900, CUL, NL Hardinge, Vol. 3.
218. Grey to Maxse, 9 Oct. 1901, WSRO, MAXSE/448.
219. Grey to Maxse, 22 Oct. 1901, WSRO, MAXSE/448. Only the first part is cited in Morris, *Scaremongers*, 42.
220. Grey to Maxse, 9 Oct. 1901, WSRO, MAXSE/448.
221. A.B.C. etc., 'British Foreign Policy', NR, 11/1901, 343–58, 357.
222. Grey to Maxse, 24 Nov. 1901, WSRO, MAXSE/448.
223. Grey to Maxse, 9 Oct. 1901, WSRO, MAXSE/448.
224. Saunders to Maxse, 23 Oct. 1901, WSRO, MAXSE/448; Grey to Maxse, 22 Oct. 1901, WSRO, MAXSE/448.
225. Tastistchev to Maxse, 29 Oct. 1901, WSRO, MAXSE/448; Dalton to Maxse, 19 Nov. 1901, WSRO, MAXSE/448.
226. Maxse, 'Episodes', NR, 12/1901, 513–25; Grey to Maxse, 24 Oct. 1901, WSRO, MAXSE/448.
227. Calchas (Garvin), 'The Crisis with Germany', FR, 12/1901, 934–48.
228. A.B.C. etc., 'Consequences of an Anglo-Russian Understanding', cited in Maxse, *Germany*, 49–51.
229. Anon., 'A Plea for the Isolation of Germany', NR, 12/1901, 703–15.
230. See Chapter 6.
231. Grey to Maxse, 24 Nov. 1901, WSRO, MAXSE/448.
232. Grey, 22 Jan. 1902, PD IV/101, cols. 608–13.
233. Anon., 'A Plea for the Isolation of Germany', RR, 10 Jan. 1902, 38; Anon., '"Isolation of Germany" – A Warning to the Cabinet', NR, 2/1903, cited in RR, 10 Jan. 1902, 83.
234. 'The whole tone of Treitschke's history is hostility to England', RR, 10 Jan. 1902, 85. In this sense Chirol demanded: 'Read Treitschke, Vol. 1!' Chirol to Spring Rice, 26 Nov. 1906, CC, CASR 1/11.
235. RR, 10 Jan. 1902, 212.
236. Crowe to Maxse, 15 Oct. 1902, WSRO, MAXSE/450.
237. Thoroughly different argues Morris: Morris, *Scaremongers*, 38.
238. Strachey, *His Life and his Paper*, 293.
239. Low to Maxse, 23 Jan. 1905, WSRO, MAXSE/453.
240. Esher to Spender, 28 Aug. 1910, BL, MSS Spender, Add. 46392.
241. Asquith to Maxse, 8 Oct. 1905, WSRO, MAXSE/453.
242. Spenser Wilkinson, 'Preparation for War', NR, 4/1902, 197–208; Maxse to Mahan, 6 Dec. 1901, Library of Congress, Mahan Papers, Reel 6.

243. MacColl, 'Russia, Germany, and Great Britain', FR, 1/1902, 21–39; Calchas (Garvin), 'The Latin Rapprochement and Anglo-Russian Relations', FR, 6/1903, 953–69; Calchas (Garvin), 'Foreign Policy of Russia', RR, 7/1907, 40; White, 'Anglo-Russian Relations', FR, 12/1904, 960–68.
244. See chapters six and seven.
245. See Rose, 'Peace Party at War'.
246. H.W. Wilson, 'The New German Navy', RR, 15 Aug. 1901, 277; see Hirst, *Six Panics*, 59–102; Mensdorff, Report, 24 Jan. 1908, HHStA, PA VIII, Kt. 140, No. 2 F.
247. *The Nation*, 25 Jan. 1908, cited in PA-AA, R 6093; *Economist*, 6 Feb. 1909; Hirst, *Six Panics*, 96.
248. *The Nation*, 29 Feb. 1908, cited in Metternich to Bülow, 29 Feb. 1908, PA-AA, R 5777. For further details, see Rose, 'The Writers, Not the Sailors', 221–40.
249. Garvin to Prothero, 12 Nov. 1908, cited in Morris, *Scaremongers*, 264. In May 1908, Spring Rice received a letter that claimed Britain would 'need another war scare like in 1887 to get the vote for the navy bill'. Anon. to Spring Rice, May 1908, NA, FO 800/241.
250. The military correspondent of *The Times* (Repington), 'Invasion', NR, 11/1907, 468–85; Anon. (Semper Paratus), 'Side-lights on German Preparations for War', NR, 4/1909, 407–14.
251. Bagehot, *Physics of Politics* (1902), 31–32.
252. Gosse, 'The Literature of Action', NAR 1/1899, 14–23; see also Langer, *Diplomacy of Imperialism*, 82–84.
253. Calchas (Garvin), 'Will England Last the Century', FR 1/1901, 20–35; RR 1/1901, 47.
254. Müllenbrock, *Literatur*, 4.
255. Schroeder, 'World War I as Galloping Gertie', 143; Steinberg, 'Copenhagen Complex', passim.
256. Maitland, 'Making of the German Civil Code', 475.
257. Mansfield, *In a German Pension* (1906), 10.
258. *Outlook*, 6 Jan. 1900, 18–19. On the formative influence of Kipling, see Wohl, *Generation of 1914*, 90–91.
259. Cited in Müllenbrock, 'Trugbilder', 303, 311.
260. Hildebrand, 'Staatskunst und Kriegshandwerk', 28; Steiner, *Britain and the Origins*, 31, 207; Williamson, *Politics of Grand Strategy*, 367.
261. See Le Queux, *The Great War in England*; Tracy, *The Final War* (1896).
262. 'Our Coming Peril', *St. James Gazette*, 12 March 1900; 'Is France Planning War?', *Daily Mail*, 20 April 1900; 'The Talk of a French Invasion', *The Spectator*, 25 Aug. 1900, 229; see Ardgah (DMI), Memorandum: A French Invasion, 11 July 1900, NA, PRO 30/40 Part II; Lyall, *Rise and Expansion*; Younghusband, *The Relief of Chitral*; Roberts, *Forty One Years in India*.
263. Stead, 'Our Great National Peril', in *War against War*, 22 Dec. 1899, 148.
264. 'English homes were ruined and burned'. Cited in Neilson, *Britain and the Last Tsar*, 86; on the image of Russia, 84–109.
265. Anon., *History of the Times*, Vol. 3, 248.
266. Müllenbrock, *Literatur*, 188; see Thies, *Literatur*, Vol. 1, 716; Clarke, *Voices Prophesying War*.
267. 'Refuse to be served by an Austrian or German waiter. If your waiter says he is Swiss, ask to see his passport.' *Daily Mail*, cited in Marwick, *British Society*, 50.

268. Hill, *Spies of the Wight*; see also Clarke, *Voices Prophesying War*.
269. On Wells, see Thies, *Literatur*, Vol. 2, 207–12; on Conrad, *The Secret Agent*, see Thies, *Literatur*, 33–34; Conan Doyle, 'Great Britain and the Next War', FR 2/1913, 219–36; Conan Doyle, *Memories*, 274–81.
270. Curtis, *A New Trafalgar*, 101. According to Corbett, Trafalgar was the foundational myth for the threat of invasion. Corbett, 'The Campaign of Trafalgar', *English Review* 10/1910, 561.
271. Amery, *My Political Life*, 158, 162, 297.
272. The charts that were included with the text were described as 'based on British and German Admiralty charts'. Childers, *Riddle of the Sands*, 13.
273. See Childers, *Riddle of the Sands*, 78; Ferguson, *Pity of War*, 1.
274. The original publication information ran *'The Riddle of the Sands.' A Record of Secret Service Recently Achieved*, edited by Erskine Childers, London 1903. 'They [Carruthers and Davies] asked for my assistance … I should edit the book.' Childers, *Riddle of the Sands*, 12; see *Times Literary Supplement*, 14 Aug. 1903, 242.
275. Childers, *Riddle of the Sands*, 336.
276. In *Spectator* and *Nineteenth Century*, William H. White ('Civis') called for sustained rearmament.
277. Selborne to Battenberg, 27 April 1904, cited in Boyce, *Crisis of British Power*, Vol. 2, No. 52, 174–75.
278. *The Spectator*, 1 Aug. 1903, 174f–175.
279. *Birmingham Post* and *To-Day*, cited in *The Times*, 23 June 1903.
280. Cited in Kerr, *Prince Louis of Battenberg*, 176.
281. Battenberg, Combined naval and military operations, 1886, USL, MSS Battenberg, MB1/T1/1; Battenberg, Manoeuvre report, May 1894, MB1/T9.
282. E.g. Wood, *Enemy in our Midst*; Oldmeadow, *The North Sea Bubble*; Griffith-Jones, *The World Peril of 1910* (1907); Cole, *The Death Trap*; Vaux and Yexley, *When the Eagle Flies Seaward*; Hislam, *The Admiralty of the Atlantic*; Curtis, *When England Slept*; Swinton, *The Green Curve and Other Stories* (1909); Townroe, *A Nation in Arms* (1909); Williams, *The Great Raid* (1909).
283. Fisher to Tweedmouth, 4 Oct. 1906, FGDN II, No. 50, 93–95.
284. See the statistics in Kennedy, *Rise and Fall of the Great Powers*, 261.
285. ADM, Report, 20 Oct. 1905; NA, ADM 116/940.
286. Garvin, 'The German Peril', *Quarterly Review* 7/1908, 264–98.
287. See Neilson, *Britain and the Last Tsar*, 84–109.
288. Brodrick, cited in Marder, *Anatomy*, 78.
289. Cited in ibid.; see also Massie, *Dreadnought*, 628.
290. Williams, *Defending the Empire*, 28.
291. Repington to Maxse, 17 Oct. 1907, WSRO, MAXSE/458.
292. Balfour to Clarke, 20 July 1907, NMM, RIC/9/1, 32.
293. See Kühlmann, *Erinnerungen*, 329–30.
294. Cited in Wilson, *Morning Post*, 26; Spring Rice to E.R. Roosevelt, 6 Sept. 1908, CC, CASR 7/30; Ware to Maxse, 13 March 1909, WSRO, MAXSE/459.
295. Minutes of discussion, 20 March 1905, 3, BLPES, ASSOC 17/MF 160.
296. James, *Lord Roberts*, 418.
297. See Judd, *Empire*, 201–13.
298. Bond, *War*, 65.

299. Ibid.
300. Cited in ibid., 77.
301. For H.G. Wells' influence, see Wohl, *Generation of 1914*, 86–87.
302. Wells, 'Anticipations', FR 11/1901, 911–27, 917.
303. Courtney, *Making of an Editor*, 157; Wells, *New Machiavelli*, 74.
304. Ibid., 75–77.
305. Ibid., 75. Meredith was a close friend of Maxse's. Thies, *Literatur*, Vol. 1, 729.
306. Wells, *In the Days of the Comet*, 101.
307. Müllenbrock, *Literatur*, 90. n. 23.
308. See 'Command of the Air – And a Forecast', *Daily Mail*, 4 July 1908; 'Germany's Air Madness', *Daily Mail*, 11 July 1908; *The Times*, 12 July 1908; *Manchester Guardian*, 14 July 1908; *Observer*, 16 July 1908; Massingham, 'The Instability of the World', *The Nation*, 24 Oct. 1908, 142–43.
309. H.W. Wilson (Ignotus) was an authority on issues of national defence, editor of the *Navy League Journals* and chief lead-article writer for the *Daily Mail*. See Hale, *Publicity*, 34. He has published in the *National Review* and was a close friend of Maxse's. See Morris, *Scaremongers*, 488.
310. *Publisher's Circular*, Notes and Announcements, 1 May 1909, 638.
311. Clarke, *Great War*, 249.
312. See Le Queux, *Things I Know*; Sladen, *Real Le Queux*.
313. Le Queux to Roberts, 28 July 1905, NAM, MSS Roberts, R 47/41; 27 Jan. 1906, NAM, MSS Roberts, R 47/48. See Le Queux, *Things I Know*, 245; Clarke, *Voices Prophesying War*, 145. Le Queux and Roberts met regularly in their club, 'The Pilgrims', of which Moberley Bell, Sydney Brooks, Arthur Conan Doyle, Lord Selborne and Henry Campbell-Bannerman were also members. *The Times*, 20 June 1904.
314. Clarke, *Great War*, 122.
315. Cited in Le Queux, *Invasion of 1910*; *The Times*, 13 March 1906.
316. *The Times*, 3 Aug. 1906; *The New London Journal*, 5/1906.
317. *The Times*, 13 March 1906; *Daily Mail*, 13 April 1906; Clarke, *Voices Prophesying War*, 145.
318. Schramm, *Deutschlandbild*, 377–81.
319. Kennedy, *Rise of Anglo-German Antagonism*, 382.
320. Northcliffe to Grey, 18 May 1909, BL, Add. 62155.
321. *The Times*, 28 Aug. 1909.
322. Kühlmann to Bülow, 4 Feb. 1909, PA-AA, R 5735; *The Times*, 29 Jan. 1909; Katherine Mansfield included mention of the play and its reception in her short stories. See Mansfield, *In a German Pension*, 12.
323. *The Times*, 29 Jan. 1909; 26 Feb. 1909; 30 March 1909; 10 March 1910. Bright, cited in *The Times*, 11 March and 5 May 1909. The phrase would be much used in interwar debates over security, and the play itself was eventually filmed. *The Times*, 31 Jan. 1920; 19 April 1926; 27 April, 1 May and 2 Oct. 1939.
324. *The Times*, 21 Sept. 1909.
325. Kühlmann to Bülow, 4 Feb. 1909, PA-AA, R 5735. The royal presence in the audience gained much attention; see *The Times*, 12 Feb. 1909. Lord Ellenborough recommended to Haldane that the author be awarded a special honour. *The Times*, 26 Feb. 1909.
326. *The Times*, 12 April 1909.
327. *The Times*, 29 Jan. 1909.

328. *Morning Post*, 6 May 1907; French, 'Spy Fever', 356.
329. 'Control of Aliens', 24 Oct. 1907, NA, WO 32/8873.
330. Cited in French, 'Spy Fever', 356.
331. *Daily Mail*, 31 Aug. 1896; 19 July 1897; 4 Jan. 1900; 11 July 1904; 10 March 1906; 9 Nov. 1906; 11 Sept. 1908.
332. *Daily Mail*, 9 Aug. 1898.
333. 'Each Pigeon Imported Should Be Registered', *Daily Mail*, 11 Aug. 1898.
334. Le Queux, *Spies for the Kaiser*.
335. French, 'Spy Fever', 357; LHCMA, MSS Edmonds III/5, Memoirs, 1 and IV/1, 1–40, passim. Subcommittee of the CID appointed to consider the Question of Foreign Espionage, Appendix 1: Cases of Alleged German Espionage, 13 April 1909, NA, CAB 16/8; Edmonds, Memorandum, 2 Dec. and 20 Dec. 1908, NA, KV 1/2; Ewart to Edmonds, 31 Dec. 1908, ibid. See also Hiley, in Le Queux, *Spies for the Kaiser*, xiii–xv.
336. Edmonds to DMO, 2 Dec. 1908, NA, KV 1/2.
337. In his comparison of the British and German fleets, Asquith had ignored the ships of the Nelson class, which some experts believed to be even more powerful than the Dreadnoughts. Anon., 'A Scare and its Makers', *The Nation*, 20 March 1909, 916–18; Anon., 'From Panic to Reason', *The Nation*, 27 March 1909, 952–53.
338. French, 'Spy Fever', 358. A study carried out in 1896 had expressed surprise at finding so few Germans, only 26,920, living in London, with a total figure for England of 50,599. There was no evidence of an explosive growth in immigration. See Shadwell, 'Germans in London', RR, 2/1896, 165; John Barlow, 24 May 1909, PD V/5, col. 812.
339. *The Times*, 28 Nov. 1903; 12 May 1905; Balfour to Clarke, 20 July 1907, NMM, RIC/9/1, 32; Balfour, 11 May 1905, PD IV/146, col. 86; Balfour, 11 May 1905, PD IV/146, col. 86; The Prime Minister and Mr Le Queux (Letters to the Editor by Ponsonby and Le Queux), *The Times*, 16 March 1906.
340. Anon., 'A Scare and its Makers', *The Nation*, 20 March 1909, 916–18.
341. Report to the FO, 11 April 1907, NA, FO 371/322.
342. Cited in Ferguson, *Pity of War*, 14.
343. Grey, Crowe, Minutes, Dumas, 4 Feb. 1908, BD VI, No. 80, 115–17, 117.
344. He told the story of a German tourist who by accident had left his briefcase, full of plans for the invasion, in the train from Hamburg to Paris. Busch, *Hardinge*, 81–82.
345. Grey, Minutes, Dumas, 4 Feb. 1908, No. 80, BD VI, 117; Grey to Lascelles, 22 Feb. 1908, NA, FO 800/61.
346. Mensdorff, 11 Dec. 1908, HHStA, PA VIII, Kt. 141, No. 66 N, fols. 129–31.
347. Mensdorff, 24 Jan. 1908, HHStA, PA VIII, Kt. 140, No. 2 F, fol. 68.
348. Secret Service, 4 Oct. 1908, NA, KV 1/1; see Secret Service, 4 Oct. 1908, NA, WO 106/6292. Plans had been drawn up in 1906 for a network of spies covering all of Germany. See Secret Service Arrangements in Northern Europe in the event of war against Germany, 1906, NA, FO 1093/45.
349. NA, CAB 2/2/1; WO 106/47.
350. MSS Kell, IWM, 10943 PP/MCR/120.
351. The attention of the British public was drawn to the activities of Trench and Brandon by the so-called 'Borkum trial' of 1910. Wile to Northcliffe, 23 Dec. 1910, BL, MSS Northcliffe, Add 62207; Wilson to Northcliffe, 24 Oct. 1910, BL, MSS Northcliffe, Add. 62201; PD IV/32, 14 Dec. 1911, col. 2502; *The Times*, 17 Jan., 20 Jan., 26 Feb.

1912; 13 May, 23 May 1913; RR 1/1911, 14; Anon., 'Military Spies', *English Illustrated Magazine* 2/1911, 503–4. For further results on espionage, see NA, ADM 344/436.
352. Dawson, *The Message*. In E.P. Oppenheim's, *A Maker of History* (1905), 'Hauptmann X' had declared that they had 290,000 young men in Britain who were militarily trained and could shoot, and that each one of them had his own task. See Ferguson, *Pity of War*, 2.
353. *New York Times*, 10 Aug. 1907.
354. Roberts to Strachey, 10 June 1907, PA, STR/12/3/33; see Clarke, *Voices Prophesying War*, 226–41.
355. James to Childe, 8 Jan. 1909, cited in Lubbock, *Letters of Henry James*, Vol. 2, 121.
356. Leonhard, 'Images', 48–65, passim.
357. Esher to Fisher, 1 Oct. 1907, CC, ESHR 10/42; see Mackay, *Fisher of Kilverstone*, 355.
358. Mensdorff, 10 Jan. 1908, HHStA, PA VIII, Kt. 140, No. 2 F, fol. 70.
359. In 1906, of the 231 liberal members of parliament, 40 were liberal imperialists.
360. Spring Rice to Chirol, 21 June 1907, GL II, 101.
361. See Lippmann, *Öffentliche Meinung*, 21.
362. Grey to Goschen, 3 Feb. 1909, BD VI, No. 152, 240.
363. Speech by Grey, February 1914, cited in Grey, *Speeches on Foreign Affairs*, 235.
364. See Fairbanks, 'The Dreadnought Revolution'; Herwig, 'German Reaction'. 'The friendship of the Power with the biggest Navy in the world ought to be worth enough to France, Italy and Russia to make them our friends. And the more Germany increases her Navy the more value will our Navy have.' Grey to Maxse, 21 June 1904, WSRO, MAXSE/452.

Chapter 2

THE POLICY OF DRIFT?
Balance of Power, Concert of Europe, or Political Power Blocs?

At the turn of the century, a new grouping, the New Liberal Imperials (Limps), emerged out of the debates over a possible change of direction for British domestic, foreign and imperial policy. As a party faction, the Limps on the liberal right as well as the radicals on the left had decisive roles to play within London's political arena, yet investigation of British foreign policy has all too often overlooked that contribution, which played out in relation to both the Unionist coalition government and, after 1906, the Liberal government.[1] Historians of the period immediately before the First World War tend to assume the existence of a fundamental continuity in foreign policy and an above party agreement between government and opposition, but closer analysis suggests that those who were directly involved saw the situation very differently. Not only did Arthur Balfour himself declare that '[t]he interests of party dialectics and those of diplomacy scarcely ever harmonize', but other contemporaries too were well aware that on occasion serious differences arose between Tories and Liberals over foreign policy concepts and doctrine, with disparities of view evident also within the parties themselves.[2]

From the mid 1890s, a group of young and ambitious liberal imperialists were able to bring the emerging discussion of foreign policy and imperialism into a general political debate about reform, and eventually they tied that conversation in with the domestic ideas of the radical liberal Gladstonians, creating a credible and comprehensive political platform. Their principal goal was to prevent another schism – the Liberal Party had not yet recovered from the rupture of 1886. The younger members wanted to form a political force that would be located between the left-liberal Gladstonians and the right-liberal imperialists and would be capable of consensus and, above all, of forming a majority and governing. In an internal party memorandum of November 1900, William

---

Notes for this chapter begin on page 118.

Harcourt, the party's leader in the House of Commons, made direct reference to the foreign policy innovation associated with the Limps: 'We are encountered by the proceedings of a section who style themselves "Liberal Imperialists" the motive of whose action is to bring about what they proclaim as a new departure both in external & domestic policy'.[3]

The Limps' colleagues on the far left of the party had been branded contemptuously, and effectively, 'Little Englanders' by the Tories during the khaki election, while their own party colleagues on the right had deemed them pro-Boer; England as a whole, according to Asquith, had thought them unpatriotic.[4] The Limps, by contrast, had little time for pacifism and even less time for 'splendid isolation'. Harcourt believed the idea machine and real force behind this faction to be his rival Lord Rosebery, who as early as 1885 had embraced the term 'liberal imperialism' as an accurate description of his political ideas.[5] A little more than a decade later, Rosebery's ideas were becoming something more than just ideas, and by the time the South Africa war was over, they formed a formal programme intended to tackle contemporary problems. For Rosebery, who had previously found his party consistently obstructive, the preservation and expansion of the Empire was key: 'We should grossly fail … did we shrink from responsibilities and decline to take our share in the partition of the world which we have not forced on, but which has been forced upon us'.[6]

Britain's European function, emphasized by Gladstone, Disraeli and Salisbury, was pushed into the background. 'Our position as an oceanic and commercial nation', Lord Rosebery reflected, 'pulled us by the coat-tails out of the European System'.[7] Rosebery was convinced that the coming century would be characterized by a global struggle for survival and that victory in that competition, which many others also deemed unavoidable,[8] would require Britain to consolidate its existing empire and move to a constructive imperialism.[9] Additionally, continued the former foreign secretary and prime minister, future foreign policy would require that public opinion be 'more guidance than stimulus', or, in other words, that greater account would need to be taken of public opinion. He found grounds for this approach in the growing democratization and speedy transformation of the British media landscape, but he also believed that as British possessions would have to be defended from the other great civilizations, the whole nation would need to be on board with that cause.[10] For Rosebery, high imperial competition between the great nations meant the end of the classic liberal and principled foreign policy of the nineteenth century.

Unlike the Gladstonians in his party, Rosebery held that collaboration with autocratic Russia and joint control of global interests in the Far East were not just conceivable but also downright desirable: 'If Russia and England can march with cordiality and without suspicion in Asiatic affairs, one great step forward towards the peace of the world will have been taken for ever'.[11] For a party whose traditional credo was absolute rejection of the autocratic system of Russia and any form of jingoism, including militarism, here was a new acid test, following on from the divisions over Home Rule of 1886. Further schism was prevented, however, not least by Rosebery's withdrawal from politics in October 1898 (for which the attitude of the radicals during the Armenian crisis was principally responsible) and by the party's long period in opposition, which provided opportunity for open debate over the party's programme, which, in turn, allowed new concepts in foreign affairs to develop. Initially, the fronts were distinctly drawn between, on one hand, the Limps' holistic approach, which emphasized the Empire and the global power system, and on the other, the attitude of the more moderate radical liberals, which turned on the classic European concert of powers. The latter came surprisingly close to the course favoured by conservative decision makers such as Salisbury and Balfour – although these two men rejected the term 'concert' and preferred to speak of a 'federation'[12] – but when it came to the fundamental ordering of international affairs, there were essential differences between Tories and Liberals. While Liberals, and not just left-liberal but also right-liberal imperialists, sought an institutionalization of security, which was to be achieved through the replacement of inherited 'balance of power' mechanisms by a concert of powers, which they believed would ensure a pre-emptive and collective security, for Conservatives the concert was above all a flexible tool that could be employed to ensure stability and maintain an equilibrium. Edward Grey, for example, not only rejected the term 'balance' but also on occasion openly ignored the concept, giving precedence to the concert alternative, for which he saw the creation of the entente bloc as a first step.[13]

The Limps included a number of young and promising individuals such as Edward Grey, Richard Haldane, Halford J. Mackinder, Herbert Asquith and Ronald Munro-Ferguson.[14] All these men largely supported Rosebery's views on future developments and the Darwinian laws according to which international relations would take shape, but they were also ready to take their practical solution a step further. In terms of the fundamental parameters of the Great Power system, Rosebery would prove typical of the beginnings of a period of transformation. He consistently emphasized the constitutive significance of the Triple Alliance for the Great Power system and excluded the possibility of Anglo-Russian cooperation in south-east Europe at the expense of the Habsburg monarchy.[15] When it came to relations with Britain's traditional partners, he proved, surprisingly, to lack a light touch. Because of his prioritization of the Empire, he was unwilling to build up credit with the Central Powers. With the reputation of the Empire in mind, he insisted that any impression must be avoided that Britain was at the beck and call of the Central Powers when it came to their security or stood in any way on a par with them.[16] In his view, the new security situation and the dominance of the Franco-Russian Dual Alliance meant that the Central Powers, not the Empire, now sat less easily; they were dependent on the good will of London. The basis on which Britain had done business with the Triple Alliance was thus reworked, but so too were the foundations of the Pax Britannica itself, whose success was grounded in Britain's reliance on Bismarck's managed equilibrium,[17] which had allowed Britain to remain on the sidelines watching over, largely passively, the European power constellations, in particular that of the Triple Alliance, and stepping onto the field to referee only in an emergency. A global power, Britain had been able to act as a silent hegemon, or as *primus inter pares*, in Europe, exercising its influence largely through coordination. Authors Frederick Greenwood and Emile Dillon were not alone in insisting that Britain therefore had the Triple Alliance to thank for its position.[18]

Although like the conservative Arthur Balfour, Rosebery was unsettled by the desperate situation of Germany and Austria-Hungary, hemmed in by Russia and France, and even declared that the situation in south-eastern Europe seemed headed for catastrophe,[19] with Britain's global responsibilities in mind, he did not believe Britain needed to provide a quid pro quo for the decades-long support it had received. Rosebery's imperial perspective meant that Britain engaged the Central Powers more frequently as an empire and less often as a partner, seeking to implement decisions independently of the European system.[20] In Berlin, Friedrich von Holstein, the '*éminence grise*' of German diplomacy who was responsible for the anglophile policy change after Bismarck's fall in 1890, had good reason to believe that Rosebery and his foreign secretary, Lord Kimberley, wanted to use Germany without giving anything in return. According to Holstein, England did nothing but wanted to devour everything.[21] That view was shared not only by Thomas Sanderson, but also, self-critically, by Cecil Arthur Spring Rice, former 'précis writer' for Rosebery.[22] Convinced of British dominance, Rosebery believed continued Anglo-German cooperation useful but no longer essential. At the same time, his greater ill feeling towards France and Russia and his doubts about the reliability of English parliamentarism and his own party prevented him from seeking an agreement with Paris and St Petersburg that would extend their cooperation beyond Asia.[23] Subsequently, too, after the establishment of the Entente Cordiale, Rosebery repeatedly voiced his opposition to that agreement, which put pressure on Balfour's government.[24]

Edward Grey, who along with Haldane proved the most dutiful of Rosebery's disciples,[25] had fewer scruples about establishing closer relations with Britain's former arch-rivals. Six months after leaving the government, in December 1895, he presented his ideas about a necessary change of course in foreign policy to Sidney Buxton. He believed the situation augured well:

> I am afraid we shall have to fight sooner or later, unless some European apple of discord falls amongst the Continental Powers, but we have a good card or hand to play and I think a bold and skilful Foreign Secretary might detach Russia from the number of our active enemies without sacrificing any material interests.[26]

Not only was Grey evidently convinced even at this early date – still before the Krüger telegram – that war was coming, but his proposal also already indicated the possibility of a more active foreign policy. Since time immemorial, London's exploitation of European tensions had proved tried and tested. Grey's acknowledgement of active involvement in creating such tension, rather than passive profiting, suggested a change of emphasis and is more reminiscent of Bismarck's 'unsolved tensions' and 'open conflicts' than of the maxim which held that balancing counterweights should serve the avoidance of conflicts. Grey even criticized Salisbury for adopting the largely traditional course of opposing Russia in the Mediterranean and instead made a case for a conciliatory and accommodating policy towards Russia, arguing, 'I have never been very devoted to the blue eyes of the Med [Mediterranean] and if old Sarum [Salisbury] has the pluck to do a bold stroke of policy and plays the dog in the manger [for Russia] there less, I for one should be glad'.[27]

On 31 December 1895, Grey had proposed that a clear demarcation of Russia's local interests could form a starting point for a general accommodation with the eastern and western continental powers. One searches in vain through his extensive commentary, however, for any reference to the international balance of powers or to possible consequences for the states system as a whole. For Grey, the opportunity was for a mutual agreement that would align the two powers' divergent global and European interests, and, he proposed, '[r]oom could easily be found for her [Russia's] wants and ours in *Asia and Europe* [my italics]. If Russia stands aside we ought to be able to deal easily with any combination ... which is possible at present'.[28]

At an early date, then, for Grey what was at stake was a definitive improvement in the security of the Empire, which came with a new approach to the balance of power. To that end, he was evidently prepared to expand Anglo-Russian cooperation into the periphery of the continent, no longer distinguishing between imperial and continental power constellations. He thus directly neglected Salisbury's advice to keep in mind the possible repercussions of an Anglo-Russian rapprochement.[29] Grey's goal was for Britain to join with the Dual Alliance to create a single dominant body, rather than for Britain to be the strongest power leaning to those lined up against the revisionist Dual Alliance. While Rosebery had in mind the weakening of the Dual Alliance by separating Russia from France, in effect a classic manipulation of the balance of power, Grey's plans went in a different direction. If necessary, he seemed even prepared to leave the eastern Mediterranean to Russia and France and to hold out to St Petersburg the possibility of access to the Persian Gulf.

Whatever the details, his primary intent was to generate tension between Russia and the Triple Alliance. While the initial paralysis of both alliances would enable England to manoeuvre into an advantageous position, the resultant balance would be precarious, a product of a state of tension and essentially military in character. That equilibrium would therefore have little in common with the universal principle of the balance of power as a method of ordering the system as a whole. Last, but not least, it would mean a new understanding of Britain's role. For Grey, that role was no longer for Britain to join temporarily with the apparently weaker power constellation in order to achieve a power balance overall. Rather than function as added weight that preserved a balance, Britain should foster, even generate, tension between the two parties in order to redirect any threat away from British interests. Without doubt, that approach brought a risky dependence on the outcome of such tension and, in the final analysis, required a permanent high-wire act taken even as far as brinkmanship.

In retrospect, Britain's withdrawal from its European commitments and gradual rapprochement with the Russian arch-enemy were often judged as a reaction to Germany and evidence that London believed Britain's position weak. Yet set in the context of Grey's broadly framed concepts, that interpretation comes up short. In 1895, the definitive issue was not Germany, which Grey does not even mention, or Britain's sense of weakness, but rather, and above all, the perceptible synergic impact of greater proximity to Russia. Relief in both the imperial and continental spheres seemed possible, with Russia more able than France to provide that assistance in both zones. Russia therefore stood ahead of France on Britain's wish list of future partners, even if Asquith was far-sighted in judging that the Fashoda crisis had cleared the air between Paris and London.[30]

In 1898, Grey had already spoken in the House of Commons in favour of 'a common ground with others',[31] with Russia in mind in particular, to the surprise of his radical liberal colleagues,[32] and he saw the period immediately after the Boer War as setting the course for the century to come.[33] His eye was on the two likely global powers of the twentieth century: the United States and Russia. He rejected Joseph Chamberlain's 'Teutonic alliance' from the outset, and deemed Chamberlain's Leicester speech a disaster.[34] While Grey, unlike Salisbury, was ready to consider the possibility of concessions to the United States and to Russia in particular, he held that Germany would play only a subordinate and instrumental role.[35] He rejected out of hand any settlement on the model of the Yangtze Agreement[36] and expressly praised Chamberlain's about-turn against Germany.[37] Grey's liberal imperial colleague Henry Norman concluded that France and Russia represented the universal solution to the problems of the Empire in the long run. Socio-political advantages might also be gleaned from the promise of financial benefits that could be of great assistance in overcoming domestic problems. For the Limps, however, an alliance with Japan, as concluded by the governing Tories during this phase, was very much the opposite of what they had in mind. While a number of current issues in the Far East could be papered over in the short term by such an agreement, both Norman and Grey were extremely critical of both the anti-Russian course that was thereby adopted and Lansdowne's habit of making concessions and arrangement without any formal agreement.³⁸ The right-liberals regretted the 'muddling through' and 'drifting' of the past.³⁹ The cyclical variations in the course of British foreign policy not only required a huge defence budget but also ran the risk of temporary isolation, and they sought greater predictability and the long-term safeguarding of Britain's interests. At the same time, their grounds for excluding possible partners had strong bipolar and even ideological character. With Germany excluded out of hand on the grounds that good Anglo-German relations would immediately mean a worsening of Britain's relationships with other powers,⁴⁰ room for manoeuvre was automatically restricted.

William Harcourt, who represented the Liberal Party's moderate wing with its high-profile members, criticized these very fixed notions and identified a nascent paradigm change in the apparatus supporting balance of power politics.⁴¹ Professor of international affairs and international law, Harcourt is best known for his biting criticism of conservative foreign policy in the 1870s and 1880s, but as an elder statesman he was not reticent in providing a commentary on foreign affairs. He admitted that Great Britain had never before experienced such isolation or been looked at with such suspicion by the other Great Powers, but he did not conclude that British foreign policy must therefore adopt a new direction. The tasks facing Britain in Europe continued to provide the principal point of reference for the strategy he advocated in foreign affairs, with the Empire of secondary import. As long as England could count on continued enmity between Germany and France, which he termed a 'positive hostility', then, he proposed, there was no need to worry about a continental alliance.⁴² The limits of that 'positive' enmity were overstepped, however, with the entry of Russia into the competition between the Great Powers, for while other powers might desire a temporary change in the continental status quo, the autocratic Russia of the tsars was a revolutionary threat not just to the states system but also to the states' social character. For Harcourt, the key to holding Russia in check was to be found not in rapprochement with St Petersburg, but in Britain's relationship with Germany. That relationship, according to Harcourt, was the determining factor of British foreign policy.

For both Harcourt and Grey, the principal concern was to prevent a renewed Three Emperor's Alliance. Both men saw Russia as the greatest threat to international peace as a whole. While Grey, the younger of the two, banked on global political concessions to Russia and included in his calculations a definite threat from future Slav imperialism, on the basis of his experience with Russia Harcourt, like Salisbury, emphasized the insecurity of the Kaiserreich and supported – for internal party considerations as well as domestic political concerns – a policy of strength in the face of the autocracy of the tsars. Where conciliation might lead when it came to Russia, Harcourt remembered all too well, for Gladstone's well-intentioned politics had resulted in the breaking of the Treaty of Berlin over Batum.⁴³ Unlike Grey, he believed that instability in European relations was a product of the well-founded assumption that Russia could take Constantinople at any time without any resistance from Britain, a threat the Central Powers would then be left to face on their own. Only Britain's withdrawal might give Russia the opportunity to overcome Franco-German antagonism by means of great pressure and force the Central Powers to join with Russia.[44] Where Rosebery and Grey stressed the Empire, Harcourt, in complete contrast, not only believed an imperial accommodation with Russia too dangerous because of the possible continental repercussions, but also pushed for such an agreement to be made with the Kaiserreich instead. He made a case for handing over Samoa to Germany and, more generally, for colonial accommodation with Berlin. Unlike in the earlier instance of Helgoland, he argued, the land at stake had not originally been British and therefore its loss was no great sacrifice. The positive effects for Anglo-German relations as a whole could hardly be overstated, and, he noted finally, non-colonial disputes were 'the grains of sand which destroy the great machinery and heat the bearings of Europe'.[45]

Rosebery had no time for such arguments. In his understanding of the global situation, against the backdrop of the competition between nations, such rapprochement could only be seen as a sign of weakness. There was absolutely no need for Great Britain to draw close to the Central Powers.[46] To mask this view, he made the exaggerated and therefore transparent claim that were Samoa to be surrendered, revolution in Australia and New Zealand might follow.[47] Harcourt, by contrast, believed it entirely in Britain's interests to come to terms with Germany and promptly accommodate that country's legitimate imperial wishes.

> There is nothing so impolitic as to irritate Great Powers on small subjects. Salisbury was very wise to make the 1890 agreement. … We cannot be surprised if the Great Powers are irritated at our advancing a claim to the exclusive possession of the Pacific Ocean and its Islands, to supremacy in the Mediterranean, to the proprietorship of Africa and the dominion of Asia. Surely a little give and take in these matters would be wise. We have already got the lion's share; why should we insist upon the tiger's also? Not to say the jackal's.[48]

Harcourt's argumentation may have been relatively untypical of its time, but it makes evident that Britain had the most with which to negotiate and therefore the greatest opportunity to influence the international order. Harcourt used information and experiences that were very similar to those deployed by the Liberals to make a recommendation that was remarkably different in two senses. First, he proposed that whatever of their former power remained, the German Empire and the Habsburg monarchy had long found themselves in the gravitational field of greater Russian interests and would only be able to hold Russia at bay as long as support from Britain remained an active option. Additionally, at the end of his political career, he again drew closer to the conservative interpretations and positions of Arthur Balfour, who similarly tended to emphasize the insecurity of the German Empire and of Austria-Hungary and was extremely critical of Russia. In terms of their analysis, both men were therefore overtaken by the Limps. Unlike Grey, Harcourt principally advocated a conciliatory and sympathetic attitude towards Britain's traditional partners and a continued demonstration of strength in the face of Russia. Every change in the British attitude towards Russia, which would have repercussions for the situation in the Far East, would only strengthen Russia's position, against which in the medium term the central European powers had nothing to play. The passivity and ignorance of Britain, Harcourt feared, could then force the Central Powers into the arms of Russia.

For each of the various proposals, a decisive role was taken by particular experiences and expectations and by whether priority was given to Empire or continent. Also significant were the varied estimations of the potential strength of the Central Powers and of Russia. From the younger Edwardian perspective, all the deliberation and cost-benefit analyses seemed to suggest that Anglo-Russian rapprochement offered the greatest likelihood that Britain's position would be immediately improved and consolidated. That argument was supported above all in the right-liberal and radical conservative media, which increasingly sought to ensure that traditional mistrust of Russia was replaced by recognition of the advantages of Anglo-Russian friendship.

From the start, this shift in emphasis gained significant support from rumours of an inherent danger to Britain from the Kaiserreich. Since 1896 at the latest, Malcolm MacColl, John Strachey, Leo Maxse and other journalists had described Germany consistently and repeatedly as Britain's greatest enemy. Their concern was not with the creation of a counterweight to an already-stronger opponent, but rather with joint, pre-emptive dominant control together with Russia and France in southern Europe, Africa and Asia.[49] The principal inference from the Armenian crisis of the mid 1890s was that in the Balkans the main threat came not from Russia but from Germany and Austria-Hungary. Liberal politician Francis Channing therefore was not alone in believing Germany to be far and away the greatest enemy of England.[50] Austro-German failure to force the sultan to initiate reforms was seen as concrete evidence in support of that interpretation. That Russia and even England also refused to put substantial pressure on the sultan on the issue of reform seemed to disturb no one and went unmentioned.[51] Nothing different could have been expected, in any case, of an autocratic state or Tory government. Henry Norman, liberal imperial Member of Parliament and journalist, spoke out in favour of an agreement between England and Russia and joint political action in both the Far East and Near East.[52] Even moderate liberals increasingly recognized benefits in rapprochement with Russia. Should Great Britain abandon its traditional animosity towards Russia over the Far East, then, they opined, the Franco-Russian Dual Alliance would very likely also be dissolved; Germany would then have its hands full and be forced to abstain from further intrigue against England on the global front.[53]

All in all, at the end of the nineteenth century a significant transition was in process in British foreign policy deliberations, with global political connections and the global advantages of an Anglo-Russian alliance given preference over more morally motivated continental concerns and responsibilities. The synergic impact was felt above all for the Far East, where even moderate Kimberley saw the relationship with Russia – not least as a link to France – as key.[54] Nowhere else did continental and imperial interests cluster so closely. Asked about the situation in the Mediterranean, Kimberley and Lord Ripon, Secretary of State for the Colonies, even saw Britain's complete withdrawal as the best solution: on one hand, they noted, Britain was already weaker than the combined force of France and Russia, and, on the other hand, Russian control of the Straits posed no direct threat to India.[55] The same principle was adopted for the Mediterranean by the Liberal foreign secretary during his short term in office, and was used by the young Edward Grey as the basis for his overall policy. Grey held that where Britain could no longer offer active opposition, it should foster disunity among other interested powers and withdraw. Where Grey hoped for Russo-German tensions in Europe, Kimberley banked on the long-term sundering of France and Russia over the Mediterranean.[56] Among the Limps, the weakening or ending of existing alliances had become an instrument of foreign policy, largely pushing the traditional balance of power into the background. On the Central Powers specifically, the liberal imperialists hoped that they would keep a low profile on the global stage but when it came to the internal politics of Europe still have sufficient strength to keep Russia and France at bay.

The challenges for the system as a whole should Britain adopt that approach were by no means unvoiced or overlooked. John Morley, editor, journalist, radical politician and an established expert on the issues, expressed his concerns to Herbert Gladstone. In light of the passivity of the Central Powers on Ottoman reforms and on Crete, Morley had come to the conclusion that Britain was now only reaping the harvest it had long being sowing: 'Her weight as an arbiter in the counsels of Europe has gone', he wrote, 'because she has shown herself rapacious and piratical these many years past. You cannot be at once a great jingo power, and a disinterested friend of humanity'.[57] He was joined in his criticism of England's attitude by Salisbury, in his correspondence with Sandars.[58] The experiences surrounding Home Rule meant that the Liberals' principal concern was now to prevent a new division. After the eventful year of 1898, even Harcourt could not fail to recognize, as he wrote, that agreement with Russia, 'who alone can injure us anywhere is of far more diplomatic importance than Germany, who cannot touch us anywhere',[59] and the radical liberals gradually moved closer to Grey on foreign policy. Leading Russians such as Baron de Staal, ambassador to London, and the Russian minister of justice and later ambassador to Italy (1905–1908) Count Nikolay Muraviev, greeted that development with pleasure and placed their hopes on up-and-coming politician Edward Grey.[60]

Two factors in particular propelled the reconciliation of the two liberal wings: the South African War and the party's loss in the khaki election.⁶¹ As early as November 1900, Rosebery used a speech in Glasgow to regain his leadership, and for the first time expressly made domestic reform an essential element of his imperial concept: 'An Empire such as ours requires as its first condition an imperial race; a race vigorous and industrious and intrepid. Health of mind and body exalt a nation in the competition of the universe. The survival of the fittest is an absolute truth in the conditions of the modern world'. What was the Empire, he concluded before students at the University of Glasgow, if it did not mean the supremacy of a single race?⁶² Following on from the election defeat, Rosebery appeared to be seeking to tie together his decidedly imperial approach and the traditional reform-oriented position of his party and to reconcile the two liberal camps. On 9 July at the Reform Club, the party leadership agreed to disagree about the South African War, which was an important step towards the party's unity.⁶³ Herbert Asquith left his mark as internal party broker when, in January 1901, he warned Grey against continuing his polemical attack on the radical liberals and at the same time called on the radical liberals' new leader, Campbell-Bannerman, at least to adopt Rosebery's line on foreign policy.⁶⁴ That same day, Harcourt demonstrated to Morley that he was prepared to come to terms with the foreign policy statements Rosebery had made in his speech at Chesterfield.⁶⁵ A truce within the Liberal Party, based on a compromise, was on the cards. While the more moderate fraction within the party adopted the Limp's position on foreign policy, the Limps in return promised to hold back and give the radical liberals the stage on domestic political reform.⁶⁶

The highpoint of this development was reached with the publication of *The Heart of the Empire*, edited by maverick Charles Masterman, in summer 1901.⁶⁷ Even socialists such as Beatrice and Sidney Webb and George Bernard Shaw found themselves in agreement with this compilation of essays, which called for a comprehensive reorganization of the Empire and dislodged Charles Dilkes' *Greater Britain* as the theoretical manifesto of the new imperial liberalism. The work was first mooted immediately after the Liberals had lost the election. Advertised in the *Spectator* on 8 June, the first edition sold out within only a week. For the *Times* and the *Spectator*, its pronouncements on empire and endorsement of the liberal imperialism of Gooch and Trevelyan did not go far enough, although they did not put this weakness down to a lack of patriotism but saw instead a reflex reaction to the recent elections. By contrast, the *Contemporary Review* and *Quarterly Review* stressed the work's geopolitical relevance and constructivist character, and although they too expressed concern about the linking of imperialism and social reform,⁶⁸ in so doing they acknowledged the particular solution being advocated.

Very rapidly, the physical decline of the nation that Masterman had highlighted had become a public watchword and a public scandal. Arnold

White followed with his polemical text *Efficiency and Empire*, in which he recorded that even in the first three months of the war, three out of every five recruits in Manchester had proved unable to perform the most basic physical requirements for soldiers in wartime and had had to be rejected on account of their lack of physical fitness. Having found similar results for York, Leeds and Sheffield, Rowntree's dramatic conclusion was that half the male population of England was incapable of performing its duty to the country in time of war.[69] When Major General John Maurice added his expert views in the *Contemporary Review* and posed the alarming question, 'Where to get men?', the political sphere could not fail to respond.[70] Here was a piece of good luck for the Liberals. The Boer War forced the largely moderate party leadership to abandon the domestic political laissez-faire attitude of Gladstone, for physical failing at home could all too easily lead to weakness abroad too. Domestic reform and foreign concerns had come together in a common cause. The war so detested by those who supported reform had itself opened the door to reform, which even the Limps now deemed necessary. Tariff reform, which could be used to finance the vital reforms – several Limps, including Mackinder, Garvin and Hewins, were won over to this idea – was now lined up against bipartisan 'national efficiency', which, it was suggested, could be achieved without raising taxes.

'Germany on the Brain': Edward Grey and the Coefficients

From the start, and unlike the radical liberals, the Limps favoured a strong empire, consolidated and served by alliances. The Empire should seek out its security partners in good time, looking not to Germany but to France and Russia. Above all, they envisaged Britain not as part of a balance of powers within Europe but as safeguarded within the circle of Great Powers. The Kaiserreich became their objective, with multiple functions. The Coefficients, a debating club founded in 1902 on the initiative of the Webbs, was representative of this approach and of the new links between liberals, socialists and the hard-to-define radical right, with its particular attitude towards Germany.[71] The Coefficients met regularly between 1902 and 1908, and following on from those meetings a number of likeminded individuals gathered in the home of later minister of war and military reformer Richard Haldane.[72] Self-identifying as a 'brains trust', this gathering, described by one member as a 'curious little talking and dining club',[73] provided 'the queerest diversity of brains' with a forum for discussing, developing and advising on the programmatic outlines of a comprehensive reform of British domestic and foreign policy. Its goals were therefore similar to those of Willoughby de Broke's Halsbury Club, the Reveille Circle and, later, the Compatriots.[74]

Members of the Coefficients, who often belonged to a number of clubs at the same time, included liberal imperialist politicians Edward Grey, Richard Haldane and Lord Milner; Halford John Mackinder, director of the newly founded London School of Economics and Political Sciences; economist William Hewins; influential editor Clinton Dawkins; journalists Leo Maxse, James Garvin, William F. Moneypenny, Leo Amery and Charles Repington; socialists Sidney and Beatrice Webb; imperial expert William Pember Reeves; politically ambitious naval officer Carlyon Bellairs; and authors Henry Newbolt and Herbert George Wells. Their meeting places included St. Ermin's Hotel and the Ship Tavern in Whitehall and they would also gather at the symposia held regularly by the Royal Geographical Society, whose president was Halford Mackinder.[75] As Wells acknowledged, these monthly gatherings enabled him to get a far better hold on the contemporary situation: 'They brought me closer than I had ever come hitherto to many processes in contemporary English politics and they gave me juster ideas of the mental atmosphere in which such affairs are managed', he recorded.[76] As philosopher Bertrand Russell confirmed in his memoirs, from the beginning of these illustrious gatherings, the liberal imperialists appeared convinced that war against Germany was inevitable.[77] Both remarkable and revealing is that the roots of that conviction were far from simplistic, unlike for Maxse, for example, where it was the product of a hate-filled, irrational Germanophobia. Their view was a complex product of Darwinist admiration of the Kaiserreich, British self-perception and a fundamental understanding of the modern states system and its dangers. According to Wells, these young imperialists were handicapped by an inability to differentiate between national vitality and patriotic bigotry. As Wells would later trenchantly observe, the younger members lacked political patience and nuanced thinking and looked instead for quick results, clear-cut solutions and global outcomes:

> Narrowing the outlook is a cheap immediate way of enhancing the effect of energy without really increasing it. They were all for training and armament and defensive alliances, and they were all careless or contemptuous of that breath and vigour of education in which the true greatness of a people lies.[78]

For Grey, Maxse and others of the Coefficients, the laws of nature determined that inevitably Germany's energies and successes would one day be turned against Britain. The Empire, they noted, had been formed through a similar process.[79] They paid little attention to fundamental differences such as Germany's geographical location or its federal structure, even though Haldane, the best acquainted with Germany among them, would later express his doubts about the policy towards Germany adopted by Grey, his colleague and friend. The young imperialists doubted neither themselves nor their arguments. They declared themselves 'fanatical devotees of the Empire', and their motto ran, 'My Empire, right or wrong'. According to Wells, the Empire was for them a divine order that must be defended through all possible means. While their attitude gave Russell reason to separate quickly from the Coefficients, Wells believed it his task to halt their imperialistic 'nonsense'.[80] He also believed Great Britain too weak to face the approaching challenge for it seemed ill prepared for its role as a world power. Oxbridge had failed to provide a modern thinking elite and instead had wasted its energies in raising future gentlemen. According to Wells, the Coefficients feared the future had been squandered, and continued to be squandered, on the cricket pitches of Eton, Rugby and Harrow: 'It [England] sacrifices intellect to character, ... its backbone is bigger than its cranium'.[81]

The discussions at this debating club contain early signs of an ambivalent, but inward-looking perception of Germany that later, in the 1930s, would develop into the concept of the 'two Germanies'. Positive views of Germany, particularly relating to German efficiency and education, could serve as models for reform in Britain, while negative perceptions were used to feed the Germany-as-enemy stereotype. Germany could be deployed to convince fellow Britons of the urgent need for reform.[82] The domestic and financial problems plaguing the Kaiserreich and the discrepancy between its global ambitions and actual modest successes paled before the admiration for oft-cited German efficiency, Germany's breathless development since 1871 and its people's close kinship with Anglo-Saxonness. It was simply unthinkable that Germany, the epitome of education, learning and military efficiency, could have no grand design for its foreign policy and was not following a fixed, rational plan.

Domestically, the unofficial discussion group formed an extra-parliamentary shadow cabinet whose members were drawn from politics, culture, business and the media, while some were authors; a number of these individuals would subsequently occupy significant decision-making positions.[83] In the 'Pentagram Circle' – the mystery-laden name Wells used to designate the club[84] – Edward Grey adopted the role of a shadow foreign secretary, who developed his approach to the European Central Power and British foreign policy further, concluding that Britain must learn from the example of Germany, invigorated by the enemy image and pooling its resources, if it wished to retain its traditional role as one of the Great Powers. Additionally, he held, a transformation of the current power constellations was necessary in order that Britain might be relieved of its responsibilities in relation to the Triple Alliance. Britain's role should not be to referee or stabilize the international system; Britain should be its beneficiary. Both in his private correspondence and in parliament, Grey welcomed the rapprochement between Italy and France, believing it opened the door on improved relations with France, 'which', he recorded, 'is much better than clutching at the skirts of the Triple Alliance'.[85] In November 1902, even without an acute crisis as his context, Grey declared 'splendid isolation' a thing of the past and that Britain's international relations were entering a period of critical transformation.

Certainly, alliances were not easily established, he continued, but all possible effort should be invested in agreements with France and Russia;[86] he was adamant, however, that any agreement with the young German Great Power be ruled out:

> Now that Austria has come to terms with Russia in regard to the Balkan Peninsula, and that Italy and ourselves are on friendly relations with France, the Triple Alliance is by no means the chief security for European peace as it once was. ... the firm friendship of France could only be secured by some far-reaching arrangement with Russia.[87]

As under-secretary of state for foreign affairs under Rosebery, his first governmental position, Grey had internalized the dangers inherent in a Franco-Russian alliance. From this perspective, he repeatedly emphasized that for Britain alliances with its most significant and most dangerous rivals might be necessary for the sake of the Empire and also of Europe.[88] A need for a balance of power influenced his position far less than the great benefits in store for the Empire and for Britain domestically. Indirectly, a new order would then also take shape, for Germany's progress and options would be curbed by the powers to its east and west. Isolated and contained on the continent, Grey emphasized to Maxse, Germany would have nothing concrete beyond its strength to offer; at best, it would be able to exploit tensions between the other powers.[89] Sooner or later, the Central Power would inevitably become embroiled in a conflict with one of its neighbours that it would be unlikely to win on land or at sea.[90] He conceded to Leo Maxse, a fellow member of the Coefficients, 'In Egypt they [the Germans] have given us quiet backing. There is some truth in this, but it is a position that is never comfortable for us and is becoming daily less comfortable and secure; the business of the British Government is to bring about a better one and the first step is an understanding with Russia'.[91] If dependency on alliances meant that Britain would have to come to terms with other powers, then the agreements into which Britain entered should at least hold out a real possibility of relief and offer some predictability. Furthermore, the Coefficients' meeting of April 1903 produced the suggestion that Russia be offered gains in the Near East in exchange for concessions in the Middle East and Far East, with the additional positive result 'that such changes in the Near East would be at the expense especially of German prestige, and would tend to divide Germany and Russia'.[92] This willingness to set interests on the continent against imperial interests provides an early taste of Grey's later Anglo-Russian convention policy.

The Conservative government categorically rejected the proposed exchange and merely accepted that the Middle East and Far East were matters for negotiation with St Petersburg. The strategy that involved ensuring potential enemies remained divided and exploiting their open tensions within the Near East had its origins in a nightmare scenario: the possible creation of a continental coalition, on the cards again since the Boer War, exerted constant pressure on Grey's foreign policy thinking. As was well known in London political circles, during the Boer War St Petersburg had looked for some form of cooperation with Germany that could be directed against Britain, making the need for rapprochement with Russia now seem all the more necessary.

Hoping to meet Maxse at the Coefficients, Grey indicated where he felt discussion necessary: 'I always thought and still think the Japanese alliance may have some very awkward consequences in the long run and I do not think it will facilitate a settlement of our outstanding affairs with Russia'.[93] The Coefficients dining club provided the future foreign minister with not only a forum in which he could develop his thoughts but also a free lesson on the domestic problems that might accompany his proposed course of action. Ultimately, his colleagues were unable to conceal their continuing mistrust of Russia. In light of the numerous imperial conflict zones, an alliance with Russia was desirable, but, Grey noted, if nothing else Salisbury's recent forays in this direction had confirmed that the Russians were not to be trusted any longer than 'the ink of the treaty was wet'.[94]

Alongside the approach to Russia, which sat uncomfortably with domestic politics and within the party, a further pillar of Grey's foreign policy concept began to form at the beginning of the new century, with greater support among the Coefficients. Grey explained to the electorate in Berwick that it was far too dangerous to risk irritating the United States and that British foreign policy must adapt to the changing conditions created by the Franco-Italian and Austro-Russian rapprochements and create greater distance from Germany. He accused the government of Balfour and Lansdowne of having moved too close to Germany, at the expense of British relations with France, Russia and the United States.[95] Possible ties with the United States were a repeated theme among the Coefficients and an idea published by H.G. Wells for the broader public.[96] The immediate context determined two specific concerns. First, during the Venezuela crisis, any suggestion of overly close cooperation with Germany was to be avoided, and secondly, continued domestic reforms were required: the minutes of a meeting held in March 1903 recorded, 'We must further republicanize our institutions. The common American opinion is that we are ruled by an effete monarchy and aristocracy'.[97] Wells viewed rapprochement with the former American colonies as an alternative to the Anglo-Russian option, which he so hated, but Grey looked not to alternatives but to the creation of a comprehensive package in which Britain would be part of an international network. France, Russia and the United States would be the cornerstones of a new security configuration whose gravitational pull countries such as Japan, Italy and Spain would be unable to escape. Here again we see an early outline of a strategy adopted subsequently.

Unlike the Conservatives and radical liberals, the largely younger liberals on the right were principally concerned with the creation of a comprehensive and absolute defence concept that would encompass Britain's most dangerous opponents and ensure that a potential, and likely, threat on the continent could be redirected or quashed by means of a defensive alliance-based policy, untypical of Britain. They hoped thereby to ensure Britain entered into the twentieth-century global struggle for supremacy already at an advantage. A partial concert among these powers could then either draw in or outvote the remaining powers. Stimulated by this new prospective course, a decidedly continental perspective now joined the domestic and imperial perspectives. The reform debate and various proposed solutions, particularly from the liberal imperialists, make evident how the so-called trinity of imperial, domestic and European politics[98] that formed the constitutive elements of British politics could at various times interrelate. As a result, in various political arenas both continuity and discontinuity could be found, even simultaneously.

The Conservatives had their eye primarily on the consolidation of the Empire by means of regional agreements, partial withdrawals and general domestic reform, while also favouring a more traditional course in relations with Europe. With their comprehensive security concept, the New Liberals went a step further, giving greater emphasis to the continental dimension of Britain's foreign policy. Here we find the roots of the quarantine policy subsequently used against the members of the Triple Alliance in the Balkans. Electoral and party concerns provided good reason to ensure the theory was backed up by action. Although even in alliance with Austria-Hungary Germany was evidently too weak to present a real threat to England, trust in the traditional reactive counterweight continued to wane. As Germany and Russia did not appear to present any threat individually, the principal concern was no longer with establishing a peaceful balance and the stabilization of the power system as a whole; now the concern was to ensure the three imperial powers were kept apart. With this new strategy, principally preventative, policy formulated in London was no longer characterized by the traditional search for a balance of power.

The Coefficient members active in the media made every effort to ensure that in public discussion of the danger from Germany their nuanced understanding of the real threat from Germany was subordinated to the need for security and for domestic reform, thereby in effect sweeping their knowledge under the carpet. Beyond parliament, the Limps generally had a strong presence in the press that was associated with members of the Liberal League, founded in 1902, including publishers such as Stuart Johnson Reid, Edward Cook, Eliot Mills and the Harmsworths.[99] Academic debate was thought too complicated to be able to mobilize the general population, who were instead presented with a blatant stereotype of Germany as the arch-enemy. The invasion theme proved particularly valuable to this approach, even though, as Haldane well knew, the threat of invasion was non-existent. The real danger from Germany was that its technical and scientific know-how might be put at the service of an alliance with Russia.[100]

Viewed close up, the attitude of the constructivist efficiency movement is not without an inner logic. For that movement, the Kaiserreich fulfilled several functions at once. First, it provided a model for a way forward and an example of efficiency and modernity for close imitation. Secondly, it served as a tool that could be used to heighten demands for reform and to emphasize the need for a change of course in both domestic and foreign policy, while also providing a goal for those reforms. And finally, surely one would want to be as well armed as possible in order to be able to take on an anticipated enemy, for conflict with Germany was inevitable, whether sooner or later.[101] 'If the British remained content with their muddling ways, they would be taught a harsh and final lesson, for the Germans were scientifically building up their strength, planning for "Der Tag", the day when their preparations would be crowned by the successful invasion and conquest of Britain.'[102]

Additionally, Germany as enemy provided an integrating and dynamic force precisely because for decades Germany had been viewed as a natural partner. That impact, hard to overestimate, was evident at the imperial level, significant for the quarrelling wings of the party and, we must take particular note, seminal for England's rich media landscape.[103] For the liberal imperialists around Grey, Asquith and Haldane, organization and efficiency became guiding principles of both domestic and foreign policy, counterweights to the 'muddling through' and 'drifting' of the past.[104] Following defeat in the khaki election, six years later, with the aid of the efficiency programme and propelled by their hunger for power, the liberal imperialists succeeded not only in overcoming the internal division between radicals and imperialists but also in bringing over a large part of labour to their side. In the contemporary press and political media, the Liberals had found a partner with its finger on the popular pulse.

Ad Hoc Politics in Place of Grand Design: Lansdowne and Balfour

The government party responded with remarkable composure to the call for comprehensive reform that would embrace foreign relations. And, indeed, why not? Had not the South African War recently confirmed Lord Salisbury's view that their very different interests meant it was nigh impossible that the other Great Powers would be able to form an anti-English coalition? Additionally, the war had made evident not just imperial weakness, but also the tremendous potential for mobilization of the Empire.[105] It was and still is always easily forgotten that no other power would have been in a position to assemble a fighting force of that ilk, bringing men from all corners of the earth thousands of miles across the seas to be deployed at the Cape and then provisioning them there for months on end. Unlike the disparate liberal wings, the two unionist wings were of one mind on foreign policy and saw no immediate need for action. Initially, Salisbury, Lansdowne and Balfour aimed to respond temperately and calmly to calls from the opposition and the media for a change of course in foreign policy. Following their election victory, their principal concern was with the consolidation of the Empire and of the financial situation. The return to imperial thinking was also intended to create unity after the heated election campaign.

In October 1900, Salisbury resolved to withdraw gradually from his various offices. His first step was to resign as foreign secretary.[106] In recent years, ill health had too often forced him to pass the work of that office over to Arthur Balfour, sometimes at very delicate moments, and Balfour now convinced Salisbury that he should reduce his responsibilities. It was not Balfour, however, who took over the Foreign Office but a friend of Balfour's from his schooldays, Henry Charles Keith Petty-Fitzmaurice, fifth Marquess of Lansdowne, who was promoted from minister of war to foreign secretary, taking up a position for which he had been considered five years earlier.[107] Like so many of his predecessors, Lansdowne was a member of the House of Lords, and Salisbury therefore appointed his own son as the new foreign secretary's parliamentary under-secretary. Additionally, Balfour's brother Gerald was made minister for trade and Salisbury's son-in-law Lord Selborne became First Lord of the Admiralty. This nepotism, which earned the title 'Hotel Cecil' from its many critics, was evidently intended to create in effect an inner cabinet, which would ensure a maximum of continuity in foreign policy. In terms of personnel at least, there was no hint of the supposed paradigm change that has often been identified in the appointment of Lansdowne.[108] Lansdowne was doubtless an ideal candidate. His family background – he was a great-grandson of Talleyrand[109] – and his political experience of the Empire meant that Salisbury and Balfour, who likely made this decision together, would have been hard pressed to find a more qualified successor among the ranks of the Conservatives.

The offspring of a long line of high aristocratic Whigs, Lansdowne had begun his political career as a liberal member of the House of Lords at the age of only twenty-three, shortly after coming down from Oxford. Although extraordinarily talented, he was handicapped by a consistent self-doubt, which had stood in the way of greater academic achievement. Although Lansdowne received only a rather unexpected and disappointing second-class degree at Oxford, Benjamin Jowett, mentor to numerous political and diplomatic great men of his age,[110] had no doubts about the political capabilities of the young lord.[111] As Lansdowne departed from Balliol, Jowett encouraged him 'to keep his mind above party feelings and motives'. He continued, 'A new era of politics is now beginning .... Freedom from personal feelings are the quality to be aimed at. ... I don't object to a touch of idealism or speculation .... But how few statesmen have these qualities in any degree'.[112]

Twelve years later, Lansdowne remained true to his convictions on Home Rule and resigned from his first governmental position, as under-secretary for war, with a brilliant speech that brought him great respect above all from the Tories.[113] Having proved himself as Governor General of Canada from 1883 to 1888, he was courted by Salisbury as a potential Conservative. Salisbury sought to lure him with a range of high offices, which included positions in the war and colonial ministries. Eventually Lansdowne accepted the position of viceroy for India, which he retained until 1894.[114] Although he had carried out the responsibilities of his offices in both Canada and India with great success, in autumn 1900 there was some doubt, especially among the public, that he was qualified for the office of foreign secretary, a concern that stemmed from his failure to achieve the reforms that he had sought as minister of war since 1895.[115] A good number of London's politically engaged held him responsible for the initial British plight at the hands of the Boers.[116] The self-doubt that had gnawed at him in his student days now raised its head again. He wrote shamefacedly to the queen of his achievements as minister for war, recording, 'I must often have seemed to your Majesty to fall short of expectations'. Queen Victoria had in fact agreed to the change in personnel under one condition: Salisbury was to continue to keep an eye on foreign policy.[117] It had likely not escaped the queen, however, that the public and some in the army had made Lansdowne a scapegoat for the failure of others. Citing cost, his sharpest critics had themselves rejected all reform of the armed forces.

Lansdowne's nature was not to engage this criticism, let alone speak out against it publicly, nor did he have a need for approval like that of, for example, his university friend Lord Curzon or his cabinet colleague Joseph Chamberlain. In the Foreign Office, he was recognized as an 'amiable' and 'hardworking gentleman', but he was not trusted to develop an own concept either administratively or politically.[118] Initially, he stood in the shadow of his great predecessor, but he was not discontent with the situation and of his own volition offered Salisbury an office within the ministry building; initially he was also somewhat reserved at cabinet meetings. The press, and specifically several foreign correspondents, were on the whole disappointed to learn of his appointment, for they had counted on the selection of either Curzon or Chamberlain for the post.[119] Their attitude has left its mark right up to the present day: even though Lansdowne is recognized as having been willing to risk ending English isolationism and adopting in its place a limited responsibility on the continent, he remains among the least studied British foreign secretaries of the twentieth century, and to date we still lack a comprehensive modern biography.[120]

Often Lansdowne is viewed simply as a placeholder, as 'postscript to Salisbury and ante-chamber to Grey'. In such accounts, he is deemed typically Edwardian – he believed his predecessor's isolationism and policy of drift needed to be reconsidered and after a number of naive forays with Germany learned his lesson and with the Entente Cordiale set a course for a balance of powers attributed to Edward Grey.[121] According to George Monger, who accepted Leo Maxse's response practically word for word, with Lansdowne's appointment the pro-German attitude within the cabinet triumphed and Lansdowne's period in office was characterized more by luck than by any real ability.[122] Lansdowne's first letter to Frank Lascelles, ambassador in Berlin, is repeatedly cited as evidence of a naive Germanophilia. Lansdowne informed Lascelles that he believed himself bound to carry out only a single essential task: 'To use every effort to maintain and, if we can, to strengthen the good relations which at present exist between the Queen's Government and that of the Emperor'.[123] That earlier assessment fails to recognize that the following day Lansdowne wrote to Edmund Monson, British ambassador to Paris, that his expressed desire to maintain good and successful relations with France contained not just empty words, but rather genuine hope.[124] He also fostered a serious desire for close cooperation with the United States and a mutually beneficial relationship.[125] Despite the evident tensions in the Far East, he wrote, he credited the Russian Foreign Minister, Count Vladimir Lamsdorff with only the best of intentions, even if the positions he adopted were rather difficult to understand. He informed Charles Scott, British ambassador at St Petersburg, that he would not be putting a foot wrong if he repeatedly emphasized 'that we wish to be friends'.[126] It would be all too easy to draw from these statements, all found in standard letters of introduction sent by a foreign minister to his ambassadors, just about any bias one might be looking for.[127] These exchanges contain no real evidence of Lansdowne's policy, which, as we will see, was largely still based on the established practice of 'muddling through', with the result that English policy was largely determined by events and experiences rather than by deliberate planning.[128] Lansdowne's letters of introduction were principally designed to make initial contact and ensure options were kept open. His first concern was to gain a sense of the international situation, for at this stage he was still finding his bearings. An approach that initially appeared pro-German would have been not in the least surprising; indeed, his predecessor had only shortly before come to an arrangement with Berlin over China that was designed to secure access to the Yangtze region and that Lansdowne still had to see through parliament. Additionally, at this date France and Russia, the two other European global powers, were not open to closer relations with Britain. While the German public fulminated against England's belligerence, the government in Berlin behaved punctiliously, but as the French and Russian publics fulminated, their governments attempted to exploit England's military entanglements by advancing into Siam and the Middle East. The American government also had no scruples about using the situation to its advantage in the Western hemisphere and attempted to force England out of the Caribbean.

High on Lansdowne's agenda was the consolidation of British possessions, on which point he was entirely in agreement with Salisbury and Balfour. The strained financial situation meant any other option was impossible anyway. As John Charmley aptly commented, 'Joe's war in fact made Joe's policy impossible'.[129] Thanks to the most expensive war in British history to date, Chancellor of the Exchequer Michael Hicks Beach had acquired such weight in the cabinet that he was able to ensure that, despite Lansdowne's and Salisbury's contrary desire, English troops were to be withdrawn from the Far East. Any consolidation and defence of the Empire was welcome, as long as it did not lead to additional costs.[130] Negotiation therefore remained the only option for reducing the burden of empire.[131] It is therefore also to consider that it was not external pressure or foreign aggression, neither from Germany nor the Dual Alliance powers, that demanded a recalibration of Britain's foreign policy, but if at all London had to pay for a war that was self-chosen.

Unlike for the liberal imperialists, for Balfour and Lansdowne the traditional principle of splendid isolation was not up for negotiation wholesale. They favoured selective imperial consolidation, or protection, that would run alongside abstinence on the continent. Although historians continue to speak of a continuity in foreign policy that ran from Lansdowne and Balfour to Grey, close examination reveals a more nuanced picture. As pupils of Salisbury, the former drew on their experiences and looked to protect the periphery without repercussions for the centre or for international constellations as a whole. Both believed developments internationally to be in a fluid phase, and they pursued neither the fostering of alliances and long-term perspective associated with Chamberlain and Grey nor the traditional isolationism associated with Disraeli and Salisbury. Their approach led in a number of directions and contained the typical attempt of a conservative political elite to combine at a time of crisis tried and tested methods with their own experiences and inferences. 'In Politics', Balfour believed, 'there is no use looking beyond the next fortnight'.[132] What was new, however, was their willingness to engage bilateral responsibilities at all; all their previous moves in that direction had been stalled by Salisbury's intransience. However, this decision was based on neither a desire to alter or reorganize international relationships from the ground up nor a desire to establish a general Anglo-Russian alliance.[133]

The conceptualization of this approach was the work of Balfour.[134] While Lansdowne could call on enormous imperial and global experience, Balfour saw international relations above all from the perspective of a European Great Power. He had gathered his initial experiences under the guidance of Salisbury at the Berlin Congress of 1878.[135] Since then, he had been as intrigued by the complexity of the pentarchy as by his philosophical studies and writings. His experiences in foreign policy and his intellectual engagement with the spirit of his age had come together to provide him with an assessment of the situation very different from that of the Limps, and also a different solution. Their initial hypothesis, however, was the same, for Balfour also believed that the creation of the Franco-Russian Dual Alliance in 1892 and 1894 against an imperialist backdrop signified a revolution in the states system that would have incalculable results.[136]

Balfour drew two conclusions: one concerned the British Empire, where, he believed, in future every disagreement with Russia would lead to tensions in central Asia,[137] while one concerned the states system as a whole, where he believed, or so we can conclude from a number of his statements, that in the long term imperial tensions among the world powers would inevitably have repercussions on the continent[138] – in other words, the alliance of the two least-saturated states presented a great threat to peace. Balfour held it undoubtedly a blessing for Britain not to be part of the European mainland,[139] but, he repeatedly stressed, it would be naive for his fellow countrymen to assume that European static was of no significance to them.[140] Balfour saw Russia as Britain's longstanding enemy, and held that Russia's drive to expand threatened the whole Empire.[141] Unusually, this reading overlapped with the views of the radical liberals around William Harcourt, for the new leader of the Conservative Party also categorically rejected the suggestion that the autocratic Russian Empire be appeased with concessions in other spheres, in the Near East for example. 'What kind of world will it be', asked Balfour, 'when Russia, which has already a hundred and twenty million inhabitants, exercises an enormously dominating influence over the whole of south-eastern Europe? What kind of Europe will it be, dominated by Slavs?'[142]

It seems unlikely that Balfour would have been drawn into war with Russia on account of the Balkans, but he certainly had no interest in encouraging Russia's Balkan ambitions, let alone in pointing Russia to potential spoils in the Near East, for such Russian expansion would not have provided lasting relief for the Empire.[143] Instead, he intended to place as many obstacles as possible in Russia's path and to make clear that its continuing expansion would come at a high cost. Without hesitation, even while facing massive protest in the House of Commons and from the English public, he admitted that he would prefer to see Balkan Christians oppressed by the Turks than Russia dominant in south-eastern Europe.[144] He was little troubled by the idea of Russian occupation of the Straits, for it could only bring Russia endless troubles. Initially, Lansdowne had appeared very optimistic about the possibility of an agreement with St Petersburg over the Middle East, and Balfour gave Lansdowne free rein, although he believed his foreign secretary was deluding himself.[145]

As a means of preventing an anti-English continental alliance, the liberal imperialists sought the creation, with the help of concessions to Russia, of a defensive bloc in which Britain would join with the Dual Alliance. Balfour, too, sought to exploit the tensions between Germany and Russia, but he favoured the traditional tool of closer ties to Germany, writing to Salisbury in April 1898:

> The real fact is that the Emperor of Germany, in spite of his air of universal domination, is in mortal fright of Russia; and especially of a maritime combination (as well

as military) combination of France and Russia. From the effects of this maritime combination we could save him – and he is prepared to buy us. If we are not for sale he will go elsewhere – to our detriment.[146]

Imperial tensions would sooner or later be played out on the continent, but why not try to delay that day for as long as possible? Experience taught that concessions to Russia only made Russia all the hungrier. An alliance with Germany, by contrast, Balfour had declared during the Boer War, was 'second only in importance to … drawing closer the English-speaking races'. Immediately after the war, when the press in London was already speaking out against Germany and Chamberlain had long since distanced himself from his projected Teutonic alliance, Metternich reported that the new prime minister was championing ties between Germany, the United States and Great Britain.[147] Six months before his appointment as prime minister, Balfour had explained his foreign policy strategy for the upcoming years, criticising the decision to enter into an overhasty alliance with Japan, not because, unlike Grey, he feared upsetting Russia, but because he would have preferred close ties with Germany. If one was to enter into an alliance at all, he opined, then one should at least do so in a cause worth fighting for.[148]

Just like the Coefficients, Balfour was convinced that in many ways England could learn from Germany. He was also enthusiastic about German culture, venerating Wagner and German scholarly and philosophical achievements. Unlike his uncle, he could even tolerate Wilhelm II well enough. He had already informed Hatzfeldt in 1898 that he thought Wilhelm far too great a man to allow himself to be disturbed by the uncouth behaviour of his uncle, the future Edward VII.[149] He did not believe the Kaiser's sense of mission a particular threat, commenting that among all the royals he had met, Wilhelm was by far the most interesting conversation partner, and noting, 'He talks like we all do'.[150]

Balfour agreed with evaluations of Germany's political weaknesses, but his conclusions were very different from those of the liberal imperialists, for he recognized the stabilization of the continent as a European responsibility and in British interests and also predicted the threat that would come from imperial tensions. He saw common concern about Franco-Russian dominance, which he deemed 'perilous'[151] for England, as unifying.

Unlike Herbert Asquith, Alfred Milner and a whole run of younger diplomats such as Eyre Crowe, Charles Hardinge and Louis Mallet, who supported a radical change of course towards rapprochement with Russia, Balfour was not a convinced Social Darwinist who allowed himself to be led by expectations for the future and assumed a fight to the death among the world powers in the course of the twentieth century inevitable.[152] While Alfred Milner invoked competition between the nations as 'divinely ordained',[153] Edward Grey, Eyre Crowe and others repeatedly spoke of an unavoidable 'struggle for existence', with Asquith convinced that continued territorial expansion was normal, necessary and inevitable, and a sign of national virility.[154] Balfour rejected not only all expansion of the Empire,[155] but also any grand theory that might give global history coherence. He had endorsed Chamberlain's 'grand design' for an imperial alliance with the United States and Germany but believed his concept utopian. As president of the Sociological Society and a keen philosopher, he had been an active participant in the debates on Social Darwinism and the future of England. His scholarly interests were genuine and he had gained much from the theory of evolution (while a student in Cambridge, he had met Charles Darwin), but his intellectual interests did not make him a Social Darwinist. His pragmatic approach to foreign policy, consistently presented with cool, clear reason – Churchill called him a new Machiavelli[156] – did not mean that he had embraced natural selection. For Balfour, a biological understanding of foreign policy[157] was only one of several legitimate explanations: 'Observe that as the world is constituted there is a struggle – sometimes industrial, sometimes military, sometimes diplomatic – going on between the leading nations of the world. I am glad to think that this is not the only way in which we can contemplate a display of civilised forces'.[158] He pointed out to journalists of the radical right, men such as Leo Maxse, Charles Repington and Rudyard Kipling, who deemed him a spineless weakling,[159] that 'congenital idiots increase faster than any other class of the population', yet their theory of natural selection implied such people 'must be deemed the fittest of our countrymen'.[160] Wearing two hats, his philosopher's and his politician's, he rejected natural selection as the dominant explanation of either society or states and insisted on the unpredictability of events.

His intensive engagement with military and defensive policy did not tell him otherwise. Ultimately, he also rejected Darwinist rhetoric that favoured bolstering Britain's fighting strength. War, Balfour commented in 1904, had never advanced the world, only inhibited its progress.[161] For foreign policy specifically, his approach left him convinced that events, perhaps unforeseeable, might yet avert seemingly inevitable conflict, or in his own words, 'An evil day put off may perhaps never come'.[162]

Sanderson, Bertie and the 'Old' Foreign Office

The course adopted by Lansdowne and Balfour was supported both substantively and administratively by Thomas Henry Sanderson. As the longest serving and most experienced diplomat at Whitehall – he had joined the foreign ministry in 1859 – Sanderson embodied the 'old' Foreign Office and its traditional approach to foreign policy. Sanderson was the institutional memory for English foreign policy of the nineteenth century.[163] Named permanent under-secretary by Salisbury in 1894, he believed his primary responsibility was to protect the foreign secretary from administrative flak. Unlike his younger colleagues, above all Francis Bertie, Charles Hardinge, Louis Mallet and Eyre Crowe, he had no interest in using overlong memoranda to make a political name for himself. Nevertheless, with his rarely expressed but therefore all the more weighty opinions, he was an *éminence grise* in the background of English foreign policy. As the last super-clerk, he oversaw the important Western and Eastern Departments, was responsible for the Treaty Department and archive, and shared responsibility with Barrington for the ever-more-important contact with the press.[164] Salisbury had trusted his judgement without question, and his influence appears even to have grown under Lansdowne and Balfour, not least as he was in accord with Balfour politically and related well to him privately.[165]

On the whole, Sanderson's recommendations were products of his decades-long experience and drew on Salisbury's criteria for a balance of power. Tensions between the Great Powers were to be diverted into the peripheries, and into the Far East in particular.[166] Sanderson opposed an alliance with Japan not out of fear of Russia but because the increased potential for conflict in the Far East would, he feared, mean its loss as leverage for the European centre.[167] He supported efforts to compensate France and Russia only if they would have no repercussions on the continent.[168]

That Sanderson had never held a posting abroad – London was always his locus of operation – was not necessarily a disadvantage. On one hand, it helped establish his fundamental sense that the European periphery was the principal frame of reference for British interests overall. On the other hand, it stopped him from adopting the preferential treatment and biases of his successors Hardinge and Nicolson, both of whom had previously been British ambassadors to St Petersburg. Additionally, although his perspective was taken from London, he believed it imperative that he place himself in the shoes of whichever foreign country he was dealing with and examine English foreign policy as that country saw it, even to the extent of expressing self-criticism.[169] Precisely in the case of Germany, that approach led to repeated accusations by both younger colleagues and some historians of Germanophilia and a certain naivety in his attitude towards the Kaiserreich.[170] In practice, however, he maintained a critical position towards Germany that overlapped entirely with that of Salisbury, complaining in particular about Wilhelm II's capricious temperament and interference in foreign policy.[171] At the same time, however, he was aware of the geopolitical weaknesses of the Central Powers and the dangers they faced,[172] and what is more, his assessment of Germany's behaviour took account of Britain's many years of negative experience with the powers of the Dual Alliance. With Britain's own behaviour as his comparandum, he repeatedly came to the conclusion that Berlin's stance on international relations was not exceptional.[173] As long as England was not prepared to support Germany as it withstood pressure on two fronts, then Germany had no real option other than to hope for continued tension between the powers to its east and west. In case of doubt, Sanderson convinced Balfour, with an eye to the Danube monarchy Berlin would always uphold the interests of Britain and, for example, advocate for the status quo at the Straits.[174] Sanderson therefore deemed all the more questionable the increasingly one-sided Germanophobia of his younger colleagues, which prevented them from making an objective comparative evaluation:

> Whereas some time ago, I had to explain often enough that there were certain things we could not expect of the Germans, however friendly they might be, I have now, wherever they are mentioned, a labour to show that the conduct of the German government has in some material respects been friendly. There is a settled dislike of them – and an impression that they are ready and anxious to play us any shabby trick they can. It is an inconvenient state of things for there are a good many questions in which it is important for both countries that we should work cordially together and of course if Bülow treads on our toes again the public will go off at once.[175]

Among the early anti-German critics was Francis Bertie, one of the three assistant under-secretaries who served under Sanderson. Only some three years younger than Sanderson, he viewed Sanderson's career jealously and, protected by Edward VII and his private secretary Lord Knollys, never missed an opportunity to plot against his superior and speak ill of him to his younger colleagues.[176] Unlike Sanderson, he voiced his opinion readily, even when not asked for it, and his overly long memoranda, which provided a model for Hardinge and Crowe in particular,[177] were characterized by a Social Darwinist conviction that a great war was unavoidable and that a policy based on strength and calculability must be adopted in place of Salisbury's 'muddling through'.[178]

At the end of October or beginning of November 1901 (the dating is inconsistent[179]), Bertie presented an extraordinary memorandum that, far more than the famous Crowe memorandum of five years later, formed the foundations of the new Edwardian policy towards Germany. The memorandum stated that in recent years the German government had repeatedly attempted to tie England to the Triple Alliance and most recently had taken a new line in threatening England with isolation should England fail to comply. According to Bertie, three issues must be borne in mind when it came to Germany: first, its Bismarckian traditions, evident in the Reinsurance Treaty, which had been agreed behind the back of Germany's most valuable partner; second, its geographical location between France and Russia; and third, its situation in relation to the British Empire. Surrounded by enemies, Germany was, he suggested, abjectly dependent on support from Britain. In light of their own internal problems and weaknesses, neither Austria-Hungary nor Italy was a reliable ally. According to Bertie's interpretation, 'These considerations have made it incumbent on Germany to create and maintain distrust between the Powers not in alliance with her, and particularly between England and Russia and between England

and France. She therefore does what she can to keep open sores. ... She is always ready with information for our consumption of Russian and French intrigues'.

Those formulating Britain's position on Germany, Bertie's memorandum continued, must be clear that a simple existential fear meant that Germany would never support England in a war against Russia: 'She will never use force ... when it may bring her into collision with Russia. Of this her interpretation of the Anglo-German Yang-tze Agreement is good proof'. Germany's trading interests meant it was interested in free access to China, while its support for the Ottoman Empire, as a bulwark against Russian expansion in the Balkans and against Austria-Hungary, continued London's traditional policy. If, however, Britain should enter into an alliance with Germany, then globally English foreign policy would have to adapt to German policy, arousing, surely, the animosity of the Dual Alliance. Bertie opined that the Boer War had provided the best evidence that isolationism would do no harm, for even during the war, it had proved impossible to create a continental coalition against England.

> In our present position we hold the balance of power between the Triple and the Dual Alliances. There is but little chance of a combination between them against us. Our existence as a great and strong State is necessary to all in order to preserve the balance of power, and most of all to Germany ... Treaty or no treaty, if ever there were a danger of our destruction, or even defeat, by Russia and France, Germany would be bound, in order to avoid a like fate for herself, to come to our assistance. She might ask a high price for such aid, but could it be higher than what we should lose by the sacrifice of our ... world policy, which would be the result of a formal defensive alliance with the German Empire?[180]

For Bertie, then, Germany's weakness, and not Germany's strength, was the real barrier to cooperation. As long as the relationship between the Central Powers and the Dual Alliance remained tense, Britain would be a significant beneficiary. If it came down to it, England would get Germany's support for nothing, so why should London consider paying for that same assistance?

Protected by the king from Lansdowne's plans for his retirement, Bertie became ambassador to Rome,[181] then deputized temporarily for Sanderson in summer and autumn 1904, and finally was made ambassador to Paris, when he was responsible for the Triple Alliance formed by Britain's joining with the powers of the Dual Alliance in order to control the Central Powers. During these years, and along with Louis Mallet and other allies, Bertie worked to prevent any reduction in the tensions between Britain and Germany.[182]

Sanderson pleaded for a different course and was particularly critical of the desire to see the Entente Cordiale widened to include Russia.[183] He, too, recognized much sooner the weakness of the Central Powers, which ran counter to the depictions of their aggressive superiority repeatedly broadcast by the press and in political novels and conveyed by several of his colleagues. Evidently roused by the anti-German media campaign that followed the Dogger Bank incident, in January 1905 Sanderson presented his superior with an equally remarkable memorandum, little noted in the literature, in which he addressed the relationship of Britain and Germany with reference to their respective media. He recorded his doubts about whether the two countries were aware of their media's transnational impact, which, he noted, could be devastating. Over the decades, British readers had become used to the style of the British press and well acquainted with domestic issues, and they could reckon for themselves which stories should be taken seriously and which not. 'But', Sanderson continued, 'the articles in the German press of which the spiciest bits are reported by the *Times* and other Correspondents at Berlin with due comments and denunciations, seem to us to have much greater significance than they probably have for the German public'.[184]

Concentration on a single type of publication that was by no means representative, Sanderson wrote, led to contorted impressions and tested bilateral relations,[185] especially as such publications conveyed emotions and not the facts of foreign policy. For example, England had completely forgotten just how precarious the Kaiserreich's position was. Before going to war against France, Berlin had had to purchase Russia's neutrality, and its geographical location meant Germany would inevitably be in the same position in the future. In the meantime, colonial ambitions had complicated the situation further. Surrounded by the Franco-Russian Dual Alliance, Germany could rely on only one of its two allies, Austria-Hungary, which was growing progressively weaker, for Rome, like London, tended to look to Paris, rather than to its ally in the Triple Alliance. These structural weaknesses should not be ignored, Sanderson insisted. No one should expect Germany to admit to these failings, for to do so would truly be 'bad politics', for Russia's limitations were only temporary, and Russia would seize on any such admission as an open invitation to attack. In Sanderson's eyes, Germany had little choice: 'Germany must feel it necessary to increase her navy and … unless she can feel sure that we will not at some untoward moment throw ourselves on the side of France, she must as a matter of precaution cultivate the goodwill of Russia far more than it is convenient for her to do'.[186]

Informed by naval expertise,[187] Sanderson thus consciously relativized the strengthening of the German High Seas Fleet, which he located in a broader historical and political framework that his younger colleagues and successors – Eyre Crowe in particular, but also Louis Mallet, Charles Hardinge, Arthur Nicolson and others – could not grasp. He did not believe that the existence of the High Seas Fleet could be explained only by characterizing Germany as the arch-enemy, nor did he hold that direct countermeasures by England were necessary. Sanderson thought the portrayal of Germany as arch-enemy was intended to bring an emotional charge to the relationship between the two countries, often to the benefit of specific interest groups. His advice was that composure, aplomb and a good dose of caution were all that was needed, just as London's existing alliances were also sufficient and did not have to be extended to include Russia.[188] Sanderson insisted that certain journalists, diplomats and politicians were determined to identify perfidious intent in every German measure, from secretive silence via public acknowledgement of the strengthening of the navy to threatening gestures, and to read any such activity as a sign of Germany's desire for closer ties with Russia. He believed, however,

> It is only natural that she [Germany] should let us know this and endeavour to keep our friendship in terms as easy to herself as possible. But I do not see that we can reasonably resent this and as a matter of fact a certain amount of friendship with Germany would be valuable for us in any bargaining with Russia.[189]

At first glance, Sanderson's analysis may seem similar to Bertie's.[190] The general mood, Sanderson agreed with Bertie, meant that a renewal of ties with the Triple Alliance was hardly realistic, but Sanderson rejected Bertie's conclusion of encirclement as a means of control, believing such pressure could only produce a panic reaction from the Central Powers. Those who proposed that policy, he believed, had failed to take into account that France and Russia were by no means saturated and would not rest content. In 1895, Sanderson had voiced his opinion that only a 'mental man' would consider Anglo-German cooperation over Constantinople, for that alliance would be a death blow first for Austria-Hungary and then for the European balance of powers. Ten years later, his position had not changed, and he therefore held that England should look for colonial agreements with Russia while maintaining its traditional role on the continent.[191] Two years later still, immediately after his departure from the Foreign Office, in a response to the much-cited Crowe memorandum, he continued to repeat that view, to Hardinge's surprise.[192] While Bertie wanted acknowledged that Germany 'has never done anything for us but bleed us, she is false and grasping and our real enemy commercially and politically',[193] the younger decision makers such as Austen Chamberlain were receptive to a scenario based on the Napoleonic power bloc. They adopted the view that Germany had only ever sought good relations with England 'for the purpose of making a better bargain with some third power'.[194] With their decades of experience of German impetuosity and sabre rattling, Lansdowne, Balfour and Sanderson were unperturbed. Yes, Germany – and other powers too – had often behaved badly towards England, but, they insisted, it was simply untrue to claim that Germany had never made any attempt to establish a mutually beneficial relationship. Against that background, Lansdowne and his permanent under-secretary refused to allow the emotions of the moment or agitation by the press to determine policy, with Lansdowne noting, 'I have perhaps become so much used to the querulous tone of the German Government that it produces less effect upon me than it does upon our colleague [A. Chamberlain]. I am at any rate more inclined to meet it with ridicule than with violent indignation'.[195] After Russia's defeat, Sanderson repeatedly advocated demonstrative calm, assurance and proportionality.[196] While his younger colleagues were largely led by their Social Darwinist expectations of imminent confrontation, Sanderson not only rejected their pessimism[197] but also emphasized English experience and reminded them that not Germany but Russia, and Muraviev specifically, had wanted to forge a continental alliance. Additionally, Monson underscored that Delcassé had been responsible for the Fashoda crisis.[198]

Sanderson was at a loss, however, when it came to the growing influence of the media. His responsibilities covered contact with Reuters and the leading organs of Fleet Street,[199] but Sanderson, too, proved unable to lead the press as Strachey had wanted.[200] Salisbury had repeatedly warned the permanent under-secretary about Chirol,[201] and any attempt by Sanderson to tone down the anti-German attitude of the *Times* led nowhere.[202] He recorded:

> The *Times* is to us a constant and fertile source of aggravation. It is always attacking some Foreign Power or lecturing it on the integrity and perversity of its ways and generally at the same moment condemning the Foreign Secretary and his unfortunate Dept. for ineptitude and weakness.[203]

Rather than tackle this new critical factor head on, Sanderson, evidently somewhat uncertain, advised caution. Lansdowne, too, preferred to lament the new involvement of the press rather than make his own views public as Balfour at times attempted. Grey and Hardinge went on the offensive with constructive attempts to work with public opinion, but for Sanderson such methods were unthinkable. His defence of the flexibility and openness of British ad hoc policy was immense, but he did little to counter its constraint by public opinion.

First Choices and Missed Chances

To bring selective relief for the Empire, Lansdowne turned first to Germany. That choice should not be seen as either a sign of naivety about German ambitions or evidence of a fundamental paradigm change, or even as the triumph of a pro-German 'Potsdam Party' within the cabinet.[204] The immediate grounds lay in the agreements that his predecessor had concluded in October 1900 in order to preserve access to the Yangtze Valley. More indirect grounds for Berlin and London's repeated discussions lay in the ongoing transformation of international relations as a whole. The Franco-Russian Dual Alliance of 1892 and its military extension in 1894 and 1899 along with the decision not to renew the Mediterranean Agreement in 1896 had wreaked havoc on the arrangements of the Bismarck era. While the Dual Alliance placed great pressure on the status quo-orientated Mediterranean powers and at the same time – as the Fashoda incident had demonstrated in 1898 – increased global political pressure on the Empire, with the end of the Mediterranean Agreement, Britain gradually withdrew from responsibility for preserving stability in Europe.[205] The Dual Monarchy compensated for Britain's withdrawal by entering into a détente with Russia in 1897, taking on an invaluable role as intermediary for the European constellations created by the Dual Alliance and Triple Alliance up until 1903, and Germany and England were forced to seek to reposition themselves. As they faced pressure from the same direction, close cooperation between Germany and Britain seemed on point, and certainly more likely than Germany's being reconciled with France or the creation of a continental alliance. London, however, had several options. As France and Russia had their eye on Britain's imperial assets but had no designs on Britain's very existence, from the start negotiation with the Dual Alliance seemed far more appealing. Additionally, for Whitehall antagonism between Germany and France was a given, which meant that at a push London would always be able to rely on Berlin.

The British leadership had been unperturbed, although not overjoyed, to see Germany preparing to become actively involved in the Far East, with the first marines landing in Jiaozhou in late 1897. Salisbury had been perfectly happy to see Russia and Germany over-extend themselves in China, and it seemed the resulting tension in German–Russian relations could only benefit the Empire for years to come.[206] As long as Russian interests were solely economic and no substantial Russian military presence was close to any British possession, Salisbury was content to leave the state of affairs as it was. In any case, he had no particular interest in China, which he had long deemed one of the 'dying nations'.[207] Once again, however, in the closing stages of his career he had underestimated both the imperial sensibilities of the English public and the determination and ambition of his younger cabinet members and Foreign Office colleagues, in particular Francis Bertie. On no account, according to Bertie, was the Empire to be sidelined.[208] The subversive under-secretary was working closely with, and perhaps even at the charge of, the 'Old-China Hands', as those involved in the China trade were described. Cecil Smith, president of the China Association, had explained to Bertie that he believed there was little reason to worry or complain, and yes, the Russian engagement might harbour a certain potential danger, but the opportunity of the moment could still be seized, as exaggerated accounts of German and Russian activities would provide reason to demand compensation.[209] As a result, on the advice of Chirol and in cooperation with MacDonald in Peking, Bertie endlessly exaggerated the inherent dangers and potential loss of prestige, increasing the already growing pressure from the London press for the 'drifting' to be brought to an end and for a rapid show of force.[210] With the occupation of Port Arthur, the pressure on the cabinet grew almost overwhelming. Under the influence of the campaigning by the press, Michael Hicks Beach even began to talk of war as a possibility should Britain be excluded from trading with the 400 million Chinese.[211] Salisbury resisted the pressure, however, demonstrating no interest in facing Russia in a duel over a few 'cartographic points of interest'.[212] As chance would have it, just as the situation came to a head over the Russian lease of Port Arthur, illness again took Salisbury out of action. On their own initiative, Balfour and Chamberlain, who was highly influential, began to sound out the possibilities for an understanding with Berlin.[213]

Just how serious the resultant Anglo-German discussions were is an issue to which scholars have returned repeatedly since the end of the First World War.[214] The current position holds that there was never any chance that these negotiations might produce an alliance. This was no 'missed opportunity' and no classic example of failure on the part of the Wilhelmstrasse.[215] But what of the suggestion that the discussions marked a 'near to sensational about-turn for English policy'?[216]

As early as 1898, Hohenlohe had made clear that in the Far East Germany was in competition, and not in accord, with Russia.[217] Convinced since taking up his position in Berlin that Britain and Germany were growing closer, since early 1898 Frank Lascelles had been reporting an improved relationship with his hosts, and with the emperor in particular.[218] Lanza, the Italian ambassador and a consistent source of information, reported to Lascelles that the German leadership was very eager to come to an agreement; Bülow was waiting only for Britain to recognize that its isolationist policy had been a mistake.[219] Under Balfour's leadership, a more active policy regarding China was launched. On the day on which the secret lease of Weihaiwei was agreed with Britain, as compensation for Port Arthur, he sat down for the first time for informal discussions with Hatzfeldt, arranged through Lord Rothschild.[220] Four days later, again brokered by Alfred de Rothschild, an additional, and apparently far more detailed, meeting took place, this time involving Chamberlain. Even with the Weihaiwei arrangement in place, Chamberlain was still attempting to torpedo Russian plans and looked to Germany for support. On 29 March, a 'very secret telegram' reached the Wilhelmstrasse in which Hatzfeldt informed his superiors of the pronouncement by the secretary of state for the colonies that the point had been reached at which Britain would have to abandon its traditional isolationist policy.[221] The report appeared all the more credible because Hatzfeldt had planned on discussing only colonial differences and had himself been surprised by Chamberlain's idea of a fundamental agreement.[222] For Chamberlain, however, such a step would be entirely in accord with his broader vision, in which the Teutonic races would stand firm against the expansion of the Slavs.[223] The German party had good reason not to dismiss the offer as diplomatic chicanery or a British testing of the waters. Parallel to the discussions, Chamberlain published a run of articles in the *Morning Post* that were intended to convince his sceptical compatriots of the economic and political possibilities of such a grand design. His articles sought to convey that the Germans, unlike the Russians, were fully trustworthy and that it was not in their interests to impede trade in the Far East. The Russians, by contrast, were no merchants; they were conquerors 'pure and simple'. A week later, when Chamberlain met Hatzfeldt for the first time, the same paper carried an article arguing that Germany was only Britain's rival because the two peoples were so similar.[224] Chamberlain's idea of a new global order based on the Teutonic races and British dominions, a concept he also spoke of in Birmingham on 13 May, represented a radical rethinking. The public response beyond the *Morning Post* was, however, somewhat disappointing, and left Chamberlain evidently somewhat uncertain.[225] For others – Chirol, for example – he was moving in the wrong direction, for Grey and Rosebery had already voiced far more extensive plans for a dual alliance.[226] Eventually, Chamberlain decided to present an alliance with Berlin to the cabinet as a proposal that had come from the German side.

Although both Bülow and Balfour were initially surprised and reticent in response,[227] the highly energetic colonial secretary was not going to let matters lie precisely during this sensitive early phase of rapprochement, and he continued to pursue his goal. The very day after Berlin had responded somewhat cautiously, he put on the table extensive economic privileges in China and even the possibility of an accord ratified by parliament.[228] Both Bülow and Balfour wanted first to see the atmosphere between the two nations improved, particularly in light of the friction of recent years stemming from the Krüger telegram and from Salisbury's Near Eastern policy, and a basis created for a potentially more comprehensive commitment.[229] With the intervention of firebrand Baron Hermann von Eckardstein in the discussions, no party was in a position to make a decision. Eckardstein drew the Kaiser into these early soundings and, if that was not enough, presented the Kaiser's position to London entirely incorrectly. Wilhelm II was interested, but he had certainly not demonstrated the euphoria that the German diplomat reported to Chamberlain and Balfour as his response. With Salisbury on the mend and back in London, Chamberlain claimed that in the interim Berlin had launched a new initiative for an alliance of the two countries.[230] In the meantime, Berlin became increasingly doubtful about London's surprisingly sudden and hastily materializing interest, and a feeling took root that England was on the search for an ally against Russia who would not cost them anything. Shortly before Lascelles was due to return to England for his summer holiday, Bülow informed him again about Germany's reservations about possibly being left to face Russia on its own.

On arriving in London, the ambassador had an immediate opportunity to convey the German concerns to the appropriate circles. At a lunch party held in Chamberlain's garden on 18 June, he was also able to converse with George

Goschen, George Hamilton and Lord Selborne. John Grenville has interpreted this event as a prearranged meeting of conspirators, led by Lascelles,[231] but the somewhat sparse surviving accounts of the gathering cast the affair in a rather more sober light. According to Lascelles, with the English ambassador sitting opposite him, Chamberlain was the first to direct the conversation, casually, to current relations. After the colonial secretary had brought up the subject of an anti-Russian alliance in Asia, a somewhat sarcastic comment from the ambassador about the Royal Navy's ability to protect Germany from an invasion by the Cossacks gave Chamberlain cause to rethink his position – he proposed a defensive alliance that would encompass and involve Europe, and the other participants in the discussion expressed their agreement. We do not know how Lascelles, the guiding spirit, responded to this suggestion, but his very pointed comment about the significance of the Royal Navy for Germany gives us reason to think that he was likely sceptical about this comprehensive agreement. While undoubtedly his prime concern was to ensure the best possible relationship between Britain and Germany, as statements he made elsewhere support, he would likely have thought it too soon for a general defensive alliance.[232] The discussions at the informal Princess Garden meeting highlight the approach that compared Russia and Germany, but they are above all significant in that not just Chamberlain but also the others present responded spontaneously but entirely positively to the idea of Anglo-German rapprochement.[233] Close examination of power relations within the cabinet as soundings were taken for a possible Anglo-German agreement suggests that there were always some who supported such an alliance and that at times that grouping was even in the majority. Precisely during these various phases, however, obstacles always emerged either in Berlin, in London or elsewhere. To conclude that there was never any chance of an alliance being formed, or to speak of that possibility as a sensational about-turn, would be to go too far.

Back in Berlin in the middle of July, Lascelles had no opportunity to test the waters or quickly inform the Kaiser of Chamberlain's concept. The Kaiser was on holiday on the *Hohenzollern*, along with Metternich and Eulenburg. Bülow was also absent from Berlin. Under-Secretary of State, Oswald von Richthofen recorded, however, that the English ambassador underscored 'after all that he had heard not only from Lord Salisbury and Mr Chamberlain, but in particular also from the other members of the cabinet, that all the ministers urgently desired the realization of an agreement with us'.[234] But was that entente to be a general agreement or a narrower response to the immediate, ongoing issue of the Portuguese colonies? For Lascelles, the context was clear: the current negotiations over inheritance of the Portuguese Empire were to prepare the ground for far closer relations between Germany and Britain. The opportunity to discuss the situation with the Kaiser, his preferred interlocutor, did not come quickly, however. As chance would have it, Lascelles and Wilhelm II narrowly missed meeting face to face. The

Kaiser was minded to visit the English ambassador at his retreat in Potsdam on 3 August, but Lascelles had travelled to Berlin in the hope of seeing the Kaiser at a memorial event for Bismarck. Much frustrated, he informed Sanderson that he would have no opportunity to see Wilhelm II before September.[235]

Chance had it that an earlier opportunity did present itself, as the Kaiser and Lascelles were both present at a reception held by Empress Friedrich at Wilhelmshöhe on 21 August, although the timing for raising the possibility of closer relations was not good, for the discussions about the Portuguese colonies had just reached an impasse, giving the Kaiser reason to complain to Lascelles that Britain was not willing to accept Germany's status as a world power. In the heat of the moment, the Kaiser accused Britain of only wanting to position Germany against Russia. For the first time, Lascelles volunteered an account of the gathering over lunch, of Chamberlain's change of mind, and of the suggested formation of a European defensive alliance. Wilhelm II responded with surprise but with great seriousness. The following day, he wrote confidently to his mother that his conversation with the English ambassador had been highly satisfying and that he was now certain that both parties could hope for a satisfying outcome.[236] Remarkably, Lascelles, to whom, as was so often her wont, Empress Frederick immediately leaked the telegram, did not comprehend this reference to changed circumstances. Rather than assume the Kaiser was alluding to his final comment on Chamberlain's idea of an alliance, Lascelles evidently believed the Kaiser was referring only to the ongoing negotiations over the Portuguese colonies, for at the time he wrote the Kaiser had not known that the negotiations over the colonies had been resumed.[237]

The whole episode of the Anglo-German exploratory discussions was characterized by a series of coincidences, misunderstandings and slip-ups by all parties; in short, a 'comedy of errors'.[238] Once Lascelles had spoken of Chamberlain's offer, the Kaiser and Berlin began to believe that in certain circumstances Britain would be willing to enter into a defensive alliance.[239] The German Foreign Office believed it could play for time in order to find the best moment to extend the Triple Alliance through the addition of Britain; in practice, however, in the course of the next two years that moment never appeared. The Samoan crisis of 1899 and German Anglophobia during the South African War hardly eased the circumstances. In place of an about-turn, at best British foreign policy was marked by increasing emancipation, particularly by Chamberlain, from Salisbury's leadership. Relations between Germany and Britain became burdened by the close watch each party kept on the other, with chance encounters preferred over official discussions, and any sign, however small, read as a signal that further negotiations were possible, or not. Overall, a willingness appears to have been present on both sides, but the pressure that might turn political concepts into political resolutions was lacking. Even during the South African War, Britain was never seriously imperilled, and therefore agreements never moved beyond regional settlements intended to relieve the burden on the Empire or protect access to China.

Two years later, on 16 October 1900, Germany, Japan and Britain entered into a mutual pact to protect free trade and the integrity of China against increasing Russian expansion. As Russia showed no signs of keeping to the promise to withdraw from Manchuria the troops sent to oppose the Boxers, Japan was on constant high alert. On 3 January 1901, the *Times* correspondent in Peking ascertained that China and Russia were negotiating over the establishment of a Russian protectorate in Manchuria. Count Hayashi, Japanese ambassador to London, immediately attempted to convince Britain and Germany to launch a protest. The Foreign Office remained unperturbed, even after Chargé d'affaires Ernest Satow had confirmed the existence of the negotiations. Francis Bertie had previously informed Japan that London had no great interest in Manchuria and would certainly not stand in Russia's way.[240] Tokyo, however, looked on the matter with far less equanimity and increased its efforts to form an anti-Russian coalition with Germany and Britain. On 12 and 15 January, Hayashi officially asked Lansdowne whether he would agree to a joint protest against Russia. Generally, Lansdowne commented to Salisbury, one should not be too pedantic when it came to China, but at the same time, for parliamentary reasons one could not simply remain on the sidelines on the Far East.[241] Essentially, Salisbury shared Lansdowne's view, but Lascelles was at least to establish whether Germany would join a possible protest.[242]

In Germany, views at the top were also divided – on one hand, a falling out with Russia should be avoided at all costs; on the other hand, as Wilhelm II commented, fluctuation between positions could not go on forever.[243] While the Kaiser and Bülow approved the idea of Anglo-German cooperation, Friedrich von Holstein recommended against it. The *éminence grise* of German diplomacy wrongly believed that Germany held all the trump cards. Britain would soon have to show its hand. But what was it playing for? For China? In Holstein's view, cooperation would benefit only Britain; Germany's position would not be any more secure. Without more extensive concessions that included Europe, he was not going to be forced into action by London. In the meantime, Eckardstein and Chamberlain, the two principal advocates of a change of course, had met at Chatsworth, and the colonial secretary had apparently held out the prospect of Britain joining the Triple Alliance.[244] At the same time, for once Wilhelm II was enjoying a positive reception by the London press, for without great ado he had rushed to be at the bedside of his dying grandmother Victoria. The conditions for rapprochement between Britain and Germany seemed far better than usual.

On 1 March, China forced the situation by requesting the Great Powers to act as mediators in the negotiations with Russia. Perhaps believing that he could thereby bring Germany on board, Lansdowne adopted a stronger position that made clear that on no account would a Russian protectorate in Manchuria be tolerated. It was crucial for the effectiveness of the warning given to Russia that the signatories of the October agreement were clearly of one accord. Britain and Japan asked the Russian foreign minister for official recognition of the intended agreement, but Lamsdorff declined on the grounds that Bülow had recently repeatedly declared that he had no interest in Manchuria. The German attitude blocked any progress, although Lascelles again attempted to bring the Wilhelmstrasse round. On 13 March, a telegram from Lascelles reported that Germany intended to abide by the 'strictest neutrality'. Even before Bülow had risen to speak in the Reichstag, Lansdowne's plan for closer cooperation in Asia, which would bring Germany and Britain a step closer to agreement on the periphery, was untenable. Once again, Germany had demonstrated clearly that it drew its map of Asia from a European vantage point. Germany had no interest in conflict with Russia – and perhaps therefore also with France – over trading interests in the Far East unless guaranteed British support on the continent.

Publicly, Whitehall appeared to have received the cold shoulder, for Bülow revealed the bluff on which British Far Eastern policy rested – London was not prepared to risk conflict over Manchuria. Internally, however, Lascelles, Lansdowne and Hamilton were aware that the imperial chancellor was not entirely wrong when he claimed that during the negotiations for the October agreement Salisbury had made clear that he did not want it to cover Manchuria.[245] Additionally, as even Lansdowne conceded, Richthofen had been justified when he complained that Britain was demanding a clear statement from Germany, prompting Germany to take an official stand against Russia, while itself intending to stay in the background.[246] The English foreign secretary noted the ongoing war in South Africa, but at the same time expressed understanding for the situation in which Germany found itself. Evidently, he had correctly assumed that Berlin would not be willing to stand alone on the front line of a defensive encirclement of Japan and Russia.[247] Lascelles only wondered whether Eckardstein was acting of his own accord,[248] but Lansdowne was sceptical. Eckardstein's suggestion of 18 March, which now envisaged a 'general alliance', went further than all previous proposals, and therefore, Lansdowne informed Eckardstein, would need to be examined closely; Lansdowne also noted that he could not act without reference to the cabinet.[249] Again, Lansdowne's actions were those not of someone determined to force through paradigm change but of someone cautiously and tentatively following the terms of reference established by his predecessor; at most, he was testing his room for manoeuvre. While the German diplomat wanted to have his government believe that the proposal came from Whitehall, Lansdowne thought Eckardstein was acting with the approval of Berlin. Nothing substantive could come from the confusion that Eckardstein's private diplomacy had created.

By mid March, Lansdowne clearly no longer placed any great hope in the exploratory discussions. Germany was demonstratively not prepared to take any risks for the sake of the Far East. For its part, Britain saw no reason to join the Triple Alliance on account of Asia. In parallel to this diplomatic venture, discussions between Moberly Bell, managing director of the *Times*, and diplomat Paul Graf Metternich, made the Anglo-German dilemma all too evident. Responding to Metternich's question of whether he could also see that the interests of the two countries were identical, Bell had noted that Britain had no interests in Europe to defend. Metternich probed, 'Have you not? Let us suppose … Germany were to be deposed from her present position … and that France and Russia could deal single handed with England, would it not be a danger that Germany should be crushed?' Bell responded, 'Yes, but … if England were crushed would not there be the same danger for Germany?'

In this moment, Metternich made a tactical error. Instead of insisting that a defeat of Britain would not affect the security of Germany, he agreed with Bell: 'Clearly, therefore our interests are identical – then why not an alliance?' Bell responded:

> Precisely because they are identical therefore there is no need of it. We should be wiser to choose that ally which can singly do us harm. That is not Germany. In the event of war, what can Germany do? She recalls you. What next? She declares war. What next? How can you touch us? We can blockade Hamburg, take Samoa, drive you out of South Africa, or try to do all three. But what can you do? Absolutely nothing.[250]

In the end, the asymmetry of Britain and Germany's relationship was always going to be decisive. London was certainly interested in maintaining the status quo in Asia, but at the same time Asia also provided a bargaining chip for negotiations with Russia. Additionally, in his final memorandum Salisbury made unambiguously clear that Britain could gain no advantages by joining the Triple Alliance.[251] He had always embraced a loose rapprochement with the alliance, but he had never favoured membership, which would have bound England to defend German and Austrian borders against Russia, a far harder task than defending the British Isles against France. Despite the oft-repeated support for the thesis that Salisbury thus laid an obstacle in the way of Lansdowne's plans that eventually derailed his foreign secretary's hopes for an alliance with Germany, beyond his suggestion of cooperation with Japan, Lansdowne never had any plans to join the Triple Alliance. Against the backdrop of Eckardstein's and Hatzfeldt's convoluted behaviour, which made clear to Lansdowne that he knew nothing of Eckardstein's private undertakings, Lansdowne had long had significant doubts about the ostensible proposals from Berlin and had never taken them entirely seriously. Like Salisbury, Lansdowne was primarily concerned to ensure that English commitments in Asia remained as limited as possible. If Germany and Russia were of no assistance on that count, then there was always Japan.

The Japanese Alliance: A Paradigm Shift?

Since the 1895 Peace of Shimonoseki, Japan had behaved very cautiously. During the Boxer rebellion, for example, it moved none of its troops without permission from the Great Powers. Japan had also hoped that its participation in the Anglo-German Yangtze Agreement would in the end produce a new triple alliance in the Far East ready to curb Russian expansion. Educated in Europe and well acquainted with Western customs and with the tensions among the Great Powers, Count Hayashi worked tirelessly – and on occasion even counter to his own government – to bring about an Anglo-Japanese union. He was not to be dissuaded by the failure of the German-English exploratory discussions or by the misunderstandings over Manchuria.[252] When the Russian-Chinese negotiations of spring 1901 introduced new tensions, he saw his chance, although it took several attempts on his part, in March, April and May, before Lansdowne responded, on 31 July 1901, shortly before leaving for a holiday. Evidently, right up to the last moment, Lansdowne had hoped that either Germany or the cabinet would relent over cooperation, but now he would need to grasp the initiative if he wished to avoid losing the Japanese option.[253] Responding to a report from Admiral Richard Tracey, for some time Francis Bertie had been recommending an alliance with Tokyo.[254] In March 1901, and again that summer, Bertie had renewed his warnings to his new superior about ignoring the favourable circumstances and possibly provoking an alliance between Japan and Russia.[255] Tokyo's hesitation suggested that Bertie's concern was not misplaced, for, much like his acquaintance Eckardstein, Hayashi had taken it upon himself to approach Lansdowne.

In spring 1901, a British agreement with Russia seemed conceivable, but London had no faith in Russian diplomacy.[256] Russia was all too ready to announce that its troops would be withdrawn from Manchuria, without following up on the ground. In March, Hamilton commented, 'The lying is unprecedented even in the annals of Russian diplomacy. ... The Russians are behaving abominably in China'.[257] In the House of Lords, Lansdowne made unequivocally clear that London would protect its interests with force,[258] and as so often, such decisiveness did not miss its mark with Russia – suddenly Lamsdorff's declarations of friendship could not come fast enough. The English foreign minister was well aware, however, that only Japan's strong stance, English resolve and Germany's participation could subdue Russia, and therefore, suspecting that the effect of his speech would be only temporary, he did not abandon his scepticism about Russia,[259] encouraged by Sanderson, who believed that even if the tsar did mean what was said, the militaristic party in Russia would attempt to force Britain out of the region as quickly as possible.[260] But, remarked Lansdowne after his first discussions with Hayashi, in Tokyo England could be confident of finding a trustworthy collaborator. He therefore commissioned Bertie to make further preparations during his absence.

In the meantime, other members of the cabinet also busied themselves with the Japanese option, with Lord Selborne, who wrote a position paper, at the fore. At the core of his considerations was a demand for a politically modified or cleansed 'Two-Power Standard'. The build-up of American forces meant, he noted, that on financial grounds the British navy could no longer be the standard against which all fleets of the world were measured; an alliance with Japan would provide valuable relief. While such an agreement would have only limited usefulness in the case of a war against France and Russia, which would likely be concentrated on the Mediterranean and Atlantic, it would still limit the alliances that might be formed in the South China Sea. A defensive alliance with Japan could therefore lead to great savings for the beleaguered British budget, and, additionally, might prove a deterrent to the Dual Alliance.[261]

Back in London after his holiday in Ireland, Lansdowne found the official proposal from Hayashi waiting for him and immediately turned to preparation of an appropriate memorandum on an alliance in accord with Selborne's ideas. On 25 October, the Foreign Office passed Lansdowne's thoughts on to the other ministers along with Selborne's own memorandum.[262]

In the meantime, a financial crisis had emerged in Persia, the second Anglo-Russian flank, providing more fodder for the idea of cooperation between England and Russia. With neither Chancellor of the Exchequer Hicks Beach, nor the government of India in Calcutta ready to provide financial support for Persia, Lansdowne was left to make a choice: lose further influence in the region or cooperate with Russia in a financial solution.[263] On 25 October, he proposed a joint loan be made to bankrupt Persia. Scholars have identified the parallel offers made to Japan and Russia as evidence that in truth Lansdowne would have preferred an alliance with St Petersburg,[264] yet that interpretation overlooks not only the general scepticism about Russian willingness to keep to the terms of any treaty,[265] but also Lansdowne's lack of any illusion, from the outset, that his proposal to St Petersburg would be successful. On 18 October, Salisbury himself had made clear to Lansdowne that he would get far less from an alliance with St Petersburg than from an alliance with Germany. In any case, Russia, Salisbury warned, would as ever fail to abide by the agreement and at the first opportunity would again betray Britain.[266] More plausible is that the parallel offers were intended to ensure that Russia's expected refusal would take the wind out of the sails of the numerous opponents in London of an Anglo-Japanese alliance.[267] In recent months and above all in the leading political publications, that wind had been blowing in favour of rapprochement with Russia, a tack now favoured by several members of the cabinet, including Michael Hicks Beach, and by diplomats such as Charles and Arthur Hardinge and Henry Drummond-Wolff.[268]

The pro-Russia and anti-Germany campaign in the *Contemporary Review*, the *Fortnightly Review*, the *Review of Reviews* and the *National Review* had reached new heights. Blennerhasset, Maxse, Garvin and others had published plea after plea for British entry into the Dual Alliance, which could then be formed into a power bloc. 'Democracy would never fight to keep Russia out of Constantinople', the press insisted, and, 'Let them have Bandar Abbas'.[269] Elements within the opposition appeared to have been warming to this thought for some time. Edward Grey declared on 26 July 1901 that a general agreement with Russia must be a highest priority.[270] From the start, that demand was tied in with rejection of Germany and, if necessary, even of the European status quo.[271] The extensive influence of this campaign is evident in the words of Valentine Chirol, still at this time more likely to be critical of Russia, who used his close contact with Charles Hardinge to report that the British public were fed up with the indecisiveness and now looked far more favourably on an alliance with Russia.[272] His attitude, however, was not deep rooted, for only five weeks later Chirol voiced a very different opinion. On 17 November, he back-pedalled on his judgement on Germany. Chirol went to the effort of attempting to verify for himself George Saunders' alarmist reports about German Anglophobia and hegemonic dreams. After a visit to Berlin, he had to concede, 'I no longer take such an unfavourable view as I did of Germany's attitude towards us on the whole. ... I am all the more disposed to credit them with a certain amount of interested sincerity'.[273]

Germany, so ran his conclusions, had behaved entirely correctly and had been repeatedly deceived by Salisbury. Berlin's position on Manchuria was, he insisted, entirely correct, and after his criticism of Lansdowne he appeared pleased that the foreign secretary was now attempting to support Japan against Russia. When it came to the constant demands for rapprochement with Russia, Chirol now confirmed Lansdowne's scepticism. The date of these comments made to Hardinge is remarkable. Chirol would have been aware for some time of the commotion caused by Chamberlain's statement about the Prussian army made on 25 October, which had caused a wave of indignation in both countries and had produced a veritable press feud. But as long as the positive impressions of his visit to Berlin stayed with him, he evidently saw no need to become part of that hostility. Three days later, however, after he had reacclimatized himself to his London surroundings, he suddenly published a furious attack on the Kaiserreich. Obviously, he was won over by the numerous reports of German Anglophobia. His sudden change of attitude is evidence of the crucial part played by the London political sphere in shaping opinion and he himself noted that the general mood had decisive influence on English foreign policy,[274] but he also went a step further in attempting to exercise direct influence on political decision makers: several times in short succession he wrote to Lascelles to convince him of Germany's hostile intentions.[275]

Lansdowne may have been more aware that public perceptions had become more pro-Russian than was his predecessor, but he was far less sensitive to that attitude than was his successor. He recorded: 'In neither case would a refusal on the part of Russia do us much harm; while in both cases our position would, I believe be strengthened, especially with the public here, by the fact that we have made proposals of this kind'.[276] His proposal that Britain would be conciliatory when it came to Manchuria and stand surety along with Russia for the Persian loan therefore seems more of a tactical tool, designed to ensure he could not be accused of having missed an opportunity, than a new strategic direction. On one hand, the concern was to present a further option, for Japan had still not yet made a definitive statement; on the other hand, Lansdowne wanted to strengthen his position both in the cabinet and in the face of external criticism. Additionally, a negative response from Russia, so ran the calculation, might even make possible a more positive and more aggressive policy on Persia.[277]

With total Russian self-confidence, Lamsdorff rejected Lansdowne's proposal as expected, although surprisingly brusquely. His response indicated that thanks to its powerful position, Russia had absolutely no need to enter into any negotiations. St Petersburg evidently had no thought of fulfilling its assurances that it would withdraw its troops from Manchuria.[278] Japanese concerns about further Russian expansion towards Korea seemed therefore completely justified.

With Lansdowne's foreign policy still finding its bearings, ideally Britain would remain similarly close to Germany, Japan and Russia. But now only Japan was still a possible partner and commitment was essential, for ambassadors MacDonald and Hardinge warned that a Japanese-Russian agreement might be imminent; Prince Ito had recently left for St Petersburg.[279] There were therefore logical grounds for Lansdowne to look again at Germany as an additional option. Awaiting Tokyo's response and able only to look on as Japan and Russia negotiated, the politically engaged in London reflected on the options. Here was the context for the exchange between Lansdowne and Bertie that we have already encountered in which the latter deemed Germany too weak to be able to help England on the global stage. On 11 November, Lansdowne addressed the same issue. He was entirely in agreement with Bertie on the essential disadvantages of an alliance with Germany, and he believed that to date the isolationist policy had been more helpful than harmful, but, he declared, 'I think, however, that we may push too far the argument that, because we have in the past survived in spite of our isolation, we need have no misgivings as to the effect of that isolation in the future'.[280] Historians have tended to see in his words clear evidence of a paradigm change for which Lansdowne was responsible, and yet the foreign secretary emphasized continuity with the policies of his predecessor and proposed a partnership along the lines of the Mediterranean Agreement of 1887 as the model for an alliance with Japan.[281] Additionally, self-critically he attempted to explain German disappointment and increasing German enmity as products of

English isolationism. Doubtless by this point he, too, had excluded any possibility of Britain joining the Triple Alliance, but in doing so he did not exclude the possibility of limited agreements.[282]

On 12 December 1901, a positive response was received from Japan after all, but Arthur Balfour continued to advocate for entry into the Triple Alliance, with its broader implications, as the best solution and criticized the Japanese course Lansdowne had set. On one hand, Balfour felt he had been overlooked in the decision-making process; on the other hand, he believed it an error to enter into an alliance without thinking through the consequences for relations between Britain and Germany. What justification could there be for entering into alliances in the Far East but not on one's own doorstep?[283] Balfour's criticism worked on two levels: he considered both the specific agreement with Japan and its advantages and disadvantages over agreement with Germany and, more generally, the role of alliances for relations between the Great Powers. Aside from his doubts that Britain should allow itself to be drawn into a war over Korea, he also believed it evident that

> if war should arise out of either a German or a Japanese alliance, the forces you have got to fight are exactly the same, namely, Russia and France, while our ally in the one case would be Japan, and in the other case the Triple Alliance. In other words, the Japanese Treaty, if it ends in war, brings us into collision with the same opponents as a German alliance, but with a much weaker partner.[284]

Britain's interests in the Far East, he continued, were marginal in comparison to its interests in Europe, and therefore in his eyes the alliance was entirely one-sided and far too risky. By contrast, a dispute involving the Triple Alliance would automatically place the most vital of British interests also at stake. His memorandum continued:

> It is a matter of supreme moment to us that Italy should not be crushed, that Austria should not be dismembered, and that Germany should not be squeezed to death between the hammer of Russia and the anvil of France. If therefore we had to fight for the central European Powers, we should be fighting for our own interests, and for those of civilization, to an extent which cannot be alleged with regard to Corea or Manchuria or Japan.[285]

While Japan would be of only limited value in a war against Russia, a war that would largely play out on land and above all in the eastern Mediterranean and Central Asia, membership of the Triple Alliance would likely inhibit France, and therefore also Russia, from even going to war. An alliance with Japan would therefore only provide 'capability aggregation', while ties to the Triple Alliance, Balfour emphasized, would have undoubtedly reinforced the system as a whole.[286]

Lansdowne completely understood Balfour's position, but believed the risks of war were far greater with an alliance with Germany. He turned Balfour's argument on its head. While for Balfour an alliance with the Kaiserreich would protect fundamental British interests, in particular when it came to European power structures, for Lansdowne the very lack of British interests in the Far East was a form of security, for there Britain would not be drawn into a war. He believed that it therefore should not be too hard to explain to Germany why agreement with Tokyo had been preferable to agreement with Berlin. Even though Lansdowne had made an agreement with a power that threatened to disrupt the status quo, he believed he had kept the risk as small as possible, convinced that even if war should break out, Britain could still choose whether to become involved.[287]

Balfour and Lansdowne's differing views on an alliance with Japan reflected differing perceptions of international politics. By no means naive about Russia's trustworthiness, globetrotter and former 'man on the ground' Lansdowne had as his first goal the protection and consolidation of the Empire. He believed it possible to form regional agreements with no implications, or at least only manageable implications, for the Great Power system. Balfour was sceptical. He did not believe that imperial and continental interests could be separated in practice, noting in particular Britain's European role as a member of the Concert of Europe. Speaking against Russia was not only that country's autocratic constitution but also its unparalleled disregard for international agreements and the lack of common interests. Additionally, Balfour believed that for the sake of international stability, any links between Britain and Russia should never be allowed to come in contact with the scaffolding around the European Great Power system, but he was convinced that as long as Russia and France were allies and sought a change in the status quo, that distinction was simply impossible.[288]

Other ministers, such as Michael Hicks Beach, Charles Ritchie and Joseph Chamberlain, preferred an association with the Triple Alliance[289] and Selborne and Hamilton were far from thrilled with the Japanese alternative.[290] Only when Lansdowne's renewed efforts with Count Metternich still proved unable, on account of Germany's unwise all-or-nothing approach,[291] to generate Anglo-German agreement[292] was Balfour's opposition to an Anglo-Japanese alliance finally broken.[293] Now much depended on Salisbury. Although in his final significant cabinet memorandum on foreign policy Salisbury had expressed similar scepticism about Japan and the proposed alliance, in the end he allowed himself to be convinced by Lansdowne, in a conversation held at Hatfield, that the agreement was far more of an insurance policy than an alliance; as Lansdowne pointed out, Britain had kept its responsibilities to provide assistance as vague as possible. On 30 January 1902, the treaty was signed, obliging each state to come to the aid of the other should it be attacked by two other powers in China or Korea.

Additionally, neither partner was permitted to enter into an independent agreement that affected the interests of the other.

Throughout the period of negotiation with Japan, repeated attempts had been made to form a closer relationship with Germany, a solution privately deemed more desirable, and even now Lansdowne was not discouraged. He confidently informed Joseph Chamberlain, who had become increasingly critical, that Lascelles' recent conversations with Bülow and under-secretary at the German Foreign Office, Otto von Mühlberg, had been productive, recording: 'Both of them think it is right to drop the idea for the present, but only for the present!'[294]

Evidently the German party had not yet given up hope that an Anglo-German agreement might yet be forged. Like Russia, the liberal imperial opposition in Britain was furious about the alliance with Tokyo. In a private letter to Maxse, Edward Grey accused the government of indolence and short-sightedness and condemned the alliance as an open attack on Russia, which would have made a better partner whatever the circumstances: 'I do not believe they [the government] have made a real effort for such an understanding [with Russia] and [I] fear they have drifted into the Japanese treaty because it was the laziest thing to do at the moment'.[295] He was backed up in parliament by fellow Liberal Party members Joseph Walton and Henry Norman, both of whom similarly favoured a global agreement with Russia, which would therefore embrace the Far East. In response, Lord Cranborne, Lansdowne's parliamentary representative, again laid out the course adopted by the government in relation to Russia: yes, the government sought friendly relations with Russia, but that association was not be bought at the expense of existing treaties.[296]

George Monger judged that the Anglo-Japanese alliance marked the unavoidable end of British isolationism.[297] Yet, as we have seen here, Britain did have other options, and the alliance must be laid at the door of imperial interests and by no means attributed to German aggression. In believing that imperial politics could be kept distinct from the Great Power relations that played out primarily on the continent, Lansdowne was taking a great risk. On learning of the Anglo-Japanese alliance, Russia immediately prepared to enter into a counter-alliance with the Kaiserreich. While in London the extra-political commentary, even from the radical liberal side, welcomed both Lansdowne's motive in securing the status quo and the open-door policy, it also recognized the danger of backing away even further from the European fellowship of Great Powers, arguing: 'By this act we are definitely stepping out of the European community … and it looks very much like pique, and a snapping of our fingers at a Europe which has discountenanced our policy'.[298] This supposed step out of isolation could have produced an even more extreme form of isolation, for in April 1901, Théophile Delcassé had already left for St Petersburg in order to discuss the possibilities for war against Britain, and in November had also tried to win over Prince Ito for that plan.[299]

In February 1902, Lamsdorff held out to the Wilhelmstrasse the possibility of an anti-English and anti-Japanese triple alliance: France and Germany would take on the Royal Navy while Russia occupied China. That scenario was again averted by Germany, which roundly rejected Russia's approaches.[300] A systemic perspective reveals that Berlin was thus both protecting the balance of power and striving to maintain peace, but Germany's interests were harmed by its response, which caused Germany's own value to fall. Britain appeared to be right: Germany could be had for nothing. Additionally, Delcassé appeared to have been given the opportunity to play the part of Russia's only true ally. On 20 March 1902, the Anglo-Japanese alliance was countered with a Russian-French declaration that effectively announced North China to be a protectorate of the Dual Alliance.[301] That declaration marked the beginning of negotiations over an Anglo-French entente, which was initially seen simply as a means of reducing tensions. German loyalty to Britain and the states system might be tied in with Germany's own interests, which could hope to benefit from Anglo-Russian tensions, but in the end that fidelity would reap Germany no rewards.

Notes

1. Matthew, *Liberal Imperialists*, 195–224. Edward Grey's early political statements remained somewhat neglected.
2. Balfour to Salisbury, 16 Dec. 1895, BL, Add. 49690; Spring Rice to Williams, 10 Sept. 1906, CC, CASR 1/70; see chapters eight and nine. Especially on liberal doubts concerning imperialism, nationalism and humanitarian traditions towards the end of the nineteenth century, see Parry, *Politics of Patriotism*, esp. 387–400.
3. Harcourt, Memorandum, November 1900, BOD, MSS Harcourt 242.
4. Asquith to Gladstone, 5 Jan. 1902, BL, Add. 45989.
5. Rosebery in Sheffield, 20 Oct. 1885, cited in Reifeld, *Empire*, 152, n. 189.
6. 'We are engaged in … pegging out claims for the future.' Rosebery, 1 March 1893; see also Langer, *Diplomacy of Imperialism*, 78; Rosebery in London, 5 July 1895, in *Speeches*, Vol. 1, 334–52, 338. For Rosebery's Foreign policy see Martel, *Imperial Diplomacy*.
7. Cairnes, 'Foreign Policy of Lord Rosebery', Part II, CR, 8/1901, 52–176, 176.
8. Rosebery in Liverpool, 14 Feb. 1902, in *Speeches*, Vol. 1, 158; Rosebery in Glasgow, 16 Nov. 1900, ibid., 200.
9. For constructive imperialism, see Sykes, 'Konstruktiver Imperialismus', 241–65.
10. Rosebery in Edinburgh, 9 Oct. 1896, in *Speeches*, Vol. 1, 158, 425.
11. Rosebery (Mansion House), *The Times*, 10 Nov. 1894; Rosebery to Sanderson, 16 April 1895, NLS, MSS 10070.
12. Anon., 'Party, Politics and the War', ER 10/1901, 503–28.
13. Holbraad, *Concert of Europe*, 176–98.
14. Other influential liberal imperialists included Henry Norman, Lord Brassey, Sidney Buxton, A.H.D. Acland, Henry Fowler, F. Lockwood, R.L. Harmsworth and Herbert Samuel.

15. Taylor, *Struggle for Mastery*, 342.
16. Ibid.
17. Stadelmann, *Hegemonie und Gleichgewicht*, passim.
18. Greenwood, 'The Wilful Isolation of England', CR 6/1895, 838–52, 842; Dillon, 'Quadruple Alliance', CR 4/1896, 457–62.
19. Rosebery to Rhodes, 27 March 1894, NLS, MSS 10130; Rosebery, Memorandum, 27 March 1898, NLS, MSS 10177.
20. See Schroeder, 'Empire vs. Hegemony', 297–305.
21. 'England leistet eben gar nichts mehr, will aber alles Fressen' ('England does nothing at all, but wants to swallow everything' [trans. A.R.]). Holstein to Hatzfeldt, 9 Oct. 1894; and 16 Nov. 1894, cited in Hatzfeldt, *Nachgelassene Papiere*, Vol. 2, 1003–5.
22. Sanderson, Memorandum, 21 Feb. 1907, BD III, Appendix B, 420–32, esp. 430–32; Spring Rice to Williams, 10 Sept. 1906, CC, CASR 1/70.
23. Reifeld, *Empire*, 32–37, 121–29.
24. Rosebery, 26 Oct. 1905, *The Times*, 27 Oct. 1905; Monger, *End of Isolation*, 260; Crewe-Milnes, *Rosebery*, Vol. 2, 581.
25. The Limp protagonists were H.H. Asquith, R. Munro-Ferguson, Lord Brassey, S. Buxton, A.H.D. Acland, H. Fowler, F. Lockwood, R.L. Harmsworth, H. Norman and H. Samuel.
26. Grey to Buxton, 31 Dec. 1895, cited in Matthew, *Liberal Imperialists*, 202.
27. Ibid.
28. Ibid.
29. Salisbury's message to Lord Rosebery on leaving the FO, 18 Aug. 1892, cited in Bourne, *Foreign Policy*, No. 119, pp. 432–33; Salisbury to MacColl, 6 Sept. 1901, cited in Russell, *Malcolm MacColl*, 282–83.
30. Asquith, 19 June 1898, PD IV/59, col. 1346; *The Times*, 14 Oct. 1898; 28 Jan. 1899.
31. Grey, 5 April 1898, PD IV/56, col. 281.
32. Grey, 3 Feb. 1899, PD IV/66, cols. 237–44.
33. Grey in Weymouth, *The Times*, 27 Nov. 1902; see also 'Party, Politics and the War': Speech of Sir Edward Grey in the House of Commons, 2 Aug. 1901, commentary in ER 10/1901, 503–28.
34. Cited in Trevelyan, *Grey of Fallodon*, 77; *The Times*, 29 Nov. 1901.
35. Grey, 26 July 1901, PD IV/98, cols. 283–86; Grey, 2 July 1902, cited in Matthew, *Liberal Imperialists*, 207; Grey in Sheffield, *The Times*, 8 Nov. 1903.
36. Trevelyan, *Grey of Fallodon*, 77.
37. *The Times*, 19 Nov. 1901.
38. Henry Norman, 13 Feb. 1902, PD IV/102, col. 1278.
39. See also the correspondence between Spring Rice and the Limps Grey and Munro-Ferguson, GL I-II, passim.
40. Grey in Berwick, *The Times*, 2 Feb. 1903.
41. Members of this wing included, in addition to Harcourt, John Morley, James Bryce, Henry Campbell-Bannerman, Herbert J. Gladstone, Lord Ripon, Lord Kimberley, A.J. Mundella and Sir George O. Trevelyan. By contrast, the most left-leaning grouping, gathered around Henry Labouchère, did not participate in the debates over foreign policy.
42. Harcourt to Kimberley, 16 Nov. 1894, NLS, MSS 10143.

43. Jelavich, 'Britain and the Russian Acquisition of Batum', 44–67; see also *Daily Telegraph*, 7 July 1886; *The Times*, 7 July 1886; *Daily News*, 8 July 1886; Rosebery to Morier, 3 July 1886, 1f. and 13 July 1886, 4–6, in HCPP, Correspondence respecting the Port of Batoum (August 1886), Cd. 4857.
44. Harcourt to Kimberley, 23 Nov. 1894, NLS, MSS 10143.
45. Harcourt to Kimberley, 6 Dec. 1894, NLS, MSS 10143.
46. 'We could of course enter the Triple Alliance or enter into a secret treaty with Italy', wrote Rosebery, but 'our hands must be free: we must cooperate but not be hand-cuffed to anyone'. Rosebery to Malet, 3 Jan. 1894, cited in Lowe, *Reluctant Imperialists*, Vol. 2, No. 99, 95.
47. Hatzfeldt to Hohenlohe, 11 Nov. 1894, GP IX, No. 2161, 156.
48. Harcourt to Kimberley, 9 Dec. 1894, NLS, MSS 10143.
49. MacColl, 'Armenia and the Transvaal', FR 2/1896, 313–29, esp. 327.
50. MacColl, 'The Crisis in the Near East', CR 10/1897, 497–509; Channing in Rushden, 25 March 1897, cited in Channing, *Memories*, 195.
51. Reifeld, *Empire*, 136–41.
52. Norman, 'Russia and England', CR 2/1897, 153–71. Henry Norman was a freelance journalist who published principally in the *Daily Chronicle* and also a liberal imperial member of parliament. MacColl, 'Turkey or Russia?', FR 12/1895, 943–59, 952. Subsequently, Norman published 'The World's Work: An Illustrated Magazine of National Efficiency and Social Progress', *The Times*, 28 Nov. 1902.
53. Shaw-Lefevre to Harcourt, 22 Jan. 1896, BOD, MSS Harcourt 91; see also Channing, *Memories*, 195.
54. Kimberley to Ripon, 21 Sept. 1896, BL, Add. 43527.
55. Ripon to Kimberley, 23 Sept. 1896, BL, Add. 43527.
56. 'I do not see how we could maintain our position there [in the Mediterranean] in the face of a combined Russian and French fleet.' Kimberley to Ripon, 26 Sept. 1896, BL, Add. 43527.
57. Morley to Gladstone, 12 Sept. 1896, BL, Add. 45988; see also letters to Harcourt, BOD, MSS Harcourt 15–36.
58. Salisbury to Sandars, 2 April 1897, BOD, MSS Sandars, MS. Eng. hist. c.730.
59. Harcourt to Morley, 17 Nov. 1898, BOD, MSS Harcourt 30.
60. Staal to Mouraview, 15 Feb. 1899, cited in Meyendorff, *Correspondance diplomatique de M. de Staal*, Vol. 2, 416.
61. Grey to Spender, 21 Dec. 1901, MSS Spender, BL, Add. 46389; Blunt, *My Diaries*, Vol. 2, 53.
62. Rosebery in Glasgow, *The Times*, 17 Nov. 1900.
63. Fry, *Lloyd George*, 52.
64. Asquith to Gladstone, 5 Jan. 1901, BL, Add. 45989.
65. Harcourt to Morley, 5 Jan. 1901, BOD, MSS Harcourt 36.
66. Churchill, *World Crisis*, Vol. 1, 46.
67. The full title was 'The Heart of Empire: Discussions of Problems of Modern City Life in England. With an Essay on Imperialism'. Subsequently, during the First World War, Masterman organized the War Propaganda Bureau in Wellington House; amongst those he engaged to write for the bureau were H.G. Wells and Arthur Conan Doyle.
68. *The Spectator*, 22 June 1901; *The Times*, 15 Aug. 1901; 'Recent Books', CR 7/1901, 147–48.

69. Rowntree, *Poverty*, 216–21.
70. Miles (J.F. Maurice), 'Where to Get Men?', CR 1/1902, 78–86; Miles (J.F. Maurice), 'National Health', CR 1/1903, 41–56. The Committee on Physical Deterioration concluded that in 1899, of 12,000 recruits only 1,200 were fit to serve. *Report of the Interdepartmental Committee on Physical Deterioration*, 1904, 123.
71. The Coefficients formed in effect a 'brains trust', with the goal of developing the foundations for policy that would be suitably imperialist and progressive, efficient and modern. The club's principal concern was the consolidation and defence of the Empire. Although the Coefficients club soon ceased to function as a body responsible, in effect, for political planning, it continued to exist until 1909 as an unofficial think tank. Müllenbrock, *Literatur*, 62–63, n. 1; see also Amery, *My Political Life*, Vol. 1, 223–30; Wells, *Experiment in Autobiography*, 761–64; Russell, *Portraits*, 76–77; Hewins, *Apologia*, Vol. 1, 65–66.
72. Gollin, *No Longer an Island*, 231. Some of the minutes of the discussions could be tracked in the papers of H.J. Mackinder now in the archive of the BLPES. BLPES, ASSOC 17/MF160.
73. Wells, *Experiment in Autobiography*, 761.
74. See Scally, *Origins of the Lloyd George Coalition*, 110–33.
75. Ibid., 79, n. 14; Ryan, *Lieutenant-Colonel Charles à Court Repington*, 49.
76. Wells, *Experiment in Autobiography*, 761.
77. Russell, *Portraits*, 77; Wells, *New Machiavelli*, 75–78.
78. Wells, *Experiment in Autobiography*, 764.
79. Milner to Maxse, 7 June 1905, WSRO, MAXSE/453; Minutes of Discussion, 27 April 1903, S. 3, BLPES, ASSOC 17/MF160.
80. Wells, *Experiment in Autobiography*, 765.
81. Wells, *New Machiavelli*, 76.
82. Minutes of Discussion, 20 March 1905, 3, BLPES, ASSOC 17/MF160.
83. The members of this 'shadow cabinet' included Richard B. Haldane (Justice), Edward Grey (Foreign Policy), Mackinder Halford (Empire), Leo Maxse (Press), H.G. Wells (without portfolio), Clinton Dawkins (Finance), Bertrand Russell (Science/Education until 15 June 1903), W. Pember Reeves (Colonies) and W.A.S. Hewins (Economy). See Scally, *Origins of the Lloyd George Coalition*, 79. Additional members of this circle included Leo S. Amery, its secretary, Carlyon Bellairs, Sidney Webb, M.E. Sadler (from 15 May 1903), H. Birchenough, Henry Newbolt and, from 1905, Viscount Milner, James L. Garvin, John H. Smith (secretary); from 1907, G.S. Barnes, Lord Robert Cecil, E.C. Grenfell, C.F.G. Masterman, L.F. Moneypenny, Theodore Morison, F.S. Oliver, Charles à Court Repington and Josiah Wedgewood. See Members List, BLPES, ASSOC 17/MF160.
84. Wells, *New Machiavelli*, 59.
85. Grey to Gladstone, 2 July 1902, BL, Add. 48495; Grey, 15 July 1902, PD IV/111, cols. 304–7.
86. Grey in Weymouth, *The Times*, 27 Nov. 1902.
87. Wells, *New Machiavelli*, 60; Minutes of Discussion, 27 April 1903, S. 2, BLPES, ASSOC 17/MF160.
88. Commenting on Grey's approach to foreign policy, Bertrand Russell noted that in 1902 Grey was already making the case for a firm alliance with France and, if possible, with Russia also. See Semmel, *Imperialism and Social Reform*, 77; Scally, *Origins of the Lloyd George Coalition*, 88. The minutes of 27 April 1903 recorded, 'it would only be good

business to come to an understanding with them rather than with Germany'. Minutes of Discussion, 27 April 1903, 2, BLPES, ASSOC 17/MF160.
89. Significantly, Curzon stated around the same time, 'It [a German Alliance] will mean the habitual and incessant surrendering to Germany on points where our commercial interests are concerned all over the world. What should we get from her in return? We do not want her army. Her Navy is not sufficiently strong enough to be of much value'. Cited in Jaeckel, *Verteidigung Indiens*, 152; see also Grey to Maxse, 12 Oct. 1902, WSRO, MAXSE/450.
90. Minutes of Discussion, 27 April 1903, 3, BLPES, ASSOC 17/MF160.
91. Cited in Wilson, *Policy of the Entente*, 109.
92. Minutes of Discussion, 27 April 1903, 2, BLPES, ASSOC 17/MF160.
93. Grey to Maxse, 21 June 1904, WSRO, MAXSE/452.
94. Ibid.
95. Grey in Berwick, *The Times*, 7 Feb. 1903.
96. See Müllenbrock, *Literatur*.
97. Minutes of Discussion, 16 March 1903, BLPES, ASSOC 17/MF160.
98. Wormer, *Großbritannien*, 283.
99. Both Harold and Cecil Harmsworth had lost their seats in the khaki election. Alfred Harmsworth assured Rosebery that the *Daily Mail* was 'independent' and 'imperial'. See Pound and Harmsworth, *Northcliffe*, 220–21.
100. Haldane, *Autobiography*, 151–55.
101. 'We must reform or perish!', cited in GL I, 301.
102. Cited in Morris, *Scaremongers*, 97.
103. Spring Rice to Ferguson, 25 May 1904, GL I, 410; to E.E. Williams, 10 Sept. 1906, CC, CASR 1/70.
104. Milner to Maxse, 7 June 1905, WSRO, MAXSE/453.
105. Beckett, 'South African War', 31–44.
106. Dugdale, *Balfour*, 313–14.
107. Crowe to Asta Crowe, 9 April 1895, BOD, MSS Crowe, MS Eng. d. 2897.
108. Shannon, *Imperialism*, 339–40.
109. His grandfather Count de Flahaut was an illegitimate son of Talleyrand. Newton, *Lord Lansdowne*, 3.
110. See Brechtken, *Scharnierzeit*, 157.
111. Newton, *Lord Lansdowne*, 10.
112. Ibid., 9–10.
113. Ibid., 20.
114. For Lansdowne's time in Canada and India, see ibid., 24–126.
115. See ibid., 130–93, esp. 148–49.
116. Lord Lansdowne's Responsibility (Letters), *The Times*, 11 March 1901.
117. Balfour to Akers Douglas, 18 Oct. 1900, cited in Buckle, *Letters of Queen Victoria*, Vol. 3, 606–7.
118. Tyrrell to Spring Rice, 27 Nov. 1900, CC, CASR 1/65; Hamilton to Curzon, 1 Nov. 1900, IOL, EUR. F. 123/82.
119. Morrison to Bland, 4 Nov. 1900, *Correspondence of G.E. Morrison*, Vol. 1, 150–51.
120. Charmley, *Splendid Isolation*, 279.
121. Kennedy, *Rise of Anglo-German Antagonism*; Steiner and Neilson, *Britain and the Origins*, esp. 42–43; Williamson, *Politics of Grand Strategy*; Rolo, 'Lansdowne', in Wilson, *Foreign Secretaries*, 159–71; Steiner, 'Last Years of the Old Foreign Office', 59–60.

122. Monger, *End of Isolation*, 21; Steiner and Neilson, *Britain and the Origins*, 42–43; Shannon, *Imperialism*, 340.
123. Cited in Newton, *Lord Lansdowne*, 196–97.
124. Lansdowne to Monson, 12 Nov. 1900, NA, FO 800/125.
125. Lansdowne to Pauncefote, 14 Dec. 1900, cited in Adams, *Brothers across the Ocean*, 18.
126. Lansdowne to Scott, 23 April 1901, NA, FO 800/140.
127. See Adams, *Brothers across the Ocean*, 17.
128. Steiner, *Britain and the Origins*, 36.
129. Charmley, *Splendid Isolation*, 299.
130. Balfour to Edward VII, 29 Dec. 1904, BOD, MSS Sandars, MS Eng. c. 716.
131. Balfour to Selborne, 25 Oct. 1901, BOD, MSS Selborne 26.
132. Balfour to Salisbury, 24 March 1886, cited in Balfour, *Chapters of Autobiography*, 160.
133. Charmley, by contrast, sees the Anglo-Russian alliance premise. Charmley, *Splendid Isolation*, 279–312; see Chapter 5.
134. Esher, National Strategy, 1904, CC, ESHR 21/6, S. 8f.; Macintosh, 'C.I.D.', EHR 7/1962, 494–95.
135. Balfour, *Chapters of Autobiography*, 103–11.
136. Balfour in Manchester, *The Times*, 23 Jan. 1894.
137. Balfour to Lansdowne, 12 Dec. 1901, cited in Bourne, *Foreign Policy*, No. 139, 471–74, esp. 472.
138. Balfour in Manchester, *The Times*, 23 Jan. 1894; in Liverpool, *The Times*, 14 Feb. 1903.
139. Cited in Tomes, *Balfour and Foreign Policy*, 39.
140. Balfour in Liverpool, *The Times*, 14 Feb. 1903.
141. Balfour to Lansdowne, 21 Dec. 1903, BL, Add. 49728.
142. Cited in Tomes, *Balfour and Foreign Policy*, 106.
143. Balfour to Lansdowne, 22 Feb. 1904, BL, Add. 49728.
144. Balfour, 10 Aug. 1903, PD IV/127, col. 696; 27 Feb. 1905, PD IV/141, cols. 1393–1394.
145. Monger, *End of Isolation*, 117.
146. Balfour to Salisbury, 22 April 1898, HH, MSS Salisbury, 3M/E.
147. Metternich to Bülow, 17 July 1902, GP XVII, No. 5089, 214–16.
148. Balfour to Lansdowne, 12 Dec. 1901, cited in Bourne, *Foreign Policy*, No. 139, 472–73.
149. Hatzfeldt to AA, 18 Aug. 1898, GP XIV, No. 3853; Hatzfeldt to Hohenlohe, 2 Dec. 1899, GP XV, No. 4401.
150. Balfour to Salisbury, 22 April 1898, HH, MSS Salisbury 3M/E.
151. Balfour to Lansdowne, 12 Dec. 1901, cited in Bourne, *Foreign Policy*, No. 139, pp. 471–74, 473.
152. Steiner, 'Views of War'.
153. Cited in Gollin, *Milner*, 129.
154. Matthew, *Liberal Imperialists*, 153.
155. 'I believe it to be undesirable that we should add another square mile to the territories we already possess … the last thing I want to see is any extension. I want to see its strengthening and consolidation.' Balfour, 6 June 1906, PD IV/156, col. 1409.
156. Churchill, *Contemporaries*, 242.
157. Mitchell, A Biologist, 'A Biological View of Our Foreign Policy', *Saturday Review*, 1 Feb. 1896, 118–20; Browne, 'Is Great Britain Falling into Economic Decay?', CR 10/1901, 492–502.
158. Balfour, 29 April 1898, PD IV/56, col. 1590.

159. Morris, *Scaremongers*, 55.
160. Cited in Tomes, *Balfour and Foreign Policy*, 25.
161. Mr Balfour on the Crisis, *The Times*, 29 Oct. 1904.
162. Balfour, cited in *The Times*, 7 May 1904.
163. *The Times*, 22 March 1923; for Sanderson, see Steiner, 'Last Years of the Old Foreign Office', 59–90; Otte, *Foreign Office Mind*.
164. Steiner, 'Last Years of the Old Foreign Office', 63.
165. Sanderson to Salisbury, 1 April 1898, cited in Steiner, 'Last Years of the Old Foreign Office', 64, n. 24.
166. Sanderson to Satow, 12 April 1901, BD II, No. 73, 55; to Lascelles, 17 Oct. 1900, FO 800/9.
167. Sanderson to Lascelles, 3 April 1901, NA, FO 800/10.
168. Sanderson to Scott, 16 Jan. 1901; 13 Feb. 1901; 24 April 1901, BL, Add. 52299.
169. Sanderson, Memorandum, 21 Feb. 1907, BD III/B, 421–31, esp. 429.
170. Wipperfürth, 'Nicht Imperialist', 31.
171. Sanderson to Hardinge, 24 Oct. 1900, CUL, MSS Hardinge, Vol. 3; to Lascelles, 10 March 1901, NA, FO 800/6.
172. Sanderson to Scott, 8 May 1902, BL, Add. 52299.
173. Sanderson to Scott, 15 March 1898, BL, Add. 52298; to Hardinge, 8 Nov. 1899, CUL, MSS Hardinge, Vol. 3.
174. Sanderson to Balfour, 20 Aug. 1902, BL, Add. 49739.
175. Sanderson to Lascelles, 5 March 1902, NA, FO 800/10.
176. Hamilton, *Bertie of Thame*, 25, 33–37.
177. Steiner, 'Last Years of the Old Foreign Office', 67.
178. Bertie to Lascelles, 16 March 1898, NA, FO 64/1347; Campbell to Satow, 2 Jan. 1900, NA, PRO 30/33; Lascelles to Salisbury, 26 Oct. 1900, FO 64/1495; Bertie, Memorandum, 13 Sept. 1900, BD II, No. 12, 11.
179. Cited in Bourne, *Foreign Policy*, No. 138, 464–69.
180. Ibid.
181. Steiner, 'Last Years of the Old Foreign Office', 71.
182. Bertie to Lansdowne, 1 May 1905; Mallet to Bertie, 2 March 1906, NA, FO 800/170.
183. 'I wish we could make the lunatics here who denounce Germany in such unmeasured terms and howl for an agreement with Russia understand that the natural effect is to drive Germany into the Russian camp and encourage the Russians to believe that they can get all they want at our expense.' Sanderson to Lascelles, 3 Jan. 1905, NA, FO 800/13.
184. Sanderson to Lansdowne, 20 Jan. 1905, NA, FO 800/145; see also Charmley, *Splendid Isolation*, 316. For Sanderson's critique of the press, see Sanderson to Scott, 27 March 1901, BL, Add. 52299; to Chirol, 3 June 1904, NA, FO 800/2.
185. Sanderson to Lansdowne, 9 Oct. 1905, NA, FO 800/116.
186. 'They [the Germans] are confronted with a Russo-French Alliance, the Triple Alliance is less effective than it was; Austria is weaker from internal dissensions and is working with Russia in the Balkans, Italy from financial and other reasons has made friends with France; and we have followed suit. France … has obstinately refused to be reconciled to her loss of territory.' Sanderson to Lansdowne, 20 Jan. 1905, NA, FO 800/145.
187. See Chapter 3.
188. Sanderson to Scott, 16 Jan. 1901, 13 Feb. 1901, BL, Add. 52299; to Balfour, 20 Aug. 1902, BL, Add. 49739; to Hardinge, 19 Sept. 1905, CUL, MSS Hardinge, Vol. 7.

189. Sanderson to Lansdowne, 20 Jan. 1905, NA, FO 800/145.
190. Sanderson to Lansdowne, 18 May 1901, NA, FO 800/115; to Balfour, 13 Aug. 1905, BL, Add. 49739.
191. 'What mental man can have dreamt of anything so foolish as a condominium of Russia and England at Constantinople.' Sanderson to Lascelles, 26 Dec. 1895, NA, FO 800/15.
192. Hardinge to Grey, 25 Feb. 1907, BD III/B, 420–33. Still in 1913: Sanderson to Lansdowne, 15 Sept. 1913, BL, LANS/NC Sanderson.
193. Bertie to Mallet, 11 June 1904, NA, FO 800/170.
194. 'When has German diplomacy ever done otherwise than to lean to Russia? In what question, where the interests of England and Russia conflict, have we ever had, or can we ever expect, the support of German diplomacy? The truth is that German policy is governed by a besetting fear of their great eastern neighbour, and I am not aware that Germany has ever made any attempt to cultivate even the appearance of good relations with England … !' A. Chamberlain to Lansdowne and Balfour, 14 Jan. 1905, BUL, AC 17/1/59.
195. Lansdowne to Balfour, 18 Jan. 1905, BL, LANS/PL 5; Sanderson to Lansdowne, 27 June 1905, NA, FO 800/116.
196. Sanderson to Rosebery, 19 May 1895, NAS, MSS 10134; to Lascelles, 22 Jan. 1902, NA, FO 800/10; to Lansdowne, 27 June 1905, NA FO 800/116.
197. Hamilton, *Bertie of Thame*, 157, 389–90; Grenville, *Lord Salisbury*, 360.
198. Monson to Lansdowne, 21 June 1901, NA, FO 800/125.
199. Steiner, 'Last Years of the Old Foreign Office', 66, n. 34.
200. Strachey, 'Public Opinion in the Conduct of Foreign Affairs', *The Spectator*, 6 April 1901, 487–88.
201. Sanderson to Hardinge, 10 Oct. 1900, CUL, MSS Hardinge, Vol. 3.
202. Sanderson to Lascelles, 28 March 1900, NA, FO 800/9.
203. Sanderson to Scott, 2 June 1903, BL, Add. 52299.
204. Steiner, *Britain and the Origins*, 28; Monger, *End of Isolation*, 21; Grenville, *Lord Salisbury*, 149.
205. The author is currently working on a major study on the Mediterranean Agreements.
206. Lascelles to Bertie, 16 Dec. 1898, NA, FO 800/17; Bertie, 18 Nov. 1897, FO 17/1330.
207. Satow, 7 Oct. 1897, NA, PRO 30/33/16/1; Salisbury to Sanderson, 23 Dec. 1897, NA, FO 800/2.
208. Chirol to Spring Rice, 10 Dec. 1897, CC, CASR 1/9; Bertie to Salisbury, 6 Jan. 1898, BL, Add. 63013.
209. Smith to Bertie, 27 Dec. 1897; Bertie to Salisbury, 30 Dec. 1897, BL, Add. 63013.
210. Chirol to Bertie, 31 Dec. 1897, BL, Add. 63013; see also Jane, 'The Problem in the Far East', CR 3/1898, 387–93; Anon., 'The Failure of our Foreign Policy', CR 4/1898, 457–80; *Freeman's Journal and Daily Commercial Advertiser*, 10 Feb. 1898 and 18 May 1898; Lowe, *Reluctant Imperialists*, 227.
211. Hicks Beach in Swansea, 17 Jan. 1898, cited in *The Times*, 18 Jan. 1898; Chamberlain to Salisbury, 4 Jan. 1898, HH, MSS Salisbury, Chamberlain Correspondence 3/119.
212. Garvin, *Chamberlain*, Vol. 3, 249.
213. Grenville, *Lord Salisbury*, 143.
214. E.g.: Canis, *Von Bismarck zur Weltpolitik*; Meinecke, *Bündnisproblem*; Schöllgen, *Imperialismus und Gleichgewicht*; Grenville, *Lord Salisbury*; Kennedy, *Rise of Anglo-German Antagonism*; Albertini, *Origins*, Vol. 1; Langer, *Diplomacy of Imperialism*.
215. Canis, *Von Bismarck zur Weltpolitik*, 396–401.

216. Schöllgen, *Imperialismus und Gleichgewicht*, 89.
217. Lascelles to Salisbury, 8 Jan. 1898, NA, FO 800/17.
218. Lascelles to Sanderson, 27 Dec. 1895, NA, FO 800/17; to Salisbury, 1 Jan. 1898, HH, MSS Salisbury, A/121/1; 22 Jan. 1898, NA, FO 800/17; 2 Feb. 1898, NA, FO 800/17; Newton, *Lord Lansdowne*, 197.
219. Lascelles to Salisbury, 22 Jan. 1898, NA, FO 800/17; 22 Jan. 1898, HH, MSS Salisbury, A/121/3.
220. Grenville, *Lord Salisbury*, 150.
221. Dugdale, *Balfour*, Vol. 3, 21.
222. Elvert, 'Anglo-German Explorations', 45. Chamberlain had already spoken in Liverpool of a fundamental settlement that would also affect the European concert. *Daily News*, 20 Jan. 1898.
223. Judd, *Radical Joe*, 204.
224. Cited in Elvert, 'Anglo-German Explorations', 57.
225. Ibid.
226. Chirol to Lascelles, 6 April 1898, CC, CASR 1/14; to Spring Rice, 7 April 1898, CASR 1/9.
227. Canis, *Von Bismarck zur Weltpolitik*, 281.
228. Dugdale, *Balfour*, Vol. 3, 24.
229. Balfour, Memorandum, 14 March 1898, BL, Add. 49746.
230. Roberts, *Salisbury*, 691.
231. See Grenville, *Lord Salisbury*, 173–76. William Langer deems these thoughts merely 'academic'. Langer, *Diplomacy of Imperialism*, 527–28.
232. Hatzfeldt to AA, 22 Aug. 1898, GP XIV/1, No. 3862, 329–31; Grenville, by contrast, suspects Lascelles was striking out on his own. Grenville, *Lord Salisbury*, 173–74.
233. For Konrad Canis, however, Chamberlain was the sole force behind the talks. Canis, *Von Bismarck zur Weltpolitik*, 282.
234. Richthofen, Aufzeichnungen, 23 July 1898, GP XIV/1, No. 3840, 304–6.
235. Lascelles to Salisbury, 2 Aug. 1898, NA, FO 800/17.
236. Tel., Wilhelm II to Empress Frederick, 22 Aug. 1898, NA, FO 800/17.
237. Lascelles to Empress Frederick, 23 Aug. 1898, NA, FO 800/17.
238. 'Komödie der Irrungen', Nipperdey, *Deutsche Geschichte*, Vol. 3, 662.
239. Holstein, Memorandum, 12 Nov. 1898, *Holstein Papers*, Vol. 4, 98–100; Lascelles to Salisbury, 3 Dec. 1898; to Queen Victoria, 9 Dec. 1898; to Salisbury, 10 Dec. 1898, all NA, FO 800/17.
240. Grenville, *Lord Salisbury*, 331–32.
241. Cited in Grenville, 'Lansdowne's Abortive Project', 205.
242. Lansdowne to Lascelles, 22 Jan. 1901, BD II, No. 28, 23.
243. Wilhelm II to Bülow, 30 Jan. 1901, GP XVII, No. 4982, 19.
244. Eckardstein, *Lebenserinnerungen*, Vol. 2, 235–37.
245. Lascelles to Salisbury, 5 Oct. 1900, NA, FO 800/17.
246. Lascelles to Lansdowne, 16 March 1901, NA, FO 800/128.
247. Lansdowne to Lascelles, 18 March 1901, BD II, No. 77, 60.
248. Lansdowne to Lascelles, 9 April 1901, BD II, No. 80, 62–63.
249. Charmley, *Splendid Isolation*, 284.
250. Cited in Anon., *History of The Times*, Vol. 3, 342–43.
251. Salisbury, Memorandum, 7 Jan. 1902, cited in Bourne, *Foreign Policy*, No. 141, 476–78.

252. Nish, *Anglo-Japanese Alliance*, 131.
253. Keith Neilson argues that Lansdowne 'jumped at this opportunity'. Neilson, *Britain and the Last Tsar*, 216.
254. Bertie to Salisbury, 30 Dec. 1897; to Bigge, 26 Nov. 1899, both BL, Add. 63013.
255. Bertie, Memorandum, 11 March 1901, BD II, No. 54, 43.
256. Sanderson to Scott, 10 April 1901, BL, Add. 52299; Salisbury to MacColl, 6 Sept. 1901, cited in Russell, 'Malcolm MacColl', 282–83.
257. Hamilton to Curzon, 15 March 1901, IOL, EUR. F. 111/148.
258. Lansdowne (Lords), *The Times*, 29 March 1901.
259. Neilson, *Britain and the Last Tsar*, 218.
260. Sanderson to Scott, 10 April 1901, BL, Add. 52299; Nish, *Anglo-Japanese Alliance*, 135–37.
261. Selborne to Lansdowne, 4 Sept. 1901, BL, LANS/PL 1.
262. Lansdowne to MacDonald, 1 Nov. 1901, BD II, No. 108, 99.
263. Newton, *Lord Lansdowne*, 233.
264. Charmley, *Splendid Isolation*, 300; Neilson, *Britain and the Last Tsar*, 220–21.
265. Sanderson to Scott, 10 April 1901, BL, Add. 52299.
266. Salisbury to Lansdowne, 18 Oct. 1901, NA, FO 800/137; see also Flood, *Ambassadorship*, 42.
267. Lansdowne, Memorandum, 25 Oct. 1901, cited in Monger, *End of Isolation*, 54.
268. Hardinge, Memorandum, 1 March 1901, CUL, MSS Hardinge, Vol. 3; Drummond-Wolff to Lansdowne, 9 Oct. 1901, BL, LANS/NC Drummond-Wolff.
269. Calchas (Garvin), 'A Plea for Peace – an Anglo-Russian Alliance', FR 12/1900, 998–1005; Calchas (Garvin), 'Russia and her Problem', FR 6/1901, 1031–44, 1031; Havelock Ellis, 'The Genius of Russia', CR 9/1901, 419–38; RR 7/1901, 40; RR 8/1901, 130–31; Anon., 'The Focus of Asiatic Policy', NR 6/1901, 624–37; Blennerhasset (Letters), *The Times*, 31 Aug. 1901. Bandar Abbas was the most important port in the Persian Gulf region.
270. Grey, 26 July 1901, PD IV/98, col. 286.
271. *The Times*, 17 June 1901; 29 June 1901; 3 July 1901; RR 6/1901, 528; An old Parliamentary Hand, 'The Causes of Unionist Discontent', NR 6/1901, 512–24.
272. Chirol to Hardinge, 11 Oct. 1901, CUL, MSS Hardinge, Vol. 3.
273. Chirol to Hardinge, 17 Nov. 1901, CUL, MSS Hardinge, Vol. 3.
274. *The Times*, 20 Nov. 1901.
275. Chirol to Lascelles, 22, 23 and 25 Nov. 1901, CC, CASR 1/14.
276. Lansdowne, Memorandum, 25 Oct. 1901, cited in Monger, *End of Isolation*, 54.
277. Steiner, 'Anglo-Japanese', 27–36, 36; Lansdowne to A. Hardinge, 6 Jan. 1902, BD IV, No. 321a, 369–72.
278. Monger, *End of Isolation*, 55.
279. MacDonald to Lansdowne, 31 Oct. 1901, NA, FO 800/134.
280. Lansdowne to Salisbury, 21 Nov. 1901, BL, LANS/PL 5.
281. Ibid.
282. Lansdowne, Memorandum, 11 Nov. 1901, BD II, No. 92, 76–79.
283. Balfour, Memorandum, 12 Dec. 1901, cited in Bourne, *Foreign Policy*, No. 139, 471–74.
284. Ibid., 472.
285. Ibid., 472–73.

286. Schroeder, 'Alliances, 1815–1945', 195–222.
287. Lansdowne to Balfour, 12 Dec. 1901, BL, Add. 49727.
288. Balfour, Memorandum, 29 Dec. 1903, NA, CAB 37/67/97.
289. Hicks Beach to Lansdowne, 2 Jan. 1902, FO 800/134; for Ritchie, see Monger, *End of Isolation*, 58–59, n. 1.
290. See Nish, *Anglo-Japanese Alliance*, 209; Monger, *End of Isolation*, 59; Charmley, *Splendid Isolation*, 303.
291. Lansdowne to Lascelles, 19 Dec. 1901, BD II, No. 94, 80–82.
292. Lansdowne, Memorandum, 11 Nov. 1901, BD II, No. 92, 76–79; 12 Nov. 1901, No. 93, 79–80.
293. Nish, *Anglo-Japanese Alliance*, 207.
294. Lansdowne to J. Chamberlain, 31 Dec. 1901, BUL, JC 11/21/16.
295. Grey to Maxse, 20 Feb. 1902, WSRO, MAXSE/450.
296. Walton, 22 Jan. 1902, PD IV/101, cols. 574–76; Norman, cols. 599–601; Grey, cols. 609–11; Cranborne, cols. 615–16.
297. Monger, *End of Isolation*, 66.
298. *The Speaker*, 15 Feb. 1902, 549; see Campbell-Bannerman's critique: 13 Feb. 1902, PD IV/102, col. 1292.
299. Langer, *Diplomacy of Imperialism*, 762–63; Hayashi, *Memoirs*, 157–62.
300. Bülow to Alvensleben, 22 Feb. 1902, GP XVII, No. 5050, 157–59.
301. Taylor, *Struggle for Mastery*, 404.

Chapter 3

SAFETY FIRST

The Politics of Defence and the Realities behind Diplomacy

Action and Response as the Dominant Interpretation

The yardstick by which Britain measured its foreign policy options was its security situation.[1] This was even more so since the Committee of Imperial Defence (CID), a non-executive body of politicians, military and naval advisors tasked with prioritizing defence problems and sifting the options, met more than twice a month from 18 December 1902 onwards. The formation of the CID in many ways exemplifies the recognition by national leadership that managing British policy through the increasing complexity of international relations required inter-departmental coordination and high-level political consideration and reflection. Neither foreign nor defence policy were any longer matters of the respective departments alone.[2]

As long as no confidential reports had been received from the imperial border zone in the Middle East, the regular meetings of the CID regularly addressed the risk of an invasion of the British Isles. As the traditional guarantor of British security, the Royal Navy functioned as a global deterrent,[3] protecting not only trade and supply routes but also the negotiating positions of British foreign policy. The Royal Navy was also the great pride of the British people and as such central to both British identity and integration.[4] Analysis of British foreign policy and its motivations cannot avoid the issue of international naval rearmament.[5]

In early December 1904, the cabinet announced the biggest naval strategic shake-up of British forces stationed around the world.[6] The basis for the shake-up was a memorandum to the cabinet by the First Lord of the Admiralty, Earl Selborne, on 6 December 1904.[7] The forces of the China Station were recalled, and the number of battleships in the Mediterranean was reduced by 30 per cent,

---

Notes for this chapter begin on page 169.

with those that remained united with part of the former Channel fleet to form a new Atlantic fleet, based at Gibraltar. The Home Fleet became a new Channel fleet backed by significant reserves.[8] According to John Arbuthnot Fisher, who had become First Sea Lord on 21 October 1904, Trafalgar Day, the Admiralty had thus ordered a total of 160 units into the vicinity of the British Isles.[9] Only two months later, on 22 December 1904, Selborne approved the appointment of a special committee to review the designs of new-model warships proposed to be laid down under the 1905–1906 construction programme.[10] As a result of this so-called 'Committee on Designs' four (later reduced to three) *Invincible*-class armoured cruisers, later battle-cruisers, were ordered and one battleship – the *HMS Dreadnought*.[11]

Both steps – the record-breaking construction, in only fourteen months,[12] of the first of the all-big-gun ships,[13] and the new strategic distribution of the British naval forces – are usually interpreted as an unavoidable response to the threat posed by the German High Seas Fleet lying at anchor at Wilhelmshaven. On the basis of Arthur Marder's pioneering research and Paul Kennedy's magisterial work on the apparently inevitable rivalry between Britain and Germany, historians have long explained Britain's policy with the aid of a model based on German action and British reaction.[14] The political leadership provided by Balfour and Lansdowne is then usually read as evidence of responses that came too late and attitudes that were either naive or overly patient. According to that interpretation, countermeasures followed only as a result of public pressure, and Lord Selborne and John Fisher were the first decision makers to recognize, prematurely, the 'singular' threat from Germany.[15] Germany's 'High Seas Battle Fleet', Kennedy writes, was 'so big that it compelled the British Admiralty gradually to withdraw almost all its capital-ship squadrons from overseas stations into the North Sea'.[16] Although a number of more recent specialist studies of British naval policy have given us reason to pause rather than accept wholesale the stimulus-response model,[17] many historians, especially diplomatic historians, continue to cling to the interpretation that claims that 'the expansion of the German fleet brought about a diplomatic revolution to the states system between 1902 and 1907'.[18]

The greatest shortcoming of this established interpretation – all the more surprising in light of the amount of ink that has been spilt on the subject – is its overwhelmingly Germanocentric perspective.[19] Like contemporaries, historians too have been much influenced by traditional attitudes and explanations. Repeatedly, their studies reveal that, much like the 'balance of power' paradigm, the classic action/reaction model as a basis of British foreign and defence policy developed from historical-political tradition into historiographical convention.[20] Even studies that look expressly at the British side and specifically at the maritime context rely too often and too readily on the established interpretation and on the records of the German Naval Office to make their case that the British response was logical and rational.[21] Their approach is explained above all by a form of scholarly thinking thought long since abandoned – the goal previously, as apparently still now, was not to explain the actions of the Royal Navy but to determine the extent of German guilt.[22]

The foundations of such largely supplemental studies undoubtedly lie in the contribution of Arthur Marder and in the work of Paul Kennedy, which built on Marder's research and appeared after the Fischer controversy. In his seminal study *The Anatomy of British Sea Power*,[23] Marder, who was particularly interested in *HMS Dreadnought* and therefore left other units, especially the at least equally important battle-cruisers, or questions of the naval policy process or other general questions aside,[24] drew the conclusion that as early as autumn 1902 and in response to German provocation, public opinion, the government and the Admiralty all agreed that the German High Seas Fleet was a far greater threat than the naval power of the Franco-Russian alliance.[25] First published in 1940, Marder's research by no means 'set standards of archival research' as is often believed,[26] but was based primarily on published source material,[27] with his section on the 'German Naval Challenge' drawing on material found in the *National Review*, the *Spectator*, the *Morning Post* and the *Daily Mail*. Marder seemed oblivious to the fact that these very publications were pushing their own agenda, riling up their readership against Germany.[28] Thus, the anti-German imperative served as a prism through which he viewed all evidence and through which he approached all questions. Needless to say that hereby First Sea Lord Fisher appeared solely focused on a showdown with the Tirpitz fleet.[29] Nevertheless, already in the *Anatomy of British Sea Power* and again years later, Marder had to acknowledge in the introduction to his valuable source collection *Fear God and Dread Nought* that even after decades spent pouring over the sources, he had not been able to establish an immediate causal relationship between German naval armament and the construction of the Dreadnoughts.[30] In the wake of the Fischer controversy, as historians tended to focus on Tirpitz's plans for the German fleet, Marder's belated self-criticism was as easily overlooked as were the more nuanced conclusions of Ruddock Mackay's path-breaking biography of John Fisher.[31] Truly, Marder's interpretation seemed all too consistent, given the fact that indeed Germany's High Seas Battle Fleet stationed in the North Sea was the primary determinant of the Royal Navy. Kennedy's work provides an ample example of this trend, for like the path-breaking studies produced by Jonathan Steinberg and Volker Berghahn, Kennedy's analysis focused on demonstrating 'that Tirpitz did indeed think of challenging the supremacy of the British Navy'.[32] Yet does that fact alone mean that the Royal Navy and British politicians had no option but to see this challenge as an acute threat that forced them to react, that demanded all concentration, led them to forget all foreign political traditions and sacrifice imperial interests?

While Arthur Marder's work still sets the standards of interpretation, Ruddock Mackay's biography has long been neglected, although he found documents directly contradicting Marder's conclusions. Therefore, already by February

1902, Fisher had thought out Selborne's later plan of fleet distribution when he thought of France and Russia as the most likely and dangerous foes. Even when Fisher became First Sea Lord in October 1904, he was not driven by any anti-German attitude.[33] Although Kennedy's ground-breaking work *The Rise of Anglo-German Antagonism* leads to the ultimately justified conclusion that German naval strategy can be termed 'exceedingly erratic and confused',[34] it remains puzzling why London should have overestimated German capability. Kennedy's explanation largely focused on reference to Alfred Thayer Mahan and the 'two-power standard', which considered only battleships and battle-cruisers, as the contemporary yardstick.[35] Calculations of tonnage may have been part of the equation, but they cannot tell us whether contemporaries were especially sensitive to such figures,[36] and Mahan's undoubted influence on the construction of the Tirpitz fleet seems too hastily extended to the Royal Navy.[37]

A further explanation is found in German behaviour, which prevented, or so runs the account, a realistic evaluation of the situation by the strongest and most experienced of sea powers, as Berlin made the mistake of hiding its weaknesses;[38] London – and here the contemporaries' conclusion is simply adopted wholesale – had no choice but to work with the worst-case scenario. Retrospectively, and in awareness of German deliberations, English naval policy can then be deemed entirely 'rational' and 'logical'.[39] The war itself, Kennedy explained elsewhere, simply proved British policy and its subsequent explanation correct.[40] For a historian of Anglo-German relations, a layered explanation of German behaviour – for example, the feeling that Germany was not being taken seriously, as in the case of Samoa, or the sense of being under threat that came from the *Bundesrath* affair and repeated seizures of German merchant ships during the Boer War – was in the end far less important than the fact that Tirpitz had turned the German fleet into an instrument of power.[41] Kennedy thus made clear that his principal concern was the German background to Anglo-German relations.

Yet this approach, a standard interpretation, only considers one side of the coin. Our picture is necessarily distorted if we fail to take into consideration the complex English background too, considering both public opinion and internal expertise. While for many historians 'the very presence of the Tirpitz battleships presented a challenge to Britain on its doorstep', and made all too understandable that London would 'respond' with the construction of the dreadnoughts,[42] Paul W. Schroeder for instance is more sceptical: in explaining international events in the run up to the war, he notes, it is 'one thing to show that Germany blundered and had dangerous aims; quite another to prove that these really caused the outcome, or that, had Germany not made them, the overall outcome would have been drastically changed'.[43]

The discussion that follows tackles especially this last issue. It presents a wider context of discussions about home defence as a further background to Selborne's memorandum of December 1904 and follows the ground-breaking results by Jon Sumida and Nicholas Lambert, that Britain's naval policy can also be explained on its own terms, without constant necessity to invoke a German peril. While Sumida and Lambert have mainly focused on technological and financial aspects of Britain's naval policy, the following considerations ask for inter-departmental questions in times of tight budgets. Eventually, it was not for nothing that the War Office and the Admiralty were described by Major General John Ardagh as 'two rival syndicates' and were primarily concerned with furthering their own interests.[44] We should also consider whether home defence really was the principal reason for London's change of course when it came to defence and foreign policy, or whether perhaps the security of the Empire required a broader adaptation of British policy. In other words, was Britain motivated primarily by the need to maintain a balance of powers in Europe, with a particular focus on Germany, as has always been argued, or were British concerns focused on a need to consolidate the Empire in the face of the challenge contained in the Franco-Russian Dual Alliance?

One further, and vital, question concerns how both the political leadership in Whitehall and the broader public responded to contemporary military expertise. In this chapter, we look first at the Conservative defence policy, using the examples of the reform of that policy after the Boer War, positions adopted on 'home defence',[45] and investigations of invasion-preparedness undertaken by the Norfolk Commission and in the Committee of Imperial Defence, in order that in a later chapter Conservative policy might be compared with the liberal approach to defence policy, on the example of the second investigation of invasion-preparedness conducted between 1907 and 1909.[46] Our interest in the political sphere and in the political possibilities during this period of transformation is good reason to set the atmosphere and general mood we have already encountered against the views of contemporary experts, which have been little explored to date. Having established the realities behind the public's sense of threat, we can then explore the relationship between perceptions and decisions.[47] As when evaluating diplomatic or journalistic judgements, again we must remain alert to the structural context, above all when political decision making ran counter to internal expertise or alternative proposals. In this age of rapid technological development, constructive exchange with experts was alone able to provide political decision makers with a sense of their room for manoeuvre, or alert them to threats: 'Naval science', wrote the naval correspondent of the *Daily Mail*, 'is not a thing to be cultivated at chance moments or odd times; it is a mistress jealous of every other pursuit'.[48] For an assessment of the actions of the decision makers that takes account of their room for political manoeuvring, their interaction with the expert knowledge available to them is of decisive importance.

Invasion Scares and Defensive Reforms

Throughout the nineteenth century, the risk of invasion generated impassioned debate within the London political sphere. That debate was part of a traditional pattern whose origins can be traced back to the Napoleonic threat faced between 1803 and 1805. Technological developments, visions for the future, or political crises tended to spur politicians and military leaders to raise their own voices. Steamships and ironclads whipped up feeling in the 1840s and 1850s,[49] while Napoleon III's coup d'état, the German wars of unification and the Boulanger crisis also stoked the fires in London.[50] With the exception of the events of 1871, the greatest apparent threats were from Britain's arch-enemies France and Russia, and even more significantly, while the army might fuel public concerns about invasion, the navy's divergent response regularly remained in house.[51] Although Napoleon had been decisively defeated at Waterloo and not at Trafalgar, throughout the nineteenth century the army leadership constantly felt a need for validation of its forces.[52] A traditional slogan recounted that not the army but 'the Navy is the Nation', with the Royal Navy deemed '1st, 2nd, 3rd, 4th, 5th … ad infinitum Line of Defence!'[53] If the British Isles' highly advantageous geography meant fears of invasion were groundless, the enemy's miracle ships, such as that found in the *Battle of Dorking* published in 1871, provided the necessary threat.[54] Other narratives completely ignored the existence of the British navy and had only the army and volunteer forces available to rescue the day. A futuristic vision of a Channel tunnel advanced by several ambitious engineers provided a way of ignoring the navy yet upturning Britain's insular identity.[55] While the Admiralty could confidently assume that the loyalty of the British people would ensure its financial requirements were met and its prestige would remain high, the army leadership believed public anxiety was the key to preserving its forces. The activities of the National Service League at the beginning of the twentieth century were also part of the army's campaign, for, unlike the Navy League, the army pressure group was very worried about recruitment rates, and it sought to assuage that concern through propaganda in support of the army.[56]

With this complex internal and inter-ministerial context in mind, we can usefully revisit traditional interpretations of British foreign and defence policy. As the very expensive recent campaign in South Africa had made evident, such policy could not be simply a matter of responding to external threats. Individual interests were to the fore when it came to the contested allocation of the somewhat scarce financial resources, the distribution of responsibilities and the apportionment of the burdens of imperial defence.[57] These debates were not contained within leading political and military circles, for they were brought by the media to a broader public. Although their significance is often overlooked by historians, these contested issues helped determine the character of British foreign policy.

In early 1900, English fear of invasion took a new turn when the traditional debate was reinvigorated by novel interventions. Yet that new dynamic was not a product, as has so often been assumed, of an extreme threat that accompanied the German naval expansion begun in 1898.[58] The *Daily Telegraph* had expressly welcomed the construction of the new German fleet, and in early January 1902 the *Observer* informed its readers that even a doubling in size of the German fleet would present the Royal Navy with no very great problem.[59] The second German Naval Law of summer 1900 was also deemed only a minor potential threat.[60] Initially, Berlin even seemed more attractive to Whitehall as a result: after France's plans for a naval fleet far larger than that of Germany became known,[61] First Lord of the Admiralty Lord Selborne, with a cautious eye on France's ally Russia and on the United States, called repeatedly for a rapprochement towards Berlin.[62] Germany may not have been deluded in reckoning that its naval forces provided Britain with an incentive to remain in discussion with Germany and might bring the two countries closer. The First Sea Lord and his admirals were at this point suffering a headache caused not only by France and Russia's open attempts to exploit Britain's predicament,[63] but also by the maritime strength of France, which led the field in a number of areas of innovation, and of Russia and the United States, which were quickly catching up.[64] At the beginning of the new century, the French navy was repeatedly practising manoeuvres at sea, and the *Revue des deux Mondes* even spread the rumour that Napoleon's Boulogne fleet was to be re-formed.[65] In July 1900, John Ardagh, Director of Military Intelligence, could report that in the course of the previous two years, signs of French planning for an invasion of Britain had been detected.[66] Edmund Monson, British ambassador to Paris, even reported that the Fashoda incident (1898) had overtaken all French thoughts of revenge for the loss of Alsace-Lorraine.[67] At the same time, the German navy had looked on helplessly as German merchant ships had been seized during the Boer War,[68] while the plans for its expansion were not only more modest than French plans for its navy but also set within a longer timeframe, reaching up to 1920, while French expansion was scheduled to be complete by 1906.[69] The German plans therefore aroused curiosity rather than consternation.[70] Soon after becoming First Lord of the Admiralty, Selborne warned, with good reason, about the realization of French and Russian plans for their navies,[71] not least because the French were concentrating on technological innovations such as torpedo boats, submarines and battle-cruisers,[72] which by then had already been recognized as the real weapons of the future.[73]

Fear of invasion did not yet grow in Britain. Full details of French and German plans for their navies were not known until summer 1900 and December 1900 respectively. A home-grown problem, along with 'Black Week' in South Africa, would have a far greater impact on Britain's feeling of imperilment. The focus on external pressures and inevitable reaction from the Empire often results in

Table 3.1. Naval planning for the period 1900 to 1920.

	England	France		Germany	
	by 1920	1900–1906	1905–1919	1900–1920	1908–1920
Battleships	60	28	36	38	45
Battle-cruisers	20	24	18	14	22
Small cruisers	35	34	20	33	14
Torpedo-boat destroyers	155	337 + (52)ᵃ	352	96ᵇ	88
Submarines	58	56	131	0	28

Source: for the figures, see Lambi, *Navy*, 85; Steinberg, *Yesterday's Deterrent*, 221–22; Ropp, *Development of a Modern Navy*, 366–67.
ᵃAlong with 337 torpedo boats, France planned 52 new torpedo-boat destroyers (TBDs); ᵇGermany did not recognize the importance of torpedo-boat destroyers before 1912, and the figures for this class are therefore not always evident.

a failure to recognize that in the heat of imperialist competition that was very much of London's own making, with the war in South Africa, Britain had manoeuvred itself into international isolation, dramatic debt and, as a result, domestic political tension. Unusually, this new anxiety was not a by-product of military or political decisions made on high and then filtered down to the general population. Essentially, the disquiet stemmed from fears of a *New Battle of Dorking*,[74] with agitation fanned and directed by the press.[75] As St. John Brodrick, at the time under-secretary in the War Office and soon after secretary of state for war, commented to Balfour, the widely experienced sense of failure was a result of Britain's own short-sightedness.[76] That tension brought a new dynamic to the existing, and not insignificant, internal societal tensions between pro-Boers and imperialists and between departments in Whitehall, which was intensified in novel ways by the media.

The War Office believed the *Times*, the leading agenda-setter in London, had thrown down the gauntlet when its lead article on New Year's Day 1900 raised doubts about the cost-benefit claims for the army, recording: 'The old idea – much cherished and zealously propagated in Pall Mall – that we must look to the army for immunity from invasion, is an exploded superstition. The protection of our shores is not the business of the Army. It is the business of the Navy, the only force we possess able to perform it'.[77] While the renowned *Times* made the case for future defence to be placed in the hands of the Royal Navy, the paper also called for a fundamental reform of the defence structures put in place in the 1860s and confirmed by the Carnarvon Commission in 1882. Ultimately, much prestige and also a large part of the army's budget were based on traditional responsibilities for coastal defence.[78]

For several years, as we have seen, the radical right that formed around Leo Maxse had been calling in the press for a fundamental change of course in foreign and defence policy, and now, like the Liberal opposition, it saw an opportunity for public political debate. Only half a decade earlier, the Liberals, above all Campbell-Bannerman together with Chancellor of the Exchequer Michael Hicks Beach, had been responsible for derailing Lansdowne's plans for military-political reform, but that did not prevent them from now seeking to make Lansdowne a political scapegoat for the disastrous performance against the irregular Boer forces.[79] Their principal goal was to counter and shake off accusations that they were pro-Boer by highlighting Britain's rapid loss of reputation globally. The war was taken as an opportunity to raise the spectre of a new Napoleonic threat, an ominous image that as the general election approached would likely overshadow the tensions within the Liberal camp involving opponents of the war and jingoists. While the Limps criticized the failure to realize reforms, with the help of William T. Stead the radical liberals sought to put the blame for Britain's position on the war itself. The Napoleonic argument was attractive not least because it could be deployed by both those who favoured disarmament and those who supported a policy of strength. Where in the course of the previous century the threat of invasion had been employed sporadically and largely as entertainment, now that same threat was instrumentalized, to be used in relation to foreign and defence policy and in light of inner-party divisions. This development was also fostered by the large number of officers of the volunteer forces who currently sat in the House of Lords, men such as Lord Wemyss and Lord Ellenborough, who found in the public defence debate an opportunity to lobby for their cause.[80]

Despite a number of highly alarming reports from Paris, the Tory leadership continued to count on being able to calm the waters.[81] Salisbury had long been sceptical, even highly pessimistic, about the political public's palpably growing influence and internal momentum.[82] He expressly warned against the reckless exploitation of his fellow countrymen's fears, commenting, 'I do not think he [Lord Rosebery] serves his country by the constant repetition of impossible apprehensions and unfounded complaints'.[83] He believed the best course of action was a demonstrative display of equanimity, with the idea of invasion exposed as preposterous. A 'collection of shooting stars', he insisted, could alone present any real danger to England.[84] This statement made in parliament was obviously intended to still public agitation, but also made evident his fundamental scepticism about the military[85] and its regular attempts to bring added drama to the defence situation with motives that were sometimes individual and sometimes structural.[86] Salisbury, on the contrary, constantly stressed the complexities and general openness of the international situation as a whole, a situation of which he had a far superior grasp. He did not invest great stock in conjecture about the attitudes and capabilities of other powers. It might well be that France was increasing its military strength and was on the search for a continental alliance, but had the Fashoda crisis not just demonstrated that Britain was prepared to take on all-comers? Had not that crisis, like the ongoing war, demonstrated that whatever the hostility towards Britain of other powers, those powers were unable to unite to strike a blow against their common enemy. Salisbury believed that Britain could depend on the enmity of Germany and France, and even count on the Kaiser himself, whose own interests would lead him to stand in the way of the creation of a continental alliance against Britain.[87]

While Salisbury could masterly play the game of the great power system, he lost his confidence when the public joined in. Unlike his long-term opponent William Gladstone or his coalition partner Joseph Chamberlain, Salisbury struggled to come to terms with the expansion of the political sphere, let alone control the political public to his own ends.[88] He maintained a Victorian equanimity that he was unable to convey to the Edwardian horizon.[89] An inability to engage public opinion would also prove a central problem for his successor's government. Equanimity was insufficient, especially as during the election the Unionists had successfully conveyed an image of themselves as the sole party up to the responsibilities of the Empire.[90]

With the retirement of Ardagh and Lord Wolseley at the end of 1900, war hero Lord Roberts, or 'Bobs' as he was popularly known, took on the military leadership at the War Office. Roberts was supported by the recalcitrant and extremely ambitious William Nicholson, Director-General of Mobilization and Military Intelligence, who by the time the war broke out in 1914 had risen to Chief of the General Staff. An additional significant member of this circle was William Robertson, Roberts' intelligence officer in South Africa, who was the new head of the Foreign Military Intelligence Division. From the start, the new leadership interpreted their responsibilities as a political mission. All three threw themselves into torpedoing their new minister's reform plans, which planned for financial cuts and a reduction of army corps, which would defend the Mother Country and form a quick reaction force for the Empire. Roberts, a war veteran himself, blamed the poor condition of the army for the loss of his son at Colenso,[91] and on his return from South Africa became very concerned about the tarnished reputation of the military forces.[92] He saw the reform plans as demoting the ground forces in their internal rivalry with the British navy, a view Nicholson shared. As one of the most stiff-necked proponents of the superiority of the army over the navy,[93] Nicholson embodied the younger generation of army officers who thought in continental terms and directly challenged the hegemony of the Royal Navy,[94] and he saw his new function as chief of military intelligence as an opportunity to thwart the minister's proposed reforms. One of his first tasks was to draw up operational plans for war against France and Russia. His principal design, he candidly admitted to Roberts, was not to answer the question as set, but rather to exaggerate the risks of such a campaign to the extent that the cabinet would be forced to back away from any idea of disarmament.[95] Threat analysis was tied directly in with reform and became the focus of discussions about a new defensive structure. While the government believed it paramount to learn the lessons of the war and ensure cooperative implementation of the necessary reforms in the cause of greater efficiency, the military leadership in the War Office had its own plans, as became evident at the first joint conference on coastal defence, an initiative of the Admiralty.[96] While their colleagues at the War Office argued that Britain's security was severely threatened, the Admiralty made its own case calmly and with composure. According to the naval specialists, in light of Britain's control of her waters, even brief and isolated forays – no mention was made of an invasion – were inconceivable. Even if the Admiralty believed the new weapons system employed by the French navy represented a threat,[97] there could still be no doubt that Britain could guarantee its own security, thanks to the Royal Navy, although only on condition that Britain kept pace with the leading nations technologically.[98]

Robertson's memorandum of 27 December 1901 left a rather different impression. Very much in accord with the wishes of his superiors, he portrayed the situation in the worst light possible,[99] although the focus of his analysis was not Germany, but rather a possible invasion by France.[100] Following a pattern by now standard, he made no reference to the navy, to maritime technology or to the problems of maritime operations. He placed France's military resources front and centre. For Robertson, France's compulsory military service was a model that Britain might learn from, and he characterized the French military as almost awe-inspiring, recording: 'France now has 3.3 Million trained men at her disposal, well armed, well led, and amply supplied with transport and war material of all kinds. … The recruiting law of 1889 will continue year by year to increase this number, to some extent, until it is in complete application in 1913'.[101] Robertson believed that France's massive increase in fighting strength was not being undertaken solely with Germany in mind; France's thoughts, he wrote, also turned to the Channel, and to its 'twenty-six ports connected by rail with the interior, and several by canal as well'.[102] French 'esprit' and French traditions convinced him that should Britain and France find themselves at war, the Grande Nation would attempt invasion.[103] This was an observation backed up by pertinent French voices, for neither the well-known *Revue des deux Mondes* nor the French naval officers who wrote for the *Revue Maritime* made any secret that plans were in place for a landing on the English coast.[104] Robertson and Nicholson had no interest in determining whether the results of French manoeuvres suggested that such an undertaking was even feasible or in recognizing that not a single French Channel port had the transportation capacity to support a land-based operation. The closely observed European manoeuvres during 1901 had in the end shown only 'how a thing [invasion] should not be done',[105] and the English press appeared to care as little about the true results as the leadership in the War Office. While the press reported on the manoeuvres as if the enemy was at the door,[106] the army leadership made no distinction between intention and realization.[107] Their goal was not simply internal, tied in with the allocation of new funds that would allow for a politically motivated military build-up;[108] evidently, they were also looking to influence Britain's foreign policy.

In keeping with the results of the conference, Robertson had characterized both France and Russia as undoubtedly the greatest threat to Britain, yet only two weeks later, in his comments on a memorandum by his colleague Lawrence, he counselled that Britain join an alliance with precisely these powers, Britain's arch-rivals. He based his recommendation – notably, his commentary closely reproduced Maxes' A.B.C. argumentation of two months earlier[109] – on the traditional balance of power and on the threat from Germany. Although the alliance of France and Russia was inimical to the status quo, and although France plotted openly against Britain, and that country's geographical position and the condition of its naval forces meant it presented the most serious threat, suddenly Robertson described the Kaiserreich as Britain's 'most persistent, deliberate, and formidable rival'.[110] The message could hardly have been clearer – by the beginning of the twentieth century, the 'balance of power' tradition was no longer the norm and no longer the standard. Germany was placed at the head of the list of threats not in order to restore the balance of existing power constellations but in an attempt to guarantee a defensive advantage over all power constellations. Robertson's thinking in this phase probably did not take him far down that political road, for his primary concern was very likely to create the drama that would bolster the realization of his military and inner-political goals. Yet the foreign policy component of his position remained noteworthy, for it was uncannily close in both military and political terms to Maxse's *National Review* or Edward Grey's thoughts of 1895 on the dominance of powers that were objectively stronger. Ensuring a power balance more passively and from a distance was evidently not on the agenda.

Robertson's approach differed fundamentally from the prevailing analytical method employed at the Admiralty, and not just in degree of political instrumentalization but also in terms of the defence-related expertise on which he drew. Army officers in the planning staff believed that if you could plan it, anything was possible, while naval officers reckoned with fluctuating factors such as tides, currents and weather and technical and practical aspects such as the challenges an invasion convoy would face and the speed at which it would need to move, as well as the capacity of available shipping. For Robertson, the facts were already clear, without any further evidence needed: an invasion carried out by between 50,000 and 200,000 French troops could be completed in only a few days, 'three days for actual embarkation, transport and landing'.[111] By the standards of land-based strategy, that figure was reasonable, especially as the army leadership interpreted the distance between Calais and Dover as negligible. With hindsight, it seems almost incredible that in analysing the risk, the planning staff made absolutely no distinction between the problems presented by a war at sea and the problems presented by a war on land. At the same time, however, it becomes all the clearer that the War Office was less concerned with a realistic assessment or with cooperation with the navy, and far more concerned with making the most dramatic impact possible on the political sphere in London. The army officers could not have been unaware that sending the first expeditionary force to South Africa, only 50,000 men strong, had presented very great logistical challenges; the preparations had taken months.[112] Brodrick himself remarked that Robertson's observations were marked by unrestrained exaggeration and therefore more likely detrimental to the goals of the conference, which lay in improving cooperation and the allocation of resources.[113] Roberts remained unperturbed. His ideal was the 'Million Men Standard', which appeared to him to be in line with the goals of the continental powers and with the wealth and status of Britain.[114]

At the same time, John Fisher, recently promoted and now one of the leading admirals in the Royal Navy, was honing his broad-ranging considerations. From his time as commander of the Mediterranean fleet, Fisher had his own experience of deliberate dramatization,[115] but he made no recourse to that persuasive device as he presented his conceptual deliberations. In close cooperation with Rear Admiral Louis Battenberg, whom he considered – at least until they fell out over the Dogger Bank incident[116] – one of the best officers in the navy,[117] he responded to Selborne in parliament[118] with three comprehensive papers on reform, in which he set out plans, based on the most recent technological developments, for possible savings by means of increased efficiency and in light of evaluation of current threats.[119] The details need not be given here;[120] it suffices to emphasize that in February 1902 Fisher had already proposed and elucidated the fundamentals of the measures he would later adopt as First Sea Lord. Although historians have consistently called upon Fisher, along with Selborne, as a key witness to the threat posed by Germany,[121] in his remarks he made very little reference to the German High Seas Fleet.[122] Aware that the war had made financial savings both necessary and politically prudent, he emphasized instead a long-term increase in efficiency that would run in parallel with a long-term reduction in costs. At the heart of his plans stood efficiency, financial management and necessary military capacity, along with self-assertion based on British strength.[123] Both Selborne and Balfour would subsequently embrace these same concerns. Fisher's appointment as First Sea Lord had much to do with his motto, 'Economy is Victory', which acknowledged the financial demands of imperial defence and war while suggesting that supremacy could be delivered at a reasonable cost.[124]

Britain's global presence was vital to Fisher's concept. Local imperial needs did not necessarily align with modern sea-based strategy. With the limited resources in mind, Fisher had no sympathy for the maintenance of naval resources simply as matter of prestige.[125] The actual and potential needs of defence were alone to determine the allocation of resources. He agreed with Battenberg that Britain's most likely opponent was France, followed closely by the Russian-French Dual

Alliance, whose global presence and preponderance in the Mediterranean was a cause of concern to Fisher. Sooner or later, the Dual Alliance would end the closing of the Straits, and Russia would force its way into the Mediterranean, where, Fisher foresaw, the 'Battle of Armageddon' would follow.[126] At least until the Dogger Bank incident, one searches in vain for an Anglo-German war on Fisher's list of foreseeable risks. And even afterwards, for example in April 1905, he thought war against France and Russia more probable and therefore by November 1904 it was decided to shift the focus of British naval power to the south, towards Gibraltar.[127] The only scenario that he until then could imagine that might leave Britain and Germany at war was a possible, but highly unlikely, war with the Triple Alliance or with a German-American alliance. Immediately before the Venezuela crisis, which we are yet to address, both Fisher and Selborne deemed war with the United States alone far more likely.[128] His catalogue of conceivable threats concluded with the purely theoretical variations of war against the United States in alliance with Russia and war against Russia in alliance with Japan and China.[129] His suggestions make clear that for Fisher, the traditional two-power standard as a measure of supremacy always included a political and temporary component and that his reckoning of potential constellations was conducted in light of political probability, not just military possibility. His evaluation of potential threats formed the core of his memorandum, 'Strategical Distribution of our Fleets'[130], on the basis of which, in turn, the cabinet ordered the redeployment of winter 1904. We should also note that while both the War Office and Admiralty demanded defence reform, they demonstrated very little willingness to work together, with each side fearing that it would lose out both financially and in terms of its popular standing. Looking back over his experiences as prime minister, Arthur Balfour pronounced, 'Hitherto the Army has run its own show, the Navy has run its own show, and there has never been any superintending authority which might bring them together'.[131] It was therefore logical that Balfour had made it one of his first tasks to remedy that situation.

The First Subcommittee on Invasion and the Norfolk Commission

As early as 1895, Balfour had proposed the creation of a body that would be responsible for the coordination of military policy,[132] and his first defence-related act on becoming prime minister was to make that suggestion a reality, with the creation of the Committee of Imperial Defence (CID). Though a non-executive body tasked with prioritizing defence questions and sifting the options, it exemplifies the recognition that managing Britain's path forward through a changing and increasingly complex international environment and revolutionary technologies required inter-departmental coordination and high-level consideration.

These were no longer matters for the service departments alone.[133] Every new proposal related to the structure of British defence was to be debated by the committee.[134] For Battenberg, Selborne and Fisher's predecessor as first Sealord, Walter Kerr, this new body provided a means 'to stereotype British defence policy', by which they understood a more concrete approach to the services and their improved coordination by means of a clearer distribution of tasks.[135] The CID met for the first time on 18 December 1902 and became part of the regular government machine, in particular when the Tories were in power. In the years up to 1914, the committee met 128 times, with eighty-four of those sessions held between 1902 and 1905, so under the Tories. Discussion, we see again, was a central element of this period of transformation in British foreign politics, along with the regular interaction of experts and political leaders.[136] Alongside the fundamental issue of reform, the committee's first concern was not the security of the Empire but the defence of the Mother Country against a threatened invasion.[137]

Its discussions were launched by two position papers, from 10 and 14 February 1903, generated by the War Office; over the following months, the War Office and the Admiralty would continue to trade memoranda.[138] As Robertson's and Fisher's positions make evident, the two ministries held entirely contrasting views on the issue of invasion. While the Admiralty was eager that there be no doubt that the navy was the first and best line of defence for Britain, the army sought to raise its profile, or at least secure its traditional position. Money loomed over all the discussions. The fiscal situation was so precarious that in February 1903, Chancellor of the Exchequer Charles Ritchie warned the cabinet of possible public commotion.[139] As a result, the Treasury tenaciously insisted on budgeting only £2,500 for the upgrading of the 'Special Service Section', the volunteer forces responsible for coastal defence.[140] For the army leadership, the refusal to provide more funds was an act of sabotage that was just another example of the general disparagement of the army after the South African war.

All the more devastating, then, would have been the news that the naval budget was to be increased for the first time since the war above army level to around £35 million.[141] At first glance, that figure seems enormous, but it represented only the planned increase, hardly exorbitant, of 2.1 per cent on the previous year's budget. Nevertheless, it was the tendency that counted and while the budgets for the army were constantly falling, those of the navy were constantly raised.[142] Balfour himself kept a close eye on the spending patterns of his government; he declared Austen Chamberlain, his new Chancellor of the Exchequer, the most important member of his cabinet.[143] Chamberlain confirmed Ritchie's view with an alarming appeal in April 1904.[144] The critical conundrum was how to pay for Britain's imperial strategic aspirations and how to divide the money between the services. While Britain was lagging increasingly far behind France and Russia when it came to new units of torpedo boats, submarines and cruisers, the allocation of means to build up the Royal Navy could not be delayed any longer. By late October 1902, the First Lord of the Admiralty, Lord Selborne, had already admitted that he was 'in despair about the financial outlook, because these cursed Russians are laying down one ship after the other'.[145] In response to the Russian threat, the Treasury even allocated an additional £1.75 million, to be used to buy two Chilean battleships from under the nose of Russia.[146]

It was a given that the War Office would resort to its traditional practice of overly dramatizing the threat to Britain in order to avoid having to come up with additional funds for the navy. Nicholson came straight to the point for Roberts: 'What I am rather afraid of is that, if all the contentions of the Admiralty are concurred in and the demands for an increase of naval strength regarded as of paramount importance, no funds will be available for the maintenance of an efficient Army'.[147] Nicholson's feeling that the army was being treated unfairly in comparison to the navy was in the circumstances entirely unfounded and evidence of a latent sense of inferiority to the navy.[148] During the war, the army had evidently become used to an unimpeded flow of resources; two years after the end of the war, the army budget was still 70 per cent greater than before the war. This spending should be seen relative to the greater expenditure and income for the Empire as a whole, but even then especially the army had benefitted in recent years from the explosion in spending.[149]

Having been turned down by the Treasury, the army lobby in press and parliament turned, as it had done so often before, to the well-established fear of a Napoleonic bloc. Both ministries had previously agreed that despite its intensified efforts, the Dual Alliance presented no especially grave threat. Now, however, the spectre of a Napoleonic continental bloc opened up the possibility of an entirely new debate.[150] As Robertson's train of thought showed, the idea of an absolute defensive solution was now in play. Calculations of probability on which past risk assessments had been based were no longer sufficient, for now concern was also directed to the 'moral effect on the public mind'.[151] The War Office and the Admiralty found themselves caught on the horns of a classic dilemma, between the allocation of the budget and the preservation of the public's confidence. When it came to engaging the public, the War Office often seemed to edge ahead of the Admiralty. Fisher commented to Leo Amery that all previous reforms of the Royal Navy had been made possible by the press, and to his taste his predecessors had been too passive in their relationship with the media.[152] Certainly, the Admiralty had long recognized the role that could be played by public opinion, but Richard Thursfield, naval expert at the *Times*, had the impression that, in contrast to the War Office, the navy leadership sought to keep him and his colleagues at a distance. As he emphasized in a letter to Selborne, the Admiralty's reservation in relation to the press was counterproductive in their power struggle with the War Office, for, he noted, 'by keeping them [the journalists] at arms length the Admiralty have no control over them at all'.[153]

In the discussions of the Committee of Imperial Defence, which now met regularly, a distinct front had emerged, with representatives of the army on one side holding up the risks of invasion and naval experts on the other advocating calm and reassurance. The younger army officers were particularly forceful, motivated, it appears, not by ambition but by the desire to see the army rehabilitated after the disaster of the Boer War.[154] Review of the minutes of these meetings also makes evident that when it came to staying on top of the particulars, Prime Minister Balfour was well able to keep pace with his department heads. Balfour never missed a meeting of the committee and appears always to have been fully prepared. He repeatedly attempted to keep the discussion to the facts, although the dogmatism and lack of naval knowledge among the army officers were challenging for Balfour's highly analytical approach.

Especially difficult was the relationship between Nicholson and Admiral Battenberg, his direct counterpart as director of naval intelligence, who was all too eager to display his brilliance. On principal, Nicholson limited himself to blocking all the factual arguments made by the naval experts,[155] but Battenberg was eager to make substantive contributions. In his clearly structured reports, he continued to insist that an invasion remained entirely impossible 'while the fleet remains undefeated'.[156] Early in his career, Battenberg had already seen the problems of 'combined strategy' in the context of amphibious operations. His Austrian origins did not make him less credible, as Marder suspected,[157] but rather, to the contrary, thanks to his frequent journeying abroad and his many foreign contacts he had excellent knowledge of continental navies, and of the sea power of the members of the Triple Alliance in particular.[158] Only when war broke out, and despite having taken British citizenship in 1868, was he forced to bow to the anti-German press campaign and, in October 1914, he resigned as First Sea Lord and left the Royal Navy. The only scenario that Battenberg believed credible, and then only under circumstances described as highly unusual, was a small raid carried out by a maximum of 5,000 men who might be able, were the political, military and meteorological conditions right, to slip through the tight net created by the British fleet. The outcome of such an attack was entirely incommensurate with the associated risks. For the defence of Plymouth, Portsmouth and Sheerness-Chatham, the most significant harbours, the Royal Navy could call on numerous units, listed individually by Battenberg, as well as new forms of submarine, which together would create the most effective barrier possible.[159]

The representatives of the army led by Nicholson refused to be drawn into any discussion of naval matters and consistently acted as if crossing the Channel to Britain and landing on the British coast was one of the easiest operations a continental army could undertake. They failed to respond to the Admiralty's arguments, let alone acknowledge the impact of technological innovations, and were, for example, entirely unwilling to accept that a raid and an invasion were different matters. Their problem was surely a mental block, for Battenberg's repeated and lucid explanations should have made clear to anyone, however militarily inexperienced, that these were two entirely distinct operations.[160]

Repeatedly, the army men fell back on the prodigious efficiency of the Prussian imperial army, which ever since 1870/71 they had believed capable of just about anything: 'We know that plans for invasion of England have been discussed in Germany and deemed by some to be a not impossible enterprise. Germany could well afford to risk in such an enterprise 80 to 100 000 men, and a dash at our Eastern Coast would be entirely in accord with her military traditions of rapid offence'.[161] Unlike in the case of French plans for an invasion, here the Committee of Imperial Defence possessed no information from the opposing government or military leadership, but neither did its facts come from its own resources. Both choice of words and style were highly reminiscent of William Stead's claims and his press campaign of early 1900, when in a number of articles Stead had warned of the dangerous repercussions of the Boer War. He had prophesized that in the not-too-distant future, the Tricolore would fly over Westminster Palace and had cited Moltke, among others, as having claimed that an invasion of England would be child's play. Sensitive to the impact of his criticism of the Boer War, Stead had withheld from his readers the information that Moltke's opinion ran completely contrary to what Stead had implied – with the example of Philip II's armada in mind, Moltke believed that an attempted landing in England would mean certain death for every man involved.[162] Those who believed an invasion was on the cards thought the opportunity ripe to use Stead's arguments to their own ends. With public opinion now increasingly hostile to Germany following the Boer War, the Venezuela crisis and the issue of the Baghdad railway, it became increasingly easy to turn the arguments initially gathered for use against France against Germany instead. Where initially Stead, Maxse, Knowles, Strachey and Conan Doyle had foreseen an invasion by France and had cited Moltke only tangentially, as a military authority on the likelihood of invasion,[163] now they interpreted France's known plans for an invasion as evidence that Germany was definitely planning to invade. Finally, in light of the wars of unification, the Kaiserreich was seen as the epitome of military preparedness and since the Krüger telegram as especially devious. Nicholson proceeded on that basis. For him, a suggestion was sufficient, without any need to investigate either its authenticity or its practicality. Political probabilities no longer mattered; military possibilities were all that counted, as the army men never tired of emphasizing.

In the course of the discussions, the War Office repeatedly accused the Admiralty of sugar-coating the reality and numbing the British public. Having deliberately chosen as his point of reference March 1900, when only 17,000 regular soldiers were stationed within Britain,[164] Nicholson claimed that at any moment the soldiers on the home front could find themselves embroiled in typical land warfare and facing a million-strong continental army. Reading the sources, one gains a sense that the English military officers longed to be part of a continental set-up, above all in terms of the respect their colleagues on the continent garnered and the independence of their command.[165] While Nicholson would have forces in place that were able to outperform the strongest armies in the world, Battenberg chose a more nuanced approach: eager to refute the whitewashing accusation, he too responded in terms of an unfavourable situation, but his starting point was a continental alliance. Although he came to the conclusion that even such an unlikely coalition would only be a real threat if the Royal Navy had been completely destroyed, he took on that scenario and based his response on the complete absence of the British battle fleet. For the unlikely event that the Home Fleet was involved in manoeuvres at a great distance from Britain, he drew on the second naval defensive line, which was never permitted to leave home waters. The only real danger would be from the French fleet, with its strongest elements assembled in the Atlantic and Channel ports of Cherbourg, Dunkirk, Brest, Lorient, Rochefort and Saint Servant for a possible operation against Britain.[166]

Battenberg was not willing to accept the army leadership's argument that only the aggressor would benefit from technological developments; for Battenberg, as for Fisher, Selborne and Arnold-Forster, precisely the opposite was the case. Steam power certainly made a crossing of the Channel faster, but it also made such a passage far more visible. The defenders could therefore have their ad hoc forces correctly positioned all the sooner. Telegraph and wireless brought additional advantages for the defenders. Rapid-firing artillery along with torpedo boats and submarines were, to Battenberg's mind, a deadly danger to any convoy, especially at night,[167] and the War Office had also long believed a landing in daylight to be impossible.[168] Once again, Battenberg demonstrated, indeed paraded, the army officers' complete ignorance of operations at sea.[169] Evidently they had prepared themselves by reading Mahan on the age of sail, which meant, Battenberg proposed, that they had also adopted the erroneous view that only battleships were of any real merit when it came to a war at sea.[170] Ostentatiously, he based his calculations on only the ocean-going torpedo-boat destroyers that were already operational.[171] Additionally, any foe could be decisively demolished by the new submarines and lighter cruisers, of which Britain had eighty-two, while France and Russia together possessed just twenty-five.

Germany had no role, indeed was not even mentioned, in Battenberg's broadly conceived and thorough calculations. He demonstrated convincingly that the anticipated combat scenario would see the enemy battleships forced to protect the convoy from repeated attacks by torpedo boats and submarines. Not only would the invasion thus be prevented, but the Royal Navy would then be in a position to launch a counteroffensive, using its own battleships, which by then would have arrived on the scene. The threatened invasion would thus have been turned into a tactical advantage.[172] In every case, the risk of such an invasion would be too great for any enemy, as the aggressor would lose not only the entirety of his convoy but also his expensive battleships, and he would also risk inciting a counterattack. Any invasion would lead of its own accord ad absurdum and was therefore out of the question.[173]

Although here we can only explore a number of examples drawn from the broad-ranging discussion, these extracts make evident the far greater nuance with which the Admiralty presented its case. While the army representatives saw threats at every turn, and added Russia, Germany and the United States to their list of dangerous foreign powers with which war seemed inevitable in the long or short term,[174] the analysis of the naval experts rested on their specialist knowledge and on the particular political possibilities. With their primarily political concerns, the army leadership, and Lord Roberts in particular, did not agree with the navy's approach.[175] Roberts emphasized the prestige of the British land forces, the allocation of resources, and reform that would move in the direction of general conscription, but he also preached of nation building and of educating English society in the ways of the military, for since the Boer War, he believed, society had become decadent and effete.[176] His views took shape in the context of a frequently expressed Social Darwinism that feared growing moral decay and waning wartime morale and that, in line with contemporary military theory, saw in moral strength and a 'nation in arms' a possible route to mastering the new technology-based character of warfare.[177]

Once more, we see the fundamental challenges of reconciling the strategies of war on land with the strategies of war at sea. While the former – evidently shaped by Mahan's work and his adaptation of the military theorist Antoine-Henri Jomini for war at sea – meant a rigid battle scenario that tied down the whole fleet, with the large battleships tipping the balance,[178] the Admiralty always assumed movement and emphasized the fighting strength of newer forces.[179] The leading army men appeared to have little comprehension of the implications of modern sea power – they saw the Channel as simply a distance that had to be negotiated.[180] Their primary concern was not whether and how the potential enemy would find their way to the English coast, but how they might increase their resource allocation and how the scenario might play out once the enemy had landed. There was no sign at all of the 'joint planning' that the political leadership had deemed desirable at the conference held in winter 1901/2.

The acute financial position, military mulishness and the service departments' unwillingness to cooperate were not the government's only defence-related problems, for the volunteer forces' lobby also brought public opinion to the table. As Lord Roberts' acquaintance Erskine Childers stirred public passions with his *Riddle of the Sands*, with edition after edition selling out in no time,[181] a parliamentary commission of inquiry met in parallel to the confidential consultations of the Committee of Imperial Defence. Exasperated by all the secrecy and entranced by the enthusiastic reception of the scaremongering, Lord Norfolk established a 'Royal Commission on the Militia and Volunteers', which was to work openly to establish the real risks of an invasion.[182] Evidently, Norfolk had little faith in the Committee of Imperial Defence, which he believed would prune Britain's land forces further and might abandon the rich tradition of volunteer regiments.[183] A public commission would offer army representatives a platform distinct from the private deliberations of the CID.

A comparison of these two bodies brings home again how important it is for historians to distinguish between 'blue water' experts and the 'bolt from the blue' invasion adherents and army lobbyists. The goals, composition, discussions and impact of the two commissions could hardly have been more different. When it came to the politics of defence, the parliamentary commission was little more than a charade. It treated all expertise with contempt and primarily sought to influence public opinion. Its members were largely more elderly members of the House of Lords, including a good number of long-retired army officers and active officers in the volunteer forces who were, in the words of the *Times*, 'dominated by the great spectre of a great invasion'.[184] Henry Spenser Wilkinson, liberal imperialist, military expert, journalist and advocate for the volunteer forces, acted as extra-parliamentary counsel and ensured the work of the commission received the desired publicity.[185] No naval officers sat on the commission, whose intention from the outset was to maintain the division of tasks between army and navy, along with their rivalry, and to exact further resources for the army.[186] Between May and November 1903, the commission met eighty-two times, and heard from over sixty-nine witnesses. All these witnesses were called, however, to confirm public speculation that the threat of invasion was acute.[187] Just how one-sidedly the commission went about its task can be seen from the example of witness Admiral Sir John O. Hopkins, who had long since retired from the navy. Hopkins was the only naval officer invited to appear before the commission, and unlike the Admiralty, he was convinced that an invasion of Britain was possible.[188]

The farcical character of the commission is only confirmed by its complete lack of effort to be objective. Its first witnesses were those who headed up the War Office, followed by Ardagh and Wolseley, who as retired officers had set aside their earlier loyalty to the political leadership and now spoke up on behalf of their military comrades and spoke out on the danger of invasion.[189] The same could be said of the next group of witnesses, focused on Lord Wemyss, Lord Harris and Sir Howard Vincent, who stressed the danger of public panic along with its advantages.[190] When the hearing of witnesses was complete, a parliamentary debate was launched that lasted until summer 1904. The argumentation of the commission's concluding report recalled the prophecies of invasion heard over past decades. Absolutely no reference was made to any maritime strategy associated with an invasion, and lessons from history were also noticeably absent;[191]

instead, the report was full of long excurses on the relevance of the army, the volunteer forces and their responsibility for the defence of the coastline. Even an officer as highly regarded and well known as John Ardagh was unapologetic about presenting a memorandum that described an invasion by 100,000 men as 'child's play'.[192] The National Service League had its own interests in an increase in the capabilities of Britain's army and heightened the scenario to an invasion by a force of 200,000 men. As was to be expected, only a 'nation in arms' was deemed capable of preventing such an invasion, and the commission demanded the creation of a conscripted army of 380,000 men.[193]

That said, however, the parliamentary commission proved neither willing to provide nor capable of providing any concrete plans for the organization of this fighting force or any definition of its future tasks. Arnold-Forster noted in his diary that the lobbyists had no interest in the realities of defence, for their only concern was that the traditional regiments should survive.[194] Evidently, they had no designs beyond ensuring that their case was made to the public through witness statements given by prominent military figures and parliamentarians. The official announcement of the creation of a parliamentary commission of inquiry bristling with the military heroes of days gone by had already been sufficient to leave the public with the impression that the enemy was already on their doorstep.

It was now all the more important that the fronts within the Committee of Imperial Defence be dissolved. In a move of incalculable significance, on 27 November 1903 Balfour addressed the public. In a speech he gave at the United Service Club, he aimed not to alarm but to calm the public, and for the first time he demonstratively took issue with all the scaremongering.

> My own view is precisely and exactly the opposite of that which was expressed by Sir Henry Campbell-Bannerman. (Cheers) I do not believe myself that home defence requires a large regular army (Hear, Hear) ... I believe the public at large have inverted the true importance of the problems with which this Empire has to deal. Our great difficulty is not home defence, the Navy can deal with home defence (Cheers) ... it is a foreign difficulty! (Hear, Hear).[195]

The newfound unity of the Committee of Imperial Defence was a product of the appointment in October 1903 of an under-secretary of state at the Admiralty as the secretary of state for war, a choice that was unexpected but in the approving words of the *Saturday Review* a 'sheer triumph of brains and industry'.[196] The presence of Hugh Arnold-Forster perceptibly altered the balance within the Committee of Imperial Defence in favour of the naval experts,[197] but only because Arnold-Forster was already acquainted with the problems faced by the War Office and was highly regarded in army circles, and because he deemed consensus and cooperation between the two service departments more important than the factual accuracy of the position of each. Thus, for example, even though he had no doubts that the 'blue water' school argumentation was correct,[198] Arnold-Forster declared himself prepared to accept a threat from Germany as a possibility[199] as long as both ministries were then prepared to work together and efficiently. The army representatives in the Committee of Imperial Defence now suddenly adopted the Admiralty's definition that stated that an invasion was a protracted landing and occupation of at least several counties. Now the Committee of Imperial Defence had a basis for a discussion that could be kept away from polemics, a basis that also supported Balfour's final memorandum of 11 November 1903. Even though the naval experts thought a comprehensive land operation would not happen, they accepted the need for an army of at least 70,000 men to face an invasion, a number that would ensure the retention and financial support of a reduced volunteer force. Arnold-Forster hoped that the navy's willingness to compromise would induce Lord Roberts, his strongest opponent in the political sphere, to accept a cooperative solution.[200] In Balfour's memorandum, France still appeared as the greatest threat to Britain – not because Balfour was ignoring Germany or because he wanted to prevent rapprochement between Britain and France,[201] but because expert opinion allowed for no other conclusion. Unanimity ruled on the belief that France, located so much closer to Britain than Germany, not only was more likely to be able to conduct a successful operation against the British Isles, but also had repeatedly boasted of that ability in carrying out military manoeuvres.

Support for Balfour's assessment could be found simply by looking at the respective fleet strengths in late 1903. Certainly, the United States and Germany were catching up in terms of battleships and battle-cruisers, the categories traditionally thought relevant, but when new technology was included, calculations suggested that France had the greatest capabilities.

If France could be kept at bay, so ran Balfour's logic, then no other country would present a threat to Britain. Just how important the political leadership believed the coordination of the two military ministries to be is evident in the willingness of this well-informed prime minister to accept the possibility, despite all the evidence to the contrary, of the scenario proposed by the invasion-theory adherents that saw the complete destruction of the main British fleets and also that France would be able to keep the whole operation secret, both its planning and its performance. In the end, the Committee of Imperial Defence still came to the conclusion that the security of the British Isles, even in this highly unlikely scenario that ran counter to all known manoeuvres and established fact, would not be seriously imperilled.

Having been educated by Fisher and Battenberg in the strategic implications of modern sea power and of the significance of the new submersible craft and new torpedo boats,[202] Balfour concluded that these innovations meant that 'Sea Command ... no longer exists within the radius of submarines and torpedo

Table 3.2. Fleet strength (September 1903).

	England	France	Germany	Italy	USA	Russia	Japan
Battleship							
First Class[a]	42 (15)[b]	19 (7)	12 (8)	12 (6)	10 (14)	13 (8)	6
Second Class	4	8 (1)	4	–	1	4	1
Third Class	2	1	12	5	–	1	–
Total	**48**[c]	**28**	**28**	**17**	**11**	**18**	**7**
Battle-Cruiser[d]							
Armoured[e]	18 (23)	9 (14)	2 (4)	5 (1)	2 (11)	8	6
Protected[f]	105 (9)	40	19 (7)	16	16 (6)	11 (5)	18 (3)
Unprotected	10	1	20	–	11	3	9
Total	**133**	**50**	**41**	**21**	**29**	**22**	**33**
Torpedo-boat Destroyer	112 (34)	14 (23)	28 (10)	11 (2)	14 (6)	48 (6)	17 (2)
Torpedo boat[g]	85 (5)	247 (43)	93	145 (8)	27 (4)	132 (7)	67 (18)
Total	**197**	**261**	**121**	**146**	**41**	**180**	**84**
Submarine	5 (14)	15 (43)	0	1 (3)	1 (7)	0 (2)	0
Modern Torpedo boat[h]	58 (9)	211 (159)	79	1 (3)	27 (6)	67 (13)	61 (14)

Source: Hurd, 'Naval Progress', NAR 9/1903, 385–92, 386.

Notes: figures in parentheses refer to ships that at this date were in construction or had been commissioned.
[a]Usually classified as battleships of over 10,000 tons; [b]see Whitaker, *Whitaker's Almanack* 1900, 222–30; [c]Hurd, Naval Progress, NAR 9/1903, 385–92, 387–88; [d]the '1st Class Cruiser' was counted as a battleship; [e]see NA, 17 Oct. 1902, CAB 37/63/142; 'the categories 'protected' and 'unprotected' are assigned by Ropp to ships of a tonnage over and under 3,500 (see Ropp, *Development of a Modern Navy*, 357); [g]this figure includes all torpedo boats, irrespective of their age; [h]data taken from NA, 17 Oct. 1902, CAB 37/63/142. This category represents the greatest technological advances.

boats'.[203] Technical advances could be interpreted as an advantage for Britain, a view that ran counter to the opinion of the press, the members of the Norfolk Commission with their propaganda interests, and representatives of the War Office. Additionally, an invading army of 70,000 men would have required a fleet of the order of 210,000 gross register tons,[204] a figure greater than the tonnage of all craft available in all the Channel ports, including the merchant fleets. Embarkation alone would take at least six days and would bring all other maritime traffic to a halt. The need to use the merchant fleet for such an invasion was also a strike against the operation's feasibility, while a crossing of the Channel at night was excluded by the sheer size of the convoy and by the need to be able to defend it, which would be an almost unparalleled challenge. And finally, the deployment of slower merchant shipping meant the crossing to the British coast could not take less than twenty hours. The extent to which Balfour had immersed himself in the complexities of the tactics and strategy of modern sea warfare is evident from his inclusion of so much exhaustive detail. He thus demonstrated that all the arguments of the invasion-theory adherents led ad absurdum. Unlike these men, Balfour also considered meteorological implications, recognizing that the very changeable weather on the British coast was an added form of defence. Even under the best of conditions, and even if the invasion went unchallenged, landing and securing the coastline would take, he reckoned, some forty-eight hours. The defenders would therefore have all the advantage on their side: 'Every shot they fired, and every torpedo they discharged, would find a victim among the thickly crowded shipping. Submarines by day, torpedo boats by night and cruisers at any time'. Even resistance offered by poorly trained riflemen would likely prove an insurmountable barrier for the enemy.[205] Selborne was not alone in being deeply impressed by Balfour's arguments.[206] George Clarke, who was highly versed in administrative affairs as well as in naval and military policy[207] – in spring 1904 Balfour would appoint him first permanent secretary of the Committee of Imperial Defence – was equally convinced, and he expressed his agreement with the prime minister in a personal letter in which he also admitted that since time immemorial his army colleagues, including even the great Wellington and his adversary Napoleon, had been out of their depth when it came to maritime issues.[208] Admiral Fisher deemed Balfour's paper 'simply splendid, … the most masterful document I ever perused'.[209]

Two days after Balfour had presented the London public with the essence of what he had learned from the Committee of Imperial Defence and drawn his own studies, Fisher stoked the fires with a memorandum on the influence of submarine technology on the risk of invasion. He had no doubt that principal responsibility for the defence of the Mother Country would fall to the Royal Navy, and with that task in mind, the navy had its own interest in the continuation of traditional defence structures. In his memorandum, Fisher also highlighted that the idea of invasion had become a traditional prop for the army, used as 'a governing condition in arranging its [the army's] strength'. Yet he also picked to pieces the gridlocked navy. History made clear, he wrote, that the Royal Navy would always oppose any change, which explained why his colleagues had for so long refused to recognize the significance of the revolutionary submarine technology. Officers of the 'bow and arrow epoch' continued to dream of famous decisive battles that would rival those fought by Lord Nelson, their great hero as young sea cadets.[210] Modern developments such as the Whitehead torpedo and submersible craft had revolutionized the very nature of war at sea, and also had a bearing for the British army, which as an imperial expeditionary force was so dependent on transportation. His memorandum continued:

> Imagine the effect of one such transport going to the bottom in a few seconds with its living freight. Even the bare thought makes invasion impossible! Fancy, 100 000 helpless, huddled up troops afloat in frightened transports with these invisible demons known to be near. Death near – momentarily – sudden – awful – invisible – unavoidable! Nothing conceivable more demoralising![211]

The leading, and therefore most dangerous power when it came to new technology was France, certainly not Germany. Recently, however, Russia had also overtaken Britain with its advances in torpedo capability. Fisher and Balfour both recognized that the submarine had not just military value but also financial advantages. Fisher calculated, for example, that Britain was wasting half a million pounds each year on mining its own harbours. A fleet of twenty-five submarines, which thanks to their constantly increasing range would soon acquire offensive capability, cost less than a single large battleship both to construct and to maintain,[212] good reason for Balfour to read Fisher's memorandum with 'the greatest interest'.[213] The submarine was the only class of ship that could not become obsolete.[214] Fisher went as far as to predict a revolution in international relations, for thanks to the new weaponry it would be possible, he opined, to win back, even without allies, the supremacy in the Mediterranean that had been lost to the Dual Alliance in the mid 1890s.[215] In correspondence with Balfour, he recorded: 'Submarines at Malta, Gibraltar, Port Said, Alexandria, Suez and Lemnos will make us more powerful than ever. The Russians are welcome to Constantinople if we bag Lemnos and infest the Dardanelles there from with Submarines'.[216] This enticing point of view likely left its impact on Balfour, who from his participation at the Congress of Berlin in 1878 and up until the conclusion of his political career was particularly interested in the eastern Mediterranean, the Levant and the Near East.[217]

Rather than exploit the public agitation in order to relieve the pressure on his government in parliament and from within his party that stemmed from continuing discussion of tariff and military reform, Balfour attempted to calm the political sphere by making public the results of the Committee of Imperial Defence's discussions in relation to defence policy. His invasion memoranda were a milestone in British defence policy. For the first time, the service departments had been allocated concrete tasks that would form the basis of future imperial strategy.[218] The Committee of Imperial Defence agreed that both Brodrick and Nicholson would search for weaknesses in Balfour's argument; both men came up empty handed. Balfour had digested all the information available, and for the time being France and Russia remained Britain's most dangerous enemies among the Great Powers – as long as Russia with its continuing expansion and apparent inviolability presented a threat, then France, tied to Russia by the terms of the Dual Alliance, was also a threat. Balfour had read himself into the complex material like no other politician, and he did not hesitate to hear advice. Yet as the Norfolk Commission demonstrated, Balfour needed to keep one eye on the unity of his party and of the government, and for that reason he was eager to find a compromise solution, within the bounds of factual accuracy, to which both army and navy could subscribe.

From 'Invasion' to 'Raid'

Adherents of the invasion theory were not going to be impressed by assessments of political prospects, nuanced argumentation or evidence of defence. Their goal remained the creation of a new role for the army and the prevention of any reduction in fighting strength.

With the Japanese torpedo attack on Port Arthur, discussion of invasion, both internal and external, entered a new phase. For the 'bolt from the blue' school, the transportation, on 8 February 1904, of 2,500 Japanese soldiers to the coast at Chemulpo was counted as an example of a successful amphibious operation that in the years up to 1914 would give ample grounds for reflection on the possibility of a similar strike against Britain.[219] Today we know that the Japanese landing succeeded only because the Russian troops had been given precise orders by the tsar, that it was 'desirable that the Japanese, and not we, open hostilities. Therefore ... you must not hinder their disembarkation'.[220] By early 1904, however, the Japanese success was not put into question. Fears already tended to be based on worst-case scenarios. The London media had developed its own style of argumentation, which tended to be simplistic and repetitive.[221] John Strachey concluded from the Japanese landing that the sea had become 'a place of dreadful mystery', a place 'from which at any moment a sudden and unexpected blow may fall'.[222] Strachey had now discovered a higher purpose in dramatization intended to support an agenda of general rearmament and moral re-education. The simplification pursued by the media and the goals of those who supported a military build-up proved complementary.

At the same time, the arguments made by those who adhered to the invasion theory gradually changed direction. Their position was no longer framed by the dispute between the services and their ministries; now it was shaped by views of society's defensive preparedness in the middle and long term. Where previously the debate had tackled task allocation for coastal defence and its financing, now the military leadership, joined by the National Service League, was far more concerned with general conscription and the creation of a million-strong army. The financial situation and tradition of volunteer forces meant these goals – especially in peacetime – could be no more than fantasy, yet they served as a useful tool for ensuring that defence continued to be debated publicly.

A fortnight after the news of the Japanese success reached London, the Committee of Imperial Defence discussed a new memorandum, composed by William Robertson. Although Britain's international situation had not changed, Robertson had rewritten the scenario such that Germany was now the threat, not France or Russia. Robertson based his evaluation on accounts that had appeared in the English press attributing intentions to invade to German military figures such as Helmuth von Moltke, Baron von Lüttwitz and Colmar von der Goltz.[223] Here we meet again the close association, even down to choice of words, between media conjecture and internal decision making and advisory.

In light of its 'well-known efficiency', Robertson concluded, the Kaiserreich was already in a position to send 150,000 to 300,000 soldiers without further ado to the British Isles. Three hundred thousand was an enormous figure – contemporary calculations suggest shipping of around 900,000 gross register tons would have been required to transport so many men[224] – and seemed the kind of calculation that would be found in a novel rather than in a sombre military assessment. The memorandum was free of any knowledge of naval strategy or any interest in the risks of a land-based operation. Its motivation was entirely political and propagandistic.[225] The same can be said of a memorandum that looked in detail at the war between Russia and Japan. Whatever its title, 'Notes on Transport by Sea and Disembarkation …', seemed to suggest, this memorandum, too, was little concerned with how troops might be landed; its only interest was in the land operation that would follow. Rather than look to the expertise of the Royal Navy, the army men looked pointedly to the assumptions of the Norfolk Commission.[226] They again demonstrated disinterest and complete cluelessness when it came to the basics of seafaring, in this case in light of the precise circumstances of the landing by the Japanese forces. Those who did consider the war in greater detail came to very different conclusions. Thus, George Clarke, one of the few army officers who, as a result of his maritime knowledge, was respected by the navy, recognized that the Japanese offensive confirmed Balfour's contention that modern torpedo boats had made an enemy landing nigh impossible.[227] Lord Ellenborough's attempt to portray the Japanese attack as evidence of the possibility of a furtive and perfidious German attack on Britain – which would be in keeping with Prussian tradition, he proposed – caused something of a sensation in parliament and among the London public; for the experts in the Royal United

Service Institute, however, it was the cause of much head shaking.²²⁸ Beyond its factual shortcomings, however, Ellenborough's report, Admirals Close and Freemantle recognized, could be useful in sounding alarm bells:

> Still, if there is a little scare, perhaps it is a very good thing, because too many of us are apt to go to sleep. If we had a few more what I venture to call scaremongers like him [Ellenborough] among us, it could be an advantage, especially if they are in such a position that they can bring their ideas prominently before the public.²²⁹

Balfour's invasion memorandum had been largely based on theoretical debates within the Committee of Imperial Defence and on Fisher's counsel, but in 1904 field tests were also performed. The Royal Navy quickly recognized that the new submarines would be a deadly threat to any enemy battle fleet.²³⁰ The traditional strategy, favoured by Mahan, of a close blockade was now out of the question, corroborating the views of Fisher, Clarke, Corbett and Balfour on the challenges of invasion and the relevance of new technologies.²³¹ In the second half of 1904, a number of small-scale and initially cooperative manoeuvres on the south coast confirmed that the idea of an amphibious operation not meeting with any resistance was sheer fantasy.²³² Volunteer soldiers and armed men with little training would be able to keep a professional army in check until regular forces arrived.²³³

Charles Repington, military special correspondent for the *Times*, now redirected the arguments of the army lobby.²³⁴ Suddenly, the concern was not with the threat of invasion but with the proven defensive capabilities of volunteer forces.²³⁵ Although in April 1903 Roberts had written of the volunteer forces as superfluous, preferring to see them replaced by a professional conscripted army,²³⁶ now he stood up in favour of the traditional 'yeomanry' and the strengthening of the volunteer support forces, flanked by much of the London press and by his friend in the House of Lords.²³⁷ The army budget was to be defended by all means possible, no matter its purposes, and the invasion issue had only been used for as long as it served that goal. Initially, adherents of the invasion theory had demanded additional resources that could be used for coastal defence or in support of conscription; following the great effort invested in the manoeuvres that had disproved their assessment of the risk of invasion and with compulsory military service out of the question on financial grounds,²³⁸ they looked now to the existing volunteer force. Their call was for an expeditionary force, whose creation would both ensure the army budget was increased, or at least kept at current levels, and bolster the country's fighting morale.²³⁹

Roberts was inspired by an image of 'nation in army'. With the budget under great pressure and demands for disarmament, tied in with technological military advances, heard constantly, financial support for a secondary defensive instrument such as the army could find little favour with 'blue water' men such as Fisher. Expressly tasked when named First Sea Lord with reducing costs, the 'essential basis … for the influence of the Admiralty over the House of Commons',[240] Fisher believed it 'simply monstrous that the bloated Army should starve the essential navy'.[241] He was supported by George Clarke, who had calculated that the maintenance of the disputed volunteer units alone cost more than a complete first class battleship.[242] In parliament, the young Winston Churchill, already with something of a reputation as a penny-pincher,[243] drew from the results of the Committee of Imperial Defence and from the manoeuvres the logical conclusion that the army had dreaded: the volunteer force of over 370,000 men should be disbanded or at least cut significantly.[244] An agreement was reached that only the superfluous elements of the traditional units would be disbanded and an imperial expeditionary force would be proposed,[245] but even then the debate rumbled on. The lobbyists for the volunteer force, numerous and vociferous in both Houses, remained active and continued to stoke the fires of the invasion threat.[246] Caught between public pressure, on one hand, and financial constraints and the strategic significance of the manoeuvres, on the other, the secretary of state for war found himself in an increasingly tight spot.[247] The political leadership had sought in vain to dispel the resistance of the army lobby and elements of the public by assuring them that Britain's security was not threatened.[248] The picture was, however, very complex, a collage made up of all the discussions of a possible invasion, the results of the manoeuvres, the precarious financial situation, Social Darwinist conceptions of what made a nation fit, animosity between, and even within, the service departments, and Britain's security, which was essentially sound but little understood by the public.[249] This melange of factors was more decisive for the redeployment of the Royal Navy that followed from January 1905 than was the widely peddled assumed threat from Germany. When it came to a comparison of the Royal Navy with all other fleets, the former was currently in a dominant position and would be for years to come. The Dogger Bank incident had done nothing to alter that assessment, with Fisher even self-confidently proposing a defensive strike against Russia;[250] he would subsequently inform his wife, with an air of disappointment, 'It has very nearly been war again. *Very nearly indeed* [emphasis in original], but the Russians have climbed down again. Balfour [is] a splendid man to work with. Only he, I, Lansdowne and Selborne did the whole thing'.[251]

The First Sea Lord was much concerned about the current deployment of French and Russian forces.[252] Fisher and Battenberg noted the possibility that Britain would be drawn into a conflict, for France was repeatedly breaching its neutrality by sheltering the Russian fleet.[253] If Britain found itself at war, then, objectively, it would most likely be at Japan's side.[254] At this date, analysis of potential risk had Germany as at most an abstract, and certainly not imminent, threat.[255] Only as a member of a continental alliance or riding on the back of another opponent might Berlin become a danger; no mention was made of an inevitable conflict with Germany. Even after the Entente Cordiale had been concluded, on 8 April 1904, Battenberg had cited France as the chief reason for the redeployment of the British fleet, and somewhat later he added that even if a continental bloc should be formed against Britain, he saw no reason for great concern.[256] Only a few days before the decision was made to redeploy the fleet, however, Selborne wrote of an 'overwhelming superiority' that had led the Committee of Imperial Defence to deal with the army independently of any rumours of invasion.[257]

Whatever symptoms the media eagerly reported, the Committee of Imperial Defence found no cause for concern about the health of Britain's defence. Britain's confidence in its naval power is evinced by the decision to use the recall of its forces from the Far East as an opportunity to reduce the size of the fleet.[258] Fisher had his eye principally on the Atlantic fleet, which he had bolstered with not only new battleships but also a good number of additional cruisers,[259] recording in February 1905: 'The Gibraltar Fleet is the germ of the new scheme! We have arranged it with our best and fastest battleships and cruisers and our best admirals … it is always instantly ready to turn the scale (at the highest speed of any fleet of the world) in the North Sea or the Mediterranean'.[260]

Yet historians seem loath to abandon the idea that there is 'little doubt that by the beginning of 1905 Germany had emerged as Britain's number one enemy at sea'. Arthur Marder wrote that the redeployment decision made in early December 1904 was 'due principally to the German navy menace'.[261] In support of his case, he cited extracts from the already-mentioned cabinet memorandum, written by Selborne and dated 6 December 1904, that a close reading shows set different priorities. In his memorandum, which as parliamentary record was published in both the *Times* and the *Naval Annual*, Selborne explained the reasons for the naval redeployment. His account bore no sense that Britain felt compelled to react or suffered any sense of weakness, nor did it focus on a threat from Germany. The First Lord of the Admiralty emphasized the Royal Navy's superiority, both quantitative and qualitative, over all other fleets.[262] The German High Seas Fleet can be counted a trigger only in as far as it appears in the memorandum as one of many new developments of the previous thirty years. For Selborne, new technologies, and not new fleets, had meant a return to the strategic drawing board. A more efficient and more affordable allocation of Britain's forces, without any loss of fighting power or prestige, had been made possible by innovations in propulsion and new means of communication. In a memorandum from March 1904 that historians have largely overlooked, army reformer Reginald Brett, Viscount Esher, had already noted all that the Admiralty could now do:

> At any hour during the day the Sea Lords are enabled to locate the position of any British or foreign vessel, and to calculate the precise effect upon our fleets of the

movements of foreign ships of war. The Naval Branch is thus able from day to day to amend and alter plans for the distribution of the Fleet, as well as schemes of naval defence, should the country be suddenly and unexpectedly plunged into war.[263]

In December, Selborne recognized that the German navy was highly efficient[264] – but he said no more and no less. He emphasized that Germany lacked bases and its forces lacked range, which suggested Germany's interests were primarily defensive and that Britain's only concerns in that quarter should address its offensive capabilities against the German coastline. The German fleet presented no direct threat to the British Isles, to the British Empire or to British supremacy.[265] Selborne's analysis was remarkably sober for a man cited as one of the few but vociferous crown witnesses to a threat from Germany[266] and had little in common with the contemporary rumours and scaremongering.[267] For Selborne, the greatest maritime threat to Britain came not from Germany but from France, which was 'always in the forefront', although Russia had recently markedly increased its own strength. He also identified a threat in the potential of the United States, which he deemed in practical terms 'limitless'.[268]

The proposed redeployment of Britain's naval power would take into account all these factors. Its goal was to distribute Britain's seaborne forces in a way that was as efficient and expansive as it was risk-free and flexible, allowing the Royal Navy to be ready for action as quickly as possible against any possible enemy and any possible combination of enemies.[269] Bases that served no practical purpose and had been retained simply on traditional grounds, and that, as was the case for Esquimalt, could not be defended in time of war, were to be closed.[270] Additionally, technological advances had made a great concentration of the British fleets for the first time not just desirable but also possible.[271] Citing efficiency, Fisher proposed that the fundamental structure of five battle fleets be retained, but mindful of issues of cost and personnel, that these fleets be brought closer to the Mediterranean and the British Isles.[272] Again, we note that Germany played no particular role in these calculations; indeed, the Atlantic fleet, not the new Home Fleet, stationed at Gibraltar and with twelve of the most modern battleships and cruisers, was to form the core of the Royal Navy. As a nod to the British public, the Channel fleet would be renamed the British Home Fleet, for the old designation had proved problematic, 'in leading the uniformed public to suppose it formed part of the Home Fleet and thus cause panic by its absence from the Channel when relations become strained'.[273]

Jean Marie Antoine de Lanessan, former French naval minister, had a firm grasp of Fisher's strategy, whose goal, de Lanessan recognized, was not supremacy over a single fleet but supremacy over all fleets. Fisher's flexible 'all-round' strategy was in accord with the political thinking of Balfour and Lansdowne, who had adopted the idea of political and military 'all-round reinforcement' for the Empire. Maximum coverage of all possible hotspots was to be achieved at minimum cost. De Lanessan underlined this flexibility, which meant that even the combination of Germany with the United States would not be a threat; the only real danger to Britain would come from a global alliance in combination with France. France above all, de Lanessan insisted, should see a clear warning in the redeployment of the Royal Navy.[274]

Remarkably, the choice of Gibraltar, far from the North Sea, as the base for the fleet at no point seems to have raised a red flag for those who suppose that Britain was forced into an inevitable response by Germany. Rather than tackle this contradiction, historians continued to toe the line established by Marder, who considered the statements about the French fleet to be 'innocuous'. Marder's position in 1940 is explained by his sources, for lacking archival material he had turned instead to reports in the media,[275] but Esher had been aware of the questionable value of the press as a reliable source on the threats to Britain. In a memorandum of March 1904, he recorded: 'It has been left to publicists, without any special knowledge which could not be gleaned from newspapers or books, to endeavour to inspire Englishmen with the spirit of inquiry'.[276] The model of the political sphere we have adopted for this investigation calls, however, for a comparison of public opinion and the specialist knowledge that was available internally and to politicians.

After the Dogger Bank incident and all the public propaganda directed against Germany, the Admiralty adopted a dual strategy, focused on Gibraltar.[277] The choice of Gibraltar was a victory for naval expertise in the internal conflict that saw specialist knowledge set against the propaganda of the invasion-theory adherents. In the meantime, however, several naval officers had recognized a potential value in the scare stories. Lobbyists around Roberts, Repington and their ilk were continuing to exploit the uncertainties in the political sphere as grounds for accusing the government of naivety and defencelessness, which meant that the government remained boxed in by the invasion theme, its room to manoeuvre restricted.[278] Evidently such was Arthur Balfour's view, but he received repeated encouragement from Fisher, Arnold-Forster and Esher not to keep the very positive results from the Committee of Imperial Defence to himself, but to use them to counter the propaganda touted by elements within the Opposition, the National Service League and individual invasion-theory adherents.[279]

In May 1905 – by which date Russia was on its way to defeat at the hands of Japan, and Kaiser Wilhelm II was steaming home from Tangiers – Balfour again tried, following on from his first attempt in 1903, to assuage English apprehensions. In a speech given in the House of Commons on 11 May 1905, he was entirely open about Britain's defensive situation, addressing the historic and strategic situation in detail, along with military and communication factors. His goal was not to justify the course he proposed – an approach that his statement of November 1903 made less likely – but to calm the waters, to which end he looked deliberately to the speeches given for similar purpose by Salisbury in

1888/89.²⁸⁰ He warned bluntly of the international complications that might result from the invasion hysteria and insisted that it was unnecessary:

> We have really endeavoured to put ourselves the problem in a very concrete form. We have not gone into generalities about the command of the sea or the superiority of our Fleet, ... we have endeavoured to picture to ourselves a clear issue ... and have shown at least to our satisfaction that ... serious invasion of these islands is not an eventuality which we need seriously consider.²⁸¹

That knowledge was a product of his intensive exchanges with John Fisher and Julian Corbett, both of whom had repeatedly pointed out that developments in torpedo boats and submarines 'drive an additional nail into the coffin of invasion'.²⁸² It was only a matter of time before the new submarines ushered in a revolution in how an offensive war was fought at sea. Even in 1905, British submarines, with a range of up to 500 nautical miles, were capable of reaching not just the opposing French coast but also the German North Sea coast.²⁸³ Despite the establishment of the Entente Cordiale and with a crisis over Morocco brewing, Balfour still considered France to be Britain's real enemy, first, because France still posed the greatest potential threat, and secondly, because he believed diplomacy of secondary importance in a fact-based analysis of the defensive situation.

Exactly three years later, as leader of the Opposition he told his successor just what he thought of the Entente Cordiale: 'I imagine that the Committee of Imperial Defence would not consider that they were doing their duty if they supposed that the safety of the country could depend upon some paper instrument or a mere entente, however cordiale it might be'.²⁸⁴ The Liberals were of an entirely different view. They had been enraged by the reference to France in Balfour's speech of 1905, and Campbell-Bannerman feared a negative response from Britain's French partner.²⁸⁵ The Tories' and Liberals' very different attitudes towards the Entente and its implications were already evident. Yet parliament could only agree with the facts put to them by Balfour and could only praise him for being so open on British defence.²⁸⁶ Selborne even termed Balfour's speech 'epoch-making',²⁸⁷ a view with which George Wyndham agreed unconditionally.²⁸⁸ John Colomb, a naval officer and member of parliament, believed himself vindicated in his long battle against the unnecessary hysteria aroused by the invasion novels and the National Service League, proposing that 'the great advantage of his speech would be its educational effect on the House and the Country'.²⁸⁹

Even during the debate, however, it was already clear that Balfour was swimming against the mood of the country and that Colomb had overestimated the ability and willingness of his countrymen to learn the lesson that Balfour was teaching them, along with their capacity for rational thought. Again, former army officers led the charge, this time Major Evans-Gordon, Major Seeley and Colonel Sandys, who, citing the Norfolk Commission, openly criticized the Committee of Imperial Defence for 'sapping patriotism'.[290] The *Times* was premature in judging that the prime minister's speech marked the final triumph of the 'blue water' school when it recorded: 'It is almost impossible to exaggerate the importance of this conclusion. It takes the problem of invasion and its possibility out of the region of opinion, conjecture and controversy, and makes its negative solution the pivot of our defence policy'.[291]

A rational grasp of the facts meant nothing to Repington. In an article that appeared in the *Times* three days later, the journalist sharply criticized Balfour's words. The prime minister, Repington wrote, had simply ignored British talents and traditions, along with the deviousness of Britain's likely opponent.[292] Over the days that followed, he presented himself as an expert on invasion who had visited and personally examined every port on both the Atlantic and the North Sea and recorded as his result, 'I would willingly undertake the invasion of England under the hypothesis of the P.M. and would lay 7 to 4 upon my success'.[293] In a number of newspaper articles, he denounced Balfour's speech in much the same tenor as a plea 'for a weak Army and a weak Navy';[294] Esher responded with an open letter to Repington rebuking him for his unfounded protests against the government.[295] Swapping out all logical considerations and factors that Britain could hope to control, Repington turned to a new argument that was, at first glance, difficult to refute rationally: the sinister character of the enemy. Balfour accused Repington and the *Spectator* of having a 'soporific effect on the nation' and of 'pernicious preaching'.[296]

The *Naval and Military Gazette* saw Balfour's speech as a serious threat to its position on defence and passed its own verdict on Balfour's attempt to calm the waters reflecting its Social Darwinist worldview: 'It is a law of nature that all life can only be maintained by a struggle, and the nation that ceases to fight must soon cease to live'. For the newspaper, Balfour's speech was evidence of 'luxory indolence, decay of morals, and degeneracy of manly fibre', the very ills that had meant the end of Rome.[297] For Spenser Wilkinson, military adviser to the invasion-theory adherents in the Norfolk Commission, the speech was nothing less than a 'national calamity', and he recommended plans be put in place for future public protest on the issue of invasion.[298] Again, commentators associated with the military and with the diplomatic corps were at the forefront of the debate, with their goal on this occasion to ensure that Balfour's speech was interpreted in a certain light. For Howell Gwynne, too, editor-in-chief at the *Standard*, it now seemed that even if the facts spoke against an invasion, the potential risk should be widely known: 'I go rather beyond perhaps the extreme probabilities of the case because I want to rouse England to the fact that she is in danger'.[299]

As Balfour's government attempted to force the defence issue – the next election was already thought lost[300] – the scaremongers believed they had a mission to fulfil. Whether Britain really was under threat was now little more than a side issue. Their real concerns were the 'martial spirit' of their countrymen, budgetary allocations that favoured the War Office, and the associated increased prestige for the army, won at the expense of the Blue Jackets, whom they judged so arrogant. With anti-German agitation growing, France, which only a few months earlier had been put to use as the impetus for calls for reform, lost something of its weight in political debate, where the words of Davies and Carruthers, the heroes of Childers' *Riddle of the Sands*, seemed to echo constantly:

> We are a maritime nation … we are unique in that way, just as our huge empire is unique. And yet read Brassey, Dilke, and those 'Naval Annuals', and see what mountains of apathy and conceit have had to be tackled. It's not the people's fault. We have been safe so long, and grown so rich, that we have forgotten what we owe it to. But there is no excuse for those blockheads of statesmen.[301]

Even Berlin's sabre-rattling could be repackaged to the benefit of Britain, for it flattered Britain's imperial self-esteem: as Childers had Davies tell Caruthers, 'Let them [the Germans] hate us, and say so, it will teach us to buck up; and that's what really matters'.[302] In the *Spectator*, Strachey pronounced:

> We shall be unworthy of ourselves if we are content to be lulled into a sense of false security by the windy consolations of abstract propositions. Let us remember that Mr Balfour has altered nothing by declaring that we cannot be invaded, and that the painful and wearisome task of securing the safety of the Empire by an adequate military preparation still lies before us.[303]

Although as secretary of state for war Arnold-Forster had reason to appreciate the protests on behalf of his army – Haldane, his successor, deemed Repington his 'Fidus Achates'[304] – he had little patience with the repeated pot-stirring. With good reason, he called Repington and Spenser Wilkinson 'the two most persistent and malicious writers whose views never go beyond their own cast iron formulas'.[305]

The impact of these views on the political establishment was not long in coming. Two months after Balfour had made his statement, fully founded in fact, his position was countered in the House of Lords with the citation of passages from an unnamed fictional account of a German landing at the Firth of Forth in parallel with the occupation of London in a joint French-Russian operation; a groaning George Clarke acknowledged the description as 'absolute nonsense'.[306] Clearly, Lord Ellenborough did not consider it beneath him to attack the Prime Minister as 'Germanophile', a judgement he based purely on Balfour's failure to identify Germany specifically as Britain's mortal enemy.[307] Lord Roberts collected £100,000 for the creation of a network of private rifle clubs and called on every man in England to arm himself without delay, as the political elites could no longer be depended upon and the enemy could be on the doorstep at any moment.[308] Speaking in the House of Lords, Roberts accused the government of inaction and claimed that the army was still no better than it had been in 1899.[309] Roberts had adopted the method so frequently flaunted by his acquaintances Strachey, Maxse, Spenser Wilkinson and Repington – first, make a claim; if parliament does not deny the claim, continue to hawk the claim; in any case, whatever parliament's response, the claim will now hang in the political air. Even though Arnold-Forster could easily refute the criticism of the army, the public remained alarmed.

Roberts toured the length and breadth of the country voicing his concerns tirelessly as he launched a career as public speaker at scientific societies, chambers of commerce, universities, schools, unions, prize ceremonies, groundbreaking ceremonies and ceremonial openings. His message was always about his efforts to ensure Britain's complete security and strengthen the country's military capabilities.[310] His appearances had such great impact that he was even invited to give a lecture tour in the United States. The political leadership was dismayed,[311] not least as Roberts, as a member of the Committee of Imperial Defence, had access to all the relevant defence-related material, while with his princely remuneration of £5,000 he was far better paid than a First Sea Lord.[312] Esher believed that Roberts was on a propaganda trail 'aiming for conscription'.[313] In early November 1905, Roberts, furious at Balfour, resigned from the Committee of Imperial Defence and accepted an offer to become president of the National Service League.[314] Further appearances followed, in the House of Lords, before the Liverpool Chamber of Commerce and at the Headmasters' Association in Manchester and Edinburgh, at school speech days at Rugby, Wellington and Reading, and at the Oxford Student Union, and so the list goes on. Where he had previously criticized the Conservative government for its equanimity, now he praised the Liberal government, with special mention of Richard Haldane for his reform of the army, which Roberts termed 'the greatest step forward in the direction of a national army'.[315] As Roberts, now aged seventy-five, continued his public addresses, the National Service League sent numerous additional speakers into the provinces, financed alarm-sounding publications such as those of Le Queux, and translated foreign-language material to provide what it claimed was evidence of hostile intent, especially from Germany. A collected edition of Roberts' speeches appeared in 1907 under the title *A Nation in Arms*.

As his engagement with the public discussion of Britain's defence after the Boer War makes evident, Balfour was cut from a very different cloth. Esher commented: 'In Mr Balfour the country possessed a Minister with a mind sharpened by dialectics, and a temper chastened by philosophic inquiry, who was peculiarly fitted for the task of shifting the often conflicting opinions of military and naval experts'.[316] While historians have criticized Balfour for showing an academic indecisiveness,[317] for Esher and Clarke Balfour's painstaking objectivity was his great strength. As his approach to the invasion issue showed, Balfour was not one for rapid-fire political decision making; he preferred to do justice to all the complexities of the situation by ensuring he acquired a sound grasp of all the information as quickly as possible and could then deliver a studied verdict. His remarkable interest in the ins and outs of defence policy, his scholarly background and his readiness to consult widely raised the discussions of defence involving army representatives and the Admiralty to a new level. In place of organizational minutiae and traditional animosities, their deliberations now tackled the redefinition of universal principles, an approach that was practically revolutionary for Britain's military thinking and a watershed between, on one side, the ad hoc crisis planning of the nineteenth century – which had meant that Salisbury and his predecessors had usually had little interest in the complexities of defence – and, on the other side, the modern analytical strategic planning of the twentieth century. Balfour's instrument of change was the Committee of Imperial Defence. What had begun as a practically unworkable cabinet committee, the Colonial Defence Committee, paralysed between the First Lord of the Admiralty and the secretary of state for war, he had turned into a defence committee responsible to the prime minister that could function as a forum for discussion and a conduit between the services and the political leadership. The invasion issue was the first hurdle the Committee for Imperial Defence faced.

We should also note Balfour's refusal to allow political options to be prescribed by public opinion. Rather than ride the wave of invasion talk in the press, Balfour went on the offensive. He was too well aware of the facts to submit to ignorance and transparent propaganda. Not only did he attempt to calm the agitation about Britain's security, but he also never pointed a finger at Germany or any other power, including France, as a potential occupier of the British Isles.

All that remained was theorizing about a possible lightning raid. For experts, the manoeuvres had made clear that even an incursion involving just 10,000 soldiers would require more than ten hours to disembark. Additionally, manoeuvres in recent years had demonstrated that a lightly trained volunteer army of 2,500 men would be able to pin down the landing forces for as long as needed, and in any case it would be essential but impossible for the invader to keep such an operation secret.[318] A German invasion was not only logistically, technically, strategically and tactically impossible, but also apparently politically out of the question. The invasion bogeyman did have political value in Britain, however, as Clarke acknowledged to Balfour: 'The raid theory in which I confess I do not believe, may be useful to serve as a peg on which to hang a justification of an intelligible organization for the Volunteers'.[319]

Drawing on the broad range of discussions about defence policy, we can conclude that the redeployment of the Royal Navy was not so much a product of defence policy and maritime contingency as an expression of a political rationale that embraced both domestic and party politics. Without the additional financial means that would have been raised through tariff reform, the only way to finance the backlog of reforms made evident by the Boer War was through increased taxation, much-reduced spending and greater efficiency. The introduction of compulsory military service in Britain was a utopian ideal, but in light of the various scenarios under discussion, even the disbandment of the expensive volunteer force seemed highly unlikely. Clarke had a compromise solution in mind. If the volunteer forces were assembled into small, regionally based groupings, costs could be saved and forces would not have to be raised and maintained permanently across the board. Distributed to sensitive locations across the British Isles – only a handful of places could really be considered possible landing sites for invading forces – the volunteer force would be able to take on any enemy and hold him at bay until regular troops arrived.[320] For Clarke, this solution seemed to hold out the possibility of removing social volatility from the debate and at the same time calming the invasion hysteria. A concession to the invasion scenario might be read, however, as a signal of willingness to move forward with the upgrading and reinvigoration of the army. The need to eliminate that possibility appears to have lain behind Balfour's decision against Clarke's plan. Clarke informed Sandars of an agreement with the prime minister that would see the raid theory aired 'in order to be able publicly to justify the maintenance of volunteer forces'.[321]

One week after his resignation, Balfour again set out his position, eager for the results of his investigations to be available to his successor. In a memorandum of 12 December 1905, he described a surprise attack as extremely unlikely.[322] This invasion memorandum was designed to counter the expected radical liberal plans for comprehensive disarmament, but the document was also intended as reassurance for all those whose ignorance made them likely to be unnerved by propagandists such as Repington and Roberts. As Clarke commented to Balfour, 'We have to consider the teaching among the masses who neither reason nor read history, and such a paper as yours is exactly calculated to allay misgivings'.[323] As permanent secretary of the Committee of Imperial Defence, where he had become the second most important figure, after Balfour, Clarke understood his role to be as an adviser on defence policy responsible for ensuring 'great and eminent people do what I think is right'.[324] With the change of government, he seriously considered offering his resignation. Especially when it came to defence policy, he expected little of a right-liberal majority, which he deemed advice-resistant and blinded by pacifism. Esher convinced him, however, that he should use his position to try to mitigate the impact of a change of course and massive disarmament and to support the liberal imperialists as a small thorn in the side of the radicals. In February 1905, Clarke had already laid out for Haldane the tasks of a future Liberal government,[325] and he hoped that those now in office would use Balfour's final memorandum as both a warning directed abroad and a means of calming the waters internally.

Clarke's hopes were dashed. Rather than make the memorandum public, the new government chose three months later to publish an entirely contradictory memorandum from the General Staff. Based on the assumption that Britain's security was in catastrophic condition, this second memorandum was of a tone entirely different to Balfour's reassuring and objective text.[326] Unlike the previous government, the new government abandoned the public to the 'malicious writers' and their rumour-mongering.[327] Rather than lead, the liberal imperial faction toyed with public discussion, manifestly siding with the War Office, whose scare-mongering Clarke had repeatedly termed 'arrant nonsense'.[328] Their response can be explained not by convincing arguments made by the army representatives or by their greater proximity to the army, but by the experience of party division and the khaki election of October 1900. Their intention was not to respond to a serious external threat but to send a signal to the majority within the party who favoured disarmament. Why else suppress a memorandum that was demonstratively credible,[329] a memorandum that served up arguments that could have been used in support of the peace dividend promised by the radicals for social reforms? We can surmise that as the new cabinet was being formed, the liberal imperialists who dominated foreign and defence policy had no desire to feed their left Liberal Party colleagues additional material in support of disarmament that might increase their cabinet profile just as decisions were being made about who would be offered which post. The fronts within the cabinet were to be clearly defined from the start. On no account were social reforms to be achieved on the back of a reduced defensive capacity that would incite a repeat of the 'little-Englander' reproaches of the Unionists. Although publicly he appeared alarmed, in private Haldane, who had little previous experience of defence issues, was very taken with Balfour's explications, which gave him the time and space to incorporate his suggestions into defence structures.[330] Additionally, Clarke and his new officer colleagues in the General Staff learned from the discussion that the army would need to redefine itself if it was to bolster its legitimacy in the eyes of the public. Investigation of the invasion threat had revealed that the risk of invasion was minimal and that the army's traditional task of coastal defence was therefore more than questionable. Two options for a redefinition of the role of the army seemed possible: emphasize the Empire, and in particular the defence of India, or promote a broad offensive capability that would encompass operations on the continent.

Balfour felt validated. In May 1905, he had stated in parliament that the investigations by the Committee of Imperial Defence 'point unmistakeably to the conclusion that the chief military problem which this country has to face is that of Indian, rather than Home Defence',[331] a public statement of what he had long been saying internally.[332] The now-evident defeat of Russia at the hands of Japan had clearly done nothing to change his opinion.[333]

Notes

1. Hamilton, *The Nation and the Navy, 1889–1914*, 12.
2. See Lambert, 'Righting the Scholarship', 278. On the CID in particular, see Johnson, *Defence by Committee*.
3. Balfour to Lansdowne, July 1904, BL, Add. 49698. See also C. Bellairs, 'The Standard of Strength for Imperial Defence', JRUSI 48/2 (1904), 995–1032, 1007–18; George. S. Clarke, 'The Navy and the Nation', JRUSI 48/1 (1904), 30–45.
4. See Rüger, *Nation*, 159–88.
5. Graham, *The Politics of Naval Supremacy*, 1; Kennedy, 'Mahan vs. Mackinder', 48.
6. *The Times*, 12 Dec. 1904; Selborne, Memorandum, 6 Dec. 1904, NA, CAB 37/73/159.
7. Selborne, Memorandum, 6 Dec. 1904, cited in Boyce, *Crisis of British Power*, Vol. 2, No. 62, 184–90.
8. Ibid.
9. Fisher, *Memories and Records*, 42; see also Campbell, 'Modern Fleet', JRUSI 50/2 (1904), 1445–76.
10. Admiralty Designs Committee, NL/15432, 22 Dec. 1904, NA, ADM 1/7737. I owe this reference to Nicholas Lambert. See also Lambert, 'Righting the Scholarship'.
11. Campbell-Bannerman, Commons, 27 July 1905, PD 162, col. 114. For the important battle-cruiser discussion, see Lambert, 'Righting the Scholarship', passim; Seligmann, *The Royal Navy and the German Threat*; see Rose, 'Review on Matthew Seligmann', 125–31.
12. *HMS Dreadnought* was laid down in early October 1905, launched in February 1906 and commissioned in December 1906.
13. See Massie, *Dreadnought*, 468–97.
14. Marder, *Anatomy*, 496; Monger, *End of Isolation*, 176; Steiner and Neilson, *Britain and the Origins*, 51–52, 219; Kennedy, *Rise of Anglo-German Antagonism*, 279; Steinberg, 'German Background', 197; Joll, *Origins*, 72; D'Ombrain, *War Machinery*, 156; Williams, *Defending the Empire*, 64; Brechtken, *Scharnierzeit*, 54–59, 369; Mombauer, *Origins*, 6; Seligmann, *Spies in Uniform*, 1. For the historiographical viewpoint, see Rose and Geppert, 'Machtpolitik und Flottenbau'; see now also Lambert, 'Righting the Scholarship'.
15. See Brechtken, *Scharnierzeit*, 82; Winzen, *Weltmachtkonzept*, 100, n. 10; Steiner and Neilson, *Britain and the Origins*, 51–63; Judd, *Balfour*, 35; Kennedy, *Rise of Anglo-German Antagonism*, 251–88, esp. 279–80, 417–20; Harris, *Britain*, 269–70; Wipperfürth, *Souveränität*, 372–73.
16. Kennedy, *Rise and Fall of the Great Powers*, 272.
17. Sumida, *In Defence of Naval Supremacy*; Lambert, *Sir John Fisher's Naval Revolution*; Hobson, *Imperialismus*.
18. Brechtken, *Scharnierzeit*, 58; Petter, 'Deutsche Flottenrüstung', 239.
19. See Lambert, *Sir John Fisher's Naval Revolution*, 102.
20. See Forstmeier, 'Flottenbau', 34–53; Stadelmann, 'Flottenrivalität', 117; Hauser, *Gegensatz*, 8; Hallgarten, *Imperialismus*, 13.
21. Brechtken, *Scharnierzeit*, 178, n. 69; 59–87, esp. 82, n. 147. On the sources: 382–86, esp. 382; Mombauer, *Origins*, 18–19, n. 8; Hewitson, *Germany*, 113–45.
22. This fundamental interpretative problem is also noted by Christopher Clark in *Wilhelm II*, 182–83.

23. Marder's study was republished in 1976 as *A History of British Naval Policy in the Pre-Dreadnought 1880–1905* in response to the numerous works on the Tirpitz fleet that had recently appeared.
24. See Marder, *Anatomy*, esp. 515–45, The same goes for Marder, FDSF, vii, 40–43.
25. Marder, *Anatomy*, 465; see also Kennedy, *Rise of Anglo-German Antagonism*, 251; Monger, *End of Isolation*, 63, 68–69, 82–83.
26. Keegan, *Face of Battle*, 27; Williamson and May, 'An Identity of Opinion: Historians and July 1914', 342; Gough, *Historical Dreadnoughts*, 8–14.
27. Lambert, 'Righting the Scholarship', 285.
28. Marder, *Anatomy*, 457–67, esp. 461–62, n. 10–18; see also Fairbanks, 'The Dreadnought Revolution'.
29. See FDSF, 367–95.
30. 'Not once in any of the Fisher papers, or the Admiralty archives or the report of the committee of designs is Germany mentioned even indirectly.' Marder, *Anatomy*, 543; Marder, FGDN II, 26; see also Lambert, *Sir John Fisher's Naval Revolution*, 104.
31. Mackay, *Fisher of Kilverstone*.
32. Steiner and Neilson, *Britain and the Origins*, 53.
33. Mackay, *Fisher of Kilverstone*, 263–70, 313–21.
34. Kennedy, 'Naval Operation', 71.
35. Kennedy, 'Mahan vs. Mackinder', 66.
36. For an extended discussion on the limited importance of tonnage and Mahanism within Britain's naval policy, see Rose, *Zwischen Empire und Kontinent*, 177–89.
37. Steiner and Neilson, *Britain and the Origins*, 52–53; Kennedy, 'Mahan vs. Mackinder', 66; see also Brechtken, *Scharnierzeit*, passim.
38. Seligmann, *The Royal Navy and the German Threat*, 172.
39. Kennedy, *Rise of Anglo-German Antagonism*, 420.
40. Kennedy, 'Maritime Strategieprobleme', 187.
41. The illegal actions of the Royal Navy in relation to German merchant shipping, which continued for months, are categorized by Kennedy as 'accidents' and 'misunderstandings'. Kennedy, *Rise of Anglo-German Antagonism*, 417. See the very different view of the British ambassador: Lascelles to Salisbury, 4 Jan. 1900, HH, MSS Salisbury, A/121/34; 12 Jan. 1900, NA, FO 800/17; GP XV, chapter CII, 439–98.
42. Hildebrand, *Das vergangene Reich*, 203; Schöllgen and Kiessling, *Imperialismus*, 84–85; Mollin, 'Schlachtflottenbau vor 1914', 168.
43. Schroeder, 'International Politics', 196.
44. Ardagh, Memorandum on the (so-called) Scheme of Authorized Defence, 19 Jan. 1897, NA, WO 32/218, 8. See also Selborne's similar viewpoint, *The Times*, 26 Feb. 1903.
45. Of particular interest here are the records of the Committee of Imperial Defence: NA, CAB 3/1, 'A Series' 1A–40A.
46. See Chapter 7.
47. See Jervis, *Perception and Misperception*, 286–304.
48. H.W. Wilson, 'The New German Navy', HMM, No. 103 (1901), 529–37, 536.
49. Palmerston, 30 July 1845, PD III/82, cols. 1223–34; *The Times*, 1, 24, 31 Dec. 1847, 8 Jan. 1848.
50. Earl of Derby, Lord Palmerston, Lord John Russell, 16 Feb. 1852, PD III/119, cols. 551–53, cols. 562–653; PD III/155, 29 July 1859, cols. 685–87; see also Cobden, *The Three Panics*, 26–33; Nugent (Colonel), 'Thoughts upon Invasion', JRUSI 32/1

(1888), 165–73; *The Times*, 17 May 1888; WO Memorandum, Defence of England, 17 April 1888, NA, CAB 37/21/6; Chesney, 'The Battle of Dorking', *Blackwood's Magazine*, 5/1871, 539–72.
51. Wharton, Memorandum: A French Invasion, 19 June 1888, NA, CAB 3/1/6A.
52. As is stated in Henry Wilson's defence memorandum of 1911, see WO 106/47.
53. Fisher, Memorandum, July 1904, USL, MSS Battenberg, MB1/T5/31, 3.
54. Clarke, *Battle of Dorking*, 314.
55. See Wilson, *Channel Tunnel Vision*.
56. Bond, *War and Society*, 74–77; Balfour, 11 May 1905, *The Times*, 12 May 1905.
57. Between 1899 and the end of the war, navy estimates rose by only 30 per cent and when more recent developments are taken into account remained relatively steady; by contrast, army estimates over the course of three years rose by approximately 300 per cent. The total cost of the war was more than £211 million. The China expedition cost a further £6 million. By comparison, the Crimean War had cost only £33 million. See Whitaker, *Whitaker's Almanack* 1904, 190–95. For a financial approach to British defence policy, see the brilliant work by Sumida, *In Defence of Naval Supremacy*, passim.
58. See Marder, *Anatomy*, 288, 296–301; Kennedy, *Rise of Anglo-German Antagonism*, 251; Steinberg, *Yesterday's Deterrent*, 18.
59. See Birchenough, 'German Ambitions over Sea', RR 2/1898, 152; *Observer*, 7 Jan. 1900 and 4 Feb. 1900.
60. Wilson, 'The New German Navy', HMM 103 (1901), 529–37, 530.
61. On the French construction programme of 9 Dec. 1900, see Ropp, *Development of a Modern Navy*, 366–67.
62. Gamble to Selborne, 9 Sept. 1901, BOD, MSS Selborne I/16; see also 'The possibility of a war between England and France', FR 5/1900, 719–29; Selborne to Lansdowne, 4 Sept. 1901, 6 Sept. 1901, 7 Dec. 1901, BL, LANS/PL 1.
63. 'Note du départment sur un projet d'accord naval entre la France et la Russie', secret, 21 Dec. 1901, DDF 2/III, Annex III, 603–6; Muraviev, Memorandum, 25 Jan. 1900, 'Zaristische Diplomatie', Berliner Monatshafte 6/1928, 638–70. For the importance of the Russian Baltic Fleet, see Lambert, *Submarine Service*, xiii.
64. Selborne to Lansdowne, 7 Dec. 1901, BL, LANS/PL 1; Henry Jackson, Report: Defence against Submarines, DNO, 5 Feb. 1900, NA, ADM 256/39; Lambert, *Submarine Service*, No. 3, 5. The United States also began to focus on building submarines, see ADM, Memorandum, Submarine Boats in the United States, 18 May 1900, NA, ADM 1/7462, cited in ibid., No. 4, 9–10; Beresford to Fisher, 12 June 1900, BL, Add. 49713. For the Russian fleet, see Rason (R.N.), 'Russian Fleet', JRUSI 42/2 (1900), 1431–38.
65. See 'Les descentes en Angleterre', *Revue des deux Mondes*, 15 March 1899, 275; 'Equipages de la flotte', *Revue des deux Mondes*, 15 July 1900, 280.
66. Ardagh (DMI), Memorandum: A French Invasion, 11 July 1900, NA, PRO 30/40 Part II; Arnold-Forster to Selborne, 3 June 1902, cited in Boyce, *Crisis of British Power*, 147 n. 50.
67. Monson to Lansdowne, 28 Aug. 1901, NA, FO 800/125.
68. H.W. Wilson, 'The New German Navy', HMM 103 (1901), 529–37, 532.
69. De Lanessan, 'French Naval Programme of 1900–1906', JRUSI 47/2 (1903), 1024–43, 1165–80, 1282–97, 1400–17, 1436–55, 1572–94; Selborne, Memorandum, 31 Oct. 1901, cited in Boyce, *Crisis of British Power*, 128–36, esp. 134–36.

70. Whitaker, *Whitaker's Almanack* 1907, 592; see also Lambi, *Navy*, 141–50; Steinberg, *Yesterday's Deterrent*, 220–21; Ropp, *Development of a Modern Navy*, 266–67.
71. Mackay, *Fisher of Kilverstone*, 245.
72. Selborne to Hicks Beach, 29. Dec. 1900, cited in Boyce, *Crisis of British Power*, 105–6. For the importance of the battle-cruiser debate, see most recently Lambert, 'Righting the Scholarship', 275–307.
73. Fisher, Memorandum, November 1903, cited in Lambert, *Submarine Service*, No. 36, 60–68.
74. This meant a new invasion fear, reminiscent of the fear in 1871, named after the book by George T. Chesney, *The Battle of Dorking*.
75. H.W. Wilson, 'The Invasion of England', NR 12/1899, 653; Wilson, 'Are We Misled about the Fleet?', NC 4/1900, 574; Cairnes, 'The Problem of Invasion', NR 4/1900, 341; Maude, *The New Battle of Dorking*; Ropp, *Development of a Modern Navy*, 345–47.
76. Brodrick to Balfour, 29 Jan. 1900, BL, Add. 49720.
77. *The Times*, 1 Jan. 1900.
78. Colomb, 'Defence of the UK', JRUSI 42/1 (1898), 456–66; see also *The Spectator*, 22 Jan. 1859, 93; 30 July 1859, 785; WO-Paper, Defences against attack by Torpedo-Boats, 10 Feb. 1903, NA, CAB 3/1/2A.
79. Lansdowne to Sandars, 1 Nov. 1900, BOD, MSS Sandars, MSS Eng. hist. c. 733; Esher, 9 Nov. 1900, JL I, p. 231.
80. Williams, *Defending the Empire*, 14.
81. Monson to Salisbury, 22 Jan. 1899, NA, ADM 1/7422A; Minute by Jeffreys (DNO), cited in Lambert, *Submarine Service*, No. 1, 3.
82. Salisbury to MacColl, 6 Sept. 1901, cited in Russell, *Malcolm MacColl*, 282–83.
83. Salisbury to Balfour, 2 April 1897, BOD, MSS Sandars, MSS. Eng. hist. c. 730,
84. Commons, 27 July 1900, PD IV/90, col. 1468.
85. Roberts, *Salisbury – Victorian Titan*, 752, 792–93.
86. Salisbury to Balfour, 29 Dec. 1899, BL, Add. 49691.
87. Salisbury (Primrose League), *The Times*, 4 May 1898; to Lascelles, 3 March 1900, HH, MSS Salisbury, A122/22.
88. Strachey, 'Public Opinion in the Conduct of Foreign Affairs', *The Spectator*, 6 April 1901, 487–88.
89. *The Times*, 10 May 1900.
90. For the Conservatives, see Searle, *Edwardian Society*, 79–96.
91. James, *Lord Roberts*, 412, 439.
92. Ibid., 414; see Lord Roberts, DNB (1912–1921), 464–70.
93. D'Ombrain, *War Machinery*, 47.
94. 'The Army is continually being exposed to hostile criticism, the Navy never.' Nicholson to Wilkinson, 16 May 1904, cited in D'Ombrain, *War Machinery*, 48.
95. Nicholson to Roberts, 8 May 1901, NAM, MSS Roberts, R 52/87; see also Altham, Memorandum, Military Needs of the Empire in a War with France and Russia, 31 May 1901, NA, CAB 3/1/1A.
96. ADM, Strategic situation, 1 Nov. 1900, NA, ADM 1/7491; Conference between Admiralty and War Office Representatives, NA, CAB 3/1/9A.
97. Selborne, Naval Estimates 1901/2, 17 Jan. 1901, NA, CAB 37/56/8; Wilson, Memorandum, 21 Jan. 1901, cited in Lambert, *Submarine Service*, No. 13, pp. 20–22; Hamilton to Selborne, 19 Oct. 1901, BOD, MSS Selborne 1/29.

98. Final Report, Feb. 1901, NA, WO 106/44; CAB 3/1/9A; Arnold-Forster, Diary, 8 Aug. 1901, BL, Add. 50294; see WO, Memorandum: Land Forces for the Defence of the UK, 14 Feb. 1903, NA, CAB 3/1/3A, 1–4; Selborne to Balfour, 12 May 1904, BL, Add. 49707.
99. Robertson, 10 Jan. 1902, NA, CAB 3/1/5A. See Notes made by Robertson on the Committee of Garrisons (13 July–11 Oct. 1901), LHCMA, ROB 1/2/2.
100. Robertson, Memorandum: The Military Resources of France, 27 Dec. 1901. CAB 3/1/4A. 'Since the above Memorandum was written the French forces have been considerably strengthened.' The issue was therefore again addressed by the Committee of Imperial Defence, 2 Nov. 1903, NA, CAB 3/1/4A, 8–10.
101. Ibid., 1–2.
102. Ibid., 4.
103. 'The only logical conclusion is that an invasion of England will be attempted.' Ibid., 9.
104. *The Times*, 29 Jan. and 11 April 1901; House of Lords Debate, *The Times*, 6 July 1901; (French Officer), 'Invasion of England an Easy Matter for France', RR 11/1901, 510; Anon., 'French Naval Manoeuvres of 1902', JRUSI 46/2 (1902), 1436–57.
105. Manoeuvres, 1901, NA, WO 32/225, 20–23, 29–34, 88–89.
106. Delauney, 'Is the Invasion of England Possible?', *Pall Mall Magazine*, 11/1901, 395–98.
107. Nicholson, 1902, NA, WO 32/225, iii; Roberts to Selborne, 8 Aug. 1901, BOD, MSS Selborne 1/29.
108. Robertson, Military Resources of France, 27 Dec. 1901, 1–2; Roberts, 17 Feb. 1902, NA, CAB 3/1/5A, 2–3.
109. A.B.C. etc., 'British Foreign Policy', NR 11/1901 [http://net.lib.byu.edu/~rdh7/wwi/1914m/abc.html, accessed 19 Nov. 2007]. See Robertson, Memorandum on a proposed alliance between Germany and Great Britain in order to forestall Russian expansion, November 1902, LHCMA, ROB 1/2/4.
110. Robertson, Minutes, Lawrence, Memorandum, 18 Jan. 1902, NA, WO 106/46; see also Robertson, *Soldiers and Statesmen*, Vol. 1, 20–23; Kennedy, *Rise of Anglo-German Antagonism*, 252–53, n. 9.
111. Robertson, The Military Resources of France, 27 Dec. 1901, CAB 3/1/4A, 9.
112. Fisher, Memorandum, November 1903, cited in Lambert, *Submarine Service*, No. 36, 60–68.
113. Brodrick, Minute, 28 Jan. 1902, NA, CAB 3/1/5A, 1–2.
114. Roberts to Brodrick, 17 Feb. 1902, NA, CAB 3/1/5A, 3.
115. Arnold-Forster on Fisher, 23 Nov. 1904, BL, Add. 50341.
116. Lambert, *Planning Armageddon*, 281–82.
117. Fisher to Balfour, 4 Jan. 1904, BL, Add. 49710.
118. Selborne, Feb. 1901, PD IV/103, Appendix I; 12 July 1900, PD IV/98, col. 238.
119. Fisher to Battenberg, 10 Feb. 1902, FGDN I, No. 115, 223–25.
120. See Mackay, *Fisher of Kilverstone*, 273–350.
121. Brechtken, *Scharnierzeit*, 82; Steiner and Neilson, *Britain and the Origins*, 51–63; Kennedy, *Rise of Anglo-German Antagonism*, 251–88, 417–20. Selborne made no mention of Germany. See Selborne on imperial defence, *The Times*, 26 Feb. 1903.
122. Mackay, *Fisher of Kilverstone*, 314.
123. Fisher, *Memories and Records*, 149–51.
124. Ibid., 88. See also Balfour to Selborne, 26 Nov. 1904, BOD, MSS Selborne 1/39; Fisher to Tweedmouth, 4 Oct. 1906, FGDN II, No. 50, 93–95; Sumida, *In Defence of Naval Supremacy*, esp. 43–46; Lambert, *Sir John Fisher's Naval Revolution*.

125. Fisher, *Memories and Records*, 41–42; Selborne to Lansdowne, 2 May 1902, BL, LANS/PL 1.
126. Fisher to Selborne, 1 Dec. 1900, FGDN I, No. 88, 167–68; to Rosebery, 10 May 1901, ibid., No. 94, 188–91.
127. Mackay, *Fisher of Kilverstone*, 318–19.
128. Fisher to Battenberg, 10 Feb. 1902, FGDN I, No. 115, 223–25. '[W]hen you consider the facts you will see that a real danger exists there [Caribbean].' Selborne to Lansdowne, 6 Sept. 1901, BL, LANS/PL 1.
129. Fisher to Battenberg, 10 Feb. 1902, FGDN I, No. 115, 223–25.
130. Fisher, Memorandum: 'The Strategical Distribution of our Fleets' (Aug. 1904), cited in Kemp, Fisher Papers, Vol. 1, 161.
131. Balfour (United Club), *The Times*, 28 Nov. 1903.
132. Macintosh, 'Role of the Committee', 492.
133. See Crowe to Asta Crowe, 25 Aug. 1900, BOD, MSS Crowe, MS Eng. d. 2900.
134. See Johnson, *Defence by Committee*, 11–165; see also Dugdale, *Balfour*, 365.
135. Minute by Battenberg, 22 Dec. 1902, NA, ADM 1/7601; Clarke to Chirol, 24 March 1903, BL, Add. 50831; Selborne to Balfour, 4 April 1902, BL, Add. 49707.
136. See D'Ombrain, *War Machinery*, 135.
137. Dugdale, *Balfour*, 365.
138. See Home Defence 'A Series', NA, CAB 3/1.
139. Ritchie, Memorandum, 21 Feb. 1903, BUL, AC 17/59. See also Satre, Brodrick and Army Reform, in Journal of British Studies 15/2 (1976), 119.
140. WO, Memorandum: Land Defences against Attack by Torpedo-Boats, 10 Feb. 1903, NA, CAB 3/1/2A, 1–2.
141. The army budget had fallen in the same year from £36.7 million to £29.2 million. See Stevenson, *Armaments*, 4–8.
142. Whitaker, *Whitaker's Almanack* 1904, 194.
143. 'Finance touches almost everything.' Balfour to A. Chamberlain, 1 Jan. 1904, BUL, AC 17/1/29.
144. 'However reluctant we may be to face the fact, the time has come when we must frankly admit that the financial resources of the United Kingdom are inadequate to do all that we should desire in the matter of imperial defence.' Chamberlain, The Financial Situation, 28 April 1904, NA, CAB 37/70/61.
145. For a shorter version, see Neilson, *Britain and the Last Tsar*, 237. Original: Selborne to Balfour, 28 Oct. 1903, BOD, MSS Sandars, MSS Eng. hist. c. 715.
146. Williams, *Defending the Empire*, 60.
147. Nicholson to Roberts, 24 Nov. 1903, cited in D'Ombrain, *War Machinery*, 31.
148. Since 1889, the navy budget of £14.3 million had grown by an average of £1.5 million each year, and by 1904 had reached £35.8 million. In light of a growth of 40 per cent in personnel and the navy's greater responsibilities, this increase appears reasonable. Whitaker, *Whitaker's Almanack* 1904, 194.
149. The War Office's budget had already been reduced significantly from its highpoint of £92.3 million, or 55 per cent of the total budget, during the war, but at £37.6 million (22.5 per cent) it remained significantly higher than the £22.3 million (23.3 per cent) of 1898. Whitaker, *Whitaker's Almanack* 1904, 195.
150. Boulger, 'Possible Addition to the Dual Alliance', NC 12/1902, 1022–32; WO, Memorandum: Land Forces for the Defence of the UK, 14 Feb. 1903, NA, CAB 3/1/3A, 1–5.

151. Memorandum: Land Forces for the Defence of the UK, 14 Feb. 1903, NA, CAB 3/1/3A, 2–4.
152. Fisher to Amery, 30 Jan. 1904, CC, AMEL 1/1/14.
153. Thursfield to Selborne, 15 Aug. 1901, BOD, MSS Selborne 1/29.
154. Marder, *Naval Policy*, 378.
155. Nicholson to Roberts, 14 Nov. 1903, NAM, MSS Roberts, R 52/113.
156. Naval Remarks on: Land Forces for the Defence of the UK, 4 March 1903, NA, CAB 3/1/8A, 1.
157. Marder, FDSF I, 406–7. For Selborne on Battenberg, see Selborne, 14 Oct. 1902, BOD, MSS Selborne 1/91.
158. Battenberg, Combined naval and military operations, 1886, USL, MSS Battenberg, MB1/T1/1; Battenberg, May 1894, ibid., MB1/T9; Correspondence with Earl Spencer, 15 Oct.–23 Nov. 1894, ibid., MB1/T1/10b.
159. Battenberg, Remarks: Land Forces for the Defence of the UK, 4 March 1903, NA, CAB 3/1/8A, 1–2.
160. Ibid.
161. WO, Land Forces for the Defence of the UK, 14 Feb. 1903, NA, CAB 3/1/3A, 3–4.
162. Stead, 'England's Peril', RR 2/1900, 124; RR 4/1900, 315–16; RR 5/1900, 541–42. For Moltke's real quotation about England, see Bucholz, *Moltke*, 91–92.
163. Knowles, 'Editorial', NC 1/1900, 1–2; Maxse, 'Episodes', NR 1/1900, 650; NR 4/1900, 126; Stead, RR 2/1900, 124–27; *St. James Gazette*, 12 March 1900.
164. WO, French Invasion, 28 Feb. 1903, NA, CAB 3/1/7A, 4.
165. Fisher to Esher, 1904, cited in Fisher, *Memories and Records*, 173–74; D'Ombrain, *War Machinery*, 147.
166. Gamble to Selborne, 9 Sept. 1901, BOD, MSS Selborne 1/16. French forces were focused on the Channel ports. ADM, Memorandum: The possibilities of Invasion, 31 March 1903, NA, CAB 3/1/11A, 1–4.
167. Fisher, Memorandum, November 1903, No. 36, cited in Lambert, *Submarine Service*, 60–68, esp. 65.
168. ADM, Memorandum: The possibilities of Invasion, 31 March 1903, NA, CAB 3/1/11A, 1–4.
169. See Intelligence Division (WO), 27 April 1903, NA, CAB 3/1/13A; Battenberg, Remarks on 13A, 14 July 1903, NA, CAB 3/1/16A; Intelligence Division (WO), 24 July 1903, NA, CAB 3/1/17A.
170. Battenberg, Memorandum, 31 March 1903: The Possibilities of Invasion, NA, CAB 3/1/11A, 2.
171. Battenberg, N.I.D. Memorandum, 31 March 1903, NA, CAB 3/1/11A, Appendix, 5.
172. Ibid., 3.
173. Ibid., 3–4; Anon., 'The Feasibility of Overseas Invasion', *Marine Rundschau* 6/1902, Translation, April 1903, NA, CAB 3/1/12A.
174. Ottley and Battenberg disagreed in a Memorandum, 6 Jan. 1905, NA, ADM 1/7807.
175. WO, Intelligence Division, Roberts, Minutes, The Possibility of Invasion, 27 April 1903, NA, CAB 3/1/13A, 2.
176. James, *Lord Roberts*, 414; Wilkinson, *Britain at Bay*, 4.
177. See Bloch, 'Lessons of the Transvaal War', CR 4/1900, 457–71; Roberts (Manchester), *The Times*, 23 Oct. 1912; see also Rose, 'Readiness or Ruin'.

178. Nicholson to Roberts, 24 Nov. 1903, NAM, MSS Roberts, R 52/107. For this view, see Hobson, *Imperialismus*, 170–71.
179. ADM, Minute, Land Forces for the Defence of the UK, 4 March 1903, NA, CAB 3/1/8A, 2.
180. Committee of Imperial Defence, Minutes of 11th Meeting, 29 April 1903, NA, CAB 2/1.
181. James, *Lord Roberts*, 439.
182. See Cd. 2062 and 2063; Corbett, 'The One-Eyed Commission', MR 7/1904, 38–49.
183. Wilkinson, *Britain at Bay*, 60.
184. *The Times*, 28 and 30 May 1904.
185. Wilkinson, *Britain at Bay*, 60–63.
186. According to Nicholson, the government should decide 'whether the naval view or the military view is correct', cited in Corbett, 'The One-Eyed Commission', MR 7/1904, 38–49, esp. 40.
187. Royal Commission (1904), Cd. 2062, Witnesses, see xi–xii; and Cd. 2061.
188. See Cd. 2062, 110–16; for earlier views, see Hopkins, 'A Few Naval Ideas for the Coming Century', 12 Dec. 1900, JRUSI 45/1 (1901), 7–38.
189. Wolseley: 'I eliminate the action of our Navy from this calculation'. Cited in Bellairs, 'The Standard of Strength for Imperial Defence', JRUSI 48/2 (1904), 995–1032, 1012. Cd. 2062, 54.
190. Report, Cd. 2062, 55, 62, 233–35, 282–83; Arnold-Forster, Diary, 25 July 1904, BL, Add. 50339. 'Lord Harris has evidently never thought the problem out at all.' Arnold-Forster, Diary, 5 Dec. 1904, BL, Add. 50342.
191. 'History teaches us exactly the reverse.' Corbett, 'The One-Eyed Commission', MR 7/1904, 38–49, 43.
192. Ardagh, Memorandum: Liability of the UK to Invasion, June 1903, NA, PRO 30/40/13.
193. Royal Commission on the Militia and Volunteers, 20 May 1904, Cd. 2061, 15–16.
194. Arnold-Forster, Diary, 3 March 1905, BL, Add. 50345; 25 July 1904, ebd., Add. 50339.
195. *The Times*, 28 Nov. 1903; *Saturday Review*, 5 Dec. 1903, 692.
196. *Saturday Review*, 10 Oct. 1903, 448–49.
197. Fisher to Sandars, 3 Jan. 1904, BL, Add. 49710.
198. Arnold-Forster to Balfour, 8 Dec. 1903, BL, Add. 49722.
199. Arnold-Forster, Diary, Aug. 1902, BL, Add. 50287; see also Kennedy, *Rise of Anglo-German Antagonism*, 253.
200. Arnold-Forster, Diary, 27 Oct. 1903, BL, Add. 50355.
201. Lord Ellenborough, PD (Lords) IV/149, 10 July 1905, cols. 19–23; Monger, *End of Isolation*, 94.
202. Fisher to Balfour, November 1903, BL, Add. 49710; Fisher to Sandars, 5 Dec. 1903, ibid.
203. Ibid.; Balfour, Draft Report on the Possibility of Serious Invasion, 11 Nov. 1903, NA, CAB 3/1/18A, 7.
204. Ibid., 11.
205. Ibid., 15.
206. Selborne to Balfour, 23 Aug. 1905, BL, Add. 49707.
207. See Clarke, *Fortification* (1892).
208. Clarke to Balfour, 11 Nov. 1903, BL, Add. 49700.

209. Selborne to Balfour, 16 Nov. 1903, BL, Add. 49703; Fisher to Sandars, 3 Jan. 1904, BL, Add. 49710; Fisher on the Balfour Memorandum, 11 Nov. 1903: The Possibility of Serious Invasion, BL, Add. 49710; Fisher, Memorandum, November 1903, cited in Lambert, *Submarine Service*, No. 36, 60–68.
210. Marder, FGDN I, 148.
211. Fisher, Memorandum, November 1903, cited in Lambert, *Submarine Service*, No. 36, 60–68.
212. Ibid.
213. Balfour to Fisher, 3 Jan. 1904, cited in ibid., No. 37, 68–69; to Selborne, 7 Jan. 1904, ibid., No. 38, 69.
214. Fisher, Memorandum, November 1903, cited in ibid., No. 36, 60–68.
215. Ardagh (DMI), The Situation at Constantinople, October 1896, NA, PRO 30/40 Part I. For Constantinople and Cairo, see Wilson, 'Constantinople or Cairo'.
216. Fisher to Balfour, 5 Jan. 1904, cited in Lambert, *Submarine Service*, No. 39, 70.
217. See Tomes, *Balfour*, passim.
218. Monger, *End of Isolation*, 94.
219. *The Times*, 27 Feb., 28 Feb. 1914. Although the award-winning analysis carried out by Lieutenant Colonel Charles Telfer-Smollett, who was a talented army officer but by no means an expert on amphibious operations or naval questions, revealed the Japanese success at Chemulpo to be 'exceptional' based on a 'thoroughly efficient organisation and preparation', he concluded that the 'immunity from disaster which has hitherto attended our arms, may, and probably will, fail us at a critical moment', C.E.D. Telfer-Smollett, 'The Best Method for Carrying out the Conjoint Practice of the Navy and Army in Embarkation and Disembarkation for War', JRUSI 49/1 (1905), 353–96, 356, 396.
220. Nicholas II to Alekseiev (Commander-in-Chief), 8 Feb. 1904, cited in Maxwell, 'The Battle of Chemulpo', *The Historian* 39/3 (1977), 491.
221. Fisher to Anon., 22 Feb. 1905, FGDN II, No. 11, 51–52; see also Koss, *Rise and Fall*, Vol. 1, 419.
222. Strachey, 'The Teachings of the War', *The Spectator*, 20 Feb. 1904, 281–82.
223. Robertson, Military Resources of Germany, 23 Feb. 1904, NA, CAB 3/1/20A, 5–6; see also Lüttwitz, 'The Invasion of England', JRUSI 2/1896, 198–202; Stead, 'England's Peril', RR 2/1900, 124.
224. Ewart (D.M.O.), Note, 1 Feb. 1908, NA, WO 106/47B, ID/8.
225. Robertson, Memorandum, 23 Feb. 1904, NA, CAB 3/1/20A; Committee of Imperial Defence, 32nd Meeting, 2 March 1904; 33rd Meeting, 4 March 1904, NA, CAB 2/1.
226. WO, Transport by Sea and Disembarkation of Japanese Troops, 27 July 1904, NA, WO 33/315.
227. Arnold-Forster to Balfour, 11 March 1904, BL, Add. 49722; Clarke to Balfour, 27 June 1904, BL, Add. 49700.
228. Ellenborough, 'The Possibility of Fleets and Harbours Being Surprised', JRUSI 49/2 (1905), 789–22, 799–807. Admirals Bowden-Smith, Mann and Freemantle and Commander Caborne argued against Ellenborough; only army officers Colonel Sandys (MP) and Major Fraser agreed. Ibid., 799–800; see also Scott to Lansdowne, 26 Jan. 1904, NA, FO 65/1684; Bompard, *Mon Ambassade en Russie*, 48.
229. Close and Freemantle, 9 May 1905, cited in Ellenborough, 'The Possibility of Fleets and Harbours Being Surprised', JRUSI 49/2 (1905), 789–822, 803–6.

230. Fisher to Amery, 17 Dec. 1903, CC, AMEL 1/1/14; Lambert, *Submarine Service*, Nos. 42–50, 82–89.
231. Custance to Selborne, 31 Aug. 1904, cited in Lambert, *Submarine Service*, No. 49, 86–87.
232. Ibid.; Kerr to Selborne, 19 Sept. 1904, BOD, MSS Selborne 1/41; see also PD IV/143, 28 March 1905, col. 1406; Arnold-Forster to Kitchener, 16 March 1905, BL, Add. 50342; Lyttelton to Balfour, 19 Sept. 1904, BL, Add. 49722; *The Times*, 12 Sept. 1904; Clarke to Balfour, 20 Sept. 1906, BL, Add. 49702; *The Times*, 13 Sept. and 9 Oct. 1904; *The Spectator*, 17 Sept. 1904, 391.
233. Lyttelton to Balfour, 19 Sept. 1904, BL, Add. 49722.
234. Repington to Hutton, 13 March 1907, RL 42, 116–17.
235. *The Times*, 8, 10, 12 and 22 Sept. 1904; Lyttelton to Balfour, 19 Sept. 1904, BL, Add. 49722.
236. Roberts to Strachey, 20 April 1903, HLRO, STR/4/10.
237. *The Times*, 7, 12, 24 and 30 May 1904; *The Spectator*, 14 May 1904, 1; and 2 July 1904, 6–7; PD (Lords), 19 April 1904, cols. 310–20; Dunlop, *Development*, 183–84.
238. For a comparison of the costs of a conscripted army and battleships, see Bellairs, 'The Standard of Strength for Imperial Defence', JRUSI 9/1904, 995–32, 1007.
239. Commons, PD IV/144, 3 April 1905, cols. 214–15, 245.
240. Cited in Mackay, *Fisher of Kilverstone*, 306–7; Sumida, *In Defence of Naval Supremacy*, 26–27.
241. Fisher to Esher, 17 June 1904, cited in Fisher, *Memories and Records*, 179.
242. Clarke to Balfour, 27 June 1904, BL, Add. 49700.
243. Massie, *Dreadnought*, 768.
244. Commons, PD IV/144, 3 April 1905, cols. 214–15, 245.
245. Monger, *End of Isolation*, 94.
246. Commons, 2 Aug. 1904, PD IV/139, cols. 605–17; 8 Aug. 1904, cols. 1410–32; Arnold-Forster to Balfour, 13 Jan. 1905, BL, Add. 49723.
247. Arnold-Forster to Fisher, 26 Jan. 1905, BL, Add. 50343.
248. Arnold-Forster, 9 March 1904, PD IV/142, cols. 606–7; Balfour, 9 March 1904, ibid., col. 623; Arnold-Forster, 28 March 1904, ibid., cols. 1403–4, 1406.
249. £5 million was lacking for the fiscal year 1904/5. A Chamberlain to Balfour, 6 Jan. 1904, BL, Add. 49735.
250. Fisher to Selborne, 29 Oct. 1904, FGDN II, No. 4, 46.
251. Fisher to Lady Fisher, 1 Nov. 1904, FGDN II, No. 5, 47. More recently, Nicholas Lambert told a different story. See Lambert, *Planning Armageddon*, 281–82.
252. Fisher to Selborne, 19 Nov. 1904, BOD, MSS Selborne 1/42.
253. Committee of Imperial Defence, 27th Meeting, 12 Dec. 1903, NA, CAB 2/1; Reconnaissance of the UK, 9 May 1904, 7, NA, CAB 3/1/23A; Balfour, Army Reform and Military Needs, 27 June 1904, NA, CAB 38/5/65, 2; Fisher to Balfour, 26 April 1905, FGDN II, No. 18, 58; Lansdowne to Bertie, 27 April 1905, FGDN II, No. 19, 58–59, n. 1.
254. Fisher to Balfour, 28 April 1905, FGDN II, No. 20, 58–59.
255. Cited in Lambert, *Sir John Fisher's Naval Revolution*, 103.
256. Battenberg, 8 Aug. 1904, cited in Marder, *Anatomy*, 495; Battenberg to Selborne, 16 Oct. 1904, cited in Boyce, *Crisis of British Power*, Vol. 2, No. 59, 181–82; Amery to Clarke, 3 Nov. 1904, CC, AMEL 1/1/14.

257. Selborne, Memorandum, November 1904, BOD, MSS Selborne 1/42.
258. See Lambert, *Sir John Fisher's Naval Revolution*, 106; for a different view, see Kennedy, *Rise and Fall of British Naval Mastery*, 258.
259. Mackay, *Fisher of Kilverstone*, 260–63; see also Hurd, 'A Dreadnought Naval Policy', FR 12/1906, 1017–30, 1019.
260. Fisher, February 1905, cited in Mackay, *Fisher of Kilverstone*, 318.
261. Friedberg, *Weary Titan*, 192; Kennedy, *Rise of Anglo-German Antagonism*, 279; Marder, *Anatomy*, 495.
262. Selborne, Memorandum, 6 Dec. 1904, cited in Boyce, *Selborne Papers*, Vol. 2, No. 62, 184–90.
263. Esher, Memorandum, 27 March 1904, BL, Add. 49718.
264. Selborne, Memorandum, 6 Dec. 1904, cited in Boyce, *Crisis of British Power*, Vol. 2, No. 62, 184–90.
265. See Greindl to Faverau, 18 Feb. 1905, BelD III, No. 2, 4–6.
266. See Kennedy, *Rise of Anglo-German Antagonism*, 252.
267. Steiner, *Britain and the Origins*, 156.
268. Selborne, Memorandum, 6 Dec. 1904, cited in Boyce, *Crisis of British Power*, Vol. 2, No. 62, 184–90; *The Times*, 16 Dec. 1904; *Naval Annual* 1905, 455–69.
269. Fisher, *Memories and Records*, 149.
270. Hurd, 'Naval Progress', NAR 9/1903, 385–92, 386; Battenberg, 6 Jan. 1905, NA, ADM 1/7807.
271. Cited in Mackay, *Fisher of Kilverstone*, 261.
272. Excubitor (Hurd), 'Our Position of Naval Peril', FR 8/1907, 241–52, 245.
273. Mackay, *Fisher of Kilverstone*, 262–63.
274. *Le Temps*, cited in *The Times*, 16 Dec. 1904.
275. Marder, *Anatomy*, 496.
276. Esher, Memorandum, 27 March 1904, BL, Add. 49718.
277. Battenberg, 14 Nov. 1904, cited in Mackay, *Fisher of Kilverstone*, 318.
278. PD IV/144, 3 April 1905, col. 239; 4 April 1905, cols. 340–76; 6 April 1905, col. 678, cols. 714–19.
279. Esher, Diary, 20 June 1904, JL II, 55; Arnold-Forster, Diary, 8 March 1905, BL, Add. 50342; Fisher to Sandars, 29 July 1904, BL, Add. 49710.
280. Hoyer, *Salisbury und Deutschland*, 328.
281. Balfour, 11 May 1905, PD IV/146, cols. 76–77.
282. Fisher to Balfour, 24 Jan. 1905, BL, Add. 49710.
283. Fisher to Balfour, 24 Jan. 1905, BL, Add. 49710; Lambert, *Submarine Service*, xxiv; Balfour (Commons), 11 May 1905, PD IV/146, col. 86.
284. Balfour, 29 May 1908, NA, CAB 16/3A.
285. Campbell-Bannerman, 11 May 1905, cited in *The Times*, 12 May 1905.
286. PD IV/146, 11 May 1905, cols. 84–87, 89–92, 99–100, 108–9, 118–21.
287. Selborne to Brodrick, 2 June 1905, BOD, MSS Selborne 2.
288. Mackail and Wyndham, *Life and Letters*, Vol. 2, 498–500.
289. PD IV/146, 11 May 1905, cols. 91–92.
290. Ibid., cols. 128f., cols. 140–41.
291. *The Times*, 12 May 1905.
292. *The Times*, 15 May 1905.
293. Repington to Esher, 18 May 1905, JL II, 125.

294. Repington, Mr Balfour to Imperial Defence, *The Times*, 22 May 1905.
295. Esher, *The Times*, 22 May 1905.
296. Repington, *The Times*, 19 May 1905. 'It constitutes a not inconsiderable danger to the state.' *The Spectator*, 20 May 1905, 737.
297. *The Naval and Military Gazette*, 20 May 1905, cited in Jaeckel, *Nordwestgrenze*, 226, n. 59.
298. Spenser Wilkinson to Roberts, 15 July 1905, NAM, MSS Roberts R 87/64; *Morning Post*, 16 and 25 May 1905.
299. Gwynne to Marker, 16 May 1905, BL, Add. 52277B.
300. G.W. Balfour to Spring Rice, 18 Sept. 1904, CC, CASR 1/2.
301. Childers, *Riddle of the Sands*, 97.
302. Ibid., 98.
303. Strachey, *The Spectator*, 20 May 1905, 737.
304. Lee, 9 April 1907, PD IV/172, col. 181; Repington to Haldane, 17 April 1907, RL 44, 118–19.
305. Arnold-Forster, Diary, 13 Nov. 1905, BL, Add. 50352.
306. Lord Wemyss (Lords), PD IV/149, 10 July 1905, cols. 4–12; Lord Newton (Lords), 10 July 1905, PD IV/149, cols. 33–36, Lord Ripon, 10 July 1905, PD IV/149, cols. 44–47; Clarke to Balfour, 8 July 1905, BL, Add. 49701.
307. Ellenborough (Lords), 10 July 1905, PD IV/149, cols. 19–23.
308. Roberts, 12 June 1905, cited in James, *Lord Roberts*, 414; Esher to Sandars, 3 Aug. 1905, BL, Add. 49719.
309. Roberts, 10 July 1905, cited in James, *Lord Roberts*, 414.
310. Ibid., 415–16; see also Roberts, *Speeches and Letters* (1906), passim.
311. Arnold-Forster, 3 Aug. 1905, cited in James, *Lord Roberts*, 417; to Lansdowne, 4 Aug. 1905, BL, LANS/PL 3.
312. Whitaker, *Whitaker's Almanack* 1900, 218.
313. Esher to Balfour, 3 Sept. 1905, BL, Add. 49719.
314. James, *Lord Roberts*, 418.
315. Roberts (Birmingham), 4 April 1907, cited in James, *Lord Roberts*, 423.
316. Esher, 'National Strategy', 1904, CC, ESHR 21/6, 8–9.
317. Macintosh, 'Role of the Committee', 494–95.
318. Ottley to Balfour, 1 March 1905, BL, Add. 49710; Clarke to Balfour, 23 March 1905, BL, Add. 49701; Balfour, Possibility of a Raid, 12 Dec. 1905, NA, CAB 3/1/34A.
319. Clarke to Balfour, 25 March 1905, BL, Add. 49701.
320. Ibid.
321. Clarke to Sandars, 16 May 1905, BL, Add. 49701.
322. Balfour, Possibility of a Raid, 12 Dec. 1905, NA, CAB 3/1/34A.
323. Clarke to Balfour, 16 Dec. 1905, BL, Add. 49702; see also Gooch, 'Sir George Clarke's Career', 558–59.
324. Clarke to Chirol, 14 Sept. 1907, BL, Add. 50832.
325. Clarke to Haldane, 6 Feb. 1905, NLS, MSS 5906.
326. Lyttelton, Memorandum, 23 March 1906: Possibility of a Raid: Remarks by the General Staff, NA, CAB 3/1/36A.
327. Arnold-Forster, Diary, 13 Nov. 1905, BL, Add. 50352.
328. Clarke, Minute, 11 Aug. 1905, NA, CAB 17/43.
329. Again in 1907. See Sydenham, *Life*, 200.

330. Clarke to Balfour, 24 Jan. 1906, BL, Add. 49702.
331. Balfour (Commons), 11 May 1905, PD IV/146, cols. 89–90.
332. Balfour to Lansdowne, 12 Dec. 1901, BL, Add. 49727; Balfour, cited in *The Times*, 26 Feb. 1903.
333. Balfour, Memorandum, 24 Feb. 1905, NA, CAB 17/3.

Chapter 4

IMPERIAL DEFENCE OR CONTINENTAL COMMITMENT?

Deterrence, balance of power or 'appeasement'

Arthur Balfour's calming assessment of the imperial security situation was based on observations made over the course of decades. Since the end of the Crimean War, the comfortable buffer zone more than 2,000 kilometres wide that separated Russia and British India had shrunk by some three quarters.[1] Donald Mackenzie Wallace, foreign correspondent for the *Times* and an expert on Russia, was not alone in believing that Britain faced invasion not only at home but also in Central Asia.[2] Forty-three of the eighty-two sessions of the Committee of Imperial Defence held under the Tories and seventy-five individual memoranda addressed this topic.[3] Alongside domestic defence, the security of India was undoubtedly central to decision making in defence policy in the pre-war decade.[4]

Up until the mid 1890s, Britain's imperial defence strategy had been predicated on the so-called 'Crimean War constellation'[5] and hence on the linking of Central Asia and the European periphery.[6] Should Russia advance towards south-eastern Europe, the Persian Gulf or India, London would respond by entering the Black Sea.[7] This strategy, however, relied on shared interests of Britain, the Triple Alliance and the Ottoman Empire as well as on the dominance of the Royal Navy in the eastern Mediterranean. The strategic connection between the Empire and the continental periphery had been frustrated by the Franco-Russian alliance and by the massive public outrage directed at the sultan's regime as a consequence of the series of pogroms against the Armenians between 1894 and 1896.[8] One result of these pogroms was that the Mediterranean Agreements that had safeguarded the status quo in the Levant and the Ottoman Empire had not been prolonged.[9] Great Power relations in the eastern Mediterranean had thus shifted in favour of

---

Notes for this chapter begin on page 207.

France and Russia. Hence, an operation at the Dardanelles could no longer so readily stand as a threat to be used against Russia and as a means of venting tensions between Russia and Britain. A strategic partial retreat to Cairo ensured that at least the Suez Canal was secured.[10] London's refusal to renew the Mediterranean Agreements meant that Britain forfeited both connections and credibility in Europe, above all in Berlin and Vienna. Without British backing, and in the face of expanding pan-Slavism, especially London's traditional ally Austria-Hungary felt it had been left in the lurch and forced into an agreement with Russia on south-eastern Europe. London, however, believed that future Russian expansionism would require case-by-case decisions on whether to prioritize imperial security in Central Asia or the stability of the Great Powers in Europe. From a global as well as European viewpoint, there seems to be much evidence suggesting that for Britain the real revolution in the states system came not with the foundation of the German Empire or the creation of its High Seas Battle Fleet but with the alliance of Paris and St Petersburg in 1892/94.[11] Succinctly, the head of military intelligence, John Ardagh, recognized that Britain had lost the final handhold that might allow it to maintain the status quo and balance of powers in the Mediterranean or to counter the growing Russian threat in Central Asia at another location through military means.[12] The Franco-Russian Dual Alliance was now unquestionably the dominant alignment among the Great Powers. 'The Triple Alliance', Ardagh noted in October 1896, represented only a 'far weaker grouping'.[13]

While Salisbury had clung to his 'buffer state' concept and the insuperable topography of Nepal and Tibet, the Himalayas and the Pamir Plateau together with Afghanistan and Persia to provide a last line of defence against the Russian tide,[14] the general technological advances in transportation threw considerable doubt on the idea of a natural *cordon sanitaire*. By the turn of the century, even the most inhospitable regions of the world seemed potentially accessible. The government of India painted a dire picture for the India Office of a huge transportation of troops as part of a Russian offensive in northern Afghanistan and through the Persian province of Sistan.[15] Additionally, both the new Emir of Afghanistan and the Shah of Persia were attempting to exploit Anglo-Russian rivalry for their own ends.[16]

This new state of affairs became acute during the Boer War. The enormous costs of the war and questionable performance of the army suggested to many observers that a land-based strategy that could defend India against the largest land army in the world seemed pure fantasy. Moreover, Russia had done more than any other country to exploit the British plight for its own advantage.[17] Barely a month into the South African campaign, Hardinge sent Sanderson alarming news of massive concentrations of troops on the northern frontier of Afghanistan.[18] While the London press focused its attention on the Anglophobia and *Schadenfreude* of the German public,[19] Russia concentrated on deeds not words.[20] The military intelligence branch reported that since early October 1899

St Petersburg had been moving munitions and an estimated 110,000 to 150,000 soldiers from the Caucasus to the northern and western frontiers of Afghanistan.[21] In early 1900, Russia also intensified its political efforts, pressing the shah to enter into an exclusive loan arrangement that ran counter to earlier agreements with London.[22] If that were not already enough, London also suspected that Russia's 'Machiavellian diplomacy' was designed to achieve concessions for the building of roads and railways that would lead towards Bandar Abbas, strategically the most important harbour in the Strait of Hormuz, as well as the right to move additional troops into the Persian-Afghan frontier region of Sistan.[23] In a region in which 'big battalions' and 'money bags'[24] were alone what counted, Russia was gradually but unmistakably seeking to establish a veiled protectorate over the whole of Persia and now seemed to have its eye also on Afghanistan.[25]

Britain was at a double disadvantage. Firstly, Russia was generally reckoned 'semi-Asiatic' and therefore thought at an advantage when it came to influence in Central Asia.[26] Secondly, Russian expansion did not depend on geographical or military conditions alone, for in Paris it had not only a friend but also a solvent and generous financier. The Quai d'Orsay made every effort to support Russian expansionism and strategic railway construction, creating its own legitimate interests in the region in the process.[27] Germany's global ambitions were still something of a puzzle to Whitehall, although the British public had long since passed its own damning verdict, but the government was well aware, from secret reports and its own observations, that the Russian General and Minister for War Aleksei Kuropatkin had in mind an offensive operation that would ensure the gradual conquest of the whole of Central Asia.[28] This offensive approach was confirmed by a Russian sense of mission, publicly articulated and widely noted, that saw the Balkans, the Straits and Central Asia as an interconnected Russian zone of interest.[29] The Russian General Staff announced publicly that if in the foreseeable future Russia was unable to fulfil its principal goal and dominate the Bosporus, then it would have no choice but to advance towards India and the Persian Gulf.[30] Russia's naval and military experts worked feverishly on how the Boer War might be used as an opportunity for a surprise attack on the Dardanelles and the Bosporus.[31] Britain, whose navy was responsible for policing the Pontus clause and safeguarding the Straits,[32] would be left to decide between ensuring the Straits remained militarily closed and protecting the Gulf. Here was a clear case of political and military blackmail of the very type that Eyre Crowe would repeatedly accuse Berlin of.[33]

In view of these alarming developments, the leadership in London quickly identified India as 'the weakest spot in the Empire'. As long as the war in South Africa continued, so ran a commonly shared concern, any open conflict would bring incalculable risks.[34] The War Office intensified the sense of danger with Curzon's and Kitchener's very disturbing reports. Having digested a memorandum by William Robertson, then working for the Foreign Military Intelligence section within the Foreign Office and a close associate of Director of Military

Operations (DMO) William Nicholson, Major Altham, who served with military intelligence, revised his concerns of summer 1902.[35] Now he predicted that the anticipated battle for India would see 292,864 British and Indian soldiers facing an army of around 3.6 million Russians.[36] Hence, only compulsory military service could save the Empire.[37]

In recent years, historians have tended to find the depictions of the potential threat posed by Russia very convincing. The action/reaction model seemed therefore as applicable to imperial defence as it was to home defence, with the pressure from Russia giving London no choice but to seek a settlement and draw closer to the tsardom.[38] Therefore, the convention of 1907 is mainly interpreted as a highpoint, with Lansdowne's discussions with Benckendorff in autumn 1903 simply a precursor of the rapprochement Grey would subsequently pursue. Britain's policy towards Russia can then be judged as a prime example of continuity in foreign policy, leading in this instance from Rosebery and Kimberley via Salisbury and Lansdowne to Grey.[39]

But a closer look raises doubts. What are we to make, for example, of the contemporary discussions on how the threatening situation in the Middle East might be alleviated with as few repercussions as possible, a heated debate that threw up various possibilities? And where is the detailed comparison of the negotiations involving Lansdowne and Benckendorff and the subsequent negotiations involving Nicolson and Izvolsky, which might tell us that the continuity conclusion has been reached somewhat precipitously? The tension between military expertise and consulting vs. politically motivated propaganda extended also to questions of imperial defence, and yet is frequently overlooked. The Indian leadership around Curzon and Kitchener deliberately dramatized the security situation in order to ensure that additional resources were made available to support the reorganization of Indian defence.[40] The War Office also saw an opportunity to raise its profile in the context of its rivalry with the navy.[41] Finally, no less a figure than Ardagh's successor as head of military intelligence, William Nicholson, was quite clear that an exaggerated picture of the Russian danger for the public would produce increased resources for the army and underline its relevance.[42] A closer examination of the evidence revealed that Russia had not transferred between 110,000 and 150,000 soldiers from the Caucasus to Persia as the Military Intelligence Department had initially reported; that figure should have read 2,300.[43] Alarming reports sent directly to the Foreign Office by military attaché Charles E. Beresford[44] nevertheless left an impression on a number of younger diplomats in particular, including Louis Mallet, Eyre Crowe and William Tyrrell and later also Edward Grey, Arthur Nicolson and Charles Hardinge.[45] While not only historians have frequently suggested that Russia had a 10:1 superiority over Britain,[46] William Robertson himself had to concede that Russia did not have a million-strong army at its disposal, ready to be deployed in Central Asia; in fact, Russia planned to draw

190,000 soldiers from the Caucasus, 85,000 from Turkestan and 112,000 from garrisons east of Lake Baikal.[47] Discipline in such a multinational force would present its own challenges,[48] and even with the railway lines already laid, the army still would have to make its way thousands of kilometres to the northern frontier of Afghanistan or into Persia before contemplating a further advance southwards.[49] As was the case with invasion concerns, when the defence of India was raised, little thought was invested in the accuracy of the Military Intelligence Department's assessment.[50] Only current perceptions, at the moment the decision was to be made, were considered important. But what if those views were far from unanimous?

Authoritative figures within the government, men such as Salisbury, Balfour, Selborne and Lansdowne, were evidently apprehensive, but they were not fatalistic.[51] After all, the alliance with Japan concluded in January 1902 had brought some relief and the situation in South Africa was no longer tense.[52] At Westminster, only the India Office under George Hamilton was much concerned by the alarming reports that continued to arrive from Calcutta.[53] Four recommendations were now in the room, three of which significantly differed from Salisbury's wait-and-see attitude. While Hamilton hoped an agreement with the central European Triple Alliance would provide some relief and a political counterpoise against Russia, Curzon and Kitchener called for an offensive strategy that would see Russia forced back behind the Oxus.[54] Power and prestige, to cite Curzon, were the pillars of English supremacy in the East, in dealing with both Orientals and semi-Asiatic Russians.[55]

When British interests in Persia were at issue, the viceroy turned directly to one of his predecessors. Lansdowne understood Curzon's concerns. The two men agreed that the division of Persia into spheres of interest was not the solution, for while Britain would be left with no say in the north, Russia would likely retain its influence in the so-important south,[56] for experience had taught both men that Russia would be unlikely to abide by any such agreement, and at the first opportunity would simply advance further towards the Gulf.[57] Lansdowne did not share, however, Curzon's exaggerated fears about Persia.[58] The Foreign Secretary, who had travelled intensively in the frontier region during his time as viceroy, considered an offensive to be neither possible nor necessary.[59] For Lansdowne, like Salisbury, the status quo in Afghanistan was sufficient, which explains why he deemed that status quo non-negotiable.[60]

All these approaches – the balancing strategy of Hamilton, the offensive strategy of Curzon and Kitchener and the continuous course of Lansdowne – differed greatly from the debate within the public sphere of London and the veritable media campaign triggered by James Garvin, Leo Maxse, Rowland Blennerhasset, Malcolm MacColl or John Strachey backed by correspondents like George Saunders or Henry Wickham Steed.[61] According to them, it was only a matter of time before Russia and Germany would come to an agreement that would be detrimental to Britain.[62] Instead of keeping the balance by joining the Triple Alliance or standing up against Russia, Britain should, they proposed, hold out a hand to Russia, a hand containing very significant concessions. St Petersburg should be offered the Straits along with ports on the Persian Gulf, a proposal that overlapped entirely with the demands of the nationalistic and notoriously anti-English *Novoe Vremja*.[63] 'Whether the future force of Slav expansion is to concentrate against Germany in the Near East or against England in Persia ... depends on our own choice.'[64] If Russia could be distracted with south-eastern Europe, the tsardom and the Central Powers would clash, leaving Britain to look on and smile. Garvin conceded with some regret that the stability of Europe would unavoidably be disturbed,[65] but the security of the Empire left no other option, a view that Edward Grey would later also voice.[66] These calculations were based less on concerns about German hegemony than on a juggling of imperial and continental interests. As things stood, at some point in the middle or long term Britain would surely have to back down before Russia, and therefore a lasting Anglo-Russian agreement seemed advisable.[67] Such a course suggested that the nerves necessary to continue Salisbury's traditional policy of 'drifting' had been lost, but it also suggested that European stability was thought of secondary importance. Such far-reaching concessions were not a variation of the usual balance of power policy; they were a sign of an entirely new approach. Only with the fashioning of a potential threat from Germany could they appear to have been designed to maintain the balance of power in Europe.[68]

What Garvin saw as politically astute foreign policy, the *National Review* turned into grounds for an Anglo-Slav agreement and a strategic build-up of Britain's land forces, to counter an apparently deadly threat from Germany.[69] In this instance, as also in the invasion debate, Germany and its policies served largely as a means to an end, rather than as a trigger.[70] Germany had made no appearance in discussions of the situation in the Middle East, but within the public debate it was given a role, as an integrating influence for Anglo-Russian relations as well as for British politics. The Kaiserreich may have been an unexpected opponent, but it was an opponent held in particular esteem because of its military efficiency. The political sphere in London had long been accustomed to thinking of France and Russia as Britain's traditional enemies, but this new role for Germany, with which London's political circles had numerous personal and family links, brought a new polarization and vigour to its debates. Selborne hit a nerve – a nerve linking domestic, foreign and imperial policy – when, in a speech on the security of the Empire given on 25 February1903, he noted that while the German model of compulsory military service was a noble matter, 'nobody has ever suggested in this or any other country that it is part of the essence of citizenship that a man should be ready to serve his country far away from it – in the tropics or India for instance. The obligation is one of home defence'.[71] Arnold-Forster also recognized that those who canvassed publicly for Anglo-Russian rapprochement were for the most part the very people who preached of the dangers of a German invasion and demanded compulsory military service.[72] This grouping had proved far more realistic than those responsible for the governance of India in recognizing that a break with traditional defence and social policy could not be made for the sake of India alone.

Moreover, onlookers saw a fundamental difference between granting concessions to a superior power because a future defeat at its hands seemed inevitable and granting concessions to a superior power in order to achieve an alliance against an even greater threat. The maintenance of the balance of power had already become a matter of tradition and a readily spouted commonplace rather than a basis for political decision making, where its role was now largely cosmetic. A frequently stated opinion argued that no power in the world could now stand in the way of an Anglo-Russian alliance.[73] Fundamental political beliefs joined forces with immediate concerns and the modern media, which worked with subjective generalizations and endless repetition, and all to Germany's disadvantage, for that country's clumsy foreign policy during the Boer War had turned Germany into an opposite and universal bogeyman. The liberal imperialists around Edward Grey and the Liberal MP for Wolverhampton, Henry Norman, also supported the idea of Anglo-Russian rapprochement. For conciliation towards Russia, they were ready to accept Anglo-German estrangement.[74] The reasoning seemed persuasive. Even a number of radical liberals, including John Morley and William Thomas Stead, were willing to put to one side for the moment their concerns about protecting the commendable Persian democratic movement because they attached greater importance to cutting the Indian defence budget in favour of social reforms.[75] Others, such as Thomas Gibson Bowles, Joseph Walton and the *Daily Mail* correspondent and member of parliament Arthur Lynch, saw the situation in Central Asia as an opportunity to criticize the Conservative government and hold it responsible for an allegedly desperate situation.[76] For the opposition, repeated failures over so many years had left considerable concessions to Russia the only option. For the government, these attacks, in particular when they came from radical liberals, would have seemed contemptible and deceitful given that the demands of the left-liberals for a morally grounded foreign policy had led to the cutting of ties with the Turkish sultan.[77]

A variety of foreign and domestic interests thus lay behind the proposed course of appeasement.[78] Again, however, hopes for the future proved more decisive than real-world experience, as demonstrated by an assessment provided by Charles Hardinge, whom Maxse had requested 'proofread' the A.B.C. articles on British foreign policy. During the five years Hardinge had spent in Teheran and St Petersburg, he had seen for himself how frequently London had been exposed to Russian intrigue. Although he acknowledged how disheartening that experience had been, he continued: 'but I still hope. … I really think there are indications of a more honest desire for an arrangement with England now than there were some time ago'. Why his hopes should be raised at just this moment remained Hardinge's secret. In any case, Britain would have to be the giver, he believed, for Russia's ambitions were evidently not yet satisfied, and, he noted, 'It is safe to say that these will never be satisfied until they have a port in the Gulf'. The motto of future policy on Russia should therefore be 'graceful concessions'. Even access to the Gulf might not suffice, he recognized, for the weight – so difficult to calculate – of Russian public opinion, which as yet lacked a focus, also had a role to play. But, in Hardinge's opinion, that very reason made it all the more important for Britain, using favourable concessions, quickly to take the wind out of the sails of the chauvinistic press, which was openly demanding a military base for an attack on India. His concrete suggestion was an extension of the Qualtah-Nuski railway to Meshed, Kerman and Bandar Abbas. Additionally, Hardinge insisted to Maxse, a policy of disinterest, no small sacrifice, would also help in south-eastern Europe.[79] Important and increasingly influential players in London were thus ready to make considerable concessions to Russia in the hope that they would not be exploited. Evidently, the real concern behind these plans was not German hegemony but supposed Russian strength. Ideally, tensions between Germany and Russia would continue to thrive and agreement between the two countries would be impossible; Britain could then seek to side with the stronger party.

Lansdowne, Sanderson and Balfour could only shake their heads at this idealistic evaluation of Russia and of the bilateral prospects and at the proposals' neglect of the states system.[80] Despite such poor experiences with the tsardom, 'out of sheer good nature', as Lansdowne emphasized, Grey and others, including the Prince of Wales, were even willing to offer Russia access to the Gulf – evidence, surely, of how little thought had been given to possible international consequences.[81] The access Grey had in mind was far from insignificant: with the Clarence Strait and Bandar Abbas, Russia would have at its disposal control of the whole Persian Gulf.[82] And on what grounds might such great trust be invested in Russia? Russia had broken the Berlin Treaty over Batumi and had repeatedly broken its word over Manchuria and Port Arthur. Russia repeatedly sanctioned pogroms against Jews and other minorities. Russia schemed and conspired when it came to the creation of an anti-English continental block, the incitement of tribal leaders in Central Asia, or loans in Teheran that violated contractual terms.[83] Even Eyre Crowe found this policy towards Russia 'abjectly servile'. The number of British attempts to reduce tensions, he informed Maxse, was greater than the latter could imagine, and yet the result had always been the same – nothing but insults, obvious lies and attempts to deceive. He called on Maxse to consider the damage he, Garvin and the others were doing to Britain's negotiating position and standing in the world, compounded by pacifist soapbox speeches made in parliament and constant currying of favour with Russia. For, he noted,

The man whose favourite exercise is to kick you is not likely to be much impressed by the kickee protesting at the top of his voice and all day that the wish of his soul is to be on friendly terms with the kicker. You imagine that by us offering a free hand to Russia in Turkey and Persia, we could conciliate them. It has been tried. The answer is that they don't want to be obliged to us for something which they believe they can in due course of time obtain for themselves.[84]

That view was shared by Lansdowne and Balfour, who called on Hardinge to keep a cool head and remain resolute. Britain's primary concern, Lansdowne noted, must be to secure a buffer zone in Persia and Afghanistan that would be 'sufficient to prevent any direct contact between the armies of Great Britain and Russia'.[85] Charles Scott, Britain's ambassador to St Petersburg, and Hamilton, secretary of state for India, believed that Lansdowne's resolution might eventually see Britain's formerly strong hand restored, but that process would take time, for St Petersburg would first have to recognize 'that they are dealing with a new man who will not accept the language and protests which they have been in the habit of handing in to the FO [Foreign Office]'.[86] In parliament, Viscount Cranborne defended the government's policy against the criticisms of Grey and Norman,[87] repeatedly rejecting any change to the status quo on the Gulf, where for both commercial and political reasons British supremacy could not be challenged.[88] Yes, he shared Thomas Sanderson's opinion that an Anglo-Russian agreement was a worthy goal, but at the same time over the course of forty years he had learned that simply coming to an understanding with Russia was insufficient, and likely to be counterproductive. Only counter-pressure and offensive deterrents had proved able to rein in the tsardom. St Petersburg was unrelenting in testing the powers' resolution, especially as concerned the Straits. Agreements made by treaty, even if guaranteed collectively, had repeatedly proved ineffectual and not even worth the paper they were written on.[89] His assessment was confirmed by diplomats including Spring Rice, O'Connor, Scott, Lascelles and Arthur Hardinge.[90] Somewhat incredulously, Curzon asked Hamilton, who favoured the granting of concessions:

> Do you really believe that it was possible to come to an agreement with Russia about any subject, any continent, or any place in the world? I know too much of her politicians, her generals, her diplomacy, and her national character to believe that any such understanding is possible, or that, if possible, it would last five years.[91]

Arthur Balfour shared this scepticism, for Russia, he noted, was led by the maxim 'that any conciliatory attitude is a weak attitude; and that Great Britain is prepared to make any concession rather than defend her rights by force'.[92] Both diplomats and journalists, including Middle East expert Valentine Chirol, tended to pass withering verdicts on the tsardom to the effect that brute force was the only language this uncivilized land understood.[93] Almost all reports suggested that Russia was a stronghold of barbarism. Even Hardinge, an earlier supporter, as we have seen, of a more benevolent policy towards Russia, the previous year had had no choice but to admit that while the Kaiser was known for his bloodthirsty speeches, the German troops for the most part had behaved correctly during the Boxer Rebellion, and in comparison Russian soldiers 'have committed horrible acts that are beyond description. The Cossack troops were savage and barbarous nomads, just like the Kurds, and the officers were as bad as the men'.[94]

Years of experience and recent events spoke a clear message: much could be expected of Russia but nothing could be guaranteed. Taking account of that reality, the Unionists' approach to Russia followed a maxim that ran, 'negotiate if possible, but stay firm and resolute'. In accord with that approach, Lansdowne, with Selborne and Balfour's full agreement, informed his ambassador at the Porte that Britain was fully committed to defending the status quo at the Straits in future, for it was as good as certain that Austria-Hungary would see the Straits as vital to its interests and if the worst came to the worst London would not be alone. More specifically, he raised the possibility of a revival of the Mediterranean Agreements, and he had already reached an agreement with Selborne regarding the scale of a possible British operation against Russia, on the basis that 'assuming that we cannot prevent Russia from seizing both the Bosporus and the Dardanelles, the best counter-move would probably be the seizure of Lemnos'.[95] He remained opposed, however, to rapprochement or any agreement with Russia, for while the advantages would undoubtedly be significant, the traditional order would be unable to bear the burden.[96]

On 19 November 1902, representatives of the Admiralty, the War Office, the India Office and the Foreign Office came together for a first joint conference on the situation in the Middle East. Its conclusion was depressing: should Russia attack, only a few central points on the Gulf and in Sistan could be secured.[97] Three months later, on 23 February 1903, the Committee of Imperial Defence launched its investigations. Even in the early stages of these meetings, Balfour proved astonishingly well informed about the strategic and political conditions of Indian security and surprisingly little disturbed by the recommendations of his military officers. He determined the structure of the meetings and core questions they addressed, with the focus on Persia and Afghanistan as buffer states. Referring back to earlier investigations, the War Office came to the alarming recognition that thanks to its transportation capabilities, Russia was in a position to move up to 20,000 new soldiers each month to any theatre of war in Afghanistan. This analysis did not consider provisioning bottlenecks, however, with problems of this sort assumed only for British armed forces.[98] Given that a massive diversionary attack elsewhere no longer seemed an option and that since the Sepoy revolt, in 1857, regional units could not be relied upon,[99] the War Office proposed that India's defence be increased dramatically with new forces,[100] advising that whatever else, Curzon's request for troops be met.[101]

Selborne and Kerr ensured that, as he wished, Balfour was fully informed about the strategic importance of the Gulf ports and their significance for the Empire as a whole.[102] Weighing in on the discussion of Gulf ports, Battenberg established that in addition to the bases in the Strait of Hormuz that were already under British control, a good many other locations – over thirty in all – might serve as military ports.[103] All the more disturbing was the discovery that Russia was continuing its strategic construction of railways in the direction of Bandar Abbas and, even more alarming, of Chabahar, which lay beyond British control in the direction of the Arabian Sea (Gulf of Oman). This port had waters deep enough for a battle fleet.[104]

Despite the outlook, and although the anti-German and pro-Russian agitation over the Baghdad railway was making waves,[105] neither Balfour nor Lansdowne, unlike public opinion, saw any reason to curry favour with the tsardom by means of special concessions. Balfour put little faith in his military experts, suspecting again that their real concern was to promote the army. Despite the railway construction at its frontier, Afghanistan remained for Balfour a 'non-conducting territory'. As long as this region remained 'un-Russianised', he declared in a memorandum, British India had nothing to fear.[106] Five years later, Balfour criticized Grey's extensive concessions to Russia as entirely unnecessary:

> The safety of India lies in the fact that before India can be touched any invading force has to go through a region of extraordinary natural difficulty, largely devoid of food, and defended by the most formidable natural barriers. And as long as we can prevent those natural difficulties being surmounted in times of peace, so long in war we shall be relatively secure.[107]

Balfour rejected the forward strategy preached by Curzon not just on financial grounds but also because it made little sense to him – he could see only greater commitments and disproportionate risks.[108] This time it was Lansdowne, no doubt sensitive to the poor handling of public opinion during the Venezuela crisis, who turned to the British public and attempted to calm the waters. His first step was a subtle attempt, via Arminius Vambéry, to moderate concerns about the Russian danger. Russia's policy and its potential implications would be exposed, with education in the facts the way to counter the widespread fatalism.[109] On 5 May 1903, after consulting with Balfour, he went a step further and in the House of Lords declared unequivocally that neither military ports on the Gulf nor any change in the status quo would be tolerated. Historians have read this declaration as a warning to Germany,[110] but its context makes evident that the veto on the stationing of foreign fleets was directed above all at Russia.[111] While the opposition proposed concessions be made and some military officers, in particular Lord Roberts, warned against a repeat of the South African disaster, the government could not bring itself to commit massive and expensive reinforcements.[112] Balfour and Lansdowne went on the offensive only rhetorically. 'We must make up our minds to face that sort of music', Lansdowne stated to Cromer, referring specifically to the demands for rearmament and the press's incitement of anti-German feeling. The lesson he had drawn from the Venezuela crisis and the issue of the Baghdad railway was that a prompt, aggressive and, above all, public statement was necessary: 'I don't want another Bagdad Railway fiasco', he admitted.[113] During the debate in the Lords, the government received unreserved support from Lord Ellenborough and Earl Percy. The latter, a junior minister in the India Office, rejected and strongly condemned the anti-German and pro-Russian agitation in the *National Review*. Addressing Russia in particular, he took the opportunity to declare the Gulf a *mare britannicum*. The *Times*, the *Daily Telegraph* and the *Daily Graphic* congratulated Lansdowne on his plainspoken words,[114] although the *Westminster Gazette* called for a decisive and dynamic policy on southern Persia,[115] while Lord Curzon patted himself on the back because he detected his own constant warnings behind the words of his university friend.[116] Norman, Grey, Strachey and Garvin expressed their disappointment.[117] Hamilton, the secretary of state for India and Percy's superior, who was prepared to let Russia have all the north-western end of the Gulf,[118] was one of the first cabinet members to distance himself from Lansdowne's declaration. 'We shall not keep Russia out of the Persian Gulf. I think the forces behind her are too strong.'[119]

Nonetheless, the timing, content and nature of Lansdowne's declaration were well chosen, for they were very much in accord with the principle that proposed readiness to come to an understanding should be demonstrated but only within narrow guidelines and traditional limits. And success followed, for on the day after the speech in the Lords, Count Benckendorff called on Lansdowne and assured him that St Petersburg harboured no intentions in Persia and that the positioning of the railways was entirely coincidental. On learning of what had taken place in the foreign secretary's office, Curzon expressed surprise that his old friend had not fallen off his chair in gales of laughter at the Russian ambassador's 'first class joke'.[120] Lansdowne's strategy ran: keep calm and make your position strong. That strength was to be reiterated by the launch of Anglo-French negotiations, which did not, as so often maintained, serve as a response to suspected German ambitions,[121] but were intended to send a further signal to Russia. At the beginning of July, Delcassé promised to exert a moderating influence on Russia, precisely as Lansdowne had hoped.[122] The subtlety of this approach distinguished Lansdowne from his successor Grey, for diplomatically it made an enormous difference whether France had a moderating influence on its Dual Alliance partner or whether Britain itself attempted to buy Russia with concessions. Lansdowne certainly also wanted an agreement with Russia, but when it came to what that agreement should look like, how it might be achieved and what it might cost, he disagreed entirely with the opposition's approach. His success in the short term appeared to justify his method, for Benckendorff now made frequent requests for an agreement on the Far East and the Middle East. Whitehall had him wait, and in the middle of October gave a further indication of how it imagined their cooperation might look. Japan was to be granted a special loan for the purchase of two battleships, a step that Lansdowne recognized could certainly be regarded by the Russians as an open declaration of war, 'but', he continued, 'she is behaving so badly to us that I should not much mind that. The result might be that she could not safely continue to flout us, and to bring about what I always wanted to see: a frank understanding between us as to Manchuria, Tibet, Afghanistan, Persia etc.'.[123]

Two weeks later – Benckendorff had recently returned to London with new instructions – the Russian ambassador formally requested exploratory talks on an agreement.[124] Lansdowne was convinced that St Petersburg had been led to commission Benckendorff to look for an agreement by Britain's resolute attitude and by the announcement of the purchase of two Chilean battleships at anchor on the Tyne. He informed Cromer, 'I do not, however, at all regret that we should have succeeded in irritating them [the Russians] and I feel pretty sure that we shall not thereby have at all diminished the prospects of an agreement'.[125]

Balfour, who was far more sceptical about Russia than was Lansdowne, did not hold out much hope for the talks, but he backed his foreign secretary completely. 'Appeasement' was not on the cards, whatever Curzon might claim as he reflected retrospectively on the negotiations held in summer 1904,[126] and historians have been far too rash in identifying these talks as a direct precursor of, or forming a continuity with, Edward Grey's later convention policy.[127] That conclusion suggests an over-concentration on the macro-level and on the simple existence of an approach between the two countries and a failure to explore the micro-level, so important in diplomatic circles, that concerned the exact form of the interaction, the content of the negotiations and the nuances of the standing and rank of those representing each party at the negotiations, the factors that determined the level of continuity for those involved. Moreover, especially in the case of traditionally hostile or suspicious powers, symbolic gestures could make all the difference.

In the last quarter of 1903, the British foreign secretary negotiated with Ambassador Benckendorff in London, although, and significantly, only at the request of the latter.[128] This situation was therefore very different from that into which Nicolson would enter three years later. Despite its financial problems, in 1903 Russia was at the zenith of its imperial might, and Lansdowne was the recipient of doom-laden prophecies from his defence experts in relation to Russia's absolute strength and Britain's relative military superiority. Three years later, Russia was on its knees while Britain was at its strongest and had never been more secure since Trafalgar. Yet it was Nicolson, British ambassador to St Petersburg, who now approached Izvolsky to request negotiations. In diplomatic terms, the status and potential advantages of a negotiating partner are signalled by such subtle indicators, often present not in the negotiations themselves but in the run-up to those negotiations and on their sidelines. Certainly, Nicolson's approach would have had a considerable effect on Izvolsky, whose reputation for personal vanity preceded him.

Lansdowne, by contrast, was negotiating with a strong, self-assured power from which a good number of his compatriots expected a declaration of war at any moment and which appeared to many to have the advantage. But Lansdowne did not retreat one inch from his demands that the status quo, and therefore Britain's position of strength, be retained in Afghanistan and the Gulf,[129] and he put Benckendorff under additional pressure with word of an official protest, yet to be dispatched, about Russian intrigue in Central Asia.[130] Balfour's position was not so much that he favoured a forward policy in Central Asia but that he was against anything that might make Britain appear to be backing down. In this region, he believed, prestige counted for more than expeditionary forces and battleships combined.[131] Lansdowne was certainly more inclined than his prime minister to look for an agreement on the buffer zone as a whole, but he left no doubt as to who would set the terms. Both politicians saw Russia's 'insidious' expansion as a 'slowly creeping tide' that could not be stopped by military or political measures alone.[132] A middle way had to be found, an approach that would take into account, on the one hand, experiences of dealing with the tsardom and its representatives and, on the other hand, the role, prestige and possibilities associated with the Empire. They saw, however, no reason to give up and certainly no reason to hand over gifts. 'Until Russia moves we remain still', as Balfour agreed to Lansdowne.[133]

Grey, Hardinge and Nicolson negotiated, as we shall see, under reverse conditions, conditions that the Russo-Japanese war had made far more favourable for Britain, and yet they lost ground and authority by turning to St Petersburg as suppliants and by hinting that the Straits could be up for debate. Lansdowne, by contrast, offered absolutely no concessions on the periphery of Europe, indeed never said a word on the subject throughout the course of the negotiations.[134] Lansdowne even spoke of the Straits to Hayashi, the Japanese ambassador, as a *casus belli*.[135] For Lansdowne, the only place concessions might be made was in the Far East, where he could grant Russia a new deadline for the withdrawal of its troops from Manchuria.[136] India might be for Russia 'too big a mouthful to swallow',[137] but in light of their very different interests in Europe, Russia still remained Britain's principal enemy. The tsardom was still reckoned the power most likely to disturb the peace of the continental states system.[138] On the whole, Lansdowne and Balfour adhered considerably more strongly to the traditional guidelines than would Grey; Salisbury too had demonstrated no great interest in the Far East. As regards Persia, Lansdowne continued down a path established by Salisbury. Lansdowne was willing to admit Russian control in the north – the situation on the Caspian Sea meant the Russian position was unassailable – but Britain must continue to call the shots in the south. Russian involvement in the south would be limited to mercantile interests; Russian ports, Bandar Abbas and railway lines were simply not on the agenda. But they would be subsequently under Grey.[139] Dominance that allowed other parties to trade was acceptable, but Balfour, so unlike the later convention, firmly rejected the division of Persia into spheres of interest. Balfour favoured instead the natural stalemate according to which London had 'nothing to give and nothing to take away'.[140] A change in the status quo in Afghanistan and Tibet was also bluntly ruled out. To delay the long-anticipated conflict with Russia, Balfour opined, Britain must stand up in good time and resolutely to the tsardom,[141] but at the same time lines of communication must be left open. His maxim decreed a policy of strength and concessions only when they had no impact on Britain's vital interests or essential arrangements. Britain's control of the Gulf region must remain absolute. Lansdowne demanded that Russia withdraw completely from Afghanistan, Sistan and Tibet, and at the end of November Benckendorff indicated that he was willing to agree.[142]

From War Games at Simla to Anglo-French Staff Talks

London may have opted for composure and resolution in dealing with Russia, but India produced its own drama. To back up its calls for massive reinforcements, the Indian military leadership planned a war game, with an operation carried out in Simla in November 1903.[143] The scenario involved some 300,000 Russian troops being transported via the Orenburg-Tashkent railway, which was on the point of completion, to Afghanistan's northern frontier and then advancing unhindered through Afghanistan to Kabul. Nine divisions were assumed to be available for the defence, and their main task would be to maintain the Kabul-Kandahar line, as the unanimous verdict held that whoever had military control of this line not only controlled the whole of Afghanistan but also secured the access route to India, the Bholan Pass south-east of Quetta and the Khyber Pass between Kabul and Peshawar.[144] The outcome of the operation was deemed clear cut: the 150,000 Indian and English soldiers had proved unable to halt the Russian forces. And the broader conclusion seemed equally clear: an invasion of India could not be prevented without additional troops from Britain. As expected, the military officers in India proposed immediate reinforcement in the form of an expeditionary force of at least 100,000 men,[145] and were soon joined in their appeal by the War Office and the Committee of Imperial Defence.[146] Neville Lyttelton, head of the General Staff, saw these events as an opportunity to demand yet again the introduction of compulsory military service.[147] In Admiral Fisher's view, the army lobby was rolling out its bogeyman once more.¹⁴⁸ Historians have largely deemed the exaggeration successful and argue that Balfour was 'overawed with Russia',¹⁴⁹ yet this view is not supported unambiguously by the sources. All that could be taken for granted was that Russia was not an open target.¹⁵⁰ Considering the Empire's vulnerable flanks, Balfour differentiated between Persia and Afghanistan, and in the latter case saw no grounds for precipitous panic. On the whole, in spring and summer 1904 he seemed not entirely convinced that the threat was real, which would explain why in April 1904, as the first reports arrived from Simla, he entrusted the intelligence branch at the War Office with carrying out its own investigation.¹⁵¹ Supported by Selborne and Lansdowne, he continued to insist on buffer zones and demonstrations of strength.¹⁵² At the end of October, in the wake of the Dogger Bank incident, he was even reckoning on a possible military conflict.¹⁵³ He was encouraged by George Clarke, his principal military advisor, who quickly and contrary to his own colleagues at the War Office advised the prime minister not to read too much into the outcome of the war games,¹⁵⁴ which he deemed 'wholly inadequate'¹⁵⁵ and saw as simply another propaganda move, especially as Kitchener was soon increasing the demand for 100,000 soldiers up to 160,000. Clarke accused the military of exploiting a purely theoretical simulation for populist and propaganda purposes, and he also noted that the Boer War had already shown that terrain was decisive for any military campaign. Clarke thus brought to the table an argument that deserves far greater attention than it has received to date, partly because the emphasis on the political angle made the accuracy of the planning staff's analysis appear irrelevant¹⁵⁶ and partly because geography as a factor in the strategic development of railways has generally been too readily dismissed.¹⁵⁷ The analysis of the operation in Simla had been based on the improved transportation that had come with the completion of the railway lines to Kushka (1899) and Tashkent (1904), which pincer-like appeared to have secured the Russian deployment zone in Afghanistan.¹⁵⁸

'The whole Central Asian question is practically one of railways',¹⁵⁹ the Intelligence Department concluded.¹⁶⁰ If the difficult geography of the region was acknowledged at all – by either contemporary army lobbyists or historians – then it was only to testify to the precarious, perhaps even impossible situation that British India faced.¹⁶¹ But does the contrary then also hold, that all the advantages were Russia's? Would not the two sides face the same climate and geography? The logistical challenges for the concentration of several hundred thousand soldiers would be enormous, and caused even General Aleksei Kuropatkin to doubt the feasibility of a Russian invasion of Central Asia.¹⁶² The majority of the Russian army would have to be brought south on the trans-Caspian railway from the Caucasus, yet not only was that line cut by the Caspian Sea, with never enough steamers available at Baku to transport several divisions across the lake, but the 1,700 kilometres from Krasnowodensk to Kushka and the 1,900 kilometres to Tashkent were single-track and plagued by land erosion.¹⁶³ Combine these factors with the standard calculation that suggests that a war-ready infantry battalion of 1,000 men together with all its equipment would require a complete military train with forty-five wagons,[164] and the fantastic nature of an attack by an army of 300,000 becomes clear. Even were this months-long deployment to run smoothly – and, of course, be kept secret – that was only the beginning. The real challenge was yet to come. Earlier studies seem to suggest that Russia would then have reached the gates of India: 'This was the great age of railway building; when the Russian network was completed', Zara Steiner and Keith Wilson agree, convinced that 'her troops and supplies could be moved through Kandahar or Kabul'.[165] In particular, the 'Kandahar access point' on the trans-Caspian railway to Kushka was 'only 483 miles from Kandahar'.[166] Yet even a quick glance at a topographical map will reveal why George Clarke emphasized that Afghanistan was 'a most difficult country on account of its natural features and a most undesirable country for occupation by any power'.[167] Transfer the distances between Kushka and Kandahar or between Tashkent and Kabul to the central European lowlands and then, indeed, they seem inconsequential. But such distances are a very different matter when they lie in their entirety more than 1,000 metres above sea level, with the route from Kushka to Kandahar running through the foothills of the Hindukush and 200 miles through a great salt desert, and that from Tashkent and Kabul crossing massifs 3,000 to 4,000 metres high that for seven to eight months of the year are covered in snow and ice and during the rest of the year can be unbearably hot and dry. Richard Temple, former governor of Bombay, who in January 1899 had looked closely at the threat on the north-west frontier, explained that the concentration of forces assumed in the Simla war game was simply not possible because the northern route over the Hindukush was only passable in the four summer months, while the track through the salt desert from the west could only be used in winter.[168]

'Only 483 miles' in a region with no passable roads[169] and therefore no possibility of maintaining smooth-running supply lines, let alone moving the vital heavy artillery, meant that an operation was impossible before it had even begun. For Britain, that same situation provided an invaluable natural defence system, which was all the more secure because Russia could not count on support from local populations. Indeed, Balfour reckoned that were Herat to fall – which would have to happen before Russia could even think of advancing further – the Russian soldiers would find themselves embroiled in a guerrilla war with local Afghan tribes,[170] and the Boer War had left no one in any doubt what that would mean.

Clarke set to work and, in consultation with Balfour, re-examined the conclusions of Simla and took a magnifying glass to the possible threat from Russia. His conclusion was unambiguous. As Afghanistan could not provision an army, any forces would be completely dependent on traditional camel caravans.[171] The Indian army would therefore be at an inestimable advantage, for it not only controlled the only hard-surfaced road over the strategically vital Khyber Pass, but it could also use the only double-track railway lines in Central Asia for transportation right up to the potential scene of the conflict, railway lines that linked Peshawar and Quetta with the most significant centres in India. As Temple concluded, compared with all the strains the Russian soldiers would face, the British soldiers might think 'they were in Hyde Park'.[172] Given the direct links with headquarters in Simla, Bengal, Bombay and Madras, there was nothing to prevent the immediate deployment of 90,000 soldiers.[173] Railways were indeed decisive, but not, as previously assumed, to Russia's advantage, but rather to its disadvantage.

On the basis of empirically established figures for Indian troops, Clarke calculated that transportation and provisioning alone for 155,000 soldiers – just half the number that had been assumed – would require over five million camels in the course of a year.[174] The scenario employed at Simla was therefore impossible simply on the grounds that so many troops could not be adequately supplied.[175] With analytical and mathematical precision, Clarke also calculated the danger British India might face in a worst-case scenario. With no railway network in Afghanistan, even under the most favourable meteorological preconditions Russia would never be able to supply more than 6,000 soldiers in Kabul in summer or more than 1,500 in the harsh winter months for any length of time.[176] With such inadequate forces, military control of the circa 500-kilometre front between Kabul and Kandahar was well-nigh impossible, to say nothing of an advance towards India.[177] The envisioned operations at division strength did not stand up to close scrutiny. Selborne, Balfour and Lansdowne had suspected from the start that other motives had determined the conclusions drawn from the war games, and Clarke provided the supporting evidence. Balfour was left in no doubt that just like the nightmare scenario predicted by the 'bolt from the blue' school, the Simla simulation said more about individual interests than about Britain's defensive realities.[178]

In Central Asia, Anglo-Russian relations were at a military stalemate, and London and Calcutta could confidently have left it at that. Natural features already provided the desired buffer zone.[179] Concessions to Britain's Russian rivals were neither indispensable nor inescapable and were firmly rejected by Balfour, who believed they would be politically counterproductive and were militarily unnecessary; in view of Britain's reputation in the region, he agreed with Curzon and other advisors who had experience of the East that they might also serve as an invitation to insurrection. At the same time, however, he had to keep one eye on the already questionable stability of his coalition government.[180] The *little Englander* reproach could be aimed at liberal pacifists, but was also much favoured by conservative publicists who demanded predictability and a strong stance in both political and military matters. Even Balfour could not in the long run ignore the repeated calls from Kitchener and other popular war heroes for a massive reinforcement of Britain's military capabilities to prevent a repeat of what had happened in the Boer War.[181] Although Balfour fundamentally agreed with Clarke that the demand for over 160,000 soldiers was absurd, his response had to be politically astute.[182] The policies favoured by Balfour, whose security memoranda were praised by Clarke as 'oases of common sense in an academic desert',[183] were determined by imperial obligations, flexible political interests, domestic and economic circumstances, and by Britain's actual security; dogmatic rules, personal vanities, unpredictable eventualities and purely theoretical projections had no place. He had good reason to turn frequently to his military advisors, yet repeatedly he was forced to recognize that their analysis had little basis in the reality that his extensive studies had revealed and was contrary to common sense. He was as little convinced that Russia would be able to cross the Hindukush as he was of an invasion 'bolt from the blue'.

Balfour's plan for the army of 19 December 1904 was therefore not an expression of weakness[184] but a compromise formulation and a political signal both external and internal. Externally, the plan documented Britain's readiness to assert its hegemony in the region. Internally, the plan indicated that Balfour was willing to move a little towards Kitchener and those responsible for the administration of India but without accommodating their demands wholesale, for the expeditionary force was to be kept to only 91,000 men, the number Arnold-Forster considered feasible.[185] In Balfour's opinion, in addition to the voluntary forces, the Empire required altogether 209,000 well-trained professional soldiers, of whom 27,000 were to defend the Mother Country, 30,000 were to man the 'thin red line' of the bases and garrisons throughout the world and 52,000 were to be stationed permanently in India; the additional 100,000 men would be held ready for deployment as a swift expeditionary force anywhere in the world.[186] Anything larger he deemed unnecessary, and certainly neither politically nor financially feasible.[187] And the best defence strategy was a policy of wait and see.[188]

For Clarke, however, now secretary at the Committee of Imperial Defence, the army plan went too far in the wrong direction. Why spend all these millions of pounds when for the next twenty years Russia would be paralysed both militarily and financially?[189] The main point of difference was that while Clarke found fault with both the internal signal to the army and the external signal to Calcutta, the prime minister was minded to send a message to Russia and the other powers. In place of concessions that might prevent the Great Powers from forming an anti-British block, Balfour counted on a 'policy of a big Navy, and efficient Indian army, and a perfectly clear intimation to Russia that the invasion of Afghanistan means war with England'.[190] When the focus was Persia, the concern was again with a demonstration of power across the whole region and for the connections with the continent. Balfour commented: 'Even if Russia found India too big a mouthful to swallow she [Russia] perhaps felt that by establishing her strategic superiority along the frontiers of India the British Government would be so much afraid of her in Asia as to become her humble servant in Europe'.[191] This precise impression, with the risk it might spur Russia into action, was to be avoided at all costs.[192] Retreat, resignation or even fearfulness were entirely absent; here was determination to face up to Russia if necessary. For Balfour, the security of the Empire was the priority, for the security of the Empire would ensure the security of Europe.

For Clarke and the new General Staff, by contrast, the role to be played by the land forces was the vital factor. As an adviser on military policy, in recent months Clarke had repudiated the invented drama of the invasion-theory adherents and disputed the exaggerated German threat, providing Balfour with arguments he could use to counter the excessive demands and Lansdowne with a self-confidence in his negotiations with Benckendorff. The maintenance of a peacetime army for an improbable emergency, which might occur only twice in any century in any case, was to Clarke's mind extremely damaging,[193] and he emphasized the need for a reconceptualization of the army and a new description of its responsibilities. Tailoring the function of the army to the defence of India might be justified on the grounds of foreign policy, but to his mind that role was not at all suited to providing the army with a new identity and sense of purpose when defence of the homeland was no longer its priority.[194] The army had to be found a new task, and in proposing that it could be actively involved on the continent, Clarke found his views in accord with those of the army leadership.

At the beginning of February 1904, with Lord Roberts' retirement and the establishment of a new General Staff, the army's attitude towards the continent had shifted. Like Clarke, the new army leadership, which was focused on Neville Lyttelton and Major General James Grierson, new director of military operations, was very concerned to see a modern army take shape and to establish its value for the defence of Britain's global empire. At the head of the army was now a new generation of 'thinking soldiers'.[195] Having fought in South Africa and grown up in 'Robert's nursery', Henry Wilson,[196] William Robertson, James Grierson, William Nicholson and Charles Repington, their mouthpiece, were all characterized by an aggressive professionalization, which they used to challenge the dominance of the Admiralty.[197] The great continental military powers were their model.[198] They looked constantly to a future conflict in which the honour of the army would be restored. Clarke might term the scenarios in the Middle East that they sketched simply 'arrant nonsense',[199] but they would not, indeed could not, set them aside, and they continued to spread the idea of a Russian invading army at least 250,000 men strong.[200] Their focus, however, was not on rearmament and the establishment of an army one million men strong; they sought a reorientation and withdrawal from regions that threatened to replicate the experiences of the Boer War and held out no real hope of victory. While Salisbury, Balfour and Lansdowne always emphasized the political and strategic connections between empire and continent, the military leadership were of one mind with the advocates of an Anglo-Russian accord on the separation, or exchange, of these zones of interest. From mid 1904, the newly appointed DMO James Grierson, in particular, sought to focus the role of the army on Europe.

India had lost much of its attraction for the younger generation of officers, partly because the dramatization of its security situation had been going on for years, but also because of the lower pay, the dependency on unpredictable auxiliary units and the less favourable career prospects. The policing of regional unrest was hardly a matter of fame and honour. Gruelling struggles for position in inaccessible mountain regions inevitably recalled de Wet's guerrilla tactics in South Africa. Moreover, the military officers were less interested in all that was impossible for the Russian army than all that was denied the British army. Repeatedly, they stressed how difficult it would be for soldiers in India to fight against Russia given the rough terrain; that the prospects for Russia were far worse was allowed to fade into the background.

One explanation may lie in the dominance, in both military and political terms, of attack strategy, an expression of the cult of the offensive evident in the fixation on the Kabul-Kandahar line. Despite the Boer War, the English planning staff evidently still thought in terms of clear fronts. A defensive strategy, a product of the terrain and limited to the small number of mountain passes, was hardly part of the officers' visions of glory and honour.[201] Additionally, the command structures for the Indian army and the British army were thoroughly unsatisfactory; with no formal means of coordination in place, competition rather than cooperation tended to be the rule.[202] The priorities set by Balfour met all the more resistance from the new members of the General Staff because in December 1903 he had informed Kitchener that the regular forces' principal purpose was not the defence of Britain: it existed, he explained, '(1) almost entirely for the defence of India, (2) the retention of South Africa, (3) conceivably (but only barely conceivably) for the defence of Canada, and (4) for the purpose of small expeditions against Naval Stations and Colonies of other Powers'.[203]

One year later, shortly before the announcement of the new plan for the army, Selborne confirmed that the investigations into the threat of invasion had made evident that the regular army was needed not for the defence of the homeland but for the defence of India.[204] Alarm bells rang for the General Staff. Now the problem was no longer just the Royal Navy but also Kitchener's army. If London complied with his demands, then Kitchener would have an authority that put the authority of the General Staff in the shade. Grierson, too, now recognized that the years of exaggerating the danger from Russia could in the end prove harmful to the British army at home.[205] Clarke got to the heart of the matter in his warning to Balfour when he spoke of India as the most important partner in the defence of the Empire.[206] The time had come, he believed, when he must support the new General Staff against the prime minister. Yet while Clarke spoke of troops that could be deployed worldwide, Grierson was already calling for a 'striking force' directed at Europe, which would be a 'projectile fired by the Navy' and come under new 'joint planning'.[207] Grierson, a former military attaché in Berlin, had already been convinced in 1900 that war with Germany was inevitable, and since then had constantly called for an army on the German model, thinking he then brought to the General Staff. On Grierson's initiative, in January 1905 a conference of the General Staff was held in Camberley, at which the army redirected its focus from Central Asia to Europe and spoke in favour of 'joint planning', and not only with the British navy, but even, and for the first time, with France. Grierson ordered a war game to be held in April and May that year, with one of its principal tasks to shed light on a Franco-German war and the neutrality of Belgium.[208] Here, then, are the origins of the much-cited interactions between the British and French General Staff that took place between December 1905 and May 1906, often identified as reaction to the Morocco crisis, which was not triggered by Germany until two months after the first exchanges.[209]

The government was still some way off viewing Germany as a probable opponent, and Lansdowne and Balfour saw the Entente Cordiale as an entirely colonial matter, and highly unstable at that. Independently and of its own accord, the General Staff found a new orientation. Right up until the preceding October, its preference had been for war against France, rather than an entente with Paris.[210] The change of thought came from within and was a product of the atmosphere in the London political sphere. German activities undoubtedly contributed but not as much as generally thought; only subsequently would German policy on Morocco have a cataclysmic impact on developments already underway. Initially decisive for the army, then, was neither the Morocco crisis nor the much-debated issue of who knew what, and when, about the initiation of the General Staff discussions.[211] What was important was that the army leadership believed itself to have a far more favourable starting position – military, psychological and political – vis-à-vis Germany than vis-à-vis Russia. In the middle of March, and therefore still two weeks before the beginning of the Morocco crisis, on his own authority Grierson assured his French colleagues of British support in the case of a Franco-German conflict.[212] The middleman between the English generals and the French military attaché was none other than Charles Repington of the *Times*, who, moreover, even presented himself at the French embassy as representing the British War Office. That Thomas Sanderson in the Foreign Office knew nothing of his role is perfectly possible, but it is inconceivable that Repington was acting completely on his own initiative, without the knowledge of Grierson and Lyttelton.[213]

None of these steps had been officially approved; indeed, to the contrary, in an addendum to his army plan, Balfour had rejected any thought of a European alignment.[214] When, somewhat surprised, Sanderson asked whether consultations had already been held or agreements been reached, Grierson simply lied.[215]

Clarke looked for retrospective approval when, in late July, he called Balfour's attention to the situation in Europe and asked that he have Belgium's neutrality examined in light of international law. Balfour was highly sceptical, and only on 19 September 1905, after Clarke had approached him repeatedly, did he agree, with great reluctance and little interest; the delay is indicative that he thought the whole business unnecessary. He had been restrained by both Sanderson and Roberts as well as by his own priorities.[216] Clarke himself admitted that whether Germany was a threat was inconsequential; the real concern was to ensure that the army was given realistic and practical responsibilities, for he noted: '*a study of this kind* [a reference to deployment in Europe] *is just what the general staff would like, and they might be able to achieve more success than in dealing with the Indian frontier*' [emphasis original].[217] The experts concluded that Germany would violate Belgian neutrality only if the situation was desperate.[218]

The change of strategy was underpinned by the interconnectedness of continent and the Empire, for the experts recognized that an alliance with France would oblige its Russian ally to observe at least a 'benevolent neutrality' on the north-west frontier of India, rendering that frontier secure.[219] At the same time, Russia's temporary weakness as a consequence of the Russo-Japanese war led to the impression of a necessary backing of France in Europe. The redirection away from the Empire and towards Europe cannot be explained simply by the action/reaction model, or by German aggression or superiority, or by a need to maintain the balance of power alone. Put simply, Europe also provided greater prospects for military success. For the army, for military organization, for propaganda purposes and for political reasons – and in light of repeated diplomatic errors such as Wilhelm II's journey to Tangiers – Germany made a far better enemy than Russia. Traditional naval strategy could be retained, while the younger army officers deemed the potential theatre of war, the likely symmetrical conduct of that war and their prospective opponent all considerably more attractive than the unpredictable Central Asian alternative. India's monopoly on Britain's military thinking would be ended. Now, without international compulsion, the General Staff adopted Germany as Britain's new enemy. An inevitable British reaction to German sabre-rattling, though reasonable at first sight, therefore seems rather insufficient on second thoughts.

Edward Grey and Richard Haldane recognized that a continental strategy would give the Entente Cordiale greater potency. Grey not only held that the talks could provide a political guideline, but also explicitly expressed that view to the French ambassador.[220] Balfour had little taste for either such candour or the proposed strategy. He trusted neither France[221] nor its army officers an inch, and with the best will in the world could see no necessity for anything more than diplomatic support for France, or for making any potential additional support public.[222] Again, his experiences were essential to his decision making, and those experiences only confirmed his scepticism about the army's advice.[223] He countered objections to the Russian focus of his army plans by insisting that the Russian-Japanese war had not altered the reality that 'a struggle with Russia being the most formidable of probable wars, calculations based upon it will suffice for any war of lesser magnitude'.[224]

In the end, Balfour only reluctantly authorized an investigation of Belgian neutrality, and his reluctance was even greater when it came to the Anglo-Russian entente demanded by Charles Hardinge, which Hardinge, anticipating Grey's later choice of words, termed a 'natural complement' to the Entente Cordiale.[225] In summer and autumn 1905, Spring Rice, too, along with publicists including Chirol, Garvin and Strachey and some of the younger staff at the Foreign Office, among them Louis Mallet and William Tyrrell, tried to convince Lansdowne and Balfour to create closer ties between Britain and Russia.[226] Even or rather because of Russia being weakened by defeat and revolution, the prime minister and foreign secretary were not to be diverted from their course. While they agreed that signs might be given that indicated British openness to such a possibility,[227] they were in no doubt about who must make the first approach and about the necessary conditions for such a lasting agreement.[228] Objectively, Russia had been weakened, but to them it remained Britain's major potential opponent. In the speech he gave in the House of Commons on 11 May on the invasion theory, Balfour also noted the reassuring situation in Central Asia, the essential background to the continuation of Conservative policy towards Russia. He ruled out the possibility of an invasion of India, a spectre that had haunted so many previous governments, even despite the new railways, whose significance, he insisted, had been greatly exaggerated 'by those who read too hastily the lessons of the war now going on in Manchuria'. And indeed, only a few weeks later diplomats MacDonald and Durand would propose that the Trans-Siberian Railway had made it possible for Russia to keep 250,000 or even 500,000 soldiers permanently in the field.[229] Balfour disagreed, to put it mildly. The comparison was not apposite, for Manchuria was very fertile – yet even there provisioning faced bottlenecks[230] – and the Trans-Siberian Railway could transport soldiers right into the conflict zone. Charles Dilke, former under-secretary of state at the Foreign Office and an acknowledged expert on international relations,[231] confirmed Balfour's views by citing Sir Thomas Holdrich, the well-known geographer, whose studies had proved that given the difficult terrain and the hostility of the local population, the construction of a railway through Afghanistan was impossible.[232] An invasion, Dilke agreed, could therefore be ruled out completely.[233]

All in all, by 1905 neither Britain's home security nor security in Central Asia gave cause for serious concern or reasons for a paradigm change in foreign policy or defence policy. Where Balfour's response to the theories about a possible invasion garnered him much criticism, his conclusions about the Empire were received with significant equanimity, although Colonel Sandys, a former officer in the Indian army, deemed India 'gone for good', while Kitchener raged against what he interpreted as Balfour's defeatism.²³⁴ Analysis of the Conservatives' foreign policy therefore has to recognize that Balfour was personally convinced that Russia would exploit any concession and that he saw no need to take action to maintain the balance of power on behalf of the weakened tsardom.²³⁵

These insights lay behind Lansdowne and Balfour's refusal at the end of October 1905 to broaden the Entente to include Russia, let alone extend it on the continent. 'Their [the Russians'] idea of an agreement with us', Sanderson declared to Charles Hardinge, the leading advocate at the Foreign Office of closer Anglo-Russian relations, 'has always been that they should have everything they wanted with our assistance, or at our expense, and that we should be content with anything we could get out of their remainder'.²³⁶ Just how correct he was is made evident by a report from Hardinge, of all people, in which he recorded of his Russian colleague Mr Wlassow that he was wont to say 'that the advocates of the Russian forward policy in the Middle East placed all their hopes in the event of a Liberal Government in England, which was sooner or later to come about'.²³⁷

The Liberal government would adopt an entirely different approach. Instead of taking Clarke's calculations into account, the new government simply ignored them. A further investigation, in which Morley and Asquith were involved, now along with Haldane and Grey as permanent members of the Committee of Imperial Defence, was undertaken from January to May 1904. The conclusions of this liberal imperial defence committee have been widely accepted by historians for decades,²³⁸ yet this was an investigation that disavowed the lessons that could be learned from the Russo-Japanese war, and even, quite remarkably, proposed that Russia without railways would do a better job of supplying its forces than Britain, with the railways of India, could manage for its troops.²³⁹ Once again, for such had also been the case for Balfour's memorandum on the invasion theory,²⁴⁰ objective conclusions were ignored or misconstrued. And yet a reassuring security situation would have meant a stronger negotiating position in relation to Russia. At the beginning of their term in office, the leadership among the Limps, who had been seeking an agreement with Russia for over a decade, were apparently happy to use a narrative of threat to internal party ends – the disarmament demands of the radicals could be defused, while an Anglo-Russian rapprochement was made to appear all the more necessary.

That inward-looking conclusion is reinforced by John Morley's reaction at the end of the Hague Conference. In 1907, Morley, who would later be critical of an excessively Russophile course, noted how useful it was that the demands of the army and the Indian government for greater military investment and the calculations of the Committee of Imperial Defence on the defence of India seemed so utopian and so horrifying; in view of Russian dominance, the War Office considered the mere existence of a British army in Central Asia to be pointless.²⁴¹ Morley saw here an irrefutable argument that favoured the supporters of an

Anglo-Russian agreement and was unhelpful to the many anti-Russian sceptics. In his view, if Britain would never be in a position to defend the Indian frontier against Russia, then at some point and at whatever price, peace would have to be made with an autocracy. 'That is the fundamental argument for the Convention', he acknowledged, 'for we have not got the men to spare and that's the plain truth of it'.[242] One would simply have to swallow the sacrifice of a stronger negotiating position with Russia, the criticism that would follow concessions to Russia, and the repercussions for the European centre.

Notes

1. CID, 30 Dec. 1902, NA, CAB 39/1/14.
2. As a result of the defeat against Japan, Wallace thought, Russia's territorial expansion 'will re-appear soon', either 'in Central Asia' or 'in the direction of the Bosporus'. Wallace, *Russia* (1905), 627, esp. 635.
3. See NA, CAB Index (18 Sept. 1902–24 Nov. 1905).
4. Beloff, *Imperial Sunset*, Vol. 1, 90; Moore, 'Imperial India', 422–46.
5. The 'Crimean War constellation' as analytical frame describes the deviation of imperial energies from the European centre to the Middle Eastern and Central Asian periphery. It was the fundamental condition for German unification and continental stability. See Hildebrand, 'Krimkriegssituation', in Dülffer et al., *Deutschland in Europa*, 37–51.
6. Temple, 'The Indian Frontier', JRUSI 43/1 (1899), 1–17.
7. Gillard, *Lord Salisbury's Foreign Policy*, 236–48; Wilson, 'Constantinople or Cairo'; Grenville, *Lord Salisbury*, 24–27, 50–51; Lowe, *Reluctant Imperialists*, Vol. 1, 19–51, 73–120.
8. Roberts, *Salisbury – Victorian Titan*, 606–11.
9. Sanderson to Lascelles, 26 Dec. 1895, NA, FO 800/15; Kimberley, 19 March 1897, PD IV/47, cols. 1009–19; Hamilton to Curzon, 6 June 1901, IOL, EUR. F. 123/83; Sanderson to Lascelles, 26 Dec. 1895, NA, FO 800/15; Kimberley, 19 March 1897, PD IV/47, cols. 1009–19. For more details on these agreements, see Lowe, *Salisbury and the Mediterranean*.
10. Wilson, 'Constantinople or Cairo'; Neilson, 'Greatly Exaggerated', 713–14; Salisbury to Rumbold, 20 Jan. 1897, BD IX, Appendix II, 774–76; Slade to Grey, 8. Oct. 1908, NA, PRO 371/551/35002.
11. Hamilton to Curzon, 9 Nov. 1899, IOL, EUR. C. 126/1.
12. Ardagh (D.M.I.), The Situation at Constantinople, October 1896, NA, PRO 30/40 Part I.
13. Grenville, *Lord Salisbury*, 24–27, 50–51.
14. Roberts, *Salisbury – Victorian Titan*, 768–70; Steele, *Lord Salisbury*, 128.
15. Hamilton to Curzon, 2 Nov. 1899, IOL, EUR. F. 111/158; see also Whitaker, *Whitaker's Almanack* 1900, 473.
16. James, *Rise*, 234.
17. See Nicholas II to Xenia, 21 Oct. 1899, cited in Langer, *Diplomacy of Imperialism*, 665; KA 66 (1934), 124–26; 'A Russia Military Agent's Dispatches on the Anglo-Boer War', KA 103 (1940), 130–59.

18. Hardinge to Sanderson, 8 Nov. 1899, NA, FO 65/1580; 16 Nov. 1899, CUL, MSS Hardinge, Vol. 3; see also Neilson, *Britain and the Last Tsar*, 207–8; Siegel, *Endgame*, 6.
19. See Geppert, *Pressekriege*, 125–77; Hamilton to Curzon, 9 Feb. 1900, IOL, EUR. F. 123/82.
20. Williams, 'Strategic Background', 361.
21. Ardagh (D.M.I.), 23 Jan. 1900, NA, PRO 30/40 Part I; Ardagh (D.M.I), Increase of Russian Forces, 5 April 1900, NA, PRO 30/40 Part I; Scott to Salisbury, 27 June 1900, NA, FO 65/1599.
22. *The Times*, 31 Jan. 1901; Curzon to Lansdowne, 5 April 1901, cited in Newton, *Lord Lansdowne*, 230–32; Lansdowne to Salisbury, 15 Oct. 1901, BL, LANS/PL 5.
23. Scott, 30 Jan. 1900; Durand, 2 Feb. 1900, in Ardagh (D.M.I) Increase of Russian Forces, 5 April 1900, NA, PRO 30/40 Part I; *The Times*, 29 Dec. 1899; 3 Feb., 10 Feb., 17 Feb. and 26 Feb. 1900. According to an agreement made with Abdur Rahman as Emir of Afghanistan in 1880, Britain acted as protecting power in exchange for a yearly payment of £80,000; the arrangement was terminated by Habib Ullah in 1901. BD IV, 855, n. 1.
24. Spring Rice, cited in McLean, *Britain and her Buffer State*, 19; Salisbury, cited in Monger, *End of Isolation*, 5.
25. Russian Embassy to FO, 6 Feb. 1900, BD I, No. 376, 306–7; Spring Rice to Lansdowne, 19 Oct. 1903, BD I, No. 377, 493–95; Hardinge to Lansdowne, 10 June 1905, BD IV, No. 321(b), 374.
26. Hamilton to Curzon, 16 Jan. 1900, IOL, EUR. F. 123/82; Vambéry to Sanderson, 14 March 1903, NA, FO 800/33.
27. Gillard, *Struggle for Asia*, 165; Lansdowne to A. Hardinge, November 1901, cited in Newton, *Lord Lansdowne*, 233; Hamilton to Curzon, 5 April 1899, IOL, EUR. F. 123/81; 1899, IOL, EUR. F. 111/141.
28. Jaeckel, *Nordwestgrenze*, 31; Hardinge to Sanderson, 16 Nov. 1899, CUL, MSS Hardinge, Vol. 3. On Kuropatkin's rather 'modest visions' compared to those of the tsar, see Lieven, *Towards the Flame*, 84–85.
29. Cited in Siegel, *Endgame*, 3.
30. Siegel's view that Russian expansion was a 'defensive reaction' was in accord with Soviet historiography. For a completely different view, see Hölzle, *Selbstentmachtung*, 89; McMeekin, *Russian Origins*, passim.
31. Neilson, *Britain and the Last Tsar*, 208; see also Russian documents: 'Die zaristische Diplomatie', BMH 7/1928, 638–70. 'We must have the Bosphorus' – Kuropatkin's words to Radolin. Radolin to Hohenlohe, 30 Jan. 1900, GP XVII, No. 5334, 520–23, 522.
32. See Treaty of London, 13 March 1871, cited in Hurst, *Key Treaties*, Vol. 2, No. 97, 467–70.
33. See Chapter 6.
34. Balfour to Lansdowne, 12 Dec. 1901, BL, Add. 49727; Robertson, November 1902, LHCMA, ROB 1/2/4.
35. Altham, Military Needs of the Empire, 12 Aug. 1901, NA, WO 106/48, E 3/2; Roberts, 10 June 1901, BDFA B/XII, No. 120, 352; Robertson, Military Resources of Russia, 17 Jan. 1902, NA, WO 106/48, G3–1.
36. Altham, Conference between Representatives of Great Britain and Japan, 2 June 1902, NA, WO 106/48.

37. See also McDermott, 'Revolution in British Military Thinking', 162.
38. See Neilson, *Britain and the Last Tsar*, 111, 122–43; Siegel, *Endgame*, 15; Steiner and Neilson, *Britain and the Origins*, 84–91; Wilson, *Policy of the Entente*, 59–84; McMeekin, *Russian Origins*. For a different view, see Lieven, *Towards the Flame*.
39. See Steiner, Review of Neilson, *Britain and the Last Tsar*, in EHR 2/1998, 223–25; Neilson, *Britain and the Last Tsar*, 370; Gillard, *Lord Salisbury's Foreign Policy*, 241; Ingram, 'Approaches to the Great Game'; Monger, *End of Isolation*, 3–4; Mahajan, 'India', 168–93; Sumner, 'Tsardom', 25–65; Williams, 'Strategic Background'; Siegel, *Endgame*, 1–20. Dominic Lieven, on the contrary, argues that Russia was a weak power and therefore implies that British diplomacy aimed at balancing Franco-Russian weakness against Germany. See Lieven, *Towards the Flame*. Both views, however, seem to go too far.
40. Jaeckel, *Nordwestgrenze*, 101–6.
41. Nicholson to Roberts, 8 May 1901, NAM, MSS Roberts, R 52/87; Robertson, 17 Jan. 1902, NA, WO 106/48.
42. Nicholson to Roberts, 8 May 1901, NAM, MSS Roberts, R 52/87.
43. Ardagh (D.M.I), Increase of Russian Forces, 5 April 1900, NA, PRO 30/40 Part I.
44. Beresford, 'The Defensive Strength of Russia', JRUSI 42/1 (1898), 299–309; Beresford, 'Transsiberian Railway', JRUSI 43/1 (1899), 61–67; Beresford, 'Manchuria', JRUSI 48/1 (1904), 533–41.
45. Scott to Salisbury, 12 Jan. 1899, and to Sanderson, 27 Feb. 1899, BL, Add. 52303.
46. Siegel, *Endgame*, 5; Friedberg, *Weary Titan*, 220; Williams, 'Strategic Background'.
47. Robertson, Memorandum, 17 Jan. 1902, NA, WO 106/48; Wilson, Memorandum, 30 Dec. 1911, NA, WO 106/47.
48. See Colonel Napier, Nos. 123, 132, 145, 205, 232, BDFA A/III.
49. Temple, 'The Indian Frontier', JRUSI 43/1 (1899), 1–17; JRUSI 43/2 (1899), 737–52.
50. McDermott, 'Revolution in British Military Thinking', 163.
51. Balfour to Lansdowne, 12 Dec. 1901, BL, Add. 49727; Memorandum, 14 Oct. 1903, BD IV, No. 465, 512–18.
52. Ripon to Malabri, 6 Nov. 1904, BL, Add. 43616.
53. Plass, *Deutschland*, 117–19.
54. Curzon to Hamilton, 23 March, 26 April, 31 May 1899, IOL, EUR. D. 510/1; see also Symposium of the Royal Society of Arts, 8 May 1902, referred to in Bennet, 'The Connection of England with the Persian Gulf', JRSA, 13 June 1902, 634–51.
55. Curzon to Balfour, 27 Nov. 1902, BL, Add. 49778; see also Major-General George Younghusband, cited in James, *Rise*, 233.
56. See Langer, *Diplomacy of Imperialism*, 666.
57. Lansdowne to Curzon, 5 May 1901, IOL, EUR. F. 111/160.
58. See GL I, 24.
59. Newton, *Lord Lansdowne*, 57–126; see also Temple, 'The Indian Frontier', JRUSI 43/1 (1899), 1–17.
60. Lansdowne to Hardinge, 31 Oct. 1902, 4 Nov. 1902, cited in FO, Memorandum, 14 Oct. 1903, BD IV, No. 465, 512–18. According to a comment from Lansdowne, the status quo in Afghanistan was essential. Scott to Lansdowne, 25 Dec. 1902, NA, FO 800/140; Lansdowne, 1 Jan. 1904, NA, CAB 37/67/1.
61. Maxse, 'Episodes', NR 3/1901, 21–24.

62. Calchas (Garvin), 'Russia and Her Problem', FR 7/1901, 124–38, esp. 126; see Gollin, *The Observer and J.L. Garvin*, 13.
63. Scott to Lansdowne, 20 Dec. 1902, NA, FO 800/140.
64. 'Russia is drawing away from Germany and nearer to us.' Calchas (Garvin), 'Russia and Her Problem', FR 7/1901, 124–38, esp. 126.
65. Calchas (Garvin), 'Foreign Policy of Russia', RR 7/1901, 40; MacColl, 'Russia, Germany and Britain', FR 1/1902, 21–39.
66. Grey (Commons), 27 Nov. 1911, PD V/32, col. 60.
67. Arnold-Forster, 'Our True Foreign Policy', NC 2/1896, 204–10; Gambier, 'A Plea for Peace – An Anglo-Russian Alliance', FR 12/1900, 998–1011; Calchas (Garvin), 'Russia and Her Problem', FR 7/1901, 124–38.
68. *The Times*, 31 Aug., 12 Sept. 1901; MacColl, 'The Foundations of Our Foreign Policy', *The Spectator*, 21 Dec. 1901.
69. Blennerhasset, 'Foreign Policy of the German Empire', NR 9/1900, cited in Maxse, *Germany on the Brain*, 36–37; Maxse, 'Pan-Germanic Idea', NR 6/1902, 64–65.
70. Maxse to Amery, 24 Dec. 1903, CUL, AMEL 1/1/14.
71. Selborne, 25 Feb. 1903, cited in *The Times*, 26 Feb. 1903.
72. Arnold-Forster, *Memoir*, 345.
73. ABC &c., 'Some Consequences of an Anglo-Russian Understanding', NR 12/1901, cited in Maxse, *Germany on the Brain*, 49–51.
74. Plass, *Deutschland*, 85–86; Norman, *All the Russians*, 379–80, 427–30; *The Times*, 20 Feb. 1903.
75. The most important exception was Henry Labouchère, who alone defended the government's course to his friends in the Liberal Party. Labouchère, 3 July 1902, PD IV/101, col. 845. Lucien Wolff was especially critical. Calchas (Garvin), 'Russia and Her Problem', FR 7/1901, 124–38; Gollin, *The Observer and J.L. Garvin*, 13.
76. PD IV/97, col. 1006–10; PD IV/98, col. 247–57; *The Times*, 22, 24 andnd 27 Feb. 1900; Calchas (Garvin), 'Russia and Her Problem', FR 7/1901, 124–38, 135.
77. McDermott, 'Revolution in British Military Thinking', 160.
78. Arthur Hardinge pointed Kühlmann to the suggestions in the A.B.C. articles and to Drummond-Wolff's letters in *The Times*, 12 Sept. 1901. Kühlmann to Bülow, 9 Dec. 1901, GP XVII, No. 5348, 537–39.
79. Hardinge to Maxse, 16 Oct. 1901, WSRO, MAXSE/448.
80. According to Count Deym, Lansdowne thought little of the A.B.C. articles and assured him 'that the Cabinet had not even thought about dealing with Russia'. Metternich to Bülow, 14 Nov. 1901, GP XVII, No. 5345, 534–35.
81. Lansdowne to Curzon, 16 Feb. 1902, NA, FO 800/145.
82. Plass, *Deutschland*, 85, 152–53.
83. A list of the Russian violations is found in Spring Rice to T. Roosevelt, 1 July 1904, CC, CASR 1/1.
84. Crowe to Maxse, 15 Oct. 1902, WSRO, Maxse/450.
85. Lansdowne to Hardinge, 6 Jan. 1902, CUL, MSS Hardinge, Vol. 3.
86. Scott to Lansdowne, 17 April 1902, BL, Add. 52303; Hamilton to Curzon, 13 March 1903, IOL, EUR. C. 126/5.
87. *The Times*, 20 Feb. 1903.
88. Cranborne, 22 Jan. 1903, PD IV/101, col. 129; 31 Jan. 1903, ibid., col. 788.
89. Sanderson to Hardinge, 19 Sept. 1905, CUL, MSS Hardinge, Vol. 5.

90. Scott to Sanderson, 18 May 1899; to Lansdowne, 17 April 1902, BL, Add. 52303; Lascelles to Lansdowne, 5 Jan. 1901, NA, FO 800/18; Spring Rice to Lansdowne, December 1904, CC, CASR 9/2.
91. Curzon to Hamilton, 25 Sept. 1901, IOL, EUR. D. 510/9. 'The next theatre of war could well be India'. Curzon to Hamilton, 8 Oct. 1902, IOL, EUR. C. 126/4.
92. Balfour, 29 April 1898, PD III/56, col. 1591f.; Balfour to Edward VII, 11 Aug. 1904, NA, CAB 41/29/31.
93. Chirol, *Middle Eastern Question*, 402–6; *The Times*, 21 April 1903; Balfour to Lansdowne, 21 Dec. 1903, BL, Add. 49728; Sanderson, 2 Nov. 1899, NA, PRO 30/67/4; Lascelles to Salisbury, 1 Jan. 1898, HH, MSS Salisbury, A/121/1; Hardinge to Lascelles, 15 Nov. 1900, CUL, MSS Hardinge, Vol. 3; A. Hardinge to Lansdowne, 27 Aug. 1902, BL, LANS/PL 5; Curzon to Lansdowne, 10 Dec. 1902, BL, LANS/NC.
94. Hardinge to Sanderson, 18 Oct. 1900, CUL, MSS Hardinge, Vol. 3.
95. Lansdowne to O'Conor, 31 Jan. 1902, BL, Add. 49727.
96. Lansdowne to Curzon, 10 April 1902, NA, FO 800/145; to Drummond-Wolff, 12 Aug. 1902, BL, LANS/NC.
97. Neilson, *Britain and the Last Tsar*, 226–27.
98. MID, Defence of India, 10 March 1903, NA, CAB 6/1.
99. MID, Memorandum, 9 April 1903, NA, FO 60/733.
100. MID, Defence of India, 10 March 1903, NA, CAB 6/1, 11–12.
101. Ibid., 14–16.
102. Selborne to Balfour, 14 March 1903, BL, Add. 49707; Kerr to Selborne, 12 March 1903, Add. 49707; Hamilton to Curzon, 5 March 1903, IOL, EUR. C. 126/5.
103. Plass, *Deutschland*, 154, 160–61.
104. CID Protocols, 19 March–10 April 1903, NA, CAB 2/1.
105. Kennedy, *Rise of Anglo-German Antagonism*, 260–62. See Chapter 5.
106. Balfour, Memorandum, 30 April 1903, NA, CAB 6/1.
107. Balfour, 17 Feb. 1908, PD IV/184, col. 552.
108. Balfour to Edward VII, 14 Dec. 1903, NA, CAB 41/28/2.
109. Vambéry to Sanderson, 14 March 1903, NA, FO 800/33.
110. Canis, *Von Bismarck zur Weltpolitik*, 396.
111. Lansdowne, 5 May 1903, PD IV/121, col. 1348; to Curzon, 16 Feb. 1903, IOL, F 111/151; Neilson, *Britain and the Last Tsar*, 229.
112. Roberts, cited in Monger, *End of Isolation*, 95.
113. Lansdowne to Cromer, 7 Dec. 1903, NA, FO 633/311.
114. *The Times*, 6 May 1903, 11. For German reactions, see GP XVII, No. 5362–5363, 558–61.
115. *Westminster Gazette*, 6 May 1903.
116. Curzon to Hamilton, 14 May 1903, IOL, EUR. D. 510/14.
117. *Manchester Guardian*, 6 May 1903; Bernstorff to Bülow, 9 May 1903, GP XVII, No. 5363, 559.
118. Hamilton to Godley, 30 Dec. 1902 and 13 Jan. 1903, IOL, EUR. F. 102/6.
119. Hamilton to Curzon, 5 June 1903, IOL, EUR. C. 126/5; Godley to Curzon, 4 June 1903, IOL, EUR. F. 111/162.
120. Curzon to Hamilton, 4 June 1903, IOL, EUR. D. 510/14; Hamilton to Curzon, 25 June 1903, IOL, EUR. C. 126/5.
121. Lowe and Dockrill, *Mirage of Power*, Vol. 1, 1; Canis, *Der Weg in der Abgrund*, 106. For a different view, see Neilson, *Britain and the Last Tsar*, 230.

122. Neilson, *Britain and the Last Tsar*, 230–31; see also Lansdowne to Monson, 26 Oct. 1903, BD II, No. 250, 217–18.
123. Lansdowne to Balfour, 23 Oct. 1903, cited in Neilson, *Britain and the Last Tsar*, 234.
124. Lansdowne to Spring Rice, 7 Nov. 1903, BD II, No. 258, 359–62.
125. Lansdowne to Cromer, 7 Dec. 1903, NA, FO 633/3. The Tibet exhibition was intended as a demonstration of strength to Russia. Lansdowne to Spring Rice, 4 May 1904, NA, FO 17/1749.
126. Ampthill to Edward VII, 16 July 1904, IOL, MSS Ampthill, EUR. E. 233/32.
127. Neilson, *Britain and the Last Tsar*, 236.
128. Lansdowne to Cromer, 7 Dec. 1903, NA, FO 633/3, No. 11.
129. Lansdowne, 1 Jan. 1904, NA, CAB 37/68/1. John Charmley paints a rather different picture, with Lansdowne in a subordinate negotiating position in relation to Benckendorff. Charmley, *Splendid Isolation*, 309.
130. Neilson, *Britain and the Last Tsar*, 236. Lansdowne rejected any change to the status quo. Lansdowne to Spring Rice, 25 Nov. 1903, BD IV, No. 182, 186–88.
131. Balfour in Glasgow, *The Times*, 16 Nov. 1895; Balfour in Norwich, *The Times*, 6 Nov. 1897.
132. Balfour to Lansdowne, 21 Dec. 1903, BL, Add. 49728.
133. Balfour to Lansdowne, 6 Sept. 1902, cited in Monger, *End of Isolation*, 89.
134. Lansdowne to Spring Rice, 17 Nov. 1903, BD IV, No. 181(a), 183–84.
135. Lansdowne to MacDonald, 11 Jan. 1904, BD II, No. 275, 233–34.
136. A. Hardinge to Lansdowne, 6 Jan. 1902, cited in Newton, *Lord Lansdowne*, 234–35.
137. Balfour to Lansdowne, 21 Dec. 1903, BL, Add. 49728.
138. Balfour, Memorandum, 29 Dec. 1903, NA, CAB 37/67/97.
139. Lansdowne to Spring Rice, 17 Nov. 1903, BD IV, No. 181(a), 183–84.
140. Balfour to Lansdowne, 21 Dec. 1903, BL, Add. 49728.
141. Balfour to Brodrick, 17 Dec. 1903, BL, Add. 49720; Balfour, Memorandum, 23 July 1904, NA, CAB 38/5; Balfour, 11 May 1905, PD IV/146, col. 83.
142. Lansdowne to Spring Rice, 17 Nov. 1903, BD IV, No. 181(a), 184–86.
143. Observations on a War Game at Simla, 1903, 5 May 1904, NA, CAB 6/1/50D.
144. On the strategic situation, see NA, WO 32/264; Kitchener, Minute, 15 Feb. 1904, Defence of India, April 1904, NA, CAB 6/1.
145. Gooch, 'Sir George Clarke's Career', 560; Maps, IOL, EUR. D. 573/37; Whitaker, *Whitaker's Almanack* 1900, 471.
146. Brodrick to Curzon, 4 March 1904, NA, CAB 6/1; Defence of India, 30 April 1903, NA, CAB, 6/1/12D.
147. CID, 37th Meeting, 24 March 1904, NA, CAB 38/4; CID, 47th Meeting, 22 June 1904, NA, CAB 38/5.
148. Fisher to Sandars, 10 June 1904, BL, Add. 49710.
149. Monger, *End of Isolation*, 139; Gooch, 'Sir George Clarke's Career', 560; Wilson, *Policy of the Entente*, 71; Charmley, *Splendid Isolation*, 308; Williams, *Defending the Empire*, 362; Steiner, 'Last Years of the Old Foreign Office', 73.
150. Balfour to Selborne, 6 April 1904, BOD, MSS Selborne 1/39.
151. Balfour to MID, 28 April 1904, NA, CAB 6/1; Selborne to Kerr, 1 April 1904, BOD, MSS Selborne 1/39; MID, Inquiry as to the vulnerability of Russia, Selborne to Balfour, 5 April 1904, ibid.

152. Balfour to Selborne, 6 April 1904, BOD, MSS Selborne 1/39; to Edward VII, 11 Aug. 1904, NA, CAB 41/29/31.
153. Balfour to Lansdowne, 20 Oct. 1904, BL, LANS/PL 5; to Clarke, 25 Oct. 1904, BL, Add. 49700.
154. Clarke to Balfour, 9 July 1904, BL, Add. 50836. For a different view, see Gooch, 'Sir George Clarke's Career', 560–61.
155. Clarke to Balfour, 19 Nov. 1904, BL, Add. 49700.
156. McDermott, 'Revolution in British Military Thinking', 171.
157. Charmley, *Splendid Isolation*, 308; Williams, *Defending the Empire*, 362; Siegel, *Endgame*, 5.
158. Balfour, Memorandum, 30 April 1903, NA, CAB 6/1.
159. Peach, Nicholson, Lord Roberts, Russia's offensive strength, 29 April, 17 May and 10 June 1901, cited in Siegel, *Endgame*, 4; Steiner, *Britain and the Origins*, 78.
160. WO, Defence of India, 30 April 1903, NA, CAB 6/1/12D.
161. Gillard, *Lord Salisbury's Foreign Policy*, 241; Neilson, *Britain and the Last Tsar*, 122–30.
162. Radolin to Hohenlohe, 30 Jan. 1900, GP XVII, No. 5334, 520–23, 521.
163. Jaeckel, *Nordwestgrenze*, 223, n. 7.
164. See Ortenburg, *Millionenheere*, 119–23, 234–36.
165. Steiner, *Britain and the Origins*, 78–79; Wilson, *Policy of the Entente*, 75.
166. Williams, 'Great Britain and Russia', 135; Siegel, *Endgame*, 5. To Peshawar it was 585 miles. Roberts, 'The North Western Frontier', JRUSI 49/2 (1906), 1349–58, 1355.
167. Clarke to Balfour, 18 April 1905, BL, Add. 49701.
168. Temple, 'The Indian Frontier', JRUSI 43/1 (1899), 1–17, esp. 14.
169. Whitaker, *Whitaker's Almanack* 1900, 471.
170. Balfour, Memorandum, 23 July 1904, NA, CAB 38/5; Balfour to Lansdowne, 26 Oct. 1904, BL, Add. 49698; Balfour, 11 May 1905, PD IV/146, col. 83.
171. Clarke, Indian Defence, 24 Nov. 1904, BL, Add. 50836; Clarke, The Military Problem of India, 16 April 1907, NA, CAB 38/8/46.
172. Temple, 'The Indian Frontier', JRUSI 43/1 (1899), 1–17, esp. 14.
173. McGregor to Lansdowne, 9 Oct. 1902, NA, WO 106/48.
174. The precise number of camels needed was 5,043,692, but no more than 100,000 were available in the whole of Central Asia. See Clarke, Required transport of an army operating in Afghanistan, 20 Nov. 1905, NA, CAB 6/3/89D.
175. Clarke, Required transport, 5 June 1905, NA, CAB 6/3/83D.
176. Clarke, Required transport, 20 Nov. 1905, NA, CAB 6/3/89D.
177. Clarke, Required transport, 5 June 1905, NA, CAB 38/9/46.
178. Balfour to Clarke, 27 Oct. 1904, BL, Add. 49700.
179. Clarke, The Afghanistan Problem, 20 March 1905, NA, CAB 38/8/26.
180. Chirol to Curzon, 23 April 1903, IOL, EUR. F. 111/162.
181. *The Times*, 14 Feb. and 22 Dec. 1903; 3 March and 23 June 1905. Lord Kitchener, NAR 4/1905, 602–13.
182. Balfour to Hamilton, 9 March 1903, BL, Add. 49778; Williams, *Defending the Empire*, 24–25.
183. Clarke to Esher, 18 May 1904, CC, MSS Esher, Clarke Correspondence, Vol. 1.
184. Monger, *End of Isolation*, 96; McDermott, 'Revolution in British Military Thinking'.
185. CID 54th Meeting, 15 Aug. 1904, NA, CAB 2/1; see also McDermott, 'Revolution in British Military Thinking', 169.

186. Balfour, Military Needs of the Empire, 19 Dec. 1904, NA, CAB 3/1/28A.
187. Balfour to Edward VII, 29 Dec. 1904, BOD, MSS Sandars, c. 716.
188. Balfour, Memorandum, 13 July 1905 CAB 38/13; see also Clarke, Note, 20 March 1905, NA, CAB 38/8.
189. Clarke, The Afghanistan Problem, 20 March 1905, NA, CAB 38/2.
190. Balfour to Lansdowne, 21 Dec. 1903, BL, Add. 49728.
191. Ibid.
192. Balfour to Lansdowne, 20 Oct. 1904, BL, LANS/PL 5; to Clarke, 25 Oct. 1904, BL, Add. 49700.
193. Clarke to Haldane, 6 Feb. 1905, NLS, MSS 5906.
194. Clarke, Invasions of India, 3 April 1905, NA, CAB 6/3/100D; McDermott, 'Revolution in British Military Thinking', 177.
195. D'Ombrain, *War Machinery*, 147.
196. After the Boer War, Wilson's principal responsibility was to prepare British forces for deployment on the continent. As head of the Staff College at Camberley (1906–1910), he encouraged his officers to travel in Germany in order to see that country's strengths and weaknesses for themselves. He himself undertook cycling tours in the Kaiserreich and worked closely with Ferdinand Foch on a common strategy to be deployed against Germany. See Deacon, *History of the British Secret Service*, 147.
197. Repington to Marker, 20 April 1905, BL, Add. 52277B.
198. Minutes, Robertson, The True Standard of our Military Needs, 1906, LHCMA, ROB 1/2/9.
199. Clarke, Minute, 11 Aug. 1905, NA, CAB 17/43.
200. General Staff, The Strength in which Russia can advance towards India, 16 Feb. 1905, NA, CAB 6/3; Ryan, *Lieutenant-Colonel Charles à Court Repington*, 54.
201. How important the prestige factor was to the General Staff is made evident by General Staff, Memorandum, 12 Aug. 1905, NA, CAB 38/1079.
202. Haig to Ewart, 28 Oct. 1909, NAS, MSS Ewart, NRAS1054/93.
203. Balfour to Kitchener, 3 Dec. 1903, BL, Add. 49726.
204. Selborne, Memorandum, November 1904, BOD, MSS Selborne 158.
205. McDermott, 'Revolution in British Military Thinking', 173.
206. Clarke, Discussion of the Indian Reinforcements, 22 Nov. 1904, BL, Add. 49700.
207. McDermott, 'Revolution in British Military Thinking', 173.
208. McDermott, 'Revolution in British Military Thinking', 170.
209. Mombauer, *Origins*, 5; Steiner, *Britain and the Origins*, 35; Strachan, 'Armee', 269. More qualified is Williamson, *Politics of Grand Strategy*, 60–88; see also BD III, No. 210–21, 160–203.
210. Wilson, Diary, 28 Oct. 1904, cited in Strachan, 'Armee', 278.
211. Coogan and Coogan, 'British Cabinet'.
212. Andrew, *Théophile Delcassé*, 286. See also Grierson, Military Forces required for Over-Sea-Warfare, 1906, LHCMA, ROB 1/2/6; Grierson to his sister, 14 Jan. 1906, cited in MacDiarmed, *Grierson*, 213.
213. Grey to Bertie, 15 Jan. 1906, BD III, No. 215, 117; Sanderson to Grierson, 15 Jan. 1906, No. 217(a), 179.
214. Balfour, Military Needs of the Empire, 19 Dec. 1904, NA, CAB 2/2/28A.
215. Grierson to Sanderson, 11 Jan. 1906, BD III, No. 211, 172–73.

216. Sanderson to Balfour, 13 Aug. 1905, BL, Add. 49739; Roberts to Balfour, 22 Aug. 1905, Add. 49725; see also McDermott, 'Revolution in British Military Thinking', 173–74.
217. Clarke to Balfour, 17 Aug. 1905, BL, Add. 49702; see also Wilson, *Policy of the Entente*, 108.
218. The Violation of the Neutrality of Belgium, September 1905, NA, CAB 38/10/73; Sydenham of Combe, George Clarke, *My Working Life*, 185–86; see also General Staff, November 1908, NA, WO 106/47.
219. General Staff, Feb. 1908, NA, WO 106/47.
220. Grey to Haldane, 8 Jan. 1906, NLS, MSS 5907; Repington to Marker, 14 June 1906, BL, Add. 52277B; Haldane, *An Autobiography*, 191.
221. Balfour to Edward VII, 8 June 1905, NA, CAB 41/30/21. See also Andrew, *Théophile Delcassé*, 287.
222. Balfour to Lascelles, 20 April 1905, BL, Add. 49747.
223. Balfour to Esher, 2 Nov. 1905, CC, ESHR 10/32; Arnold-Forster, 5 Feb. 1905, BL, Add. 50344.
224. Balfour, Memorandum, 24 Feb. 1905, NA, CAB 17/3.
225. Hardinge to Sandars, 21 July 1905; to Sanderson, 21 July 1905, CUL, MSS Hardinge, Vol. 6.
226. Spring Rice to Lansdowne, 4 Oct. 1905, NA, FO 800/116; Durand to Lansdowne, 10 Aug. 1905, NA, FO 800/144; Strachey to Spring Rice, 2 Oct. 1905, PA, STR/13/14; Chirol to Hardinge, 22 Aug. 1905, CUL, MSS Hardinge, Vol. 7.
227. Lansdowne to Hardinge, 21 Oct. 1905, NA, FO 800/141; to Cromer, 10 Oct. 1905, FO 800/124.
228. Lansdowne to Salisbury, 13 June 1905, BL, LANS/PL 3; to Hardinge, 4 Sept. 1905, CUL, MSS Hardinge, Vol. 7; to Nicolson, 18 July 1905, NA, FO 800/336; A. Chamberlain to Lansdowne, 29 Oct. 1905, BUL, AC 17/1/73.
229. WO, Memorandum, 16 Feb. 1905, NA, CAB 38/8/9; see also Wilson, *Policy of the Entente*, 75. Totally different conclusions can be drawn from later assessments: WO, Memorandum, 22 Oct. 1906, NA, WO 106/182; WO, Russian Railway Communications, 1911, NA, WO 106/58.
230. Clarke, Memorandum, 5 June 1906, NA, CAB 38/9/46.
231. See Dilke's evaluation of international relations in the *Fortnightly Review* 1–6/1887.
232. *The Times*, 12 May 1905; see also Holdich, *The Indian Borderland* (1901).
233. Balfour, 11 May 1905, PD IV/146, col. 81f.; Dilke, ibid., col. 81–84.
234. Jaeckel, *Nordwestgrenze*, 40.
235. Balfour, 28 April 1898, PD IV/56, col. 1591–92; Balfour to Edward VII, 11 Aug. 1904, NA, CAB 41/29/31.
236. Sanderson to Hardinge, 19 Sept. 1905, CUL, MSS Hardinge, Vol. 7; Hardinge to Lansdowne, 15 Oct. 1905, NA, FO 800/141; Lansdowne to Hardinge, 17 Oct. 1905, CUL, MSS Hardinge, Vol. 7.
237. Hardinge to Lansdowne, 10 June 1905, BD IV, No. 321(b), 372–74, 373.
238. Wilson, *Policy of the Entente*, 76.
239. CID, Military Requirements, 1907, NA, CAB 16/2, 175f.; see also Sydenham of Combe, George Clarke, *My Working Life*, 200.
240. See Chapter 2.
241. The Military Resources of the Russian Empire, 1907, NA, WO 33/419, 295.
242. Morley to Minto, 19 Sept. 1907, IOL, EUR. D. 573/2.

Chapter 5

FOREIGN POLICY UNDER LANSDOWNE AND BALFOUR

'A blessing in disguise': The Venezuela Crisis of 1902/1903

The provisional end to the exploration of possibilities with Berlin was not as tragic to Lansdowne and Balfour, who were aware of Britain's relative security, as it has often seemed to historians.[1] Both men were understanding of the difficult geopolitical position Germany faced.[2] Viewing the international picture as a whole, they, unlike Chamberlain, also saw no need to turn their backs entirely on the possibility of an agreement. A single maxim governed their approach to every power: make concessions where possible and signal strength as required by Britain's essential interests. The situation in the Far East and South Africa had hardly quieted when a new opportunity to act in concert with the Wilhelmstrasse arose, this time in the Caribbean.

The joint blockade of Venezuelan ports from 9 December 1902 to 13 February 1903 is often treated from a German or American perspective,[3] but makes only a rare appearance in studies of British foreign policy.[4] Berlin is usually identified as the driving force, with the suggestion that in the course of its expansive 'grip to world power' the Wilhelmstrasse not only risked an aggressive challenge to American pre-eminence in the western hemisphere but also, in order to sunder the Anglo-Saxon powers permanently, urged London to take a similar line.[5] Such analysis falls back on contemporary explanations that appeared in the press, without close scrutiny of the press's own possible motives.[6] For example, Leo Maxse and others were convinced that Wilhelm II would do anything to 'bamboozle the British public' as long as the High Seas Fleet remained under strength; Paul Kennedy's assessment has the cooperation intended solely to bypass German naval rearmament. Was London really

---

Notes for this chapter begin on page 259.

infected by Prussian sabre-rattling and drawn into the crisis by Berlin, as Emile J. Dillon, Leo Maxse, George Saunders and Rudyard Kipling's poem *The Rowers* proposed to the broader public?[7] The most recent studies agree with their conclusion, proposing that in the first Venezuelan crisis, in 1895/96, Britain had learned its lesson when it came to the Monroe Doctrine and six years later followed a non-confrontational course with Washington, with the lack of Anglo-American coordination in the run-up to the crisis generally attributed to oversight and misunderstanding.[8] But could it not also be that London pursued its own interests in South America? Did Lansdowne's plans really take account of US sensibilities from the start,[9] or are we perhaps dealing here with British self-assertion in the face of a former colony that during the first Venezuelan crisis had demonstrated a lack of respect for London? Certainly, shortly before, in taking possession of the strategically significant island of Patos, the Empire had demonstrated that it was not wasting any time on Washington's illegitimate claims to power in the region.[10] What role was played by London's political sphere and its press? After the fact, in February 1907, Eyre Crowe judged that during the Venezuela Crisis in particular, but also on the question of the Baghdad railway, the public opinion moulded by the press had directly influenced the government's foreign policy,[11] a view that suggests the increased relevance of the political sphere for decisions made by Whitehall.

Here, then, is good reason to give the Venezuelan episode more attention than it usually receives. Despite all the complexities of the specific South American circumstances, the background to the crisis is quickly recounted. Throughout the nineteenth century, Latin America provided foreign investors, in the City of London in particular, with an enticing investment opportunity.[12] Diversified across a range of projects, British direct investment in the Caribbean rose to over £750 million.[13] In second place among the numerous investors, although some way behind, was Germany.[14] Yet investment in this region faced problems still familiar today – chronic political instability and disastrous local management of invested funds.[15] Vacillating throughout the nineteenth century between despotism and chaos, Venezuela alone soon owed debts in London of more than £7.19 million, excluding interest.[16] In early 1901, Cipriano Castro, a dictator as unpredictable as he was brutal, summarily declared all foreign debts void; he also repeatedly harassed European settlers. The patience of the creditor nations snapped.[17] German and British creditors joined forces and repeatedly called on their respective governments for assistance.[18]

The Committee of Foreign Bondholders (CFB) became the principal recipient of British complaints. The committee had close ties to the political establishment at Westminster, and its members were key financial players in the City. Having floated several articles in the press, in November 1901 the board of directors consulted the government directly.[19] Their correspondence reveals that the committee was not only in regular contact with the highest governmental circles,[20] but also acted transnationally, having some time earlier made its own preparations for a joint demonstration along with the German Diskonto-Gesellschaft.[21] Evidently, the pressure on the London leadership to take action was to be heightened by the subtle hint of a concerted response along with Germany.[22] British interests must be safeguarded, however, the committee insisted, before Germany or other creditor nations acted pre-emptively, leaving British investors empty handed.

A cautious, unilateral operation against Caracas formed one option, but in light of the continuing problems in South Africa, that course seemed hardly prudent. Another possibility, proposed since September 1901 by Sir William Haggard, the highly engaged British minister in Caracas, was that Whitehall remained in the background, allowing Germany to force Venezuela to pay the outstanding debts. Haggard's suggestion was that Britain could then use the most-favoured creditor clause to collect its dues as *tertius gaudens*[23] – France would adopt much this strategy at the conclusion of the operation.[24] Additionally, without informing Lansdowne,[25] Haggard repeatedly attempted to propel Gisbert von Pilgrim-Baltazzi, his German colleague in Caracas, in this direction and rouse Berlin.[26] Ultimately, as a third option, London could wait for a favourable moment at which to join Berlin, and together they could teach Venezuela a lesson. That method would provide London with diplomatic safeguards, particularly against the United States, and enable Britain to show its colours, and it would also allow the thread of the conversation with Berlin to be taken up again.

Initially, Lansdowne chose to play for time. Hasty decision making was not his friend, for he needed to bear in mind various considerations, global, Great Power and domestic. Whitehall attempted a balancing act: on one hand, it was important to retain an impression of independence and sovereignty; on the other hand, any sense that the government was indifferent to justified complaints from within its leading circles and, in the end, to its prestige in the region was to be avoided. While Lansdowne informed the representatives of the Committee of Foreign Bondholders that he took their problems seriously, from January 1902 he waited for a 'favourable opportunity for further action, possibly in the form of joint action'.[27] In practice, the pressure on the government grew enormously precisely in spring 1902, with the various interest groups up in arms.[28] The *Financial News* and other organs of the press had long deemed the passivity of the government scandalous, while the opposition saw its chance and also increased the pressure.[29] With so many voices raised, it would have been impossible to stay immune to the protests.[30] The economic possibilities and literally golden natural resources of Venezuela[31] appeared too significant to be left to a despot or other rivals. Castro's repeating effrontery was also all too evident.[32] In the course of the summer, Caracas had seized or destroyed seven ships flying the British flag.[33] The ongoing revolutionary unrest now threatened 6,000 British and 1,000 German settlers.[34] An example could be made of Venezuela, sending a message to the indebted countries of South America and to the dominant but inactive regional power.[35]

Germany also had good reason to complain about its treatment at the hands of Caracas.[36] With its first show of power and the world looking on, Berlin discovered that it was not being taken seriously. In winter 1901/1902, Germany had sought to send a signal by having three small cruisers patrol the coastline at La Guaira, but, as Haggard reported, Venezuelan officials had responded by making fun of Germany.[37] Even in these preliminary stages, the possibility of profiting from an intervention by Germany had proved illusionary. In fact, in the German Admiralty only Admiral Diederich recommended force be used, while even Tirpitz, Bülow and the Kaiser wanted to avoid conflict.[38] For Berlin, it seemed all too obvious that a political-military response in the zone covered by the Monroe Doctrine would be possible only, if at all, as an ally of Britain. Haggard informed the foreign secretary that Germany was simply not in a position to make a show of force.[39]

When Caracas not only ignored the official British communication protesting the seizure of English merchant ships[40] but also began to open diplomatic post, Lansdowne's patience was at an end.[41] The Foreign Office balked at going it alone,[42] and Lansdowne named Germany as a desired partner.[43] On 23 July, the Wilhelmstrasse signalled its willingness to enter into a joint venture, and on 29 July Lansdowne sent a telegraph to Haggard communicating that Castro's behaviour would no longer be tolerated.[44] The British sources say nothing of Berlin having to urge London into action.

The two countries were linked by mutual interests and by a desire to use these shared concerns to help ease bilateral relations.[45] Both countries were eager to see a warning shot fired, but whether that would happen depended on Britain. When Caracas let pass the final ultimatum over the payment of compensation, the Foreign Office approached the Admiralty to ask that it contribute its expertise for a shared demonstration against Venezuela.[46] Only a week later, Whitehall was able to present a first detailed plan of action, to take place the following November.[47] Metternich and the Wilhelmstrasse were astonished, for they had not reckoned on their initiative proceeding nearly so quickly, and they were particularly concerned about upsetting Washington. Metternich therefore requested that Lansdowne invite the United States to participate in the reprimand, but the British foreign secretary refused – to the surprise of the German ambassador, he believed that it would be sufficient to inform the United States later, immediately before the operation was launched.[48] Although often accused of having behaved recklessly in the face of the Monroe Doctrine, Germany was taken by surprise by the speed with which London was now pushing forward issuing a second ultimatum.[49] Seeing that Britain was able to advance alone, and aware of how fraught the relations between the two countries had become due to the Boer War, Berlin feared being deserted at the last moment.[50] In order that the long-sought rapprochement not be endangered, the Kaiser demanded 'great patience and discretion – also in the Foreign Ministry – and our press to keep its trap shut'. He continued: 'Germany is much too weak', and warned, 'Take care, here there are thirty-five armoured vessels against our eight'.[51] In just a few words, Wilhelm II summed up the relative strengths – no less, but also not necessarily more. When it came to the reprimand for Venezuela, Britain, and not Germany, determined its objective, course, means and even timing.[52]

Whitehall pressed ahead. On 12 October, Lansdowne had informed Balfour that the German government was hesitating, while he himself was in such a rush that, he noted, 'We can hardly wait until the Cab of the 21st'.[53] Asked about the United States, he told the cabinet, 'It will not be necessary to say anything as to our intention ... to the US Govt., until we see the effect of the ultimatum'.[54] On 21 October, the cabinet voted unanimously in favour of a joint operation.[55] From this point on, the pace was set largely by diplomat Francis Villiers. Villiers had been the first to establish official contact with the Wilhelmstrasse, on 2 January 1902,[56] since when he had attempted to convince Lansdowne not only that the other European creditors stood behind London, but also that the United States would raise no objections. Villiers' knowledge was based, admittedly, not on direct inquiry but on conclusions he had drawn from Roosevelt's New Year's address and from queries made by Germany in Washington – the American government had repeatedly made clear that it would not provide backing for a dictator such as Castro. Lansdowne did not believe it necessary, however, to consult Washington at all,[57] which historians have repeatedly attempted to explain away as a 'misunderstanding'.[58] The discrepancy between German sensitivity and British ignorance seems, however, too stark to be explained by a simple oversight. Since the first Anglo-American crisis at the latest, London had been well aware of American interests; it had been only six years since Henry Cabot Lodge had informed Arthur Balfour that Venezuela was a point of principle for the United States.[59] Not by chance had Selborne, as First Lord of the Admiralty, warned Lansdowne of the possible consequences of a British operation in the area covered by the Monroe Doctrine.[60]

Just as Venezuela was about to be reprimanded, Germany, it seemed to Villiers, was shying away because of American interests. In two memoranda – one was addressed directly to Lansdowne – Villiers urged action be taken soon, for, he noted, two weeks had already passed and Germany still had not made a final decision. 'The time for best naval action was running out', he warned Lansdowne,[61] noting in the second text: 'If the Germans want to associate themselves with us in this preliminary step [the sending of an ultimatum], they can do so'.[62] Only when the two monarchs, Wilhelm II and Edward VII, specifically required that official notice be given to Washington[63] did the British foreign secretary let the United States know of the upcoming operation, somewhat casually and without mentioning the cooperation between Britain and Germany.[64] This was clearly not the best way to treat a country that was supposedly a natural partner. At the same time, by insisting that action be taken as soon as the ultimatum expired,⁶⁵ Lansdowne put Germany in a difficult situation.⁶⁶ Only when, at the end of November, Graf von Quadt, the German chargé d'affaires in Washington, again confirmed that Washington had agreed to action being taken did Berlin dare to join in,⁶⁷ and after a meeting at Sandringham the Germans agreed without objection to the British plans.⁶⁸

British haste and Germany's naval and financial limitations make evident which party held the upper hand within the cooperation between the two nations.⁶⁹ The London press, followed by historians, claimed that as a member of an unholy alliance, Britain had been drawn into an even less holy operation, yet Haggard commented to Lansdowne that the Kaiserreich had to take its cue entirely from England.⁷⁰ But Britain also saw the advantages of collaboration with Germany, especially in light of their encumbered relationship since the Boer War.⁷¹ Additionally, London knew from experience that an operation undertaken within the radius of the Monroe Doctrine could never be overly diplomatically safeguarded.⁷²

We know that the Kaiserreich not only sought to protect itself politically but also evidently planned for a worst-case scenario; its 'Operationsplan III' even considered the possibility of a regional war against the United States. The discovery of this plan has fed the continuing controversy over whether Germany was only planning for the most radical of possible outcomes or whether Germany expected war. In light of subsequent events, most commentators have tended to adopt the latter position, proposing that while Berlin may not have set a course for war, they did not run from the possibility.⁷³ Here, then, they argue, was a model for the calculated risk of the July Crisis, providing Wilhelmine foreign policy with a strategic continuity. But the War Office in London also believed that there was a good chance of war, or at least declared that it would be very foolish 'to eliminate the serious contingency of war with the US'.⁷⁴ Only a few weeks before the operation, and shortly before Edward VII required that Washington be informed, the Colonial Defence Committee considered the security situation in the west Atlantic, and recorded:

> The Country from which most risk was to be apprehended in those waters is the United States. ... The CDC [Colonial Defence Committee] have no reason to doubt that the defensive arrangements are sufficient to fulfil the purpose required in the event of war with the United States, provided that the neutrality of all other powers were assured.⁷⁵

Even before the joint action was approved, the Admiralty and War Office had long been concerned about the risk of jeopardizing the relationship with the United States, a concern that continued after the decision had been made.⁷⁶ Against the expectations raised by the oft-cited special relationship between the Anglo-Saxon powers, the United States has no prominent place in the records of the Foreign Office or Lansdowne's private papers during this phase.

Neither Germany nor Britain sought a military conflict, but both were concerned to assert their claims or rights as creditors. The Monroe Doctrine had no legal standing and should not be viewed retrospectively as self-evidently legitimate. It was a product of a typical imperialist claim of the type asserted by Great Britain in Africa and India, by Austria-Hungary in the Balkans, and by Russia in the Far East and Middle East. For once, in the case of Venezuela, German diplomats proved significantly more professional and more cautious than their British colleagues. Berlin had taken to heart Theodor von Holleben's warning, given in late 1901, that American sensitivities must be heeded, which explains why Berlin sent two memoranda and numerous other enquiries to the White House to explain the tensions in the relationship with Caracas and to guarantee that the occupation of Venezuelan territory was not envisioned whatever the circumstances.[77] No similar reassurance was given at any point by London. Lansdowne had clearly rejected Metternich's wish that the United States be informed at least during the run-up to the operation.[78] In light of the bitter, and at times even scathing undertone to Haggard's diplomatic correspondence, in which he commented on the lack of support from Washington, it would not seem out of the question that the British position was also intended to demonstrate to the United States that Britain was willing not only to award itself rights in the western hemisphere, but also to take on responsibilities. Britain allowed a year to go past after Germany had requested permission from the United States before deigning to inform Washington of the planned operation.

Running counter to the established view, the suggestion that Britain was sending a message to Washington might appear at first glance somewhat daring. Yet the ignoring of American interests is in line with the foreign policy approach adopted by Lansdowne and Balfour, and therefore this suggestion seems more coherent than the idea of simple oversight. Whether with France, Germany, Russia or, indeed, the United States in mind, the course adopted by the Conservatives was consistently characterized by a combination of carefully measured concessions and equally considered demonstrations of strength. All the Great Powers had attempted to exploit the tensions during the Boer War, but next to Russia the United States had been at the forefront, attempting to use Britain's entanglements to pry concessions from London on the Isthmus question and on various border conflicts in the north. Even before Lansdowne became foreign secretary, in order to reduce the burden in the western hemisphere[79] the cabinet had made significant concessions on the Panama Canal and on the Clayton-Bulwer Treaty of 1850.[80] In February 1900, the Hay-Pauncefote treaty had recognized the United States' sole right to build, regulate and administer the Panama Canal, an enormous concession as the war against Spain had made the strategic relevance of the Panama Canal very evident to Washington. Yet that was still not enough for Washington. While Britain had hoped to leave open the possibility of using the Panama Canal at times of war, the United States had insisted on exclusivity.[81] In light of the pressures in South Africa and the Far East, the Salisbury administration had had no option but to back down.[82]

When he entered office, Lansdowne had not forgotten Washington's ungracious behaviour. It was, in his eyes, a matter of principle. Although in the current circumstances Britain was not in a position to put up great resistance, he believed it obvious that the situation could soon change again.[83] Like Salisbury, Lansdowne did not think the issue of the canal in the end sufficiently important to be grounds for conflict with the United States. At the same time, however, he wanted to teach the former colonies a lesson in manners. He may have spoken of 'brothers across the Ocean',[84] but in light of his constant bemoaning of the lack of willingness to cooperate on the canal question, his words should be attributed to politeness and not over-interpreted as evidence of an agenda.[85] When it came to Venezuela, Lansdowne's demonstrative disregard for America was entirely in line with that attitude. Mindful of his experiences on the canal issue, he saw no need to remind Washington of London's well-known rights or to inform Washington of how those rights were to be safeguarded. To his mind, Germany's very different response had nothing to do with any perfidious plans being hatched in Berlin and everything to do with the precarious broader situation in which Germany found itself.[86]

Britain's active leadership was also evident during the blockade itself, which began on 9 December 1902, after Castro had ignored the allies' ultimatum. With British forces double the strength of those sent by Germany, London had an evident numerical superiority. Commodore Robert Montgomery summarized the operation neatly when he recorded: 'When boys are naughty, they should be spanked'.[87] Commodore Scheder, his German colleague, was cut from the same cloth. As Montgomery had not yet arrived in the Caribbean, it fell to Scheder to initiate the blockade. When, as planned, he seized the first Venezuelan gunboats, Castro responded by summarily taking two hundred German and British citizens in Caracas as hostages. By this point, the *Panther*, a new German gunboat with a troubled story ahead of it,[88] already had two ships, largely obsolete, in tow – the *Totumo* and the *General Crespo*. News of the hostage taking arrived at the *Panther* along with orders to make for La Guaira as quickly as possible, in order to protect the German consul, his family and the German citizens resident there from the same possibility of being taken hostage. Having received no specific word on what was to happen to the two ships in tow, Scheder ordered them immediately sunk, with the *Panther* then to make for La Guaira at full steam. In retrospect, and in light of the indignation expressed by the *New York Times*, the sinking of the two gunboats was judged evidence of typical German ruthlessness, yet that decision was entirely in accord with military practice of the time.[89] Additionally, the outcome bore out Scheder's decision, for the intimidation led to the immediate release of the hostages. The German navy was not alone in adopting such decisive action, for Montgomery was anything but bashful when it came to having the Royal Navy flex its muscles. Only four days later, he had the coastal fortifications at Puerto Cabello levelled, demonstrating that, unlike Scheder, he was willing to risk the possibility of both military and civilian casualties. What was termed an 'outrageous' affront to the Union Jack provided justification for the bombardment – an excited mob had forced Captain Davison of the *Topaze*, a British merchant ship lying at Puerto Cabello, to haul down the British flag. Montgomery immediately demanded satisfaction. The Venezuelan government in Caracas failed to respond within the thirty-minute ultimatum, and therefore on Montgomery's command at '5.07 p.m.' the *Charybdis*, supported by the *Vineta*, opened fire. The bombardment destroyed the strongholds of Libertador and Vigia.[90] Just how thorough the Royal Navy was is evident in Montgomery's order that units should land to complete the work of the naval bombardment. The Admiral's report to London left no doubt as to who had been in command of the operation: 'The German Commodore backed me up most loyally', Montgomery related.[91] And indeed, Berlin had instructed the German forces to act as back-up: 'Let the British go first', Wilhelm II had commanded.[92]

The message in the Anglo-Saxon press was completely reversed. Although the events had been part of a joint Anglo-German operation, the American press, joined two days later by the London press, pointed the finger at Germany as the sole culprit. For the *New York Times*, the sinking of the two gunboats on 9 December was a disproportionate act of aggression. To Herbert's surprise, that newspaper also attributed the bombardment of Puerto Cabello solely to German expansionism, and he viewed with 'malevolent satisfaction the explosion of feeling against Germany'.[93] It was certainly the case, the New York newspaper reported, that several European powers did not acknowledge the Monroe Doctrine, but, it continued, Britain was 'surely not one of these Powers'.[94] The crusading character of the article is reinforced by the general absence of press reports on the bombardment of Puerto Cabello in both the United States and London. The *Daily Mail* had limited itself to protesting against any cooperation with Berlin, and 4 December had attempted to put Lansdowne and Balfour under pressure by insisting, 'under no circumstances would [we] forgive a Ministry which drifted into strained relations with the United States to oblige Germany'.[95] The leading Fleet Street editors had initially indicated their satisfaction at seeing an example made of the corrupt Castro at last,[96] but two days later, when the response of the American press had been digested, their reaction moved in a radically different direction. Their indignation was directed solely at Germany, partly because of the existing attitudes of certain opinion makers, as already discussed,[97] and partly because of fears that the relationship with the United States could be used as reason to attack Balfour's government.[98] This latter issue proved of far greater interest to the British and American public than to their governments. On 11 December 1902, the *Daily News* warned of American maritime movement in the Caribbean,[99] and subsequently campaigned against what it termed the 'bumbailiff expedition', which, the paper insisted, Britain had been induced by the Kaiserreich to join. The *Daily News* cited several American cabinet members and congressmen as its principal witnesses to the potential and significant threat to Anglo-American relations.[100]

Other liberal publications concurred. The *Manchester Guardian* had initially campaigned in favour of the alliance against Venezuela[101] but abruptly changed its tune and was now dead set against any cooperation between Britain and Germany. Its criticism had two targets, for it was directed against both Germany and the Balfour government, a model repeated in the *Westminster Gazette* and the *Daily Chronicle*.[102] One day later, a storm of indignation was unleashed as Campbell-Bannerman, leader of the opposition, claimed in parliament, 'We are bound hand and foot to Germany'.[103] Now the Sandringham pact between Berlin and London was vilified as an 'ironclad agreement' because of the risks it brought in its wake. 'An energetic Emperor has stolen our independence',[104] the *Daily News* insisted, continuing three days later: 'This barbed hook Lord Lansdowne cheerfully bolted, so that England is bound by a pledge to follow Germany in any wild enterprise'.[105] The *Westminster Gazette* feared that Castro could prove even more unmanageable than feared, and that Britain faced another loss of prestige, compounding the harm done by the Boer War.[106] Concerns about resistance from Castro were combined for the Liberals with the headache of the American attitude.[107] Grey agreed with his friend Spender that conflict with Washington must be avoided at all costs.[108] In parliament, he joined with Campbell-Bannerman in pressuring the Balfour government to separate Britain from Germany at last.[109]

By contrast, the *Times* believed that even after that first operation, a blockade was still necessary and mocked the over-sensitive Americans and their Monroe Doctrine. Venezuela must be brought to its knees. Yet with American anger directed solely at Germany, from 15 December 1902 the *Times* suddenly began to emphasize that it would be better to forgo cooperation with Germany.[110] While Washington had no legal right to get involved, such cooperation could still create the wrong impression, the paper opined.[111] Again, the suspicion raised its head that Berlin's real purpose was to establish outposts throughout the world in order that Germany might be ready to take over from the Empire.[112] The *Daily Mail* was in its element. The scandal sheet insisted that Germany could never be England's friend and should never be treated as such. No mention was made of the fact that only a few months earlier, that same paper had advocated for an attempt to win Germany over for a joint operation against Castro. Now, suddenly, structural differences meant that rapprochement was precluded: economically, its identical interests made Germany Britain's rival; politically, Germany's geographical location between Russia and France was precarious, even deadly; psychologically, Germans envied Britain the Empire. For these reasons, Britain must take a stand against the young Reich and, the *Daily Mail* insisted, the best means of doing so was by turning the skills, knowledge and efficiency shown by Germany into weapons of its own. The dispatch of Prince Henry of Prussia to the United States was seen by the press as a perfidious act designed to position Britain and the United States against one another. Luckily, however, declared the *Contemporary Review*, the American government would not allow itself to be fooled as Lord Lansdowne had been.[113]

Again, we see how the press employed rumour mongering – the newspapers talked, for example, of the dispatch of an American fleet and the threat of war – as a means of exerting influence.[114] Transatlantic and transnational connections came to the fore as the crisis was reflected in the public spheres moulded by the British, American and German press.[115] From mid December, the leading British newspapers were increasingly united in claiming the relationship with Washington as a fundamental pillar of British foreign politics.[116] At the same time, however, the United States showed no evidence of willingness to deal with Castro; much to the contrary, in offering to act as mediator, the White House clearly placed itself on the side of the dictator, for only damages from the time of the revolution would be considered, with all other claims annulled, in keeping with the decree issued by Castro in January 1901. The supposedly special relationship between the two Anglo-Saxon nations appeared very lopsided. Fleet Street was far more concerned with American public opinion than with American policy. Maxse, in particular, but joined by Strachey and other likeminded commentators, saw it as his task to convince his readership of the damage that would be wrought by an alliance between Britain and Germany.[117]

A first climax to that cause was provided by Kipling's poem *The Rowers*, published in the *Times* on 22 December 1902, with cooperation with the 'shameless Huns' the focus of the campaign. Kipling's way with words galvanized London's political sphere. The conservative *Spectator* declared cooperation with Germany to be the greatest diplomatic failure of recent years, and numerous other newspapers and journals agreed.[118] Again, the most virulent attacks on Germany came from the *Spectator*, the *National Review* and Northcliffe's *Daily Mail*, all of which reviled Whitehall's strategy as a 'Germanization of British foreign policy'.[119] Herbert Wilson (Ignotus) sharply attacked the government: 'No minister', he insisted, 'has a right to conclude an alliance which departs from the settled and recognised line of national policy, in defiance of public opinion. No Minister has the right to pledge his country, without consent of Parliament, to responsibilities of which he knows nothing'. Suddenly, Wilson claimed that the whole press had warned against cooperation with Germany, 'and we all know', he wrote, 'that the press answers to and represents public opinion'.[120]

Although Lansdowne and Balfour resisted the public criticism, found the American willingness to mediate impertinent[121] and even considered extending the blockade,[122] in the face of criticism Whitehall was eventually forced to turn its back on cooperation with Germany. As George Saunders had prophesized,[123] as the pressure from the press grew, so too did the pressure within the cabinet, with not just Austen Chamberlain but also Joseph Chamberlain and George Hamilton pushing for a renunciation of the partnership with Germany.[124] Only now, over the New Year, did a brisk exchange between Washington and London begin. London's change of course could be detected in its departure from the united front on which the two parties had originally agreed when it came to demands for compensation. Again, Berlin tied its demands to the demands made by London,[125] but to Berlin's surprise Lansdowne now reverted to the original terms presented at the time of the revolution.[126] Lascelles, the British ambassador in Berlin, and Lansdowne knew that Germany had little choice but to agree: 'The German Government have been frightened by the tone of the English press. They certainly do not wish to increase our difficulties with public opinion in England'.[127]

London now unilaterally abandoned its demands to Caracas and signalled a willingness to negotiate.[128] As the American chargé d'affaires in Caracas, representing Venezuelan interests, attempted to divide the powers responsible for the blockade, Roosevelt played his trump card: he offered London the long-sought-after agreement on the Alaskan border, an issue that had burdened Anglo-American relations for decades. John Hay, US secretary of state, even openly threatened that a belligerent Senate resolution might take the package deal for Alaska and Venezuela off the table.[129] To reinforce the severance of Britain and Germany, at the beginning of 1903 the American Diplomat at Caracas, Herbert Bowen, proposed that the British demands, reduced to £5,500, be given preferential treatment.[130] Additionally, the wishes of non-participating nations, and France in particular, would also be taken into account.[131] The significantly higher demands from Germany, at £66,000, would be deferred to an unspecified later date.

This new course generated irritation in Berlin.[132] When the scale of German demands was discussed in parliament, Lansdowne failed to clarify the facts, leaving the impression that when it came to the repayments, Germany planned to go behind Britain's back and was making unduly high demands. In practice, because the two parties had never agreed differently, Germany was simply reiterating its original claims, the very claims for which the operation had been launched in the first place. Fearing an escalation of the situation from the start, Germany would hardly have risked an international crisis for the negligible sum of £5,500, all that Berlin was to be granted. Finally, Balfour proposed that £5,500 be accepted for the moment, with guarantees provided for the remainder. Germany finally relented.[133]

According to Metternich, Edward VII, who wanted to be rid of the whole matter as quickly as possible, was responding entirely to pressure exerted by the British press,[134] where again, having replied in kind to fire from the fortress of San Carlos on 21 January 1903, Germany had been portrayed as the sole aggressor.

Even the Prince of Wales had to admit that any English naval captain would have done just the same,[135] but that corrective, part of an internal exchange with the German ambassador, was not made public.[136] Lansdowne repeatedly stressed that the German government had behaved entirely correctly throughout the whole crisis,[137] noting: 'The anti-German feeling here has been furious and unreasoning and has, I think, produced a profound impression on the German mind. It has, however, been allowed to go much too far. Kipling's poem was an outrage'.[138] Two weeks later, he commented that the German behaviour as a whole had been trustworthy and fair.[139] He could hardly have made any clearer the growing influence of public opinion on his foreign policy.

At the conclusion of the Venezuela episode, the *National Review* published 'A Warning to the Cabinet', with a demand, indeed practically an ultimatum, that future British foreign policy 'must work for the isolation of Germany, as the most dangerous and aggressive enemy of the Status quo in Europe'.[140] Lansdowne and Balfour, however, held the anti-German campaign to be 'outrageous' and 'abominable', for Berlin and London 'had acted in complete harmony'.[141] Yet a very different impression took hold not only among contemporaries but for many historians too. One reason may lie in Roosevelt's subsequent election campaigning that in the midst of the First World War declared his 'big stick diplomacy' the only means to tackle Wilhelmine aggression.[142] The episode also demonstrated that Germany's principal problem lay less in an exaggeratedly aggressive attitude but rather in its structural weakness. For Leo Maxse, who for years had put the case for renouncing ties with the Kaiserreich, the crisis was unquestionably a 'blessing in disguise'[143] that made very evident the 'virility and vigour' of the campaign to shape public opinion.[144] While in late January 1903 the *Daily News* identified a definite 'parting of the ways'[145] for Germany and Britain, in the *Fortnightly Review* Spender confirmed that interpretation and summarized the lesson that could be learned from the crisis: 'An agreement with Germany is no longer possible as a basis for British policy abroad. ... The countries, in short, are natural rivals and not natural allies'.[146]

The Public as a Political Handicap: The Case of the Baghdad Railway

Spender's conclusion was not limited to transatlantic relations; it also embraced European power constellations. As 'mischief-maker of the world', the Kaiserreich was to be excluded from the realignment of the powers. Edward Grey also found the core of that argument attractive. Even before the Venezuela Crisis, he had compared an alliance with the Kaiserreich to a costly investment that tied up British capital without Britain ever receiving a dividend. Financial parallels also inspired Maxse. A Conservative government had already backed the wrong horse once, he noted, and every politically aware contemporary was clear about his allusion to the famous 'wrong horse' speech made by Salisbury only a few years earlier.[147] If the government should actually attempt to establish a relationship with Germany of any kind, Grey wrote privately to Maxse, he could see no one within the opposition that might stand in its way; public opinion alone had that capacity.[148]

Only a few weeks after the Venezuela job had been so botched, a new opportunity arose to torpedo Anglo-German cooperation by means of a media campaign, with the added advantage of the promotion of closer links with Russia.[149] In and of itself, the Baghdad railway seemed to hold out great advantages for all those involved. In November 1899, and again, together with the *Morning Post*, in summer 1902, the *Times* had welcomed the railway as a counterweight to Russia's continuing advance towards the Gulf. Both papers expressed their full support for the Conservative leadership.[150] In 1899, the sultan had granted the Anatolian Railway Company, which was under German control, the right to construct a railway to the Persian Gulf, but the company was not able to raise the necessary financing on its own and therefore looked to French and British investors.[151] The City initially responded cautiously, wary of the instability of the Ottoman Empire. With Disraeli's purchase of shares in the Suez Canal in mind, Lord Rothschild and Lord Revelstoke called on the British government to buy into the project. Lansdowne preferred, however, to entice private investors by offering generous subventions.[152] Like his predecessor Salisbury, and like Sanderson and Balfour, and along with O'Conor, Lascelles and de Bunsen, all experienced diplomats, the foreign secretary had a soft spot for the project.[153] Firstly, it offered a good and extended opportunity for improved relations with the Kaiserreich.[154] Secondly, while it might be possible to delay such progress, the railway would certainly happen at some point, and standing in its way would only push Britain onto the sidelines, excluded from all the benefits, or, worse still, allow space for Russia to come up with its own plans.[155] Participation, it seemed, was the only way to secure at least a degree of influence.[156] The exclusion of all other powers from the region, a plan repeatedly advocated by Lansdowne's somewhat over-eager university friend Curzon,[157] appeared simply impossible. Thirdly, participation and the concomitant internationalization of the project held out a possibility of being able to control not just Russia's advance but also all the other participating nations. At a ministerial conference held in early February, the participants were of one mind that as long as Britain received its fair share, it would be remiss not to be involved in the construction, for a railway from Constantinople to Baghdad, they agreed, would form 'the most effective check to Russian progress towards the Persian Gulf' and would also bring Turkey and Germany into position.[158] Even Hamilton, who as secretary of state for India tended to pessimism and was practically resigned to pressure from Russia, took heart and attempted to convince Curzon that Britain might regain its prestige and former role as arbitrator.¹⁵⁹ He detected a new opportunity in Lansdowne's tone towards Russia, noting: 'He has not only used firm but at times very strong language. By his attitude and language, he is doing a great deal to regain the positions that have been lost'. Nevertheless, he wrote to Curzon, it would be some time before the Russian government realized that it was dealing with a new and more assertive course adopted by Britain.¹⁶⁰

Lansdowne commissioned financiers Lord Revelstoke, Clinton Dawkins and Sir Ernest Cassel with participation at the negotiations in Paris, where the British goal was to ensure the railway and its terminus at the Persian Gulf were equitably internationalized, which would keep the ambitions of the participating nations in check. After a number of taxing discussions, they were able to report complete success. Germany had yielded on all points, and Dawkins reported that the Anatolian Railway had been included in the terms of the treaty and therefore was also to be internationalized.¹⁶¹

Although the German party had met the demands made of it, there was still no agreement. The delay was caused by politicking in London. For many journalists and for the opposition, Lansdowne's foreign policy had become too complicated, and the whole business of the Baghdad railway was evidence that the government was allowing too many variations to its original concept. Dawkins would recall that Lansdowne 'manifested great pleasure' at the outcome of the negotiations, but at the beginning of April Metternich noted, 'the *Spectator* and the *National Review*, which have made much capital out of anti-German feeling and preach of an understanding with Russia, violently opened fire on the whole Baghdad scheme'.¹⁶² Only a few weeks after all the campaigning against Lansdowne's South American policy, Whitehall seemed about to come under pressure again.¹⁶³

Following a private recommendation from Grey, Strachey and Maxse had agreed to a joint attack on the planned cooperation between Britain and Germany.¹⁶⁴ They already rejected every possible agreement with Berlin as a matter of course, and this specific plan was also diametrically opposed to their desired Anglo-Russian alliance. It is impossible to establish how they knew of the secret negotiations – perhaps their close friend Chamberlain, secretary of state for the colonies, was deliberately indiscreet, or perhaps word reached them through diplomatic channels.¹⁶⁵ There is no doubt, however, that during his recent journey to Russia, Strachey had noted with great concern that the Russians were not taking Britain especially seriously,¹⁶⁶ which he found all the more unsettling as Cecil Spring Rice had informed him of the sensitivities of the situation in the Middle East associated with Russia's presence in the region.¹⁶⁷ Adding in further information from Mallet and gleaned from the Russian press, in an article that appeared in the *Spectator* on 4 April Strachey issued a warning about the plans for possible collaboration with Germany. Although he did not know the details and was working only from various reports that had appeared in the *Novoe Vremja*, he claimed: 'The Germans under the present scheme will at any moment be able to make over their whole interest in the railway to Russia'.[168] Having been filled in by Saunders in late 1901,[169] Maxse made much the same case, although with much greater vehemence.[170] Only chance and his good relationship with Jean Constans, the French ambassador to Constantinople, he recorded, had meant he had even heard anything of the outrageous discussions between Germany and Britain.[171] The Foreign Office must be lacking in any instinct if it really was prepared to enter into an agreement with Berlin, whose only goal ever since the time of Bismarck had been to embroil Britain and Russia in a war.[172]

The argumentation of the various articles on the Baghdad railway carried in the *Spectator* and *National Review* had the British public clearly in mind. The horror of closer ties with Germany was used as the hook, while the newspapers' actual objective was to convey subtly the need for rapprochement with Russia.[173] In May, Emile Dillon repeated his colleagues' arguments in the *Contemporary Review*, emphasizing the overlap with the views and protestations of Witte and the *Novoe Vremja*.[174] And indeed, Strachey and Maxse had based their articles not on their own research but, as they explicitly acknowledged, on rumours spread by the leading Russian newspaper. Maxse repeatedly made reference to his well-informed contacts in Paris who had informed him of a secret agreement between Germany and Russia directed against British interests. The reports sought to bring home the impact of any such agreement, which 'kills the prospect of any Anglo-Russian agreement', 'will arouse lasting feelings of bitterness among Russians' and 'means good-bye to the possibility of coming to terms with Russia'.[175]

For some historians, the press's opposition was motivated by a political desire for a balance of powers,[176] but Dillon had a rather different explanation: 'Russia can harm us very seriously without actually going to war – Germany will not and cannot take sides against her neighbour'.[177] Spring Rice had previously explained to Strachey that Germany or Turkey could not be relied upon to contain Russia; indeed, their own weakness suggested that in the short or long term they were more likely to ally with Russia against Britain. Spring Rice not only kept Strachey abreast of the British dilemma but also bolstered his conviction that Britain lacked the strong and trustworthy partners necessary to maintain the traditional balance of power policy. It was more sensible in the long term, he suggested, to ally, even with a heavy heart, with Russia, at the expense of Germany, and establish a system based on hegemonial power blocs.[178] As Maxse admitted to Mahan, and as the tenor of the numerous articles in his journal confirmed, Germany's geopolitical weakness in relation to Russia was the deciding factor for the foreign policy priorities advocated by the press.[179]

The press campaign in favour of appeasement increasingly addressed, even targeted, liberal imperial politicians. Hardly had the rumours begun to circulate in the political sphere when Henry Norman and Edward Grey protested against any

Anglo-German discussions and demanded an agreement between Britain and Russia instead.[180] Maxse wrote in his monthly column for May 1903 that one could hope that not only independent unionists such as Chamberlain but also influential politicians such as Lord Rosebery, Herbert Asquith and Sir Edward Grey would now make their presence known. As long as Lansdowne failed to grasp the 'ABC' of British foreign policy, it would be 'inevitable' that he would 'find himself in perpetual conflict with British public opinion, and such a conflict can only end in one way'.[181]

Lord Esher soon suspected that nothing good could come of the growing pressure from the press, and he feared that the government would prove unable to stand its ground. With his memories of the Suez Canal and his awareness of the benefits to Russia, he believed adoption of the policy advocated by the press would be a great mistake, especially as it was apparent that the rumours and accusations were nothing but transparent and untenable attacks motivated by the fact that the Baghdad railway was a German project.

> Stupid fools! There is no pacificator like a railway. We ruled the Punjab more by the locomotive than by the sword. Also the Sudan. … The Government will flinch. They are very timid … The Germans will go on just the same and the Railway will ultimately be made, only we shall be out of it. We never learn by experience.[182]

Esher's prediction about the government's response proved correct. Only three days after the first two articles appeared, Balfour found himself facing a parliamentary question from Gibson Bowles, who was critical of the government, and required to make a public statement. He sought to calm the waters with an assurance that the government would not enter into any agreement that did not give Britain equal rights over the railway.[183] Lansdowne played for time, and Dawkins recalled[184] that he and Revelstoke were summoned to an enraged Foreign Office. Confronted with the massive opposition from the media, Lansdowne back-pedalled on the negotiations because of what he identified as a serious attempt to disparage his foreign policy, along with the plans for British participation, solely on the grounds that Germany was also involved. The negotiations, which had been going well, would not be concluded for the moment, so that opponents would not have even more to complain about.[185] Any hope that the disquiet could be dispelled, however, proved abortive. In Liverpool, Balfour sought one more time 'with all earnestness in my power' to convince the public 'that these international animosities' in South America and in the Near East or Far East 'are a great source of international weakness'. They limited Britain's foreign policy down to only a single possibility and yet only mere trifles were at stake. What of the implications if a real crisis should develop? 'Nations foolish enough to cherish grudges risked greatly aggravating any real controversy which might arise', he noted, insisting that public opinion, 'however provocative, must not be allowed to warp British policy'.[186] On various occasions, Balfour had demonstrated great enthusiasm for the German plan for the Baghdad railway,[187] but that response now conjured up the opposition of anti-German and pro-Russian activists.

Maxse in particular saw himself as herald of the British public, who, he believed, understood foreign policy far better than those tasked with conducting it.[188] He was delighted to recognize that only 'several Jews' – the reference was to Iwan-Müller of the *Daily Telegraph* and Lucien Wolf of the *Daily Graphic* and *Standard* – had not responded to the rallying cry against an Anglo-German agreement. The great majority of the press criticized Whitehall sharply, and even the *Times*, Maxse noted, was now 'on the fence'.[189] Those who had launched the campaign expressed their pleasure at its success:

> The *Spectator* is magnificent on the Baghdad Railway. If we had not blown the gaff, the British Public would have been presented a fait accompli in the beginning of April, and the war between Russia and England, for which Germany has worked for the last twenty years, would have been brought a step nearer. We are by no means out of the woods, but I think we have a chance of defeating Lord Lansdowne's latest.[190]

On 23 April, Balfour finally announced an about-turn.[191] Shortly before, the agreement between Germany and Turkey had been published, given by Arthur Gwinner, head of the Deutsche Bank and the Anatolian Railway, to the *Times* in the hope of calming the situation. Rather than employ it to that end, however, the *Times* had used the text to incite the public further. Skilfully, attention had been directed away from the relatively mundane content of the agreement and onto an accompanying two-page lead article that portrayed the treaty as a Machiavellian power play and openly accused Balfour of dissembling.[192] Together with the lobbying of his fellow cabinet members by Joseph Chamberlain, who was in regular contact with Saunders, Maxse and Strachey, the publication of this article was decisive in destroying the original majority in favour of the railway plan, ensuring that Balfour and Lansdowne were outvoted. Both men had been taken by surprise by the attitude of the *Times*, for they had thought Valentine Chirol, as a responsible editor-in-chief, at least neutral on the Baghdad railway.[193]

The prime minister and his foreign secretary had had to give way under the combined impact of internal and external pressure.[194] The press also left a lasting impression on Chamberlain, whose responsibilities meant he had never developed a particular interest in the Middle East[195] and who was if anything anti-Russian.[196] As Dawkins credibly reported, the secretary of state for the colonies never decided anything 'without an eye on the electorate'. Additionally, Chamberlain had become an outspoken opponent of cooperation between Britain and Germany, and his opposition may well have been another opportunity to vent his annoyance that during his absence Britain had been part of a joint action with Germany in South America. Dawkins also interpreted

Chamberlain's veto as tit-for-tat directed at Brodrick, secretary of state for war, who originally had similarly supported the railway project but had previously opposed Chamberlain's proposed build-up of South Africa as a military base. According to Dawkins, internal cabinet animosities and his public reputation were the real grounds for Chamberlain's objection.[197]

Dawkins' fascinating account gives us access to the situation immediately before, during and shortly after the decisive cabinet meeting. 'With great ardour' Balfour and Lansdowne together countered their critics with the argument that sooner or later the railway would be built, whether or not Britain was involved, that railways were an achievement of civilization, and that Britain must not be allowed to isolate herself. Additionally, the railway provided a one-time opportunity to legitimize and anchor British interests in the Gulf, which would be beneficial not only because of the ambitions of other powers but also because British trade and industry constantly complained about a lack of political support.[198]

After the British withdrawal and the experiences of the winter, Lansdowne appears to have been generally shocked by the vehemence of the anti-German campaign, which put his policy under considerable pressure and limited his room for manoeuvre: 'We are still suffering from an insensate hatred and suspicion of anything which can be described of German origin and these feelings will not die out in a hurry – it is ridiculous and to my mind humiliating', he recorded.[199] Lansdowne was not alone in believing the animosity and the incitement of the public extremely damaging – he was joined by other influential figures, such as Selborne and Sanderson, who were not themselves even especially pro-German.[200] The precise nature of the press campaign's impact on the eventual outcome cannot be known, but most of those who were involved were apparently convinced that the media was responsible for derailing the agreement between Germany and Britain.[201] With disappointment, the British foreign secretary explained the decision to his ambassador at the Porte, along with the limits to the government's ability to determine foreign policy that it demonstrated, as a product of the 'violence of the outburst of public opinion'.[202] Esher also deemed the government's back-down disastrous:

> It is a pity. The Defence Committee are strongly in favour of the line ... it is well for us to have a joint control ... there can be no doubt. But the German Emperor is a bogey just now in certain quarters, and the English People led by the foolish half informed press, are children in foreign politics.[203]

Dawkins believed the whole episode evidence of political ineptitude. Like Revelstoke, he was convinced that Germany would even have agreed to further concessions. But how, he wondered, could they possibly have kept face if their government, under pressure from the press, had again retreated at the last moment and under the thinnest of pretexts: 'There would have been another unmotivated withdrawal, and we should have been once more left in the lurch! The whole muddle again'.[204]

In the meantime, Chirol assessed Lansdowne's attitude as 'wobbly'.[205] He wanted to see Curzon made foreign secretary, as only Curzon and Chamberlain had remained resolute and shown backbone. Yet Chirol's verdict appears highly cynical. As recently as September 1899, he had expressly encouraged Germany, via Saunders, to become involved in the Middle East, emphasizing that London would welcome a counterweight to the Dual Alliance.[206] In summer 1902, he had repeated that attitude in the *Times*, emboldening the British government. Then, in spring 1903, he suddenly changed sides, joining with Maxse, Strachey and his colleague Saunders to launch an all-out attack on his own government on account of its plans for cooperation with Germany and to demand the very retreat that he now presented as evidence of the government's weakness.

As had also been the case with Venezuela, journalists had become political actors with no real concern for nuanced reporting; their goal was to whip up public passions. As both Chirol and Strachey admitted in private, it was of little interest to the journalists that far greater concessions had been wrestled from Germany than had been expected.[207] Chirol was far more interested in the threat from Russia than in the threat from Germany. He informed Saunders two years after the fact that in November 1902 he had had a conversation with Bülow that had left him convinced that should it come to it, Germany would be too weak to be of any assistance against Russia. German interest in the railway was therefore, he believed, either evidence of a secret German-Russian agreement or intended to bind Britain to Russia.[208] Although he had not been at all in favour of looking to Russia, gradually, he wrote, he had come to accept that option as the best of a bad lot.[209] While the Germanophobes argued that should it come to an agreement with Germany, Britain would appear 'so abject in its attitude towards Germany ... that the more offensively it is treated the more obsequious it becomes',[210] Lansdowne recognized that a very similar signal might be sent to Russia. In using information gleaned from the *Novoe Vremja*,[211] the two leading organs of the press indirectly confirmed Lansdowne's view that 'Strachey and Maxse are doing worse still by preaching a throw-yourself-into-the-arms-of-Russia-at-any-price-doctrine'.[212] And indeed, their arguments appeared to be based only on the vague hope that Russia 'appreciates our action'.[213] The differing approaches of the two sides could hardly have been clearer. Even Dawkins recognized that the campaign could mean, on one hand, liberation from the Kaiserreich, but, on the other hand, the risk that Britain would serve itself up to a far stronger opponent, and he recorded: 'The Russians ... disliked the whole affair. And they found an English Editor, whose passion is to throw us into the arms of Russia blindfold'.[214] As Dawkins informed Gwinner that the British press campaign could be traced back to Russian influence, Wilhelm II's suspicion that Russian correspondent Wesselitzki lay behind what had happened is not unsurprising.[215]

In Hamilton's mind, London had a choice between seeking to counter the Russian advance in the Gulf or following an appeasement strategy, which might win time but would allow Russia to exploit the situation. A traditional approach based on a balance of powers would be handicapped by the London public. Whenever British interests were at stake, the public adopted a resolute, almost truculent attitude towards France and Germany, but, he noted, 'when we come to deal with Russia, the whole conditions are reversed. France and Germany [are] both vulnerable to naval attack, both [have] Colonies and both [have] a large commerce. Russia is impenetrable to attack'.[216] Inevitably, his essential scepticism about the parliamentary system was reinforced by the recognition that with the House of Commons and public opinion 'perpetually interfering and exercising an influence on the trend of our foreign policy', Britain was not in a position to try its luck and take on a seemingly invincible enemy.[217] Apparently for that reason, he had in the end voted against the project. Hopes for a new British assertiveness in the face of Russia were too faint. He was convinced that while the public campaign had made such an aggressive stance impossible, it had opened up a new opportunity for an alliance with Russia.[218]

Lansdowne and Balfour continued to try to convince their fellow Britons of the benefits of participation in the Baghdad railway.[219] Both the Venezuelan crisis and the discussions surrounding the railway project had highlighted the press's self-assigned role as a political actor and its influence over foreign policy, which significantly constricted Whitehall's options. Those around Maxse and Strachey demanded nothing less than a change of course.[220] The assessment of Drummond-Wolff, Lansdowne's advisor, was astute: the vehement opposition to agreement between Britain and Germany was directed at Berlin, but viewed more closely that opposition did not adopt the traditional pattern in calling for a counterweight to Germany, but was instead a product of 'the disinclination to offend Russia'.[221]

Morocco and Anglo-French Rapprochement

Drawing a lesson from the public opposition to Anglo-German cooperation, in May 1903 the *Fortnightly Review* proposed a 'Latin rapprochement' with France, which would rework existing international constellations and encompass a closer relationship with Russia.[222] Less than a year later, in April 1904, the Anglo-French convention presaged that precise transformation of Great Power politics. During the Boer War, Théophile Delcassé had repeatedly attempted, via Russian Foreign Minister Muraviev, to draw the German Reich into a continental league directed against Britain.[223] Yet despite the anti-English hysteria among the German public, Berlin would not countenance any thought of such Machiavellian games unless German possessions within Europe were secured against the Dual Alliance. As Christopher Andrew has correctly observed, after Fashoda and the unsuccessful attempt to woo Berlin, for the first time the French foreign minister recognized that Paris had to accept British occupation of Egypt and British control of the Suez Canal.[224]

In Britain, however, there was no sense that Germany should be compensated for its neutrality. Bertie's assessment that the services of Berlin could be acquired at no cost had already proved correct. At the same time, abetted by the nascent pro-Russian and anti-German campaign and the international tensions that followed, for the British public the traditional threat from France and Russia was now upstaged by the 'German peril'.[225]

That development did not go unnoticed at the Quai d'Orsay. A fundamental change of direction was introduced to French policy, on the initiative not of Delcassé but of his ambassador Paul Cambon, who, as he interacted on a daily basis with the political mood in London, thought in broader conceptual terms. Earlier, in January 1901, he had raised the possibility of an Anglo-French agreement on Morocco, an offer he repeated to Lansdowne in March 1901 and summer 1902.[226] Anxious to reach an agreement, he repeatedly gave the French foreign minister the impression that the British, and specifically Lord Lansdowne, were eager to enter into talks.[227] Metternich, the German ambassador, reported with apprehension that discussions involving Chamberlain and Cambon had taken place, but he did not know for certain what topic they had addressed. A week later, Eckardstein was able to throw some light on the issue, for during a banquet held at Marlborough House on 8 February, he overheard the terms 'Morocco' and 'Egypt' being used during a secretive exchange.[228] The foreign secretary refused to be drawn into the horse-trading proposed by the French, taking a definitive stand in August 1902.[229] He noted that he was not opposed to a colonial exchange in principle, for Newfoundland, West Africa, the New Hebrides or Siam, for example,[230] but the situation was fundamentally different for Morocco, where the European Great Powers collided openly. Longstanding German interests in Morocco had been expressly acknowledged by Lansdowne.[231]

With good reason, Lansdowne feared that on learning of the plan proposed by France, the sultan would request assistance from Germany, which could produce an international crisis involving the signatories of the Madrid convention of 1880. Britain would be required to take an unequivocal stand, but should Berlin and Paris come to a bilateral agreement, Britain would still in all likelihood lose out the most. He initially made clear to Cambon that he was only interested in a demarcation of interests in Siam,[232] continuing the model of his predecessor, who had established that when a colonial-related agreement was made with another Great Power, it must have no potentially explosive impact on Britain's relationship with a third power, above all in the form of repercussions in Europe itself. When it came to Morocco, Lansdowne was in agreement with

Balfour when, with German interests in mind, he declared the best solution to be internationalization.

Lansdowne's initial intention to leave everything in Morocco as it was[233] had been turned on its head by December 1902. Following a rebellion against the sultan and the defeat of his troops, who were under British command, the North African state seemed at risk of collapse.[234] The parallels with the situation in Venezuela were striking: the Royal Navy was dispatched to transport British citizens to safety; arrangements were made should the sultan need to flee; and Morocco was bankrupt.[235] Lansdowne received a request from Paris that the advantageous situation might be used to settle the Morocco issue without reference to any other power, excluding Germany in particular. The massive public criticism of the unholy alliance over Venezuela evidently influenced the interactions of the European Great Powers. Reluctantly and with great hesitation, but under heavy fire for continuing to cooperate with Germany over Venezuela,[236] Lansdowne finally agreed to the French proposal. Official word from Whitehall suggested that he believed it sensible to keep the number of intervening powers to a minimum,[237] but as only Berlin and Vienna were thereby excluded, the real intention was not easily concealed.

The foreign secretary had moved away from the established model of collective treaties, but there was no thought (at least in London) at this point of establishing a counterweight to Berlin. In light of the vehemence of the anti-German campaign being conducted in London, defence of the legal position, which would mean further support for Berlin, was simply unthinkable. To do so, on one hand, would have likely – perhaps definitely – ensured that the existing problems with Russia in Persia and China would have been compounded by further complications with France, and on the other hand would have led to massive criticism in London that could have imperilled the governing party, already teetering under tariff reform. Lansdowne preferred to follow the path of least resistance. That decision would ease the way to entente, but in the first months of 1903 such was not yet Lansdowne's specific goal.

In several reports, Lord Cromer, British Consul-General of Egypt, explained to the British foreign secretary that only an agreement among the Great Powers could guarantee the orderly reform of Morocco's finances and the stabilization of that country. Despite warning from Balfour, who insisted that Europe's treaty law be respected and therefore an international conference called,[238] in his answer to France, Lansdowne held out the prospect of Morocco's division between France and Spain, with Berlin excluded entirely, *conditio sine qua non* for French agreement.[239] That response was not intended to set a new course for the long term, for, as Lansdowne explained to Cromer, his goal was only to create space for a possible solution to the Morocco issue.

These initial ideas only took on more concrete form at the beginning of July, against the background of the possibility of a conflict in the Far East with potentially global implications,[240] a situation that eventually produced a worldwide barter. On 3 July 1903, with a French delegation already present in London for exploratory discussions, the foreign secretary unexpectedly received word from Hayashi that Japan was no longer willing to accept Russian policy in Manchuria without responding. Lansdowne had evidently underestimated Japan and now had to recognize that Balfour had been right to advise against entering into an alliance with the ambitious Asian power.[241]

Now Lansdowne needed a new approach that would ensure Britain was not drawn into the issues in Asia, not least as just at this moment a likely temporary, but certainly inglorious, end to Britain's involvement with the Baghdad railway had put the Anglo-Russian conflict zone in the Middle East back on the agenda. Delcassé's presence in London provided a good opportunity to turn to the French foreign minister in an attempt to lessen the tensions. Although there had been no plans for the two foreign ministers to meet, they now assured each other that their differences were of little consequence when set alongside the global implications of the looming conflict, and they agreed to a joint settlement of the problems in Egypt and Morocco. France would be responsible for ensuring stability returned to Morocco, under the condition that the Mediterranean coast was kept neutral, Spanish interests were respected and British trade protected. In exchange, Lansdowne received assurances that the problems in Egypt would be resolved as he had intended.[242]

The chronology of events makes clear that these agreements were made against the backdrop of a possible conflict in the Far East. Only the thought of a looming global political crisis meant that Lansdowne was willing to accept Delcassé's promises on Egypt, which the British foreign secretary recognized were rather indistinct. The indirect approach to France via North Africa was intended to loosen Paris's ties with St Petersburg and thereby make it less likely that, should conflict break out in the Far East, Britain would face a *casus foederis*.[243] Impressed by the efforts made by his French colleague with regard to the Russian ambassador,[244] the British foreign secretary also recognized that an understanding with France might also improve Britain's relationship with Russia.[245] There was talk of a 'stepping stone to a general understanding with Russia',[246] at least from Cromer. Both Cromer and Lansdowne were also aware, however, that Delcassé was eager to see the Kaiserreich entirely isolated and with its back against the wall: as Cromer wrote to Lansdowne, 'I fancy that Delcassé hopes that we shall come to terms with Russia, and thus isolate Germany … It is manifestly in French interest that we fall out with Germany'.[247] Yet is that evidence strong enough to suggest that the Entente Cordiale should be understood as a measure intended to ensure a political balance of power in Europe?[248]

Ultimately, Cromer and Lansdowne hoped that Berlin would remain calm. According to Lansdowne, France could at least help relax the tensions in the relationship between Britain and Russia. Lascelles was therefore to make clear to the Wilhelmstrasse that Britain's alliance with France was not directed against Germany and that Germany now had a golden opportunity to earn Britain's gratitude.[249] Only Cromer was looking ahead, and he attempted to convince the foreign secretary that he should consider an Anglo-Russian rapprochement,[250] writing: 'I gather from what I have read that you are not sanguine about the possibility of arranging with the Russians. For you it is impossible to rely on Russia, [but] it is still worth an effort. ... I do not think I ever remember such an opportunity'.[251]

To Lansdowne's relief, in light of the public pressure of recent months and the beginnings of a cabinet crisis, for once the London press welcomed the course adopted by Whitehall.[252] Chirol was downright enthusiastic, for every dispute with Paris came with the added danger of a duel with invincible Russia,[253] while Saunders expressed his relief that as rapprochement between Britain and France might well cause the government to distance itself further from Germany, he would no longer have to put so much effort into anti-German campaigning; 'this would be a great relief to myself and a saving of the space and the money of *The Times*', he noted.[254] Additionally, the Liberal opposition gave the course adopted by Lansdowne its unanimous support.[255]

Germany had little, indeed nothing, with which to counter. London therefore had no scruples about disregarding Berlin's interests of an 'open door' policy for Morocco. Lansdowne appeared also deeply impressed by the value of the rapprochement with France, for in autumn 1903 Paris extracted from Lamsdorff, the Russian foreign minister, a promise to take greater account of British sensitivities in future.[256]

Lansdowne was not prepared, however, to let France get away with its excessive demands, not least because Paris was evidently attempting to use French mediation as grounds for extorting as large concessions as possible from London.[257] On 2 April, he complained vociferously to Balfour about the arrogance of the French, who were again calling into question British occupation of Egypt and were also proving completely unwilling to accept any compromise on fishing rights off Newfoundland. The negotiations appear to have been far more difficult than is often portrayed. Again, the London leadership was negotiating from a position of strength. The implications of Lansdowne's willingness to allow the negotiations to collapse over commercial issues only six days before the agreement was signed have often been overlooked by historians,[258] yet they show that in the Anglo-French negotiations, as in the Anglo-German and Anglo-Russian exploratory talks on Persia, Lansdowne was not prepared to carry on with talks for their own sake. Historians have repeatedly failed to recognize that, well aware of the strength of the British negotiating position, Lansdowne was no typical Edwardian peering pessimistically into the future.[259] Evidently, the foreign secretary was clear how far he would go and which concessions were worth making for the price of a political alliance, and which were too costly. Thus, for example, despite the very significant internal political problems Delcassé was currently facing, and despite Francis Bertie's repeated intercessions on his behalf, London was not prepared to come to Delcassé's aid against his critics and deviate from its own course.[260] That reality was again evident when, after Russia's catastrophic defeat in the Battle of Mukden, the French foreign minister appealed to London to intervene. The request was declined. Lansdowne roundly refused to recognize the good services of the French minister by seeking to placate Britain's Japanese allies. Bertie's depiction of the dangers of an anti-British continental alliance and the arguments about the creation of a bridge between France and Russia also left Lansdowne unmoved.[261]

Strikingly, this phase was characterized not so much by an end to Britain's isolation and integration into a European network as by targeted consolidation at various levels and by various means. When bilateral agreements were in play, the new constellations they might form were to remain firmly under the direction of Britain. Additionally, Lansdowne's confident negotiating style made evident the extent of British room to manoeuvre and the fluid state of international relations. The first defeats of Russia appeared to grant him greater political scope, and he could view the consolidation of the Dual Alliance with greater equanimity than in the previous summer. The Entente Cordiale was in intent and content a colonial alliance, a temporary agreement intended to relieve current pressures on Britain, both global and domestic. Germany's role was at most indirect. The differences from a general alliance intended to ensure a balance of power were underscored, and Whitehall emphasized to Paris the limits of British support rather than elaborate on the possibilities and opportunities associated with the agreement.

Mallet and Grey suspected that Lansdowne and Balfour had simply failed to recognize the fundamentally new situation that they had conjured up with the Entente Cordiale.[262] In fact, that assessment could better have been applied to those who, like they themselves, had had more in mind with the Entente. Lansdowne and Balfour had been fully conscious of the dangers and Delcassé's intentions. Not for nothing had the prime minister insisted on the internationalization of the Morocco issue and limited the Entente to colonial concerns. The opportunity of the moment appeared in the end more important. Cromer emphasized the significance of the rapprochement, while Cranborne wondered if he would not have preferred the role of *tertius gaudens*. Lansdowne, by contrast, congratulated himself on his policy, which had left it to another power to deal with as helpless and as hopeless a country as Morocco. What more would come of it all, he noted, would become clear of its own accord.[263]

For the first time in over a year, the London press responded positively to Lansdowne's foreign policy. Even his sharpest critics at the *Times*, the *Spectator* and the *National Review* were full of praise, identifying in the rapprochement with France a lesson directed against Germany.[264] The radical liberal press read the situation very differently but still responded equally positively – they saw nothing anti-German in the alliance and recognized instead a possible end to traditional Anglo-French enmity and perhaps even, the *Manchester Guardian* suggested, the beginning of a new era for a global Great Power concert embracing democratic states.[265]

Edward VII, Charles Hardinge, Maurice Bompard and Paul Cambon seized the opportunity, however, to seek to extend the Entente Cordiale, against the will of Lansdowne and Balfour,[266] to include autocratic Russia.[267] Even if the Entente was not initially directed against Germany, the Kaiserreich was still the principal loser, and yet, again Germany had not breached any law, indeed much to the contrary. While the other signatories at Madrid in 1880 had received compensation, Berlin and Vienna had been left empty handed. An oft-repeated claim in the literature proposes that Lansdowne's intention was to test Germany's friendship.[268] In Lansdowne's eyes, however, Germany had been Britain's friend both in Venezuela and over the Baghdad railway and yet had repeatedly been left with nothing – later Spender would even talk of Germany having been abandoned – which makes evident that this new test was not a sign of Germanophilia but rather evidence that Lansdowne's principal concern was for Britain's own interests.[269] He did not see the Entente, however, as a safeguard to the balance of power.[270]

The Russo-Japanese War

Rapprochement with France was one option for limiting the risks that might arise from Britain's alliance with Japan. Grappling with Britain's position in the Far East was a rather different matter. Put simply, no one could be sure whether the agreement for North Africa would extend to the other side of the world, and, if so, for how long. In December 1903, as a clash between Russia and Japan appeared increasingly likely, intensive discussions were launched in London. While the British military favoured direct intervention,[271] the strained financial situation ruled out that option from the start.[272] Lansdowne, Selborne, Austen Chamberlain and Balfour were far from being of one mind on either the prevention of a war or how Britain should act.[273] Selborne held that a conflict could hardly be avoided and that neither Britain's interests nor Britain's responsibilities permitted the country simply to look on while Japan was attacked; then again, he feared the firestorm that might result, for if Britain attacked, France would surely go to Russia's aid.[274] Austen Chamberlain, who had recently joined the cabinet, feared the government might be forced to intervene by the British public. If Russia should be victorious, it would surely be all the harder to find a diplomatic means of protecting British interests. He therefore recommended Britain follow a 'selfish but national game'.[275]

Initially, Balfour and Lansdowne did not agree. Lansdowne insisted that nothing that might prevent a conflict should go untried. While St Petersburg was ready to recognize the status quo in Manchuria and Korea, Tokyo sought to extend its authority permanently into Korea. Lansdowne therefore proposed that Japan should be forced to enter into negotiations.[276] Balfour was not convinced. Rather than bewail the alliance, of which he had been critical from the start, he insisted that Britain must stand by its decision, especially as he had always believed Russia to be the greater threat to global stability and in any case had no faith in negotiations with the tsardom. Historians have always seen the debate that took place in the last week of December 1903 as evidence of a fundamental difference of opinion and serious conflict between peace-loving and accommodation-favouring Lansdowne, who might even be deemed to some extent 'pro-Russian', and the Machiavellian Balfour, a judgement that appears to be supported by Lansdowne's comment to Balfour: 'I attach I think more importance to averting war than you do'.[277]

Arthur Balfour had been troubled for longer than his colleagues by the risks associated with the alliance with Japan. In October, he had expressed his concern about developments: 'If Japan goes to war, who is going to lay long odds that we are not at loggerheads with Russia within six months?'[278] Now, two months later, he was more confident, writing to Selborne: 'I detest all war, but if any war could be conceived as being advantageous to us this is one. Both, before, during and after it is likely to do wonders in making Russia amenable to sweet reason. ... We are only required to "keep the ring"'.[279] While Lansdowne and Selborne wavered over whether Britain could remain on the sidelines, Balfour had no doubts about his own position.[280] Unlike his foreign secretary, he looked beyond the specifics of the current situation, adopting a broader perspective and remaining unruffled. As he wrote to Edward VII, the status quo in China had been one reason why he had opposed entering into an alliance with Tokyo, for in light of the identities of the competing powers, it was always going to be impossible on the ground, let alone from London, to find a permanent solution using diplomatic means.[281] Buoyed by the positive and ultimately reassuring results from the Committee of Imperial Defence, he was convinced that Britain would be under no threat as long as it kept calm and played its cards right. Yes, negotiations might be launched, but what could that really achieve, he asked. Japan and every other potential partner would question British loyalty, which could only burden future negotiations. He responded to Selborne's concerns by noting that France would certainly not dig up the hatchet again for the sake of Russian interests in Manchuria as long as Britain retained a well-intentioned neutrality.[282] He agreed that direct intervention was precluded on financial grounds,[283] but he opined that in any case Britain could confidently limit its role to that of onlooker. In several detailed statements, he made clear his views on the approach Britain should take.

Balfour did not reckon on a Japanese victory, although he did not think the conflict would be a walk in the park for Russia. Again, Balfour demonstrated that he was primarily concerned with Britain's security, as a politician who had learned much from his experts in the Committee on Imperial Defence and now brought that knowledge into a much larger political arena. To Balfour's mind, Japan was weaker than Russia, at least in terms of its naval strength, and would likely not be able to send a secure expeditionary force to Korea, or rather to maintain lines of communication and supply between Japan and the Asian mainland. But at the same time, it would similarly be impossible, he believed, for Russia to conquer Japan, and he therefore deemed a Russian invasion of Japan improbable, recording: 'a war therefore would not "smash" Japan in the sense of whipping it out as a military force: nor need it greatly damage her fleet'. As a student of modern naval warfare, Balfour had learned from Fisher and Corbett about the tactical significance of cruisers and torpedoes, and he therefore thought that Japan's real advantage lay in its dominance in these areas. Japanese warships were inferior to Russian warships in firepower, but a war would not seriously threaten Japan itself, only Japanese interests in Korea.[284] An expensive victory by the tsardom was, Balfour therefore believed, probable, although by no means certain. Morally, he was clear it would certainly be wrong to encourage Tokyo to go to war, but from a British standpoint it would be equally wrong to use all possible means to keep Japan from taking that step. If the conflict could be limited geographically and to only these two parties, a war between Russia and Japan would be anything but an 'unmixed curse'.[285] Japan might be forced out of Korea, but even then, there could be nothing better for London than that Russia exhaust itself in Korea. The best-case scenario saw Russia win one more useless, expensive and hard-to-secure province, and that would only guarantee that 'whenever she [Russia] went to war with another Power ... Japan would be upon her back'.[286]

Overall then, for Balfour, Russia's value to France as an ally in case of a conflict with Britain was almost negligible and all Russian diplomatic efforts for the whole area from the Black Sea to the Oxus would have to be based on 'sweet reasonableness'.[287] Germany, he stressed, thought similarly and hoped for a pyrrhic Russian victory, which would banish the spectre of a war on two fronts.[288]

Lansdowne was of a different opinion. He reported that experts within the Royal Navy had given him to believe[289] that Japan's military power was currently greater than Russia's[290] – a surprising claim as historians have normally assumed that naval experts expected Russia to be victorious[291] – but that personally he believed that in the long term Russia would more likely prove the superior power. Lansdowne held that by the following autumn, Russia might well be in control in the region, which would be fatal for Britain's local interests.[292] Rather than await an uncertain military outcome,[293] Lansdowne favoured a negotiated solution, for with war came three significant risks:

1. The possibility that our ally may be crushed.
2. That we ourselves may become implicated, not on account of Treaty rights but because the British public will not sit still while the crushing is being done.
3. The aggravation of our present financial difficulties, already grave enough.[294]

All in all, Lansdowne certainly had greater interest in the Far East than Balfour, but unlike in the case of the alliance, he was unable to persuade the majority of the cabinet to follow his lead. Selborne showed some sympathies for his point of view,[295] but Chamberlain even hoped that Japan would declare war as soon as possible.[296] Edward VII was convinced by Balfour's argument that the alliance with Japan brought no responsibilities on Britain as long as the war remained limited.[297] As this exchange of views made evident, the real debate was not over a fundamental political orientation but rather on how Russia might be most effectively contained.

On 29 December, the prime minister announced the course to be taken. Only British interests had any bearing. An invasion of Japan and Japan's defeat had to be prevented. With the possibility of a Japanese defeat practically nil, he sought to reassure Lansdowne that it was extremely unlikely that the British public would require Britain to go to war.[298] In the worst-case scenario, Tokyo would have to abandon its claims to Korea.[299] As French involvement was unlikely, London would only have to keep to the letter of the treaty. While victory might allow Russia to emerge as a regional power in the Far East, Balfour noted, that outcome should cause Britain no great concern. Balfour stressed that Russia need only be feared 'chiefly as (a) the ally of France; (b) the invader of India; (c) the dominating influence in Persia, and (d) the possible disturber of Europe'. In all instances, Russia's involvement in a costly war or Russia's defeat could only be to Britain's advantage.[300]

The new year began with extensive deliberations in the Committee of Imperial Defence on the various scenarios for British involvement.[301] In the first week of January, the Japanese ambassador posed an interesting question to Lansdowne, whose answer sheds light not only on his mindset but also on the central interpretative issues for Conservative foreign policy: continuity or discontinuity and continental or imperial primacy. On the question of what the British government would do should the Black Sea Fleet enter the Mediterranean – an issue that was not addressed in the alliance treaty – Lansdowne responded in diplomatic terms but entirely on point: London would have to see that action as a 'serious breach of international law'.[302] In other words, even without a cabinet resolution and before the Committee of Imperial Defence had come to a clear conclusion, Lansdowne had identified a possible *casus belli*. Neither Lansdowne nor Balfour had any doubts about the significance of that event. During his negotiations with Russia, it had not crossed Lansdowne's mind to include the Far East; those discussions turned on Afghanistan, Tibet, Persia, Sistan and Manchuria.[303]

The traditional British position on the eastern Mediterranean and south-eastern Europe was not up for discussion. A similar attitude was evident in his approach to the Macedonian question, where he only stepped in as intermediary between Vienna and St Petersburg and otherwise maintained the traditional line of non-involvement or a balance of the regional powers.[304]

Immediately after his conversation with Hayashi, Lansdowne drew up a memorandum on the Far East in consultation with Balfour, Selborne and Admirals Kerr and Battenberg. The outcome was unambiguous. Secure in the assumption that Russia might well ignore its legal obligations – secure, because it had so often happened before – Lansdowne believed that the undoubted impact on Britain's allies would be decisive, but also that the legal and traditional basis for the British response was unequivocal.[305] His proposal, accepted by Balfour, was that should war break out, Britain must immediately declare that a violation of the terms of the treaty regarding the closure of the Straits would be seen as a declaration of war.[306] On 27 January, Hayashi received official word that the cabinet had unanimously declared its support for Lansdowne's earlier position. The British ambassadors at St Petersburg and the Porte were instructed that should Russia breach the terms of the treaty, diplomatic relations were immediately to be broken off.[307] The decision was to be backed up with both a reinforcement of the British naval presence in the eastern Mediterranean and repeated unambiguous warnings to St Petersburg.[308]

Although at the end of April Lansdowne restated this position to Monson,[309] in almost the same moment at the Foreign Office a conceptual shift seemed to be forming, behind Lansdowne's, and also Balfour's, back, that contradicted the official position of the government. Charles Hardinge feared Britain would be drawn into the conflict, and for some time he had been calling for closer ties with Russia, very much in line with the ideas advocated in Garvin's published pieces and in the A.B.C. articles. In April 1904, together with Edward VII, he established parallel private diplomatic links with Alexander Izvolsky, who would subsequently become Russian foreign minister. Lansdowne only found out about Garvin's activities four years later.[310] In the spring, Edward VII had visited Copenhagen, together with Hardinge, who had very recently been appointed as British ambassador to St Petersburg as the result of efforts by the king.[311] In the course of an uninhibited discussion with Izvolsky, Edward VII had made clear just how greatly he wished for an alliance between Britain and Russia that could bring global peace.[312] In direct contradiction of his government, together with Hardinge the king summarily declared the Straits up for discussion, stating that 'there did not appear to be any reason for preventing the passage of the Dardanelles by Russian warships as we have endeavoured to do in the past'.[313] For the monarch and Hardinge, his loyal companion on all his foreign travels, the Straits appeared a useful quid pro quo for future negotiations involving Britain and Russia. Only a few weeks after election of the new government, Grey held out to the Russian ambassador Benckendorff the possibility of a solution to the Straits issue, a decision Hardinge would justify as the continuation of a course already established in February 1903. Evidently, Hardinge was confusing his own position and the official position, although historians keen to identify a continuity in policy have simply brushed aside that distinction.[314] Hardinge was not alone in his interpretation. Along with journalists already cited here, a growing number of diplomats were convinced that the goal must be an Anglo-Russian alliance. Hugh Arnold-Forster and George Clarke also believed the Straits a matter for negotiation, the former because he had decided Russia's advance was unstoppable, and the latter because he believed agreement in the Middle East to be more important than the European status quo.[315] The political leadership, however, and Balfour and Lansdowne in particular, were well aware of what that position could mean for the system as a whole, and they ranked the issue of the Straits as more consequential than Britain's interests in the Far East.[316] They pointedly ignored any suggestion that would have repercussions for the international system, and they continued to reject any such plans as long as they were in government, and beyond. They did not deviate from this line despite Clarke's repeated proposals or when, in summer 1905, as the alliance with Japan was being extended temporally and geographically, Mallet informed Lansdowne that Witte's greatest desire was an agreement on this very issue.[317]

In the end, what almost led to Britain's involvement in the war was neither the issue of the Straits nor France's repeated breaches of its neutrality,[318] but the so-called 'Dogger Bank incident', which occurred on the night of 21/22 October 1904. As it crossed the North Sea on its way to the theatre of war, the Russian Baltic fleet misidentified several English trawlers as Japanese torpedo boats and opened fire, killing a number of English sailors. Numerous politicians rode the wave of public indignation that followed and demanded satisfaction. Selborne, Balfour and his brother Gerald Balfour all immediately considered a declaration of war. Admiral Fisher believed that the real culprit was the Kaiserreich,[319] but saw a great opportunity to dispose of the greatest of all Britain's rivals at a single stroke, for the Russian Pacific fleet already lay on the seabed.[320] A bellicosity infected numerous groupings, and confident of the outcome, Clarke announced that it would not even be necessary 'to send a single man to India!'[321] Only when the British press turned its sights on Germany did Fisher suddenly begin to argue for a defensive strike on the German High Seas Fleet.

The government's initial response had been uncompromising. Lansdowne demanded not just an immediate apology but also a detailed explanation and the punishment of those responsible.[322] For over a month, Russia and Britain seemed on the brink of war. Russia doggedly refused to meet the British demands, while the British fleet began to shadow the Russian fleet from a distance of only five sea miles.[323] Alongside the diplomatic and precarious military manoeuvres, which we do not need to go into in detail here,[324] the crisis was played out above all in the London press. The incident itself had only a bit part, during the first few days, for soon the outrage was directed entirely at Berlin, which yet again, and incorrectly,[325] was thought to be pulling the strings.[326] Those who had advocated a strategic change of course feared that a war would prevent the planned rapprochement with Russia. In the November issue of the *Fortnightly Review*, Garvin published an article entitled 'The Limits of Japanese Capacity', in which he again spoke of the advantages of closer ties between Britain and Russia.[327] Having remained remarkably quiet since the beginning of the war,[328] Chirol, Maxse and other journalists with whom we are now well acquainted attempted to defuse the potentially threatening situation by declaring their suspicions that the Kaiserreich was its driving force.[329] Foreign correspondents had quickly helped redirect the sense of outrage against Germany. 'My own practice with the Germans', so Steed wrote from Vienna, 'is "poignez vilain". With Saunders I have a sort of understanding and with Lavino [in Paris] also'.[330] Chirol, their superior in London, confirmed that the *Times* thought Germany an international troublemaker to whom no allowances should be made: 'The Germans deserve no mercy'. Readers of the *Times* were to be left in no doubt that Germany was behind the Dogger Bank incident.[331] Chirol's conviction stemmed not only from the now-established stereotypical image of Germany as perfidious troublemaker but also from the Russian newspaper *Novoe Vremja*, which had published a report by General Klado that put the blame squarely on Berlin and that Spring Rice had sent on to Mallet as an assertion that was all too likely true, while backing up that position by citing a French friend who spoke very positively of Klado.[332]

The collaboration between these journalists and a number of likeminded diplomats is evident. Mallet suggested that while the government did not recognize the advantages of an alliance between Britain and Russia, 'the country does and public opinion will keep them straight',[333] and therefore made sure the journalists received a hearing not just through the articles they wrote but also, via unofficial channels, among the highest echelons. The configuration that had Spring Rice in St Petersburg, Saunders in Berlin and Chirol and Mallet in London proved especially useful. For example, Mallet denounced Ambassador Lascelles – long a thorn in the side of those around Hardinge, Bertie and Crowe – for being overly German-friendly, for Lascelles always demanded evidence in support of allegations against Germany and refused to believe the alarming reports of German intrigue.[334] While experienced minds such as Lascelles or Sanderson were critical, and at times self-critical,[335] Bertie, Hardinge, Mallet and Spring Rice remained convinced that all blame lay with the Kaiser, 'the central telephone office in which all wires meet'.[336] Maxse again noted with delight the influence of the press on the Foreign Office, recording: 'There is a complete estrangement ... between the highest circles in Germany and in Britain, at which I frankly rejoice'.[337] The media campaign had indeed defused the calls for Russia to provide satisfaction. The liberal imperial opposition gathered around

Lord Rosebery had played a particular role in ensuring that the public anger at Russia was vented instead at Germany. In the course of several public appearances, Rosebery called on his audience to put themselves in Russia's position, for obscure German informants, he suggested, had warned the Russian fleet of Japanese torpedo boats in the North Sea.[338]

Although Germany, rather than Russia, was now the public's target, the government was not to be diverted. In vain, France and the Unites States sought to convince Britain to commit to a joint intervention.[339] Perhaps, Ian Nish muses, Lansdowne endorsed the continuation of the conflict because Japan was already on a path to victory.[340] Lansdowne himself explained his resistance to mediation with Britain's Japanese ally's wish not to be deprived of a hard-fought victory.[341] A closer look at their exchange suggests that MacDonald's account of Japanese wishes was not as unambiguous as Lansdowne had Bertie believe,[342] for previously, on 10 February 1905, MacDonald had reported that the Japanese government was not opposed to a brokered peace. Additionally, the Japanese representative in Paris had signalled to Théophile Delcassé that Japan was becoming exhausted by the war. The United States and Russia were therefore not without grounds for believing that Lansdowne wanted to extend the war in order to increase British capital.[343] Balfour came straight to the point with his foreign secretary: 'I am, on broad moral ground very anxious that we should do everything we can to put an end to the war. But I have to admit that, from a narrowly national point of view, the balance of advantage, I suspect, is on the side of continued hostilities'.[344] Lansdowne's pre-war attitude had evidently changed. After the stormy autumn, by spring 1905 Britain no longer seemed about to be drawn into the war at any moment, and Japan was rushing from one victory to another. Lansdowne was eager to make the most of the opportunity, and he now sought an early renewal of Britain's alliance with Japan, with its scope extended.[345]

For Balfour, the great advantage of the new alliance, signed on 12 August 1905, was that it was no longer directed against two aggressors, but against Russia alone.[346] Balfour had joined Lansdowne in pushing for a renewal of the alliance, making clear in the process who he believed would be the most likely adversary, even after the defeat of Russia. In a memorandum, he recorded: 'It is, of course, clear that the new alliance will be regarded by the Russians as directly aimed at them, and in a sense they will be right'.[347] The prime minister wanted to be sure that British interests in the Middle East were permanently protected, and he was able to correct what he had criticized in the first alliance while ensuring that the next government would also be bound by the treaty.[348]

Historians have often drawn a direct line from the end of the Russo-Japanese war to the Anglo-Russian Convention of 1907. There is much to be said for that interpretation in that in 1907 Russia became part of an alliance for which it had previously thought itself too powerful. Historians have fallen prey, however, to the temptation to find a continuity in attitude towards Russia running from

Lansdowne to Grey, overlooking in the process that traditional positions were surrendered not by a weakened Russia, but by Britain.

After the war, Balfour believed Russia now in a position that meant he could, at last, deal confidently with the tsardom. His goal was to ensure the perpetuation of the buffer state concept, that Persia would not be divided, British dominance in Afghanistan would be recognized, and Russian agents would not be allowed to operate in Afghanistan or Tibet, that no separate trading concessions would be allowed to operate in Tibet or Persia, and that all railway construction would cease for ten years. In 1907, Persia was divided, Russian agents were permitted to operate in Afghanistan, and plans were afoot for joint railway projects that would give access to the strategically important ports on the Gulf and beyond.[349] Where Balfour and Lansdowne had limited themselves to colonial concerns, with the possibility, for example, of a limited exchange of interests in the Far East for interests in the Middle East, their successors even put the Straits on the table.[350] After his discussions with Benckendorff, Lansdowne had commented that Russia had absolutely no expectations of receiving Constantinople.[351] Following the war, Hardinge pressed increasingly vehemently for a general settlement that would also cover the European periphery, while Bertie went as far as to adopt Delcassé's idea that Britain could join with France and Russia in encircling Germany, and even brought south-east Europe into play. He advised Lansdowne to concentrate on those areas where Japan had no interests but Russia and Germany rubbed up against each other; if Britain and Russia could agree on these issues, he wrote, 'the German eagle's claws would be clipped – perhaps his wings too!'[352]

If we are to talk of continuity, then we must do so only in terms of a course advocated within the political sphere by those who set the agenda for the British public and by individual decision-making groupings within the Foreign Office. The political leadership had not approved that course, just as they had not approved the discussions involving the British and French General Staffs. Right to the last, Balfour, Lansdowne and Sanderson ignored or opposed the idea that rapprochement with Russia might embrace the European periphery.[353] That suggestion overstepped a boundary,[354] a boundary that was already not in accord with the standards laid down by Salisbury, who, in September 1901, had expressly warned about the construction of a bridge between France and Russia.[355] If the separation of empire and continent were abandoned, especially in dealings with Russia, colonial tensions would automatically be channelled into the continent, where they might intensify into existential crises.

In 1895, Edward Grey had proposed the creation of a triple alliance involving Britain, France and Russia that would be able to control the states system. Ten years later, his proposal was finding an increasingly enthusiastic audience when the *Spectator* announced that it no longer believed it in British interests for the integrity and independence of the Ottoman Empire to be maintained and suggested that there was no longer any reason to oppose Russian control of the Straits.[356]

The First Moroccan Crisis and a Change of Government

Consequently, in spring 1905 Britain found itself in an extremely advantageous position. The Entente Cordiale had defused Anglo-French enmity; in late 1904, the United States had been informed of Britain's intention to keep out of the western hemisphere;[357] and in the Far East, following events at Port Arthur and the Battle of Mukden, a decisive Japanese victory seemed in the offing. The Russian Baltic fleet was still making its fateful way towards Tsushima, but any chance that it would change the course of events had seemed unlikely for some time. In each instance, Balfour's prognosis seemed vindicated. The war had brought Russia to the point of collapse, and in upcoming years that country would be preoccupied with its own problems.[358] Its ties to Paris had undoubtedly helped ensure that Britain had not been drawn into the war, fulfilling their principal purpose. Whitehall kept at arm's length all other efforts by Delcassé, as he tried, for example, to launch negotiations together with Britain in order to bring the war to an end. Britain's alliance with Tokyo evidently took priority,[359] for negotiation of its prolongation and possible extension to include India was now on the agenda. For the first time since the Crimean War, Britain did not need to fear Russian expansionism, a situation that Britain wished to see last as long as possible, to which end signals were sent to Russia that its internal problems must not be allowed to spill over into its foreign affairs, neither in the Middle East nor in the Near East. The ties with Paris had provided a useful communication channel for warnings addressed to St Petersburg, and as a result were spoken of by their supporters as a first step towards a long-term understanding between the two countries. At the same time, those bonds were by no means always cordial,[360] even though they are often seen as part of a grand plan for paradigm change – and even as the answer to the strengthening of the German fleet – that Edward Grey had continued, thereby maintaining the policy of his predecessor.[361] With that interpretation, historians have embraced too closely the particular views and wishes of a growing group of principally younger British diplomats who demanded Lansdowne adopt a pro-Russia course, a very plausible finding from the perspective of the imperial administration.[362] John Brodrick, who had succeeded George Hamilton as secretary of state for India, stated openly that 'another six or nine months may exhaust Russia to a degree which will render her innocuous to us for many years to come'.[363] The majority of historians are of one mind in believing that Lansdowne failed to understand the implications of the Russian defeat, continued to adhere to a policy of 'muddling through', had more luck than judgement, and proved himself highly naive about the

German threat.[364] Yet that assessment is predicated on the assumption that from the start his policy had been to set a new course and that the Entente Cordiale was intended as a means of maintaining the power balance to the detriment of Berlin. Historians have largely also adopted the criticism of 'muddling through' that emerged shortly before the Boer War. And yet is it not possible that this ad hoc diplomacy actually guaranteed the success of British foreign policy, opening up unexpected room to manoeuvre, providing flexibility and, finally, helping to stabilize the states system precisely by keeping it in flux?

At the beginning of 1905, with Russia's defeat becoming evident, neither Lansdowne, who thought principally in global terms, nor Balfour, who thought principally in terms of the continent, had reason to rethink his position. An extended Entente Cordiale with wider European utility did not appear called for, and there was certainly no apparent need for a Triple Entente that included Paris and St Petersburg.

Having observed the cyclical movement of the states system for more than four decades, Sanderson appeared far more unsettled by the weakness of the Central Powers, and in particular Germany, than by their supposed dominance and aggression.[365] Balfour and his foreign secretary did not judge Anglo-German relations and the Kaiser's erratic behaviour as particularly remarkable. They did not take Bülow and Holstein too seriously,[366] nor did they believe war between the two countries inevitable. Repeatedly – and the comparison with later years is striking – they sought to imagine themselves in Berlin's shoes. Thus, for example, Gerald Balfour commented that Germany repeatedly seemed to ignore good opportunities to realize the hegemonial plans that Berlin was accused of harbouring.[367]

And so Wilhelm II's journey to Tangiers, without which the significance of the Entente Cordiale after the end of the Russo-Japanese war would in all probability have decreased all the more, initially caused little stir. Balfour judged it a further example of Berlin's usual 'mischief-making' and saw no reason for any great alarm. Lansdowne appeared equally unconcerned. Immediately after the incident, he demonstratively ignored Delcassé's appeal, with its warning that Germany might exploit Russia's temporary weakness.[368] Similarly, we know of no troubled reaction from Sanderson. It fell to Louis Mallet and Francis Bertie in particular to raise the alarm and warn of an imminent war. Every day they wrote to the foreign secretary with warnings and objections. To each other and in private, they welcomed the development warmly.[369]

Lansdowne did not want to burden the cooperation between France and Britain unduly, but he was not prepared to countenance any display of power, let alone any belligerent action.[370] The issue was not sufficiently important for such a response, and when it came down to it, Paris, or the French foreign minister, was the real cause of the quandary, having been advised repeatedly since the previous April to come to an understanding with Germany.[371] To Lansdowne, an amicable solution seemed possible, for compensation was still on the cards. He instructed Mallet to establish with the Admiralty whether a German port would to British eyes be acceptable compensation. Only now, and as a result of forces in the Foreign Office already set against Germany, did the actual crisis begin. Mallet, aware of Fisher's yearning for a defensive surgical strike against any sea power, expressly requested that the Admiral compose a highly dramatic report for Lansdowne. Personally, the First Sea Lord deemed it completely irrelevant whether Germany receive Mogador, and Britain, in return, receive Tangiers, recording: 'Of course it would not matter to us whether the Germans got Mogador or not but I am going to say so all the same'. Mallet knew how he might get Fisher to make the desired statement, and candidly admitted to Bertie, 'He [Fisher] is a splendid chap and simply longs to have a go at Germany. I abound in his sense and told him I would do all I could with Lord L'.[372]

From the letter he received from Fisher, Lansdowne knew that the Admiralty believed the issue of a German port to be 'vitally detrimental'. That same day, he telegraphed Balfour with the Admiralty's evaluation and recommended the French government be supported as long as the French kept London fully informed.[373] The context seems to be that Lansdowne wished to prevent a bilateral agreement between France, on its own, and Germany. France, he recorded, had manoeuvred itself into a 'bad mess' and Russia was no longer in a position to help, and, he continued, 'Nor am I at all sure that we ought to do so except in certain eventualities'.[374] Evidently, Lansdowne thought a delicate warning to Paris entirely appropriate. On the other hand, the Entente Cordiale could suffer as a result, for Delcassé might fall, allowing the pro-German approach of French Premier Maurice Rouvier to move ahead, without the involvement of Britain.

As a solution based on compensation had been dismissed by the Admiralty, Lansdowne resolved together with Balfour to pledge British support to the French government.[375] The telegram, whose contents Bertie was to translate and convey to the Quai d'Orsay, spoke of 'strong opposition to a German demand of a port' and of giving 'all the support we can'. Cambon and his colleagues in the French Foreign Ministry took the telegram to be a clear commitment to an alliance.[376] Certainly, the context for Delcassé's receipt of Bertie's aide-mémoire is also relevant, for in light of the massive criticism of his failed Morocco policy, which had simply bypassed Germany, a signatory at Madrid, the French foreign minister feared for his political future. Cambon was alarmed by Delcassé's potential successors, who evidently favoured reducing tensions with Germany, and he therefore read more into the contents of the telegram than Lansdowne had intended. We should also not overlook the role played by Bertie as translator.

Lansdowne and Balfour's principal purpose was to prevent France from striking out on its own, and therefore the French party was to make no concessions 'without giving us a full opportunity of *conferring* with them as to the manner in which the demand might be met' [italics added].[377] One day later, Bertie, who had always favoured an alliance, translated the telegram as a memorandum for Delcassé. His first draft contained the terms 'conférer' and 'discuter', providing as close a translation as possible of the original English, as authorized by Balfour and Lansdowne.[378] The final version, submitted to Delcassé, contained, however, the wording 'concerter avec le Gouvernement Français les mesures', which could convey a very different impression for recipients eager to discern any sign of support, as 'concerter' could mean not just 'take counsel' but also, with added nuance, 'prepare', 'arrange' or even 'rig'.[379] These variations were unlikely to be evident to Lansdowne who, in the midst of his hectic daily business, did not check over his colleagues' translations word for word. It is not possible to establish whether Bertie's version contained an unintentional faux pas or whether a somewhat sharper nuance had been deliberately included. In light of Bertie's desire for as close as possible an alliance with Paris, it is not impossible that a degree of premeditation played its part. Delcassé immediately seized on the message and reported joyfully to his assistant Maurice Paléologue, 'England supports me thoroughly; she too would go as far as war. I repeat, England will support us thoroughly, and she will not sign peace without us'.[380] Britain, it appeared, would do its utmost, even to the point of war, to support France. As a result, Delcassé was somewhat disappointed and irritated by Edward VII's rather unforthcoming attitude during his flying visit to Paris on 29 April.[381] Lansdowne's suspicions were still not aroused when, on 3 May, Cambon effusively thanked him for the message sent via Bertie.[382] This new conversation gave Cambon no grounds to report to his superior that Britain was prepared to provide support, but Delcassé joyfully concluded that, 'if there is war, we will have England with us'.[383] Three weeks later, with Lansdowne recognizing that the exchanges and mutual assurances were slipping out of his control, he used a further letter to state Britain's position – the two governments were to continue 'to treat one another with the most absolute confidence' and to keep each other fully briefed.[384] To make his point absolutely clear to his counterpart, Lansdowne added that he was talking not of consultations in the case of unprovoked aggression but simply of situations where France had the impression that such an unprovoked attack was in the offing. Four days later, Cambon conceded to Delcassé that a misunderstanding had taken place, using in the process the term 'discuter' rather than 'concerter'. Yet he concluded that on this occasion Lansdowne had even gone somewhat further: 'It is no longer an agreement in case of aggression that England invites us to, it is to an immediate discussion and an examination of the general situation'.[385]

Following Delcassé's resignation, rumours of an agreement to enter into an alliance continued to circulate, passed on to the press by Delcassé himself and giving some historians cause to assume a continuity from Lansdowne to Grey.[386] But just as no authorized military discussions had been held under Lansdowne, as Sanderson highlighted,[387] so too had no such commitment been made. The real hallmarks of Lansdowne's diplomacy were that he left France in the dark over his warning to Germany and thus keeping control of the Entente.[388] Moreover, he rejected any extension of the mere colonial understanding.[389]

The foreign minister's apprenticeship was over. He had come to favour frightening off Germany over cultivating the Entente Cordiale and receiving further unsolicited interventions from Maxse, Strachey and others. The decision Lansdowne made was thus not the decision of his successor, a distinction that would prove characteristic of the fundamental differences in both the style and the content of their foreign policy. Grey sought both publicly and internally to convince Paris and St Petersburg of London's unconditional loyalty. Even before he had been confirmed in office by the election, in early January 1906 he informed Cambon that he had sent a warning to Germany in the name of the Entente,[390] marking a subtle but striking difference from his predecessor that was surely registered by contemporary diplomats. Following Delcassé's resignation, Balfour and Lansdowne concluded that France no longer would be taken so seriously within the broader international context,[391] which makes it all the more surprising that neither man believed that France should therefore be supported all the more resolutely. Lansdowne instead saw the opportunity to use a conference on Morocco to Britain's advantage, noting: 'If the French are really on the run, we might perhaps extract a not unsatisfactory settlement out of such a conference'.[392] Unlike his successor, Lansdowne was operating without reference to the Entente Cordiale and to a long-term Anglo-French alliance. For Lansdowne, expectations counted for far less than his recent experiences with France, principally during the Boer War. The specifics of contemporary circumstances also allowed Britain to leave France in the dark or even to squeeze France to Britain's benefit. The Tory government gave no sign of a latent dependency on France produced by a fear of isolation. In summer 1905, the Entente Cordiale was not half as cordial as it would become under Grey; Lansdowne even expressly opposed its augmentation.[393]

Lord Salisbury, too, had never taken the threat of a Napoleonic bloc particularly seriously, even when British troops were ensnared in South Africa and France and Russia sought to persuade Germany to join with them in forming such a bloc. He counted on tensions within Europe and on the secure knowledge that Britain's integrity was in Germany's interests. In summer 1905, the situation was certainly no worse, and what was more, France needed Britain, while Russia, thought to be the greatest threat to the Empire, was on its knees. Panic appeared just as unnecessary as a fundamental change of course. It was the case, Salisbury's son admitted, that the circumstances of recent months had meant that Britain had moved closer to France than had even been intended, but he also testified that Balfour, his cousin, had acted in accordance with his father's intentions, for the alliance with France was by no means 'a departure from our previous foreign policy, but strictly in accordance with it'. He also noted, 'For the last twenty years we have been engaged with different Powers, notably with

Germany and with France'. Lansdowne, together with Balfour, had not altered course dramatically; rather, he had agreed to more limited accords 'in adjusting conflicting claims, and in bargaining so as to get rid of causes of friction'.[394] After the Morocco crisis, the 4th Marquess of Salisbury continued, it had been necessary to keep things flowing and redirect them as necessary, and also to separate off from France. For the stability of international relations as a whole, it would have been extremely questionable and dangerous to let Germany believe that rapprochement with Britain was impossible, he continued, noting that a panic reaction could not be ruled out, not least as France would always try to exploit the situation.[395]

Lansdowne did not believe Anglo-German rivalry a fundamental law of nature, but that did not mean he was a naive Germanophile who ignored the dangers presented by Germany. During his last months in office, he tried again to find some kind of agreement on the Baghdad railway, and again recognized that the greatest obstacle to his foreign policy as a whole was found not in Germany but in British public opinion, which was entirely irrational and uncontrollable.[396]

During the Morocco crisis, for the first time – and not to be overlooked in light of the policy of the next government and its options – support for a rapprochement with Germany came from an unexpected source. The inclusion of Britain in a network of ententes and alliances with its former arch-enemies France and Russia could not come quickly enough for the radical liberal press, a vocal supporter of a fundamental reorientation of British foreign policy thought more likely to be critical of Germany. Yet this press chided the political leadership for its one-sided, pro-French attitude after the Kaiser's visit to Tangiers. French behaviour made German anger entirely legitimate in its eyes, for, after all, Britain and France had decided the fate of Morocco without any regard for the rights of other states.[397]

At the end of July, the *Manchester Guardian* even went so far as to reprimand the government for its cooperation with Delcassé, noting that it was well known that the French foreign minister's goal was nothing less than the complete isolation of Germany, and insisted that London must not become the stooge who enabled a new destabilization of the continent.[398] This criticism is all the more remarkable in light of the traditional pro-French orientation of English liberalism. With the Morocco crisis in mind, the radicals feared losing ties with the Central Powers, with which Britain had previously been friendly, and declared that 'to rush into a hostility to Germany' would be 'as improvident as our former hostility to the Dual Alliance'.[399] When, in the autumn, Delcassé began to plant the idea of an Anglo-French military alliance against Germany in the newspapers *Matin* and *Libre* even as the official British position continued to deny the existence of an agreement,[400] the radical liberal press believed its warnings justified, even if Massingham did not want to believe that the government had actually gone so far: 'I believe the story that France was offered definite military and naval support against Germany to be untrue, but I am afraid the whole incident shows the gross mischief and injury already caused to France by the bent of anti-Germanism in foreign policy. There are obvious errors in *Le Matin*, but it is not all error'.[401]

Liberal doubts about Paris stemmed from two causes. On one hand, those who supported free trade were not convinced by France's 'open door' guarantee. On the other hand, and of particular interest in light of the later Liberal government, the Liberals, and above all Henry Massingham, saw potential risks for the stability of the Great Powers, for Delcassé had been all too clear that he wished to see Germany isolated in order then to be able to tackle the status quo on France's eastern border. The leader writers for the *Manchester Guardian* and the *Speaker* questioned whether an Anglo-French agreement was worth the complications for the broader power arrangements that would surely follow. The Entente Cordiale could on no account be allowed to stand in the way of other alliances, even with Germany, and should serve instead as the starting point for a whole network of treaties. 'Unless our understanding with France is treated as the nucleus for a wider understanding embracing all the Powers, its value is greatly mutilated', the *Manchester Guardian* opined in November 1906,[402] giving expression to the classic idea of the concert favoured by the Gladstonians, which had little in common with secretive 'balance of power' policy and even less with an open policy based on the formation of power blocs, which threatened to leave cornered the Central Powers, core members of the states system. Cecil Spring Rice, who had long kept a close eye on developments in the press, saw in this argumentation evidence of the old radical liberal politics of weakness and unpredictability, and therefore urged Spender to take action against these pro-German tendencies.[403]

Two months later, as Spender explained his thinking to Strachey, he was surprisingly self-critical in agreeing with Sanderson's objections to the excessive position taken on Germany, for the anti-German campaigns had made a new rapprochement with the Kaiserreich more difficult than ever. That challenge, in Spender's estimation, had less to do with Germany and more to do with the behaviour of the London press in recent years. Spender noted in particular the propaganda published during the Venezuela Crisis and in relation to the Baghdad railway, recording: 'I have always felt as those two things turned out, they must necessarily have been regarded as fresh wounds in Germany'. According to Spender, Germany must have come to believe that trustworthy cooperation with the British government was impossible. 'Is this surprising?', he asked, continuing:

> Our Government pledged to the Germans and then backed out and left the Germans to suppose that the anti-German feeling over here is so strong that nothing could be done against it. ... I don't see how we can expect Germans to put these affairs [Baghdad and Venezuela] to our credit. It is the backing out the Germans will remember. The belief apparently is in Germany that we promised our cooperation as part of the price for Germany's extreme official correct attitude during the Boer War and for

turning Mr Krueger away from the gates of Berlin, and they keep saying that when they have done their part, we failed to deliver ours. Bear this in mind!'[404]

Although Spender had shared the anti-German attitude in the past, with the experience of Morocco he began to wonder whether the public protest might be doing more harm than good. A change of climate could only be good for Anglo-German relations. The stimulus for these surprising insights would appear to have been a sense that Britain was becoming too dependent on Paris. Paris, Spender noted, had registered Britain's attitude towards Germany and now required Britain's complete loyalty; otherwise, fearing being deserted at the last minute, France would no longer trust Britain at all.

All the more surprising, then, is his principal recommendation, which did not seek to resolve the problems that he had identified, but instead agreed to a change of course and the complicated policy of 'drifting', for, Spender wrote, 'we can't live perpetually on this razor's edge between doing too much and doing too little'. For Spender, a close friend of Grey's, there was only one way out of the dilemma Britain had created: Britain must openly treat the Entente Cordiale as if it were an alliance. 'The French will ask if the inconvenience is worth it', he noted, but Britain must repeatedly make clear that the answer was yes. Above all, London should do all it could to create closer ties with Russia, as Paris thought the connection essential. Whether in the long term or short term, the chance of rapprochement was fair.[405]

Shortly before the new government took office, the liberal press therefore seemed of one mind on domestic policy but deeply divided over foreign policy, between, on one hand, a variant of the classic Concert of Europe and, on the other hand, a progressive alliance-based concept. Within the government coalition, the case was completely reversed. When it came to foreign policy, Balfour and Lansdowne were firmly in charge, while the divisions were most evident on issues of tariff reform and on educational and social policies.[406] The continuing conflict between free traders and protectionists and the growing lethargy among Conservatives,[407] who no longer had the energy to counter the constant criticism from the press and the opposition, made the differences within the unionist camp so impossible to bridge that Balfour believed he should resign. In terms of domestic policy, his resignation proved a tactical error, for he had nothing left with which to counter the Lib(eral)-Lab(our) constellation in the election that followed. He may have hoped that the Liberals too would be divided, as his resignation had given him the opportunity to influence who filled the most important positions, for it fell to the departing prime minister to advise the king on the appointment of an interim government. He could expect that the liberal imperialists around Asquith, Haldane and Grey would at least continue the course he had set, and indeed, in October Grey had publicly voiced his support for such continuity.[408] By contrast, on account of their pacifist and idealistic attitudes and their consistent calls for disarmament, he deemed the radical liberals entirely unsuitable. Then again, he was certain that in terms of foreign policy, no changes were needed.

In 1894, on learning of the creation of the Franco-Russian alliance, Balfour had feared that the coming years would form an era of war. Eleven years later, he prophesized an era of peace, pronouncing in his Guildhall speech: 'So far as human foresight can go, I see no prospect of any calamity to Europe'.[409] Soberly and by no means euphorically, as was his way, he declared that it would be impossible 'to find a decade of more essentially successful British foreign policy than the preceding ten years'.[410] Only four years after its darkest hour, the Empire was again at its zenith, threatened by no external dangers or measures.[411] Yet despite Grey's avowal of continuity, a fearful and almost hectic search for means to be used to protect and promote Britain's vested rights appeared as the motivating force for his foreign policy. In October 1905, when the Russian ambassador officially raised the possibility of an Anglo-Russian agreement analogous to the Entente Cordiale, Lansdowne and Balfour had decisively rejected the possibility;[412] two months later, the new foreign secretary personally approached Count Benckendorff with just such a proposal.[413]

Notes

1. See Grenville, *Lord Salisbury*, 342–43, 421; Taylor, *Struggle for Mastery*, 392–402; Kennedy, *Rise of Anglo-German Antagonism*, 244.
2. Balfour to Lansdowne, 12 Dec. 1901, cited in Charmley, *Splendid Isolation*, 301.
3. See Hase, *Lateinamerika*, 846–1044; Herwig, *Politics*, 76–80; Collin, *Roosevelt's Caribbean*, 95–123; Mitchell, *Danger of Dreams*, 64–107.
4. Monger, *End of Isolation*, 104–7; Steiner and Neilson, *Britain and the Origins*, 22; Kennedy, *Rise of Anglo-German Antagonism*, 256–61.
5. Kneer, 'Britain', 11; Monger, *End of Isolation*, 104–7; Livermore, 'Theodore Roosevelt'; Parsons, 'German-American Crisis', 436–52; Hendricksen, 'Venezuelan Controversy', 482–98; Seed, 'British Reactions', 254–72; Burton, *Roosevelt*, 12–34; Herwig, *Germany's Vision*, 223.
6. Holbo, 'Perilous Obscurity', 447.
7. Dillon, 'Foreign Affairs', CR 1/1903, 130–42; Maxse to Mahan, 25 June 1902, LoC, MSS Mahan, Reel 6; Saunders to Maxse, 22 Dec. 1902, WSRO, MAXSE/450; Maxse, *Germany on the Brain*, 77–84; Kipling, The Rowers, *The Times*, 22 Dec. 1902. See also Kennedy, *Rise of Anglo-German Antagonism*, 257–58; Hase, *Großmachtkonflikt*, 529; Kneer, 'Britain', 11.
8. Brechtken, *Scharnierzeit*, 34, 235–42, 262, n. 609–10; 293.
9. Adams, *Brothers across the Ocean*, 37–63.
10. See Mitchell, *Danger of Dreams*, 79; Villiers, 24 Jan. 1902, NA, FO 80/468. For Patos, see Haggard to Lansdowne, 1 Oct. 1902, NA, FO 420/206. Villiers saw no reason 'to communicate with the USA about Patos'. Minutes, Lucas to Villiers, 24 Jan. 1902, NA, FO 80/468.

11. Crowe, Minutes, Sanderson, Memorandum, 21 Feb. 1907, BD III, App. B, 420–33, 429.
12. Hobsbawm, *Industry*, 125–26, App. Table 32b; see also Knight, *Latin America*, 122–45.
13. Platt, 'British Bondholders', 3; Bernstein, 'Foreign Investment', 6.
14. Bernstein, 'Foreign Investment', 8; Whitaker, *Whitaker's Almanack* 1900, 591–92, 703.
15. Oakes, Memorandum, 27 Feb. and 10 March 1898, BDFA I/D, Vol. 6, No. 70/6753, 74–89.
16. The precise figure was £7,195,040. Together, the Caribbean states of Costa Rica, Columbia, Guatemala, Honduras, Santo Domingo and Venezuela owed £22,456,687, or £23,210,454 when interest is included. GL, 29th Annual Report of the CFB (1901), 455, App. 31.
17. Ibid., 444; Haggard to Lansdowne, 1 Aug. 1902, NA, FO 420/206.
18. Castro revised the debt down five times. Avebury, 3 March 1903, PD III/118, cols. 1054–59.
19. CFB, Deputation to Lord Lansdowne, 26 Nov. 1901, NA, FO 15/344.
20. Platt, 'British Bondholders', 25.
21. GL, 30th Annual Report of the CFB (1902), 415–19.
22. CFB, Deputation to Lord Lansdowne, 26 Nov. 1901, NA, FO 15/344.
23. Haggard to Lansdowne, 13 Dec. 1901, NA, FO 80/443.
24. Sternburg to AA, 3 Feb. 1903, GP XVII, No. 5145, 285–86.
25. Adams, *Brothers across the Ocean*, 39.
26. Herwig, *Germany's Vision*, 93; Haggard to Lansdowne, 27 Oct. 1901, NA, FO 420/206.
27. CFB, Memorandum, 26 Nov. 1901, NA, FO 15/344; 30th Annual Report of the CFB (1902), 415–19; FO to CO, 16 Jan. 1902, NA, FO 80/443.
28. CFB to FO, 3 Jan. 1902, NA, FO 80/443. According to Platt, the lobbying started not before 23 Sept. 1902. Platt, *Finance*, 341; Atlas Trust to Lansdowne, 28 Jan. 1902, NA, FO 80/443. From 17 February to 30 June, Whitehall was approached nearly every day. See NA, FO 80/443.
29. *Financial News*, 3 Jan. 1902, NA, FO 80/443; PD III/116, col. 1263, 1267, 1273; PD III/118, col. 1070; Lansdowne to Buchanan, 17 Nov. 1902, NA, FO 80/445.
30. Platt, *Finance*, 347; Knight, *Latin America*, 140.
31. Haggard to Lansdowne, 23 Sept. 1902, NA, FO 420/206.
32. Haggard to Lansdowne, 30 April; 8 June 1902, NA, FO 80/443; 12 Sept.; 4 Oct. 1902, NA, FO 80/439.
33. Larcom, Memorandum, 20 July 1902, NA, FO 420/206; Haggard to Villiers, 19 April 1902, NA, FO 80/438.
34. See Blue Book, Affairs of Venezuela, Part I, 1901–1902, NA, FO 420/206; *Daily Telegraph*, 4 Dec. 1902.
35. Haggard to Lansdowne, 30 April 1902, NA, FO 80/443.
36. Herbert to Lansdowne, 8 Oct. 1902, NA, FO 5/2487.
37. The German chargé d'affaires, Gisbert von Pilgrim-Baltazzi, was demonstratively frustrated by his government's weak response. Haggard to Villiers, 23 Feb. 1902, NA, FO 80/443.
38. Hase, *Lateinamerika*, 458; Holstein, Diary, 11 Jan. 1902, cited in Rich and Fisher, *Holstein Papers*, Vol. 4, 245–46.
39. Haggard to Lansdowne, 4 April 1902, NA, FO 80/443; 21 Sept. 1901, FO 80/427; 15 Sept. 1901, FO 80/435.

40. Adams, *Brothers across the Ocean*, 41; Haggard to Lansdowne, 30 June 1902, NA, FO 80/443.
41. De Lemos to Haggard, 12 July 1902, NA, FO 420/206; Haggard to Lansdowne, 30 June 1902, NA, FO 80/443.
42. Lansdowne to CO, 16 Jan. 1902, NA, FO 80/443.
43. Lansdowne, 2 March 1902, PD III/104, cols. 1060–61; Lansdowne to Lascelles, 22 April 1902, NA, FO 800/11.
44. Lansdowne to Buchanan, 23 July 1902, BD II, No. 171, 153–54. 'We clearly cannot let this pass.' Lansdowne to Haggard, 29 July 1902, NA, FO 420/206.
45. Lascelles to Lansdowne, 1 March 1902; to Buchanan, 8 June 1902, NA, FO 64/1551.
46. Lansdowne to Haggard, 29 July 1902, NA, FO 420/206; Lansdowne to ADM, 8 Aug. 1902, NA, FO 80/444; Bertie to ADM, 8 Aug. 1902, NA, ADM 1/7690; Lansdowne to Lascelles, 19 Aug. 1902, BL, LANS/PL 5.
47. ADM to FO, 14 Aug. 1902, NA, FO 80/444.
48. Bülow to Wilhelm II, 1 Sept. 1902, GP XVII, No. 5107, 244–46, 245; FO, Memorandum, 16 Aug. 1902, NA, FO 80/444; Lansdowne to Lascelles, 19 Aug. 1902, BL, LANS/PL 5.
49. ADM to FO, 10 Oct. 1902, NA, FO 80/445; Lansdowne to Lascelles, 22 Oct. 1902, BD II, 172, 154. For a different view, see Adams, *Brothers across the Ocean*, 41.
50. Metternich to AA, 11 Nov. 1902, BD II, No. 5111, 250–52; Lansdowne to Buchanan, 11 Nov. 1902, BD II, No. 174, 156–57; Lansdowne to Buchanan, 23 July 1902, NA, FO 420/206.
51. '[V]iel Geduld, Takt – auch im AA – und "Maul halten" unserer Presse'; 'Deutschland ist viel zu schwach!'; 'Vorsicht, hier 35 Panzerschiffe gegen unsere acht.' Wilhelm II to Bülow, 12 Nov. 1902, GP XVII, No. 5031, 115–17. See also Prochnow, *Deutsche Kriegsschiffe*, Vol. 1, 26–51; see the contrasting exaggerated figures for German ships in Hallmann, *Schlachtflottenbau*, 337.
52. Metternich to AA, 11 Nov. 1902, GP XVII, No. 5110, 250–54.
53. Lansdowne to Balfour, 12 Oct. 1902, BL, LANS, Vol. 5.
54. Lansdowne, Memorandum, 17 Oct. 1902, NA, CAB 37/118/63.
55. Balfour to Edward VII, 21 Oct. 1902, NA, CAB 41/27/31.
56. Herwig, *Germany's Vision*, 223. See also Bülow to Wilhelm II, 20 Jan. 1902, GP XVII, No. 5106, 241–43.
57. Lansdowne to Balfour, 12 Oct. 1902, BL, LANS/PL 5.
58. Adams, *Brothers across the Ocean*, 37–62.
59. Lodge to Balfour, 1 Feb. 1896, BL, Add. 49742.
60. 'You will see that a real danger exists there especially since the American Govt. is beginning to take such a close interest in Central America.' Selborne to Lansdowne, 6 Feb. 1901, BL, LANS/PL 1.
61. Villiers to Lansdowne, 8 Nov. 1902, NA, FO 80/445.
62. Villiers to Haggard, 11 Nov. 1902, NA, FO 80/445.
63. Wilhelm II to Bülow, 12 Nov. 1902, GP XVII, No. 5031, 115–17, 117.
64. Metternich to AA, 13 Nov. 1902, GP XVII, No. 5113, 254.
65. Bernstorff to AA, 17 Nov. 1902, GP XVII, No. 5114, 254–55.
66. Bülow to Metternich, 12 Nov. 1902, GP XVII, No. 5112, 253–54.
67. Quadt to AA, 25 Nov. 1902, GP XVII, No. 5116, 256.
68. Richthofen to Metternich, 5 Dec. 1902, GP XVII, No. 5118, 257.

69. Mitchell, *Danger of Dreams*, 64.
70. Haggard to Lansdowne, 22 Nov. 1902, NA, FO 420/206.
71. Lascelles to Lansdowne, 1 March 1902; to Buchanan, 8 June 1902, NA, FO 64/1551.
72. 'The Germans are working fairly well with us.' Lansdowne to Herbert, 4 Dec. 1902, NA, FO 800/144.
73. Herwig, 'Politics', 13–92; Lambi, *The Navy*, 226–31; Hase, *Lateinamerika*, 428–72.
74. Cited in Bourne, *Balance*, 376.
75. Strategical Considerations in the Caribbean Sea, 10 Nov. 1902, NA, CAB 8/3, C.D.C. 300M.
76. WO, Military Resources of the United States, 1904, NA, WO 33/327. Roosevelt only pronounced the Monroe Corollary, which stated that the United States would intervene in the Latin American states to prevent the involvement of the European Great Powers, on 2 December 1904.
77. Cited in Guthrie, *Venezuela*, 21.
78. Lansdowne, Memorandum, FO, 16 Aug. 1902, NA, FO 80/444.
79. Pauncefote to Salisbury, 9 June 1900, NA, FO 5/2428.
80. See Hurst, *Key Treaties*, Vol. 1, No. 46, 282–85.
81. Cited in Adams, *Brothers across the Ocean*, 24.
82. Ibid., 25.
83. Ibid., 26. 'It is not really in the interest of Great Britain that it [the canal] should be constructed.' Lansdowne to Pauncefote, 14 Dec. 1900, NA, FO 800/144.
84. Cited in Adams, *Brothers across the Ocean*, 34.
85. Ibid.
86. Lansdowne to Herbert, 4 Dec. 1902, NA, FO 800/144.
87. Montgomery to ADM, 16 Dec. 1902, NA, ADM 1/7620.
88. The *Panther*, launched on 1 April 1901, helped cause the Agadir crisis in 1911, when it called at the port of Agadir to load coal while on its way to Germany.
89. Metternich to Balfour, 17 Nov. 1902, BL, Add. 49747.
90. Ship's log, *HMS Charybdis*, NA, ADM 53.
91. Montgomery to ADM, 16 Dec. 1902, NA, FO 420/206.
92. 'Let us give the British precedence', Wilhelm II, Minute, Bülow to Wilhelm II, 12 Dec. 1902, GP XVII, No. 5120, 258–60.
93. Herbert to Lansdowne, 16 Dec. 1902, cited in Adams, *Brothers across the Ocean*, 49.
94. *New York Times*, 12 Dec. 1902, cited in ibid.
95. *Daily Mail*, 4 Dec. 1902, cited in Brex, *Scaremongerings*, 31.
96. *Daily Mail*, 9, 12 Dec. 1902; *Daily News*, 11 Dec. 1902; *Pall Mall Gazette*, 27 Nov. 1902; *The Times*, 3, 9, 10 Dec. 1902; *Daily News*, 1, 4 Dec. 1902; see also Koss, *Rise and Fall*, 365; Mitchell, *Danger of Dreams*, 250, n. 97.
97. Maxse, *Germany on the Brain*, 77–84; Spender to Strachey, 21 Oct. 1905, PA, STR/13/13/6.
98. Saunders to Maxse, 22 Dec. 1902, WSRO, MAXSE/450.
99. *Daily News*, 11, 12 Dec. 1902.
100. *Daily News*, 13, 15, 16, 17, 18, 19 Dec. 1902.
101. *Manchester Guardian*, 9 Dec. 1902.
102. *Manchester Guardian*, 12, 13, 16, 17 Dec. 1902; *Westminster Gazette*, 12 Dec. 1902; *Daily Chronicle*, 11 Dec. 1902.
103. Campbell-Bannerman, 15 Dec. 1902, PD III/116, col. 1270.

104. *Daily News*, 13 Dec. 1902.
105. *Daily Mail*, 16 Dec. 1902.
106. *Westminster Gazette*, 12 Dec. 1902.
107. Grey to Rosebery, 7 Jan. 1896, NLS, MSS 10028.
108. For Grey, Germany was Britain's 'worst enemy and our greatest danger'. His position stemmed not from the actions of Germany but from the attitude of other powers: 'Close relations with Germany mean for us worse relations with the rest of the world'. Grey to Newbolt, 5 Jan. 1903, cited in Kennedy, *Rise of Anglo-German Antagonism*, 259; *The Times*, 7 Feb. 1903.
109. *Morning Post*, 11 Dec. 1902.
110. *The Times*, 25, 29 Nov. 1902; 15, 18 Dec. 1902; Metternich to AA, 13 Dec. 1902, GP XVII, No. 5122, 261–62.
111. *The Times*, 17, 19 Dec. 1902.
112. *The Times*, 18 Dec. 1902; Tweedmouth, 2 March 1903, PD IV/118, col. 1049.
113. CR, 17 Dec. 1902, cited in Brex, *Scaremongerings*, 31.
114. *The Times*, 10 Nov. 1902; 3, 5, 6 Dec. 1902.
115. See Geppert, *Pressekriege*, 183–89.
116. Lee, *Origins of the Popular Press*, 160.
117. Selborne to Curzon, 4 Jan. 1903, cited in Monger, *End of Isolation*, 110.
118. *The Spectator*, 27 Dec. 1902, 3 Jan., 7 Feb. 1903; *St. James Gazette*, 22 Dec. 1902; *Daily Mail*, 17 Dec. 1902; *The Times*, 22 Dec. 1902.
119. Geppert, *Pressekriege*, 221; Brex, *Scaremongerings*, 31–34, Maxse, *Germany on the Brain*, 77–84; Kennedy, *Rise of Anglo-German Antagonism*, 251, 267.
120. Ignotus (Wilson), 'A Lesson to Lord Lansdowne', NR 1/1903, 710–14.
121. Balfour, 18 Dec. 1902, cited in Adams, *Brothers across the Ocean*, 51; Lansdowne to Balfour, 1 Jan. 1903; Balfour to Lansdowne, 2 Jan. 1903, BL, Add. 49728.
122. Durand to Lansdowne, 29 Jan. 1903, BL, LANS, Vol. 5.
123. Lansdowne even thought of taking steps against his former diplomat Rumbold and his agitation in the *National Review*. Rumbold to Maxse, 4, 8 and 10 Nov. 1902, WSRO, MAXSE/450; Verney to Saunders, 8 Nov. 1902, BL, Add. 49727.
124. Hamilton to Curzon, 24 Dec. 1902, IOL, EUR. F. 123/84; Newton, *Lord Lansdowne*, 256.
125. Holleben to AA, 16 Dec. 1902, GP XVII, No. 5124, 264.
126. Metternich to AA, 16 Dec. 1902, GP XVII, No. 5125, 265–66.
127. Lascelles to Lansdowne, 27 Dec. 1902, NA, FO 800/18.
128. White to Hay, 18 Dec. 1902, FRUS III, 456.
129. Herbert to Lansdowne, 19 Dec. 1902, NA, FO 800/144.
130. Quadt to AA, 24 Jan. 1903, GP XVII, No. 5136, 276.
131. Sternburg to AA, 3 Feb. 1903, GP XVII, No. 5146, 285–86; 4 Feb. 1903, No. 5147, 287.
132. Metternich to AA, 27 Jan. 1903, GP XVII, No. 5137, 277–78.
133. Richthofen to Metternich, 28 Jan. 1902, GP XVII, No. 5139, 279–80.
134. Metternich to AA, 15 Dec. 1902, GP XVII, No. 5123, 262–64.
135. Richthofen to Quadt, 24 Jan. 1903, GP XVII, No. 5134, 274–75.
136. Quadt to AA, 20 Jan. 1903, GP XVII, No. 5123, 273–74.
137. Lansdowne to Lascelles, Feb. 1903, NA, FO 800/129.
138. Lansdowne to Herbert, 2 Jan. 1903, NA, FO 800/115.

139. Lansdowne to Herbert, 20 Feb. 1903, NA, FO 800/144.
140. Cited in Maxse, *Germany on the Brain*, 83–84.
141. Lascelles to Lansdowne, 30 Jan. 1903, NA, FO 800/129.
142. Roosevelt to Thayer, 21 Aug. 1916, cited in Hase, *Großmachtkonflikte*, 540.
143. Maxse to Mahan, 6 March 1903, cited in Morris, *Scaremongers*, 54. For an extended analysis on the Venezuela Crisis, see Rose, *Zwischen Empire und Kontinent*, 279–99.
144. Maxse to Mahan, 6 March 1903, cited in Morris, *Scaremongers*, 54.
145. *Daily News*, 23 Jan. 1903; *Daily Express*, 23 Jan. 1903.
146. Spender, 'Venezuela Crisis', FR 2/1903, 197–205, 205. For George Saunders, it appeared necessary 'to cooperate with our most important European and Asiatic neighbours, Russia and France'. Saunders and Maxse, 17 June 1902, WSRO, MAXSE/450.
147. See Roberts, *Salisbury – Victorian Titan*, 646.
148. Grey to Maxse, 12 Oct. 1902, WSRO, MAXSE/450.
149. See Hale, *Publicity and Diplomacy*, 261–62; Earle, *Turkey*, 180–82; Chapman, *Baghdad Railway*, 45–70; Francis, 'British withdrawal from the Baghdad Railway', 168–78; Schöllgen, 'Germanophobia'; Monger, *End of Isolation*, 118–23.
150. *The Times*, 30 Nov. 1899; 16 Aug. 1902; *Morning Post*, 13 Dec. 1899; 19, 22, 27 Aug. 1902.
151. *The Times*, 18 July 1899.
152. Ferguson, *Rothschilds*, Vol. 2, 465–66; Lansdowne, Minutes, O'Conor to Lansdowne, 10 April 1902, BD II, No. 205, 178–79; Lansdowne, Minutes, 18 June 1902, NA, FO 800/145.
153. 'We wish it [Baghdad railway] well as a buttress against Russia. It will show that the maintenance of Turkey is now worth to Germany the bones of many Pomeranian Grenadiers.' De Bunsen to his father, 22 Dec. 1902, MSS De Bunsen, BOD, 7dd; Lansdowne to Drummond-Wolff, 12 Aug. 1902, BL, LANS/NC Drummond-Wolff; Balfour, 8 April 1903, PD IV/120, cols. 1373–74; see also Hoyer, *Salisbury und Deutschland*, 315.
154. Sanderson, Memorandum, 4 Jan. 1901, NA, FO 78/5249.
155. Hamilton to Curzon, 2 Nov. 1899, IOL, EUR. F. 111/158.
156. Lansdowne to Lord Hillingdon, 7 March 1902; Memorandum, 9 June 1902; Minutes, 18 June 1902; Sanderson, 19 March 1902, 23 April 1902, 23 March 1903, NA, FO 800/145.
157. Curzon to Dawkins, 3 April 1903, IOL, EUR. F. 111/182.
158. Conference result, 4 Feb. 1903, cited in Lansdowne, Memorandum, 14 April 1903, NA, FO 800/145.
159. Hamilton to Curzon, 8 Oct. 1902, IOL, EUR. F. 123/84; 6 Jan. 1903 and 27 Feb. 1903, IOL, EUR. C. 126/5.
160. Hamilton to Curzon, 13 March 1903, IOL, EUR. C. 126/5.
161. Dawkins to Curzon, 4 March 1903, IOL, EUR. F. 111/182; Lansdowne, Memorandum, 4 Feb. 1903, NA, FO 800/145; Cassel to Lansdowne, 5 Feb. 1903, ibid.; Sanderson, Memorandum, 24 Feb. 1902, ibid. The treaty gave Britain an equitable 25 per cent of the shares and eight seats on the board; 15 per cent of the shares were to be diversified while 10 per cent would remain with the Anatolian Railway Company. Sanderson, Memorandum, 23 Feb. 1903, ibid.; O'Conor to Lansdowne, 9 March 1903, ibid.; Gwinner to Revelstoke, 18 March 1903, ibid.; Revelstoke, Memorandum, 20 April 1903, ibid.

162. Dawkins to Curzon, 15 April 1903, IOL, EUR. F. 111/182; Metternich to Bülow, 4 April 1903, GP XVII, No. 5257, 436–37.
163. Maxse, 'Episodes', NR 1/1903, 669–80; NR 2/1903, 845–57; NR 3/1903, 15; Ignotus (H.W. Wilson), 'A Lesson to Lord Lansdowne', NR 1/1903, 710–14; Blennerhasset, 'The Rise and Character of Prussian Power', NR 2/1903, 906–20; Scrutator (Canon MacColl), 'The Kaisers', NR 3/1903, 28–43.
164. Maxse to Strachey, 21 April 1903, PA, STR 10/9/6.
165. Morris, *Scaremongers*, 55; Dawkins to Curzon, 26 April 1903, IOL, EUR. F. 111/182.
166. Strachey to Harmsworth, 15 Feb. 1903, PA, STR/11/4.
167. Spring Rice to Strachey, Easter 1903, PA, STR/13/14/3.
168. *The Spectator*, 4 and 18 April 1904, cited in Dillon, 'The Baghdad Railway', CR 5/1903, 732–51, 743.
169. Saunders to Maxse, 19 Nov. 1901, WSRO, MAXSE/448.
170. Maxse, 'Episodes', NR 4/1903, 166–67.
171. 'These notes were the fruit of a lucky conversation in Paris with the then French Ambassador in Constantinople [Jean Constans]. The *National Review* sounded the alarm and the Press was able to destroy a project which would have placed Asia Minor under the Mailed Fist.' Maxse, *Germany on the Brain*, 90.
172. Maxse, Episodes, NR 4/1903, 165–71; Maxse, *Germany on the Brain*, 90–92.
173. Maxse, *Germany on the Brain*, 90–92; *The Spectator*, 4, 11, 18 and 25 April 1903.
174. Dillon, 'The Baghdad Railway', CR 5/1903, 732–51, 741–45.
175. Maxse, Episodes, NR 4/1903, 165–71; Maxse, *Germany on the Brain*, 90–92.
176. See Schöllgen, 'Germanophobia', 424.
177. Dillon, 'Foreign Affairs: The Baghdad Railway', CR 5/1903, 743.
178. Spring Rice to Strachey, Easter 1903, PA, STR/13/14/3.
179. See Chapter 1. See also Geppert, *Pressekriege*, 195.
180. *The Times*, 19 Feb. 1903. See also Grey (Commons), cited in *The Times*, 7 Feb. 1903.
181. Cited in Maxse, *Germany on the Brain*, 98–102.
182. 'Do you see that some of the newspapers are attacking it because it is a German project, and wish us to block it – or keep out of it – as we did when the Suez Canal was made? In that case we had to buy our way in later, at an enormous cost; and it did not prevent the canal being made.' Esher to Brett, 6 April 1903, JL I, 396–97.
183. *The Times*, 9, 18 April 1903; *The Spectator*, 11, 18 April 1903; *Saturday Review*, 18 April 1903. Cited in Schöllgen, 'Germanophobia', 421; Metternich to Bülow, 9 April 1903, GP XVII, No. 5258, 437.
184. Dawkins to Curzon, 15 April 1903, IOL, EUR. F. 111/182.
185. Lansdowne, Memorandum, 7 April 1903, NA, FO 800/145.
186. *The Times*, 14 Feb., 10 Nov. 1903; see also Balfour (Guildhall), 10 Nov. 1902, ER 1/1903, 253–72.
187. Metternich to Bülow, 12 April 1903, GP XVII, No. 5259, 438f.; Balfour, Memorandum, 28 Nov. 1899, BL, Add. 49691; Note of Conversation between Kaiser and Balfour, 1 Dec. 1899, cited in Tomes, *Balfour and Foreign Policy*, 131.
188. Maxse, 'Episodes', NR 8/1900, 879.
189. Balfour to Lansdowne, 14 April 1903, BL, LANS/PL 5. See also *Daily Mail*, 4, 16, 21, 24 April 1903; *The Times*, 9, 18, 20, 24 April 1903; *Pall Mall Gazette*, 9, 22 April 1903; *Manchester Guardian*, 23 April 1903; *Speaker*, 18 April 1903, 53–54.
190. Maxse to Strachey, 21 April 1903, PA, STR/10/9/6.

191. PD IV/121, cols. 220–22.
192. *The Times*, 22 April 1903.
193. Lansdowne to Balfour, 17 April 1903, BL, Add. 49728; see also Fritzinger, *Diplomat without Portfolio*, 188.
194. Kennedy, *Rise of Anglo-German Antagonism*, 261; Geppert, *Pressekriege*, 198.
195. Ripon to Malabri, 6 Nov. 1904, BL, Add. 43616.
196. Neilson, *Britain and the Last Tsar*, 239.
197. Dawkins to Curzon, 15 April 1903, IOL, EUR. F. 111/182.
198. Ibid.
199. Cited in Newton, *Lord Lansdowne*, 254.
200. Selborne to Curzon, 24 April 1903, IOL, EUR. F. 111/229; Sanderson, Memorandum, 21 Feb. 1907, BD III, App. B, 420–31, 429.
201. Lansdowne to Curzon, 24 April 1903, cited in Newton, *Lord Lansdowne*, 254.
202. Lansdowne to O'Conor, 6 May 1903, NA, FO 800/143.
203. Esher, Diary, 24 April 1903, JL I, 397.
204. Dawkins to Curzon, 26 April 1903, IOL, EUR. F. 111/182.
205. Chirol to Curzon, 23 April 1903, IOL, EUR. F. 111/182.
206. Chirol to Saunders, 4 Sept. 1899, NIA, FELB IV/428.
207. 'Finally … they had got from the Germans all the concessions that the Govt. had hitherto asked for.' Chirol to Strachey, 26 April 1903, PA, STR/4/9/1; 29 April 1903, STR/4/9/2.
208. Chirol to Saunders, 9 May 1904, NIA, FELB IV/868.
209. Chirol to Strachey, 26 April 1903, PA, STR/4/9/1.
210. Maxse, *Germany on the Brain*, 92.
211. Dillon, 'The Baghdad Railway', CR 5/1903, 732–51, 741–44.
212. Lansdowne to O'Conor, 6 May 1903, NA, FO 800/143.
213. *The Times*, 24 April 1903; Saunders to Maxse, 26 April 1903, WSRO, MAXSE/451.
214. Dawkins to Curzon, 26 April 1903, IOL, EUR. F. 111/182.
215. Dawkins to Gwinner, 23 April 1903, GP XVII, No. 5262, 442–44.
216. Hamilton to Curzon, 8 April 1903, IOL, EUR. C. 126/5.
217. Hamilton to Curzon, 14 April 1899 and 2 Nov. 1899, IOL, EUR. F. 123/81.
218. Hamilton to Curzon, 24 April 1903, IOL, EUR. F. 123/81.
219. Balfour (Commons), 7, 8 April 1903, PD IV/120, cols. 1247, 1373–74; 23 April 1903, PD IV/121, col. 222; Balfour to Edward VII, 23 May 1905, NA, CAB 41/30/19.
220. Calchas (Garvin), 'The Latin Rapprochement and the Baghdad Imbroglio', FR 5/1903, 732–51.
221. Drummond-Wolff to Lansdowne, 4 May 1903, BL, LANS/NC Drummond-Wolff.
222. Calchas (Garvin), 'The Latin Rapprochement and Anglo-Russian Relations', FR 6/1903, 953–69.
223. Sanderson to Hardinge, 8 Nov. 1899, CUL, MSS Hardinge, Vol. 3.
224. Andrew, *Delcassé*, 179.
225. See chapters one and two.
226. Lansdowne to Monson, 2 Jan. 1902, NA, FO 800/125; see also Weiner, *Cambon*; Newton, *Lord Lansdowne*, 267; Monson to Lansdowne, 31 Dec. 1903, cited in ibid., 270–71. For the French diplomats, see Keiger, *Origins*, 25–43; Hayne, 'Foreign Office', 9–28.
227. Charmley, *Splendid Isolation*, 307.

228. Metternich to Bülow, 30 Jan. 1902, GP XVII, No. 5186, 342–43; Charmley, *Splendid Isolation*, 306.
229. Monger, *End of Isolation*, 39; Lansdowne to Monson, 6 Aug. 1902, BD II, No. 322, 264–66; Newton, *Lord Lansdowne*, 268; Rolo, 'Lansdowne', 135.
230. Lansdowne to Cambon, 17 July 1902, to Monson, 18 July; 6 Aug. 1902, NA, FO 800/125.
231. Lansdowne to Monson, 6 Aug. 1902, NA, FO 800/125; Lansdowne to Lascelles, 8 June 1905, BD III, No. 117, 92–3.
232. Lansdowne to Monson, 6 Aug. 1902, NA, FO 800/125.
233. Lansdowne to Balfour, 1 Jan. 1903, BL, LANS/PL 5.
234. Lansdowne to Monson, 28 Dec. 1902, cited in Newton, *Lord Lansdowne*, 269–70.
235. Monger, *End of Isolation*, 111.
236. Lansdowne to Herbert, 2 Jan. 1903, NA, FO 800/115.
237. Lansdowne to Monson, 31 Dec. 1902, BD II, No. 330, 274–75.
238. Balfour to Lansdowne, 2 Jan. 1903, BL, Add. 49728.
239. Lansdowne to Monson, 19 May 1903, BD II, No. 352, 289; to Cromer, 8 June 1903, NA, FO 800/124; Nicolson to Lansdowne, 13 May 1904, NA, FO 800/142.
240. For a different view, see McKercher, 'Diplomatic Equipoise', 313.
241. See Chapter 2.
242. Lansdowne to Monson, 7 July 1903, BD II, No. 357, 294–97; Newton, *Lord Lansdowne*, 279–80; Cromer to Lansdowne, 17 July 1903, BD II, No. 359, 298–301.
243. Hamilton to Curzon, 9 July 1903, IOL, EUR. C. 126/5.
244. Andrew, *Théophile Delcassé*, 229.
245. Lansdowne, Memorandum, 10 Sept. 1903, cited in Monger, *End of Isolation*, 133.
246. Cromer to Balfour, 15 Oct. 1903, NA, FO 633/6; to Lansdowne, 22 Oct. 1903, NA, FO 800/115.
247. Cromer to Lansdowne, 27 Nov. 1903, NA, FO 633/7.
248. McKercher, 'Diplomatic Equipoise', 301, 303, 338.
249. Lansdowne to Lascelles, 23 March 1904; 18 April 1904, NA, FO 800/129.
250. Cromer to Lansdowne, 17 July 1903, BD II, No. 359, 298–301.
251. Cromer to Lansdowne, 27 Nov. 1903, NA, FO 633/7.
252. Cromer noted in particular the support from the *Standards* and its Morocco expert Harris. Cromer to Lansdowne, 27 Nov. 1903, NA, FO 633/7.
253. Chirol to Fullerton, 4 June 1903, NIA, FELB IV/818–19.
254. Saunders to Bell, 26 April 1903, NIA, MSS Bell.
255. *Speaker*, 17 Oct. 1903, 57; *Blackwood's Magazine* 5/1904, 743; *The Times*, 7 Oct. 1903; RR 12/1903, 596; Lee, 'Promoters of the Anglo-French Amity', FR 7/1903, 132–40.
256. Andrew, *Théophile Delcassé*, 229. For Tibet, see Lansdowne to Spring Rice, 4 May 1903, BD IV, No. 184, 189–90.
257. Andrew, *Théophile Delcassé*, 212.
258. 'We ought in my opinion to break off and I have told Cambon that if we cannot come to terms over Nfoundland [sic] the whole arrangement will have to go.' Lansdowne to Balfour, 2 April 1904, BL, Add. 49728.
259. Neilson, *Britain and the Last Tsar*, 235; Monger, *End of Isolation*, 133.
260. Monson to Lansdowne, 18 Nov.; 9 Dec. 1904, NA, FO 800/125; Lansdowne to Monson, 5 July 1904, BD III, No. 6, 8–9.

261. Bertie to Lansdowne, 17 Jan. 1905, NA, FO 800/125; Lansdowne to Bertie, 21 March 1905, NA, FO 800/126.
262. Monger, *End of Isolation*, 160.
263. Lansdowne to Monson, 26 Dec. 1904, NA, FO 800/126.
264. Calchas (Garvin), 'The Bankruptcy of Bismarckian Policy', FR 5/1904, 765–77; see also Dillon, 'The Anglo-French Convention', CR 5/1904, 609–13; Maxse, 'Episodes', NR 5/1904, 440–48; Doumer, 'The Anglo-French Agreement', NR 6/1904, 556–62; Harris, 'The Anglo-French Agreement', NR 5/1904, 494–99; Dicey, 'The Anglo-French Compact', FR 5/1904, 778–89; *The Times*, 24 March; 6, 9, 11, 12 April 1904.
265. *Manchester Guardian*, 10 April 1904.
266. Lansdowne to Balfour, 2 April 1904, BL, Add. 49728.
267. Monger, *End of Isolation*, 160.
268. McKercher, 'Diplomatic Equipoise', 321.
269. Spender to Strachey, 21 Oct. 1905, PA, STR/13/13/6.
270. Lansdowne to Monson, 11 Dec. 1903, BD II, No. 259, 224.
271. Brackenbury to Arnold-Forster, 23 Dec. 1903, BL, LANS/Working Files 14.
272. Chamberlain, Memorandum, 7 Dec. 1903, NA, CAB 37/67/84.
273. McKercher, 'Diplomatic Equipoise'; Neilson, *Britain and the Last Tsar*, 238–66.
274. Selborne to Lansdowne, 24 Dec. 1903, BL, Add. 49728.
275. A. Chamberlain to Lansdowne, 21 Dec. 1903, BL, LANS/Working Files 14.
276. Lansdowne to Balfour, 22 Dec. 1903, BL, Add. 49728.
277. Lansdowne to Balfour, 24 Dec. 1903, BL Add. 49728; see also Monger, *End of Isolation*, 147–55.
278. Balfour to Brodrick, 28 Oct. 1903, BL, Add. 50072.
279. Balfour to Selborne, 23 Dec. 1903, BUL, AC 17/1/19.
280. Balfour to Spenser Wilkinson, 3 Jan. 1904, BL, Add. 49747.
281. Balfour to Edward VII, 14 July 1903, NA, CAB 41/28/14.
282. Balfour to Edward VII, 11 Dec. 1903, NA, CAB 41/28/26; 28 Dec. 1903, BL, Add. 49683; Balfour, Memorandum, 22 Dec. 1903, NA, CAB 37/67/92.
283. Balfour to Edward VII, 14 Dec. 1903, NA, CAB 41/28/27. Cited in Williams, *Defending the Empire*, 60.
284. Balfour, 22 Dec. 1903, BL, LANS/PL 5.
285. Balfour to Lansdowne, 22 Dec. 1903, BL, Add. 49728.
286. Balfour, Memorandum, 22 Dec. 1903, NA, CAB 37/67/92.
287. Balfour, Memorandum, 27 Dec. 1903, NA, CAB 37/67/97.
288. Balfour to Lansdowne, 11 Feb. 1904, BL, Add. 49728.
289. Bridge to Selborne, 14 Jan. 1904, Boyce, *Crisis of British Power*, Vol. 2, No. 48, 166–67.
290. 'I understand that Japan is at this moment considerably stronger at sea than Russia in the Far East. … Even when the Russian ships now in the Mediterranean have reached the Far East, Japan will still be stronger than Russia.' Lansdowne to Balfour, 24 Dec. 1904, BL, LANS/Working Files 14.
291. Monger, *End of Isolation*, 147–55; Grenville, *Lord Salisbury*, 393; Busch, *Hardinge of Penshurst*, 68–69.
292. Lansdowne to A. Chamberlain, 22 Dec. 1903, BUL, AC 17/1/17.
293. Selborne to Lansdowne, 24 Dec. 1903, BL, LANS/Working Files 14.
294. Cited in Monger, *End of Isolation*, 148.
295. Selborne to Lansdowne, 27 Dec. 1903, BL, LANS/PL 1.

296. A. Chamberlain to Lansdowne, 25 Dec. 1903, BL, LANS/Working Files 14. 'Let the Japs decide for themselves. Let us only promise to do our best to keep a ring fence round the combatants, ... If they fight and win, tant mieux. If they fight and lose, Korea is gone, but Japan will remain.' A. Chamberlain to Lansdowne, 30 Dec. 1903, BL, Add. 49735.
297. Balfour to Edward VII, 28 Dec. 1903, BL, Add. 46893.
298. Balfour to Lansdowne, 26 Dec. 1903, BL, LANS/PL 5.
299. 'All this is to the good; but if Lansdowne's suggestion is followed none of these things would happen.' Balfour to Selborne, 23 Dec. 1903, BUL, AC 17/1/19.
300. Balfour to Lansdowne, 31 Dec. 1903, BL, Add. 49728.
301. CID 29th Meeting, 4 Jan. 1904, NA, CAB 2/1.
302. Lansdowne to MacDonald, 11 Jan. 1904, BD II, No. 274, 232–33, 233.
303. Lansdowne, Proposed Agreement with Russia, 1 Jan. 1904, NA, CAB 37/68/1.
304. Lansdowne to Balfour, 24 Sept. 1903; 23 Dec. 1903; 18 March 1905, BL, LANS/PL 5; to Hardinge, 4 Sept. 1905, CUL, MSS Hardinge, Vol. 7.
305. Lansdowne, Memorandum, 11 Jan. 1904, NA, CAB 37/68/11.
306. Ibid.; Selborne to Lansdowne, 11 Jan. 1904; Kerr, Memorandum, 12 Jan. 1904; Battenberg, Memorandum, 13 Jan. 1904; Balfour, Memorandum respecting the Russian Black Sea Fleet and the Passage of the Dardanelles, 19 Jan. 1904, NA, CAB 37/68/11.
307. Lansdowne to MacDonald, 30 Jan. 1904, BD IV, No. 40, 48; to Scott, 30 Jan. 1904, BD II, No. 285, 241f.
308. Neilson, 'A Dangerous Game', 69–74.
309. Lansdowne to Monson, 29 April 1905, BD IV, No. 43, 50.
310. Temperley to Lansdowne, 9 Sept. 1920, NA, FO 800/130.
311. Knollys to Hardinge, 17 Dec. 1903, CUL, MSS Hardinge, Vol. 7.
312. Lee, *Edward VII*, Vol. 2, 285–87.
313. Ibid., 289–90.
314. Hardinge, Memorandum, 16 Nov. 1906, BD IV, 58–60, 60.
315. Arnold-Forster, Diary, 21 Nov. 1904, BL, Add. 50340; Clarke to Sanderson, 17 Jan. 1905, NA, FO 800/116.
316. Sanderson to Hardinge, 19 Sept. 1905, CUL, MSS Hardinge, Vol. 7.
317. Mallet to Lansdowne, 25 July 1905, BL, LANS/PL 5.
318. Balfour to Lansdowne, 31 Dec. 1904, BL, LANS/PL 5; *The Times*, 13 Jan. 1905.
319. Geppert, *Pressekriege*, 251; McKercher, 'Diplomatic Equipoise', 326.
320. Fisher to Selborne, 29 Oct. 1904, FGDN II, No. 4, 46; to Lady Fisher, 1 Nov. 1904, FGDN II, No. 5, 47. See also Steinberg, 'Copenhagen Complex', 23–46; Lambi, *The Navy*, 247–48; Monger, *End of Isolation*, 176.
321. Mallet to Spring Rice, 20 Dec. 1904, CC, CASR 1/49.
322. Neilson, *Britain and the Last Tsar*, 255.
323. Sanderson to Hardinge, 10 Jan. 1905, CUL, MSS Hardinge, Vol. 7.
324. Neilson, *Britain and the Last Tsar*, 255–60; Monger, *End of Isolation*, 172–80; BD IV, Nos. 5–31, 5–40.
325. Brian McKercher suspected Wilhelm II was playing a leading role. McKercher, 'Diplomatic Equipoise', 326.
326. See Geppert, *Pressekriege*, 246–56.
327. Calchas (Garvin), 'The Limits of Japanese Capacity', FR 11/1904, 783–99, 799; X (Garvin?), 'Japanese Barbarism', MR 11/1904, 1–14.

328. See *The Spectator*, 9 Jan. 1904, 40; Calchas (Garvin), 'The New German Intrigue', FR 9/1904, 385–402.
329. Geppert, *Pressekriege*, 251.
330. Steed to Chirol, 24 Oct. 1904, NIA, MSS Steed, LB/II/1–499.
331. Chirol to Lascelles, 21 Sept. 1904; 27 Sept. 1904, NA, FO 800/12; to Spring Rice, 1 Nov. 1904, CC, CASR 1/10.
332. Spring Rice to Mallet, 5 Nov. 1904, BL, Add. 49747.
333. Mallet to Bertie, 2 June 1904, NA, FO 800/163.
334. Mallet to Sandars, 11 Nov. 1904, NA, FO 800/163.
335. Sanderson to Hardinge, 29 Nov. 1904, CUL, MSS Hardinge, Vol. 7.
336. Bertie to Hardinge, 28 Nov. 1904, CUL, MSS Hardinge, Vol. 7; Spring Rice to Chirol, 7 Dec. 1904, CC, CASR 1/20.
337. Maxse to Spring Rice, 15 Nov. 1904, CC, CASR 1/50.
338. Anon., 'Rosebery's Public Counsel', RR 12/1904, 598–601.
339. Lansdowne, 14 Feb. 1905, PD (Lords) IV/149, col. 28; Lansdowne to Hardinge, 3 April 1905, NA, FO 800/141; to Delcassé, 17 June 1905, FO 800/127.
340. Nish, *Anglo-Japanese Alliance*, 131.
341. MacDonald to Lansdowne, 2 Feb. 1905, NA, FO 800/134.
342. Lansdowne to Bertie, 21 March 1905, NA, FO 800/126; 27 March 1905, FO 800/163.
343. Th. Roosevelt to Spring-Rice, 16 May 1905, NA, FO 800/141.
344. Balfour to Lansdowne, 24 Jan. 1905, BL, Add. 49729; Lansdowne to Durand, 25 Jan. 1905, NA, FO 800/116.
345. Lansdowne to Balfour, 16 Jan. 1905, BL, LANS/PL 5.
346. Balfour to Cooper, 11 Sept. 1905, BL, Add. 49747.
347. Balfour, Memorandum, 27 May 1905, NA, CAB 37/77/98.
348. Nish, *Anglo-Japanese Alliance*, 307–24.
349. See Chapter 8.
350. Balfour to Clarke, 11 Oct. 1905, BL, Add. 49720; see also Monger, *End of Isolation*, 217–20.
351. Lansdowne to Bertie, 8 Oct. 1905, NA, FO 800/127.
352. Bertie to Lansdowne, 17 Jan. 1905, NA, FO 800/125.
353. Clarke to Balfour, 7 Oct. 1905; 14 Oct. 1905, BL, Add 49720; Clarke, Memo, 16 Oct. 1905, NA, CAB 17/60.
354. Sanderson to Hardinge, 19 Sept. 1905, CUL, MSS Hardinge, Vol. 7.
355. Salisbury, 6 Sept. 1901, cited in Langer, *Diplomacy of Imperialism*, 755.
356. *The Spectator*, 16 Sept. 1905, 753; Metternich to Bülow, 14 March 1902, GP XVII, No. 5351, 542–44.
357. Wells, 'Withdrawal', 336–41.
358. See the reports by Spring Rice, GL II, 1–52.
359. Lansdowne to A. Chamberlain, 31 Jan. 1905, cited in Monger, *End of Isolation*, 221.
360. Lansdowne to Bertie, 21 March 1903, NA, FO 800/126.
361. McKercher, 'Diplomatic Equipoise', 299–339; Marder, *Anatomy of British Sea Power*; Steiner, *Britain and the Origins*; Neilson, *Britain and the Last Tsar*; Kennedy, *Rise of Anglo-German Antagonism*; Grenville, *Lord Salisbury*. For a different view, see Wilson, *Policy of the Entente*; Charmley, *Splendid Isolation*.
362. Monger, *End of Isolation*, 184–85. As early as 1904, Mallet held: 'Entre nous, I do not think that Mr Balfour at all realizes what may be expected from the Anglo-French

understanding and would be ready to make an arrangement with Germany tomorrow'. Mallet to Bertie, 2 June 1904, BL, Add. 63016.
363. Brodrick to Ampthill, 17 March 1905, cited in Monger, *End of Isolation*, 184.
364. See in particular Steiner and Neilson, *Britain and the Origins*, 34.
365. See Chapter 2.
366. '[A]u grand sérieux', Lansdowne to Balfour, 18 Jan. 1905, BL, LANS/PL 5.
367. G.W. Balfour to Spring Rice, 2 May 1905, CC, CASR 1/2.
368. Bertie to Lansdowne, 17 Jan. 1905, NA, FO 800/125; Lansdowne to Hardinge, 3 April 1905, NA, FO 800/141.
369. See Monger, *End of Isolation*, 186–88.
370. Fisher to Lansdowne, 22 April 1905, FGDN II, No. 30, 55.
371. Andrew, *Théophile Delcassé*, 269–73.
372. Cited in Monger, *End of Isolation*, 189.
373. Lansdowne to Balfour, 23 April 1905, BL, Add. 49729. For the navy's view, see Ottley to CID, 10 May 1905, NA, FO/1630; Seligmann, *Naval Route*, No. 63, 242.
374. Monger, *End of Isolation*, 190.
375. Balfour joined Clarke in believing that Fisher had exaggerated and that a German port would present no danger. Clarke to Balfour, 29 April and 4 May 1905, BL, Add. 49701.
376. Monger, *End of Isolation*, 191.
377. Ibid., 189.
378. For the difficulties of translation see also Wilson, 'Found and lost in translation', 38–9.
379. Lansdowne to Bertie, 22 April 1905, BD III, No. 90, 77–78; Bertie, 24 April 1905, BD III, No. 91, 78; Anderson, *First Moroccan Crisis*, 210–11.
380. 'L'Angleterre me soutient à fond; elle aussi, elle irait jusqu'à la guerre ... je vous répète, l'Angleterre nous soutiendrai à fond, et elle ne signerait pas la paix sans nous', cited in Paléologue, *Grand tournant*, 307–8.
381. Ibid., 315.
382. Lansdowne to Bertie, 3 May 1905, BD III, No. 86, 69–70.
383. '... s'il y a guerre, nous aurons l'Angleterre avec nous'. Cambon to Delcassé, 3 May 1905, DDF 2/VI, No. 390, 410; Delcassé, 10 May 1905, DDF 2/VIII, 557. For a different view, see Monger, *End of Isolation*, 191.
384. Lansdowne to Bertie, 31 May 1905, BD III, No. 95, App. 2, 77–78.
385. 'Ce n'est plus à une entente en cas d'aggression qu'il nous convie, c'est à une discussion immédiate et à un examen de la situation générale'. Cambon to Delcassé, 29 May 1905, DDF 2/VI, No. 465.
386. See Williamson, *Politics of Grand Strategy*, 34–38; Andrew, *Théophile Delcassé*, 281–83; Monger, *End of Isolation*, 199.
387. 'As a matter of fact the emergency of a rupture with Germany was never discussed at all.' Sanderson to Lansdowne, 9 Oct. 1905, NA, FO 800/145.
388. Metternich to Bülow, 28 June 1905, GP XX/2, No. 6860, 168–70; Lansdowne to Lascelles, 5 Aug. 1905, NA, FO 800/130.
389. Lister to Lansdowne, 30 June 1905, NA, FO 800/127.
390. Grey, *25 Years*, Vol. 1, 72–74; Grey to Bertie, 10 Jan. 1906, BD III, No. 210(a), 170–71.
391. Balfour to Edward VII, 8 June 1905, NA, CAB 41/30/21; to Esher, 23 July 1905, CC, ESHR 10/37; Lansdowne to Bertie, 12 June 1905, NA, FO 800/164.
392. Lansdowne to Bertie, 12 June 1905, NA, FO 800/163.

393. Lister to Lansdowne, 30 June 1905; Lansdowne to Lister, 10 July 1905, NA, FO 800/127.
394. Salisbury to Balfour, 9 Nov. 1905, BL, Add. 49758.
395. Ibid. Only the last part is quoted in Monger, *End of Isolation*, 226.
396. Lansdowne to O'Conor, 23 May 1905, NA, FO 800/143.
397. *Manchester Guardian*, 8 April 1905.
398. *Manchester Guardian*, 29 June, 5 July and 9 Aug. 1905.
399. *The Speaker*, 17 June 1905, 271.
400. *Manchester Guardian*, 13 and 14 Oct. 1905.
401. *The Speaker*, 14 Oct. 1905, 37.
402. *Manchester Guardian*, 16 Nov. 1906.
403. Spring Rice to Spender, 11 Aug. 1905, BL, Add. 46391.
404. Spender to Strachey, 21 Oct. 1905, PA, STR/13/13/6.
405. Ibid.
406. Spender, 'The Liberal Party', CR 7/1902, 153–65.
407. G.W. Balfour to Spring Rice, 18 Sept. 1904, CC, CASR 1/2. 'I never go upstairs to bed without thanking heaven that, in a very brief period, I shall have left my official residence and gone back to the comfort and repose of my own house.' Balfour to Chamberlain, 2 Nov. 1905, BL, Add. 49774.
408. Grey (City), *The Times*, 21 Oct. 1905.
409. Balfour, Guildhall-Rede, *The Times*, 10 Nov. 1905.
410. Cited in Tomes, *Balfour and Foreign Policy*, 127.
411. Chirol to Spring Rice, 19 Sept. 1905, CC, CASR 1/11.
412. 'It would be a mistake to attempt transaction analogous to that which had taken place between France and Britain.' Lansdowne to Hardinge, 3 Oct. 1905, BD IV, No. 194, 205.
413. Grey to Spring Rice, 13 Dec. 1905, BD IV, No. 204, 218.

Chapter 6

THE MYTH OF CONTINUITY
Foreign Policy under Edward Grey

The change in government in Britain preceded a general change of direction and leadership in international relations.[1] Within only a few months, new individuals with new ideas were at the helm not only in Whitehall but also at the Ballhausplatz in Vienna and at the Choristers' Bridge in St Petersburg.[2] On 7 February 1906, the change in London, which had already been effected the previous December, was confirmed by the general election. After more than a decade, the Liberals again formed the government, headed by Henry Campbell-Bannerman.

Initially, however, the appointment to the post of foreign secretary gave rise to internal divisions.[3] Internal party politics, personal reasons and power politics had led Campbell-Bannerman to attempt to put a stop to the conspiratorial Relugas Compact[4] formed by a number of younger party members: Herbert Asquith, Richard B. Haldane and Edward Grey. As part of an effort to limit the influence of liberal imperialists in his cabinet, Campbell-Bannerman sought to prevent Grey from becoming foreign secretary. Their personal animosity stemmed from the many years of scheming by Grey against Campbell-Bannerman.[5] The internal party strife was a direct consequence of the long time in opposition. Since the Liberals' failure at the polls in the khaki election, the party had been beset by internal wrangling, not only across generations but also over political orientation. As the representative of the established Gladstonians, the designated prime minister's desire to try to block Grey's path was not so surprising. Charles Hardinge, newly appointed permanent under-secretary, even thought it impossible that Grey would be appointed his superior at the Foreign Office.[6] Grey himself was hardly optimistic, suspecting that he, Asquith and Haldane, his liberal imperialist comrades in arms, had gone too far, and that it was therefore all too likely that he would be left empty handed when appointments were made.[7]

Notes for this chapter begin on page 297.

What has often been identified as a logical development was therefore rather a product of unexpected circumstances and chance. First, Lord Rosebery exited the race, having disqualified himself with his controversial stance on the long-running issue of Ireland.[8] While potential alternative candidates were not scarce, there was hardly a flood of applicants. Lord Elgin, former viceroy of India and a candidate of choice, preferred the post of proconsul in Egypt; Charles Dilke and James Bryce, both radical liberals and well qualified for the Foreign Office, were ruled out, the former because he still carried the stigma of adultery from a highly public case in the 1880s,[9] and the latter because he was valued by his colleagues more for his encyclopaedic knowledge than for his leadership qualities.[10] John Morley, an eminent authority on foreign and global policy, ruled himself out, according to John Spender, who usually knew what he was talking about, because of his doctrinaire radical liberal attitude, which, in the wake of the khaki election, was little welcome and would not help integrate the two wings of the party.[11] How little enthused the prime minister was at the idea of Grey as his foreign secretary is made evident by his fruitless attempt to win Lord Cromer, a Conservative, for the office; Cromer refused the offer, noting his regrets and citing his worsening arthritis.[12] William Harcourt favoured Edmond Petty-Fitzmaurice, Lansdowne's younger brother, for his expertise,[13] and Asquith introduced Lord Robert Crewe into the discussion as a compromise candidate, but neither man was a good party-political fit.[14] The game continued right up until the last moment: Esher recorded in his diary, 'On Thursday night at 8 Grey wrote six pages to C B finally declining to join the Government. At 11 he went to Belgrave Square with Haldane, and said he had changed his mind. Haldane to the WO, Grey to the FO'.[15]

How are we to understand Edward Grey, on whom opinions have always differed?[16] In terms of domestic policy, he appeared a moderate radical liberal, but when it came to foreign policy, as he was parliamentary under-secretary of state for foreign affairs (1892–1895), his views were largely conservative and focused on power politics.[17] Nevertheless, he hardly seemed a strong candidate for high office. Rusticated several times from Balliol College for 'incorrigible idleness' by Lansdowne's mentor Benjamin Jowett, Grey possessed neither an outstanding intellect nor linguistic skills.[18] Moreover, he had no administrative experience at all.[19] His practical knowledge of foreign policy issues was limited to parliament and party politics, as was frequently evident in his later policy decisions. Although the power balance within the party between radicals and liberal imperialists initially impeded his progress towards the Foreign Office, in the long run it would prove key to his becoming foreign secretary, for Herbert Gladstone and Arthur Acland made the case that the majority of other posts had gone to radical liberals.[20]

Grey's appointment rested first and foremost on his reputation as a party politician, in which he was markedly different from his mainly aristocratic predecessors, whose natural home was the House of Lords.[21] Although he avoided public appearances, his impact on the Commons when he did speak was deemed almost hypnotic.[22] While Lansdowne and Balfour had frequently dared to counter the panic-mongering, Grey, according to George Trevelyan, aimed to please his public.[23] His liberal approach to domestic policy and imperial orientation for foreign policy allowed him to hold the two wings of the party together.[24] The demands of party and parliament, to which he claimed he sacrificed half his energies, often kept him from his immediate ministerial responsibilities.[25] He frequently found himself defending his liberal imperial course, and especially his promotion of rapprochement with the autocratic tsardom, against the radical majority.[26] Thus, in early 1905, no less a figure than Charles Dilke avowed that he would stand in the way of the pro-Russian course expected of Grey, recording: 'Grey has always favoured the deal with Russia [although] I hope I may be able to stay outside the next Govt. to kill it'.[27] All the more reason, then, for the liberal imperialists to hold the most influential foreign affairs posts.[28]

Grey the foreign secretary was very much Grey the parliamentarian. His weekly duties in the House of Commons, limited to when parliament was sitting, corresponded more comfortably with his regulated lifestyle than did the often unpredictable tasks of Whitehall. Shortly after the Bosnian Annexation Crisis, he complained, very characteristically, of the unwelcome interruption to his private life: 'It is degrading to be an Englishman and then to get into a position in which one's holiday is dependent upon the doings of foreigners. I tried for ten days in Scotland. I got three and was then dragged back'.[29] He may not have been blessed with the diplomatic genes and political experience of his immediate predecessors, he may not even have spoken proper French, but he was regarded as extremely meticulous, level-headed and conscientious.[30] Retrospectively in particular, his predecessor was credited with an excessive naivety towards Germany, and his flexibility was tarnished with the negative connotations of 'muddling through',[31] while what was seen as 'single-mindedness'[32] was praised as Grey's great virtue. Grey has long been considered a moral authority, a steadfast politician true to his principles who stood for peace and the balance of power.[33] Today, the failure of his foreign policy to prevent war is still mainly laid at the door of others.[34]

Yet, although the predominant interpretation is positive, historians have still to come up with a conclusive judgement. While the majority reject the admittedly harsh judgement of Lloyd George, who, at the outbreak of war, described Grey as one of those principally to blame,[35] especially Niall Ferguson and John Charmley have turned a rather critical eye on the specifics of Grey's foreign policy.[36] Thomas Otte, on the contrary, has convincingly argued against the background of growing international complexities that Grey was rather driven by circumstances than being himself a driving force. His policy, as Otte highlights, was appropriate to British interests and it was successful as it allowed him to avoid any firm commitments.[37] The questions, however, remain whether Grey was not too dependent on his permanent under-secretaries, Charles Hardinge and Arthur Nicolson, who both favoured an Anglo-Russian rapprochement irrespective of the systemic consequences and impressions on the Central Powers, whether Grey's diplomacy proved flexible enough, especially in his assessment of Germany and Austria-Hungary, and whether what served British interests also promoted international stability.

In the end, he was criticized not only by Lloyd George, his rival within the party, who accused him of inflexibility,[38] but also by close friends and companions. Looking back, Richard Haldane could not help reproaching Grey for his complete ignorance of other countries, and of Germany in particular. When that obliviousness was combined with the anti-German mood at the Foreign Office, the result, in Haldane's estimation, was toxic for bilateral relations.[39] In light of his inexperience and obstinacy when it came to the complexities of foreign policy, Alfred Gardiner and Arthur Ponsonby held Grey to be a danger to the future and overly dependent on his advisors.[40] 'From beginning to end', his confidante John Spender assessed, 'he steered the same steady and simple course'.[41] As Ponsonby confirmed, Grey's political powers of imagination were limited to a few basic and generally preconceived notions. His readiness to accept advice functioned only within this narrow framework.[42] All in all, these were hardly the best qualifications for the top foreign policy position in the pre-eminent global power, especially when that power's key concern was active and formative contact with the continent.

We have no extensive account of the rationale behind Lansdowne's thinking, largely because he tended to respond instinctively and on an ad hoc basis in light of traditional practice and the immediate circumstances. Edward Grey, however, drew on the conceptual framework that he had established in the mid 1890s. Moreover, Grey came to a ministry that was significantly shaped by men of his own generation, providing homogeneity in both experiences and expectations. Thanks to the earlier reforms, he had at his back a whole phalanx of young, ambitious and highly talented diplomats. For the conceptual development and practical realization of his fundamental ideas on foreign policy, Grey appears to have depended greatly on these young career diplomats, and in particular on Charles Hardinge, Arthur Nicolson and his influential private secretaries Louis Mallet and William Tyrrell.[43] His desire to see an end to the fluctuation in policies was on the whole in accord with the views of the majority of the younger elite at the Foreign Office, and in many instances there was therefore no need to steer the foreign secretary in a particular direction. Close examination reveals that the traditional British policy directed at maintaining a balance of power was abandoned.[44] Where the credo of Grey's predecessors had run 'consolidate the Empire but steer clear of tensions on the continent', Grey and Hardinge emphasized from the beginning that Britain's principal concern was Britain's security, and to that end Britain was required to be an active player in the European system of alliances. In the paper of 31 December 1895 in which he had laid out his conceptual thinking, Grey had already determined the side that Britain must join, for the sake of both imperial and continental interests.[45]

On 20 October 1905, he had made clear that he believed his plans must become government policy. In a keynote speech given as foreign policy spokesman for the Liberals, he assessed Britain's international position and informed his audience of the necessary goals, and risks, of Britain's foreign policy. He declared his support for the alliance with Japan, for the Entente Cordiale and for an Anglo-American friendship, which together formed what he believed to be the essential framework for that policy. Historians have tended to see here a clear continuity in British diplomacy and Britain's balance of power policy,[46] but that conclusion seems rather premature. While Grey's 'cardinal features' included one alliance and two agreements that closely resembled an alliance, he made no mention of a higher goal defined by international stability and did not use the term 'balance of power'. His change of direction is particularly evident in a passage that tends to be overlooked. Like Campbell-Bannerman,[47] he was perfectly aware of the difficulty of extending the Entente cordiale in writing. But with reference to the Entente Cordiale, he noted that what was important was not just its specific content but also, and above all, its spirit. In his opinion, and this was also made clear to Paul Cambon,[48] should the next government seem disloyal to Japan or France, it would risk appearing as an 'example of fickleness and folly'.[49] He insisted that such alliances must not be simply a matter of protecting the participants' interests; they represented a far broader task, a common mission even.[50] Grey regarded the Entente Cordiale as the inviolable core of his foreign policy that demanded absolute loyalty.[51] Subsequently, in his memoirs, he even spoke of the Entente Cordiale as a 'point of honour'.[52] This approach had nothing in common with the policy adopted by Lansdowne and Balfour or with much-cited British pragmatism. With his insistence on such 'spirit', Grey brought an indefinable and unfathomable consideration to his foreign policy, and an emotional factor that was impossible to control. The agreement with Paris, repeatedly spoken of as 'most important',[53] could readily be packaged in this light, and his interpretation of the Entente Cordiale became a press stereotype, alongside the inevitable 'German peril' – to which Grey frequently alluded and which he discussed with Maxse[54] – and the long-term answer that was a three-way alliance of London, Paris and St Petersburg.[55] Evidently, for Grey, treaties and rational argument no longer sufficed to maintain good relations with France. However, the revolution in the states system came not from the Anglo-French relationship, which throughout the long nineteenth century had alternated between tension and dependency. The crucial issue in Grey's speech was his attitude towards Russia. For the first time, Russia, Britain's traditional enemy, was no longer perceived above all in light of the threat the tsardom represented for the Empire or the states system; now, Russia was a potential ally for Britain, and even on the European continent.[56]

On 13 December 1905, only a week after Balfour had resigned (and not in March 1906[57]), Grey assured Benckendorff, the Russian ambassador, that his first intent was to secure a close agreement between Britain and Russia.[58] The speed with which he set his sights on negotiations with Russia, a possibility rejected by his predecessor only two months earlier, puts a spoke in the wheel of arguments for continuity,[59] and is entirely in line with his conviction that the Entente should actually be transformed into a triple agreement for which he had been advocating since the mid 1890s.[60] His attitude was so well known that particularly Russian politicians had set their hopes on him in 1899.[61] In his conversation with Benckendorff, he named the Entente Cordiale as the model for Anglo-Russian relations, and recounted that his strategy was to ensure that as soon as possible Britain enter into a close and lasting relationship with the Dual Alliance.[62] Grey even spoke publicly of a 'natural complement of the agreement with France',[63] whereas his predecessors had hoped only for partial rapprochement in the Middle East and Far East.[64] For Grey, however, the settlement would be much further reaching, and, for that reason, he was prepared to make concessions that his predecessors had consistently rejected. In summer 1904, in a private letter, he had confided in Leo Maxse that he considered France, and the Entente, simply a staging post on the way to St Petersburg, but he had thought the government of the day incapable of making that link, or even of recognizing the possibility. By contrast, he noted, he had long been speaking of this possible development, and in August 1905 had declared that were the Balfour government to approach Germany again, 'I will oppose it openly at all cost'.[65] The young foreign secretary was candid with both Maxse and the Russian ambassador, but in diplomatic terms he was impatient and his behaviour inept. After promising Benckendorff a formal entente, in March 1906 he went a step further, of his own accord, noting that 'every arrangement of this kind must have two sides on the table'.[66] While it is true that Salisbury, Lansdowne and Grey already preferred an Anglo-Russian rapprochement, they too had been aware of the possible systemic consequences. If at all, they therefore could only imagine a rapprochement limited to colonial questions in Central Asia. Edward Grey's emphasis, however, seemed to lay in a combination of his policy of backing France against Germany and his policy towards Russia.[67] While Lansdowne had rejected the King's and Charles Hardinge's idea of using the straits question as 'a useful quid pro quo',[68] Grey doubted 'whether any complete arrangement with Russia can be made unless it included the Near East'.[69]

Although in October 1905 Grey publicly indicated that he hoped for improved relations with Germany, he had long since resolved to invest no real effort in that direction. Were Britain and Germany to move closer, he feared 'the French will never forgive us ... Russia would not think it worthwhile to make a friendly arrangement with us ... and we should be left without a friend and without the power of making a friend'.[70] Precisely this fear of isolation would, notoriously, both determine and characterize his foreign policy,[71] limiting his room for manoeuvre from an early stage. As Hardinge commented, a future alliance between France, Germany and Russia[72] could now be prevented only by British forestalling.[73] To make the case that the isolation of Britain would lead inevitably to German hegemony required both the attribution of aggressive aspirations to Germany and enormous exaggeration of Germany's ability to make those wishes come true. Even the Björkö agreement, never realized, had not been directed against Britain but was intended as a defensive alliance and applied merely 'to Europe'.[74]

This narrow twofold conceptualization, focused on the isolation of Britain and the easily achieved hegemony of the Kaiserreich, is indicative of the growing ideological character of London's foreign policy and had deep psychological roots in, on the one hand, the formative experience of the Boer War and associated crisis of British self-confidence and, on the other, a desire for self-assertion. In the debate over the modernization of domestic politics and during the longstanding invasion fever, a finger had repeatedly been pointed at Germany, as a means to galvanize the British population, and much the same pattern could be seen among diplomats. Using similar argumentation, they sought to demonstrate Britain's value for the continent as an alliance partner. Whitehall had its reasons when it repeatedly emphasized that only the Royal Navy and an association with the Dual Alliance could block German hegemony and a new Napoleonic threat.[75] Under Grey, the stylization of Germany as the greatest enemy since Napoleon[76] could meet several goals of domestic and foreign policy at once. The peril from Germany was effective across the board, including within the Liberal Party, reducing radical liberal inhibitions about rapprochement with the autocratic tsardom and also countering the disarmament plans of the radicals. In foreign policy terms, its effect was integrative and to a striking extent in accord with the tenor of public opinion.

The passive, and in part also active, encouragement of public debate provides a further criterion for the evaluation of Grey's policy, and is a factor that to date has received less attention. The extent to which Grey deviated from his predecessors in method, direction and objective is evident in his engagement of the ongoing debate over British security.[77] Although he, unlike Lansdowne, had become a permanent member of the Committee of Imperial Defence on taking up office, he never showed any particular interest in the complicated details of military and naval policy. All the more decisive, then, became the advice he might receive and from whom it might come, and also the attitude he adopted in relation to the public. While his predecessors had used public appearances to try to convince the British people that Britain was not at risk, while a member of the opposition Grey had not joined that public stance and had instead shared in the public's sense of unease, which, through his contacts in the press, he had even heightened.

The security that came with Japan, France and friendly relations with the United States, which Clarke had described to Haldane as entirely sufficient,[78] was still not enough for Grey once he had become foreign secretary. Grey and Haldane had their reasons when they sanctioned the General Staff discussions with France, and it was no coincidence that in June 1906 the Committee of Imperial Defence set its seal on a change of direction with the decision against Fisher and the Admiralty and in favour of an offensive land-based strategy.[79] In Grey's opinion, once a shattered Russia recognized the relief it could garner from close ties with Britain, it would certainly, sooner or later, agree to a close mutual arrangement, and the resultant three-way alliance would be able to hold the Central Powers in check. To that end, the door must never be closed on an Anglo-Russian alliance, for, he noted, 'an entente between Russia, France and ourselves would be absolutely secure'. If it had to come to war, then, Grey opined, it would be a great mistake 'to let Germany choose the moment which best suits her'.[80]

Here was a succinct summary of the aims of future policy and also evidence of the fundamental conviction that war was inevitable and of the break from his predecessors. Whereas Salisbury, Lansdowne and Balfour believed international relations to be in constant flux and had understood the Entente Cordiale primarily as a balancing of colonial interests and as a means to an end,[81] Grey saw an entente that included Russia and had global reach as the objective and *conditio sine qua non* of British foreign policy. Established facts played a more minor role in shaping his approach than his fatalist expectations of a major war. In November 1908, Grey recorded:

> After a big war a nation doesn't want another for a generation or more, but after 40 years of peace, if a nation is strong it begins spoiling for a fight. It was so with us between 40 or 50 years after the Crimean War, and it was so with Russia; and it was so with the United States nearly 40 years after her Civil War. And now, it is 38 years since Germany had her last war, and ... I don't think that there will be a war at present, but it will be very difficult to keep the peace of Europe for another five years.[82]

The idea of absolute security, a motif found repeatedly in contemporary sources, ran counter to diplomatic set theory and to the flexible equilibrium-based system.[83] At Whitehall, a flexible response had been replaced by anticipation, which meant a balancing of blocs and a pre-emptive strategy intended to ensure victory in the anticipated conflict.

Nominally, European stability and peace remained London's goal, but the path to be taken now led to a bloc-based system that could both control and be controlled. London aimed to stay ahead of the expected provocation, but in so doing acted counter to the interests of the stability that was its real goal. A lack of objectivity was paired with an almost pathological fear of isolation and, by the same token, of a German invasion. Under Grey, that fear seemed to become integral to British diplomacy. The Boer War had raised the vision of Britain standing alone against the continent, and Britain needed a good starting position in the twentieth-century competition between the Great Powers – for these reasons, Grey was prepared, for example, to support 'offensive' and 'aggressive' actions by France over Morocco that were covered by neither the Entente nor international agreements.[84] The gauge of his readiness to stand by Paris is provided not only by the Algeciras conference but also, and in particular, by the secret military talks, whose extent he even sought to keep from the cabinet until 1912.[85] That concealment is further evidence of his fear that he might not find support in either his own ranks or from the public. While it is right that as early as 1905 plans for a sea blockade of Germany had been safely stored in a drawer at the Admiralty,[86] these plans, however, represented a rather flexible foreign policy strategy independent from French behaviour and without encouraging the Quai d'Orsai. Considering an expeditionary force or joint Anglo-French military action, as the political leadership did from early 1906 onwards, went in the direction of brinkmanship.[87] Even though Grey would later claim that he had inherited the discussions from his predecessor, stimulating the myth of continuity, that position does not stand up under close examination. He was almost euphoric when he got wind of the early contacts between British and French officers that they had launched on their own initiative,[88] and was determined that these links should be formalized and coordinated with his foreign policy.[89] Certainly, German sabre-rattling and Berlin's clumsy and irresponsible diplomacy during the first Morocco crisis were a catalyst for the rapprochement of the Entente powers, just as the temporary weakening of Russia as a result of the disastrous defeat by Japan and the revolutionary movement furthered Anglo-Russian rapprochement, but we must not overlook that Grey had long before identified tripartite rapprochement as the ideal solution. His principal goal was less the creation of a stabilizing force; his intention was rather to safeguard the Empire in the long term and to limit the demands on the budget to allow funds to be diverted to social reforms. Furthermore, it is commonly held that German diplomacy for instance is always interpreted not only by its goals, motives, options and conduct, but also by the impact on others. British diplomacy also needed to be interpreted by its effect upon the Central Powers and especially on France and Russia.

Keith Robbins has described Edward Grey as the last foreign secretary in the tradition of the nineteenth century.[90] Yet in light of Grey's conciliatory approach to Russia, his vision of collective security via Entente diplomacy and his essentially modern use of ties to the press, he might rather be described as the first foreign secretary of the twentieth century.

In dealing with the continent, Grey no longer demonstrated the detachment, composure and flexibility of his predecessors. Germany, repeatedly characterized as being 'in mortal terror' of the Dual Alliance,[91] was not only abominated as a potential hegemon but also exploited in the cause of bringing Britain closer to its greatest rivals.[92] With its competitors now its partners, Britain would be able to retain its global supremacy and its dominance of the seas and be able to face the possibility of a continental alliance with composure. Rapprochement with Germany, which had rejected the role of junior partner,[93] had been deemed too costly by Grey and his allies.[94]

For Grey, there was no question that all foreign powers must have the omnipresent Empire in their sights,[95] and in his mind the only solution was to divert that attention into consistent tension between the continental powers instead.[96] Grey continued to insist that the Limps pursue a European policy.[97] By January 1903 – and thus much earlier than Lansdowne or Balfour and unlike most security experts – he had come to the conclusion, which he believed irrefutable, that Germany was Britain's worst enemy and greatest threat,[98] a position that accorded with the need for London to stay on good terms with its arch-rivals. Lord Rosebery thought Grey on the wrong track, with a counterproductive, overhasty and one-sided approach, but Grey was not to be dissuaded.[99] Lansdowne and Balfour's attempts to keep their foreign policy options as open as possible were hindered and thwarted by the political press in London; Grey had already narrowed down his possibilities himself, through the rigidity of his approach.[100] As a result, foreign policy took shape less often in Whitehall and more often at the Quai d'Orsay,[101] which did not go unnoticed in St Petersburg.

Pro-Russianism and Anti-Germanism:
The New Foreign Office and the Race for Russia

The support that Grey received from Charles Hardinge was critical.[102] During the new foreign secretary's first two years in office, Hardinge's experience and advice did much to set the political course. Grey's ministerial inexperience and recent administrative reforms at the Foreign Office also played their part, along with Hardinge's dominant character and specialist knowledge.[103] Whether Hardinge was in effect functioning as the foreign secretary, as contemporaries suspected,[104] must remain an open question. More important for our purposes is that Grey and Hardinge were in complete agreement. The uncompromising course that they adopted brought a new direction and new emphasis to traditional English diplomacy. Charles Hardinge had previously been stationed in Teheran and St Petersburg, and for the first time the most influential post in the Foreign Office was occupied not only by a career diplomat but also by someone with excellent knowledge of Russia. He replaced Thomas Sanderson, an expert on Germany and Europe, who had retired at the beginning of February 1906 after forty-seven years of service.[105] Having returned from St Petersburg specifically, and directly, to take up his new post, Hardinge immediately threw himself into the creation of closer ties with Russia,[106] which came with a surprising openness with St Petersburg. Shortly before his departure, he had confided in the tsar that he believed he would have even more opportunities in London 'to realise my hope of an Anglo-Russian Agreement than if I were to remain Ambassador in St. P'.[107]

Although Lansdowne's appointment of Hardinge as his permanent under-secretary at the Foreign Office has been seen by historians as another indicator of continuity in British foreign affairs running from Lansdowne to Grey, Lansdowne's decision appears to have been principally a product of Hardinge's close friendship with Francis Bertie and Edward VII.[108] Compared to Lansdowne's very modest attempts to improve relations between Britain and Russia, Hardinge's Russophilia fell into a whole new category, especially since his aim was not to ease international tensions but to create a deliberate rival to the Central Powers.[109] The timing and circumstances of Hardinge's appointment are also revealing. We have good reason to assume that Lansdowne had had in mind not far-reaching consequences for foreign policy but rather the future radical liberal government, for in Hardinge he recognized a possible counterweight to his probable left-liberal successor. Too much more should not be read into Lansdowne's choice. Nevertheless, Hardinge's move to Whitehall marked a significant break for the diplomatic corps and for British foreign policy.

An established diplomat and close friend of the monarch, Hardinge, ten years older than Grey, was already exerting considerable influence as under-secretary by the time Grey was appointed.[110] That influence extended over both the running of the Foreign Office and the conceptual redirection of British foreign policy. Both the how and the what of the role of permanent under-secretary were radically redesigned. Much in contrast to Sanderson, Hardinge's highly energetic personality meant that he could not confine himself to an advisory capacity when it came to Britain's relationship with Russia. His correspondence with Leo Maxse reveals that the two men's views overlapped almost entirely and both understood their roles as a form of mission.[111] Just how important that responsibility was to Hardinge is evident in his willingness to surrender such a lucrative post in order to return to Whitehall. In St Petersburg, he had been paid a princely £7,800 annually, but his starting salary as permanent under-secretary was only £2,000 per annum. Although that salary would increase by £500 after the conclusion of the convention with St Petersburg,[112] Hardinge's excellent contacts with the London press and political circles via Maxse and Chirol as well as his personal contact with Edward VII via Lord Knollys, the king's private secretary, were advantageous for his ambitions, as was the new allocation of political responsibility within the Foreign Office. The Foreign Office reform of 1904 had rejuvenated and restructured the whole staff. Mallet, Tyrrell, Spicer, Montgomery, Villiers and Crowe had all been stamped in the late 1890s and at the turn of the century by the much the same experiences. There was little to distinguish their argumentation or their expectations of Germany, and they competed to be recognized by their new superior as Berlin's greatest adversary.[113] Even Langley and Campbell, old colleagues of Salisbury's, would finally be persuaded over to their way of thinking. The only exceptions were Edmond Petty-Fitzmaurice and Frank Lascelles, who criticized the anti-German invasion hysteria as 'preposterous' and 'ill-grounded' and were the only individuals to speak up at the Foreign Office in favour of Haldane's attempts to reach an understanding, and they repeatedly recommended that Grey should visit Berlin.[114]

The majority view seems to have been largely a product of the homogenous experiences and impressions of a single generation and of their career ambitions. Any younger diplomat eager to make a name for himself had to have the Hardinge seal of approval. The new administrative system and well-received annotations in the margins of incoming diplomatic post could provide a springboard into a sought-after foreign posting or a career at Whitehall. Eyre Crowe, Walter Langley and Gerald Spicer, for example, all sought to enhance their standing through their minutes, as did Louis Mallet and William Tyrrell,[115] Grey's two private secretaries. Like their superiors and many of their colleagues, Mallet and Tyrrell believed that complete loyalty to Paris bolstered by attempts at rapprochement with Russia was a *sine qua non* of British foreign policy. Unlike Eric Barrington, their predecessor in the foreign secretary's office, they saw themselves not merely as assistants but as additional foreign policy advisors.

Tyrrell's influence on Grey and within the political sphere can scarcely be overestimated, for he believed himself responsible for the public image of the Foreign Office. He had outstanding connections not only to journalists but also to various members of parliament. According to Harold Nicolson, Tyrrell 'believed in personal relations and relied upon atmosphere'.[116] Moreover, his diplomatic skills were remarkable, and he was reputed to possess fine diplomatic instincts. After the war, H.G. Wells would describe him as completely inflexible and narrow-minded; he was for Wells the embodiment of pre-1914 British diplomacy, which was 'run to a very large extent by little undeveloped brains such as Tyrrell's, ... immensely protected from criticism and under no control from educated opinion'.[117] Grey's almost blind trust in Tyrrell was characteristic. The foreign secretary valued what seemed to him his private secretary's exceptional ability to put himself in the shoes of foreign powers.[118] For Wells, however, Tyrrell's views were often sweeping and stamped by his Social Darwinism, which meant that he spoke in national stereotypes and believed that there were peoples with whom Britain could get along, and peoples with whom Britain could not get along. In his view, the Germans and their young Kaiserreich would fold at any demonstration of power by Britain, and he recorded:

> Our best policy is as far as I know the German official character to sit tight, never to miss an opening for giving them a knock on their knuckles and wait for them to come to us hat in hand. I am certain that time will come, because I don't believe that France

will ever be brought into line against us with Germany and Russia ... Bülow is a very vain peacock and thoroughly understands the art of flattery.[119]

Edmond Fitzmaurice, under-secretary of state for foreign affairs, Lansdowne's brother and an established expert on the Balkans, was a lonely voice at Whitehall warning about an open anti-German or anti-Austrian policy in south-east Europe and noting the possible consequences for the system as a whole. Fitzmaurice certainly mistrusted Russia and the tsar, but he was even more suspicious of Alexander Izvolsky and all his vanities. He made a case for pursuing the traditional friendly approach to the Central Powers or, at a minimum, for adopting a neutral position on the complex Balkan situation, insisting: 'I have always a profound doubt how far Russia is able to control her own agents, civil as well as military in foreign parts ... Therefore, we must not rely too much on a Russian understanding – at least according to my view – and in any case it ought not exclude good relations with Germany'.[120] Together with Lascelles, Fitzmaurice regretted the very evident anti-German tendency within the Foreign Office, which he thought in the long run, would do more harm than good, not least because it blinded the policy makers and their advisers to the danger from Russia.[121] In October 1908, just as the simmering tensions in the Balkans reached their first crisis point, he left Whitehall for good.

Frank Lascelles, who dedicated such energy to bringing London and Berlin together,[122] was looked on with suspicion by Hardinge and, especially, by Crowe, who attacked him sharply in his commentaries and on occasion in person;[123] the two men believed Lascelles' position untenable, and in summer 1908 he too had to leave his post, against his wishes, sending a clear signal that was understood even in neutral Europe.[124] Hardinge had Fairfax Cartwright, the British envoy in Munich, in mind as Lascelles' replacement. Cartwright and his Germanophobia had already left their mark in various memoranda and minutes. Presumably in order to advance his career, Cartwright had even fabricated tales of hostility towards Britain in the German press.[125] Although Berlin, which greatly regretted Lascelles' departure,[126] was able to prevent the appointment of this 'coarse German-eating joker',[127] it got instead Edward Goschen, former ambassador in Vienna – a piece of very poor casting, for the role of British ambassador to Berlin required exceptional skills and tact, given the family ties between the two courts. Berlin would have preferred Cecil Spring Rice or Gerald Lowther as Lascelles' successor, and would even have taken Nicolson over Goschen – the former's anti-German and pro-Russian sentiments had been all too evident since Algeciras,[128] but the Wilhelmstrasse had no desire to see his notorious Germanophobia ensconced in Paris or St Petersburg.[129]

The best that can be said of Goschen's actions in Berlin is that he was entirely passive, although that meant he made not the slightest attempt to improve relations between Germany and Britain. Whereas Lascelles had spoken with conviction of closer ties, Goschen was cold and sceptical and made little effort to conceal his deep dislike of Germany. Goschen, like many of his colleagues and peers, had been profoundly affected by the events at the turn of the century and had taken to heart the opinions found in the press, which we examined earlier. When his Italian colleague congratulated him on a temporary improvement in relations, he replied that the Krüger telegram had made such relations impossible, for while Germany was happy to forget it, Britain never would.[130] His antipathy towards Germany was no less than that of Cartwright, or of Bertie in Paris or Nicolson in St Petersburg. Yet while Bertie and Nicolson used Germany in order to promote closer ties with the countries to which they had been sent, Goschen simply refused to cooperate.

Whitehall's poor choice in Goschen was not made necessary by a lack of alternatives. Lascelles had not asked to be recalled, and British diplomats were not anti-German to a man. Cecil Spring Rice or the promising Andrew Ryan and Ralph Paget, who were waiting for an ambassadorial post to become free, would have been far better choices, even though they too were not uncritical of Germany. Yet Hardinge seemed to wish to neutralize those whose views were more moderate or at least more sensitive – after he had been critical of the Anglo-Russian convention, Paget was, for example, sent to Belgrade, while Spring Rice, so well informed on Russia and Germany, found himself twiddling his thumbs in Stockholm.[131] In financial terms, Spring Rice had been demoted: as second secretary at the legation in Teheran, he had earned more than he did as consul general in Sweden.[132] Without exception, all vacant postings significant for Anglo-German relations were filled with men whose attitudes towards Germany ranged from the critical to the hostile, while those whose views were more nuanced were moved on. The evidence suggests not negligence but intent. Berlin, and other powers, received the British signal loud and clear, not least because other Great Powers such as the United States, Russia and France made distinct efforts to appoint diplomatic representation that would foster good bilateral relations.[133]

Alongside Hardinge, Arthur Nicolson, his friend and successor in St Petersburg, became a key figure for British foreign policy. His appointment was a brilliant move for British relations with Russia. Again, we can see Anglo-Russian rapprochement and Anglo-German animosity as two sides of the same coin. Hardinge cited as evidence of Nicolson's suitability for the St Petersburg posting that the new ambassador was disliked in Berlin.[134]

The consensus that, in light of all the rumours circulating about the imminent formation of a new German-led continental alliance,[135] Russia too should be drawn onto Britain's side seems to have been founded on stereotypical assumptions rather than hard fact. In order to promote the desired but controversial rapprochement with the tsardom, Hardinge and Nicolson allowed known falsehoods about German machinations during the Boer War to circulate, with the suggestion that in 1899/1900 the Kaiser had made every effort to forge a Napoleonic bloc together with Russia and France. William Thomas Stead had made this claim during his invasion campaign of 1899, and it continued to be taken up by journalists such as Maxse, Garvin and others. Yet Hardinge would have known better, for his diplomatic posting had taken him to St Petersburg in precisely these years. The reality had been turned on its head: Russia had sought the alliance, and Germany had opposed it.[136] When, following the Crowe memorandum, in 1907, Hardinge went on to spread these claims himself, through Mallet, Bertie and Nicolson,[137] those who knew the truth of the matter, men such as Edmund Monson, who had been ambassador in Paris, Thomas Sanderson and Lord Lansdowne, had either retired, were no longer in office or, as was the case for Frank Lascelles, were deliberately not consulted or even defamed as pro-German.[138] Grey, who would surely have been informed of what had actually happened, participated in the historical falsification, aware of the potential political advantages of the idea of Germany as the enemy, whether in relation to the contested rapprochement with the tsardom or the radicals' demands for disarmament.[139] The rumour was just too good to pass up.

What evidence was used by the Foreign Office to assess the possibilities and make its prognoses? The political decision makers surely had to have had something more conclusive than the stereotypical assumptions and dubious predictions used by the press and the authors of the invasion literature to conjure up their apocalyptic notions and nightmare scenarios. Perhaps the answer can be found in the Crowe memorandum, so often cited as the 'blueprint' of British foreign policy.[140]

Eyre Crowe and Thomas Sanderson

The attitude of senior clerk Eyre Crowe is symptomatic of the qualitative change in foreign policy under Grey and Hardinge. His approach can be read from his minutes,[141] as extensive as they were numerous, his famous memorandum and his response to Sanderson's detailed counter-memorandum. Released on New Year's Day 1907, Crowe's memorandum has never ceased to arouse the interest of historians. Likely at his own instigation,[142] it was published as part of the first three volumes of the *British Documents on the Origins of the War* and reprinted in the *British Documents on Foreign Affairs*,[143] and it appears often as the standard for British foreign policy, seen in hindsight as a 'concept for Europe' or a 'milestone' in British analysis of the Kaiserreich.[144] 'In the light of historical evidence', Thomas Otte commented, the memorandum had proved to be 'one of the most insightful, intelligent and precise analyses' of the pre-war period; for Otte, it was 'a balanced and accurate judgement of German Weltpolitik'.[145] Crowe wrote of a continuity running from Frederick the Great, via Bismarck, to Wilhelmine *Weltpolitik*; in 1940, Robert Vansittart, his most prominent pupil, continued that line into his present age, drawing a German 'Sonderweg' from the eighteenth century until well into the twentieth.[146] That interpretation often provided a frame of reference for historians, for it was adopted with little alteration by Fritz Fischer and by Fischer's pupils, such as Imanuel Geiss.[147]

However, a closer examination finds few traces of balanced or historically accurate analysis in Crowe's thinking, and his view of the Kaiserreich in 1907 was not the sole possibility. Crowe always had a penchant for simplification, along with a tendency to over-interpretation that might be attributed to personal motives.

With Sanderson's retirement, Crowe, the most industrious commentator and author of memoranda on Britain's task on the continent,[148] became the leading expert on Germany in the Western Department of the Foreign Office. Crowe had excellent social and political contacts with the Kaiserreich, for his British father had been a commercial attaché and his mother was from the Ribbentrop family; Crowe himself had grown up in Leipzig until 1882, and he had married a German cousin. His colleagues in Whitehall thought him different and not at all 'clubable', not least on account of his family background, his strong accent and his pronounced Prussian work ethic.[149] He had close links with liberal groupings in Germany – his father had been a member of Frederick III's circle of advisors – and he expressly rejected all that was Wilhelmine. His views on foreign policy had, from an early stage, aligned closely with those of the liberal imperialists, with the idea that the structures of international relations were essentially confrontational, and he agreed on the need for planning that would put an end to Salisbury's 'muddling through'.[150] In his eyes, Germany should become Britain's junior partner, with no strings attached. Anything else, and above all Germany's wish to be treated as an equal, he rejected as 'impertinent'.[151] His private correspondence strongly suggests that in his youth in Germany, Crowe had internalized Germany's desire for greatness and recognition. He came to Britain for the first time as an eighteen-year-old and, thanks to his father, immediately became part of the elite of the greatly envied Empire, a feeling he savoured when judging the country of his birth.

Convinced that a war for survival was imminent and that a display of strength was imperative, with conciliation a sign of weakness, he was soon exerting his influence on his colleagues in Whitehall via his numerous minutes. As senior clerk, he was the first to read all press reports, ambassadors' reports and legation reports sent from Germany; he was then required to sort and filter them according to their relevance and to add a preliminary comment.[152] From the start, he evidently intended to convince the new foreign secretary of his own abilities and to put Lascelles, an experienced ambassador, in the shade. Crowe succinctly brushed aside all Lascelles' endeavours to maintain good relations with Germany as 'empty talk'.[153] While he believed good relations with France and Russia to be in Britain's interest, he could see no point in good relations with Germany; indeed, Germany, he was convinced, would always try to exploit any friendship. So while he deemed Britain's rivals in the Dual Alliance to be Britain's equals according to the classic *do ut des* principle, he reproached Germany for its self-interest.[154] Crowe evidently shared the opinion of the young hawks in the Foreign Office gathered around Hardinge, Nicolson and Grey. Hardinge, for example, set little store by Lansdowne's attempts to speak to Metternich in a spirit of consensus, and Grey said much when he commented that the Germans should recognize that they had nothing to complain about.[155] That assertion soon became a guiding principle for the young and ambitious Crowe.

No doubt, as has recently again been demonstrated, Crowe's demonization as an evil spirit at the Foreign Office was misguided and cannot be allowed to stand.[156] Yet it would be equally negligent to describe him as merely the 'ablest servant', to suggest that his observations found no echo in political circles,[157] or to relativize or dilute his impact on his colleagues by noting how widespread the antagonism towards Germany already was.[158] Crowe's memorandum was without doubt a key document of British pre-war foreign policy. Its significance lies not so much in its quality[159] as in its reception, where striking comparisons are to be made with Sanderson's response. The many historiographical assessments of Crowe's text serve to demonstrate how often reconstruction of the past is determined by knowledge of what came next. Close examination of the memorandum reveals not a prophetic prognosis about Germany but the hesitant strategic recommendations of an alleged German expert. In scale, his memorandum was an impressive achievement, but at many points the content is contradictory, even confused. More than three quarters of the text is devoted to the classic stereotypical image of Germany as also found, for example, in the *National Review*, a paper Crowe regarded highly and supported actively.[160]

The memorandum cannot be considered genuine political analysis. In some passages, Crowe provided almost word for word a summary of a piece of popular scientific propaganda written by his brother-in-law Spenser Wilkinson and published ten years before. In 1897, Wilkinson, Crowe's model and mentor with whom he had regularly exchanged ideas in earlier years,[161] had called on the nation to wake up to the inevitable threat from Germany, from which he deduced a need for compulsory military service.[162] In his commentaries, Crowe frequently referred to information, rumours and claims that had appeared in the press rather than to established facts or the views of experts. His claims to the contrary, there was no documented evidence that as great an authority as Moltke believed an invasion of England possible;[163] the Prussian general had, to the contrary, warned against an amphibious operation, believing the 'natural elements' too unpredictable.[164] Crowe was far too ready to believe, and frequently be deceived by, friends in the press, in this case by Charles Repington.

In the case of the Edelheim article, published in the *National Review*, Crowe's trust in his friend Leo Maxse led him to assume that the report of a secret plan by the German General Staff was true, yet the article was based on an unauthorized pamphlet written by a somewhat insignificant officer in 1901,[165] when Germany had long abandoned its somewhat vague intellectual play with the idea of possible invasion of the British Isles, which had even been reported in the journal published by the Royal United Service.[166] Ironically, Britain's supposed friend France, and not Germany, had dedicated most energy to the possibility of an attack on Britain, continuing its deliberations even when the Entente Cordiale was in place. In January 1906, when the French military attaché travelled to Paris to bring news of intensive military cooperation with Britain, he found his colleagues on the General Staff 'deeply engaged upon the elaboration of an academic plan for the invasion of England, and when he told them of the friendly British invasion, which some of us [Repington, Maxse etc.] contemplated their jaws dropped, their pens fell from their hands and they were positively transfixed with surprise'.[167] Instead of turning to naval experts for information that was readily available, Crowe preferred to follow his preconceived opinions, bolstered by useful commonplaces drawn from Darwin and Mahan and by claims made by the press. He likewise lost no opportunity to circulate as proven fact the rumour spread by Stead, Garvin and Maxse about the efforts made by Kaiser Wilhelm II during the Boer War to form a continental alliance against Britain.[168] Short memories could prove very useful, Bertie noted.[169]

Within the Foreign Office, Crowe took a leading role in the campaign against the troublesome ambassador to Berlin, as his constant criticizing of the content of Lascelles' reports[170] became a call for the foreign secretary to take disciplinary action against the ambassador, who was far above a senior clerk in the diplomatic hierarchy. Grey and Hardinge's assent to that proposal is indicative of the great influence exerted by Crowe, a young senior clerk at Whitehall, and provides a striking comparison with the impact of an ambassador serving abroad.[171]

Immediately distributed by Grey and Hardinge to Campbell-Bannerman, Lord Ripon, Asquith, Morley, Lascelles, Cartwright, General French, Haldane and Edward VII, Crowe's memorandum found a broad audience.[172] Although now retired, Sanderson, an expert on Germany, felt compelled to respond. His counter-memorandum and Hardinge's and Grey's approaches to it are both very revealing. Hardinge expressed his surprise[173] at Sanderson's contradictory, and level-headed, assessment of the young Kaiserreich, in which he had respectfully termed the Germans 'les Juifs de la diplomatie',[174] seeing them as tough but honourable negotiating partners. For Grey, the matter was over and done with,[175] and he made no effort to include Sanderson's counter-evaluation in the diplomatic debate,[176] although due diligence alone should have led this still rather inexperienced minister to examine Sanderson's opinion closely, not least because it differed from Crowe's memorandum at vital points. Whereas

Lansdowne and, above all, Balfour tended to soak up all available information before they permitted themselves to express an opinion or make a decision, Grey apparently categorized information according to the extent to which it confirmed his preconceived views.

Although Crowe's memorandum is often termed a 'State Paper',[177] its comparison with Sanderson's memorandum shows how little of substance it contained. Crowe launched his discussion with thirty pages of historical background, mainly on Prussian militarism, before, eventually, presenting two hypotheses to account for German behaviour. In light of Germany's Prussian and militaristic past – Sanderson countered with the hardly more peaceable history of the British Empire[178] – Crowe proposed that Germany now was looking for either general political hegemony and maritime supremacy or mere protection of its rightful position as a Great Power.[179] Crowe did not argue for one conclusion over the other or propose that the current situation favoured one interpretation, which is all the more surprising as the memorandum is often judged as evidence that London had seen through German ambitions. Under the new government, Crowe did lay particular emphasis on Germany's expansionism, but he could not have forgotten a comment he had made in October 1902, on reading Maxse's A.B.C. article, when he had criticized his friend's pro-Russian attitude and pleaded the case for confronting both Russia and Germany with a show of strength. However, after the appointment of a new foreign secretary, Russia's wrongdoings had been swept under the Whitehall carpet, leaving only Germany the object of his attack. Even if the Kaiserreich should desire an alliance, it would never settle for an equal distribution of obligations, 'because in a conflict she is the one really exposed to great danger whilst we are much less so, and that therefore she will always ask for something in addition', an assessment that suggested that ties between Britain and Germany were structurally problematic not because of German intentions, as he taught Leo Maxse, but because of the geopolitical constraints faced by the Kaiserreich.[180]

Yet Crowe's memorandum of January 1907 breathed this very spirit. Page after page he recited Germany's misdemeanours, making not the slightest attempt to take the geopolitical situation or political alliances into account. The significance of the memorandum lay not in unambiguous statements but in the various interpretations that it left open to its readers, and also to historians. In light of the attitudes we have seen dominating the Foreign Office at the time the memorandum was composed, the conclusions were predictable. More sober deductions would surely have ensued from a factual analysis of the situation that examined the strengths and weaknesses of both the German position and the British position and that considered the international context as a whole before attempting to recommend a strategy. Even eyewitnesses critical of Germany could not overlook the diplomatic defeats experienced by the Kaiserreich.[181] As evident from his minutes, for Crowe, impact, and not analysis, was the prime concern. He constantly criticized Lascelles' reports without first exploring their author's arguments, and his comments repeatedly proposed that Lascelles be summoned home or disciplined.[182] Crowe believed himself on a mission.

His memorandum should have recommended a strategy, a challenge that Crowe overcame in a typically Social Darwinist manner by stating that Britain did not have to know how German policy was being implemented or what its goals were; the very existence of Germany was a threat to the integrity of Britain. Konrad Canis recently proposed that Crowe emphasized German capabilities and deemed German intentions of secondary importance.[183] In fact, Crowe argued in both directions. While he emphasized the military strength of Prussia-Germany, the evidence of his communications with Maxse shows that he was also privately aware of the geopolitical weakness of his old homeland. But as soon as diplomats such as Lascelles, Sanderson or Dumas, the naval attaché, mentioned German disadvantage, he fled to stereotypes based on national character and empty phrases about 'German' traits, which he listed as efficiency, a desire for hegemonic power, immoderation and militarism. Yet his argument had an obvious flaw that caused him something of a headache. Was it not in Germany's interests to remain on friendly terms with Britain until the German navy was stronger than the Royal Navy? Yet, instead of following the strategic imperative to disguise its ambitions for global hegemony, Germany seemed dead set on standing up to Britain. Perhaps, he suspected, Germany did not really know what it wanted,[184] but that possibility seemed too fantastic, not least in light of the German efficiency so admired in Britain.

Crowe deployed his rhetorical style to avoid coming to a conclusion. As a clear conceptual recommendation, the memorandum was thus practically worthless, for it was left to the individual reader to evaluate German policy. It was thus possible and, in light of the increasingly widespread attitudes that we have noted, highly probable that no matter what Germany did, whether openly aggressive or conciliatory, it would be judged to be behaving badly. We see evidence of that reality in the minutes that Crowe provided subsequent to the memorandum and the tendentious treatment of reports received from Dumas, Trench, Russell and other attachés.[185] On 14 January 1908, Cartwright's annual report from Munich arrived. In an unusually long commentary that practically turned Cartwright's text into a joint report, Crowe once again explained why the Kaiserreich could not be trusted. Cartwright had already internalized Crowe's argument that any amicable or cooperative action by Berlin was simply a smokescreen 'for the purpose of gaining time for the necessary preparations ... for the inevitable violent collision'. Any doubts Crowe might have had about his claim that Berlin had to act in a friendly manner to avoid arousing suspicions were gone – Berlin's plan was to lull London into a false sense of security.[186]

As John Charmley recognized, Berlin faced a diplomatic dilemma. Whatever Berlin did – reaching out, sabre-rattling, even nothing – could be interpreted as a part of a grand plan aimed at hegemony.[187] A year later, Cecil Spring Rice argued in much the same vein. He judged Germany's apparent reticence to be a deliberate deception by the Berlin government, in order that it might realize its invasion plans – dismissed by the experts as impossible – 'in darkness and in silence'.[188] That politicized approach could be deadly for European crisis management. At the end of the Bosnian Annexation Crisis, Goschen, who certainly harboured no pro-German feelings, had to admit that Germany was displaying no evidence of any bitterness towards Britain, and that an agreement might even be possible. Yet Crowe deemed that it would be extremely regrettable if such thoughts caught on in London, and concluded his comments by observing that Germany would try to trick Britain with false and non-binding assurances.[189]

In contrast, Sanderson set Anglo-German relations within the broad historical and international context that he had helped create. He responded to each element of Crowe's argument individually and in turn. Germany had declared its interests in Morocco in good time, he noted, while Britain had unilaterally sided with France. Germany's heated reaction was no surprise to an expert on Germany, for it was surely typical of a young ambitious power, and as also on other occasions, the German response led nowhere as the necessary political preconditions were again lacking. Berlin's response made sense to Sanderson particularly because Delcassé had demonstratively ignored the well-established interests of the Kaiserreich, which were covered by the Madrid Convention. Sanderson had no doubt that Delcassé's actions were the product of a desire to see Germany isolated. Crowe's argument that the Morocco issue was really an economic matter was in Sanderson's eyes evidence that again Crowe was unilaterally favouring Britain's partner in the Entente.[190] Moreover, Crowe's blind trust in Delcassé was indicative of a joint course of action by the Entente, of which, when responding to Sanderson, Mallet was already convinced. Although two years earlier Mallet had informed Lansdowne that the French foreign minister was making diplomatic preparations for an unavoidable clash between Britain and Germany,[191] now, in his critical response to Sanderson, Mallet wanted to know no more of this idea. Instead, he revived the myth of foreign policy continuity by maintaining that Lansdowne had never doubted Delcassé's good intentions.[192] In fact, Lansdowne had not only been informed by a variety of sources about Delcassé's plans for the isolation of Germany,[193] but had also greatly mistrusted his French colleague, for he assumed, correctly, that the French foreign minister was seeking to encircle Germany with alliances.[194] The fact that Delcassé, whom neither Monson, Salisbury nor Roosevelt trusted an inch,[195] was now fashioned by Crowe into a man of peace says everything. Crowe no longer even acknowledged the very great British concerns about the Russian-French Dual Alliance, which Balfour and Selbourne had judged 'perilous',[196] and turned their agreement into a defensive, peace-oriented alliance. The only explanation is surely that he felt bound by a loyalty to Britain's partner in the Entente.[197]

Unlike Crowe, Sanderson tried to put himself in Berlin's shoes. While he was frequently accused of being a Germanophile as a result, in fact he was simply doing what any good diplomat would do. For every action taken by Germany or any other power, he asked himself, directly or indirectly, if Britain could have reacted differently. In most cases his answer was in the negative. He admitted quite soberly that of course Germany had endeavoured to split the Entente; Germany had not been especially aggressive in doing so, for here was merely a logical consequence of the humiliating indifference to German rights.[198]

When it came to German colonial policy, Crowe had accused Bismarck of deceit and of being the cause of outrageous affront to Britain. Sanderson countered Crowe succinctly, maintaining that German policy was a perfectly understandable reaction to years of arrogant English behaviour and that Crowe was obviously confusing cause and effect[199] – a view with which historians examining the evidence today, especially as regards colonial policy, would concur.[200] For a brief time in 1884 and 1885, domestic concerns and election propagandizing had led Bismarck to approve German colonial efforts, but only if they were carried out in close accord with Britain. Bismarck had even consulted with ambassador Odo Russell in hope of receiving the blessing of the largest global empire, but London had flatly ignored the German request, snubbing the Kaiserreich and turning instead to expanding its own empire. According to Sanderson, and backed up by what we know today, Crowe's description of a sudden and completely unexpected annexation of Angra Pequena and his accusations of deceit on the part of Bismarck were unfounded.[201] No government could really have been expected to do more than ask London if it claimed the coastal area of Angra Pequena for the British Empire. London's failure to reply was not only a grave diplomatic omission but also provided justifiable cause for accusations of imperial arrogance. According to Sanderson, the real question was not why Germany dared lay claim to colonies,[202] but why, two decades later, Britain read a request about the British stance on a potential German claim, a type of request that was no longer even usual among imperial powers, as evidence of aggression. Crowe also wanted to pass the blame for the Samoan crisis to Germany, but Sanderson again cited British failings, for Britain had not behaved properly towards Germany. His reference was to Salisbury's attempt, contrary to agreement and eventually uncovered by Germany, to line up the United States against Germany.[203] Unlike Sanderson, Crowe took for granted that in all colonial matters anywhere around the globe, including the issue of Zanzibar, the British Empire had first bite.[204] Today we can see that any colonial commitments – in relation to Samoa, for example, or as found in the resolutions of the Congo Conference – were interpreted by Britain as British interests saw fit, and, if necessary, simply ignored.[205] Where Britain acquired new colonial lands, Crowe saw British 'business'; where Germany sought to acquire lands not yet under a colonial power, Crowe identified German 'blackmail'. Crowe saw fit not to mention the former Portuguese colonies in South Africa: as had been the case with Samoa, Britain at first had appeared conciliatory towards Germany, but in this instance, in October 1899 then came to a very different agreement with Lisbon, with the secret Windsor Agreement,[206] which guaranteed the integrity of the Portuguese possessions.[207] Yet Crowe claimed that before the Boer War, German friendship had come only at a high price.[208]

Turning to Europe, Sanderson was clear that British interests had not been sold out with the Mediterranean entente; on the contrary, the protection of the status quo in the Mediterranean had been very valuable to Britain over the years.[209] While Sanderson was able to understand Germany's disappointment at London's lack of gratitude for Germany's protective role, he had little reason to trust Delcassé's claims about German attempts to create a continental league.[210] Crowe had not been aware that Sanderson had been told by Hardinge of the Russian scheming that had taken place during the Boer War and therefore knew all about Muraviev's attempts to persuade Germany to form an anti-British league.[211] Sanderson now also pointed out not only the Kaiser's demonstrative refusal to give President Krüger the usual honours of a state visit, but also Britain's illegal and disproportionate behaviour in impounding German passenger ships, mail ships and cargo ships, an act that, according to the former administrative head of the Foreign Office, 'if practised on ourselves would have certainly been denounced as intolerable'.[212] In the case of China, with the best will in the world, Sanderson could likewise not see 'that the [Yangtze] Agreement … was in any way detrimental to our interests'.[213] Overall, looking back on the history of 'German policy towards this country', Sanderson could not detect the 'unchequered record of black deeds'[214] found in Crowe's memorandum and Hardinge and Grey's commentaries.

Sanderson's assessment of German policy was by no means uncritical, and he thought Germany's attitude excessive not only on the Morocco issue.[215] At the same time, he made every effort to avoid judging Germany by standards any different from the standards that might be applied to another Great Power, including Britain itself. In so doing, he demonstrated a matter-of-fact and typically Victorian composure, replicating an attitude we have already encountered in Salisbury, Balfour and Lansdowne. After an unprecedentedly long career in the Foreign Office, he was well positioned to assess Germany's actions and compare German behaviour with that of other powers. Additionally, he evidently believed it essential to take specific interests and particular constraints into account:

> In considering the tendencies and methods of German policy, we have to remember that the Empire took its present place among the Great Powers of Europe only 35 years ago, after 50 years of helpless longings for united national existence. It was inevitable that a nation flushed with success which had been obtained at the cost of great sacrifices, should be somewhat arrogant and over-eager. … The Government was at

the same time suffering from the constant feeling of insecurity caused by the presence on the East and the West of two powerful, jealous and discontented neighbours. It is not surprising that with the tradition of the Prussian monarchy behind it, it should have shown itself restless and scheming and have had frequent recourse to tortuous methods, which have not proved wholly successful.[216]

Seen in this light, Sanderson continued, German *Weltpolitik* was anything but surprising and merely a logical development. While he advised caution, he also recommended Germany be given time and not be plunged unnecessarily into even greater insecurity. If that were not enough, he considered the burden of Germany's sins since 1871 'light in comparison to ours'. Set against German ambitions, the British attitude, evident in Crowe's words and actions, that saw every change as a threat to British current or potential interests and on that basis made 'claims to interference or compensation' was at least equally deserving of criticism.[217]

A comparison of the memoranda by Crowe and Sanderson sheds light on the qualitative changes in policy that came with the new government. Unlike Sanderson's classic counter-memorandum with its wealth of information, the views that flowed from Crowe's pen were not based on objective material addressing the German situation or international context; Crowe's text was full of leaps in the dark, with pertinent imaginings, stereotypes and perceptions of Germany his only guide. His account was not forged in light of pressures and realistic possibilities, but spoke of putative potential and vaguely assumed intentions. Crowe's evaluation had its own roots in its author's German roots. Having grown up in Germany, Crowe was presumably more receptive than his English countrymen to Wilhelmine propaganda that spoke of finding a 'place in the sun' and left no doubt that this goal was achievable.[218] For Crowe, Germany's dreams were no different from its realizable goals,[219] for this nation had already overcome all the challenges that lay in the way of unification, and its renowned efficiency had long been admired in Britain as exemplary. Crowe shared that conviction with Milner, who had been born in Giessen and had grown up in Germany, with Haldane, who had studied philosophy in Göttingen, and with William Tyrrell, who had been educated in Germany. All these men respected, and even overestimated, German achievements, and their experiences abroad, which in their case were not limited to the British colonies, made them sensitive to British shortcomings. And yet, moulded by the optimism of the *Gründerzeit*, they overlooked the continuing pressures on Central Europe. The realities and the obstacles still confronting the Kaiserreich faded into the background, along with the opportunities that Britain had retained.

Sanderson did not share Crowe and Tyrrell's experiences or German contacts and was therefore also less prone to be swept up in their mood and by their expectations. His judgements were made in light of forty years of observing the world from London and on the basis of cold facts. Sanderson is often considered pro-German because he paid little attention to the German naval build-up,[220] but perhaps his more profound knowledge simply inspired composure rather than exaggeration.

London was perfectly aware of Germany's dread of encirclement and fear of a 'Copenhagening'.[221] Goschen, who also had German roots, had good reason to worry that the Kaiser might feel forced into a corner.[222] Zara Steiner and Keith Neilson saw the stereotypical assessment of Germany as a product of a widespread British sense of helplessness that made the threat from Germany seem all too real.[223] Sanderson was of a different opinion. His response was in line with the warning he had given Lansdowne two years earlier: 'Their [the Germans'] naval inferiority is therefore now a serious matter not to be ignored'.[224] For Hardinge, too, Germany was already 'generally recognised as the one disturbing factor owing to her ambitious schemes for a "Weltpolitik"', although in the same memorandum, from autumn 1906, he had admitted that on account of its evident geopolitical and financial weakness, the Kaiserreich would present 'no naval threat' in the foreseeable future.[225] Edward Grey bragged of planning to keep the High Seas Fleet in port without losing a single ship or sailor, or even firing a single shot. The radical liberal *Nation*, which, unlike other newspapers and journals worked not with projections and plans but with figures and facts, expressed serious reservations about the widely broadcast tales of a German peril, which it saw as promoting stereotypes,[226] which bolstered a system that made selective use of the facts.[227] Although nominally a strategy document, the Crowe memorandum was cavalier with historical facts and when it came to commenting on relative British and German strength, tended to speak in vague platitudes. Yet we still need to consider what impact the German High Seas Fleet could have on the established structures of international relations, and how the political decision makers investigated that possibility. In May 1907, Admiral Arthur Wilson, a naval expert, assumed that it was barely conceivable that Britain and Germany could do each other any serious harm.[228] Six months later, that apparent impossibility preoccupied the experts in the Committee of Imperial Defence.

Notes

1. Hildebrand, *Das Vergangene Reich*, 222; Kennedy, *Rise of Anglo-German Antagonism*, 282.
2. Spring Rice to Grey, 29 March 1906, GL II, 71.
3. *The Times* (Letters), 9 Dec. 1905; Stead, 'C.-B.', RR 5/1908, 442–43; Amery, *My Political Life*, Vol. 1, 223. Henry Labouchère thought the appointment of Grey as foreign secretary an 'invention of the press'. Labouchère to Campbell-Bannerman, 30 Nov. 1905, BL, Add. 52521.
4. Grey, *25 Years*, Vol. 1, 62–63; Haldane, *An Autobiography*, 170–73; Lee, *Edward VII*, Vol. 2, 443–45.

5. Crewe to Gladstone, 30 Nov. 1903, cited in Pope-Henessy, *Lord Crewe*, 55; Grey to Gladstone, 24 Dec. 1901; Gladstone to Grey, 28 Dec. 1901, BL, Add. 45992; Campbell-Bannerman on Grey, cited in Fyfe, *Liberal Party*, 169; Grey (Glasgow), *The Times*, 29 Nov. 1901.
6. Hardinge to Maxse, 5 Dec. 1905, WSRO, MAXSE/453.
7. Grey to Rosebery, 3 Dec. 1905, NLS, MSS 10028; see also *The Times*, 9 Dec. 1905; Grey to Margot Asquith, 11 Dec. 1905, M. Asquith, *Autobiography*, Vol. 3, 112.
8. See Wilson, 'Grey', 173; *The Times*, 21 Oct. 1905. On Rosebery's deficits as a leader and on his stance towards the Irish question, see Malcom MacColl, *Memoirs and Correspondence*, e.g. MacColl to Gladstone, 19 Sept. 1896, 165.
9. Campbell-Bannerman to Gladstone, 14 Jan. 1900, BL, Add. 45988; see also Nicholls, *The Lost Prime Minister*, 177–233; Jenkins, *Sir Charles Dilke*, 215–371, esp. 404.
10. Robbins, *Sir Edward Grey*, 127.
11. Spender, *Life, Journalism and Politics*, Vol. 1, 132.
12. Robbins, *Sir Edward Grey*, 120–24; Boyle, 'Campbell-Bannerman', 283–302; Wilson, *Policy of the Entente*, 22.
13. *The London Gazette*, 12. Jan. 1906.
14. Asquith, *Memories and Recollections*, Vol. 1, 195.
15. Esher, Diary, 10 Dec. 1905, JL II, 126.
16. See Palmer, *Glanz*, 353; Rowland, *Liberal Governments*, 170; Steiner, *Foreign Office and Foreign Policy*, 94.
17. Balfour described Grey as 'a curious combination of the old fashioned Whig and the Socialist', cited in Jenkins, *Balfour's Poodle*, 44; see also *The Times*, 4 March 1898.
18. Balliol Minute Book, 19 Jan. 1884, cited in Trevelyan, *Grey of Fallodon*, 20.
19. See Trevelyan, *Grey of Fallodon*, DNB, 367–75.
20. Wilson, *Policy of the Entente*, 22.
21. Taylor, *Struggle for Mastery*, 436.
22. Gardiner, *War Lords*, 69.
23. Trevelyan, *Grey of Fallodon*, 191; Amery, *My Political Life*, Vol. 1, 393; Spender, *Public Life*, Vol. 1, 115–16.
24. See Taylor, *Struggle for Mastery*, 436.
25. Grey, *25 Years*, Vol. 1, 71; see also Steiner, *Foreign Office and Foreign Policy*, 83–91; Robbins, *Sir Edward Grey*, 125.
26. Anon., 'The Foreign Policy of Sir Edward Grey', *The Nation*, 3 Aug. 1907, 822–23. Contemporaries spoke of a 'veiled coalition'. According to Churchill, 'There was a very distinct line of cleavage between the Radicals on the one hand and the Liberal Imperialists on the other'. Churchill, *World Crisis*, Vol. 1, 26.
27. Dilke to Fitzmaurice, 2 Feb. 1905, cited in Gwy, *Dilke*, Vol. 2, 502–3; Spring Rice to E.E. Williams, 10 Sept. 1906, CC, CASR 1/70.
28. Haldane to Beatrice Webb, cited in Rowland, *Liberal Governments*, 18. n. 39.
29. Grey to Thursfield, 30 April 1909, NIA, MSS Thursfield.
30. *The Times*, 3 Jan. 1906.
31. Kennedy, *Rise of Anglo-German Antagonism*, 251, 267; Steiner, 'Last Years of the Old Foreign Office'.
32. Amery, *My Political Life*, Vol. 1, 393; Spender, *Public Life*, Vol. 1, 115–16; Steiner, 'Grey, Hardinge and the Foreign Office'.
33. Taylor, *Struggle for Mastery*, 437; Steiner, *Foreign Office and Foreign Policy*, 94.

34. See Albertini, *Origins of the War*, Vol. 3, 368; Barnett, *Collapse of British Power*, 54; Steiner, *Britain and the Origins*, 255; Bridge, *Great Britain and Austria-Hungary*, 15, 222, 228; Bridge and Bullen, *Great Powers*, 159; Vagts, *Balance*, 100, n. 34; Bernstein, *Liberalism and Liberal Politics*, 167; Wormer, *Großbritannien*, 70, 172; Otte, *July Crisis*.
35. Lloyd George, *War Memoirs*, Vol. 1, 98; Steiner, 'Grey, Hardinge and the Foreign Office'; Massie, *Dreadnought*, 590–93; Hinsley, *British Foreign Policy*; Otte, *July 1914*.
36. Ferguson, *Pity of War*, 56–68; Charmley, *Splendid Isolation*.
37. See Thomas Otte, '"Postponing the Evil Day": Sir Edward Grey and British Foreign Policy', in Jones and Smith, 'Edward Grey' (special issue) IHR 2016, 250–63.
38. Lloyd George, *War Memoirs*, Vol. 1, 99.
39. Haldane, *An Autobiography*, 229–30.
40. Cited in Ferguson, *Pity of War*, 56–57; Ponsonby, January 1913, cited in Steiner, *Foreign Office and Foreign Policy*, 84–85.
41. Spender, *Public Life*, Vol. 1, 116.
42. Ponsonby, January 1913, cited in Steiner, *Foreign Office and Foreign Policy*, 84–85.
43. See Gall, *Hardinge*, 19–22; Ferguson, *Pity of War*, 56–68; Steiner, *Foreign Office and Foreign Policy*, 84–85.
44. Taylor, *Struggle for Mastery*, 437; Steiner, *Foreign Office and Foreign Policy*, 94.
45. See Chapter 2.
46. Conwell-Evans, *Foreign Policy*, 44; Read, *Edwardian England*, 243.
47. According to Campbell-Bannerman 'the sentiment of the English people would be totally averse to any troops being landed on the continent under any circumstances'. Cited in Jones, 'Anglo-French negotiations', 225; Grey to Bertie, BD III, No 219, 180–2; 'Disposition du Gouvernement britannique au sujet d'une coopération militaire et navale avec la France' Cambon to Rouvier, 31 Jan. 1906, DDF IX/1, 149–53.
48. Cambon to Rouvier, 31 Jan. 1906, DDF IX/1, 152.
49. Grey (City), *The Times*, 21 Oct. 1905; Grey to Lascelles, 1 Jan. 1906, NA, FO 800/61.
50. Kennedy, *Rise of Anglo-German Antagonism*, 283, Lowe and Dockrill, *Mirage of Power*, Vol. 3, 426–28.
51. Trevelyan, *Grey of Fallodon*, 108.
52. Grey, *25 Years*, Vol. 1, 104.
53. Cited in Trevelyan, *Grey of Fallodon*, 108.
54. Grey to Maxse, 24 Nov. 1901, WSRO, MAXSE/448; 21 June 1904, MAXSE/452.
55. See Robbins, 'Grey', JICH, 213–21, 217; see also Anon., 'The Unwisdom of Sir Edward Grey', RR 9/1901, 280; Grey to Maxse, 22 Oct. 1901, WSRO, MAXSE/448; Morley to Minto, 13 Dec. 1906, IOL, EUR. D. 573/1.
56. Grey (City), *The Times*, 21 Oct. 1905.
57. Siegel, *Endgame*, 17.
58. Grey to Spring Rice, 13 Dec. 1905, BD IV, No. 204, 218; Hardinge to Edward VII, 13 March 1906, CUL, MSS Hardinge, Bd. 9.
59. Williams, 'Great Britain and Russia', 133; Monger, *End of Isolation*, 260.
60. See Chapter 2; Grey (Berwick), *The Times*, 7 Feb. 1903; Grey, 18 Feb. 1903, PD IV/118; 18 Feb. 1903, col. 245; 23 July 1903, PD III/136, cols. 128–30; Grey (Coventry), *The Times*, 9 Nov. 1904.
61. Staal to Mouraview, 15 Feb. 1899, cited in Meyendorff, *Correspondence diplomatique*, Vol. 2, 416.

62. Trevelyan, *Grey of Fallodon*, 82–83; Searle, *Quest for National Efficiency*, 75; Grey to Spring Rice, 19 March 1906, NA, FO 371/124.
63. Grey, *25 Years*, Vol. 1, 152–53; Asquith, *Ursprung des Krieges*, 67.
64. Lansdowne Memorandum, 10 Sept. 1903, NA, FO 27/3765.
65. Grey to Ferguson, 13 Aug. 1905, cited in Trevelyan, *Grey of Fallodon*, 84.
66. Grey to Spring Rice, 19 March 1906, NA, FO 371/124.
67. Grey, Memorandum, 28 Apr. 1908, NA, FO 800/92.
68. Hardinge, Memorandum, 16 Nov. 1906, BD IV, 58–60; Lee, *Edward VII*, Vol. 2, 285–90. For Lansdowne's rejection see: Sanderson to Clarke, 10 Nov. 1905, NA, CAB 17/60.
69. Grey to Nicolson, 16 Nov. 1906, NA, FO 800/72.
70. Grey, Memorandum, 20 Feb. 1906, BD III, No. 299, 266–69; *The Times*, 21 Oct. 1905.
71. See Gade, *Gleichgewichtspolitik*; Morley to Minto, 13 Dec. 1906, IOL, EUR. D. 573/1.
72. Grey, Memorandum, 20 Feb. 1906, NA, FO 800/53.
73. Hardinge, Memorandum, 16 Aug. 1908, BD VI, No. 117, 184–90.
74. Hildebrand, *Das Vergangene Reich*, 229–30.
75. See Wilson, *Policy of the Entente*, 115.
76. *Morning Post*, cited in Canis, *Von Bismarck zur Weltpolitik*, 405.
77. See Strachey, 'Public Opinion in the Conduct of Foreign Affairs', *The Spectator*, 6 April 1901, 487–88.
78. Clarke to Haldane, 6 Feb. 1905, NLS, MSS 5906.
79. Military Conference, 1 June 1906, NA, CAB 38/11/4; see also Taylor, *Struggle for Mastery*, 438.
80. Grey, Memorandum, 20 Feb. 1906, BD III, No. 299, 266–68.
81. See Charmley, *Splendid Isolation*, 315–17; Monger, *End of Isolation*, 329–30.
82. Grey to Ella Pease, 8 Nov. 1908, cited in Trevelyan, *Grey of Fallodon*, 154–55.
83. See Kissinger, *World Restored*, 240.
84. Wilson, *Policy of the Entente*, 86.
85. See Coogan and Coogan, 'The British Cabinet'; McDermott, 'Revolution in British Military Thinking'; Williamson, *Politics of Grand Strategy*, 284–85. See also Chapter 2.
86. Offer, *World War*, 223–24; Taylor, *Struggle for Mastery*, 441.
87. Hayes, 'Admiralty's Plans', 75–76; McDermott, 'Revolution in British Military Thinking'.
88. Grey to Haldane, 8 Jan. 1906, NLS, MSS 5907; to Campbell-Bannerman, 9 Jan. 1906, cited in Grey, *25 Years*, Vol. 1, 114.
89. Grey to Bertie, 10 Jan. 1906, cited in Grey, *25 Years*, Vol. 1, 70–71.
90. Robbins, *Sir Edward Grey*, 372.
91. Bertie to Mallet, 11 June 1904, BL, Add. 63016. On Germany's dependence on Russia, see, for example, Crowe to Asta, 26 April 1895, BOD, MSS Crowe, MS Eng. d. 2897; Currie to Victoria, 6 Nov. 1895, Royal Archives, MSS Victoria, Film 1448, H 37/67; Clarke to Sandars, 18 Aug. 1904, BL, Add. 49700; Spring Rice to Morley, 7 Nov. 1906, BOD, MSS Morley, MS Eng. d. 3581.
92. Schroeder, 'World War I as Galloping Gertie', 143.
93. See Wells, *New Machiavelli*, 75–80; Spring Rice to Adams, 7 Nov. 1897, cited in Burton, *Cecil Spring Rice*, 108–10; Sanderson to Lansdowne, 18 May 1901, NA, FO 800/115; *The Spectator*, 18 May 1901, 728.
94. Grey to Maxse, 12 Oct. 1902, WSRO, MAXSE/450.

95. See Remak, *Third Balkan War*, 89–90; Otte, 'Almost a Law of Nature', 88.
96. Grey to Buxton, 31 Dec. 1895, cited in Matthew, *Liberal Imperialists*, 202.
97. Ferguson, *Pity of War*, 57–58.
98. Grey to Newbolt, 5 Jan. 1903, cited in ibid., 58.
99. Steiner and Neilson, *Britain and the Origins*, 42.
100. Grey, *25 Years*, Vol. 2, 43.
101. Grey to Lascelles, 1 Jan. 1906, NA, FO 800/61; Chirol to Strachey, 3 July 1906, HLRO, STR/4/9/9.
102. Busch, *Hardinge*, 122.
103. See Ferguson, *Pity of War*, 56–60; see also the character sketch from Stumm, 30 Dec. 1907, PA-AA, R 5962.
104. See Steiner, *Foreign Office and Foreign Policy*, 102.
105. On Sanderson's poor health, see Spicer to Spring Rice, 9 Jan. 1906, NA, FO 800/241.
106. Hardinge to Nicolson, 4 Sept. 1907, BD IV, No. 520, 580.
107. Hardinge, *Diplomacy*, 97.
108. Bertie to Hardinge, 28 Nov. 1904, 5 July 1905 and 27 Aug. 1905, CUL, MSS Hardinge, Vol. 7.
109. Hardinge, *Diplomacy*, 146; Hardinge to Maxse, 16 Oct. 1901, WSRO, MAXSE/448.
110. On Hardinge, see Otte, *Foreign Office Mind*, esp. 240–59, 314–23.
111. Hardinge to Maxse, 2 July 1900, WSRO, MAXSE/447; 16 Oct. 1901, MAXSE/448; 8 Dec. 1905, MAXSE/453; to Lansdowne, 2 July 1904; 13 July 1904, CUL, MSS Hardinge, Vol. 46.
112. Steiner, 'Last Years of the Old Foreign Office', 84; Whitaker, *Whitaker's Almanack* 1910, 189.
113. Steiner, *Foreign Office and Foreign Policy*, 103.
114. 'Your views coincide with mine … a good understanding with Russia … certainly should not exclude good relations with Germany.' Lascelles to Fitzmaurice, 2 June 1906 and 28 Sept. 1906; to Haldane, 27 Sept. 1906, NA FO 800/19; Fitzmaurice to Lascelles, 21 Sept. 1906, NA, FO 800/13.
115. See Steiner, *Foreign Office and Foreign Policy*, 24.
116. Nicolson, *Carnock*, 328.
117. 'Tyrrell was a compact self-assured man, … and delivered a discourse on the "characters" of France and Germany, that would have done credit to a bright but patriotic schoolboy of eight.' Cited in Wells, *Experiment in Autobiography*, 704–5.
118. 'He did more than any man to increase the prestige of the FO in circles which had hitherto regarded Diplomacy as mysterious and aloof: he was on excellent terms with journalists and Members of Parliament. … His influence with Ministers was exceedingly great.' Cited in Aston-Gwatkin, 'Tyrrell', DNB Vol 19, 893–96.
119. Tyrrell to Spring Rice, 3 Nov. 1897, CC, CASR 1/65.
120. Fitzmaurice to Lascelles, 31 May 1906, NA, FO 800/13; Lascelles to Fitzmaurice, 2 June 1906, NA, FO 800/19.
121. Monger, *End of Isolation*, 260, 290; Fitzmaurice to Lascelles, 21 Sept. 1906; Lascelles to Fitzmaurice, 28 Sept. 1906, NA, FO 800/19.
122. Philippi, 'Botschafter', 174.
123. See the criticism proffered by Crowe, which was often harsh and ill-founded but generally followed by Grey and Hardinge. For example, Minutes, BD VI, No. 81, 118–31, 132; No. 85, 227; No. 88, 138.

124. Greindl to Davignon, 18 July 1908, BelD III, No. 50, 142–44. Cartwright to De Bunsen, 1908, BOD, MSS De Bunsen 7dd.
125. Fay, 'Influence of the Pre-war Press', 20f.; Cartwright to Hardinge, 22 Feb. 1907, NA, FO 371/257.
126. Bülow to Metternich, 4 June 1908. 'Am liebsten wäre es, wenn Lascelles verlängert würde, so dass Spring Rice zum Nachfolger heranreifen könnte.' (It would be best if Lascelles' term was extended, in order that Spring Rice had time to mature into his successor.) Cited in Philippi, 'Botschafter', 174.
127. '[U]ngehobelten deutschfresserischen Flätz', comment by Wilhelm II on Bülow's report to the Kaiser of 2 July 1908, cited in ibid., 178; see also Szögenyi to Aehrenthal, 22 Dec. 1908, HHStA, PA VIII, Kt. 142, Bl. 183.
128. Crowe, Minute, 6 Feb. 1911, NA, FO 371/1123.
129. Philippi, 'Botschafter', 175–76. See also Kühlmann, *Erinnerungen*, 315. The Belgian ambassador also believed that Britain had done all it could to turn Algeciras into a humiliating lesson for Germany. Greindl to Faveraux, 5 April 1906, BelD II, 46–48.
130. Cited in Bülow, *Denkwürdigkeiten*, Vol. 4, 667.
131. Spring Rice to Lady Spring Rice, 8 Oct. 1908, GL II, 127.
132. See Whitaker, *Whitaker's Almanack* 1907, 472, 581.
133. By, for example, sending McCormicks to St Petersburg. Durand to Lansdowne, 5 Feb. 1905, NA, FO 800/116.
134. See Neilson, 'My Beloved Russians'; Pribram, *Austria-Hungary and Great Britain*, 83–84; Nicolson, *Sir Arthur Nicolson: Lord Carnock*, passim.
135. Note by Hardinge on Grey's Memorandum, 23 Feb. 1906, BD III, No. 299, 266–67.
136. Hardinge to Sanderson, 29 June 1899; 2 Nov. 1899; 1 Nov. 1900, CUL, MSS Hardinge, Vol. 3.
137. Mallet, Memorandum, 25 Feb. 1907, BD III, App. B, 431–32; Hardinge to Nicolson, 30 Oct. 1907, NA, FO 800/341.
138. Crowe and Corp, *Ablest Servant*, 120–23; Grenville, *Lord Salisbury*, 271.
139. Hardinge to Sanderson, 29 June 1899, CUL, MSS Hardinge, Vol. 3; Hardinge, 30 Oct. 1899, NA, FO 65/1580; Hardinge to Nicolson, 30 Oct. 1907, NA, FO 800/341.
140. Gooch, *Diplomacy*, 91–93.
141. The change in these years is evident above all in the minutes of Crowe, Langley, Villiers, Spicer, Hardinge and Grey, and others that are of direct relevance for the politics of the day. See BD VI, passim.
142. See Mombauer, *Origins of the First World War*, 64.
143. Extract in BD I, No. 342, 276–77; BD II, No. 170, 152–53; BD III, App. A, 397–420; BDFA F/XIX, No. 282, 367–86. Original in NA, FO 881/8882Z.
144. Monger, *End of Isolation*, 313; Hale, *Publicity and Diplomacy*, 284–85; Steiner, *Britain and the Origins*, 44–45; Kennedy, *Rise of Anglo-German Antagonism*, 433.
145. Otte, 'Eyre Crowe and British Foreign Policy', 24–25; for Steiner, the Memorandum was a 'brilliant, if not entirely accurate survey'. Steiner, 'Last Years of the Old Foreign Office', 79.
146. Reinermann, *Kaiser*, 303; see also Crowe, Memorandum, 1 Jan. 1907, BD III/A, 403–5.
147. Geiss, 'Weltpolitik', 148–70, 168–69; Fischer, *Krieg der Illusionen*, 112, 125, 496–97, 704, 730; Crowe, 1 Jan. 1907, BD III/A, 397–420, 402. For a different view, see Neitzel, *Kriegsausbruch*, 122.
148. Crowe's minutes even appeared as shorter memoranda. See Minutes in BD VI.

149. Otte, 'Eyre Crowe and British Foreign Policy', 17.
150. Crowe to Asta, 21 Jan. 1895, BOD, MSS Crowe, MS Eng. e. 3019; 26 April 1895, BOD, MS Eng. d. 2897; see Otte, 'Eyre Crowe and British Foreign Policy', 17–19.
151. Crowe to Asta, 14 Jan. 1895; 5 Jan. 1896, BOD, MSS Crowe, MS Eng. e. 3019.
152. Fay, 'Influence of the Pre-war Press', 19.
153. Crowe, Minutes, 11 Feb. 1907, Lascelles to Grey, 6 Feb. 1907, BD VI, No. 4, 14–15.
154. Crowe, Minutes, 28 May 1906, Lascelles to Grey, 24 May 1906, BD III, No. 416, 357–58.
155. Ibid.
156. Otte, 'Eyre Crowe and British Foreign Policy', 14. See also Lutz, *Crowe*, passim; Remak, *Origins*, 37; Fay, *Origins of World War I*, Vol. 1, 557–58.
157. Steinberg, 'Diplomatie', 269.
158. Monger, *End of Isolation*, 315; Cosgrove, *Crowe*, 193–205; Crowe and Corp, *Ablest Servant*. For Crowe's influence, see Nicolson, *Sir Arthur Nicolson: Lord Carnock*, 327–28; Vansittart, *Procession*, 45–46.
159. Kissinger, *Diplomacy*, 192–93.
160. Crowe to Maxse, 29 Sept. 1902, WSRO, MAXSE/450; 15 Oct. 1902, MAXSE/450; 16 May 1907, MAXSE/457.
161. MSS Eyre Crowe, BOD, MS Eng. d. 2897–2902; e. 3019. Wilkinson, *Thirty-Five Years*, 316–19.
162. Wilkinson, *Nation's Awakening*; see also Review in *Spectator*, 1 Aug. 1896, 149–50.
163. Crowe, Minutes, 10 Feb. 1908, Dumas to Lascelles, 3 Feb. 1908, No. 80, BAD VI/1, 193–97, 197.
164. Bucholz, *Moltke*, 91–92; see also Moltke's speech in the Reichstag, cited in Ferguson, *Pity of War*, 8.
165. Dawkins to Amery, 2 April 1905, CC, AMEL 2/5/4.
166. While Germany had halted all thoughts of an invasion of England by 1903, France continued to contemplate that possibility up until 1906. See BA-MA, RM 5/1609–1610. See also Steinberg, 'Copenhagen Complex', 28; Ritter, *Staatskunst*, Vol. 2, 195; Repington, 27 Nov. 1907, Subcommittee of the CID to reconsider the Question of Overseas Attack, NA, CAB 16/3A, 33–34; Lüttwitz, 'The Invasion of England', JRUSI 2/1896, 198–202.
167. Cited in Repington, *First World War*, Vol. 1, 10.
168. Crowe, Memorandum, 1 Jan. 1907, BD III/A, 397–420; Crowe, Minutes, BD III/B, 426.
169. Cited in Crowe, Crowe and Corp, *Ablest Servant*, 122.
170. Crowe, Minutes, 9 April 1906, Lascelles to Grey, 5 April 1906, BD III, No. 398, 332–34, 334; Crowe, Minutes, 28 May 1906, Lascelles to Grey, 24 May 1906, BD III, No. 416, 358; Crowe, Minutes, 3 Feb. 1908, Lascelles to Grey, 30 Jan. 1908, BD VI, No. 78, 111–13.
171. Crowe, Minutes, 3 Feb. 1908, Lascelles to Grey, 30 Jan. 1908, BD VI, No. 78, 112–13.
172. Crowe, Memorandum, 1 Jan. 1907, BD III/A, 397–420; Cartwright to Hardinge, 22 Feb. 1907, NA, FO 371/257; Hardinge to Grey, 2 Jan. 1907, NA, FO 800/92; Hardinge to Lascelles, 29 Feb. 1907, NA, FO 800/15. 'Crowe's Memo should go to the PM, Lord Ripon, Mr Asquith, Mr French, Mr Haldane with my comment upon it. This Memo by Mr Crowe is most valuable. The review of the present situation is both interesting and suggestive, and the connected account of the diplomatic incidents of past years is most helpful as a guide to policy. The whole Memo contains information and

reflections which should be carefully studied.' Grey, 28 Jan. 1907, NA, FO 371/7. 'I think there is something to be said on the other side.' Lascelles to Hardinge, 1 Feb. 1907, NA, FO 800/19; Mallet, 25 Feb. 1907, BD III/B, 431–33.
173. Hardinge to Grey, 25 Feb. 1907, BD III/B, 686.
174. Sanderson, Memorandum, 21 Feb. 1907, BD III/B, 421–31, 429.
175. Ibid., 420.
176. Grey, 28 Jan. 1907, NA, FO 371/7.
177. Hildebrand, *Das Vergangene Reich*, 238; Crowe and Corp, *Ablest Servant*, XI, 115–35; Spenser Wilkinson, 'Eyre Crowe', DNB, Vol. 5, 219-21.
178. 'The sins of Germany since 1871 are light in comparison to ours.' Sanderson, Memorandum, 21 Feb. 1907, BD III/B, 430.
179. Crowe, Memorandum, 1 Jan. 1907, BD III/A, 680; see English version: BD III/B, 417.
180. Crowe to Maxse, 15 Oct. 1902, WSRO, MAXSE/450.
181. Schroeder, 'World War I as Galloping Gertie'.
182. Crowe, Minutes, 3 Feb. 1908, Lascelles to Grey, 30 Jan. 1908, BD VI, No. 78, 111–13; Crowe, Minutes, 4 Feb. 1908, Bertie to Grey, 3 Feb. 1908, BD VI, No. 79, 113–15, esp. 114–15.
183. Canis, 'Außenpolitik im letzten Jahrzehnt', 111.
184. Crowe, Minute, 21 Jan. 1907, NA, FO 371/257.
185. See, for example, Spicer, Minutes, 16 Sept. 1907, Bertie to Grey, 12 Sept. 1907, BD VI, No. 35, 55–58; Hardinge, Grey, Minutes, Lascelles to Grey, 24 Oct. 1907, BD VI, No. 39, 63–66, 66; Crowe, Minutes, 10 Feb. 1908, Dumas to Lascelles, 3 Feb. 1908, BD VI, No. 80, 115–17; Crowe, Minutes, 1 March 1908, Dumas to Lascelles, 12 Feb. 1908, BD VI, No. 81, 117–32; for Trench, see NA, FO 371/75.
186. Crowe, Minutes, 14 Jan. 1908, Cartwright, 8 Jan. 1908, BD VI, No. 108.
187. Charmley, *Splendid Isolation*, 347.
188. Spring Rice to Maxse, 3 June 1908, WSRO, MAXSE/458.
189. Crowe, Minutes, 25 March 1909, BD VI/1, No. 158, 416–17.
190. Crowe, Memorandum, 1 Jan. 1907, BD III/A, 398–99; Sanderson, Memorandum, 21 Feb. 1907, BD III/B, 420.
191. 'La guerre entre L'Angleterre et l'Allemagne n'est qu'une question de temps. Elle doit fatalement venire.' (War between England and German is only a matter of time. It must inevitably happen.) Delcassé in conversation with Mallet, Mallet to Lansdowne, 13 July 1905, NA, FO 800/145.
192. Mallet, Memorandum, 25 Feb. 1907, BD III/B, 431–32.
193. Cromer to Lansdowne, 27 Nov. 1903, NA, FO 633/311; Bertie to Lansdowne, 17 Jan. 1905, BL, Add. 63017; Sanderson to Lansdowne, 9 Oct. 1905, NA, FO 800/145.
194. Lansdowne to Monson, 6 Aug. 1902, NA, FO 800/125; to Lascelles, 11 April 1904, NA, FO 244/636.
195. Monson to Salisbury, 9 Dec. 1898, BD I, No. 238, 196–97; Roosevelt to Spring Rice, 1 Nov. 1905, GL II, 10.
196. Balfour to Maxse, 5 Dec. 1898, BL, Add. 49853; Balfour, Memorandum, 29 Dec. 1903, NA, CAB 37/67/97; to Selborne, 6 April 1904, BOD, MSS Selborne 1/39; to Amery, 14 July 1904, BL, Add. 49775.
197. See Kennan, *Alliance*, 251–52.
198. Sanderson, 21 Feb. 1907, BD III/B, 420–31, passim.
199. Ibid., 687–88.

200. Cited in Bismarck, *Gesammelte Werke*, Vol. 8: Gespräche, 646; see Canis, *Von Bismarck zur Weltpolitik*, 209–30.
201. Fitzmaurice, Minutes, BD III/B, 420; Sanderson, 21 Feb. 1907, BD III/B, 421–22.
202. Hildebrand, *Das Vergangene Reich*, 87; Kennedy, *Rise of Anglo-German Antagonism*, 79.
203. Crowe, 1 Jan. 1907, BD III/A, 409; Sanderson, 21 Feb. 1907, BD III/B, 692; see English version: 'We have not an absolutely clear record.' BD III/B, 421–22.
204. BD III/B, 409, 424–25.
205. Ibid., 426; see also Canis, *Weltpolitik*, 53–70.
206. Text of Contract, 30 Aug. 1898, GP XIV/1, No. 3872, 347–55.
207. See Porter, *War*, 155–57; Grenville, *Lord Salisbury*, 177–97; see also GP XIV/1, No. 3872; BD I, Nos. 90–92.
208. Crowe, 1 Jan. 1907, BD III/A, 409; Sanderson, 21 Feb. 1907, BD III/B, 423–24.
209. BD III/B, 409, 423–24.
210. Mallet, 25 Feb. 1907, BD III/B, 432.
211. Sanderson, 21 Feb. 1907, BD III/B, 425–26; see also Kazemzadeh, *Russia and Britain*, 332–40.
212. Sanderson, 21 Feb. 1907, BD III/B, 426.
213. Ibid., 428; see also Canis, *Weltpolitik*, 338–55.
214. Sanderson, 21 Feb. 1907, BD III/B, 428.
215. Ibid., 421–23, 426–28.
216. Ibid., 429–30.
217. Ibid., 430.
218. Crowe, Memorandum, 1 Jan. 1907, BD III/A, 404–5.
219. For a different view, see Canis, 'Außenpolitik im letzten Jahrzehnt', 111.
220. Niedhart, *Geschichte Englands*, 144.
221. Fisher to Esher, 21 March 1909, cited in Fisher, *Memories and Records*, 189–90.
222. Goschen to Lascelles, 16 June 1907, NA, FO 800/13.
223. Steiner and Neilson, *Britain and the Origins*, 54.
224. Sanderson to Lansdowne, 18 May 1901, NA, FO 800/115; 20 Jan. 1905, FO 800/145.
225. Hardinge, Memorandum, 25 Oct. 1906, NA, ADM 1/7904. Cited by Zara Steiner with the date 30 Oct. 1906. See Steiner, *Foreign Office and Foreign Policy*, 94. Fisher to Edward VII, 3 Nov. 1906, FGDN II, No. 57, 105–7. See Chapter 2.
226. Anon., 'Two German Legends', *The Nation*, 30 Nov. 1907, 294–95.
227. 'Wenn erst ein System von Stereotypen gut verankert ist, wendet sich die Aufmerksamkeit den Tatsachen zu, die es stützen und von den anderen, die ihm widersprechen ab.' (When a system based on stereotypes is firmly anchored, attention is given to the facts that support it and diverted away from those that contradict it.) Luhmann, cited in Lippmann, *Öffentliche Meinung*, 87.
228. Cited in Wilson, *Policy of the Entente*, 106.

Chapter 7

THE COMMITTEE OF FOUR
The German Peril Revisited

Repington, Fisher and the Invasion Inquiry

Although the Committee of Imperial Defence under Balfour had established that the idea of invading the British Isles was impossible, in November 1907 a new invasion subcommittee was formed; it would continue to meet until July 1908.

Historians have long identified the construction of the Tirpitz fleet as the immediate impetus for the new investigation, an interpretation that is made very plausible by the causal and temporal concurrence of the disappointing conclusion of the Hague peace conference in October 1907, Berlin's Fourth Naval Bill in mid November 1907, and the first meeting, ten days later, of the new subcommittee in London.[1] Although scares and scaremongering were recognized for precisely what they were,[2] they are frequently taken to have been a logical response to German sabre-rattling,[3] a position usually supported by material largely German in origin. Count Metternich, the German ambassador to London, naval attaché Wilhelm Widenmann and Under-Secretary of State Wilhelm von Stumm had no doubt that the public disquiet had been caused by news of the new German naval law. 'In November 1907', Ivo Lambi wrote without any qualms, 'Britain reacted to the publication of Germany's Fourth Naval Bill'.[4]

By contrast, however, British sources indicate that months before the German proposals had become public knowledge, demands for a new inquiry were already being voiced and that the decision to launch an investigation had been made by August 1907 at the latest.[5] At the Hague peace conference held between June and October 1907, domestic political interests had been of greater significance than external purposes, for the Liberal government's principal concern was to reduce the financial burden.[6] Eyre Crowe, a member of the British delegation at The

---

Notes for this chapter begin on page 333.

Hague, had reported that the disappointing outcome should not be blamed on Germany's brusque rejection of proposals, but laid instead at the door of highly deficient British diplomatic preparations.[7] In advance of the conference, Grey had pointedly launched preliminary discussions with all the Great Powers and had even sent James Bryce as a special envoy to Washington to sound out the views of the US government.[8] Although Berlin had proposed a bilateral agreement, Germany had been left largely ignored. Such pointed disregard meant that rebuff by Germany in turn had always been on the cards. Against the background of the outright rejection of the disarmament proposals of the radicals by the liberal imperial minority in the cabinet,[9] Grey had good reason to assume that the marginalization of Germany might mean the failure of the conference.[10] A statement he had made six months earlier suggests Grey had already resolved to use the Hague conference as a prime opportunity to portray Germany as the greatest threat to plans for peace: in November 1906, he had declared clearly, 'I want people here and in Germany to realise that it is he [Wilhelm II] who had forced our hand in spite of our wish to limit expenditure'.[11]

Count Mensdorff, whose diplomatic role had given him good knowledge of Britain, suspected that the tensions evident in London in autumn 1907 had entirely domestic causes. In the ambassador's mind, the public mood was closely tied to the knotty political position into which the Liberal government had manoeuvred itself with its election promises,[12] a thesis that deserves greater attention from historians. Objectively, Britain's security was 'in every little particular magnificently splendid', according to First Sea Lord John A. Fisher. He therefore insisted not only to Lord Tweedmouth and Arnold White, but also to Edward VII and his heir in August 1906, noting specifically:

> The present naval force in full service at sea is greater in power than at the time of the Dogger Bank incident, and we considered our naval strength then amply sufficient. Now Russia is annihilated, France our friend, and Germany our only possible foe, many times weaker than ourselves; so how can we support or justify keeping up our strength at sea at a higher pitch than then?[13]

Fisher evidently saw Germany as Britain's only remaining threat, but also as a threat very unlikely to be realized, illuminating the scope for interpretation of the classic issue of German naval armament and the British response. Although so frequently characterized as Germany's arch-enemy par excellence,[14] at least during this phase Fisher never lost an opportunity, either internal or public, to call for caution. He continued to share the position Balfour had adopted at the time of the first invasion investigations of 1905, and he had made very clear to all the various British decision makers that German shipbuilders required nine months longer than an English shipyard to construct a modern battleship[15] and that Britain could therefore forgo the construction planned for 1907/8.[16] One year later, in November 1907, the first German dreadnoughts were already laid down;[17] Fisher instructed an alarmed public, 'Sleep quiet in your beds!'[18] With his penchant for publicity, Fisher was always ready to rally journalists to his cause.[19] Yet while well aware of the potential inherent in mobilizing the public,[20] as his concerns about the reputation of the navy as Britain's first line of defence demonstrate, he also knew just how hard, even almost impossible, it was to channel and calm public hysteria once it had been unleashed.

The framing of the public discourse is therefore worthy of attention. Gustav Schmidt and Jonathan Steinberg have highlighted the discrepancies between intention, or views expressed internally, and the public's response to the printed word, and both hold that studies based solely on official sources come up short,[21] a view that is valid for both analysis of international relations and interpretation of the internal conduct of British foreign, defence and press policy. At the same time, we must be wary of studies that are based primarily on accessible press material but focus in on textual patterns, for they too easily overlook the press's own motives as well as the press's intrinsic value and increasing contribution as a political actor.[22] For evaluating the impulses and context of Whitehall's decision making, and for illuminating the complexities of domestic and foreign policy,[23] understanding of the differences between public mood and internal experts, and of the political ties between the services and among the political parties, is invaluable. The contours of the frequently cited 'relative autonomy' of London foreign policy are then clearer and can be set against the earlier course adopted by the Conservative leadership, already discussed here in the context of the first invasion debate.[24] Only five days before the new subcommittee met for the first time, Edward Grey commented, 'the Germans are a long way behind'.[25] Why, unlike Balfour in 1905, he should have expressed this opinion only to his inner circle and made no attempt to calm the public awaits explanation.

The construction numbers and periods of construction corroborated Fisher's confident assessment. In a comparison of international naval strengths published in late November 1905, the *Times* could only confirm France's 'crushing superiority' over Germany, an advantage that was especially evident in the category of 'destroyers, torpedo-boats, submersibles, and submarines',[26] where the French navy's pre-eminence was almost overwhelming.[27] In the category covering warships and battle-cruisers, when French ships that were not part of the Atlantic Fleet were included, France also had a significant lead over Germany, despite the unwillingness of the *Times*'s Paris correspondent to believe such was the case. While the German navy had completed just four of the more recent armoured cruisers, the strategic planning of the *Jeune École* meant that France already had eighteen ships of this class. The *Times* had listed France as having twenty-one 'pre-dreadnoughts', but according to figures provided by Paris in July 1903, France already had twenty-nine such ships. The new French fleet law also planned for additional modernization of French naval forces, with the navy to

Table 7.1. 'Effective Fighting Fleets of the Nations' (31 March 1906).

	England	France	Germany	Italy	USA	Russia	Japan
Battleships							
First Class	55 (6)[a]	31 (4) 6a[b]	18[c] (6)	14 (4)	14 (11) 2a	11 (4)[d]	9 (4) 2a
Second Class	4	9	4	–	1	3	2
Third Class	2	1	9	2	–	1	–
Coast Defence	–	9	11	(2)	11	10	3
Battle-Cruisers							
Armoured	28 (10)	19 (5)	6 (2) 1a	6	7 (8)	3 (4)	9 (3) 2a
Protected	21	7	6	–	3	12 (1)	2
Second Class	48[e]	14	14	5	17	12	11 (1)
Third Class	19	16	12	13	2	1	7
Unprotected	–	1	9	1	6	3	7
Scouts	12	–	–	–	3	–	–
Torpedo-Boat Destroyers	143 (18)	33 (23) 10a	43 (6) 12a[f]	13 (4)	20	58 (29)	29 (25)
Torpedo Boats	108	263 (41)	72[g]	139 (20)	34	59[h] (172)	82
Submarines	25 (15)	39 (39) 20a	1 Experiment	2 (4)	8 (4)	13 (15)	5 (2)

See Whitaker, *Whitaker's Almanack 1907*, 198, 585, 592, 616; Dumas, Report 3/07, 29 Jan. 1907, cited in Seligmann, *Naval Intelligence from Germany*, No. 24, 59–74, 60; *The Times*, 24 Jan. 1907, counted 19 French battleships. See Dilke, Fleets, HCPP, AP 184, 10 June 1907, 885–957.

Bracketed figures indicate ships under construction; (a) indicates ships that were ordered or would be completed during the 1906/7 fiscal year.

[a]Whitaker, *Whitaker's Almanack 1900*, 222–30; Excubitor (Hurd), 'British Reply', FR 3/1908, 456–69; [b]Whitaker, *Whitaker's Almanack 1907*, 585; [c]These contain pre-dreadnoughts from the Brandenburg Class (1890–1893), Kaiser Friedrich III Class (1895–1901), Wittelsbach Class (1899–1903), Braunschweig Class (1901–1906) and Deutschland Class (1903–1908). Prochnow, *Deutsche Kriegsschiffe*, Vol. 1, 33–64; Dumas, Report 3/07, 29 Jan. 1907, cited in Seligmann, *Naval Intelligence from Germany*, No. 24, 59–74, 60; [d]Whitaker, *Whitaker's Almanack 1907*, 616; [e]Dumas, Report 3/07, 29 Jan. 1907, cited in Seligmann, *Naval Intelligence from Germany*, No. 24, pp. 59–74, 60; [f]Whitaker, *Whitaker's Almanack 1907*, 592; [g]Only 47 were 'up to date'. Ibid.; [h]Jane, *Imperial Russian Navy*, 428.

reach a total of 486 ships.[28] Even though these forces would be divided between the Atlantic and the Mediterranean, as a result of Britain's withdrawal from the Mediterranean, France now had greater scope for concentrating its forces, with Italy and Austria-Hungary hardly presenting a serious threat. The plans drawn up by the German Naval Office for the period up to 1920 were downright modest by comparison; while the German fleet would grow markedly, the increase would take place over a longer period and prestigious capital ships were favoured over innovation. But especially these 'old testament' battleships Fisher and his experts thought less important than is usually assumed.[29]

Thinking qualitatively, in late January 1907, naval attaché Philip Dumas established that just half of Britain's battle-cruisers had the same fighting strength as half of Germany's battleships, and noted: 'In every case we have undoubted superiority both in speed and armament'. Even while undertaking a distant blockade across the whole North Sea, Britain would still have the offensive capacity to destroy the German navy's ports.[30] 'At this moment', opined Archibald S. Hurd, who wrote on naval matters, in reference to December 1906, 'there is absolutely no danger from the German Fleet'. According to Hurd, Britain's position, secured by diplomacy and defensive policy, had never been stronger and far exceeded the two-power standard. Above all, he insisted, too much must not be read into any redeployment of forces.[31] In light of the tense relations with Germany, it was not surprising, he recognized, that every precautionary or organizational rearrangement was understood by the public as a reaction in that context, but, he continued, internally it was acknowledged that such measures had less to do with Anglo-German relations and more to do with new friendships, British strength and British economic and domestic policy. The replacement of the inflexible and purely military two-power standard, which the rise of the United States had made financially impossible, with the political power standard long demanded by the Conservatives was very overdue. Hurd also insisted that it was entirely pointless to include in the power calculations states with which Britain was allied to, or entirely improbable constellations such as an alliance between France and Germany or between the United States and Germany. He believed that Fisher's policy suggested not a higher state of alert in relation to Germany, but a greater focus on minimum requirements, and indeed overall Britain's naval forces had been reduced. In December 1906, Hurd had declared: 'Of all the great powers the Germans possess the Fleet which contains the weakest units in offensive power',[32] and nothing had changed on that front by the time the Committee of Imperial Defence launched its second invasion investigation.[33] In October 1907, Fisher recorded:

> England has 7 *dreadnoughts* and 3 *invincibles*,[34] in my opinion better than Dreadnoughts, built and building, while Germany in March last [March 1907] had not begun one![35] Even if in May last a German Dreadnought had been commenced! ... We have 123 destroyers and 40 Submarines, the Germans have 48 Destroyers and one Submarine.

The whole of our Destroyers and Submarines are absolutely efficient and ready for instant battle and are fully manned, and they are all constantly exercised.[36]

Why, then, was a second investigation of the invasion risk even thought necessary, with historians up to the present generally writing of the German High Seas Fleet as an 'unprecedented challenge to Britain's security'?[37] An answer to that question requires detailed examination of various interconnected factors and different phases and opinions within British arms policy, foreign policy and defence policy.

That exploration reveals that, to a significant extent, Whitehall was responding far less to German plans for military expansion than to domestic public disquiet that had begun in early 1906. As Mensdorff had suspected, that public alarm was a product of the ambitious election promises of disarmament, financial relief and social and defence-related reforms. The new Liberal leadership was being observed particularly closely by the wings of its own party.[38] While the left-liberal majority was particularly keen to see cuts in the defence budget, the imperial-liberal wing had learned from the khaki election that a future majority would be secure only if it committed to an increase in security and prestige. As the fascinating correspondence between Fisher and the First Lord of the Admiralty, Lord Tweedmouth, demonstrates, the overdue organizational reform of the military also remained a concern. Fisher wished to see any savings by the navy reinvested in greater efficiency and not necessarily redirected to social reform, while the army continued to call for compulsory military service. Here we encounter just a few of the issues facing British defence policy during these years, and they have in common a limited connection to any external threat.

With the reassurance on the invasion risk aired in May 1905, the campaign for reform of the army took on a new quality. The cause was led by neither the Conservative opposition nor the Royal Navy. Once Balfour had spoken out against the over-dramatization of the situation and had publicly declared the current defensive situation satisfactory, the army lobby, along with a number of Conservative newspapers, had disparaged the Tories as a 'dead party in a military sense';[39] it had even less faith, however, in the military policy of the largely pacifist Liberals. Fisher continued to do all he could 'to smash forever the invasion bogey'.[40] The rumours now gained a new dynamic. For Hugh O. Arnold-Forster, Balfour's secretary of state for war, the domestic, foreign and defensive context had been clear: 'The man who believes in invasion believes in conscription'.[41]

The driving forces were Lord Roberts and, once again, Charles Repington. Having resigned from the defence committee in exasperation in November 1905, as president of the National Service League (NSL) Roberts launched a press campaign designed to put pressure on the government.[42] In the meantime, as military expert at the *Times*, Repington had extended his reputation as a media and propaganda personality. His declared goal was to support Haldane, who notwithstanding the radical liberal majority in the House of Commons, continued to call for the creation of a professional army 300,000 men strong.[43] Thanks to the National Defence Association (NDA), which Haldane himself had founded, Repington was soon able to recruit for a joint propaganda campaign a number of highly influential supporters of the volunteer army, including John St. Loe Strachey, Leopold J. Maxse, Lord Northcliffe, Lord Wemyss, Arthur Gwynne of the *Standard* and that newspaper's owner, Cyril Pearson, who also owned the *Daily Express* and a majority share of the *Westminster Gazette*, as well as liberal imperial member of parliament John Seeley.[44] The National Defence Association demanded a long-term military policy of 'universal military service for Home Defence'.[45] First, however, the British public was to be armed psychologically, for as Repington declared at Aldershot, 'The Nation must be a Nation in Arms or it must perish'.[46] With tradition, political constellations and the current financial situation all running counter to comprehensive military reform, Repington called first for a concentrated, targeted and extended propaganda campaign. The army would at last overcome the ignominy of the events of the turn of the century and gain a new sense of purpose that would allow it to catch up with, and even outstrip, the standing of the Royal Navy among the British public. For Repington, the threat of invasion provided 'the blueprint for reducing the value of the Navy to the equivalent level of the 500 bayonets put on it by Henry Wilson!', with the Prussian army the most worthy opponent of a 'national army'.[47] For the status of the army to be increased, and to ensure sufficient means were made available to support a new expeditionary force, the British people would need to be convinced that the navy was no longer able to guarantee their safety. Repington may have cited Field-Marshall Henry Wilson, but later Wilson would record privately, in his diary, that talk of invasion had been nothing more than a means to an end and was essentially 'a lot of nonsense'.[48] Yet Wilson proved just as unwilling as the other members of the General Staff around John French and Secretary of State for War Richard B. Haldane to forgo the unprecedented ability of the German threat to mobilize the public[49] – a capability evident, for example, in the remarkable success of William Le Queux's *The Invasion of 1910*.[50]

In spring 1906, Repington and Roberts joined Lord Lovat and Samuel Scott, both financially powerful and officers in the volunteer forces, to create an informal committee that would soon be known as the conspiratorial-sounding 'Committee of Four'. Their goal was to ensure funds were made available to support the military and to showcase the German threat in order that the Committee of Imperial Defence would undertake a new investigation.[51] Roberts' principal function was as a gateway to what Repington termed the 'big people',[52] for the 74-year-old war hero could contribute little to the committee's conceptual thinking. 'Bobs' struggled to come to terms with the demands of the modern media.[53] According to Repington, his arguments lacked force and the necessary focus on a single enemy. To make the case for a standing army of one million men, a nightmare scenario would need to be hammered home. Memories of distant colonial wars were not what was needed, and in light of discussions between Britain and Russia and Britain and France, Roberts' references to Russia were not helpful.[54] In military circles, Russia had long been deemed invulnerable, and any plans in that direction therefore seemed unlikely to draw much enthusiasm. That left only one credible enemy. At the latest as a member of the Coefficients, Repington had become convinced that the real bogeyman was Germany.[55]

With his close personal ties to the new General Staff, Repington was motivated by a number of factors: (1) the idea of a powerful, offensive British army that would be the equal to the armies of the continent; (2) the conviction that this new army should be formed at the expense of the Royal Navy, which had dominated imperial defence to date;[56] he stated openly to Esher, 'Until we have put an end to all the damned nonsense that is written about sea power, we shall never get our national army';[57] (3) the desire to see the 'martial spirit' of his fellow British bolstered; and (4) his pursuit, as an unofficial facilitator of the discussions between the British and French General Staff,[58] of a foreign policy firmly directed at the creation of a security bloc that included Paris and St Petersburg. Repington believed Britain's arch-enemy Russia to be the country's only long-term threat, despite Russia's devastating defeat by Japan and irrespective of whether Germany built up its High Seas Fleet. Britain neither could nor should stand in the way of Russia's relentless advance into Slav lands; instead, he opined, London should seek to appease Russia with political concessions and to draw Russia in via France in order to keep the tsardom under control – at least until Britain had made the necessary military preparations for what might come.[59] For Repington, Germany was the ideal enemy to serve up to the British public and to his army friends,[60] and he had no qualms about falsifying information to Germany's disadvantage. He had learned, for example, from his French interlocutors that despite the Entente Cordiale, France was continuing its usual planning for an invasion of Britain;[61] he took that information back to his fellow countrymen but plugged in Germany as the schemer in place of France, even though by the turn of the century Berlin had already established that an invasion of Britain was not a realistic option.[62] In their numerous public appearances, which included panel discussions, articles in the *Times*, the *National Review* and the *National Defence*, and anonymous contributions in other newspapers and journals, Repington and Roberts, now supported by Leo Maxse, John Strachey and James Garvin, sought to use the risk of invasion to put pressure on the government to carry out a reform of the army and to criticize what they believed was the misguided policy of the Admiralty.[63] The latter approach automatically built ties to Fisher's critics within the Admiralty, and to Charles Beresford in particular.[64]

Exploiting the commotion created by Le Queux's novel *The Invasion of 1910*, from late summer 1906 Repington generated an upsurge in agitation with a run of supposedly new and certainly sensational revelations in the *Times*.[65] Again, his principal goal was to demonstrate the relevance and necessity of the army, first as an instrument of defence and secondly, and very much in line with the ideas of the General Staff, as, in Edward Grey's words, a 'projectile fired by the Navy'.[66] The army was to be thought of as an expeditionary weapon. Repington's claims were downright absurd. In an article in the *Times* entitled 'Moltke and Overseas Invasion', he cited as clear evidence of German plans for Britain the Prussian occupation of the island of Als in 1864, during the war between Prussia and Denmark. He claimed the Prussian military leadership had seen that operation as an opportunity to practise for a future conquest of Britain and that it now served the Prussian General Staff as a model for an impending landing on the British coast.[67] The article, so he had informed his friend, Colonel Raymond J. Marker, in advance of its publication, would be a 'nasty jar for the Blue Water fanatics', and, he suggested, 'the only way out for them will be to declare that Moltke was an ass'.[68]

Over the following months, an at times heated debate was staged, in which 'no periodical, great or small' could fail to participate, encouraging the publication of further fictional accounts of invasion and spying.[69] A contemporary record described how 'the newspapers of the breakfast table, the reviews of the clubs, even the "society" journals teem with articles of more or less interest on naval topics'.[70] Repington's dispute with the representatives of the Blue Water School was conducted in the august pages of the *Times*,[71] as blows were exchanged in the letters to the editor and in op-ed articles. The nature of the arguments, and the intentions and expectations that lay behind those arguments, could hardly have been more different. Repington missed no opportunity to voice his theories and to demand a new investigation by the Committee of Imperial Defence, whether at events organized by the National Defence Association, as a member of the Marlborough Club, where he dined regularly with the Prince of Wales and Haldane, secretary of state for war,[72] or in other newspapers and journals, with the support of Garvin, Strachey and Maxse.

Repington's critics – foremost among them were Arnold-Forster, George Clarke, who was secretary to the Committee of Imperial Defence, and a colleague of Repington's at the *Times*, Richard Thursfield, alias 'Navalis', who was that newspaper's naval correspondent – approached the various claims as objectively as possible.[73] They demonstrated down to the last detail just how grotesque and historically inaccurate were Repington's claims that the crossing of the 700-yard-wide Alsenfjord had been a test case for an invasion of Britain.[74] Yet all their detailed objections could apparently do nothing to stem the impact of his claims, and their meticulous refutations served instead only to prolong and intensify the debate.[75] For months, the *Times* continued to provide the broader public with a very one-sided debate, with the Blue Water party's increasingly complex arguments tackling issues such as water depths, tides and tonnage capacities,[76] while the other party parried with a highly suspect employment of historical facts and unproven claims[77] based solely on the public mood.[78] Repington adopted the style of the *National Review* and made no secret that his main aim was to ensure that the public remained up in arms.[79] To that end, he willingly admitted, he practically coveted the vehement refutation by Richard Thursfield, his colleague at the *Times*.[80] His efforts generated a massive sense of outrage that could not be reversed, even for members of the Foreign Office, by subsequent clarification.[81] Masterfully, Repington deployed his crass simplifications to boost initial suspicions, and in November 1906 he noted to Roberts: 'We are greatly in need of a strong civilian pen to back us up. ... The more frock coats and mutton-chop whistlers we can whip up the better'.[82]

The new government was surprisingly quiet. Neither Asquith nor Grey was much concerned with military issues, and the new secretary of state for war, Richard B. Haldane, who was equally inexperienced, saw the general alarm as primarily a political opportunity for his reform plans. Balfour, former prime minister and defence politician, was a very different matter. Having invested so much energy in his own investigations of the invasion risk two years earlier, he wondered if the situation was really now so essentially different.[83] Clarke assured him, 'Nothing has happened or is likely to happen which will in any way invalidate the reasoning of your speech'.[84] In the meantime, however, the discussion had developed a momentum of its own, such that even the construction of the dreadnoughts could not allay the widespread unease. For Clarke, rearmament by Germany or any other state was not to blame; rather, as he acknowledged in the foreword to a new edition of his standard text *On Defence*,[85] those concerns were solely attributable to deliberate campaigning by a number of writers and politicians.[86] Roberts and others – deemed by Clarke to be no more than troublemakers – had, he wrote, developed a habit of jumping to any conclusion that appeared quickly, pithily and effortlessly to support the cause of a wholesale increase in Britain's military strength. In the political sphere, they had, he noted, an automatic advantage over more sober discussions, which were handicapped by appearing overly complex and seeming to require too much time and effort. Clarke was exactly right when he described the problematic nature of the modern popular press, which was making it increasingly difficult to base decisions on the facts alone.[87] As Clarke searched for objectivity and warned of the unforeseeable results of such public hysteria,[88] Roberts and Repington continued their campaign undaunted. When it came to the media, their detractors had been fighting a losing battle from the start.[89]

At the turn of the year 1906/7, the tone of the debate sharpened perceptibly. Renowned publications now took their own stand for[90] and against[91] the idea that Britain was under threat. Admiral Fisher for one was deeply concerned by the rekindled campaign. The greatest secret of a successful government, he had once declared to Balfour, 'is an intelligent anticipation of agitation',[92] and on that basis he now deemed it vital that Repington's assertions not go unrefuted, left to spread unhindered. The best response, he insisted, was a publishing broadside directed against 'uninformed and ignorant editors'.[93]

> I enclose a copy of the report of our invaluable and trustworthy Naval Attaché at Berlin [Dumas.]. ... Four points should be reiterated all over the country:
> 1. Not a single battleship had been laid down by a European Power in the past twelve months;
> 2. In the same period England had built the Dreadnought and had laid down three *invincibles* which were practically *dreadnoughts*;
> 3. The Navy was preparing to lay down three more *dreadnoughts*;
> 4. There was no foundation for stories that the Germans were building larger and more powerful *dreadnoughts*.[94]

Coming from someone so eager to use every potential threat as a chance to commission new ships, these instructions are all the more remarkable. Fisher also used the opportunity to congratulate Arnold White on his creation of the term 'Blue Funk School', which he thought a wonderful riposte to Repington's attack on the naval leadership: 'It's splendid! ... The Blue Funk School want to spend more money on soldiers in the ridiculous delusion, fostered by military quill drivers, who predominate in the press, that invasion is possible'.[95] Fisher was so impressed by Clarke's series of articles under the heading 'The Bolt from the Blue School' that he had them distributed as a memorandum to the Admiralty.[96]

The First Sea Lord had nothing but contempt for views on naval issues provided by unqualified 'nincompoops'.[97] He held that party politics pure and simple lay behind the current anti-German press campaign,[98] and he believed the circle around his arch-enemy Admiral Charles Beresford to be the guiding spirit of the invasion hysteria. His suspicions would soon be proved correct, for not only was Beresford scheming internally against Fisher, but he had instructed his chief of staff Frederick Sturdee to pass on to the Committee of Four secret information about the allocation of forces and the strengths and weaknesses of individual units.[99] Fisher also believed Hardinge, who, he knew, was also making the case for a threat from Germany, entirely wrong in his assumptions for, Fisher insisted, 'The real truth is we have enormously increased both our readiness for war and our instant fighting strength'. Yet, when combined with government party's disarmament demands, making public the details of Britain's impressive military strength could be suicide for reform plans and naval politics.[100]

In his correspondence with Tweedmouth from late September to mid October, Fisher set down his impressions,[101] recording that he believed the public outcry had nothing to do with external developments but was a product of party interests above all.[102] In light of generally positive developments and the advance of reforms, he even recommended to Tweedmouth that the dreadnought production planned for the current fiscal year be put on ice, as long as his ambitious construction plans had not been replicated abroad. Appointed by the Tories to keep a close eye on the budget, he had resolved to take a demonstrative stand against public scaremongering and at precisely this juncture insisted that parliamentary approval of the budget did not mean that the Admiralty could spend its funds however it wanted. Certainly, he had one eye on his own reform policy, for joining in with the chorus of invasion adherents would have meant an enormous loss in prestige and trust for the Royal Navy and for Fisher himself, as its supreme commander. His assessment, however, was founded on the figures.

> Again *and this requires to be most prominently and emphatically reiterated, ad nauseam*: We are not going to be frightened by foreign paper programmes (the bogey of agitators) ... when foreigners actually build, *then* we will double. ... Our present margin of superiority over Germany (*our only possible foe for years*) is so great as to render it absurd in the extreme to talk of anything endangering our naval supremacy, *even if we stopped all shipbuilding altogether!!!* [All italics original][103]

Alongside construction, Fisher invoked international constellations. Surprisingly, of his own accord he rejected the pure two-power standard, giving preference to the politically adjusted power-balance model favoured by the Tories.[104] For the years to come, the Kaiserreich appeared, he wrote, 'the only possible foe', but in practical terms this scenario was highly unrealistic: 'For years and years to come it is simply impossible for Germany to cope with us single handed and she has no naval ally'. Neither Austria-Hungary nor Italy would ever join Germany against Britain. In light of their new ties, France was also eliminated as a possible opponent of Britain, while Japan was out of Germany's range and was in any case more likely to be a threat to Germany's interests in the Far East than an ally.[105] In other words, in light of Downing Street's promises on social policy, it was a stroke of good luck that Germany, and not France or another sea power, was seen as Britain's potential enemy, for money could be saved while Britain's supremacy was maintained. With their concentration on the Anglo-German naval arms race, historians have often overlooked that such tensions involving British military policy, defence policy and party politics were essential to London's foreign policy.[106]

Appointed as a reformer by Balfour and Selborne, Fisher achieved his greatest savings after the Boer War. Redeployment and concentration on a single opponent, instead of several, also contributed, saving £250,000 annually.[107] Fisher saw in a Liberal government, which he had always feared, the risk that these successes would prove a Pyrrhic victory.[108] He believed his worries confirmed in autumn 1906 when the new government failed to protect him from attacks or to take a stand on Repington's blatant propaganda. Fisher's overall concept was based on an increase in efficiency by means of, for example, innovation, flexible regroupings, new training structures and the nucleus-crew system, which doubtless saved enormous sums. Expensive election gifts had no place, and he was therefore all the more frustrated when the Liberal government, which had come to power on the back of a Lib(eral)-Lab(our) campaign, wished to show its gratitude to a clientele that was ready to support striking.[109] Via an employment programme that was in part justified by the 'German peril', the government ensured that the state-run shipbuilders had 'spasmodic entries of Dockyard workmen'. Where the previous government had urged the workers on with calls for greater savings, now thousands of new workers were subsidized although the situation was not precarious and no new orders required them to be hired. According to Fisher, the additional costs for the new shipyard workers could have paid for the construction and maintenance of three of the most up-to-date battle-cruisers. In terms of the economy as a whole, in the long run it would be 'simply ruinous to the private shipbuilding trade to reduce the work that can be given to them by swollen numbers of workmen at Government Dockyards'.[110] In Britain, too, it seems, invented risks were used to generate artificial orders. The German peril thus not only preoccupied the people but also created actual work for them.

Fisher was fighting battles on numerous fronts, external as well as internal. To characterize him as a supporter of the invasion theory and an enemy of Germany therefore seems too simple and too rash. Certainly, he expressed his scepticism and on occasion even his plans for a pre-emptive war, but his thoughts were not directed just at Germany, for he stated similar concerns about Russia and France. More importantly, he ensured that Berlin knew his thinking, as a means to scare off German thoughts of further adventures. Repeating a model Lansdowne and Balfour had used for the Wilhelmstrasse during the Morocco crisis, Fisher sought to convey and demonstrate Britain's strength, admitting in July 1905: 'I've taken means to have it whispered in the German Emperor's ear!'[111] He was, however, opposed to a secret amphibious attack that would be carried out in cooperation with France.[112]

Again, the differences between Fisher and Repington or between Fisher and the new political leadership could hardly have been greater.[113] Fisher repeatedly emphasized the strength of the Royal Navy,[114] a reflection, naturally, of his concerns for his own programme of reform and for his own prestige and for the prestige of the navy in relation to the land forces, although the data also supported his arguments. But the greater the advantage, all the greater would be the radicals' demands for some form of peace dividend. British strength was a fact, but in early January 1907, Fisher responded to the continuing attacks in the *National Review* and *Spectator* by noting that there was another truth to consider: 'The real truth is, we don't want anyone to know the truth'.[115] Tirpitz and Wilhelm II were well aware that the British navy was far stronger than the German navy, but Fisher's concern was not just that the public abroad be left in the dark, for, as he noted, 'we don't want to parade all this, because if so we shall have parliamentary trouble'. The 150 radical liberals led by John Brunner and

Henry Campbell-Bannerman already had a very good grasp of the facts, and had sent Fisher what he termed 'one of the best papers I have read ... convincingly showing that we don't want to lay down any new ships at all – *we are so strong*. It is quite true!' [italics original].[116] In light of British strength, and with Germany now Britain's only likely enemy, the Admiralty recognized it was a 'common sense conclusion that the outlying Fleets no longer require to be maintained at the strength which was admittedly necessary a year ago when France and Russia were our most probable opponents'.[117]

The supporters of the invasion threat needed the invasion threat, as Arnold-Forster acknowledged: 'If they were to propose conscription only for foreign service they would utterly fail to move public opinion'.[118] Britain's security was kept to the fore, but at the same time the traditional anti-Russian resentments of the radical liberals and a number of Conservatives took the discussion in other directions.[119] Repington himself admitted that the agitation was not really about Germany and its High Seas Fleet. The Channel Fleet, he noted,

> is by itself a match for the German fleet, and reinforced by the Atlantic Fleet, it has an overwhelming superiority in the world. ... The truth is ... our superiority over Germany is so overwhelming and the superiority of our personnel and of our gunnery practice is so great, that the Germans know it would be madness for them to provoke war.[120]

In summer 1907, the Committee of Four got its wish – a new fact-finding committee was set up.[121] Its creation cannot be rationalized by the traditional action/reaction model, and is explained instead by the complex inner workings of British foreign policy. Fisher had been unable to convince the British people that the British defensive situation was excellent, and the very creation of the new investigation was a vote of no confidence and marked a lasting defeat at the hands of the army lobby. Clarke confirmed that impression. If agitators like Repington were able to shake the people's faith in the Royal Navy, he warned Balfour, 'then clearly we have no possible basis for military organisation except compulsion'.[122] But, he also noted, 'numerous writers in this country have been endeavouring for some time to create a German Scare ... It is clear that this propaganda has produced a certain feeling of uneasiness and suspicion of which it is necessary to take account'.[123]

Although both Balfour and Clarke remained convinced that Britain was in no danger, in the end they agreed to a new investigation – Clarke because, much as in 1905, he hoped that the publication of its conclusions would calm the situation and perhaps even lead to joint planning by the two services,[124] and Balfour because as the leader of the opposition he recognized an opportunity to draw out the new government onto the terrain of defence policy and perhaps even cause a renewed split.[125]

The Second Inquiry: 'Blue Water' versus 'Blue Funk'

Right up until the last moment, John Fisher, Julian Corbett and Admiral Edmond Slade, the new director of naval intelligence, attempted to avert a renewed investigation of the danger from Germany, which would be, they believed, a 'master piece of funk'[126] and 'waste of time'.[127] Although all the results presented by the Committee of Four had been refuted in detail both internally and publicly,[128] on 27 November 1907 a second investigation of the threat to the British Isles was launched by the Committee of Imperial Defence.[129] The new inquiry had not been made necessary by a change in Britain's situation; indeed, Corbett and other experts believed that Britain had even less to worry about than three years earlier.[130] Repington's offer to end the invasion-scare campaign if Fisher would support universal military service speaks for itself.[131] The real reasons for the inquiry lay in an increasingly complex convergence of domestic factors: the continuing conflict between the navy and army lobbies,[132] the increasingly vociferous campaign by the press against Germany and in favour of rearmament, and the feud between Fisher and Beresford,[133] which threatened to divide the Royal Navy, for Beresford never missed a chance to discredit the First Sea Lord, even going as far as open insubordination and the betrayal of secret information.[134] The decisive factor, however, was a paradigm change, a product of the change in government, in how the public debate over Britain's security was handled. Where, largely as a result of Balfour's interest in defence, the Conservative government had worked closely with Fisher, Battenberg and Clarke and had attempted to counter the scaremongering, the liberal imperialists in particular were eager to use the continuing debate to their own advantage – in foreign policy terms it highlighted the relevance of the navy and the advantages of having Britain as an ally, while internally it legitimized closer ties with Britain's former arch-rivals and could be used to counter the radical liberals' thoughts of disarmament.[135] Asquith, Grey and Haldane pointedly refrained from contradicting the invasion-related rumours. Most notably, the government also made no effort to protect Britain's most senior admiral from outrageous defamation and what was in effect a smear campaign, which came to a climax when Leo Maxse repeatedly branded Fisher 'a traitor to his country and a panderer to Germany' and a man 'who ought to be hung at his own yard arm'.[136] Rather than put a halt to Beresford's transparent tactics, Asquith even took his side publicly, and he repeatedly threatened to join with the radical liberals and to use his popularity to split the party and divide the Royal Navy.[137]

Lord Esher was undoubtedly one of the most significant supporters of the adherents of the invasion theory.[138] As was typical of his generation, he believed a major war in the course of the twentieth century inevitable, whoever Britain's opponent might be. A military reformer who had played a decisive role in the introduction of the General Staff and the continental orientation that ensued, he saw it as his duty to ensure that Britain and the British people were ready for war. As long as the Conservatives were in power, led by a prime minister well versed in defence policy and a foreign secretary who had previously been secretary of state for war, he had believed it safe to declare, both internally and publicly, any invasion of the British Isles, even if the Royal Navy were defeated, completely impossible.[139] Since then, however, Fisher's public assertions of the outstanding strength of the Royal Navy had seemed to him too much.[140] He therefore called for a new inquiry, even though internal discussions suggest that he remained convinced that the idea that Britain faced any real danger was absurd.[141]

For Esher, however – and he also convinced Clarke – what was really at stake was the broader political reality under Liberal leadership, and in particular party unity and an end to the rivalry between the services. Solidarity across the armed forces was key to countering the disarmament demands being voiced by the radical liberal majority.[142] To Esher's mind, the First Sea Lord now needed to think in political terms, and rather than worry about how the debate over a possible invasion might harm the reputation of the navy, he should look to how to exploit the hysteria. Yes, he admitted to Fisher in mid October 1907, the German threat was a 'bogey. Granted'. But, he continued, 'it is a most useful one'. For Esher, it was only of peripheral significance that, in light of naval strategy and the tactics demanded by war at sea, the First Sea Lord preferred a completely different weapons system and therefore had to put his case very differently. For Esher, the realities of the security situation were also only a matter of detail. A nightmare scenario would not only awaken the 'martial spirit' of the nation, but would also ensure that the construction of additional dreadnoughts was included in the budget.[143] That nightmare scenario would also work in favour of the army,[144] as Roberts had stressed to the committee of inquiry, for Balfour's reassurance had been counterproductive when it came to finding new recruits.[145] Esher saw in the fashioning and instrumentalization of the German threat an opportunity for the long-overdue reforms of Britain and its aging social and political structures.[146] In a letter to Roberts, he drew on Darwinist principles to explain his ideas for a professionally organized propaganda machine that could be deployed in peacetime:

> There is but one solution – i.e. to convince the English people, much against their will, of their peril ... If history has any teaching for us, it is that *our* day of trial must come, and that without adequate preparation we cannot avoid the fate of other nations. ... We require writers and lecturers, *not* labelled as paid agents, but with an appearance of independence. These men *have* to be paid, because those who are most capable are not wealthy enough to do the work gratis, and the work is one of converting the nation to an idea which it is anxious to put aside as long as possible; and time presses. When we consider the vast sums which men spend on their pleasures, on 'works of art', and

futilities of all kind, it would not be asking much of a few rich men ... to enable us to carry through a systematic cause of 'education' of the country before the next general election. [Emphasis in original][147]

Esher found in the Committee of Four, in journalists such as Strachey, Maxse and Garvin, and in novelists such as Childers and Le Queux, propagandists willing to work for free in the cause of militarization.

While the diplomatic performance of Germany proved disastrous, the German military machine was expected to perform miracles. In all seriousness, Repington, Roberts, Lovat and Scott spoke to the advisors on the Committee of Imperial Defence of Germany's ability to transport 150,000 solders, 200 guns and 7,000 horses to their ports in complete secrecy, have them embark within only a few hours, and then have them land on the coast of England, largely unnoticed, at a rate of 20,000 infantrymen an hour.[148] When we consider the standard time required by an army corps to deploy in the field,[149] the problems faced by the Japanese in their amphibious operations against Russia, and the results of the British manoeuvres that indicated that even under the best conditions 12,000 soldiers would require over thirty hours for a landing, their depiction is revealed to have been sheer fantasy.[150]

Their claims could not stand up to detailed examination. Alfred Vagts, an expert on landing operations undertaken throughout history, was not alone when he declared them 'shockers'.[151] With their knowledge of the logistical and meteorological challenges that amphibious operations faced, George Clarke, Julian Corbett and Admirals Slade, Battenberg and Colomb were highly dubious of the findings that had been presented to them.[152] These narratives made no mention of tides or of problems that might be faced during the crossing, and they were silent on how such an operation could possibly be kept secret.[153] It would take at least thirty hours to cross the 360 nautical miles that lay between Hamburg and the English coast, and the smoke produced by such an invasion fleet would be visible 30 nautical miles away.[154] How could either the requisitioning of a merchant fleet of at least 250,000 gross register tons or the embarkation of so many men and so much equipment be kept secret, with the latter requiring normal operations in a number of large ports and centres that handled goods from throughout the world to be brought to a halt simultaneously and for days on end.[155]

Carried away by their own descriptions, Repington and Lovat believed they had left a lasting impression on their audience.[156] And indeed, the politicians present were impressed by the potential German threat.[157] The experts, however, had no difficulty in dissecting their claims, showing their information to be full of fabrications and making Repington and Roberts, with their ignorance of amphibious operations, seem very foolish.[158] Roberts, who has continued to be seen as an eminent authority on all things military,[159] left an especially poor impression. He proved entirely out of his depth when it came to the specifics of an amphibious operation and was unable to answer a single question. Repington, although undoubtedly a brilliant propagandist and self-publicist, was unable to make up for Roberts' failings.

Corbett recognized that Repington had simply swallowed Mahan's conclusions for the eighteenth century.[160] Repington and Roberts had not the least understanding of strategic or tactical concerns, let alone of the relevance of the modern technology found, for example, in torpedoes, the telegraph, submarines or of the greater speed at which battles at sea were now fought.[161] According to Corbett, over-reliance on Mahan meant that it was now common for 'Clausewitzian land theories' to be transferred wholesale for 'sea purposes'.[162] An expression of that problem, he noted, could be found in the exaggerated weight placed by both the public and politicians on decisive battles, the inner line, large battle fleets, battleships or tonnage, and 'command of the sea', a term too easily banded around to describe Britain's superiority at sea. As his publications demonstrate, Corbett thought very differently. For him, the task of a large fleet was to keep enemy battleships at bay.[163] The decisive role in defending against an invasion would be played not by battleships but by individual flotillas operating independently.[164] The future of sea power was all about new technologies and the intelligence advantage. Temporary loss of 'command of the sea', which for Corbett meant control of communications and contacts at sea, did not mean that the opponent then automatically had the upper hand. In three out of five of the great sea battles of the past, England had lost that command entirely, he noted, but had still won the war. The idea that if Britain lost command of the sea, then Britain too was lost ignored the effectiveness of strategic defence, whose value had been increased tenfold by new developments, and was based far too closely on strategy on land.[165] When Corbett turned specifically to Germany, it was to emphasize Germany's geographical challenges. While in the past Britain's enemies had always had access to nearby ports on the Atlantic, Germany was dependent on a narrow, and easily blockaded, exit to the Atlantic.[166] Corbett thus repeated Balfour's earlier arguments and even anticipated the use of the distance blockade.[167]

Corbett and the committee of inquiry got to the heart of the matter. Yet with their concentration on British concerns about the German High Seas Fleet, historians continue to overlook those same facts. Today's research makes too little distinction between statements by diplomats, politicians, journalists and army officers on invasion theory and navy size and, taking all such information too readily for contemporary expert opinion, they too easily conclude that London had no choice but to respond to the German challenge. Simply because they spoke about naval matters, Roberts and Repington are seen as naval experts.[168] To the historical analysis it makes a difference whether the challenge from Germany 'was seen as a real one',[169] whether the German striking power was a real one or whether it was overestimated. Although misperceptions do matter and belong to the whole decision-making process,[170] it falls short not to look beyond mere (mis)perceptions and ask about inner motives and their causes.[171] For Matthew Seligmann, by 1906 naval and army representatives alike were 'harbingers of the German menace'.[172] Yet these interpretations take no account of the motivations that might lie behind such conclusions or the context in which they were made. Naval advisors deemed the danger far smaller than did their army rivals. The rivalry between the services could have definitive impact on the positions adopted by each party. While the representatives of the army were primarily interested in proving the existence of a threat that would legitimize the creation of a far larger army, Fisher was eager to defend his reforms, his reputation and the role of the Royal Navy as the first line of defence. Corbett and Slade introduced much more plausible arguments and highlighted the differences between the navy and land forces. Corbett's well-founded counterarguments, especially his relativizing explanations of the concept of the 'command of the seas' and of the value of innovations and strategic defence – ideas that can only be noted here and certainly deserve further study[173] – provided the political decision makers with an alternative to participation in a race to re-arm, which provides in turn an alternative to the usual reading that says Britain was bound to respond to the challenge and enter the naval race and to depictions of widespread militarism before 1914.

The existence of that alternative was grasped by Balfour, who had sought to make sense of the available information for himself. In May 1908, when he appeared as a witness at the inquiry being conducted by the Committee of Imperial Defence, he was still unperturbed. His statement was described as 'lasting about an hour, quite perfect in form and language, and most closely reasoned', and Esher recorded privately in his diary: 'not a question was put to him. Asquith, Grey, Haldane, Crewe, Lloyd George. All were equally dumbfounded'.[174] In essence, Balfour abided by his position of May 1905. Britain's security continued to be guaranteed by the Royal Navy and new developments would only benefit Britain and reinforce its supremacy at sea.[175] Although the convention with St Petersburg had been concluded since the last enquiry, Balfour continued to identify Russia as Britain's most likely opponent.[176] He thought Germany would try invasion only if it had its back to the wall and was fighting for its survival.[177] Slade was so impressed that he designated Balfour's speech 'most excellent' and recounted that Balfour had 'summed up the whole situation in a most remarkable manner';[178] Esher, too, had to admire Balfour's 'masterly knowledge'.[179] In light of the overwhelming evidence, Esher and Haldane could only admit that Britain had nothing to fear even from an alliance between Germany and France.[180] Haldane described Corbett's memorandum, which has been completely ignored by historians, as 'one of the most important state papers that he had ever seen'.[181]

Table 7.2. 'British Fighting Fleet Compared' (31 March 1909)

	England	France	Germany	Italy	USA	Russia	Japan
Battleships							
First Class	49 (8)	26 [33][a]	32[b]	8 (1)	26 (6)[c]	13 (4)	14 (4)
(Pre-Dreadnought Class)							
Semi-Dreadnoughts[d]	2	(6)	0	0	0	0	0
(Lord Nelson Class)							
Dreadnought-Class	2 (6)	0	(10)	0	(6)	0	0
Battle-Cruisers	3 (1)	(2)	(2)	(3)	0	(2)	(2)
Invincible-Class							
Armoured (1st Class)	38	20	8[e]	7	15	14	11
Protected (2nd Class)	72 (5)	28	33 (7)[f]	16	21	11	20 (1)
Unprotected (3rd Class)	(2)	–	11	–	10	2	7
Torpedo-boat destroyers	146 (25)	56 (21)	73 (24)[g]	17	20 (15)	97	55 (3)
Torpedo boats	30[h]	269	77 (30)	66	32	154	77
Submarines	45 (23)	49 (55)	4 (4)[i]	7	12 (16)	24 (11)	9 (2)

Whitaker, *Whitaker's Almanack* 1910, 473, 615, 646–47; Excubitor (Hurd) 'British Reply', FR 3/1908, 461; Dilke, Fleets, HCPP, AP 137, 6 May 1909, 577–649. Figures in parentheses indicate ships under construction.

[a]This is the number of ships if one adopts the same counting method as in the German case; [b]The figure 32 is reached only by including 15 pocket battleships built since 1870 and partly obsolete as well as the 'Große Kreuzer'. The real number was 24, including the pre-dreadnoughts since 1890. Prochnow, *Deutsche Kriegsschiffe*, Vol. 1, 23–52; Dumas, Report, 3/07, 29 Jan. 1907, cited in Seligmann, *Naval Intelligence from Germany*, No. 24, 59–73, 60; [c]See Dilke, Fleets, HCPP, AP 137, 6 May 1909, 577–649, 579; [d]In contrast to the 'all-big-gun-ships' of the dreadnought type, this class of ship carried a mixture of gun type; [e]See Seligmann, *Naval Intelligence from Germany*, 100–108; Breyer, *Hochseeflotte*, 12; [f]See Prochnow, *Deutsche Kriegsschiffe*, Vol. 2, passim; [g]See Prochnow, *Deutsche Kriegsschiffe*, Vol. 3, passim; [h]See Dumas, Report, 3/07, 29 Jan. 1907, cited in Seligmann, *Naval Intelligence from Germany*, No. 24, 59–73, 60. According to *Nauticus*, in May 1909 England possessed 204 torpedo-boat destroyers and 55 submarines; see *Nauticus* (1909), 566; [i]See Prochnow, *Deutsche Kriegsschiffe*, Vol. 4, passim.

The expert opinions could be confirmed by a comparison of figures for naval construction drawn up at the time of the great invasion panic one year later. Germany had turned its efforts to new forms of torpedo boat and submarine, but we should not overlook the qualitative implications. For Germany, ships of this class were of too small tonnage to be employed other than in a defensive capacity, positioned close to the German coastline.[182]

Impressive for contemporaries and historians alike, the explosive growth in the number of German battleships – from eighteen in March 1906 to thirty-two three years later – has a single explanation: the statisticians were not immune to the general hysteria. They were evidently founded not on confirmed data but on future expectations, with some figures apparently drawn from thin air. In late 1906, the Kaiserreich had twenty ships of the pre-dreadnought era commissioned, not the thirty-two supposed. By 1913, Germany had twenty-three built and building instead of twenty-six, as is often assumed, while the Royal Navy had forty-four instead of forty-two.[183] Therefore, by 1914 the Royal Navy has reached a reassuring numerical margin over the next biggest naval powers, Germany and the United States, combined and more than 60 per cent over Germany alone.[184]

Although the facts should have been comforting for Britain, neither political agreement on military strength nor a reduction in tension in the London political sphere materialized. Attempts to come to an understanding with Germany failed repeatedly: in the run-up to the second Hague Convention;[185] in December 1907 when Germany sought a North Sea convention with Britain and France;[186] in February and March when Tirpitz[187] and Wilhelm II denied any challenge to British supremacy;[188] or in summer 1908 when Hardinge met the Kaiser at Kronberg.[189] According to the established view, right up until 1914, all opportunities for an understanding between Germany and Britain were blocked by the former's refusal to accept any limitation on a military build-up at sea. The fleet issue had been identified as *the* decisive obstacle.[190] Even with their improved knowledge of facts, the liberal imperial political leadership does not seem to have felt a call to calm the atmosphere, which could, in turn, have created foundations on which an understanding with Germany might have been constructed.

The evidence suggests that the leadership's lack of inclination to pursue an understanding with Germany was united with awareness of the potential usefulness of the current atmosphere. Although Haldane and Grey knew exactly how things stood, they continued to bluster about an imminent loss of British supremacy. While Haldane was eager to defend his army reform from the radicals and their enthusiasm for disarmament, Grey was thinking of France, and later Russia, and about the legitimization of his Entente policy and military expansion.[191] Asquith, as prime minister designate, was concerned about the makeup of his cabinet. Support for this interpretation is provided by the Tweedmouth affair, staged in March 1908 by Repington in combination with the *Times* and the *National Review*. Although often treated in light of Wilhelm II's damaging 'personal rule' and ill-conceived travels,[192] the event was above all an indication of the influence a single propagandist could now have on relations between Germany and Britain. Ostensibly, the turmoil was a product of Wilhelm II's tactlessness in sending a private letter to Lord Tweedmouth in which he denied that Germany had plans on British supremacy.[193] Tweedmouth was unwise enough to indulge his vanity and announce proudly to the London political world that the Kaiser had written to him personally. It was not long before the news reached Repington, who with all his media savvy immediately saw an opportunity to get back at his arch-enemy from the committee of inquiry. Tweedmouth was to pay for his 'impertinence' in exposing Repington and Roberts' ignorance of naval matters before the Committee of Imperial Defence:

> Yes, I hope my calculated indiscretion may do good to the cause we have at heart. We shall see how Tweedmouth gets out of it, but I fancy he may regret his impertinence to you, and his description of our little party as a 'ring of wild and self convinced alarmists'.[194]

After discussions with Esher, Repington launched his campaign in the *Times* on 6 March 1908 with the heading 'Under which King?' and flanked by articles by Buckle and Chirol and supported by Maxse's *National Review*. The correspondence was refashioned into the 'greatest outrage that has happened in our time'.[195] The argumentation adopted the standard character of the day, with Germany presented as up to its usual scheming,[196] although in practice the content of the letter was mundane.[197] Letters from enraged readers enabled the *Times* to make the impression, according to a note Slade made in his diary, that 'the whole of England and the Court is buzzing like a hive of bees'.[198] Asquith admitted that the letter had been composed 'in an entirely friendly spirit',[199] but he was taken with the fortuitous opportunity[200] to undermine Fisher's Blue Water group and 'to put "Cousin Reggie" [Reginald McKenna] in Tweedmouth's place'.[201] Grey, and not Wilhelm II, vetoed the publication of the correspondence, which would have done much to clear the air.[202]

Damage control, we should note, was a concern not just for Grey's colleagues on the left of the party, but also for Conservatives. While the radical press criticized the *Times* as a 'mischief-maker',[203] despite all their best efforts the conservative newspapers, and the *Morning Post* and the *Daily Telegraph* in particular, struggled to take offence at Germany's attitude. In the House of Commons, the *Times*'s campaign was criticized as 'mischievous'. Lansdowne, Balfour and numerous other Tory politicians took a stand against the *Times*, and George Hamilton, Lansdowne's brother-in-law, voiced his suspicions that the real roots of the affair lay in the tension within the Admiralty between those in Fisher's camp and those who stood behind Beresford and believed in the risk of invasion.[204] Even Edward VII, who tended to be very sensitive when it came to Britain's defence, called Repington's article the work of a propagandist with no principles, and he deemed it irresponsible that someone of Repington's ilk should have access, via the Committee of Imperial Defence, to secret papers.[205]

Again, Asquith, Grey and Haldane were noticeably quiet, hiding themselves behind less-than-convincing claims about an independent press.[206] When it came to defending Russian and French feelings, they had proved to have no scruples about calling Chirol and the *Times* to heel.[207] Lord Esher even noted his delight at Repington's propaganda success.[208] Unmerited by the occasion, these individual interests poisoned the well for relations between Berlin and London,[209] as was recognized by Slade, Ewart and Corbett, who were now eager, like Esher, to see the rivalry between the British army and Royal Navy halted, and identified in the German navy a way to bringing the services onto the same page, as long as the Royal Navy did not lose out in the process.[210] Slate recorded:

> The more I think of this invasion business the more I am pleased that it should have come up, and we ought now to have a very good chance of showing that the Army and the Navy are not two separate forces, but only divisions of one which should never have been thought of as apart from each other.[211]

Slade repeatedly took the sting out of Fisher's wild attacks as they were recorded in the committee's minutes, and together with Ewart sought to convince the naval secretary of the CID, Captain Charles Ottley, and the chief of staff, General William Nicholson, of the benefits of joint planning.[212] In order that a way forward for the two services might be found, the final record of the committee did not accurately reflect the results of its inquiries. It declared the possibility of a surprise attack to be 'not sufficiently remote to be ignored' and made the case for an army that would be large enough and well enough equipped 'not only to repel small raids'.[213] The Admiralty fell into line with public opinion, hoping to avoid further conflict with the army and with the public.[214]

The public disquiet continued even after the committee had concluded its work, and was evident throughout the summer and autumn in the London public sphere.[215] Against the background of increasingly apparent international tension, Balfour had advised Asquith to work to neutralize the anti-German propaganda, and he recommended that the prime minister announce as the official result of the investigative committee that Britain was militarily fully prepared to counter any threat to its security. The goal, Balfour explained, must be to avoid a public inquiry and further discussion in parliament, along with any incitement of public panic.[216] Yet that outcome appeared to be precisely what the Liberal government apparently did *not* want, and there remained 'an attitude of mystification and concealment'.[217]

Lord Roberts' invasion-focused speech given in the House of Lords in November 1908 created something of a sensation and was the polar opposite of what Balfour had recommended. Roberts made explicit reference to the fictional invasion literature, fantasized about '80,000 Germans in the United Kingdom, almost all of them trained soldiers' and just waiting to cut loose,[218] and demanded the creation of a 'risk army' that even the strongest armies in the world would not risk engaging. Rather than take on Roberts – Balfour had specifically asked Asquith to prevent Roberts from giving his speech, while Lansdowne and even Edward VII had appealed to Roberts to consider the international tensions and call off his plan[219] – Asquith, Grey and Haldane were in the audience, drawing even more attention to the event.[220] In the debate that followed, Lansdowne, Crewe and Cromer were left on their own to counter Roberts' absurd claims,[221] which even Repington, Roberts' speech writer, had admitted in private were so ridiculous as to be funny.[222] With the support of Lord Midleton (Brodrick), Cawdor, Lovat, Wemyss and Milner, the final vote approving the engagement of 150,000 additional soldiers was passed, with seventy-four votes in favour and thirty-two against.[223] Mensdorff suspected that the parliamentary debate had been designed to advertise Britain as an appealing partner for an alliance against the Central Powers and to persuade the British public to see Britain join such an alliance.[224] Fleet Street rejoiced and treated any response by Germany or Austria-Hungary that sought a compromise as further evidence of Berlin's perfidious plans.[225]

The Foreign Office had already resolved to fall into line with the now-widespread image of Germany. In February 1907, when Philip Dumas reported that Tirpitz had no intention of launching an invasion of England, the Foreign Office, and Edward Grey in particular, read his words as evidence that the German Grand Admiral planned precisely such an invasion but wanted to lull the nation into a false sense of security.[226] Again, the stereotyping so ingrained in British perception of Germany was evident. It counted for nothing that British experts, including Fisher, confirmed Dumas's report.[227] The pervasive image of Germany dovetailed too neatly with the British government's domestic and foreign policy. According to the conventional interpretation, the reality only became evident subsequently,[228] and only hindsight could reveal that the navy scare of 1909 was largely an invention by the new First Lord of the Admiralty, Reginald McKenna, that fell far short of the mark.[229] That position implies that Britain *had* to assume that Germany was being duplicitous.

Undoubtedly, the Central Powers, and in particular the Kaiserreich and its monarch, blundered and failed miserably and were always eager to make a strong and self-assertive impression, but that the impression and the reality did not align was hardly news. Reports of Germany's massive domestic and financial problems sent home by British envoys and the British ambassador in Berlin were too numerous not to have landed on the desks of Hardinge and Grey.[230] In summer 1906, Goschen had reported Germany's dependence on Austria-Hungary,[231] while in March 1907 he discovered just how unhappy German naval officers were about the German navy's precarious financial position.[232] Fairfax Cartwright, minister to Bavaria and Württemberg, and Ambassador Frank Lascelles, joined by charge d'affaires and counsellor in Berlin, John de Salis, from autumn 1907, also reported on the domestic difficulties facing the Kaiserreich.[233] While Lansdowne and Balfour had taken account of similar reports in their policy decisions,[234] such revelations appear to have been of little interest to the new political leadership or to the younger generation at the Foreign Office.

When it came to the German fleet, Whitehall surprisingly invested greater faith in Colonel Frederick Trench, who was the military attaché, than in Philip Dumas, the naval attaché.[235] For Trench, one of the most anti-German officers and military diplomats, the German General Staff seemed to be capable of anything.[236] Sanderson and Lascelles suspected that German ambitions were largely a product of the combination of an ideological surrogate construct that had followed on from German unification, wishful thinking and deliberations that lacked both financial and geopolitical foundations. Trench was not prepared to go an inch in this direction. While he deemed anti-British sentiments expressed in France and Russia entirely normal and increasingly less worthy of attention, his reports progressively made more of similar voices raised in Germany.[237] Trench's assessment of German capabilities appears to have been a product of his lack of faith in British potential, a result in turn of the traumatic experience of the Boer War. That attitude can be identified in his conjectures about the German General Staff's plans for an invasion of Britain, with even the idea that such a successful and secretly admired institution might consider such a plan eliciting a fatalistic response.[238] Trench was among those who did not place a great deal of faith in the British army, who saw every German holidaymaker in Britain as a reserve lieutenant tasked with spying, and who believed a lightning attack out of the blue all too possible and general conscription therefore essential. Even though the risk of invasion had been repeatedly rebutted, those who thought like Trench still found an audience in the liberal imperial leadership or in the Foreign Office. This grouping was fully convinced that since the time of Helmuth von Moltke, the German military had been committed to a conquest of Britain.[239] Although Edward VII had previously described the one-sided views of the invasion-theory supporters as forming a 'vicious circle',[240] he came to a rather different conclusion before his meeting with the Kaiser at Kronberg in summer 1908, when he suggested that Wilhelm II might 'throw a Corps d'armée or two into England'.[241]

According to Wolfgang Mommsen, at Kronberg Wilhelm 'harshly dispatched' Hardinge, thereby depriving German diplomacy of a 'great opportunity'.[242] Yet the stereotypes so beloved of British diplomacy when it came to Germany were very evident at Kronberg, along with a lack of pressure from London to come to any agreement, which meant that 'opportunity' was surely illusionary. Appearing to ignore the expertise available to the Committee of Imperial Defence over the previous months, Hardinge claimed that all England was well aware that in only a few years the German fleet would be superior to the Royal Navy.[243] Wilhelm II attempted to convince his interlocutor that no reasonable person in Germany had any thought of attacking Britain, and the Kaiser had the facts on his side when he spoke of Britain's navy being already far superior to the two-power standard and noted that in 1909 the Royal Navy would have sixty-two battleships to Germany's twenty-four.[244] Even if Hardinge disputed that comparison, evidently with figures proposed by Repington in mind – in Repington's fantasies Germany would have seventeen dreadnoughts to Britain's twenty[245] – the numbers cited by Wilhelm II were accurate.[246] Ambassador Metternich would also be entirely honest when, in February 1909, he informed Fisher in full detail about the German ships under construction or in planning.[247] The German programme of naval construction, the Kaiser sought to make clear to Hardinge, should give Britain no reason for nervousness. Certainly, viewed retrospectively, it was diplomatically inopportune that the Kaiser protested against interference in German armament plans, but that stance was hardly 'harsh'. Roosevelt similarly rejected any comment on or involvement in US plans for military construction, which were no less ambitious, and France and Russia would hardly have been amenable to demands from Britain to limit production. In the course of his discussion with the emperor, Hardinge pointedly ignored the data that was presented to him, deeming it entirely arbitrary and refusing even to glance in its direction. He was not to be moved from his longstanding conviction that the British coast lay exposed to an invasion by the largest military force in the world. Hardinge adopted almost line by line the arguments made by the Committee of Four, and believed that he was up against an 'immense German fleet'. Although he was well aware of the massive financial problems that Germany faced, and at a time when Germany had just launched the first dreadnought and not even started another one and the Royal Navy were seven dreadnoughts in advance, he believed it a 'common notoriety' that within only three or four years Germany would have more dreadnoughts than Britain.[248] Hardinge had no real expectation that Germany might back down, but he had good reason to see a positive in his dismissal by the Kaiser, for it justified for parliament and to the world any countermeasures that Britain might adopt.[249]

Subsequent initiatives also all came to nothing: in 1909 and 1910, Bethmann-Hollweg proposed to Ambassador Goschen that a naval convention might be held;[250] in March 1911, Kaiser Wilhelm II suggested an agreement on limiting military expenditure;[251] in February 1912, Haldane undertook his famous mission to Berlin;[252] in 1913, Churchill proposed a caesura in the building of battleships; and in summer 1914, Ernest Cassel and Albert Ballin made their final, and ultimately fruitless, efforts.[253] In ascribing the principal responsibility for the failure to reach an agreement on the German and British fleets to the Kaiserreich alone, the standard interpretation tells only part of the story, as is evident from Grey's correspondence with Lord Ripon, the leader of the liberal imperialists in the House of Lords. Grey repeatedly noted his concern that the discussions between Germany and Britain might anger the French.[254] When Germany proposed a convention in 1907, Ripon endorsed Grey's apprehension. Although Germany had already enquired in Paris whether France would have any objections to an Anglo-German understanding, and had even invited France to participate in a joint North Sea convention, Ripon noted that there was still danger 'of some misunderstanding arising if we enter into negotiations'. His worry was not for French feelings; a rather different explanation lay behind the desire to stymie any long-term rapprochement: 'It does not seem to me', Ripon confided, 'that a North Sea Convention would do us any good, and it might hamper us inconveniently in the future. All that we need in the North Sea is to have our hands quite free as they now are'.[255] Once again, it is evident that what really lay in the way of closer relations between Britain and Germany was not so much Berlin's naval laws as Berlin's inability to bring much to the table. London was therefore only prepared to negotiate if Britain seemed about to lose, or had already lost, its free rein. Neither Grey nor Ripon saw any need to deal with Germany on an issue where Britain already had the upper hand.

The discussions repeatedly stumbled because the parties involved had such different views – as a sovereign power, Germany refused, for example, to accept that the speed at which it might build up its military capability could be dictated by another power, while London rejected any suggestion that Britain might distance itself from the possibility of an unprovoked attack on the Central Powers – and were derailed by flashpoints such as the Tweedmouth affair. Personal vanities and tussles over jurisdiction, as in the cases of Beresford and Fisher or Repington and Tweedmouth, could be just as detrimental to potential rapprochement as were wishes to revive a 'martial spirit', budgetary or technological issues, or party-political debates between the pacifist and imperial wings of the governing Liberals. Additionally, the spectre of British dominance at sea and across the globe haunted discussions, and Britain, well aware of that superiority, felt no great pressure to make an alliance happen. Fisher repeatedly acknowledged that Germany's greatest fear was a pre-emptive strike against its expensive fleet. The negotiations therefore failed not so much because the weaker partner was too stubborn to allow itself to become any weaker, as because, and principally because, as American Andrew Carnegie observed, the stronger British party refused to compromise.[256] Grey believed it 'comparatively simple' to make foreign policy when he had the Royal Navy at his back.[257] To destroy the whole maritime and commercial efforts of Germany, Arthur Nicolson bragged in a minute, 'an afternoon's fight' might be enough.[258]

The German High Seas Fleet did not have the revolutionary impact on the stability of the Great Power system that has always been attributed to it. First of all, a strong navy was nothing exceptional and even the fundamental basis of being accepted as an imperial power. Secondly, it missed its revolutionary impact because British decision makers and their advisors already knew better, and thirdly because Britain had many options at hand. Militarily, technically and financially, London at any time was able to put on a quick burst of speed as the 'we want eight and we won't wait' (1909) debate showed[259] and diplomatically the Empire proved to be the gravitating force of the states system which had the biggest bargaining power at hand. The naval arms race and the views of British naval advisors served only to confirm that the members of the Entente had the greatest room to manoeuvre and the most extensive options, and therefore were in a position to control the international system. Anyone in the London political sphere, whether from the Foreign Office, the cabinet or the press, who examined the available evidence would have readily discovered that the German High Seas Fleet presented no real challenge to the island nation. The Germans were hardly in a position to invade Britain; they were more fearful of the loss of their fleet through a 'Copenhagening' – a seizure of the High Seas Battle Fleet by a surprise attack of the Royal Navy.[260] External strategic constraints were at least as decisive as domestic calculations when it came to Britain's diplomatic relationships with other powers. In order to exploit the German threat in order, in turn, to rally and mobilize the British population, the Liberal Party and the divided service departments, the Limps, who held the political reins, allowed the largely outrageous claims of the Blue Funk School to circulate unchallenged. Increasingly, they adopted the most basic judgements of public opinion. Bilateral solutions to the naval arms race were burdened just as much by that public pandering as by the lack of pressure from Whitehall to find a path to an alliance. The main goal, as described by Cecil Spring Rice, was always 'to create a new people, a people which thinks of its duties before its rights and which is ready to die'.[261] The German danger, Spring Rice insisted, must serve to maintain the British people 'warlike in spirit' and to ensure that the necessary funds were funnelled in that direction.[262]

Notes

1. See Steiner and Neilson, *Britain and the Origins*, 51–52; Williamson, *Politics of Grand Strategy*, 91–92; D'Ombrain, *War Machinery*, 220–24; Kennedy, *Rise of Anglo-German Antagonism*, 442–43; Charmley, *Splendid Isolation*, 350; Seligmann, *Naval Intelligence from Germany*, 105; Marder, FDSF I, 136; Dumas, Navy Bill, 2 Dec. 1907, BDFA F/XX, No. 75, 142–48.
2. Morris, *Scaremongers*.
3. Steiner and Neilson, *Britain and the Origins*, 51.
4. Lambi, *The Navy*, 290; Kennedy, *Rise of Anglo-German Antagonism*, 443; Steiner and Neilson, *Britain and the Origins*, 51–55; Woodward, *Great Britain and the German Navy*, 157–58; Padfield, *Great Naval Race*, 181–82; Berghahn, *Germany and the Approach*, 67; Williams, *Defending the Empire*, 89.

5. See Notes on Invasion supplied to Mr Balfour, June 1907; Note by Secretary, August 1907, NA, CAB 3/2/1/42A; Esher to Haldane, Campbell-Bannerman, Fisher, 24 Aug. 1907, JL II, 247; Dumas, 3 Oct. 1907, BDFA F/XX, No. 59, 121–22.
6. Steiner and Neilson, *Britain and the Origins*, 52; Lowe and Dockrill, *Mirage of Power*, 30–31.
7. Crowe to Dilke, 15 Oct. 1907, NA, FO 800/243. See also Crowe's private reports from the conference: BOD, MSS Crowe, MS Eng. d. 2901. For a different view, see Hewitson, *Germany*, 183–84.
8. Crowe to Dilke, 15 Oct. 1907, NA, FO 800/243; Anon., 'The Anglo-German Tension', *The Nation*, 6 Feb. 1909, 701–2.
9. See Charmley, *Splendid Isolation*, 350.
10. Stead to Campbell-Bannerman, cited in Stead, 'C.-B.: In Memoriam', RR 5/1908, 442–43.
11. Grey to Knollys, 12 Nov. 1906, cited in Lowe and Dockrill, *Mirage of Power*, 30.
12. Canis, '*Außenpolitik im letzten Jahrzehnt*', 110–11.
13. Fisher to Tweedmouth, 4 Oct. 1906, FGDN II, No. 50, 93–95.
14. See e.g. Kennedy, *Rise of Anglo-German Antagonism*, 251–88, esp. 279–80, 417–20; Steiner and Neilson, *Britain and the Origins*, 51–63; Harris, 'Britain', 269–70; Brechtken, *Scharnierzeit*, 82; Judd, 'Balfour', 35.
15. Seligmann, *Spies in Uniform*, 197.
16. Fisher to Tweedmouth, 26 Sept. 1906, FGDN II, No. 49, 90–93; Williams, *Defending the Empire*, 89–90.
17. Dumas, German Ships Laid down, Nov. 1907, cited in Seligmann, *Naval Route*, No. 82, 268 69. *SMS Nassau, Westfalen, Posen* and *Rheinland* were laid down between June and August 1907.
18. *The Times*, 11 Nov. 1907.
19. See, for example, his extensive correspondence with J.A. Spender.
20. Massie, *Dreadnought*, 445–46.
21. Schmidt, 'Rationalismus und Irrationalismus', 286, n. 6; Steinberg, 'Diplomatie'.
22. See Niedhart, 'Selektive Wahrnehmung', 141–57; Jervis, *Perception and Misperception*, passim.
23. See Schroeder, 'Embedded Counterfactuals', 165–81.
24. See Schmidt, 'Rationalismus und Irrationalismus', 283–95.
25. Grey, Minute, Bertie to Grey, 22 Nov. 1907, BD VI, No. 73, 105.
26. *The Times*, 23 Nov. 1905; Hurd, 'A Dreadnought Naval Policy', FR 12/1906, 1017–30, 1017.
27. Ropp, *Development of a Modern Navy*, 357; *The Times*, 23 Nov. 1905. The increase was in torpedo boats, destroyers and submarines. Only Germany had not geared up to follow that pattern, and in the short term even reduced its number of torpedo boats from eighty-four to seventy-two. See *The Times*, 17 April 1905; 23 Nov. 1905; see also Naval Intelligence Notes on German Submarines, 1902–1912, NA, ADM 137/3905; Prochnow, *Deutsche Kriegsschiffe*, Vol. 3, 8–54.
28. Ropp, *Development of a Modern Navy*, 357.
29. Fisher to Esher, 13 Sept. 1909, cited in Fisher, *Memories and Records*, 192–94.
30. Dumas, Report 3/07, 29 Jan. 1907, cited in Seligmann, *Naval Intelligence from Germany*, No. 24, 59–74, 60; Dumas, Report 7/07, 6 March 1907, No. 26, cited in ibid., 75–82, 81.

31. Hurd, 'A Dreadnought Naval Policy', FR 12/1906, 1017–30, 1017; see also Cd. 2335 and Cd. 2430.
32. Hurd, 'A Dreadnought Naval Policy', FR 12/1906, 1017–30, 1019–20; Dumas to Lascelles, 21 March 1907, BDFA F/XX, No. 11, 12–13. For Hurd, see Coerper to Tirpitz, 28 Nov. 1906, PA-AA, R 5578.
33. Grey, Minutes, Bertie to Grey, 22 Nov. 1907, BD VI, No. 73, 106.
34. *HMS Dreadnaught* commissioned, *HMS Bellerophon* launched, *HMS Temaire* launched, *HMS Superb* building, *HMS St Vincent*, *HMS Collingwood*, *HMS Vanguard* building and *HMS Invincible*, *Inflexible* and *Indomitable* launched.
35. That was incorrect: *SMS Nassau* was laid down on 22 July 1907.
36. Fisher to Edward VII, 4 Oct. 1907, FGDN II, No. 90, 139–43.
37. Stevenson, *Armaments*, 165; McKercher, 'Diplomatic Equipoise', 314–15.
38. Steiner and Neilson, *Britain and the Origins*, 52.
39. Repington to Marker, 14 April 1907, RL 43, 117. Again, the *National Review* was their mouthpiece in the media. H.W. Wilson, 'The Command of the Sea in Danger', NR 3/1905, cited in Maxse, *Germany on the Brain*, 156–58.
40. Fisher to Balfour, 29 Nov. 1907, BL, Add. 49712.
41. Arnold-Forster, *Memoir*, 345; Selborne, *The Times*, 26 Feb. 1903.
42. 'An Invasion … is always possible.' Roberts, 29 Jan. 1906, cited in Roberts, *Speeches and Letters*, 52.
43. Repington to Haldane, 17 April 1907, RL 44, 118–19; 19 April 1907, NLS, MSS 5907.
44. Roberts had previously been attacked by Strachey and Wemyss. See *The Times*, 15 March 1906.
45. Cited in Mills, *Decline and Fall*, 128.
46. Repington at the Aldershot Military Society, cited in Repington, *Peace Strategy* (1907), 13.
47. Repington to Marker, 19 July 1906, cited in D'Ombrain, *War Machinery*, 219–20, n. 35.
48. Wilson, Diary, 19 Jan. 1910, cited in D'Ombrain, *War Machinery*, 222.
49. Callwell, *Sir Henry Wilson*, Vol. 1, 93, 120; *Daily Mail*, 10 March, 13 April 1906; General French, cited in *Daily Mail*, 12 May 1906; Anon., 'Leading Books of the Month', RR 8/1906, 204.
50. See Chapter 1.
51. Repington to Maxse, 15 Oct. 1907, RL 48, 126.
52. Repington to Roberts, 22 Nov. 1906, NAM, MSS Roberts, R 62/9.
53. Repington to Marker, 5 July 1906, BL, Add. 52277B.
54. Repington to Marker, 2 Jan. 1906, BL, Add. 52277B.
55. Ryan, *Lieutenant-Colonel Charles à Court Repington*, 49–50.
56. Repington, *Vestigia*, 277.
57. Repington to Esher, 22 Nov. 1906, CC, ESHR 4/2.
58. Sanderson to Grey, 11 Jan. 1906, BD III, No. 210(b), 171–72; see also Ryan, *Lieutenant-Colonel Charles à Court Repington*, 68–85.
59. Repington to Marker, 15 Dec. 1905, RL 18, 68–70, 70.
60. Repington to Hutton, 13 March 1907, RL 42, 116–17; to Marker, 14 April 1907, RL 43, 117; Repington to Maxse, 11 March 1908, WSRO, MAXSE/458; to Garvin, 15 March 1908, RL 63, 145.
61. Repington to Roberts, 20 Nov. 1907, RL 51, 129–30.

62. See Steinberg, 'Copenhagen Complex', 28; Ritter, *Staatskunst*, Vol. 2, 195; Repington, *First World War*, Vol. 1, 10; Repington, 27 Nov. 1907, Sub-Committee of the CID, NA, CAB 16/3A, 33–34. One of Repington's informants was Major Huguet; see Repington to Roberts, 20 Nov. 1907, RL 51, 129–30; see also BA-MA, RM 5/1609–10.
63. Repington to Roberts, 28 July 1906, NAM, MSS Roberts, R 62/3. 'I am delighted to hear that you are still on the war path and I wish you success in your whole crusade with all my heart. It is most important that some of the leading civilian statesmen should support you for my reading of our modern history is that people of this country will not follow a soldier however eminent unless he is backed by the great guns of the Parliament.' Repington to Roberts, 15 Aug. 1906, NAM, MSS Roberts, R 62/6. For Spender, see Repington to Roberts, 29 Jan. 1908, RL 58, 139.
64. Fisher to Esher, 7 Oct. 1907, FGDN II, No. 91, 144–46.
65. *The Times*, 29 Aug. 1906.
66. Fisher, Notes, 22 Aug. 1907, NMM, CBT/6/4, 27.
67. *The Times*, 29 Aug. 1906.
68. Repington to Marker, 25 July 1906, BL, Add. 52277B.
69. In the course of the next six months there appeared: Wood, *The Enemy in our Midst*; Cornford, *The Defenceless Islands*, Oldmeadow, *The North Sea Bubble*; Vaux, *The Shock of Battle*; Vaux and Yexley, *When the Eagle Flies Seaward*. See also *Times Literary Supplement*, 5 Oct. 1906, 339. Hundreds of invasion stories were published in the period up to 1914.
70. Anon., 'The Truth about the Navy', ER, 1/1907, 169–91, 170.
71. *The Times*, 29, 30 Aug. 1906; 1, 4, 5, 7, 8, 15, 17, 20, 22 Sept. 1906; 4, 8, 9, 13, 16 Oct. 1906; 27, 28 Dec. 1906; 8 Jan. 1907; NR 11/1907, 468–84; USM 12/1907, 248–51; QR 7/1908, 295; *The Spectator*, 29 Sept. 1908, 438–40; Sydenham, *My Working Life*, 153.
72. See Nicolson, *George V*, 96.
73. Clarke to Thursfield, 22 Oct. 1906, NIA, MSS Thursfield; Dilke, 'Clarke on Defence', *The Nation*, 13 July 1907, 733.
74. Navalis (Thursfield), *The Times*, 4. Sept., 4, 9, 16 Oct. 1906; Arnold-Forster, *The Times*, 5 Sept. 1906; Hannay (Letters), *The Times*, 15 Sept., 8 Oct. 1906. For the failed Alsen operation (1–2 April 1864), see Moltke and Theodor von Bernhardi's discussion from 13 Feb. 1865, in Kessel, *Moltke Gespräche*, No. 18, 43–48. For Moltke's motives and the success of the second attempt (29 June 1864), see Bucholz, *Moltke*, 91–92, 97–100; see also WO, Note, 10 Dec. 1907, NA, WO 106/47B, ID/ 8.
75. *The Times*, 5, 14, 20 Sept. 1906; 4, 8, 9 Oct. 1906; Repington, *The Times*, 13 Oct. 1906.
76. *The Times*, 27, 28 Dec. 1906; 8 Jan. 1907.
77. Clarke to Ewart, 16 Oct. 1906, NAS, MSS Ewart, NRAS 1054/81/C.
78. *The Times*, 27, 28 Dec. 1906.
79. Edelsheim, 'The Future of the German Navy', NR 4/1905, 242–50; Maxse, 'Episodes', NR 5/1905, 394–96.
80. Repington, The Blue Water School, *The Times*, 1 Dec. 1906; (Letters), 8 Jan. 1907.
81. Crowe, Minutes, 10 Feb. 1908, BD VI, No. 80, 115–17, 117. For Hardinge, see Fisher to Edward VII, 23 Oct. 1906, FGDN II, No. 56, 102–5.
82. Repington to Roberts, 28 Nov. 1906, NAM, MSS Roberts, R 62/10.
83. Balfour to Clarke, 14 Sept. 1906, BL, Add. 49702.

84. Clarke to Balfour, 20 Sept. and 15 Nov. 1906, BL, Add. 49702.
85. Dilke, Clarke on Defence, *The Nation*, 13 July 1907, 733.
86. Clarke to Balfour, 20 Sept. 1906, BL, Add. 49702; to Thursfield, 22 Oct. 1906, INA, MSS Thursfield.
87. Clarke to Balfour, 20 Sept. 1906, BL, Add. 49702.
88. Clarke to Balfour, 15 Nov. 1906, BL, Add. 49702.
89. Repington to Roberts, 8 Nov. 1906, NAM, MSS Roberts, R 62/8.
90. See, e.g., Crutchley, 'Lest We Forget, *Daily Mail*, 21 Oct. 1907; Kennedy, *The German Danger*; Ross, *Problem of National Defence*; Shore, 'Home Defence', USM 7/1907, 373–84; Oppenheim, *The Secret*.
91. See, e.g., Radcliffe-Cooke, 'The Invasion-Scare: A New View', NC 3/1907, 395–405; Hennell, 'Organization of Power Traction', JRUSI 4/1907, 413–14; Dilke, 'Official Opinion on Defence', USM 10/1907, 31–33.
92. Fisher to Tweedmouth, 16 Oct. 1906, FGDN II, No. 55, 101; to Amery, 1903, CC, AMEL 1/1/14.
93. Fisher to Thursfield, 25 Dec. 1906, FGDN II, No. 59, 107–8; Thursfield to Buckle, 30 Dec. 1906, ibid., n. 2.
94. Fisher to White, 3 Dec. 1906, FGDN II, No. 60, 109.
95. Fisher to White, October 1906, FGDN II, No. 52, 97–98.
96. Clarke, The Bolt from the Blue School, *The Times*, 19 Feb., 15, 29 March 1907; ADM, Memorandum, n.d., BL, Add. 49711.
97. Fisher to White, 25 Dec. 1904, FGDN II, No. 10, 50; '"XYZ" who is Sir John Wolfe-Barry, writes in *The Times*, and he knows no more about marine engines than this sheet of paper.' Fisher to Prince of Wales, 15 April 1906, FGDN II, No. 37, 78–79.
98. Fisher to Fortescue, 24 April 1906, FGDN II, No. 33, 71–72.
99. Repington to Roberts, 22 Oct. 1907, RL 49, 127–28; Beresford to Repington, 17 Nov. 1907, NAM, MSS Roberts, R 62/23.
100. Fisher to Edward VII, 23 Oct. 1906, FGDN II, No. 56, 102–5.
101. Fisher to Tweedmouth, 26 Sept. 1906, FGDN II, No. 49, 90–93; 4 Oct. 1906, ibid., No. 50, 93–95; 5 Oct. 1906, ibid., No. 51, 95–97; 11 Oct. 1906, ibid., No. 53, 98–99; 16 Oct. 1906, ibid., No. 55, 101.
102. Fisher to Tweedmouth, 26 Sept. 1906, FGDN II, No. 49, 90–93.
103. Ibid.
104. PD IV/171, 27 July 1906, cols. 114–19.
105. Fisher to Tweedmouth, 26 Sept. 1906, FGDN II, No. 49, 90–93.
106. 'Of course economy must never be allowed to clash with fighting efficiency – in this case it does not! IT INCREASED IT!' [emphasis original]. Fisher to Tweedmouth, 4 Oct. 1906, FGDN II, No. 50, 93–95.
107. Fisher to Tweedmouth, 11 Oct. 1906, FGDN II, No. 53, 98–99. Under the unionists, the budget fell from £124 million in 1901 to £59 million in 1906; it would rise again under the Liberals. See Butler, *Political Facts*, 230.
108. Fisher to Tweedmouth, 4 Oct. 1906, FGDN II, No. 50, 93–95.
109. Weinroth, 'Left-Wing Opposition', 114–15; on the strikes, see *Political Facts*, 211, 217.
110. Fisher to Tweedmouth, 26 Sept. 1906, FGDN II, No. 49, 90–93; see also Bacon, Memorandum, 26 Aug. 1905, No. 62, cited in Lambert, *Submarine Service*, 120–22; Fisher to Tweedmouth, 26 Sept. 1906, FGDN II, No. 49, 90–93.

111. Fisher to Corbett, 28 July 1905, FGDN II, No. 24, 63.
112. Fisher to Edward VII, 4 Oct. 1907, FGDN II, No. 90, 139–43. Instead he favoured a Copenhagening. Ibid., 168, n. 2. His consistent opposition to an amphibious operation led to a break with Churchill during the war, over the disastrous events at Gallipoli. *The Times*, 12 July 1920.
113. Grey to Haldane, 8 Jan. 1906, NLS, MSS 5907; Repington to Marker, 14 June 1906, BL, Add. 52277B.
114. Fisher to Beresford, 30 April 1907, FGDN II, No. 74, 122.
115. 'We shall have 4 Dreadnoughts ready to fight before a single foreign Dreadnought is launched. But we don't want to say this. We have 3 Invincibles building, which some people think stronger than Dreadnoughts – this is also a secret – and we have a pledge to lay down 3 more Dreadnoughts next year. Practically 10 Dreadnoughts. … *We are more than equal to any combination*' [italics added]. Fisher to Anon., 3 Jan. 1907, FGDN II, No. 61, 110–12.
116. Fisher to Edward VII, 4 Oct. 1907, FGDN II, No. 90, 139–43. For Wilhelm II's knowledge, see Fisher to Tweedmouth, 26 Sept. 1906, FGDN II, No. 49, 90–93.
117. ADM, The Home Fleet, December 1906, cited in Marder, FDSF I, 71.
118. Arnold-Forster, Diary, 21 May 1907, BL, Add. 50353.
119. Repington to Marker, 14 April 1907, RL 43, 117; to Mrs. Haldane, 27 Feb. 1908, RL 60, 141–42.
120. Repington to Hutton, 13 March 1907, RL 42, 116–17.
121. Roberts, Memorandum, 17 Nov. 1907, NMM, RIC/9/1, 36–37.
122. Clarke to Balfour, 15 Nov. 1906, BL, Add. 49702.
123. Clarke, secret, Distribution of our Naval Forces, early 1907, BL, Add. 50836.
124. Clarke, August 1907, NA, CAB 3/2/1/42A, 1.
125. Balfour to Clarke, 2 July 1907, NA, CAB 3/2/1/42A, 6–8; Arnold-Forster, Diary, 5 Dec. 1907, BL, Add. 53535.
126. Fisher to Corbett, 28 Sept. 1907, No. 88, FGDN II, 137–38.
127. Fisher to Edward VII, 4 Oct. 1907, No. 90, FGDN II, 139–43; Slade to Corbett, 5, 14, 18, 21 Nov. 1907, NMM, CBT/6/5; Fisher to Corbett, 7 Nov. 1907, NMM, RIC/9/1; Slade, Sub-Committee of Imperial Defence, 22 Oct. 1908, NA, CAB 16/3A, 226; Fisher to Spender, 11 Feb. 1908, BL, Add. 46390.
128. See the exchange in *The Times* between 10 Sept. and 21 Oct. 1907; Fisher to Clarke, 12 Sept. 1907; Clarke to Fisher, 14 Sept. 1907, NA, ADM 116/3108.
129. Along with Asquith, Grey, Lloyd George, Haldane, Lord Tweedmouth, Lord Crewe and Lord Esher participated. The Admiralty was represented by Fisher and Slade (DNI), Admiral Colomb and Julian Corbett; the army by General Chief of Staff Lyttelton and generals Nicholson, French and Ewart. Sub-Committee of Imperial Defence, 22 Oct. 1908, NA, CAB 16/3.
130. Fisher, Memorandum, 22 Aug. 1907, NMM, CBT/6/4, 25.
131. Fisher to Leyland, 22 Sept. 1907, FGDN II, No. 87, 13–17.
132. The driving force was Repington, 'a man who had been kicked out of the Army and turned out of all his Clubs'. Arnold-Forster, Diary, 5 Dec. 1907, BL, Add. 50353.
133. Fisher to Esher, 8 Nov. 1907, CC, ESHR 10/42; Fisher, Memorandum, 22 Aug. 1907, NMM, CBT/6/4, 25.
134. Beresford to Fisher, 16 July 1907, FGDN II, No. 80, 127, n. 2; to ADM, January 1908, NA, ADM 116/3108; for the cooperation with Repington, see Ewart, Diary, 7 May

1907, NAS, RH4/84/2 [NRAS 1054/124]; Beresford to Repington, 17 Nov. 1907, NAM, R 62/23; for the Beresford-Fisher feud, see Massie, *Dreadnought*, 515–43.
135. Grey to Maxse, 21 June 1904, WSRO, MAXSE/452; Nicolson to Hardinge, 9 Feb. 1910, cited in Wilson, *Policy of the Entente*, 115; Anon., 'The New Scare about the Navy', *The Nation*, 6 Feb. 1909, 700–701.
136. Fisher to Esher, 7 Oct. 1907, JL II, 145.
137. Fisher to Cawdor, 4 Dec. 1907, FGDN II, No. 97, 151–52.
138. Arnold-Forster to Maxse, cited in Morris, *Letters of Repington*, 'Introduction', 19.
139. Esher: 'In absence even of the main Fleets invasion is impossible'. *The Times*, 31 May 1905. Recently, Niall Ferguson proposed that this recognition came only in 1911. Ferguson, *Pity of War*, 23.
140. Esher to Morley, 8 Oct. 1907, JL II, 250.
141. Esher, Memorandum, 27 March 1904, BL, Add. 49718. 'The Bolt from the Blue upon which Lord Roberts' case is founded, is absurd.' Esher, 16 Nov. 1907, JL II, 257.
142. Esher to Ewart, 9 Oct. 1900, NAS, MSS Ewart, NRAS 1054/3.
143. Esher to Fisher, 15 Oct. 1907, JL II, 251; 1 Oct. 1907, CC, ESHR 10/42; Mackay, *Fisher of Kilverstone*, 355.
144. Invasion, Note by Lord Esher, 23 July 1908, NA, CAB 1/37, 2.
145. Notes on Invasion supplied to Mr Balfour, Balfour to Clarke, 2 July 1907, NA, CAB 3/2/1/42A, 10; Report of the Sub-Committee on Invasion, 15 July 1908, NA, CAB 1/37, 2.
146. Esher to Knollys, 6 Nov. 1908, JL II, 357.
147. Esher to Roberts, 28 Aug. 1907, NAM, MSS Roberts, R 29/15.
148. Notes on Invasion, 2 July 1907, NA, CAB 3/2/1/42A, 6–8, 10–13.
149. See Ortenburg, *Millionenheere*, 208–9.
150. *The Times*, 27 Dec. 1906.
151. Vagts, *Landing Operations*, Foreword.
152. Balfour to Clarke, 20 July 1907, NMM, RIC/9/1, 32; Clarke, 33; Slade, 16 Aug. 1907, NMM, CBT/6/5, 17.
153. Slade, 16 Aug. 1907, NMM, CBT/6/5, 1–2; Notes on Invasion, 2 July 1907, NA, CAB 3/2/1/42A, 12–13.
154. Slade, Sub-Committee of Imperial Defence, 22 Oct. 1908, NA, CAB 16/3A, 226.
155. Clarke, August 1907, NA, CAB 3/2/1/42A, 2–4.
156. Lovat to Repington, 1 Dec. 1907, cited in Lindlay, *Lord Lovat*, 117; Repington to Roberts, 27 Nov. 1907, NAM, MSS Roberts, R 62/27.
157. Esher, Diary, 27, 29 Nov. 1906, JL II, 263.
158. Slade to Corbett, 27, 28 Nov. 1907, NMM, CBT/6/4. 'What fascinates me is that the Committee as a whole don't seem to take the point that the whole case of Roberts rests on an absolute naval surprise, which is really a sheer impossibility.' Fisher to Esher, 12 Dec. 1907, cited in Fisher, *Memories and Records*, 183.
159. Wipperfürth, *Souveränität*, 368; John Röhl sees Repington as the principal witness to the German peril. Röhl, *Wilhelm II*, 650.
160. Luvaas, *Education of an Army*, 299; Ryan, *Lieutenant-Colonel Charles à Court Repington*, 59.
161. 'He [Roberts] does not understand navy attitude and he does not understand naval strategy.' Corbett, 9 Dec. 1907, NMM, RIC/9/1, 38, 43; Fisher, Memorandum, 22 Aug. 1907, NMM, CBT/6/4, 25.

162. Corbett, Minutes, Roberts, Memorandum, 17 Nov. 1907, NMM, RIC/9/1, 37; see also Mahan, *Naval Strategy*, 113.
163. Corbett, *Some Principles of Maritime Strategy*.
164. See Lambert, 'Admiral Sir John Fisher'.
165. Corbett, *Some Principles of Maritime Strategy*, 95; 'Great Britain, Germany and limited War, Review of Corbett's "Principles" in comparison to Mahan's "Naval Strategy"', ER 4/1912, 485–514. See also Freedman, *War*, No. 64, 225–27.
166. Corbett, 12 Dec. 1907, App. XVI: Memorandum by the DNI, NA, CAB 16/3A, 21–22.
167. Ibid., 20.
168. Weinroth, 'Left-Wing Opposition', 97, 107.
169. Steiner and Neilson, *Britain and the Origins*, 52–53; Kennedy, *Rise of Anglo-German Antagonism*, 251; Weinroth, 'Left-Wing Opposition', 107.
170. Seligmann, *Royal Navy and the German Threat*, 164, 173.
171. In the case of Germany, we have for a long time not been satisfied by references to the mere existence of Berlin's encirclement phobia as the basis for decision making.
172. Seligmann, *Spies in Uniform*, 159–213; Hyam, *Empire*, 55.
173. See Corbett, *Some Principles of Maritime Strategy*; Mahan, *Naval Strategy*.
174. Esher, 29 May 1908, JL II, 317–18; Arnold-Forster to Balfour, 28 Sept. 1908, BL, Add. 49723; Selborne to Brodrick, 14 Jan. 1908, BOD, MSS Selborne 3.
175. Mr A.J. Balfour before the Sub-Committee on Invasion, 29 May 1908, NA, CAB 3/2/143A, 3–5.
176. Balfour to Esher, 25 May 1908, BL, Add. 49719.
177. Mr A.J. Balfour before the Sub-Committee on Invasion, 29 May 1908, NA, CAB 3/2/143A, 3–5.
178. Slade, Diary, 29 May 1908, NMM, MSS Slade, MRF/39.
179. Esher to Balfour, 29 May 1908, JL II, 317–18.
180. Esher, Note, 23 July 1908, NA, CAB 1/37; see also Fisher to Edward VII, 4 Oct. 1907, FGDN II, No. 90, 139–42; Slade, Memorandum, 16 Aug. 1907, NMM, CBT/6/4, 28–29.
181. Fisher to Balfour, 23 Dec. 1907, BL, Add. 49712.
182. Dumas to Lascelles, 12 Feb. 1908, BD VI, No. 81, 117–32, 132.
183. Like Hallmann's erroneous assumptions, many studies are still based today on the German programmes on paper rather than on the actual numbers. See Hallmann, *Schlachtflottenbau*, 337; Prochnow, *Deutsche Kriegsschiffe*, Vol. 1, 26–120. As a matter of fact, if one sees the calendar year as Epkenhans does, one has to include *HMS Resolution* and *HMS Ramillies*, both laid down in November 1913. Furthermore, Epkenhans exaggerates the German battleships and battle-cruisers by two. See Michael Epkenhans, 'Was Peaceful Outcome Thinkable? The Naval Race before 1914', in Afflerbach and Stevenson, *An Improbable War*, 113–29, 128. See also Sumida, *In Defence of Naval Supremacy*, Table 19.
184. This relates to the ships started, launched or completed. See Sumida, *In Defence of Naval Supremacy*, Tables 19–21, 361–63.
185. Crowe to Dilke, 15 Oct. 1907, NA, FO 800/243.
186. Grey, *25 Years*, Vol. 1, 149.
187. Dumas to Lascelles, 3 Feb. 1908, BD VI, No. 80, 115–17.
188. Berghahn, *Germany and the Approach*, 67; Ferguson, *Pity of War*, 70–71; Hildebrand, 'Staatskunst und Kriegshandwerk', 30–31; Halpern, *Naval History*, 7–10; Steiner and Neilson, *Britain and the Origins*, 51–61.

189. Neilson, *Britain and the Origins*, 68; Grey, Memorandum, 23 July 1908, NA, FO 800/92; for Kronberg, see Röhl, *Wilhelm II*, 677–88; Wilhelm II to Bülow, 11 Aug. 1908, GP XXIV, No. 8224, 124–25. For a new interpretation, see Rose 'The Writers, Not the Sailors'.
190. Geiss, *Weltpolitik*, 167; Kennedy, *Rise of Anglo-German Antagonism*, 450–52; Berghahn, *Germany and the Approach*, 134–35, 175; Mommsen, *War der Kaiser an allem Schuld*, 140.
191. Weinroth, 'Left-Wing Opposition'.
192. Balfour, *The Kaiser*, 139–41; Reinermann, *Kaiser*, 325–32; McLean, *Royalty and Diplomacy*, 128–30.
193. Cited in Morris, *Scaremongers*, 142–43.
194. Repington to Roberts, 7 March 1908, NAM, MSS Roberts, R 62/47; Repington to Dilke, 10 March 1908, BL, Add. 43920; see CID, 12 Dec. 1907, NA, CAB 16/3A.
195. Repington to Esher, 5 March 1908, CC, ESHR 10/53; to Maxse, 11 March 1908, WSRO, MAXSE/458; Maxse to Harmsworth, 16 March 1908, BL, Add. 62175.
196. Cited in Reinermann, *Kaiser*, 326.
197. Wilhelm II to Tweedmouth, 16 Feb. 1908, GP XXIV, No. 8181, 32–35; see also Lascelles to AA, 28 Feb. 1908, GP XXIV, No. 8184, 36–37.
198. Slade, Diary, 7 March 1908, NMM, MSS Slade, MRF/39.
199. Asquith, cited in FGDN II, 166, n. 3.
200. Metternich to AA, 6 March 1908, GP XXIV, No. 8189, 40–41.
201. Asquith to Stanley, 31 Oct. 1914, cited in Asquith, *Letters to Venetia Stanley*, 300; Massie, *Dreadnought*, 745–47.
202. Metternich to AA, 9 March 1908, GP XXIV, No. 8194, 47.
203. *The Nation*, cited in Morris, *Edwardian Radicalism*, 134.
204. Metternich to AA, 7 March 1908, GP XXIV, No. 8190, 41–42.
205. Edward VII to Fisher, 10 March 1908, FGDN II, No. 117, 168.
206. Asquith and Grey, cited in Weinroth, 'Left-Wing Opposition', 107.
207. Hardinge to Chirol, 3 June 1905, CUL, MSS Hardinge, Vol. 6.
208. Repington, *Vestigia*, 291; see also Esher, 12 March 1908, JL II, 295.
209. Morris, *Scaremongers*, 135; Fisher, FGDN II, 163; Kennedy, *Rise of Anglo-German Antagonism*, 443–44.
210. Slade, Diary, 27 April 1908, NMM, MSS Slade, MRF/39.
211. Slade to Corbett, 1 Dec. 1907, NMM, CBT/6/5.
212. Slade, Diary, 1, 5, 8 April 1908, NMM, MSS Slade, MRF/39; Ewart Diary, 27 July 1908, NAS, RH4/84/3 [NRAS 1054/125].
213. Sub-Committee to reconsider the question of overseas attack, 22 Oct. 1908, NA, CAB 3/2/1/44A, 3–9, 7.
214. ADM, War Plans: anticipated German Actions of War, 18 June 1908, NA, ADM 116/1043B, Part II, 9.
215. This agitation was largely the work of Repington, Maxse, Garvin and Baden Powell. Between 30 July and 5 September, the *Morning Post* published eight articles by Spenser Wilkinson on the German invasion threat in which he attacked the naval experts for their arrogance and excessive optimism. At the same time, Hyndmann and Blatchford, socialist politicians and journalists, caused a stir with rumours about an invasion they published in the *Clarion*. Maxse, 'Episodes', NR 9/1908, 3, 6, 19; NR 7/1908, 880; PD IV/188, 13 May 1908, cols. 1122–23; 25 May 1908, cols. 742–45; Garvin, 'The

German Peril', QR 7/1908, 295–305; Anon., 'The Insecurity of Home Defence Today', NC 8/1908, 877–89; Baden Powell, *German Plans for Invading England*, London 1908; Hyndmann, 'The Coming War against Great Britain', *The Clarion*, 31 July 1908; Blatchford, 'The Danger of War', *The Clarion*, 7 Aug. 1908; Anon., 'England and Germany: The Case for Scaremongers', *The Clarion*, 21 Aug. 1908.
216. Balfour to Asquith, 5 Nov. 1908, BL, Add. 49725.
217. Repington to Roberts, 16 Nov. 1908, NAM, MSS Roberts, R 62/56.
218. Roberts, 23 Nov. 1908, PD (Lords) IV/196, cols. 1679–92; Lovat: cols. 1696–704.
219. Roberts to Lansdowne, 24 Oct. 1908, NAM, MSS Roberts, R 122/11/19; Edward VII to Roberts, November 1908, cited in James, *Lord Roberts*, 434; Balfour to Asquith, 5 Nov. 1908, NAM, MSS Roberts, R 8/29; Lansdowne to Roberts, 18 Nov. 1908, R 34/469; Crewe to Roberts, 21 Nov. 1908, R 46/154.
220. *Daily Express*, 24 Nov. 1908.
221. Report (London), 28 Nov. 1908, PA-AA, R 5634.
222. 'I am inclined to think it is 80,000 cocks and bulls.' Repington to Maxse, 20 Oct. 1908; Chirol to Maxse, 13 Nov. 1908, WSRO, MAXSE/457.
223. Hale, *Publicity and Diplomacy*, 340; Mensdorff, 27 Nov. 1908, HHStA, PA VIII, Kt. 141, No. 61 K, fols. 82–83.
224. Mensdorff, 17 Dec. 1908, HHStA, PA VIII, Kt. 142, fol. 109.
225. *The Times*, 24–27 Nov. 1908; *Daily Mail*, 24 Nov., 7 Dec. 1908; *Daily Express*, 24 Nov. 1908; *Morning Post*, 24 Nov. 1908; Hale, 'What of the Night?', NC 12/1908, 924–33; Anon., 'The Danger of Invasion', *The Spectator*, 28 Nov. 1908, 865–66; Anon., 'Lord Roberts' Warning', *Saturday Review* 12/1908, 521–25.
226. Grey, Minutes, 10 Feb. 1908, Dumas to Lascelles, 3 Feb. 1908, BD VI, No. 80, 115–17, 117.
227. Fisher to Esher, 21 Feb. 1908, FGDN II, No. 113, 164; to Corbett, 11 March 1908, FGDN, 164, n. 2.
228. Massie, *Dreadnought*, 623.
229. Weinroth, 'Left-Wing Opposition', 111.
230. Goschen, Report 1906, BDFA F/XXXIV, No. 94, 122–59, 122–26; Report 1907, ibid., No. 123, 191–255, 123–30; Cartwright, Report 1908, ibid., No. 137, 268–91, 268–76; Goschen to Grey, 23 June 1906, ibid., No. 77, 100–101; see also NA, FO 371/75/711.
231. Goschen to Grey, 23 June 1906, BDFA F/XXXIV, No. 77, 100–101.
232. Dumas to Lascelles, 4 March 1907, BDFA F/XX, No. 9, 7–8.
233. Cartwright to Grey, 20 March 1907, BDFA F/XX, No. 10, 8–11; Lascelles to Grey, 21 March 1907, ibid., No. 12, 13–14.
234. Lascelles to Lansdowne, 6 May 1904, BDFA F/XIX, No. 157, 174; 25 May 1904, No. 159, 176; Whitehead, Memorandum, 26 Jan. 1905: German Imperial Estimates 1905, ibid., No. 180, 224–29.
235. Seligmann, *Spies in Uniform*, 69–70.
236. See ibid., 165–73; Seligmann, 'A view from Berlin',114–47. A typical example of his bias is his report on German motor balloons: Trench to de Salis, 14 Dec. 1908, BDFA F/XX, No. 188, 217–18.
237. Trench to Lascelles, 6 Jan. 1908, BD VI, No. 75, 108–10; 12 Aug. 1908, ibid., App. to No. 113, 176–78; to Goschen, 8 Jan. 1909, ibid., No. 145, 228–32; 21 Feb. 1909, App. to No. 149, 234–36.
238. Trench 27 April 1908, BD VI, App. to No. 94, 147–49.

239. Trench, Report, 24 June 1909, NA, KV 3/1. See also Seligmann, *Spies in Uniform*, 172; Crowe, Minutes, 10 Feb. 1908, Dumas to Lascelles, 3 Feb. 1908, BD VI, No. 80, 115–17, 117.
240. Edward VII to Fisher, 10 March 1908, FGDN II, No. 117, 168.
241. Blunt, 7 Aug. 1908, *My Diaries*, Vol. 2, 218; Burgoyne, *The War Inevitable*; Anon., 'The Invasion of Britain', *The Spectator*, 29 Sept. 1908, 438–40.
242. Mommsen, *War der Kaiser an allem Schuld*, 140–41; Röhl, *Wilhelm II*, 677–88; see also Rose, 'The Writers, Not the Sailors', 221–40.
243. Wilhelm II to Bülow, 11 Aug. 1908, GP XXIV, No. 8224, 124–25; see also Hardinge (Letters), The Kronberg Interview. Lord Hardinge's Report, *The Times*, 10 Nov. 1924.
244. Wilhelm II to Bülow, 11 Aug. 1908, GP XXIV, No. 8224, 124–25; 12 Aug. 1908, ibid., No. 8225, 125–26.
245. Repington to Roberts, 26 March 1909, RL 70, 151.
246. Bellairs (MP), 6 Dec. 1906, 'The Standard of Naval Strength', JRUSI 51/1 (1907), 123–83, 135. For a German evaluation of that article, see Coerper to Tirpitz, 8 Dec. 1908, PA-AA, R 5578.
247. Fisher to Churchill, 28 Feb. 1909, FGDN II, No. 163, 226.
248. Hardinge, Memorandum, 16 Aug. 1908, BD VI, No. 117, 184–90, 186–87.
249. Wilhelm II to Bülow, 13 Aug. 1908, GP XXIV, No. 8226, 126–29; see also Hardinge, Memorandum, 16 Aug. 1908, BD VI, No. 117, 184–90.
250. Goschen to Grey, 21 Aug. 1909, NA, FO 800/61; Grey to Goschen, 31 Dec. 1909, NA, FO 800/62.
251. Craig, Report, 31 Aug. 1909, NA, FO 800/93; with Nicolson's response: 'Were we to fall in with this plan we should be unfaithful to our friend'. Goschen to Grey, 4 March 1911, BD VI, No. 442, 593–96, 595. Crowe interpreted the Kaiser's proposal as another attempt at hegemony. Goschen to Grey, 12 March 1911, Crowe, Minutes, 20 March 1911, BD VI, No. 446, 600–602, 602.
252. See BD VI, Nos. 492–594, 666–761; Kennedy, *Rise of Anglo-German Antagonism*, 334–35, 451–53; Langhorne, 'Britain and Germany', in Hinsley, *British Foreign Policy*, 288–314, 290–93.
253. See Berghahn, *Germany and the Approach*, 140; Ferguson, *Pity of War*, 70–71.
254. Grey to Ripon, 13 Dec. 1907, cited in Grey, *25 Years*, Vol. 1, 149.
255. Ripon to Grey, 15 Dec. 1907, cited in Grey, *25 Years*, 148–49.
256. Carnegie, The Cry of Wolf!, NC 8/1906, 224–33, 229.
257. Cited in Wilson, *Policy of the Entente*, 8.
258. Grey to Buchanan, 9 Dec. 1912, Nicolson, Minute, BD IX/2, 270.
259. 'The Admiralty had demanded six ships; the economists offered four; and we finally compromised on eight.' Churchill, *World Crisis*, Vol. 1, 23.
260. See Hayes, 'Admiralty's Plans'. In February 1905, the *Review of Reviews* also emphasized that Germany's fear of England was greater than England's fear of Germany. RR 2/1905, 183. In the second battle of Copenhagen (1807), the Royal Navy had bombarded Copenhagen and captured the Danish fleet.
261. Spring Rice to Chirol, 21 June 1907, GL II, 101; to Maxse, 3 June 1908, WSRO, MAXSE/458.
262. Spring Rice to Williams, 10 Sept. 1906, CC, CASR 1/70.

Chapter 8

AT THE COST OF STABILITY
The Anglo-Russian Convention and its European Implications

In many ways the outcome of the war between Russia and Japan was a stroke of luck for London.[1] Emile J. Dillon, an experienced commentator on foreign affairs, believed the work of two generations of Russian diplomats had been sunk at Tsushima along with much of the Russian fleet, and the conflict had not spread, which would have forced Britain to rethink its own position.[2] While George Saunders, Leo Maxse and Charles Hardinge argued that Germany was the greatest beneficiary and drew alarming pictures with German hegemony on the cusp of realization,[3] Dillon described an alternative scenario: the political order had been given a new start, and Britain was in the best possible position to serve as broker for the various power groupings.[4] Edward Grey also noted the favourable circumstances for setting diplomatic relations on a new footing. Unlike Dillon, however, and also unlike his Conservative predecessors, who had seen a renewal of the Anglo-Japanese alliance (1905) as a bulwark against Russia,[5] Grey planned to widen the Entente Cordiale to include St Petersburg.

Before Arthur Nicolson began the long journey to St Petersburg, he received instructions in Grey's private London flat on his new role as British ambassador to Russia. For more than four hours on 24 April 1906, he discussed 'entente in and out, up and down' with the foreign minister, the prime minister, the secretary for war and the India secretary.[6] Two related goals were pressed upon him. Future British policy on Russia would be focused on an imperial settlement in the Indian North West Frontier, in Baluchistan and in the Persian Gulf, as the previous government had also been minded.[7] That was, however, only the starting point – an enduring broader agreement with Russia would now also be sought, to cover the Near East, the Straits and south-east Europe.[8] Balfour and Lansdowne had taken a hard line on Russia and had sought to keep the continental and imperial spheres

---

Notes for this chapter begin on page 385.

distinct,[9] but now the new government sent clear signals to the Russian ambassador, Alexander Benckendorff, that accommodation with Russia was on the table.[10] Edward Grey fundamentally agreed with King Edward VII and Charles Hardinge who thought especially the Straits question 'useful asset in the event of general negotiations'[11] and the foreign secretary discovered in this question even 'the original cause of the hostility and friction between Russia and us'.[12]

Scholarship is divided on whether imperial or continental interests predominated in the convention politics that followed. The majority of historians have seen Britain concerned to restore the balance of power by supporting the weakened Russian Empire.[13] More recent studies propose that the convention was largely about resolving points of conflict in Asia, driven by Russia, with the repercussions for the continent an unwanted secondary consequence.[14] Both interpretations bear elements of truth, yet each tends to spend more time messaging the details than considering the implications for international stability. Thus, for example, we see a rush to identify a continuity running through Conservative and Liberal policy on Russia, with too little attention paid to the immediate contexts. The military stalemate on the North West Frontier of India as well as the limitation of the German peril hardly suggests any compulsion to come to a balancing agreement with Russia.[15] Hardinge thought a new League of the Three Emperors unlikely,[16] while in autumn 1906 Grey was seriously concerned that a realignment of the powers might cause panic in Berlin.[17] After the secret meeting at Björkö, Balfour and Lansdowne, for instance, did not believe it necessary to extend the Entente Cordiale, let alone offer any support to Russia in the Balkans, of all places.[18] Decisions were based on counterfactual expectations in relation not just to Germany, but also to Russia and the international system more broadly. We need to look particularly closely at how Britain approached the issues of south-eastern Europe, the most fraught geographical area within the Great Power system, a subject that to date has been surprisingly neglected.[19] Here, it is assumed, one can find the roots of the so-called 'Balkan inception scenario' that triggered war in 1914.[20]

In citing Persia and the Straits, Grey had pointed to a path all previous British governments had kept barred. Since time immemorial, Russia had longed for an ice-free, all-year point of access. Now Grey beckoned with two: an economically lucrative and strategically important gateway to the Gulf[21] and the possibility of a change to the terms for the gateway to the Black Sea and thus to the eastern Mediterranean and the Balkans.[22] The objections of John Morley, the radical liberal secretary for India, were brushed aside. The liberal imperialists explicitly refused to make any mention of previous experiences with Russia or Russia's expansive ambitions; instead they highlighted their optimism that the Russian revolution would bring positive change.[23] The difference between the Conservative and Liberal approaches to Russia can be seen very clearly in the Liberals' willingness to plan on the basis of vague hope, an enthusiasm that often ran counter to the information and recommendations provided by diplomats and other sources on the ground, men such as Cecil Spring Rice and Arminius Vambéry.[24] For both domestic and international reasons, the liberal imperialists spoke of the changes in Russia as being far more profound than they actually were.[25] The foreign secretary tended to draw on views he had formed during his years in opposition, producing an overlap with the pro-Russia press campaign and the 'A.B.C.' articles that is almost astonishing.

Publicists were also integrated practically into the process of rapprochement. Thus, for example, Donald Mackenzie Wallace of the *Times* was to assist Arthur Nicolson by 'obtaining information from sources generally closed to diplomatists'.[26] The tone would be set as the circumstances demanded, although Spring Rice explicitly warned:

> The Russians still think that we are dying to have an arrangement with them and would pay anything to have one. ... We must be most careful ... and say that we don't want a thing and therefore will give it. That is the worst bargaining. So about the Dardanelles. We ought to say that it is impossible. ... What I should say is: wait till Russia has declared herself, and the constitution is working. Before then, don't identify yourself with any man or any party.[27]

But Grey thought he had no time to lose. He spotted a first opportunity in December 1905, when the Persian government asked London for a loan of £800,000. Should he help Britain's old ally Persia and at the same time demonstrate continuing interest in the region to Britain's old enemy Russia? The previous government and the India Office had seen an opportunity to buy back lost influence and at the same time support the Persian democratic movement,[28] but Grey refused to grant the loan, determined that Russia should be given no grounds for protest. Instead, he proposed to Britain's arch-enemy that they might make the loan together, and that Russia should get access to the Gulf.[29] Count Vladimir Lamsdorff, Russia's foreign minister, was astounded. Out of the blue, he had been given something previously denied him by the London government.[30] And as if that were not enough, Grey had acknowledged that the physical connection of the Transcaucasian railway to the neutral Baghdad railway could provide Russia with additional compensation.[31] George Curzon had already used the term 'appeasing' in relation to Lansdowne's negotiations; what must he have thought now?[32] For those on the ground who for decades had competed with Russian agents for influence in Persia, here was a paradigm shift that for Persians and Asian Russians would surely seem the equivalent of capitulation.[33] The mutual loan, with each party paying one half, was designed to deny any third power access to the Middle East.[34] London had repeatedly demanded that Berlin maintain an 'open door' policy, but now, as on Morocco, Britain sought to close the door.[35] Benckendorff and the Russian leadership were most surprised by Britain's change of heart.[36]

There was no sign of a classic balance of power reaction to German aggression. From the start, Britain's policy had been all about imperial exclusivity and nurturing alignments, first with France and now with Russia, as was made clear by the openness with which Grey let Paris and St Petersburg know that he thought it natural that the Entente Cordiale should be expanded to include Russia. The French chargé d'affaires in St Petersburg began to dream of the creation of a political bloc that would oppose Germany.[37] For Grey, the flexible balance of power approach had been a matter of 'fickleness', and this new policy, which would come with proactive evidence of loyalty, was 'the only practical alternative to the old policy of drift, with its continual complaints, bickerings, and dangerous friction'.[38] At the very moment when the defeat of Russia had given Britain the opportunity to reinforce its role as an anchor of international stability, Grey declared that there was no alternative to rapprochement with the tsardom, the greatest enemy of the status quo.[39]

The idea of a diplomatic arrangement 'similar to that which we had concluded with France'[40] came with complex domestic and defence considerations, which meant that while internally Grey and Haldane displayed no concerns about the security of India, externally they gave the impression that only the Anglo-Russian rapprochement had banished a deadly threat.[41] The new political leadership did nothing to deflate the arguments of the Indian military, who described their part of the Empire as almost inevitably vulnerable, even though George Clarke's expertise impressively contradicted that claim.[42] For one, their arguments bolstered the public case for the redefinition of the army as a continental expeditionary force and for military cooperation with France, now sanctioned, by Grey, for the first time as a political instrument. Additionally, exaggerated demands for disarmament voiced within the liberal camp could be countered, with the endangerment of India, the crown jewel among all imperial possessions, providing a substantial argument in favour of Anglo-Russian rapprochement. Finally, that rapprochement promised to relieve the burden on the British budget, and even on the Empire as a whole.[43]

Whether Russia actually represented a threat to India was however of increasingly less importance, for a new course had already been set with the Anglo-French General Staff discussions.[44] For the political leadership, the expansion of the Entente Cordiale was the key concern, while the military leadership was principally concerned about its reputation with its French partners and with the augmentation of the army as a fighting force at a time when the radical liberals were calling for costs to be cut. To that end, the General Staff was ready to overestimate the strength of the German army massively, and to underestimate the strength of the Entente just as dramatically. By the time of the legendary British 'War Council' of 23 August 1911,[45] detailed plans had already been drawn up for the eventuality of a German attack on France through Belgium,[46] with Henry Wilson, director of military operations, calculating that Germany had over 121 divisions to launch against its neighbours, but under-counting the fighting strength of France and Russia.[47]

Although during the conflicts over Morocco Berlin had not proved itself a European hegemon but rather isolated, during the early phase of liberal foreign policy the balance of power argument against possible threats seems to have become rather a tool to be used against internal critics, and was no longer the fulcrum of British foreign policy. Grey was fully aware of how effectively the threats from Russia for conciliation or Germany for countermeasures[48] could be used against his critics,[49] with whom he always had to tread gingerly. So, for example, his suggestion that alleviation of Anglo-Russian tensions could benefit internal reform won over leading radical liberals Henry Campbell-Bannerman[50] and John Morley.[51] Nevertheless, right up until 1914, the cabinet, especially Morley, remained an incalculable factor when it came to closer ties with Russia.[52]

Like Hardinge, Arthur Nicolson actively promoted an Anglo-Russian entente,[53] and both men found Persia a very suitable subject to raise. Before Grey became foreign secretary, he had made a very similar argument: if Russia were to accept that Britain intended to secure its possessions in Asia peacefully, 'then I am quite sure', he continued, 'that in this country no Government will make it its business to thwart or to obstruct Russia's policy in Europe'.[54] His words already suggested a division of interests. Only three and a half months later, in October 1905, he repeated them when explaining his position to the City of London.[55] Officially, Whitehall spoke of the 're-establishment' of Russia in the 'Councils of Europe',[56] a reference not only to Russia's recovery and its balancing status after its defeat by Japan but also to the revival of Russian interests in south-eastern Europe. Every observer of Russia – whether Spring Rice, Curzon, Nicolson, Hardinge or Vambéry, or a publicist such as Maxse or Garvin, an expert on Russia such as Dillon, or an Orientalist, spy and journalist such as Graham Bennet or Valentine Chirol – was aware of the extended pan-Slavic line that ran from St Petersburg straight to the Balkans.[57] At the same time, virtually every report sent from the Austrian-Hungarian monarchy expressed doubts about the stability of the multi-ethnic state in that particular region.[58] While at first glance the negotiations and the text of the convention appear to have been purely concerned with a settlement of imperial interests,[59] both diplomats and London press were clear from the start that the real concern was to lay the foundations for a new political system for Europe.[60] Ultimately, that could mean only one thing: relations between the Central Powers and Russia in south-eastern Europe must become more tense.[61] 'The Grouping of the Powers', the *Daily Telegraph* concluded, 'has begun'.[62]

On 12 May 1906, a few days after Nicolson's arrival at St Petersburg, Alexander Izvolsky succeeded Lamsdorff as foreign minister. Here was a further stroke of luck,[63] for only three weeks later he entered into negotiations with the British ambassador.[64] Grey remained patient, believing, 'we must avoid raising in M. Isvolsky's mind the suspicion that we wish to force the pace in order to take advantage of Russia's present situation'.[65] The appointment of Izvolsky signalled a political change of course in Russia, now redirected towards Europe.[66] Previously, Count Witte, the Russian finance minister, had determined the political attitude in Russia, and he had rejected closer ties with Britain on the grounds that the consequences for the power system were incalculable.[67] Matters were different with Izvolsky. In 1904, he had seemed decidedly Anglophile,[68] and Edward VII explicitly counselled his nephew the tsar to appoint Izvolsky his foreign minister.[69] In London, however, Izvolsky had also cut an unsympathetic figure, appearing an over-achiever eager for personal glory.[70] He now sought to make up for the Russian loss of prestige at Tsushima with new arrangements at the Straits. In the short term he was willing to let pan-Slavic interests in the Balkans wait, but his middle-term and longer-term goals are evident in an interview he gave in late summer 1906 to Alexej Suvorin, owner and editor-in-chief of the *Novoe Vremja*. To Suvorin he noted that events were moving apace in Europe, and that if Russia was to have its hands free for Europe, it would need to secure its back. Russian greatness could be restored only with a victory in war; whom that war was fought against was inconsequential. Ensuring no doubt would be left, he added: 'in the future we will be the heirs of Austria. We will join with Bulgaria in the Balkans'. Asked about the Straits, he shared with Suvorin presciently: 'in this question England is with us', but noted, 'I say this to you, Alexej Sergejevitch, and not to the journalist'.[71]

London wanted to exploit Izvolsky's ambition to British ends. For the moment, however, Persia's need for a loan brought Russia and Britain to the negotiating table,[72] with a total loan of £2.15 million up for debate. Despite Germany's chronic financial weakness, although only 3 per cent of all trade in the region was in German hands,[73] and while neither the German government nor the German banks had any desire to form a wedge between Russia and Britain,[74] Grey used Germany as a means to draw closer to Russia, proposing that the Kaiserreich be excluded entirely.[75] Grey was particularly concerned to send to Russia a signal of loyalty,[76] and he refused to be swayed by the warnings offered by Lord Minto, Spring Rice and Morley that he was whetting Russian appetites for what might follow.[77]

Morley recognized that Russia was recovering far more quickly from its defeat and from the revolution than had been anticipated,[78] and he was concerned for Britain's European position in the Balkans, for if agreement was reached on the Middle East, then Russia, he predicted, would inevitably be forced to look to south-eastern Europe. Morley and Fitzmaurice concurred that the traditional British role as the sole power protecting against expansive pan-Slavism would automatically fall to Germany.[79] Moreover, Fitzmaurice held that rapprochement with Russia would undermine not only the British position in the Gulf, but also the British relationship with the Muslims of the Empire.[80] Lansdowne, Fitzmaurice's brother, had always stood with the shah in advocating for all powers to be excluded from the Gulf, and the Persian government now protested vehemently against the change in policy and allowed the loan to fall through.[81] Even Edward VII, who cannot be suspected of harbouring any particular concern for Germany, found Grey's orientation had become overly pro-Russian and 'anti-German'.[82] Yet Asquith, Grey and Hardinge held the line.[83] Despite what had been said previously at the Committee of Imperial Defence, suddenly they began to talk of the deadly danger for the Middle East that Russia presented, noting Britain's strained financial position and insisting that the course they were following was therefore inevitable.[84] At this stage, 'inevitability' became something of a pet concept for the liberal imperialists. They excused their failure to look for alternatives with domestic and international constraints, when, in reality, at the time no European Great Power had greater latitude when it came to foreign policy.

In November 1906, Nicolson proposed a revolutionary move: should Britain and Russia form an alliance, London, or in other words Grey, would declare its willingness to discuss how the Russian situation at the Straits might be improved and how Russia might return to the status of a European power.[85] If the offers related to Persia and the Gulf were insufficient for Izvolsky, and he required a further quid pro quo, then, Grey noted, it was 'for him to say what he wants!'

> If it is access to the Persian Gulf, that is a matter which should be referred to us for discussion. But I doubt, myself, whether any complete arrangement with Russia can be made unless it includes the Near East as well. It is the differences in the Near East that have been the original cause of the hostility and friction between Russia and us.[86]

Of all the possible concessions contemplated by Grey during the negotiating phase – a share in customs revenue, involvement with the Baghdad railway, access to the Gulf, and the opening of the Dardanelles[87] – the appeal to Russia of a deal on the Straits was greatest. For decades, Russia had considered the closing of the Straits the key issue for its empire. A port on the Gulf was relatively meaningless as long as British torpedo boats still controlled the Strait of Hormuz, and Izvolsky therefore did not find it too difficult to forgo, generously and temporarily, the realization of the Russian dream of a railway line to the Gulf, although Nicolson was happy to present that concession as evidence of his negotiating skills. Michael von Taube, a member of the Russian Council of Ministers, later recalled that this offer helped to convince Izvolsky that British support for Russia in Europe was a certainty. In response to Taube's comment that Izvolsky had originally had in mind a peaceful coexistence in Europe for which such support would have been superfluous, Izvolsky insisted that questions of huge significance could flare up very suddenly in Europe and for their resolution Russia would need the support of Britain; he cited specifically the Åland islands and the Straits.[88] In terms of access to the Gulf, the British government could hold out the possibility of further concessions and a railway line to the port at Chabar, in the Strait of Hormuz.[89] On this issue, too, the British negotiators encouraged Russian aspirations. London seemed to have lost any overview of the individual offers it was willing to make.

Historians have argued that Nicolson's exchanges with London in November 1906 indicate that the agreement with Russia was focused above all on regional concerns. The British ambassador appeared to have offered a package of compensation that was based 'particularly in the Middle East', an area that would be so prominent in the later convention.[90] Yet closer examination reveals that the real debate was not only about the Middle East, which Nicolson had deemed lost to Russia in 1886.[91] Unlike in the case of the Entente Cordiale, Britain could not enter into a straight quid pro quo, and the day after Grey sent his instructions, Nicolson counselled that concessions be made on the European periphery, taking up his superior's idea: 'I think we should be prepared for some proposals as to deal over the *Near East*. [italics added]'[92] Edward Grey agreed.[93] Nicolson explicitly stated that Izvolsky had not made any demands of this ilk, a sign of where the momentum lay in the negotiations.[94]

Hardinge's return to the issue of British responsibilities on the Straits reveals how important it was to be able to legitimize, or conceal, the rapprochement with Russia. In a memorandum on the Straits dated 16 November 1906, Hardinge gave the impression that the Balfour government had already approved concessions for Russia, noting specifically the February 1903 meeting of the Commission of Imperial Defence that had addressed the topic. The security experts had indeed discussed the strategic consequences of opening the Straits, but their deliberations at this early stage had been purely academic. Hardinge's conclusion, in which he has been joined by historians, that the decision to grant Russia concessions had been made at this early date not only reads too much into that specific event, but also, in light of Lansdowne's memorandum from January 1904 and the attitude of the government even up to late 1905, appears to have been a distortion of the facts.[95] By no stretch of the imagination could an internal strategic military report composed *in camera* and suggesting that concessions were a possibility be counted as a political resolution. Indeed, Balfour, Lansdowne and Curzon's continued scepticism about Russia and repeated concerns about Russian pressure in south-eastern Europe, evident in Lansdowne's attempts to revive the old Mediterranean entente, suggest that no political decision had been taken. And even if a decision had been made in case of emergency, the Tory leadership's optimistic assessment of relative strength suggests that that decision would have involved waiting to see what transpired. Again, Hardinge had reinterpreted a theoretical opinion from the Committee of Imperial Defence such that it corresponded with the views of the new political leadership, thus providing support for his personal agenda, which sought an Anglo-Russian agreement that included the Near East. His manipulation is made all the more evident by his keeping secret other findings by the Committee, such as the deadlock on the North West Frontier or concerns about the Orenburg-Tashkent railway. The facts were not his real concern; above all, he wanted to ensure that British resentment of Russia was reduced, and, as he confessed to his friend and supporter Francis Bertie, to deliberately unsettle Germany.[96] In his exchanges he made no secret of his desire that Britain and Russia should together dominate the international scene.[97]

The continental implications of the planned convention, with its conceptual change of direction, could hardly have been more evident. London tended to respond before Russia had even opened its mouth. At this point, the Russian Council of Ministers had not even dared to hope for any progress on the Straits,[98] while any agreement that was not in Japan's interests seemed ruled out, which greatly limited Russia's room for manoeuvre.[99] As the threat in northern India was not acute, the only possibility for a deal seemed to be to interest St Petersburg in Europe again, diverting the pressure from the periphery onto the centre. The possible impact on the international system was not thought a cause for concern. As Nicolson succinctly noted, for Grey the Near East was also part of the picture, a suggestion that appeared to make the Russian foreign minister very happy.[100] Nicolson's negotiating tactics were successful.[101] He and Grey had dangled British support for longstanding Russian aspirations at the Straits before Izvolsky, but in the process, they failed to recognize that they were themselves now dangling from the foreign minister's hook. During the negotiations, Izvolsky repeatedly retreated in order to draw Nicolson out in turn. On 16 May 1907, Benckendorff progressed and Hardinge reported,

> Benckendorff opened yesterday the Straits question … I personally am in favour of making concessions upon this point if we can obtain a quid pro quo.[102]

Hardinge could see that Austria-Hungary and Germany had good reason to object, but unless it included concessions on the Straits and in the Gulf, he opined, 'no agreement with Russia can be said to be complete or on a solid basis'.[103] For some time now, Grey had been convinced that the traditional position on the Straits would have to yield.[104] The German bogeyman could be deployed to prepare the way to that final step both for the majority within the Liberal Party who remained critical of Russia and for the political public.[105] For Izvolsky, Grey's positive response was 'a great revolution in the relations of the countries'.[106] And he was not wrong, for Grey briefed Nicolson: 'If Asian things are settled favourably the Russians will not have any trouble with us about entrance to the Black Sea'.[107] Only Fitzmaurice again expressed concern, noting that the Russian Foreign Ministry was giving the impression that there was a conspiracy designed to damage the states system, and Austria-Hungary in particular.[108]

At the moment of greatest Russian weakness, caused by war and revolution, Britain had failed to summon the will to continue its traditional role as guarantor of the status quo. The revolution in international relations was not simply a product of an imperially oriented settlement, but was caused by Britain's neglect of its responsibility for the integrity of the states system as it pointed its old rival to spoils in the Orient.[109] That approach had little in common with the attitude of the previous government. While Salisbury had made the Straits part of the conversation, he had done so as part of a far more extensive plan to resolve the eastern issue with a victory over the Ottoman Empire, realized with a consensus of all the powers, and Germany and Austria-Hungary in particular; Lansdowne's strategy had been limited to a resolution of colonial conflicts that would encompass the Far East.[110] All such plans had vanished. Humiliated in the Far East, unburdened in Persia and weighed down by unrest at home, it was only a matter of time before Russia sought a new outlet. Encouraged by Britain, Russia turned its gaze on the Baltic and south-eastern Europe. For in the medium term, the goal of the convention was 'to begin an understanding with Russia which may gradually lead to good relations in European questions also'.[111]

Following the approval of the Russian Council of Ministers in February 1907 and the visit of the Russian fleet to Britain in March, on 31 August the Anglo-Russian Convention on Tibet, Afghanistan and Persia was signed. Tibet became a buffer state, while Persia was divided into spheres of influence – the north to Russia, the middle neutral, and the south-east to Britain. Both parties agreed to the status quo in Afghanistan, but at the same time laid the foundations for its partition. Russia received the right to enter into a relationship with Kabul and to send its agents there, agents that London's experiences with Russia in Persia left no doubt would be political, rather than commercial.

Significantly, Whitehall was very interested to see Berlin's reaction.[112] Shortly before the conclusion of the negotiations, Izvolsky had noted that of all the Great Powers, the Kaiserreich would be most affected.[113] The official German reaction was initially muffled,[114] but what Lascelles found entirely appropriate, Fairfax Cartwright, his colleague in Vienna, identified as perfidious intrigue.[115] Bülow, who had been kept informed throughout the negotiations by Izvolsky, reacted with the same restraint he had shown on the occasion of the Anglo-French entente, and he accepted the convention as what he termed a purely colonial matter. But that did not mean that Germany was oblivious to the implications. Three weeks after the convention was signed, Hans von Miquel, charge d'affaires at St Petersburg, spoke of a 'syndicate of powers formed against Germany'.[116] For too long, Germany had counted on the antagonism between Britain and Russia being fundamentally insurmountable. Completely misjudging the situation, following the disappointing Algeciras conference, Germany had refused to place a Russian bond in Berlin,[117] and Britain and France had happily jumped into the breach. In autumn 1906, the *Times* and the Parisians crowed that

Germany had finally been excluded as an 'honest broker', a response repeated after the agreement had been made.[118] Cambon and Clemenceau thought it self-evident that the convention was the precursor of an alliance of Britain with Paris and St Petersburg.[119] In private, Berlin could only respect Britain for its clever manoeuvre,[120] but Wilhelm II grasped the full structural implications of an alliance between powers that lay on either side of Germany and agreed with his ambassador to the tsar, Friedrich Pourtalès, noting, 'yes, altogether it is directed against us'.[121] The agreement may have appeared simply a colonial matter, but because its signatories were the two poles of the states system, it inevitably had implications for that system as a whole.[122]

Without question, the Anglo-Russian Convention was the culmination of imperial foreign policy before the First World War. For Britain, it meant an end to the separation of colonial and continental interests and indicated that London had fallen for the temptation to exploit the continent and was no longer ready to prioritize its peacekeeping role. Although clearly a minority position among diplomats, Dillon's idea that Europe had been given an opportunity for a new beginning, with Britain as the continent's political broker, suggests a possible alternative course, which makes evident in turn the limits of British Realpolitik at the beginning of the twentieth century. The message that the British attitude had sent to St Petersburg is also revealing, for with the convention concluded, Alexander Savinsky, who was chief of the Russian Cabinet of Foreign Affairs, believed he could count on an 'alliance with England' in European matters too.[123]

New Alignments and the Åland Question

The convention certainly introduced a new factor into Great Power relations,[124] but it was also part of a broader message that had been being broadcast since the change of government in London. The convention marked the conclusion of a development that could only be a cause of concern to the Central Powers. Between early 1906 and the summer of 1907, Whitehall had been exploring the formation of a fundamental new grouping on the continent and of a network of alliances and agreements globally, with the Central Powers deliberately excluded. An agreement, often overlooked, had, for example, been made with Rome.[125] France had concluded a pact with Japan in 1906 over the Far East and was there also indirectly bound to London. To explain why Germany had not been part of these arrangements, Garvin provided a spurious argument in the *Fortnightly Review* in which he proposed that German acquisition of Kiautschou in 1897 was still too fresh in everyone's mind to permit the Kaiserreich a return to international relations.[126] Paris also proved clever enough to demand that Japan come to an agreement with Russia over Asia, a requirement that Tokyo and St Petersburg met later the same year.[127]

The Hague Peace Conference also adopted the principle of deliberately ignoring Germany. What is mostly remembered today is that in an apparent gesture of good will, London proposed that Britain would build only three capital ships and would postpone the construction of a fourth for several months, while Germany brusquely refused any limitations on armament, delivering a further example of its clumsy and aggressive foreign policy.[128] Meanwhile, independently of Berlin's short-sighted diplomacy, the Liberal government was much less altruistic than this gesture might suggest. Its primary concern was to cut back on the Conservative-supported Cawdor programme, which had planned for the construction of four new battleships each year, in order that the government might meet social promises made during the election.[129] According to conference participant Eyre Crowe, in the run-up to the event Berlin had proposed a bilateral agreement, but London had roundly refused, concerned about 'what would have been said by France?'[130] Instead, Britain had first consulted the other Great Powers.[131] Germany became the scapegoat for the failure of the negotiations over disarmament,[132] yet Crowe confessed in his private correspondence that the German negotiators had shown themselves to be unfailingly fair and capable and ready to meet all Britain's wishes when prizes were distributed. The French, by contrast, had been very difficult to deal with, for they were 'slippery and crooked' and 'dreadfully suspicious of everybody and everything'.[133]

As a result of all these endeavours, by 1907 a new and comprehensive system of alliances and treaties with global reach had taken shape, with the Central Powers left at a disadvantage. The Mediterranean Agreements had previously tied Britain to the interests of the Triple Alliance and had been designed to secure the status quo in the Mediterranean; discontinued in 1898, they had been replaced by a treaty signed by Spain, France and Britain and limited to the western Mediterranean.[134] This agreement was an idea first voiced by Grey and Hardinge at the Algeciras conference and then realized by Nicolson and Cambon. The impetus for the alliance had been provided by the well-advanced negotiations of the Cologne firm of Feltern and Guillaume with Spain for the establishment of a telegraph connection that would run from Emden to the Canaries. Although from a British perspective Grey had no reason to object, he informed the Quai d'Orsay that his agreement was dependent on France.[135]

Where Lansdowne had always been careful to ensure that France did not think British support a given, Grey was almost fawning in his repeated expressions of loyalty and even handed Paris partial control over Britain's policy towards Germany.[136] In January 1907, the Swiss chargé d'affaires in Paris described the impact of this attitude to a high-ranking French general:

> The actions of British policy led by Edward VII against his nephew Wilhelm II have never stopped since the crisis of Tangier, and they are now more active than ever.

England has everything to gain and nothing to lose in a war against Germany with the assistance of France.[137]

Certainly, Lansdowne had also had an Anglo-Spanish agreement in mind, but his primary concern had been Gibraltar and the threat to its security from France, as the Admiralty confirmed.[138] Grey's concern, by contrast, was first the relationship with Paris, which was to be cemented, and second the broad political constellation.[139] With his unerringly accurate readings of Grey's foreign policy that appeared in the *Fortnightly Review*, Garvin got right to the heart of the matter when he wrote that the Entente Cordiale was the crux of a system around which all other powers, excluding Germany, were to take up position.[140] The colonial-focused arrangements of April 1904 had become something much more. The goal was to prevent Spanish concessions to Germany at any cost, even if they were purely economic, and to bind the Iberian Peninsula more securely to Britain and France.[141] Strict secrecy was declared a 'chief object' – surely a sign that Britain had a bad conscience – for otherwise, Hardinge noted, 'It would be seriously resented by Germany who would regard it as aimed at her; it would appear as a tightening of the net spread around German political activity; and might act as a sufficient provocation to drive her into hostile action of some kind'.[142] Cambon proposed that the agreement be extended to cover the 'status quo in respect of their respective maritime possession in the Mediterranean basin and in the part of the Atlantic in front of the European and African coasts.[143] Italy would also be invited to participate.[144]

St Petersburg made full use of these developments. Although Izvolsky complained to the French ambassador about the very evident encirclement of Berlin, he only enhanced that impression when he explained to the German ambassador that here was now another link in the chain that Britain was using to encircle Germany.[145] At the same time, the French foreign minister Stephan Pichon informed Bertie that Rome was unable to give the Central Powers any further active assistance against France, and that it was now in the interests of Italy to look to France and Britain, rather than to Germany.[146] The international community did not see the new web of alliances as an inevitable response to German aggression. Belgian observers shared the views of their Swiss colleagues in believing that the new arrangements reflected the actual relationship between the various powers, with control of such international relationships now entirely in the hands of Britain, France and Russia, the gravitational core for all the other powers, including Italy, Spain, the Scandinavian states and Greece. Globally, that bloc also encompassed Japan and the United States, as either allies or friends. To neutral Belgium and Switzerland, it seemed that the real goal was to ensure that the Central Powers were entirely isolated.[147]

London wanted to take matters into its own hands and ensure that it was no longer tied down by an ailing states system, and to that end it was willing to accept that the demarcation of interests in Asia would transfer Russian pressure elsewhere. With the tensions on the margins of Europe now again central to Europe, the Entente Cordiale shifted in character from a dual to a Triple Entente. That shift can be seen in particular in relation to Russia, once Britain's arch-enemy and now Britain's friend. The Anglo-Russian entente was certainly no love match.[148] The problems on the Indian border remained, put on ice in the short term and downplayed in public. Russia had little interest in abiding by the terms to which it had committed, whether in Persia or in Manchuria. British observers demonstrated a tolerance towards Russia that they did not replicate for the Central Powers. Anything Berlin did became shameless presumption in Fleet Street and Whitehall, but nothing else had apparently been expected of Russia.[149] Grey wanted to offer his domestic critics as little purchase as possible and above all sought to minimize the implications for Europe, limiting himself to a 'business-like' discussion of the definition of spheres of interest in Asia.[150] Benckendorff informed Izvolsky that the focus was therefore on regions of which, to Russian eyes, it seemed the British foreign secretary 'knew nothing'.[151] And indeed, Grey even confused the Persian Gulf and the Red Sea.[152]

Britain proceeded cautiously and vigilantly. Izvolsky's post-convention attempt to come to an agreement with Germany over the Baltic was viewed with suspicion,[153] and even Grey curbed his initial enthusiasm. The rapprochement had first to prove its worth on the continent. Only when Russia fully understood the value of a friendship with Britain would the alliance pay off.[154] Early mistrust soon seemed justified, for despite having been asked directly, in autumn 1907 Izvolsky said nothing to either his new British partner or his French allies about the existence of a German-Russian status quo agreement on the Åland islands,[155] snubbing his new allies, both of which had been guarantors of the Åland convention of 1856.

At stake was the status quo in the Baltic, which was supposed to be assured by the demilitarization of this strategically located island group, which lay between Finland and Sweden. In summer 1906, the *Times* had warned on several occasions[156] that Russia intended to exploit ongoing issues with Finland as a pretext for bringing the islands permanently under its control. With Kronstadt, Sveaborg and Libau already in Russian hands, the newspaper noted, the tsardom would then undoubtedly be in a position to control the whole of northern Europe, which, the *Times* insisted, was precisely the goal of Grand Duke Mikhailovich, who was responsible for Russian policy on the Baltic but not England's friend.[157] As Nicolson prepared for the first talks in St Petersburg about an Anglo-Russian rapprochement, London generously ignored the issue, along with other developments, including the oppression of its Finnish friends and the many anti-Semitic outrages in Russia.[158] While the foreign secretary was determined to see no cause for disquiet in Russia's actions, the *Times*, despite its concerns and traditionally critical approach to Russia, suddenly decided that Russia's potential treaty violation gave no real cause for alarm. The paper soberly accepted that Russia saw no link between the status quo and observation of the Åland convention and, adopting an empathetic tone, at the behest of Valentine Chirol proposed to its readers that St Petersburg must have found the terms of the agreement on Åland humiliating and therefore was surely justified in unilaterally terminating the treaty.[159] The close relationship between Hardinge and Chirol lay behind this change of heart. Well acquainted with the situation in Central Asia, the Foreign Editor at the *Times* tended to be critical of Russia,[160] which repeatedly led Hardinge to encourage him to make his reports more positive than the facts warranted:

> I think you have hardly any idea of the position in which *The Times* is regarded in this country, its power for good or evil as a political weapon, and the harm that it has done our country and our individual countrymen during the past few months in embittering our relations with the Russians. It is useless to try to dissipate from the mind of the foreigner the idea that *The Times* is officially inspired and reflects the views of the Govt.

In order that an agreement with Russia that would be 'beneficial in every way to our country' might be reached, Hardinge continued,

> it is necessary to lose no time in preparing public opinion for it and I venture to say from my knowledge and experience ... that if *The Times* still continues to maintain its present tone of hostile criticism the difficulty of my task will be infinitely greater and may become impossible.[161]

Ever since the Boer War, the Kaiser and the German public had been frustrated by the bad press Germany received in Britain, but their concerns had been countered with references to press freedom and expressions of surprise that such great weight should be ascribed by the German press to what appeared in the London *Times*. The standards applied to Russia were clearly very different.

Hugh O'Beirne, embassy counsellor at St Petersburg, reported to Grey that Izvolsky planned to use the Åland issue to launch a horse-trading over the Straits. According to Maurice Bompard, the French ambassador in St Petersburg, there could be no doubt that the principal aim of Izvolsky's political plans was to see 'the regime at the Straits' revised, and he therefore tasked the French representative in London with establishing where Grey stood. Grey had responded, 'that England doubtless no longer attaches to the question of the straits the same importance as in the past'. Bompard saw that Izvolsky was 'delighted at the answer'.[162] Although Bertie and Nicolson agreed that Izvolsky's behaviour was questionable,[163] it was both more satisfying and more useful for the London press and the Foreign Office to claim that they could detect German machinations behind his actions.[164] Such, however, was far from the case. Concerned about being ignored as in the Mediterranean, Germany had proposed that Paris, as a guarantor of the Åland convention, participate in a new status quo agreement on the Baltic,[165] while France's ally Russia had not even thought it necessary to inform Paris that it was moving ahead unilaterally.[166] Peeved by the German involvement, Nicolson insisted that he could not see how Germany, which had not even been part of the 1856 convention, could have any interest in the islands,[167] and suggested that Britain had far greater reason for involvement in the issue than the islands' Baltic neighbours. Ultimately, the Kaiserreich recoiled from a course that appeared to be directed against Britain – it would have turned the Baltic into a *mare clausum* for the Baltic powers – and rejected Izvolsky's plans. In place of a bilateral convention, Berlin favoured an international agreement on the model of the old Åland convention or the Mediterranean Agreement.

Although Clemenceau was gradually losing patience with Izvolsky, the London leadership continued to show great forbearance with the Russian foreign minister.[168] On 23 December 1907, Clemenceau communicated to Bertie that a German-Russian rapprochement in the Baltic would not be tolerated by France and that he was very aware that St Petersburg, and not Berlin, was behind these plans. Hardinge and Nicolson felt compelled to act, for while the British diplomats continued to count on the Russian foreign minister for the improvement of Anglo-Russian relations, the French premier proposed ways 'for getting rid of him [Izvolsky]'.[169] Suddenly, the plans for a Triple Entente seemed threatened not by Germany but from within. Out of concern for its *amour propre*, Hardinge complained to Nicolson and the advisor at the French embassy in London Leon Geoffray, France was willing to advocate the removal of Izvolsky and put at risk the closer ties between Russia and Britain.[170] Apprised of the situation by Geoffray, a few days later Clemenceau rowed back. Hardinge had been able to defuse the tensions between Russia and France.[171] The unexpected support from Britain was taken so seriously in St Petersburg that in early 1908 the *Novoe Vremja*, a newspaper traditionally hostile to Britain, believed that it could generate support for an Anglo-Russian alliance in the Balkans directed against Germany and Austria-Hungary, with the convention identified as the natural starting point.[172]

With the retirement of Thomas Sanderson, the principal voices in the Foreign Office had become much more harmonious.[173] London was determined to keep the entente system together, even, if necessary, in opposition to France. Although aware of Izvolsky's double dealing – he was acknowledged to have been the mastermind behind the German-Russian agreement, and not just an accomplice[174] – Britain was willing to excuse him on the grounds of his 'inexperience of les grandes affaires'.[175] With his long involvement in working with Izvolsky, Michael von Taube was well aware just how far short of the mark that description fell.[176] Yet, once more, the resentment was directed at Germany, which was again branded a troublemaker.[177] Grey wished to ensure that Germany was fully aware of its isolation and of Britain's blossoming friendship with Russia, and Whitehall was also concerned to appease France. Hardinge suggested to Cambon that a good will visit by Edward VII to Reval would send all the right signals.[178]

British actions should not be read as a complex attempt to ensure European stability,[179] for they ran in one direction only, aimed simply at remaining on good terms with Russia. As Sweden, which was friendly with Britain, and neutral Belgium and Switzerland were aware, London used two different measures when it came to determining international rights.[180] Paul W. Schroeder, so well able to turn a phrase, summarized: 'Some men steal horses to great applause, while others are hanged for looking over the fence'.[181] Lord Minto was equally aware of just how two-faced the British response was, commenting:

> I cannot believe in the sympathy of the English people with the most abominable rule I ever heard of [Russia]. The 'sick man' commits some atrocity and the whole of Europe holds up its hands in holy horror, but the Russian government can instigate wholesale massacres or wink at them, and we are for worldly advantages to shake them by hands? In respect to Russia's diplomacy I know you told me that I must accept her good faith as a hypothetical assumption, so I must say no more.[182]

Britain had abandoned its mandate to oversee the balance of power and had become guardian of the ententes that now formed a system within the states system.[183] Its commitment to international law was increasingly seeming little more than empty words, as the flouting of the Madrid convention in the first Moroccan crisis demonstrated. In the Åland question the British position finally won through, with the Admiralty insisting that violation of Norway's neutrality remain a possibility.[184]

Britain's plan was to work with Russia to dominate the Near East and prevent what had been identified as a 'Germanization' of the Balkans. The Eastern Department of the Foreign Office appears to have been as little concerned about the cooperative agreements with the two stabilizing powers in south-east Europe – arrangements that may have been inconvenient but remained valid – as it was with the instability that would surely accompany the involvement of a further Great Power in the already volatile Balkans. While the available sources might give no indication of a deliberate systematic encirclement of the Central Powers,[185] Britain's agreements on the Mediterranean, its indulgence of Russia on the Baltic – at Germany's front door – and its subsequent policy on the Balkans all suggest that the Concert of Europe and the balance of power were overburdened and simultaneously neglected. In drawing closer to Russia, London had elected to encourage the very power that in 1899 had already consulted with France on how the Austrian-Hungarian monarchy might be destroyed and thereby committed to a massive change to the status quo.[186] And that power had also long been denounced as autocratic precisely by English Liberals.

'Between Two Fires': The Convention and Its Critics

With the Anglo-Russian Convention and Britain's inclusion in a network of new alignments, widely held concerns about British isolation were put to bed and hopes grew that an end to the decades-long 'great game' was in sight. At the same time, however, Grey's distinct pro-Russian course also came in for harsh criticism. Valentine Chirol believed that from the start Grey's policy on Russia had to shift 'between two fires' – the Conservative opposition and the radical liberal majority within his own party.[187]

Although the conservative newspapers are generally considered to have been pillars of Grey's foreign policy, we need to distinguish more clearly between the conservative media and the parliamentary opposition in the early stages of his time in office. Members of parliament felt Grey had gone much too far in his wooing of Russia and with the terms of the agreement itself. While the radicals were principally distressed by Russia's autocratic constitution, which led to frequent anti-Semitic persecution, the Tory leadership believed that British interests had been sold out.

Left-wing politicians were particularly critical of the agreement. Months before the treaty was ratified, the *Times* had received an appeal from a number of established journalists and parliamentarians that called on the government not to undermine the democratic movement in Russia and Persia by entering into a rapprochement with St Petersburg.[188] Among the signatories were Ramsay MacDonald, George Bernard Shaw, John Hobson and George Cadbury.[189] Subsequent protests against any alliance with the 'most brutal and diabolical autocracy in Europe' came primarily from the London working class, organized by the Independent Labour Party (ILP) and various unions, and included numerous rallies and a public boycott of Russian goods.[190] Newspapermen such as Henry Brailsford and Lucien Wolf used letters from readers and their own articles to speak out against closer ties with Russia.[191]

Similar, if less voluble voices could be heard within Grey's own party, which makes evident again just how difficult it was for the Liberal foreign minister to balance a general desire for great predictability in foreign relations and the demands of the left-liberal majority within the party for an independent foreign policy with moral and democratic standards. Right up until the July Crisis, Grey continued to insist, particularly in the face of objections from radical cabinet colleagues such as John Morley and David Lloyd George, that he had not been constrained by his Russia-friendly course.[192] Where commentators on Grey's foreign policy have often seen a continual avoidance of alliances, a closer gaze will detect constricting party structures and concerns about renewed splits in the party.[193] Here, then, is an explanation for the professions of loyalty made to Paris and St Petersburg, which his predecessors would never have contemplated.[194] Uncertain about the impact within his own party, Grey postponed the conclusion of the convention until shortly before the end of the parliamentary session, leaving no time for extensive debate in the House of Commons but more time to talk round those who were not yet on board. Again, it is very revealing that he was so open to the Russian ambassador about his motives[195] and yet kept his radical liberal colleagues in the cabinet in the dark.

Loyal to the government, the *Times* expressed its public support for Grey. Although traditionally somewhat critical of Russia,[196] Chirol complied with Hardinge's repeated requests and demands and avoided any criticism of the policy towards Russia.[197] Privately, Chirol judged the convention a 'tremendous give away',[198] but broader political considerations led him to believe public support for the liberal imperialists within the government of greater importance. Ultimately, he held radical liberal pacifists responsible for the lack of patriotism and self-sacrifice among the British people that meant the Empire could no longer hold its own without assistance. In light of what Chirol termed 'the present state of public feeling in this country and the reluctance to make any patriotic sacrifices for our national defences', the convention was the only way to hold Russia at bay for a while at least.[199] For the moment, Britain could still benefit from Russia's temporary weakness and from its traditional reputation for pugnacity, but Chirol believed that in the long term his fellow countrymen lacked the resolution to stand firm against Russian expansionism.[200]

Chirol's observations are invaluable for historians precisely because he looked so closely at such a range of complex domestic and international concerns. Strikingly, in this phase he made no mention of a balance of power solution for the problem of a weakened tsardom and an overly strong Germany. He believed the choice Britain faced was between continuing independence and increased but expensive military strength, on one hand, and salvation in an alliance, and not with the Central Powers but with its greatest rivals, on the other. Singularly well informed, he was able to welcome the agreement with Russia with something close to euphoria even before it had been announced officially on 26 September 1907, identifying in its contents the long-awaited revolution in international affairs. As he defended the government's course against critical readers with unusual dedication, he pronounced that the world had been freed at last from the longest and most profound enmity between the United Kingdom and Russia.[201]

The Foreign Editor of *The Times* countered the accusation that Grey had merely wanted to further isolate Germany by suddenly refuting the idea that such isolation was necessary, even though he had previously proposed that it was.[202] According to Chirol, despite its defeat, Russia required no reinforcement. He also sought to make clear to his readers that the convention had brought no harm to the Persian independence and democracy movement,[203] while in terming the convention a 'requisite for universal peace',[204] he automatically allocated it a continental function. The support for the convention expressed by the *Times* enabled

Chirol to prevent a media campaign by Kitchener against the convention, and the critical *Pall Mall Gazette* and John Morley committed to the pro-Russia course, with the latter specifically invoking the *Times*.[205]

Among the liberal press, the *Westminster Gazette* in particular defended the rapprochement. Spender made great effort to correct Russia's very poor reputation as a brutal autocracy. In a series of lead articles that appeared over a number of weeks, he sought to place Russia in the most positive light possible,[206] aided by Russian expert Bernard Pares, who, like Spender, belonged to Grey's circle of advisors.[207] The overlap in Spender's and Grey's argumentation suggests that the two men must have consulted with one another. Thus, Spender emphasized that thanks to the agreement, Russian influence at the North West Frontier had been contained, India had been freed from the threat of invasion, and a war that appeared imminent had been avoided at the last moment,[208] observations clearly addressed to the radical liberals.

On the conservative side, the government was supported, as would be expected, by the *National Review* and the *Spectator*.[209] Surprisingly, however, Spenser Wilkinson and the *Morning Post* had reservations. The European character of the ties with Russia was bluntly pointed out, and the convention deemed checkmate for the German Empire.[210] At the same time, the *Morning Post* complained that the agreement served only Russia and that 'it left Russia just as free to quarrel with Great Britain as she was before'.[211] For the *Morning Post*, the implications of the agreement lay not in its detail but in the handshake that sealed it,[212] which had implications far beyond its local arrangements and affected the Great Power system as a whole.[213] Similarly, the *National Review* saw in the agreement the foundations of a new triple alliance of global import, the very alliance that for so long it had thought necessary and that would be able to dominate the nations of the world.[214]

A number of leading Conservative politicians were of a very different opinion. On the issue of Persia, they tended to overlap with the views expressed in the radical liberal press. Shortly before the parliamentary debate, Asquith sought to take the wind out of the sails of his critics by placing the 'spirit' of the agreement centre stage.[215] But even Balfour and Lansdowne, who had also sought a rapprochement with Russia, had their concerns. Balfour and Lansdowne focused on the outcome of the negotiations and on the possible consequences. The majority of the Tories were disappointed that despite the favourable circumstances, Grey had not been able 'to make a better bargain especially if, as we were told, the arrangement was sought by Russia', and noted, 'Both in Afghanistan and Tibet we seem to be rather worse off than before'.[216] Balfour was especially upset to see that when it came to Persia, Grey had not even managed to get Izvolsky to recognize the status quo at the Gulf.[217] With a view to the far more favourable negotiating conditions his successors enjoyed, Lansdowne noted that the Liberals repeatedly attempted to represent their policies as merely a continuation of those in place when he was in office, but, he insisted, such was not the case. Much to the contrary, the agreement covered none of the issues that had previously been deemed essential; in Lansdowne's opinion, it was entirely new.[218] Rather than see access to the Gulf as a *casus belli*, Grey seemed to have thought the status quo of little importance, and at the negotiations Izvolsky had stubbornly resisted recognition of the status quo, feeding the general mistrust.[219] Additionally, Grey had endorsed Russian claims to a portion of the customs revenue in the region. Grey had to admit in parliament that his predecessors would never have consented to this division of Persia, but he declared it had been made necessary by new strategic considerations, which, however, he failed to spell out. His argument was clearly spurious, for the situation in the Middle East had not changed since the time of Lansdowne's negotiations with Benckendorff. The repeated claim that the convention had helped improve the 'atmosphere' between Britain and Russia on the continent was far more effective.[220] In the end, Lansdowne and Balfour demonstrated a statesman-like restraint that should not be interpreted as broad acceptance of the convention; their response followed the principle that proposed one not be unduly disapproving of one's successors, with criticism left to others.

Privately, however, Lansdowne gathered together the reports on the convention that appeared in the press and highlighted the passages that appeared to him most significant. Their essential message was that the alliance was about far more than just an agreement on Asia, and could readily give the impression 'that the agreement has been concluded to isolate Germany'.[221] Although Lansdowne had also sought a settlement of colonial disputes that would lighten the burden on the Empire and on the British taxpayer, he had abided by the fundamental maxim, encouraged at times by Balfour, that British support must never be taken for granted, not even by France. In this respect, the negotiating situations in 1903 and in 1906/7 could not have been more different. Earl Percy, Lansdowne's former deputy, spoke on his behalf, complaining that the convention required real sacrifices by Britain, but Britain appeared to gain very little in return, and John Morley concurred that Russia had so far given no reason to be trusted and that the convention was an advance payment that St Petersburg had still to earn.

George Curzon spearheaded the conservative critics. In Oxford in early November 1907, he had already described the agreement as a diplomatic disaster. In his maiden speech in the House of Lords, given in February 1908, he made his mark with a speech against Liberal policy on Russia that was both knowledgeable and eloquent. For nearly two hours, the former viceroy of India spoke of his experiences with Russia in order to attack the convention as an 'absolute surrender'. He denounced its content, which he saw as signalling unnecessary sacrifice and a loss of prestige, its timing and its complete disregard for regional evaluations and expertise. The sphere of influence in Persia that Grey had secured for Britain had, Curzon declared, no commercial value. And indeed, the Russian sphere of influence allocated in the convention encompassed seven of the eleven major trade routes and eleven of the twelve largest cities and trading centres, each with over 30,000 inhabitants.[222]

Overall, Curzon was appalled with the results of the negotiations, which gave Russia the prime land and the principal communication and trade routes, while Britain had to be content with desert. Curzon demanded to know how the British colonial administration could expect to secure the popular respect that was so essential for dealings in the east when Britain was willing to allow itself to be so thoroughly hoodwinked by Russia. Here was one reason, he told the House of Lords, why with all his decades of experience in the Middle East he held the claims about the vaunted strategic implications of the convention and its supposed spirit to be misleading, and even fraudulent. In Berwick-upon-Tweed, Grey had insisted that Britain's economic interests had been in no way compromised. Curzon found it all the stranger then, that Buchar, the headquarters of British commercial representation in the Gulf, the whole of the Karun and Baktiari regions, and large cities and trading centres would all land in the Russian sphere of influence. And even more significantly, Russia had not provided a specific commitment to maintain the status quo in the Gulf. Curzon pronounced a stark judgement: 'We have thrown away to a large extent the efforts of our diplomacy and of our trade for more than a century'.[223]

Curzon suspected Grey was attempting to appease Russia. Under pressure from his colleagues and the Indian government, on 6 June 1907 Grey had finally resolved to include a clause on the status quo of the Gulf, but Izvolsky simply refused to recognize it. Nicolson caved.[224] Without waiting for a response from London, he took the opportunity 'to make the graceful concession at once'.[225] Russia would never sign a clause attached subsequently.[226] The accuracy of Curzon's prophecy about the loss of influence in the Gulf would be confirmed by his biographer, Harold Nicolson, who was a son of Arthur Nicolson.[227]

Finally, the former viceroy of India seized on a criticism voiced by the radical liberals when he accused Grey personally of having left both parliament and the country in the dark during the negotiations. For Curzon, it was a 'blunder of the first magnitude'[228] that Grey was so resistant to hearing the advice of those experts who knew the region and knew Russia. Ten days later, Percy called for an investigation by a Royal Commission,[229] while the Earl of Ronaldshay viewed it as fatal for international stability for Russia to be lined up against Germany.[230]

Grey did not manage to convince his critics. He avoided making any reference to the content of the agreement and evoked instead a spirit of rapprochement. As foreign secretary, he continued to operate like a parliamentary spokesperson, spending more time trying to persuade his fellow countrymen[231] than grappling with his Russian negotiating partners. Campbell-Bannerman primarily had his hopes set on relief for the budget,[232] for the agreement promised 'to remove the danger of an Asiatic avalanche and will make things easier in Europe', at least for a while.²³³ Hardinge sold the convention as a triumph of British statesmanship, with what was important being 'that it prepared the ground for future eventualities'.²³⁴

Opposition politicians were not alone with their excoriating criticism, for they were joined by Lord Minto, the new viceroy,²³⁵ and by Cecil Spring Rice, who had been stationed in Teheran for many years. Spring Rice's accusations against his superior were unusually pointed.²³⁶ 'My dear Liberals at home', he remarked sarcastically, were vying for the tsar's approval, yet in the end would only succeed in leaving their Persian allies subjugated.²³⁷ Beyond the political criticism, Spring Rice continued, it was actually highly likely that Russia would use the agreement as an opportunity 'to carry on her old designs under a new cover'. In Central Asia, Britain was now 'worse off than the Russians because we are not feared as they are, and because we are regarded as having betrayed the Persian people',²³⁸ and he emphasized to Chirol that the new course seemed an excellent thing only at first glance.²³⁹ Spring Rice demonstrated that he was well aware of the high price that Britain had paid for the agreement and the close ties between the policy towards Russia and the attitude towards Germany. The agreement had been brokered at the cost of Anglo-German alienation: 'It has been done by painting the German devil on the wall. We are all hard at work at that job, including the Germans themselves and one of the reasons why I hate them [the Germans] most is that they are forcing us into an agreement with Russia'.²⁴⁰ The benefit lay only in the ability 'to prepare for what will come',²⁴¹ and he was under no illusions about what that would be, for counter to the general tenor among his superiors and to the views of historians who have characterized him as notoriously anti-German, Spring Rice believed Russia to be the real threat: 'Iswolsky has Mongolia, wants the Åland Islands and the Bosphorus, predominance in Persia, equality in Afghanistan and Thibet, and all within two years of the most disastrous war Russia ever waged. Do you really believe Russia has ceased to be aggressive?'²⁴² Spring Rice could see no balance of power advantage for either the Middle East or Europe; the only pleasure he could take from the convention was in the short-term security of the Empire.

Spring Rice feared the consequences for Europe could be calamitous,²⁴³ and even Nicolson and Hardinge, who had advocated closer ties with Russia, shared his pessimistic assessment. The convention had simply bought five, or a maximum of ten years in which to prepare for the expected conflict with Russia; the only alternative was to hope for an international development that would head off this outcome.²⁴⁴ Hardinge thought the Near East might provide such an eventuality:

> Confidence has to be established and mutual prejudices have to disappear. ... I do not think that Russia more and more will be drawn in the German orbit. Russia will

inevitably be drawn into paying greater attention to her position in the Near East, bringing her into conflict with the central powers.[245]

As an explanation sent to the India Office makes evident, the leadership at the Foreign Office was now setting continental concerns against imperial concerns.[246] Although usually judged to have had no real understanding of the international community, the radical liberal press identified a systematic problem in this approach,[247] and was alarmed, and anything but 'sanguine',[248] about the conspicuous isolation of Germany and Austria-Hungary. The *Manchester Guardian*, for example, was worried about the effects of the Japanese-French alliance in the Far East; the paper noted that although the inclusion of Germany would provide 'an additional guarantee of peace ... it appears that Germany is to be kept aloof while other Powers strike their compact'.[249] A few weeks later, the principle of imperial powers to exclude all newcomers from their share of the colonial cake, a concept well known in the Far East, was causing the *Manchester Guardian* serious concerns because it seemed to be being expanded to cover Europe also. The newspaper could see the alliance between Spain, France and Britain concluded shortly before the convention only as inherently anti-German, and asked, 'What are the unforeseen contingencies? What is the treaty getting at?', replying to its own question, 'At Germany, says Matin'.[250]

In his lead articles, Charles P. Scott expressed his horror at the evident appeasement of St Petersburg. The smallest act by the Central Powers provided ammunition for an extended smear campaign, Scott pointed out, yet Russia was treated with great leniency.[251] By granting Russia a loan in April 1906, Scott argued, London had helped the Russian regime against its own (revolutionary) people, and now the convention further guaranteed that the tsar could extend that war, first against Britain's Persian democratic allies, then across the Near East, and finally to take on Austria-Hungary. Here was Russia's real goal, and it meant that the Great Powers were now affected directly, and not just indirectly, via the periphery, as had previously been the case. Scott spelled out his suspicions that Grey's goal was to build up a power bloc, and warned of the consequences. The convention must be the limit of Anglo-Russian cooperation, for the stability of international power relations was assured only 'so long as we don't become allies'.[252] When the details of the convention became public three days later, however, to many it seemed that limit had been overstepped. While rapprochement with France, another parliamentary-based state, was generally deemed accepted, collaboration with Russia seemed to compromise Britain's political and moral stance, while also running counter to the common-sensical rules of international politics.

Within the political press, the charge against British foreign and defence policies and their consequences was led by Henry Massingham's *The Nation*. Politically an alternative to the *National Review* and with a similar circulation, this radical liberal paper also concluded that the convention was an astonishing development, noting that it represented a disproportionate evaluation of German and Russian actions and meant collaboration with an autocratic and brutal system.

According to *The Nation*, conclusion of the Anglo-French entente had given everyone the hope that came with the peaceful combination of two liberal states. But in recent years a Liberal foreign secretary had taken this hope *ad absurdum*. As a result, London had damaged its relationship with its traditional partners, without gaining control over its new partners, on whom it had allowed itself to become increasingly dependent. France and Russia were in no way to blame – they had simply followed their own interests. With its constant and partially unfounded agitation against Berlin and its ingratiation with its traditional rivals, London had limited its own options.[253] The newspaper provided no wild pacifist fantasies or amateurish political suggestions; it proved itself well informed and its analysis overlapped internal expert views remarkably closely, in revealing, for example, that the threat of an invasion by Germany was no more than a myth.[254] *The Nation* insisted the problem was not Germany, its legitimate ambitions or the expansion of its navy, whose threat had repeatedly been refuted. The real problem, the paper insisted, was Britain's lack of willingness to treat Germany as it treated other powers and to return to being the non-partisan arbitrator of Europe. *The Nation* called on its readers to compare the *Times*'s coverage of Germany and Russia 'in such parallel incidents as that of Casablanca on the one hand, and the besetting of our Legation in Teheran by Colonel Liakhoff's men on the other'. In the first instance, the paper noted, a trivial episode in which 'our friends' had not been entirely innocent had been blown up into a *casus belli*, while 'in the second an open affront to our own agents is passed over in silence'.[255]

The inclusion of Russia to form a 'triple pact' had crossed a limit. Persia had been 'sold', given in exchange for a dubious friendship with Russia, an enormous price, for which Germany could also easily have been acquired. Yes, Germany was a conservative power, but Russia was unquestionably reactionary. 'German diplomacy has often been tortuous and Machiavellian', the paper admitted, 'but it has never revealed quite the same chaos of intrigue as Russian policy has exhibited in the Balkans, and exhibits in Persia today'.[256] If the tsardom had been kept at a distance and a carrot-and-stick policy adopted, then Britain might have been able to exert a modicum of influence on Russian domestic arrangements. From the moment the Russian government felt it had become integral to British global politics, British interests were bound for better or worse to the defence of the integrity of Russia. As a consequence, *The Nation* recognized, political decisions made in London had to align with St Petersburg, whatever the prevailing political system.[257] The repeated balance of power arguments made by Ripon or Grey could not persuade the paper otherwise, and *The Nation* continued to deem the idea of a renewed Three Emperors' League far-fetched, made highly unlikely by the tensions between Germany and France and by Germany's financial weakness, which meant that 'Russia cannot well abandon the French alliance, for the simple reason that Germany cannot act as her banker'.[258]

In its analysis of the Liberals' imperial policy and the issues of the moment, *The Nation* always considered the broader context, which included the liberal concert tradition and liberal moral principles, the international system and Britain's sense of purpose and authority derived from its imperial status, as well as the impact on and hopes of its global rivals and partners. Its intricate argumentation proved too complex, and sometimes even confusing, for some readers, who were required to have a detailed understanding of the situation and an ability to ponder both international and national developments. Overall, *The Nation* found Grey's course far too dogmatic and based on fixed ideas that were now very dated, with the fundamental concepts on which they were based constantly changing, and very different in 1906/7 from earlier years. Despite ongoing disagreements – with France or over Persia, for example – neither Russia nor Germany was currently a threat per se. British policy, the newspaper noted, would only increase the tensions with Germany and play down the tensions with Russia, making the situation a whole lot worse and forcing Germany into a corner. The German Empire could then justifiably claim it needed its fleet; any other power that found itself similarly surrounded would feel the same. But cause and effect were too often overlooked in London, *The Nation* recognized, which meant that Britain had been highly indulgent of Russia and France.[259]

At least for the phase between 1906 and 1908, the interpretation provided by Massingham's *Nation* was entirely in accord with the facts, as Gregor Schöllgen has been able to demonstrate on the example of German consideration for British interests in Persia.[260] The left-liberal paper did not deny that Grey wanted peace; the problem, as it saw it, was that Grey hated war so much that he was willing to do anything to secure peace, but in the end that meant following a security policy that was so stubborn and so full of absolutes that the Central Powers were left in a state of permanent uncertainty. This interpretation is surprising for a newspaper that as a rule historians have rarely consulted on international affairs,[261] largely because they have joined with contemporaries in ascribing the paper a radical liberal and unworldly idealism.[262] Yet *The Nation*'s striking analysis suggests that it adopted a detailed and nuanced approach not replicated by other political periodicals of the time. With their monocausal argumentation and established stereotypes of German danger and Russian good will, the *National Review* and the *Spectator* could not match the quality of the commentary provided by *The Nation*. Only the *Fortnightly Review* could provide something similar on occasion, thanks above all to the large number of authors who appeared in its pages.

Like several authors who wrote for the *Fortnightly Review*,[263] *The Nation* arrived at the interesting conclusion, which has been overlooked to date, that

Lansdowne's conservative diplomacy embodied the liberal tradition far more than Grey's approach. Only a passive and uncritical attitude, the paper claimed, could think there was any continuity. 'It [Grey's diplomacy] has been a loyal and zealous partisan, but it has shown no fertility of ideas, no inspiration of method'. According to *The Nation*, an *idée fixe* that circulated in the numerous myths about the German High Seas Fleet and Germany's supposedly exceptionally Machiavellian ambitions – which closer examination reveals to have been entirely comparable with the pretensions of other powers – was used by Whitehall to justify a policy towards Germany of boycotts and isolation. And yet, the paper was convinced, that policy repeatedly undermined the stability of Europe.[264]

For *The Nation*, the convention with Russia provided a clear example of that threat. The journal was the first publication to express serious concerns about the continental implications of the rapprochement, recognizing a 'mobilisation of powers with England and France at its centre and Germany outside of it'.[265] In entering into league with Russia, London had unnecessarily forced a state of alarm on the Central Powers. For *The Nation*, the question now was whether the alliance of the encircling powers would so paralyse the Central Powers that they would be unable to do anything to disrupt the peace or whether that alliance would in fact achieve precisely the opposite. The paper even insisted that 'a risky game of isolating Germany is at the bottom of the Entente with Russia, much more than a question of Asiatic frontiers'.[266] According to the *Daily News*, the creation of the new groupings over recent years suggested that there had been no real grounds for the convention with Russia unless Persia was to be used as bait to bring Russia into the Entente camp.[267] Why otherwise would Britain offer up something that it had refused for decades – and to a power that was for the moment on its knees?

In the period immediately after the convention was signed, the British government tended to indulge Russian agent activity and public wrongdoings. For the pan-Slavic *Novoe Vremja*, that was only right:

> Russian action in Europe is being restored by means of a widening of the Franco-Russian Alliance, by a development of that 'Einkesselungs' [encirclement] policy, which has already wasted so much blood for German policy. The further this policy is extended, the more isolated will become that power which at present is the sole serious threat to European peace, and which is called the German Empire.[268]

Both radical liberals and Conservatives recognized in the convention a caesura in British foreign policy and in the states system. The details of the agreement were less significant than the symbolism and impact of the negotiations and the fact that Britain and Russia were now bound to one another. While the radicals rejected a close friendship with Russia in either Persia or Europe, the Tories believed that any rapprochement – in particular after past experiences,

Russia's catastrophic defeat and the revolution – must involve Russia coming cap in hand to Britain, and not the other way around. As experts such as Curzon, Hamilton and Spring Rice repeatedly sought to make clear, all that Britain had ever achieved in the Middle East had been based on strength and prestige.[269] Together, the arguments made by Conservatives and radical liberals against the convention and the way in which it had come about largely mirrored the views of the majority Russia-critical public.[270] Foreign policy decision makers always had to bear in mind this intersection of views as they sought to justify their actions publicly.[271] If we focus on the Middle Eastern content of the convention, we risk overlooking the goals that Grey had been pursuing since the 1890s as well as the complex domestic political situation, evident in the criticism of the convention.[272] That broader picture not only highlights the domestic pressures on foreign policy, but also helps us determine whether Liberal foreign policy was qualitatively new or whether it ran with a baton grasped from its predecessors.

'Spectator of Events'? Great Britain, the Macedonian Reforms and the Sanjak Railway

In early 1908, Hardinge was very confident that closer Anglo-Russian ties in Europe were on the cards.[273] Together with Nicolson, he encouraged Grey to ignore the Austro-Russian détente in the Balkans and use the Macedonian reform question, a case he had been making since 1903,[274] as leverage to ensure Russia went hand in hand with Britain on the continent.[275] The results of the convention, he was persuaded, would be felt first in the Balkans. Any Russian animosity against the Central Powers, whatever form it took, was only an advantage for Britain.[276] It was in British interests to nurture the easily wounded vanity of Izvolsky as a means of inserting a wedge between Russia and the Central Powers.[277]

In January 1908, such an opportunity arose, fostered by, of all people, Count Alois von Aehrenthal, the foreign minister of Austria-Hungary. Aehrenthal, notoriously choleric and ambitious, had not been produced from the same mould as his somewhat lethargic predecessor Agenor Goluchowski, whom he had succeeded in October 1906.[278] He immediately began to roll out his ambitions for south-eastern Europe. In October 1906, Vienna seized the initiative for the construction of a railway line, as approved by the Treaty of Berlin, through the Sanjak of Novi Pazar.[279] This expression of Vienna's Balkan ambitions marked the beginning of the end for the Austro-Russian partnership established by the Mürzsteg agreement. The Foreign Office had no objections per se to Vienna's project; indeed, the opposite was very much the case, for just as attempts were being made to draw Britain and Russia closer together, the railway plans opened up an opportunity to come between Vienna and St Petersburg.[280]

Anglo-Russian collaboration first played out on Macedonia.[281] In November 1906, and in parallel to the efforts being made by Nicolson, the first Anglo-Russian attempts had been made to find a common language on Macedonian reform, primarily on British initiative. Since 1903, the European powers had been trying in vain to have the local sultan introduce social and political reforms and halt the activities of terrorist bands supported from Bulgaria.[282] With tension between Vienna and St Petersburg increasing again, London faced a choice: mediate between Austria-Hungary and Russia, as Balfour's government had attempted to do, or detach Austria-Hungary from its Russian partner.

Various models of reform for Macedonia were available, and Anglo-Russian discussions were protracted, spanning many months. The British goal was not so much to influence Russia as to convince Russia of Britain's loyalty as a new partner. Evidence of just how seriously this change of course was taken in London is found in a complaint, received by Lansdowne, from a group of radical MPs that formed the Balkan Committee to safeguard the interests of the Balkan nations. This noted that although Grey had become the unofficial leader of the Concert of the Great Powers, he made no efforts to use his influence for the cause of regional stability; quite the contrary.[283] Balfour also considered Grey responsible for Britain's one-sided Russophile policy in the Near East. For Balfour, it was essential that British intervention in this region was directed at the broad maintenance of order; anything else, especially anything partisan, should be avoided at all costs,[284] yet, recalling the situation with Persia,[285] London allowed the opportunity for a broadly framed realignment on the Macedonian question to evaporate.[286] Stéphen Pichon, the French foreign minister, was delighted, for he already held that international relations would now be determined by the 'rapprochement anglo-russe' and hoped that a triple alliance was the model of the future.[287]

Although Vienna fell into line with the wishes of both St Petersburg and London by adopting a harsher stance in its political relations with the sultan, the response in London was not as expected. London suddenly procrastinated on the Macedonia question and delayed the instruction that was to be sent to the British embassy in Constantinople. Nicholas O'Conor, British ambassador at the Porte, rounded off the confusion by deliberately disobeying the outdated instructions from London and following his own pro-Turkish line. His goal was to win back British influence with Turkey at the expense of Germany.[288] Any delay was an advantage only to Britain. The Mürzsteg agreement had been made in 1903 and was to last only five years, but a breakthrough in Macedonia might have brought Vienna and St Petersburg closer. London became very alarmed at any sign, however small, of a tighter bond between Austria-Hungary and Russia,[289] and delighted in every revelation of friction between the two powers. Attitudes towards Bulgaria are also very revealing. George Buchanan, the envoy to Bulgaria, had noted in a memorandum that the unresolved situation and lack of independence stood in the way of further reforms, which for London was only one more reason to torpedo Bulgarian independence,[290] for as long as the troubles of south-eastern Europe continued, Russian ambitions could be fed there, and London could use this to edge closer to Russia and to widen the rift between Russia and Austria-Hungary.

That broader objective explains British procrastination. At first, Britain expressed its support for Austrian reform plans, but subsequently it withdrew that initial agreement. In September, Paris urged London to support only Russia, which Pichon hoped would help break up the partnership formed at Mürzsteg.[291] London entered into a game of cat and mouse with Vienna: in late September O'Conor was instructed to accept the Austrian reform plans; following Vienna's agreement, they were simply rejected a second time. Vienna and Berlin were baffled by London's unpredictable behaviour. In mid December, Germany's former secretary of state and representative at the second Hague conference, Adolf Marschall von Bieberstein, was warned by Aehrenthal that 'England and Russia are outdoing each other with sharp demands for reform and they are supported in doing so by France and Italy'. It would not be long, Aehrenthal suggested, before the two Great Powers came to their own agreement on the Near East too.[292]

Vienna had initially been unperturbed by the Anglo-Russian Convention with its implications for the Near East[293] but was now forced to re-evaluate that response. The first doubts were raised during a flying visit to Vienna by Izvolsky, when the Russian foreign minister not only made clear his conspicuous happiness about the situation with the Straits but in the same breath termed the London government Russia's partner. Greatly alarmed, Aehrenthal recognized a need to be especially cautious when it came to the Mürzsteg agreement. Berlin assumed that Russia was continuing to accommodate British wishes for the Balkans, and a fear grew that the western powers together with Russia would soon grab the reins from the Central Powers.[294] His prediction proved accurate. As a result of Aehrenthal's offensive Balkan policy, British prospects for closer collaboration with Russia seemed good, or, in Nicolson's words, 'The stars in their course are bringing Iswolsky closer to us'.[295] Hardinge already hoped to repeat the model of Algeciras with Macedonia.[296] For Hardinge and Grey, it was most important that relations between the two Mürzsteg signatories should continue to worsen,[297] and they were therefore overjoyed when Izvolsky not only rejected Aehrenthal's reform proposals but also announced to Nicolson that Russia would no longer work together with Austria-Hungary and intended to look for other partners.[298] His reference could only be to the Entente Cordiale.

By early 1908, Nicolson was confident. By his reckoning, Izvolsky would try to stay on good terms with the Central Powers for as long as possible, but in the long term Russia would turn to Britain. Britain must be ready to fill the void created by friction within the alliance between Russia and Austria-Hungary as soon as it appeared.[299] Nicolson correctly believed that the key would be Britain's attitude on south-eastern Europe, and he went as far as to hold out to Izvolsky the prospect of British support should conflict break out over the Balkans.[300] Even before London had been officially informed about the railway project,[301] Hardinge believed that there were signs of a significant estrangement of the Central Powers and Russia, and he was certain that Izvolsky would be forced into the arms of London and Paris. During January, he informed Cambon, the French ambassador, that much hung on this sensitive stage in the rapprochement and that whenever possible France and Britain should together support the Russian foreign minister's plans.[302] Shortly before, Hardinge had written to Nicolson: 'Germany is driving Russia into our arms ... if Great Britain played the game quite straightly with Russia in Persia ... we ought to have her ... in Europe also'.[303]

Encouraged by disturbing reports received from Count Mensdorff, the Austrian-Hungarian ambassador in London, Aehrenthal was eager to avoid any further delays in the implementation of his Balkans plans, which were designed to safeguard the multi-ethnic state.[304] Should London really be prepared to make concessions on the Straits, then no time must be lost in securing Austrian-Hungarian interests on its own doorstep. The Treaty of Berlin had specifically given the Austrian-Hungarian monarchy the right to 'to control the military and commercial routes'[305] in the Sanjak of Novi Pazar. The Mürzsteg agreement had in the meantime repeatedly proved unable to halt the westward drive of the small Balkan states. At the same time, however, the Austrian-Hungarian foreign minister was eager to ensure that his offensive actions did not force Britain and Russia closer together and cut the cord that bound Russia and Austria-Hungary together.

In the end, the attempt to separate legal reforms in Macedonia from the railway in Sanjak proved an error. Initially, London had not believed British interests would be compromised by the railway. Hardinge had officially given his approval in Constantinople, and parliament concurred on 25 February 1908, noting that as a trading nation Britain contemplated the railway's construction with benevolent neutrality.[306] Vienna received only encouragement from Montenegro, Bulgaria, Greece and Italy, but Nicolson's hope that the Turkish railway concessions would undermine Izvolsky's trust in Austria-Hungary to Britain's advantage proved well founded.[307] Russia charged Austria-Hungary with blatant disregard of the Mürzsteg agreement, an accusation that was sufficient to bring Russia's entente partners onto the stage. France had originally given its support to the railway plan, but now, suddenly and without hesitation, Paris jumped aboard the Russian bandwagon. Before Vienna knew what was happening, sharp criticism was also raining down from the far side of the English Channel, to everyone's surprise.[308] The nature of the criticism provides a first indication of the consolidation of the Triple Entente. Although their real intentions were masked by a sudden concern about Vienna's advance towards

Salonika,[309] in cooperation with Russia over the Balkans Grey and Hardinge had discovered a means of banishing for the long term a new League of Three Emperors.

For Louis Mallet and William Tyrrell, Germany was again the guiding spirit, this time as the force behind the Austrian-Hungarian railway plan, and they sought to prevent a 'Germanization' of the region.[310] Hardinge's calculations continued, and he commented on the margin of a report from Nicolson: 'The struggle between Austria and Russia in the Balkans is evidently now beginning, and we shall not be bothered by Russia in Asia'.[311] A long-desired hope now seemed to be realized, with Russia not only withdrawing from Asia but also backing away from the understanding with the Dual Alliance on the Balkans. Five days later, Hardinge commentated on another communication from St Petersburg: 'The action of Austria will make Russia lean on us more and more in the future. In my opinion this will not be a bad thing'.[312] Britain's delay over Macedonian reform had begun to pay off, for the issue could now be used to draw London and St Petersburg closer together.

Power politics in this instance came down to alliances. The British government hoped that the Mürzsteg agreement would be dissolved, with Britain ready to step into the breach and form an alliance with St Petersburg that would cover continental affairs.[313] British correspondence from this period says nothing of a British offer to mediate and makes not even a brief mention of the balance of power, or more specifically the implications for stability in the Balkans. Grey noted only that Germany was alarmed, as Berlin had hoped to see the concert of powers, in the form of discussions among ambassadors to Constantinople, hold together.[314] Austria-Hungary was of secondary importance to Britain[315] and in light of its domestic problems would, according to British reports, sooner or later implode.[316] After the experiences of the last two years, a systemic perspective would have given Berlin cause to identify a clear danger.[317]

When it came to assessing the Russian position, the Foreign Office could rely on Hardinge and Nicolson as its Russia experts, but the lack of German expertise was fatal for its ability to anticipate Berlin's response. Some voices could be heard warning about a panicked knee-jerk reaction by Wilhelm II or by the German or Austrian-Hungarian government. Grey feared the German fear of encirclement.[318] And yet these concerns played no part in shaping British policy on the current problems in the Balkans. London assumed that if the Habsburgs were blocked in the Balkans, Germany would also be forced to back down. Above all, Nicolson expected that in future Izvolsky 'will be disposed to march as far as he dare with us in all questions'.[319] Britain's concern was not to see Germany encircled, but to force Germany to consult *à quatre* on all issues and to ensure Britain had the upper hand politically, although for Berlin it made no difference. That approach reflected neither a return to traditional concert diplomacy, as demanded by the radical liberals, nor the classic and flexible balance of power-based policy that had been adopted by Salisbury and Lansdowne; instead, the system was to be weighted in favour of the Triple Entente.[320]

With relations between Vienna and St Petersburg rapidly deteriorating over the railway issue, with great satisfaction Hardinge came to the conclusion that Mürzsteg was dead in the water.[321] The possibility of a new League of Three Emperors receded over the horizon.[322] For Grey, Macedonia was a 'comfortable anchorage'[323] for attempts to draw closer to Izvolsky. 'Ten years hence a combination of Britain, Russia, and France may be able to dominate Near Eastern Policy; and within that time events will probably make it more and more clear that it is to the interest of Russia and us to work together: but we must go slowly.'[324] No foolhardy sabre-rattling by Germany was required to keep the entente together. The Belgian envoy to Berlin sensed that Germany and the Austrian-Hungarian monarchy in particular, with its direct interests in the Balkans, were in effect automatically sidelined in the Balkan issue and treated as 'quantité négligéable'.[325] In mid July, Grey spoke candidly to Benckendorff about Britain aligning with Russia, provided that St Petersburg dropped Vienna and accepted London instead as its partner in the reform plans.[326]

Grey's real concern was neither international treaties nor the stability of the Balkans and Macedonian reforms that his radical liberal colleagues wanted.[327] Above all, Grey hoped to make collaboration with London palatable to Izvolsky. While Grey still held the London–Paris–St Petersburg axis to be the weaker combination than the Triple Alliance, that situation was, he believed, only temporary. Unlike Maxse,[328] Grey remained concerned about the British public's opinion of Russia. In the short term, he felt it would make sense from a balance of power perspective for Britain to have ties to both France and Russia. At a time when alliances were becoming increasingly permanent and forming a lasting component of foreign policy design,[329] the British change of course acquired a particular quality. Grey also followed longer-term goals, for Russia would need to recover from its military setback against Japan before it could pull its weight in Europe. And Nicolson reported that although Izvolsky was seriously annoyed by the Danube monarchy, he was not yet ready to break with his Mürzsteg partner.[330]

The evidence does not suggest that London simply reacted to external circumstances, feasting on the corpse of the Austro-Russian relationship.[331] Whitehall, and Hardinge in particular, were far more methodical than that interpretation implies.[332] Significantly, neither Hardinge, Grey nor Nicolson talked of long-term repercussions for the stability of the Balkans or of the states system; their repeated concern was instead for the direct and indirect benefits that London might garner from the growing rifts and alienation experienced by Austria-Hungary, the Dual Alliance and Russia. While London justifiably complained about German attempts to drive a wedge into the Entente Cordiale and thereby throw international relations into turmoil, Britain was itself playing a very similar game; the real question was who would come out ahead. Britain's moves were guided by fear, fear of a three emperor's alliance, of isolation, especially in the global arena, and of the invasion that seemed a logical consequence. Between 1894/96, with the conclusion of the Franco-Russian alliance and Britain's renunciation of its traditional policy in the east, and 1907, with the signing of the Anglo-Russian Convention, a new 'global formation' had taken shape that bypassed Germany and the Dual Alliance.[333]

From Reval to the Annexation of Bosnia

Excitement and nervousness prevailed in the House of Commons when, in February 1908, the new entente with Russia was debated. The *hear, hears* from the opposition benches were matched by anguished silence and sudden mutterings from the government backbenches. Edward Grey declared: 'I stand by that [Anglo-Russian Convention] and if the House rejects it or makes it impossible I fall with it'.[334] Grey seemed to be willing to put his career on the line, as he had also done in the rather ridiculous episode involving the Coldstream Guards and an alleged wounding of French feelings,[335] by linking his own fate to the deepening of the Anglo-Russian friendship. His threat of resignation – he was, admittedly, aware of his strong position within the cabinet – showed, on the one hand, just how great his commitment was to a Triple Entente and, on the other hand, just how aware he was of the critical pressure from members of his own party. His threat to resign, which he would repeat during the July crisis, was targeted at the majority of radicals. They were to focus their attention on the demands of domestic political reform, leaving foreign policy and security policy to the liberal imperialists and, above all, to Grey himself. His confrontational course took him where he wanted to go[336] – a success whose significance for the future direction of British foreign policy must not be underestimated. Aware that Grey's resignation could bring down the government and might split the party again, the radicals balked at his political blackmail.

The meeting of crowned heads, very much Hardinge's work, that took place at Reval inspired further debate. The implications of the rapprochement were evident at this remarkable first meeting of Edward VII and Nicholas II. Grey had originally spoken of his wish to proceed slowly on the issue of Anglo-Russian rapprochement on the continent, but in February 1908 Hardinge began to force the pace,[337] explaining: 'We are quite hopeful. If we can only come to terms with Russia we shall be able to secure the co-operation of France and Italy also'.[338] He was aware that the context for developing closer ties with Russia was more favourable than ever before.[339] In November 1907, in response to suspicions that Germany and Russia were working together to find a solution to the Åland issue, he had suggested that the ruling heads of Russia and Britain might meet.

Positive press coverage of such an event was practically guaranteed; even reports on meetings between Wilhelm II and his uncle Edward VII tended to be neutral at worst, and on the whole they were polite. Positive reports about the tsar, who had previously appeared as a despot in the pages of the British press, could only help promote understanding between the two peoples. If the entente was to become a closer bond, then external impressions were everything. Hardinge was not especially anxious, although the liberal radicals continued to cause him a headache.[340] He instructed Nicolson to filter negative domestic news out of his reports and to paper over Russia's problems with Finland and with the Duma.[341] Additionally, he kept word of the upcoming meeting between king and tsar from the cabinet for as long as possible,[342] an act that was all the more controversial when we recall that Hardinge accompanied Edward VII and that he did so completely unsolicited.[343]

In addition to Hardinge and Nicolson, the royal entourage included the British military leadership, so John Fisher, the First Sea Lord, and John French, chief of the General Staff.[344] The encounter clearly was not a social visit, and its effect both in Russia and abroad could hardly have been greater.[345] Those in Britain who appeared surprised by expressions of mistrust in the foreign press and in foreign policy despite the eminence of the travellers, as was predominantly the case for the London press, were either naive or irresponsible.[346] Even neutral countries less directly affected set the encounter alongside the visit by French president Armand Fallières to London and identified a new triple alliance that had the Central Powers surrounded,[347] while both Russian journalist Wesselitzki, who, as the London correspondent of the *Novoe Vremja* was on the payroll of Izvolsky,[348] and British agent Arminius Vambéry spread the rumour that the king and the tsar had come to an agreement directed against Austria-Hungary. For the left-liberals, the meeting was evidence of a 'transition from entente to a military alliance à trois'.[349]

Hardinge used the occasion to make the first follow-up suggestions 'for joint action aimed at countering German advances in the Middle East'[350] and, often overlooked, 'in the Balkans'.[351] His proposals are all the more significant because Hardinge had decided that war with Germany in 1913 was inevitable. The German press panicked at the apparent expansion of the Anglo-Russian Convention to south-eastern Europe, and 'encirclement' became the *mot du jour*.[352] The mark left in Russia was even more powerful than the impression made in Germany and Austria-Hungary. Although no written agreement on a common foreign policy had been drawn up, Hardinge's impact on his Russian interlocutors can hardly be overestimated. One member of the Austrian-Hungarian embassy openly surmised, 'Izvolsky thought he would shove and ended up being shoved'.[353]

Although Russia remained an autocratic country, Britain under a Liberal government indicated that it was willing to cooperate with the tsardom beyond the limits of the convention, on the continent itself. Izvolsky could not have been happier.³⁵⁴ Domestically, too, Stolypin's government gained ground as a result. The Kadets were already pressing the tsar's regime to form an alliance with Britain.³⁵⁵ The hopes that Britain had raised in Russia were evident in the Russian press, where the meeting was deemed 'historic', for it marked 'the beginning of a return of our foreign politics to the Balkans and Europe'.³⁵⁶ In connection with the meeting at Reval, the Kadet press, joined by the pan-Slavists, pushed for Russia to form an alliance with Britain and celebrated the new power grouping in Europe. In their opinion, the Anglo-Russian rapprochement was dictated by the need to have 'a counterweight to the triumphs of German diplomacy on the Bosphorus and of the Central Powers in the Balkans'.³⁵⁷ Britain could not direct these sweeping interpretations, but Whitehall played with the sentiments they contained, exacerbating and instrumentalizing them through its actions. During the various dinners, Fisher was often seated between Stolypin and Izvolsky, and he reported that on being asked by Stolypin what he believed Russia most needed, he had answered, 'Your western frontier is denuded of troops and your magazines are depleted. Fill them up, and then talk of fleets'.³⁵⁸ We may well wonder about the impact of such advice. Shortly after the meeting, the British banker Sir Ernest Cassel confirmed to Otto Hamann, the chief of the German Press Bureau within the German Foreign Office, that Russia had been urged on at Reval and had been advised to increase its military capability to take on Germany.³⁵⁹

During what was an 'entirely unpolitical encounter',³⁶⁰ as Whitehall was never tired of emphasizing, Hardinge explicitly and repeatedly encouraged Russia 'to prepare militarily', for a situation might arise 'in seven or eight years' in which Russia could be granted the role of 'arbiter of Europe'.³⁶¹ In his own version of this statement, Izvolsky was more confident about Russia's future, for he cited Hardinge as having said, 'Then Russia without doubt will be the arbiter of the situation'.³⁶² Instead of taking the role of arbiter for itself, London sought to give that position to Russia, which was hostile to the status quo.³⁶³ Whichever the case, Izvolsky felt he had been expressly encouraged, and he read Hardinge's statements as the official position of the cabinet in London.³⁶⁴

Hardinge's goal was to secure Russia's friendship in advance of the imminent conflagration.³⁶⁵ While Lansdowne and Balfour had made great efforts not to reveal their cards to their partners, Hardinge could hardly restrain himself. Izvolsky crowed that on several occasions Hardinge had emphasized how very much Britain wished for Russia to be as strong as possible both on land and at sea, and according to Izvolsky Hardinge had made clear that he was expressing not a personal view but the official position of the London cabinet.³⁶⁶ British comparisons with the meeting in Paris in 1904 say much about the intentions of both British diplomats and British journalists. One of the first of the well-wishers in this mould was the influential editor of the *Spectator*, who congratulated Grey 'heartily upon the success of the Reval meeting', noting how impressed he was that the foreign secretary had prevailed against his radical liberal critics.³⁶⁷

Germany's shock at the meeting at Reval[368] is explained when we note the commentary and expectations the event engendered in the British press. For Spender and Strachey, Reval was a 'proclamation to the world' that Russia, France and Great Britain, their powers now combined, now controlled the international system.[369] Maxse was already writing of a new 'triple alliance',[370] and Spenser Wilkinson observed: 'There will be no need for a formal alliance, for when three such powers are bound together in the ties of close and intimate friendship no one is likely to attempt towards any one of them a policy of aggression which would bring that friendship into active evidence'.[371] Additionally, Chirol, whose reputation as the official mouthpiece of Whitehall extended beyond Berlin, proposed that as a result of its dominance this 'Triple Entente' would be able to resolve all the outstanding issues of international relations as it saw fit, a possibility he naturally couched in positive terms: 'A Triple Entente of this kind is not only a sure pledge of European peace, but will also find many opportunities for fruitful work in promoting the useful interests of the three powers in finding solutions of the difficult and dangerous problems with which European Diplomacy is constantly confronted'.[372] Only a year earlier, Emile J. Dillon had been sceptical, even negative, about the convention, but now he commented that in Reval that arrangement had become a 'solid, positive and permanent entente'.[373] 'A partnership of Great Britain, France and Russia', Maxse added, 'working as custodians of the peace would undoubtedly be a boon to Europe'.[374] Charles Scott, however, was more apprehensive and hoped that Edward VII had at least also shown the tsar the limits of their friendship,[375] while Lucien Wolf doubted whether continual collaboration with Russia was even possible.[376]

Historians have long puzzled over what agreement was in fact made at Reval. In practice, the meeting did not have the intentions ascribed to it in the German and Austrian press and in diplomatic circles.[377] Nonetheless, British foreign policy makers would have had to be highly negligent to think that such an event would not raise a red flag for the Central Powers. Mistrust of the government was evident even in the House of Commons and in the left-liberal press,[378] and it is hardly surprising that London was concerned that Berlin would look in future for an opportunity to disrupt Anglo-Russian harmony. The Central Powers' fear that they were now facing a new triple alliance[379] does not speak of hegemonic desires, military strength or a menacing supremacy; it is evidence instead of a self-perceived weakness in comparison to a triple alliance so long thought an impossibility but now taking shape.

Hardinge was relaxed about attempts to cause a rift in the Triple Entente, noting that he was persuaded that the friendship with St Petersburg ran deep.[380] It was unimportant for him that the arrangements on the Macedonian issue did not produce a 'Morocco of the East'[381] and that in any case the Young Turks' revolution made them irrelevant – he was even delighted to be free of the Macedonian millstone.[382] For Whitehall, Reval was a sign of improved relations with Russia and a shot across the bows of Germany. The outrage expressed in the German press was sign enough of the meeting's worth. The stronger the opposition from Germany, the greater the benefit reaped by the still somewhat shaky bond.[383] For Fisher, the agreement was a 'phenomenal success', and he opined: 'the King has just surpassed himself all round. Every blessed Russian of note he got quietly into his spider web and captured! The whole lot of them are now all dead-on for the Emperor coming to England, but he said: don't let us hurry too much; we might spoil it'.[384]

The shock waves from the meeting reverberated through the Balkans and all the way to Constantinople, where the Young Turks similarly read more into the good-will visit and feared that the spoils of the failed Ottoman Empire had been divided up. The demonstration of Anglo-Russian unity caused commotion throughout the whole of south-eastern Europe and returned the tensions of the periphery back to the heart of the continent. From behind closed doors, London pondered the developments of the last months with satisfaction,[385] and had good reason to do so, for even the Young Turks' unexpected revolution after the meeting at Reval had a positive impact on the British position. Fearing that the Anglo-Russian meeting at Reval was a harbinger of the dissolution of the Ottoman Empire, in July the Young Turks revolted. The overthrow of Abdul Hamid II, who was also hated in London,[386] suddenly generated a positive assessment in Britain, both popular and political, of the Turks.[387]

After the arrival of Gerald Lowther, Britain's new ambassador, had been celebrated on the streets of Constantinople, London summoned the hope that its painful loss of influence in Turkey might be reversed.[388] At the same time, Germany's dominant influence seemed to collapse overnight. After these 'marvellous events', in Grey's exuberant words,[389] Britain's goal became to join with France in replacing the economic and financial might of Berlin with an Anglo-French financial hegemony, and to expel Germany from Central Asia,[390] for which reason London now invested great effort in ensuring the consolidation and prestige of the new Turkish regime, stepping in as, apparently, protector of Turkish interests in the Geschow case which caused some diplomatic trouble between Turkey and Bulgaria[391] and on the Orient railway.[392]

While this pro-Turkish line was principally determined by colonial interests that were not just economic but also ethnic-religious, the repercussions for the change of direction already adopted by London could not be hidden for long. Whitehall seemed to have lost an overview of its options. In parallel to the implications of the newly formed friendship with Turkey, the first European consequences of the Anglo-Russian Convention became apparent as Russia became more involved in the Balkans and set about inserting itself between the Central Powers, on one side, and the Ottoman Empire, on the other. The situation could hardly have been more complex. How was Britain to protect Turkish prestige and yet at the same time stand back to let Russia become involved in the Balkans? Any pressure exerted by Russia would inevitably have an impact on Constantinople. Before the situation could become acute, Bulgaria threatened to declare its independence. Britain's evidently pro-Turkish involvement in the Bulgarian question and its revived interests on the Bosporus have led some historians to conclude that at this point London's foreign policy did an about-turn. According to this interpretation, British policy affirmed its established approach in preserving the traditional sick man of Europe as a cornerstone of the European concert, defending the European balance of power in the process.[393] That assessment, however, does not paint the full picture. Whitehall's diplomats and the radical liberals within the cabinet indeed faced traditional choices,[394] although in light of new options the Foreign Office tended to adopt a dual strategy that meant that preferences were only temporary and did not imply an underlying change of emphasis.

Although the Anglo-Russian agreement on the Macedonian question had been overtaken by events at the Golden Horn, the prospect of a common Balkan policy had strengthened London's resolve to maintain its ties with St Petersburg, whatever the cost.[395] Baron Greindl, Belgian ambassador to Berlin, was convinced that London wanted to seize the opportunity and treat Austrian-Hungarian involvement in the Balkans entirely as a 'quantité négligéable'.[396] Developments had bolstered Grey's position within the government in two respects.[397] The revolution of the Young Turks had provided him with relief from the criticism of his radical and anti-Russian cabinet colleagues and from pressure from the Balkan Committee, which in recent years had repeatedly urged the government to intervene against the despotic regime of Abdul Hamid II,[398] while at the same time his foreign policy options grew. In early August 1908 he outlined his two-fold strategy:

> We must be careful not to give Russia the impression that we are reverting to the old policy of supporting Turkey as a barrier against her ... The delicate point will presently be Russia – we cannot revert to the old policy of Lord Beaconsfield, we have now to be pro Turkish without giving rise to any suspicion that we are anti-Russian.[399]

Bulgaria was key. On one hand, it could embody the pro-Turkish line within British policy that promoted the status of the Young Turks. On the other hand, however, any engagement with Bulgaria had to bear Russian sensibilities in mind, along with Britain's own calculations in the Balkans, for Hardinge recognized that in the long term Russia intended to draw Sophia into its sphere of influence.[400]

To the pleasure of the anti-German Diplomats at the Foreign Office, in late summer 1908 all the signs told of a reordering of the powers at the expense of the Central Powers.[401] Britain's approach to the continent appeared affirmed. On 13 August, Nicolson returned to St Petersburg confident that 'unless he [Izvolsky] is deceiving me he is earnestly desirous of laying Russian foreign policy entirely alongside that of England'.[402] Britain as yet knew nothing of Izvolsky's plan to use Vienna to have the rules on the Straits rewritten; London foresaw Britain's ties to Russia and France and their mutual dominance of the situation at the Bosporus eventually ensuring Britain's position was unassailable. The flagrant weakness of Italy meant that the Triple Alliance could now only really function as a dual alliance, and after the meeting between Franz Josef and Edward VII at Bad Ischl in August 1908, even Austria-Hungary believed itself well on the way to being able to exert its authority over Italy as an ally. For a moment, it seemed as if London was enjoying a situation similar to Bismarck's Bad Kissinger ideal of 1877, with in this instance all powers except Germany cooperating with Britain.[403] In keeping with this assessment were much-circulated but never confirmed rumours that Austria-Hungary[404] was being forced out of the Austro-German alliance by Britain, a story that can evidently be traced back to Cartwright.[405] The suspicions were not without substance. A number of diplomats in Whitehall had raised the possibility of 'detaching' the Austrian-Hungarian monarchy from Germany. While Hardinge saw an opportunity to put 'a check on her ally [Germany]',[406] Walter Langley recorded:

> While the persuasion of Austria is in progress we should be in some danger, for if Germany resents and is frightened at our friendly relations with Russia, any overtures to Austria which might be on the ears of Germany would be calculated to produce on her a much greater effect.

Even Grey hesitated when he read these thoughts from Cartwright, his ambassador. He too thought it dangerous for Berlin to feel surrounded, although he also believed war was inevitable sooner or later.[407] In the end, unemotional cost-benefit analysis won out in London. The refusal to make any attempt to detach Vienna from Berlin is therefore explained not only by surviving traces of balance of power thinking, but also, and simply, by Britain's failure to see any advantage in doing so, for with the Anglo-Russian entente the Austrian-Hungarian monarchy had lost its remaining geopolitical strategic value as an ally. Years earlier, Curzon had decreed: 'Austria can give us nothing and might entangle us in a fight over the Balkans'.[408] While cooperation with Russia certainly brought its own risks, as a 'rich bride'[409] the tsardom had its compensations. But detaching Austria-Hungary from the Dual Alliance would have brought few benefits and potential fallout. Britain's own phobia about isolation brought home the reality of German fear of encirclement.[410] In August 1908, shortly before Edward VII and Franz Joseph I met at Bad Ischl, Grey commented on the margin of a report from Vienna: 'At present there is a fair equilibrium and we should not try to make a breach between Germany and Austria'.[411] But London's idea of a 'fair equilibrium' is revealed by Hardinge, who thought Italy dependent on the good will of the Entente Cordiale and a valuable point of vulnerability, a backdoor that during a conflict might be accessed to demolish the Triple Alliance.[412] Militarily, Britain bought into the doctrine of the defensive advantage, while politically it turned its back on the multipolar and flexible balance of power. Whitehall's principal goal was not so much to retain the Triple Alliance for the sake of the balance of power as to ensure that the Triple Alliance was as strong as possible in the moment but as weak and vulnerable as possible for a conflict. It did not help to have Grey repeatedly cite his own calculations for the equilibrium, according to which Germany had two allies, while France had only one.[413] In British calculations, Italy did not count and in any case the Austrian-Hungarian monarchy seemed unlikely to survive very much longer. In late 1906, the *Times*, perused daily by Grey, had cited the Italian ambassador to Vienna and the concerns of the Triple Alliance on the possibility of a 'Franco-Russian-English bloc', noting: 'The best will in the world could not guarantee loyalty to the old Triple Alliance against such a compelling force of facts'.[414] By 1908, by contrast, Britain was already counting for more on the continent than made the cabinet comfortable, excepting Grey, Haldane and Asquith. According to Hardinge, Rome was only a 'source of weakness' to the Triple Alliance,[415] mistrusted by Germany and seen by Austria-Hungary as practically its enemy. For Britain, that 'fair equilibrium' was naturally one in which Britain had first choice and the upper hand,[416] although Hardinge was silent on precisely the form it should take. Perhaps he believed in a return to the traditional balance of power policy. Perhaps he was counting on Britain being able in the foreseeable future to get out of its current alliances, in particular that with Russia.

Too late it was evident that a well-timed move to break off these ties could have been a blessing for the continent, for it might have sent everyone back to the drawing board; admittedly, however, it could also have weakened one side to such an extent that the whole business could have come crashing down. Between 1906 and 1909, that split would most probably not have been peaceable, but it might have had geographically limited implications, and might not have led to a global conflagration. The formations taking shape did not yet have the fatalistic destructive force of opposing alliances that they would acquire when the powers involved placed their alliance-worthiness above their freedom of action,[417] but a move in that direction was already evident, especially, since the change of government, for Britain.

Under Grey, a qualitative change in Britain's alliances took shape because his concern was not the stability of the system but the security of Britain. Although this shift has been explained as a response to Germany's Dreadnoughts or as a product of the need to be able to offset Russian weakness after the tsardom's defeat in the Far East, neither the Admiralty's evaluation nor Britain's own interests appear to support that reasoning, which appears a subsequent or supplementary rationale. This new course became a problem because the entente with

Russia drew Britain further into the explosive mixture in the Balkans and tied Britain to a power that not only wanted the status quo in the Balkans changed in its own favour but also was not prepared to wait.[418] British diplomats believed it made good sense to stand in the way of the Central Powers as a whole, for since Algeciras the Austrian-Hungarian monarchy had been thought simply 'a shadow of Berlin'.[419] Britain hoped that quarantining the Balkans would constrict Germany, halting the 'Germanisation of the Balkans'[420] and the German advance towards Salonika. Yet this reading of Germany and Austria-Hungary's alleged goals is surely based on an overestimation of the intentions of the Central Powers that was much influenced by stereotypes. Certainly, London was concerned to ensure that the Central Powers had no further points of contact with Russia, and British policy was focused on the prevention of a new three-emperor alliance on the continent. To that end, Whitehall was even prepared to allow the unpredictable and ambitious Izvolsky to believe that Britain would stand by his side in a conflict over the Balkans. Such was indeed the impression he garnered, as is made evident by his offer to Aehrenthal to bind together their particular interests in the annexation of Bosnia and Herzegovina and access at the Straits.[421]

After all the tensions of recent months, London thought the best way to replace Vienna as Russia's partner had been found.[422] That undiluted optimism is evident in British evaluation of the imminent meeting at Buchlau, when Aehrenthal and Izvolsky would carry out the horse-trading[423] that led to the Annexation Crisis.[424] The meeting should have been taken as a warning, but instead it was read as a sign of a growing rift between Vienna and St Petersburg.[425] On 23 August, William Edward Goschen, the king's ambassador in Vienna, had confidently reported from Vienna that the personal vanities of Izvolsky and Aehrenthal made renewed rapprochement between the two countries unlikely.[426] Britain also thought that after the successful meeting between Edward VII and Franz Joseph at Bad Ischl, Vienna was very unlikely to act without reference to Britain.[427] After that meeting, Hardinge had described the future fate of Bosnia and Herzegovina as a purely internal matter for Austria-Hungary.[428] Immersed in the attempt to create long-lasting ties with Russia, London appeared to have lost all sense of the possible consequences, and dangers, in the Balkans.

Notes

1. Roosevelt to Spring Rice, 16 June 1905, NA, FO 800/116.
2. Dillon, 'Foreign Affairs', CR 7/1905, 130–48.
3. Saunders to Maxse, 2 Oct. 1905, WSRO, MAXSE/457, fol. 119; Hardinge to Knollys, 13 Sept. 1905, CUL, MSS Hardinge, Vol. 6; Chirol to O'Conor, 19 Aug. 1905, CC, MSS O'Conor, OCON 5/3/2.
4. Dillon, 'Foreign Affairs', CR 7/1905, 130–48.

5. Salisbury to Lansdowne, 12 June 1905; Lyttelton to Lansdowne, 31 July 1905, BL, LANS/Private Letters, Vol. 3; Esher to Sandars, 23 July 1905, BL, MSS Balfour Add. 49719.
6. Williams, 'Great Britain and Russia', 133. Morley to Minto, 25 May 1906, IOL, EUR. D. 573/1; Morley, *Recollections*, Vol. 2, 168.
7. Lansdowne to Balfour, 17 Dec. 1905, BL, MSS Lansdowne, LANS/Private Letters, Vol. 5.
8. Nicolson, *Verschwörung*, 228.
9. Cited in Williams, 'Great Britain and Russia', 135; see also Grey, *25 Years*, Vol. 1, 56.
10. Grey to Nicolson, 16 Nov. 1906, NA, FO 800/72; Williams, 'Strategic Background', 362.
11. Lee, *Edward VII*, Vol. 2, 289-90.
12. Grey to Nicolson, 16. Nov. 1906, NA, FO 800/72; Hardinge to Nicolson, 28 Nov. 1906, BD IV, No. 241, 254.
13. As a reaction to Germany, see Lowe and Dockrill, *Mirage of Power*, Vol. 1, 15–28; Kissinger, *Diplomacy*, 192; Fischer, *Krieg der Illusionen*, 101. For a more qualified view, see Steiner, *Britain and the Origins*, 81–83; Charmley, *Splendid Isolation*, 342–45. As 'isolating Germany', see Neitzel, *Kriegsausbruch*, 92–93.
14. See Neilson, *Britain and the Last Tsar*, 267–316; Siegel, *Endgame*, 1–20; Williams, 'Strategic Background'; McLean, *Britain and Her Buffer State*, 73–105.
15. CID, Minutes of 85th Meeting, 9 March 1906, NA, CAB 38/11/11, 2; NA, CAB 2/2/1 and PD IV/153, col. 675; Grey, *25 Years*, Vol. 1, 154.
16. Hardinge to Sanderson, 21 July 1905, CUL, MSS Hardinge, Vol. 6; to Lansdowne, 15 Oct. 1905, NA, FO 800/141.
17. Grey, 18 Sept. 1906, BD III, No. 439, 389–90.
18. Hardinge to Lansdowne, 26 Sept. 1905, BD IV, No. 192, 199–202; Lansdowne to Hardinge, 3 Oct. 1905, BD IV, No. 194, 204–5; Sanderson to Clarke, 10 Nov. 1905, NA, CAB 17/60.
19. See Adam, *Großbritanniens Balkandilemma*.
20. Clark, *Sleepwalkers*, 559.
21. Minto to Morley, 2 May 1906, 12 June 1906, IOL, EUR. D. 573/8; DDF 2/II, No. 9, 811; No. 10, 42; Spring Rice to Grey, 26 Jan. 1906, BD IV, No. 208, 222–24; Grey to Spring Rice, 26 March 1906, BD IV, No. 213, 229.
22. Grey, *25 Years*, Vol. 1, 56, 160; Grey to Spring Rice, 13 Dec. 1905, BD IV, No. 204, 218.
23. Morley to Minto, 25 May 1906, IOL, EUR. D. 573/1.
24. See Spring Rice to Mallet, 31 Jan. 1906, GL II, 61f.; Hardinge to Vambéry, 5 Jan. 1909, NA, FO 800/33.
25. See Canis, 'Außenpolitik im letzten Jahrzehnt', 110.
26. For Wallace's role, see Anon., *History of the Times*, Vol. 3, 480.
27. Spring Rice to Mallet, 31 Jan. 1906, GL II, 61–62.
28. Minto to Morley, 28 Dec. 1905, 5 Feb. 1906, IOL, EUR. D. 573/7; for a contrast, see Grey, Memorandum, 18 Dec. 1905, NA, FO 800/92; see also McLean, *Britain and Her Buffer State*, 87; Plass, *Deutschland*, 173–74.
29. Grey, Note, 18 Dec. 1905, NA, FO 800/53.
30. Spring Rice to Grey, 7 Feb. 1906, BD IV, No. 326, 378–79.
31. Minto to Morley, 2 May 1906, 12 June 1906, IOL, EUR. D. 573/8.

32. Ampthill to Edward VII, 16 July 1904, IOL, MSS Ampthill, EUR E. 233/32.
33. Scott, Diary, 19 June 1900, BL, Add. 52305; Hamilton to Curzon, 8 April 1903, IOL, EUR. C. 126/5; Chirol to Hardinge, 20 Aug. 1904, CUL, MSS Hardinge, Vol. 7; Lascelles to Lansdowne, 14 Sept. 1905, NA, FO 800/130. 'Russia should be thought of as an enemy, but in respect of Grey and Nicholson, Russia is being approached as a friend.' Morley to Minto, 13 Dec. 1906, IOL, EUR. D. 573/1.
34. Grey to Spring Rice, 11 May 1906, BD IV, No. 329, 382–83.
35. Grey to Nicolson, 6 Nov. 1906, cited in Grey, *25 Years*, Vol. 1, 160–62.
36. Grey to Nicolson, 3 Oct. 1906, NA, FO 800/72.
37. Charge d'affaires to Rouvier, 10 Jan. 1906, cited in Hölzle, *Die Selbstentmachtung Europas*, 139. See also DDF VIII, 496–97.
38. Cited in Grey, *25 Years*, Vol. 1, 152–53.
39. Grey to Lascelles, 1 Jan. 1906, NA, MSS Grey FO 800/61.
40. CID, 85th Meeting, 9 March 1906, NA, CAB 38/11/11, 2; PD IV/153, col. 675; Grey, *25 Years*, Vol. 1, 154.
41. Busch, *Hardinge*, 70; Grey, *25 Years*, Vol. 1, 165–66.
42. CID, Military Requirements of the Empire, 1907, NA, CAB 16/2, 175–76; Sydenham, *My Working Life*, 200.
43. Morley to Minto, 19 Sept. 1907, IOL, EUR. D. 573/2; Duff, Memorandum, 1907, NA, CAB 16/2; Hardinge to Nicolson, 7 Aug. 1906, BD IV, No. 226, 241.
44. Macintosh, 'Role of the Committee'. Kitchener, like Minto, still held an anti-Russian attitude on the Straits. Minto to Morley, 13 Dec. 1905, IOL, EUR. D. 573/7; Minutes, 85th Meeting of the CID, 9 March 1906, NA, CAB 6/3.
45. See Ferguson, *Pity of War*, 64–65.
46. Massie, *Dreadnought*, 745. See also Grierson to Barnardiston, 27 Feb. 1906, BD III, No. 221(c), 187; Barnardiston to Grierson, 3 March 1906, BD III, No. 221(c) 1, 187–88.
47. In fact, Germany in 1910 had not more than 97 divisions while the French forces were reduced from 93 divisions to 75 and the Russian forces from 142 to 78. Wilson, 20 Sept. 1911, NA, WO 106/47; see also Fiedler, *Taktik*, 113; Ehlert et al., *Schlieffenplan*, 443.
48. CID, 88th Meeting, 25 May 1906, CAB 6/3.
49. Anon., 'Our Relations with Russia', *The Nation*, 8 June 1907, 552–53; Anon., 'The Foreign Policy of Sir Edward Grey', *The Nation*, 3 Aug. 1907, 822–23; Grey, *25 Years*, Vol. 1, 155–56; Morley to Minto, 22 June 1906, IOL, EUR. D. 573/1.
50. Campbell-Bannerman to de Novikoff, 27 Feb. 1907, cited in Spender, *Sir Henry Campbell-Bannerman*, Vol. 2, 363.
51. Campbell-Bannerman to Grey, 3 Sept. 1907, cited in Trevelyan, *Grey of Fallodon*, 214; Morley to Minto, 26 Sept. 1907, IOL, EUR. D. 573/2; Morley to Minto, 6 July 1906, IOL, EUR. D. 573/1.
52. Grey, *25 Years*, Vol. 1, 333; see also Morley, August 1914, BOD, NL Morley, MS Eng. d. 3585.
53. Neilson, 'My Beloved Russians'.
54. Grey to Maxse, 6 July 1905, WSRO, MAXSE/453.
55. Grey (City), *The Times*, 21 Oct. 1905.
56. Grey, cited in Trevelyan, *Grey of Fallodon*, 90–92, 103–4; Grey to Spring Rice, 22 Dec. 1905, GL II, 54; *Westminster Gazette*, 2 Sept. 1905.

57. Dillon to Spring Rice, October 1900, CC, CASR 1/41; Dillon, 'Foreign Affairs', CR 6/1903, 876–98; Balfour to Lansdowne, 21 Dec. 1903, BL, Add. 49728; Bertie to Mallet, 11 June 1904, BL, Add. 63016; Buchanan to Hardinge, 11 Dec. 1907, CUL, MSS Hardinge, Vol. 10; Spring Rice to Grey, 16 Jan. 1906, GL II, 60; Morley to Minto, 5 Feb. 1906, EUR. D. 573/7; Chirol to Spring Rice, 2 Oct. 1906, CC, CASR 1/11.
58. Prorok, 'The Breaking of the Austrian Empire', CR 2/1898, 153–73; Anon., 'The Isolation of Germany', *The Spectator*, 4 Jan. 1902, 4–5; Dillon, 'A New Grouping of the Powers', CR 9/1904, 281–88; Spring Rice to Hay, June 1904, CC, CASR 9/1; Plunkett to Lansdowne, 3 Nov. 1904, NA, FO 800/117; 5 May 1905, NA, FO 7/1362; Bell to Steed, 10 July 1906, NIA, MSS Bell.
59. See McLean, *Britain and Her Buffer State*, 73–77, 101–5.
60. The *Times* saw the convention as a new basis for 'the whole domain of international politics'. *The Times*, 8 Oct. 1908. Anon., 'The Price of the Russian Agreement', *The Nation*, 7 Sept. 1907, 980–81. 'It will lead to closer and more intimate relations all over the world.' *The Times*, cited in The Anglo-Russian Convention, *The Nation*, 28 Sept. 1907, 1078–79, 1078. Only the *Westminster Gazette* thought the convention had 'no European motive', cited in The Nation, 28 Sept. 1907, 1078.
61. Grey to Spring Rice, 19 March 1906, NA, FO 371/124; Lansdowne, Notes, 10 Sept. 1907, BL, LANS/Working Files 17; Mensdorff to Aehrenthal, 29 May 1907, cited in Walters, 'Unpublished Documents', in SEER 30, 228.
62. *Daily Telegraph*, 3 May 1906; Anon., *History of The Times*, Vol. 3, 499.
63. Spring Rice to Grey, 29 March 1906, GL II, 71.
64. Nicolson to Grey, 7 June 1906, BD IV, No. 224, 289–90.
65. Grey, *25 Years*, Vol. 1, 156.
66. Chirol to Spring Rice, 16 May 1906, CC, CASR 1/11; Tscharykow, *High Politics*, 268.
67. See Siegel, *Endgame*, 21–22.
68. Edward VII to Nicholas II, 12 May 1904, cited in Lee, *Edward VII*, Vol. 2, 289.
69. Gooch, *Before the War*, Vol. 1, 290.
70. Cambon to Delcassé, 29 May 1905, DDF 2/VI, No. 465, 557–59; Hardinge to Edward VII, 1 Sept. 1907, CUL, MSS Hardinge, Vol. 9; Spring Rice to Grey, 24 May 1906, GL II, 72–74.
71. Izvolsky to Suvorin, 19 Aug. 1907, cited in Suvorin, *Geheimtagebuch*, 274; Iswolski, *Memoirs*, 83.
72. Nicolson to Grey, 31 Aug. 1906, BD IV, No. 336, 386–87.
73. Lascelles to Lansdowne, 31 Oct. 1903, BDFA F/XIX, No. 142, 158; Buchanan to Lansdowne, 3 Dec. 1903, ibid., No. 146, 162–63; Whitehead, Memorandum, 26 Jan. 1905: German Estimates for 1905, ibid., No. 180, 224–29; Lascelles to FO, German political situation, 21 March 1907, BDFA F/XX, No. 12, 13.
74. Schöllgen, *Imperialismus und Gleichgewicht*, 226–33, 226–27.
75. Grey to Campbell-Bannerman, 13 Sept. 1906, BL, Add. 41218; *Daily Mail*, 28 June 1906; Grey to Nicolson, 3 Sept. 1906, BD IV, No. 337, 387.
76. Jaeckel, *Nordwestgrenze*, 179.
77. Minto to Morley, 19 Sept. 1906, IOL, EUR. D. 573/9; Morley to Minto, 20 Sept. 1906, IOL, EUR. D. 573/1.
78. Morley to Minto, 22 June 1906, 23 March 1906, IOL, EUR. D. 573/1.
79. Morley to Minto, 29 June 1906, IOL, EUR. D. 573/1; Asquith to Grey, 23 Sept. 1906, NA, FO 800/62; Fitzmaurice to Grey, 22 Sept. 1906, NA, FO 800/53.

80. Cited in Monger, *End of Isolation*, 290.
81. Plass, *Deutschland*, 183.
82. Lee, *Edward VII*, Vol. 2, 569; Monger, *End of Isolation*, 329.
83. Morley to Minto, 2 Nov. 1906, IOL, EUR. D. 573/1.
84. See Hardinge, *Diplomacy*, 70.
85. Nicolson to Grey, 5 Nov. 1906, NA, FO 800/337; Grey to Nicolson, 6 Nov. 1906, NA, FO 800/338.
86. 'Some change in the direction desired by Russia would be admissible.' Grey to Nicolson, 6 Nov. 1906, cited in Grey, *25 Years*, Vol. 1, 160–62.
87. Grey to Nicolson, November 1906, BD IV, No. 370, 413–15.
88. Cited in Taube, *Der großen Katastrophe entgegen*, 128.
89. McLean, *Britain and Her Buffer State*, 120; Morley to Minto, 30 Nov. 1906, IOL, EUR. D. 573/1.
90. Neilson, *Britain and the Last Tsar*, 281.
91. 'This part of the world is lost to us', cited in Nicolson, *Sir Arthur Nicolson: Lord Carnock*, 65.
92. Nicolson to Grey, 7 Nov. 1906, NA, FO 800/337.
93. Grey to Nicolson, 16 Nov. 1906, NA, FO 800/72.
94. 'M. Isvolsky has not foreshadowed this to me, even in the most indirect way, but … he might ask us. Do not think I am coming under the influence of my local atmosphere.' Ibid.
95. Monger, *End of Isolation*, 295; Hardinge, Memorandum, 16 Nov. 1906, BD IV, 58–60; Plass, *Deutschland*, 51; Grey to Nicolson, 16 Nov. 1906, NA, FO 800/72. See also Lansdowne, Proposed Agreement with Russia, 1 Jan. 1904, NA, CAB 37/68/1; Lansdowne to MacDonald, 11 Jan. 1904, NA, CAB 37/68/11.
96. Cited in Monger, *End of Isolation*, 295.
97. Hardinge to Sanderson, 21 July 1905, CUL, MSS Hardinge, Vol. 6; to Lansdowne, 15 Oct. 1905, NA, FO 800/141.
98. Grey, *25 Years*, Vol. 1, 163–64; Russian Council of Ministers, 1 Feb. 1907, BDS I, No. 1, 1–9.
99. Nish, *Anglo-Japanese Alliance*, 359–60.
100. Nicolson to Grey, 23 Aug. 1907, BD IV, No. 283, 301–2.
101. See Nicolson, *Sir Arthur Nicolson: Lord Carnock*, 239.
102. Hardinge to Edward VII, 16 March 1907, CUL, MSS Hardinge, Vol. 9.
103. Hardinge to Bertie, 18 March 1907, BL, Add. 63020; to Nicolson, 19 March 1907, NA, FO 800/339.
104. Grey, 15 March 1907, BD IV, No. 257, 279; Grey to Nicolson, 19 March 1907, BD IV, No. 258, 280–81.
105. Grey to Nicolson, 1 May 1907, BD IV, No. 269f., 291–92.
106. Nicolson to Grey, 25 March 1907, BD IV, No. 259, 463–64.
107. Williams, 'Great Britain and Russia', 146.
108. Fitzmaurice, Minutes, Nicolson to Grey, 14 April 1907, BD IV, No. 265, 287–88.
109. Minutes, O'Conor to Grey, 30 April 1907, BD IV, No. 267, 289.
110. Salisbury, 19 March 1897, PD IV/47, cols. 1009–19.
111. Cited in Williams, 'Great Britain and Russia', 147.
112. Bertie to Grey, 22 Oct. 1906, BD IV, No. 230, 243; Nicolson to Grey, 7 Nov. 1906, BD IV, No. 236, 411–13.

113. Goschen to Grey, 5 Sept. 1907, BD IV, No. 522, 582.
114. See Carroll, *Germany and the Great Powers*, 563–64, for Vienna, see Goschen to Grey, 5 Sept. 1907, BD IV, No. 522, 582.
115. Lascelles to Grey, 1 Oct. 1907, BD IV, No. 540, 599–600.
116. 'Syndikat der Mächte gegen Deutschland', Miquel to AA, 27 Sept. 1907, GP XXV/1, No. 8536, 42–45, 44.
117. Spring Rice to Grey, 6 April 1906, NA, FO 371/124.
118. *The Times*, 5 and 20 Oct. 1906; *The Times*, 2 Sept. 1907.
119. Grey to Nicolson, 18 Sept. 1907, BD IV, No. 537, 596–97.
120. Delbrück, Preußische Jahrbücher No. 130 (1907), 197.
121. 'Ja, insgesamt ist es gegen uns gerichtet', aside by Wilhelm II, GP XXV/1, No. 8537, cited in Nicolson, *Verschwörung*, 279.
122. See Miquel to Bülow, 19 Sept. 1906, GP XXV, No. 8518, 23.
123. Savinsky, *Recollections*, 139.
124. 'Anyone behind the scenes knows that what we have gained strategically in Europe is real, while the sacrifices we have made are not real.' Grey to Nicolson, 24 Feb. 1908, NA, FO 800/341.
125. Cartwright to Grey, 11 March 1907, BD VIII, No. 17, 32; FO, Memorandum, 11 Dec. 1905, BD VIII, No. 9, 24–25.
126. Garvin, 'Foreign Affairs', FR 7/1907, 1118–30, 1122.
127. Morley to Minto, 7 March 1907, IOL, EUR. D. 573/2; Minto to Morley, 2 April 1907, IOL, EUR. D. 573/11.
128. Kennedy, *Rise of Anglo-German Antagonism*, 442–43; Hewitson, *Germany*, 183–84; Charmley, *Splendid Isolation*, 350.
129. Steiner and Neilson, *Britain and the Origins*, 52.
130. Crowe to Dilke, 15 Oct. 1907, NA, FO 800/243; Lascelles to Grey, 16 Aug. 1906, BD VIII, No. 163, 192–94.
131. Anon., 'The Anglo-German Tension', *The Nation*, 6 Feb. 1909, 701–2.
132. Calchas (Garvin), 'The Kaiser and the Future', FR 12/1907, 889–1004.
133. Crowe to Clema, 17 July 1906, BOD, MSS Crowe, MS Eng. d. 2901. For a different view, see Hewitson, *Germany*, 183–84. See also Marder, FDSF I, 130–31; Woodward, *Great Britain and the German Navy*, 155; Anon., 'Foreign Affairs', FR 11/1907, 850–70; Lawrence, 'The Hague Conference', JRUSI 52/1 (2/1908), 479–509, 491.
134. Hamilton, *Bertie of Thame*, 127–39.
135. Grey to Campbell-Bannerman, 27 Dec. 1906, cited in Hamilton, *Bertie of Thame*, 130.
136. Cambon to Quai d'Orsay, 2 Jan. 1907, DDF 2/X, No. 383, 401.
137. 'Les agissements de la politique anglaise dirigée par Edouard VII. contre son neveu Guillaume II. n'ont jamais cessé depuis la crise de Tanger, et ils sont, aujourd'hui plus actifs que jamais. L'Angleterre a tout à gagner et n'a rien à perdre dans une guerre contre L'Allemagne avec le concours de la France'. Specher to Forrer, 10 Jan. 1907, DDS V, No. 160, 344.
138. Grey to De Bunsen, 7 Feb. 1906, BD VII, No. 11, 11–12; ADM, 25 Feb. 1907, NA, CAB 38/13/11.
139. Grey to De Bunsen, 13 Feb. 1906, BD VII, No. 12, 20–21.
140. Garvin, Foreign Affairs, FR 7/1907, 1118–30, 1122.
141. Hardinge, Memorandum, 25 March 1907, BD VII, No. 19, 17.
142. Ibid.

143. 'status quo en ce qui concerne leurs possessions maritimes respectives dans le bassin de la Méditerranée et dans la partie de l'Atlantique qui baigne les côtes de l'Europe et de l'Afrique'. Cambon, 14 Feb. 1907, BD VII, No. 13, 21–22.
144. Grey to Bertie, 14 Feb. 1907, BD VII, No. 14, 22–23; see also Nos. 39–41, 52–55.
145. Schoen to Bülow, 19 June 1907, GP XXV/1, No. 8544, 60–62; Bertie to Grey, 31 March 1907, BD VII, No. 22, 19–20.
146. Bertie to Grey, 31 March 1907, BD VII, No. 22, 19–20, 20.
147. De Cartier to Favereau, 28 March 1907, BelD III, No. 25, 64–66; Lalaing to Davignon, 19 June 1907, BelD III, No. 34, 96.
148. See Siegel, *Endgame*; Benckendorff to Izvolsky, 3 June 1909, BDS I, No. 79, 110.
149. Anon., 'The Foreign Policy of Sir Edward Grey', *The Nation*, 3 Aug. 1907, 822–23; Diplomaticus, 'Sir Edward Grey's Stewardship'; Sidney Low, 'An Anglo-French Alliance in der *Fortnightly Review*', both cited in Anon., 'The Policy of Sir Edward Grey', *The Nation*, 2 Dec. 1911, 366–67.
150. Nicolson, *Sir Arthur Nicolson: Lord Carnock*, 207; Williams, 'Great Britain and Russia', 137.
151. Cited in Iswolski, *Au service*, 339–40.
152. Blunt, *My Diaries*, Vol. 2, 250.
153. Nicolson to Grey, 21 Oct. 1907, BD IV, No. 544, 604–5; Hardinge to Nicolson, 12 Nov. 1907, NA, FO 800/340.
154. Hardinge to Nicolson, 30 Oct. 1907, NA, FO 800/340.
155. Luntinen, *Baltic*, 147–82. For the Åland question, see Hurst, *Key Treaties*, Vol. 1, 332–33; Hardinge to Nicolson, 5 Feb. 1908, NA, FO 800/341.
156. The *Times*, like the Foreign Office, wanted to believe Russia's explanation that its actions had been made necessary by Finnish arms smuggling. See Maude, 'Finland', 557–81, 568.
157. *The Times*, 25 June and 6 Aug. 1906.
158. Maude, 'Finland', 557–81; Feldman, 'British Diplomats'.
159. *The Times*, 10 Aug. 1906, 3. As the Åland agreement was an extension of the Treaty of Stockholm of 21 Dec. 1855, this interpretation is hard to maintain. See Treaty of Stockholm, 21 December 1855, in Hurst, *Key Treaties*, Vol. 1, 315–16.
160. Chirol to Hardinge, 14 June 1903, CUL, MSS Hardinge, Vol. 7.
161. Hardinge to Chirol, 3 June 1904, NA, FO 800/2; Hardinge to Chirol, 3 June 1905; 20 June 1905, CUL, MSS Hardinge, Vol. 6; Chirol to Hardinge, 22 Aug. 1905, ibid., Vol. 7.
162. 'que l'Angleterre n'attachait sans doute plus à la question des d'étroits la même importance que par le passé'. Bompard, *Mon Ambassade en Russie*, 267–70; O'Beirne to Grey, 18 May 1908, NA, FO 371/529.
163. See Bertie to Grey, 9 July 1907, BD VIII, No. 106, 130–32.
164. Luntinen, 'Baltic', 183–84; Grey to de Salis, 4 Dec. 1907, BD VIII, No. 113, 137–38; Tyrrell to Grey, 5 Dec. 1907, NA, FO 800/92; Grey to Bertie, 6 Dec. 1907, NA, FO 800/51.
165. Nicolson to Grey, 11 Dec. 1907, BD VIII, No. 123, 146–47; 16 Dec. 1907, ibid., No. 130, 258–60, 260.
166. See esp. DDF 2/XI, Nos. 222, 224, 225; Grey to Lister, 11 Dec. 1907, BD VIII, No. 120, 144–45.
167. Nicolson to Grey, 16 Dec. 1907, BD VIII, No. 130, 152–53.

168. Bompard, *Mon Ambassade en Russie*, 281–82; Taube, *Politique Russe*, 102; Nicolson to Hardinge, 4 Dec. 1907, BD VIII, App. II, 722–23.
169. Bertie to Grey, 23 Dec. 1907, NA, FO 800/117; Bertie to Grey, [2.?] 6 Dec. 1907, BD VIII, No. 115, 140.
170. Bertie to Grey, 25 Dec. 1907, BD VIII, No. 134, 156–57.
171. Hamilton, *Bertie of Thame*, 146.
172. *The Times*, 18 Feb. 1908.
173. Nicolson to Grey, 28 Oct. 1907, BD IV, No. 544, 604–5.
174. Neilson, *Britain and the Last Tsar*, 292.
175. Hardinge to Nicolson, 24 Dec. 1907, NA, FO 800/340.
176. 'Au point de vue machiavélique, on serait donc même tenté de dire que, pour son premier début diplomatique a Pétersbourg. M. Iswolsky avait remporté une éclatante victoire en faisant accroire à ambassadeur étranger juste le contraire de ses véritables sentiments.' 'From a Machiavellian point of view, we would be tempted to say that for his first start at Petersburg. Mr Iswolsky won a resounding victory by making foreign ambassadors believe just the opposite of his true feelings' [Transl. AR]. Taube, *Politique Russe*, 102.
177. Hardinge to Villiers, 7 Jan. 1908, NA, FO 800/24.
178. Hardinge to Nicolson, 12 Nov. 1907, NA, FO 800/340.
179. Neilson, *Britain and the Last Tsar*, 291–92.
180. *The Times*, 24 Feb. 1908; (Letters), 3 March 1908; Spring Rice to Grey, 3 Aug. 1909, NA, FO 371/745; Specher to Forrer, 10 Jan. 1907, DDS V, No. 160, 344; De Cartier to Favereau, 28 March 1907, BelD III, No. 25, 64–66.
181. Schroeder, 'Stealing Horses', 25.
182. Minto to Morley, 12 June 1906, IOL, EUR. D. 573/8.
183. For entente policy as synonymous with balance of power policy, see Wormer, *Großbritannien*, 73–75.
184. Hardinge to Nicolson, 5 Feb. 1908, NA, FO 800/341.
185. Hildebrand, *Das vergangene Reich*, 236.
186. Walters, 'Franco-Russian Discussion', 184–97.
187. Chirol to Spring Rice, 12 April 1906, CC, CASR 1/11.
188. For protest in Russia, see Crisp, 'Russian Liberals', 497–511.
189. *The Times*, 11 June 1907.
190. Foreign Office Report, 19 July 1907, NA, FO 371/324.
191. Beloff, *Lucien Wolf*, passim; BL, LANS/Working Files, September 1907; *The Times*, 7 July 1907; Terror in Russia, *Manchester Guardian*, 6 Nov. 1905. For the Bialystok massacre against Jews, see *Manchester Guardian*, 11 May 1906; *Daily Graphic*, 12 Jan., 10 March, 11 June, 3 July, 13 July and 7 Sept. 1907; see also Murray to Grey, 25 June 1906, NA, FO 371/125; Commons, 21 June 1906, PD IV/159, col. 360.
192. Morley, August 1914, BOD, MSS Morley, MS Eng. d. 3585.
193. See Wilson, *Policy of the Entente*, 85–99.
194. Bernard Porter even speaks of a 'proto-alliance … very similar to Britain's arrangement with France'. Porter, *Britain, Europe and the World*, 75; Palmer, *Glanz*, 356; McLean, *Britain and Her Buffer State*, 73–75; Neilson, *Britain and the Last Tsar*, 267, 287–99; Monger, *End of Isolation*, 295. 'We were not committed, he [Grey] always said.' Morley, August 1914, BOD, MSS Morley, MS Eng. d. 3585.
195. Benckendorff to Izvolsky, 25 July 1907, cited in Iswolski, *Au Service*, Vol. 2, 81.

196. *The Times*, 14 Feb., 16 July and 31 Aug. 1907; Chirol to Strachey, 10 June 1903, PA, STR/4/9/3; Sanderson to Hardinge, 11 June 1903, CUL, MSS Hardinge, Vol. 7; Hardinge to Chirol, 20 June 1905, ibid., Vol. 6.
197. Chirol to Hardinge, 3 April 1905, CUL, MSS Hardinge, Vol. 7; 3 Oct. 1905, ibid.; Chirol to Nicolson, 27 Nov. 1906, NA, FO 800/340; *The Times*, 14 March and 27 April 1907; PD IV/131, cols. 1253–54; PD IV/141, cols. 1076–77; Chirol to Bouchier, 29 Nov. 1907, NIA, FELB 5/341.
198. Chirol to Morrison, 2 Sept. 1907, cited in Morrison, *Correspondence*, Vol. 1, 430–31; Anon., *History of The Times*, Vol. 3, 502–3.
199. Anon., *History of The Times*, Vol. 3, 502–3.
200. Ibid.
201. *The Times*, 2, 6, 14 and 25 Sept. 1907; *The Spectator*, 26 Sept. 1907.
202. *The Times* (Letters), 10 and 14 Sept. 1907.
203. *The Times*, 14 Sept. 1907.
204. *The Times*, 25 Sept. 1907.
205. Jaeckel, *Nordwestgrenze*, 270, n. 3; *Morning Post*, 4 Aug. 1905; *Pall Mall Gazette*, 7 Feb. 1906; Morley to Minto, 5 April 1906, IOL, EUR. D. 573/1.
206. *Westminster Gazette*, 2, 16 and 30 Sept. 1907; see also Stead, 'Russia Revisited', RR 9/1908, 225–32; Dillon, 'How Peace Was Brought About', CR 2/1907, 270–83.
207. Spring, 'Trans-Persian Railway Project', 62.
208. Grey, *25 Years*, Vol. 1, 165–66; *Westminster Gazette*, 25 Sept. 1907.
209. Maxse, *Germany on the Brain*, 229–35, 239–40; *The Spectator*, 26 Sept. 1907.
210. *Morning Post*, 2 Sept. 1907.
211. *Morning Post*, 20 Sept. 1907.
212. 'The significance of the Convention is not to be found by the study of its details.' *Morning Post*, 26 Sept. 1907.
213. 'Having the game entirely in our hands, we have surrendered every political and commercial advantage we enjoyed.' *Blackwood's Magazine*, cited in RR 1/1908, 59; *Daily Telegraph*, 25 Sept. 1907.
214. Maxse, 'Episodes', NR 8/1907, 813–15.
215. Asquith, 7 Feb. 1908, PD IV/183, cols. 141–42.
216. G.W. Balfour to Spring Rice, 11 Feb. 1908, CC, CASR 1/2.
217. Balfour 17 Feb. 1908, PD IV/184, col. 552.
218. Lansdowne, 7 Feb. 1908, PD IV/183, col. 1325.
219. The wording from the first draft, 'Grande-Bretagne a un intérêt spécial au maintien du statu quo au Golf Persique', was omitted in the final version; see BD IV, App. I, 618–20; App. IV, 624–25.
220. Grey (Commons), 17 Feb. 1908, PD IV/184, cols. 478–96; *The Times*, 18 Feb. 1908.
221. Lansdowne, Press Cuttings (Anglo-German Convention), 10 Sept. 1907, BL, LANS/Working Files 13.
222. Grey to Nicolson, 8 March 1907, BD IV, No. 393, 435; Nicolson to Grey, 10 March 1907, BD IV, No. 395, 487–89.
223. Curzon, 6 Feb. 1908, PD (Lords) IV/183, cols. 31–33.
224. Nicolson to Grey, 24 and 28 June 1907, BD IV, No. 429, 477–81; No. 431, 481–82.
225. Nicolson to Grey, BD IV, No. 433, 484.
226. Grey to Nicolson, 21 Aug. 1907, BD IV, No. 501–2.
227. Nicolson, *Curzon*, 126.

228. *The Times*, 7 Feb. 1908.
229. *The Times*, 18 Feb. 1908.
230. Ronaldshay (Lords), 25 Feb. 1908, PD IV/184, col. 499.
231. Grey to Nicolson, 24 Feb. 1908, BD IV, No. 550, 616–17.
232. Campbell-Bannerman to de Novikoff, 27 Feb. 1907, cited in Spender, *Sir Henry Campbell-Bannerman*, Vol. 2, 363.
233. Campbell-Bannerman to Grey, 3 Sept. 1907, cited in Trevelyan, *Grey of Fallodon*, 214.
234. Hardinge, *Diplomacy*, 146.
235. For Minto, the convention had 'no value at all'. Morley to Minto, 19 Sept. 1907, IOL, EUR. D. 573/2; Morley, Memorandum, 1908, IOL, EUR. D. 573/37.
236. Spring Rice to Grey, 11 April 1907, BD IV, No. 409, 450–53.
237. Cited in Greaves, 'Some Aspects of the Anglo-Russian Convention', 80.
238. Spring Rice to Grey, 13 Sept. 1907, GL 2, 103–5.
239. Spring Rice to Chirol, 21 June 1907, CC, CASR 1/21.
240. Ibid.
241. Ibid.
242. Ibid.
243. Spring Rice to Chirol, 13 Sept. 1907, CC, CASR 1/21.
244. Nicolson to Grey, 24 Sept. 1907, NA, FO 371/312.
245. Hardinge to Nicolson, 25 Nov. 1907, NA, FO 371/312.
246. FO, Memorandum resp. the Anglo-Russian Convention, 2. Sept. 1908, IOL, PS/18/C/140.
247. Weinroth, 'British Radicals'.
248. Siegel, *Endgame*, 22.
249. *Manchester Guardian*, 27 May 1907.
250. *Manchester Guardian*, 19 June 1907.
251. *Manchester Guardian*, 2 Sept. 1907.
252. *Manchester Guardian*, 26 Sept. 1907.
253. See Spender to Strachey, 21 Oct. 1905, PA, STR/13/13/6.
254. 'It was the German Navy which caused *The Times*, *The Spectator* and the *National Review* to make the sudden discovery that Germany is an enemy. The legend that our supremacy was challenged became with them a fixed idea.' Anon., 'England and Germany', *The Nation*, 19 Oct. 1907, 74–75.
255. Anon., 'The Anglo-German Tension', *The Nation*, 6 Feb. 1909, 700–701. For Russia violating the convention, see Siegel, *Endgame*, 38–39.
256. Anon., 'The Price of the Persian Agreement', *The Nation*, 7 Sept. 1907, 501.
257. Ibid.
258. Anon., 'Our Relations with Russia', *The Nation*, 30 Oct. 1907, 552–53.
259. Anon., 'The Price of the Persian Agreement', *The Nation*, 7 Sept. 1907, 501.
260. Schöllgen, *Imperialismus und Gleichgewicht*, 226–33.
261. An exception is the early work by Heinz-Joachim Müllenbrock, *Literatur und Zeitgeschichte*.
262. Weinroth, 'British Radicals'.
263. Landon, 'Views on the Anglo-Russian Agreement I', FR 11/1907, 726–33, 729; Hamilton, 'Views on the Anglo-Russian Agreement II', ibid., 739–43, 739.
264. Anon., 'The Anglo-German Tension', *The Nation*, 6 Feb. 1909, 700–701.
265. Anon., 'The Foreign Policy of Sir Edward Grey', *The Nation*, 3 Aug. 1907, 822.

266. Ibid.
267. *Daily News*, 4 Sept. 1907.
268. Cited in Jaeckel, *Nordwestgrenze*, 207.
269. Curzon, 'Russia in Central Asia in 1889 and the Anglo-Russian Question', ER 1/1890, 179–208; Curzon to Lansdowne, 10 Dec. 1902, BL, LANS/NC Curzon 1; Minto to Morley, 28 Dec. 1905, IOL, EUR. D. 573/7; Hamilton to Curzon, 6 June 1901, IOL, EUR. F. 123/83.
270. See Neilson, *Britain and the Last Tsar*, 51–110; Dillon, 'Anglo-Russian Convention', CR 6/1904, 800–829.
271. Grey to Nicolson, 1 May 1907, BD IV, No. 270, 292; 27 June 1907, BD IV, No. 430, 481–82; Hardinge to Nicolson, 29 June 1907, NA, FO 800/339; Anon., 'The Foreign Policy of Sir Edward Grey', *The Nation*, 3 Aug. 1907, 822–23.
272. Neilson, *Britain and the Last Tsar*, 292.
273. Hardinge to Nicolson, 21 Jan. 1908, NA, FO 800/341.
274. Hardinge cited in Gall, *Hardinge*, 51.
275. See Steiner, *Britain and the Origins*, 86–87; Mensdorff, 10 Jan. 1908, HHStA, PA VIII, Kt. 140, No. 1 B, fol. 9; Taube, *Der großen Katastrophe entgegen*, 160.
276. Hardinge to Nicolson, 25 Nov. 1907, NA, FO 800/340.
277. 'He will not easily get over these annoyances over Germany and therefore he is a Minister who should be supported as much as possible by England and France since his tendency will be to lean more and more to us than to Germany.' Hardinge to Nicolson, 21 Jan. 1908, NA, FO 800/341.
278. See Wandruszka and Urbanitsch, *Habsburgermonarchie*, Vol. 6/1, 309–10. For Austrian Balkan views, see Goluchowski to Aehrenthal, 2 March 1899, cited in Walters, 'Unpublished Documents', in SEER 32, No. 5, 206–13.
279. May, 'Novibazar Railway Project', 496; Angelow, *Kalkül und Prestige*, 151–74.
280. Aehrenthal to Goluchowski, 31 Dec. 1898, cited in Walters, 'Unpublished Documents', in SEER 32, No. 4, 196–206.
281. Neilson, *Britain and the Last Tsar*, 294. See also Izvolsky to Benckendorff, 18 June 1908, BDS I, No. 3, 13; for the Macedonian question, see Fikret, *Makedonische Frage*.
282. See Fikret, *Makedonische Frage*.
283. W.A. Moore to Lansdowne, 28 June 1907, BL, LANS/Working Files 17.
284. Hewins, *Apologia*, Vol. 1, 225; Balfour to Lansdowne, 10 Sept. 1903 and 22 Feb. 1904, BL, LANS/PL 5.
285. Lansdowne to Curzon, 16 Feb. 1902, IOL, EUR. F. 111/151.
286. Parker, Memorandum, 29 July 1909, BDFA F/XXXIV, No. 155, 324–411, 329.
287. Pichon to the embassies at Rome, St Petersburg and Constantinople, 24 Feb. 1908: 'C'est sur l'affaire des réformes en Macédoine que l'Angeterre et la Russie porteront sans doute d'un commun accord leur effort le plus prochain ... Il suffira que, là comme ailleurs, nous facilitons autant qu'il dépendra de nous, le rapprochement anglo-russe.' DDF 2/XI, No. 297, 507.
288. Bridge, *Great Britain and Austria-Hungary*, 67; Moore to Lansdowne, 28 June 1907, BL, LANS/Working Files 17.
289. Mensdorff to Aehrenthal, 29 and 31 May; 1, 4, 7 and 17 June 1907, cited in Walters, 'Unpublished Documents', in SEER 30, 228–47; see also Asquith, *Ursprung des Krieges*, 68.
290. BD V, Nos. 266, 275, 278, 279, 280.

291. Pichon to Cambon, 21 Sept. 1907, DDF 2/XI, No. 173, 284–86, 285.
292. Marshall to Bülow, 14 Dec. 1907, GP XXII, No. 7719, 466–71, 471. See also Aehrenthal, January 1908, in Friedjung, *Geschichte in Gesprächen*, Vol. 2, 72–77.
293. For Vienna's reaction, see Hantsch, *Berchtold*, Vol. 2, 83.
294. Cited in Angelow, *Kalkül und Prestige*, 160.
295. Nicolson, 2 Feb. 1908, cited in Cooper, 'British Policy in the Balkans', 261.
296. Cited in ibid.
297. Neilson, *Britain and the Last Tsar*, 294.
298. 'Russia is now asking for our co-operation in the Near East.' Nicolson to Grey, 10 Feb. 1908, NA, FO 800/73.
299. Nicolson to Grey, 12 Feb. 1908, NA, FO 800/73; 26 Feb. 1908, cited in Cooper, 'British Policy in the Balkans', 261.
300. Taube, *Der Großen Katastrophe entgegen*, 160. See also Pourtalès to Bülow, 16 Jan. 1908, GP XXV/2, No. 8761, 385–87.
301. See Bridge, *Great Britain and Austria-Hungary*, 79.
302. 'He [Izvolsky] is a minister who should be supported as much as possible by England and France since his tendency will be to lean more and more on us than on Germany.' Hardinge to Nicolson, 21 Jan. 1908, NA, FO 800/341. 'Clemenceau is quite satisfied to knock on the head of the possible Russo-German agreement.' Bertie to Grey, 2 Jan. 1908, ibid.
303. Hardinge to Nicolson, 7 Jan. 1908, NA, FO 800/341; O'Conor to Grey, 24 Jan. 1908, NA, FO 371/531; Nicolson to Grey, 18 Feb. 1908, NA, FO 371/531.
304. Bridge, *Great Britain and Austria-Hungary*, 65; see also Walters, 'Unpublished Documents', in SEER 30, 213–31.
305. Cited in Bridge, *Great Britain and Austria-Hungary*, 77.
306. Lord Fitzmaurice, 25 Feb. 1908, cited in Delbrück et al., *Schultheß' Geschichtskalender*, Vol. 24 (1908), 309; see also O'Conor to Grey, 5 Feb. 1908, BD V, No. 229, 330; Parker, Memorandum, BDFA F/XXXIV, No. 155, 324–411, 329. For Mensdorff, see Angelow, *Kalkül und Prestige*, 165; May, 'Novibazar Railway Project', 523.
307. Nicolson to Grey, 12 Feb. 1908, BD V, No. 233, 335–36.
308. May, 'Novibazar Railway Project', 522.
309. Brussels, 16 March 1908, BelD IV, No. 8, 56–58. Identified as the inspiration behind this plan, Germany was accused of having egotistical motives. Brussels, 20 March 1908, ibid., No. 9, 58–59.
310. Tyrrell to Spring Rice, 22 Oct. 1908, NA, FO 800/241.
311. Nicolson to Grey, 30 Jan. 1908, NA, FO 371/581; Bridge, *Great Britain and Austria-Hungary*, 80.
312. Nicolson to Grey, 4 Feb. 1908, cited in NA, FO 371/581.
313. Nicolson to Grey, 18 Feb. 1908, BD V, No. 188, 232–33.
314. Grey to Nicolson, 25 Feb. 1908, NA, FO 800/341.
315. Nicolson to Grey, 18 Feb. 1908, BD V, No. 188, 232–33; Cartwright to Grey, 1 Aug. 1908, NA, FO 371/399.
316. See Reports in BDFA F/XXXIV (1905–1909).
317. See Weinroth, 'British Radicals', 665.
318. *Manchester Guardian*, 27 May and 19 June 1907.
319. Nicolson to Grey, 13 Feb. 1908, BD V/1, No. 234, 336.
320. Grey to Nicolson, 2 April 1909, NA, FO 800/342.

321. Hardinge to Lascelles, 19 Feb. 1908, NA, FO 800/11.
322. Grey to Nicolson, 24Feb. 1908, NA, FO 800/341; Grey to Nicolson, 17 March 1908, BD V, No. 192, 235.
323. Nicolson to Lascelles, 24 Feb. 1908, NA, FO 800/11.
324. Nicolson to Grey, 26 Feb. 1908, NA, FO 800/73. Identical words were used by Hardinge in a letter to Nicolson. Hardinge to Nicolson, 24 Feb. 1908, NA, FO 800/341; see also Grey, 25 Feb. 1908, PD IV/184, cols. 1692–708.
325. Greindl to Davignon, 12 June 1908, BelD III, No. 48, 134–38.
326. Grey to Benckendorff, 15 July 1908, BD V, No. 254, 353–54.
327. 'His [Grey's] influence is the sole force which can at once secure reform and ensure peace.' *Daily News*, 9 May 1908. See also Noel Buxton (Letters), *The Times*, 4 June 1908; Lucien Wolf in *Illustrated Graphic*, 18 April 1908; Strachey, *The Spectator*, 4 April 1908.
328. Maxse, 'Episodes', NR 5/1908, 339.
329. See Gade, *Gleichgewichtspolitik*, 46.
330. Nicolson to Grey, 26 Feb. 1908, NA, FO 800/73; Izvolsky to Benckendorff, 18 June 1908, BDS I, No. 3, 13.
331. Palmer, *Glanz*, 357–63.
332. Hardinge to Nicolson, 25 Nov. 1907, NA, FO 800/340.
333. A 'weltpolitische Formation der Kräfte', Miquel to Bülow, 29 July 1907, GP XXV/1, No. 8537, 45–47, 47.
334. Cited in Cooper, 'British Policy in the Balkans', 262. See also G.W. Balfour to Spring Rice, 11 Feb. 1908, CC, CASR 1/2; PD IV/190, cols. 211–13.
335. See Kennedy, *Rise of Anglo-German Antagonism*, 283; Monger, *End of Isolation*, 328.
336. PD IV/190, cols. 223–27, 246–53; for the vote, with 212 Liberals abstaining, see cols. 266–67; *Daily News*, 5 June 1908; *The Times*, 5 June 1908; *The Spectator*, 5 June 1908, 61; Maxse, 'Episodes', NR 7/1908, 679–83.
337. 'I have insisted with him [Edward VII] very strongly that he ought to pay a yacht visit … but nothing must be said for the time being.' Hardinge to Nicolson, 5 Feb. 1908, NA, FO 800/341.
338. 'The visit is in my opinion the thing to work for now and it provides the solution of many questions by pleasing the Emperor of Russia and getting him to work with us in the Near East.' Hardinge to Nicolson, 13 April 1908, NA, FO 800/341.
339. Hardinge to Nicolson, 12 Nov. 1907, NA, FO 800/340.
340. Hardinge to Nicolson, 5 Feb. 1908 and 13 April 1908, NA, FO 800/341.
341. Hardinge to Nicolson, 1 April 1908, NA, FO 800/341. 'If you agree with me *I hope you will not be alarmist to Grey about Finland or the Duma. … the visit may be the key to the solution of many questions by pleasing the Emperor and the Russians and getting them to work with us in the Near and Middle East*' [italics added]. Hardinge to Nicolson, 13 April 1908, NA, FO 800/341.
342. Asquith to Edward VII, 6 May 1908, NA, CAB 41/31/50. For the 'staff talks', see Williamson, *Politics of Grand Strategy*, 284–85.
343. Taube, *Der großen Katastrophe entgegen*, 167–70.
344. Sweet, 'The Baltic in British Diplomacy'.
345. For the Russian impression, see Taube, *Der großen Katastrophe entgegen*, 167–70.
346. *The Times*, 1 Aug. 1908. For Edward VII's entourage, see Anon., 'The Motives of German Policy', *The Nation*, 27 March 1909, 955–56; Stead, 'Progress', RR 7/1908, 4;

Grey to Goschen, 9 June 1909, NA, FO 800/61; Strachey to Grey, 12 June 1908, PA, STR/7/8/5; Metternich to Bülow, 13 June 1908, GP XXV/2, No. 8809, 457–58.
347. Aehrenthal to Mensdorff, 10 Jan. 1908, HHStA, PA VIII, Kt. 142, fol. 30. For *Le Temps*, see Weinroth, 'British Radicals', 670. 'L'opinion publique en Russie n'avait pas d'abord accueilli favorablement l'idée d'un rapprochement politique avec l'Angleterre. Elle est aujourd'hui revenue de ses préventions. Bien qu'ayant à peine huit mois d'existence, l'entente des deux Gouvernements [Russia and England] est devenue unfacteur de la politique internationale.' Report (St Petersburg), 3 July 1908, BelD III, No. 16, 82–84. For Bülow, the meeting was a 'central incident'. Bülow, *Memoirs*, Vol. 2, 351; Metternich to Bülow, 7 Jan. 1909, PA-AA, R 6093.
348. Fay, *Origins of World War I*, 270.
349. Spring Rice to Chirol, autumn 1907, CC, CASR 1/21; *Manchester Guardian*, 29 May 1908; *The Nation*, 13 June 1908. For *Le Temps*, the meeting reflected an 'entente permanente'. *Le Temps*, 8 June 1908; Tschirschky to Bülow, 2 June 1908, GP XXV/2, No. 8801, 442–43.
350. See Cooper, 'British Policy in the Balkans', 262, n. 14.
351. Hardinge, 12 June 1908, BD V, No. 195, 237–46; see also GP XXV/2, Nos. 8798–829, 439–94; Lee, *Edward VII*, Vol. 2, 586–96.
352. Hardinge, *Diplomacy*, 155.
353. Ratibor to Bülow, 28 May 1908, GP XXV/2, No. 880, 442.
354. Taube, *Der großen Katastrophe entgegen*, 167–70.
355. See Rede M.S. Adzemov (Duma), 4 April 1908, cited in Giertz, 'Die außenpolitische Position Miljukov', 83.
356. Cited in ibid., 84.
357. *Rec* (a Russian periodical), 9 May 1908, cited in ibid.
358. Fisher to Esher, 8 Sept. 1908, cited in Fisher, *Memories and Records*, 187.
359. Hamann about Cassel, 22 June 1908, GP XXIV, No. 8199, 52–54; see also Fisher to Esher, 8 Sept. 1908, cited in Fisher, *Memories and Records*, 187.
360. Grey (Commons), 28 May 1908, cited in Delbrück et al., *Schultheß' Geschichtskalender*, Vol. 24 (1908), 315.
361. Hardinge, Memorandum, 12 June 1908, BD V, No. 195, 237–46; Izvolsky to Benckendorff, 18 June 1908, cited in Siebert, *Entente Diplomacy*, 479–80.
362. Ibid., 479.
363. Nicolson to Grey, 26 Feb. 1908, NA, FO 800/73.
364. Taube, *Der großen Katastrophe entgegen*, 170; KA, Bd. IV, 128.
365. Cooper, 'British Policy in the Balkans', 262; Protocol of the Russian Council of Ministry, 2 Feb. 1908, cited in Pokrowski, *Drei Konferenzen*, 17–20; Pourtalès to Bülow, 19 Feb. 1908, GP XXV/2, No. 8762, 387–88.
366. Izvolsky to Benckendorff, 18 June 1907, BDS I, No. 3, 12.
367. Strachey to Grey, 12 June 1908, PA, STR/7/8.
368. Trench to Lascelles, 17 Aug. 1908, cited in FDSF I, 148.
369. *Westminster Gazette*, 11 June 1908. 'Reval is in effect a proclamation to the world that the three Powers, Russia, France and Great Britain, are determined to do all they can to maintain the peace of the world and to maintain it in the right way.' *The Spectator*, 13 June 1908, 61.
370. Maxse, 'Episodes', NR 7/1908, 679–83: 'There is now good cause to speak of a defensive triple alliance'.

371. *Morning Post*, 11 June 1908.
372. *The Times*, 11 June 1908.
373. Dillon, 'A New Era for England and Russia', CR 7/1908, 107–9.
374. Maxse, 'Episodes', NR 7/1908, 684–85.
375. *Manchester Guardian*, 11 and 12 June 1908.
376. *Graphic*, 13 June 1908.
377. Hildebrand, *Das vergangene Reich*, 241.
378. See Delbrück et al., *Schultheß' Geschichtskalender*, Vol. 24 (1908), 315; see also *The Nation*, 13 June 1908.
379. Metternich to Bülow, 30 May 1908, PA-AA, R 5962. See also Nicolson to Grey, 2 Nov. 1908, BDFA F/XX, No. 186, 292.
380. Hardinge to Nicolson, 19 Feb. 1908, NA, FO 800/341.
381. Hildebrand, *Das vergangene Reich*, 263.
382. Hardinge to Blocker, 21 Sept. 1908, CUL, MSS Hardinge, Vol. 11.
383. Hardinge to Bertie, 17 June 1908, NA, FO 800/170; Strachey to Grey, 12 June 1908, PA, STR/7/8/5; Minute by Mallet: O'Beirne to Grey, 2 June 1908, NA, FO 371/571.
384. Fisher to Edward VII, 14 March 1908, FG II, No. 118, 169.
385. Goschen to Grey, 12 June 1908, NA, FO 371/517.
386. See Feroz, *Young Turks*.
387. See Heller, *Ottoman Empire*; Kent, 'Great Britain and the End of the Ottoman Empire'.
388. 'Hardinge told me the Germans were utterly flattened out at Constantinople and the Bagdad Railway as dead as a doornail and England predominant.' Fisher to McKenna, 11 Aug. 1908, FG II, No. 135, 186–88.
389. Grey to Lowther, 11 Aug. 1908, BD V, No. 207, 266.
390. See Sweet, 'Bosnian Crisis', 178.
391. There was much hard feeling in Bulgaria when Geschow, a Bulgarian diplomatic agent, was not invited to an official banquet in honour of the sultan because he was the representative of a Turkish vassalage.
392. Tscharykow, *High Politics*, 273.
393. See Cooper, 'British Policy in the Balkans', 258–79; Miller, *Straits*, 39–40; Dockrill, *Formulation*, 53–84.
394. Fisher to McKenna, 11 Aug. 1908, FG II, No. 135, 186–88.
395. See Neilson, *Britain and the Last Tsar*, 296.
396. Greindl to Davignon, 12 June 1908, BelD III, No. 48, 134–38.
397. Lowe and Dockrill, *Mirage of Power*, Vol. 1, 86–89.
398. Robbins, 'Public Opinion', 85–86; see also Stavrianos, 'Balkan Committee', 258–66. 'Le comité balkanique qui fonctionne à Londres fait de la propagande presque exclusivement en faveur de la Bulgarie.' Report of the Belgian Consulat in Belgrad, 12 June 1908, BelD III, No. 17, 85.
399. Grey to Lowther, 11 Aug. 1908, BD V, No. 207, 266.
400. Nicolson to Grey, 30 Jan. 1908, BD V, No. 227, 328–29.
401. Wilson, 'Question of Anti-Germanism'; Neilson, *Britain and the Last Tsar*, 296.
402. Nicolson to Grey, 13 Aug. 1908, NA, FO 800/337; see also Neilson, 'My Beloved Russians', 521–554.
403. 'We have now agreements with nearly all great powers, with the exception of the two powers of the Triple Alliance.' *Observer*, 1 Sept. 1909.

404. 'Wir sollten abgekreist werden' ('We should be headhunted', Transl., AR). Karl Frhr. von Werkmann, cited in Gall, *Hardinge*, 250, n. 193. See also Verosta, *Theorie*, 591; Specher to Forrer, 23 Jan. 1907, Annex I (December 1906), DDS V, No. 163, 353–57, 354; Brockdorff-Rantzau to Bülow, 19 Aug. 1908, GP XXIV, No. 8230, 133–35.
405. Friedjung, Diary, 7 Feb. 1909, in *Geschichte in Gesprächen*, Vol. 2, 196–99, 199.
406. Hardinge to Goschen, 28 June 1908, CUL, MSS Hardinge, Vol. 11. 'Cartwright, just before he was sent to Vienna, had in a despatch, openly advocated the policy of detaching Austria from Germany and thus completing the latter's isolation.' Rumbold, 9 March 1909, BOD, Journal, Vol. 3.
407. Minutes, Langley and Grey to: Cartwright to Grey, 1 Aug. 1908, NA, FO 371/399.
408. Cited in Jaeckel, *Nordwestgrenze*, 152.
409. Taube, *Der großen Katastrophe entgegen*, 3–41, 18.
410. Brailsford, 'The Hush in Europe', ER 7/1907, 779–93; Dilke, 'Foreign Affairs', ER 10/1909, 495–500.
411. Cartwright to Grey, 1 Aug. 1908, NA, FO 371/399.
412. See Wilson, *Policy of the Entente*, 112; see also Grey to Egerton, 1 March 1906, NA, FO 800/64.
413. Mensdorff, Report, 26 June 1908, HHStA, PA VIII, Kt. 141, No. 32 D, Bl. 68f.; Grey to Nicolson, 10 Nov. 1908, BD V, No. 441, 494–95.
414. 'I heartily hope he [Bülow] may spare Germany the splendid isolation which, through no fault of his, threatens to become a reality against which he is now working with German tenacity.' *The Times*, 29 Nov. 1906.
415. Cited in Wilson, *Policy of the Entente*, 112.
416. 'A far more formidable combination might take its place.' Minutes Hardinge's: Lascelles to Grey, 25 March 1908, NA, FO 371/469.
417. Hildebrand, 'Zentrum', 87.
418. Greindl to Davignon, 30 May 1908, BelD III, No. 47, 130–32.
419. Mensdorff to Aehrenthal, 28 May 1909, HHStA, PA VII, Kt. 143.
420. See Holbach, The Germanisation of the Balkans (Letters), *The Nation*, 19 Dec. 1908, 470–71; see also Metternich to Bülow, 2 April 1906, PA-AA, R 5627.
421. In the 1870s, Russia had already agreed to an annexation. See the secret agreements made at Reichstadt, 26 June 1876; Budapest, 15 Jan. 1877; and Berlin, 13 July 1878. See Taube, *Der großen Katastrophe entgegen*, 180–81.
422. See Dockrill, *Formulation*, 52; Geindl to Faverau, 5 April 1906, BelD III, No. 16, 46–48.
423. According to Nicholas de Basily, it was Izvolsky who proposed the deal over the Near East. See Basily, *Diplomat of Imperial Russia*, 83. See also Tscharykow, *High Politics*, 269; Taube, *Der großen Katastrophe entgegen*, 167–70. See Aehrenthal's notes about his talks with Izvolsky, Buchlau, 16 Sept. 1908, ÖUA I, No. 79, 86–92; Aehrenthal to Francis Joseph I, 17 Sept. 1908, ÖUA I, No. 80, 92.
424. Aehrenthal, 16 Sept. 1908, ÖUA I, No. 79, 86–92; to Franz Joseph I, 17 Sept. 1908, ÖUA I, No. 80, 92.
425. Aehrenthal thought of winning Britain over from Russia. GP XXVI/1, No. 9004; Berchtold to Aehrenthal, 18 Oct. 1908, ÖUA I, No. 327, 252–54.
426. Goschen to Grey, 28 Sept. 1908, BD V, No. 269, 366–67.
427. Anon., *History of The Times*, Vol. 3, 611. By summer 1906, Steed had already heard rumours about an intended annexation. Steed to Chirol, 9 July 1906, NIA, MSS Chirol.
428. Brockdorff-Rantzau to Bülow, 19 Aug. 1908, GP XXIV, No. 8230, 133–35.

Chapter 9

'MORE RUSSIAN THAN THE RUSSIANS'?
British Balkan Diplomacy and the Annexation of Bosnia 1908/9

Looking back, Henry Wickham-Steed recognized the crisis year of 1908/9 as a watershed moment that had seen the course set towards the catastrophe of 1914. The two groupings that faced each other as a result of the persistent tensions in the Balkans would meet again six years later for a showdown in the trenches of the Great War. 'However', Wickham-Steed continued, 'I have always held that the tangible beginnings of trouble date rather from 1907',[1] the year in which a bridge had been constructed between the competing powers on the eastern and western edges of the continent. Wickham-Steed was by no means the only one to see the Annexation Crisis as a direct consequence of Anglo-Russian rapprochement, for his colleagues James Garvin, Henry Spenser Wilkinson and Valentine Chirol also grasped that link, along with the wider implications of the complexities surrounding Bosnia and Herzegovina. Again, in what seemed practically a reflex action, Leo Maxse attempted to win Alfred Harmsworth over to the idea of a new campaign against the Central Powers.[2]

Within the diplomatic corps, the crisis left a deep impression not only on Alwyn Parker but also on Charles Hardinge and others. They all foresaw profound and lasting consequences for the system of alliances and ententes.[3] By February 1909, David Beatty, naval advisor to the Army Council, was already thinking in terms of joint planning by army and navy and assumed that a great war was imminent in which Britain would participate on the side of the Franco-Russian Dual Alliance.[4] Prime Minister Asquith and Foreign Secretary Grey were able to see – with hindsight, admittedly – signs that appeared to support the view that Aehrenthal's fait accompli was a prelude to the July Crisis,[5] a judgement that historians have long taken for granted, above all when tackling the policies adopted in Vienna, Berlin and St Petersburg.[6] When it comes to the British approach to

---

Notes for this chapter begin on page 447.

the crisis, in which the *Times* identified the first fruits of the new power grouping,[7] the research is surprisingly thin. Despite the many contemporary commentaries on the Balkan crisis, works on British pre-war diplomacy seldom deal with the Balkan region as it seems of no primary concern for Whitehall. Nevertheless, it was of neuralgic importance for the whole states system and it shows the British attitude towards the system of Triple Entente and Triple Alliance and it indeed provides the dilemma Edward Grey and his diplomacy had to face between Russian ambitions, systemic interests and nurturing the bonds of the new alignments. Thus, London faced the same dilemma as did Berlin with its Austrian partner.[8] The cursory investigation of British Balkan diplomacy has suggested that London merely continued its hereditary role as disinterested and honest broker. In what remains the only, and rarely cited, comparative study of the crisis, undertaken by Bernadotte Schmitt in the 1930s,[9] and in subsequent works too, Whitehall is depicted as following its traditional reactive policy, intended to keep the peace and maintain the balance of power. That policy, the studies suggest, was shaped by concert thinking until forced by the aggressive attitude of Berlin and Vienna to turn to strengthening, reluctantly, the entente with Russia.[10]

Although Arthur Nicolson has been identified by historians as an influential proponent of an Anglo-Russian alliance, little additional research has been undertaken on motivations, the imperial or domestic background, or the implications for the power system.[11] Nicolson's failure to achieve an alliance with Russia, and the cabinet's refusal to consider the Straits as part of a deal with St Petersburg, are usually presented as proof that for as long as possible Britain maintained the continuity of its foreign policy, which meant keeping its distance from any continental commitments. In short, that interpretation proposes that Britain continued its exemplary performance as arbiter and protector of the European law and status quo.[12] Historians have tended to overlook, however, the constraints to which these decisions were subject, in the cabinet, within the Liberal Party and in relation to domestic policy, which meant they cannot necessarily be attributed to a simple commitment to the idea of maintaining the balance in Europe. Additionally, even before the crisis, the relationships that would make up the Triple Entente were already an accepted part of international structures and practice, created, distinct from treaty obligations, by external pressures and by diplomatic norms and oral agreements. London's policy was less a matter of treaties and more a matter of fundamental convictions and the communication of those convictions. Thus, in summer 1908, Count Mensdorff, the Austrian ambassador to the United Kingdom, realized that at the Foreign Office the ambassadors of France and Russia, Paul Cambon and Alexander von Benckendorff were commonly referred to in a single breath as representatives of the 'nations amies et alliées'.[13] Already by 1907, even neutral states such as Belgium and Switzerland thought the Central Powers entirely isolated, an interpretation that meant the crisis in the Balkans was in turn seen as an unambiguous confrontation between two power blocs.[14] As soon as Britain began to work on generating closer ties with Paris and St Petersburg, therefore, the Balkan region also became a field of experiment for Anglo-Russian relations. British diplomacy's impact on the Triple Entente and on the wish for predictability, repeatedly identified by Grey as a 'question of honour', gained an importance that cannot be underestimated.[15]

A question mark therefore hangs over Britain's characterization as a disinterested mediator or mere spectator of events. The mere suggestion that Britain's intention in supporting Russia diplomatically was to serve the balance of power falls short. Not only did London suspect the Russian foreign secretary, Alexander Izvolsky, had been the major driving force behind the horse-trading agreement with Aehrenthal about the annexation made at Buchlau;[16] British observers also knew only too well about the importance of the Habsburg Monarchy as a traditional regional power and Russia's ambitions in the Balkans. Moreover, the Foreign Office already reckoned with a reinvigorated Russian army.[17] The crisis undoubtedly put the whole of Grey's policy to the test. It is therefore all the more revealing that the Foreign Office from the start dismissed Germany and Austria-Hungary alike as liars and scoundrels, equally complicit in violating the Berlin Treaty of 1878. Neither at Whitehall nor at Fleet Street were there the slightest doubts that Germany was the real author of Austrian diplomacy.[18] Only Cecil Arthur Spring Rice, who knew Aehrenthal personally from his time as chargé d'affaires at St Petersburg and who is generally thought essentially anti-German, raised the possibility of cooperation with Berlin, which he saw as a means of preserving or restoring Britain's flexibility within the free play of the powers. As an experienced diplomat, especially as concerns Russia, he thought the situation in south-eastern Europe an opportunity for containment of the tsardom and for prioritizing mediation over the nurturing of British ententes.[19] Surprisingly, also radical liberals relegated the protection of smaller states like Serbia or Montenegro, one of their traditional principles, in favour of a concert solution.[20] Others, like Arthur Nicolson and Charles Hardinge, saw themselves confirmed in their bias against Germany. For them, the Dual Monarchy was only a cat's paw of Berlin. London's policy stood at a crossroads. Were imperial interests or continental interests to be prioritized, or what of an integrated solution that would embrace both spheres of interest? The distortion inherent in the anti-German perception of the Austro-German alliance from now on played a crucial part in British diplomacy towards the continent and it hampered any German efforts to work together with Paris and London as well as to appeal to Vienna. Both powers, Germany and Great Britain, now sought to rationalize the behaviour of their partners, to strengthen their alignments and not to lose control of a strategically vital partner by any means. Thus, the role of a necessary 'third party', an essential element of any crisis management within the modern European states system, was considerably aggravated if not lost completely. While M.B. Cooper and David Sweet agreed in essence with Bernadotte Schmitt on the British role in the balance of powers,[21] in their view London was most concerned not with Russia but with regaining its former standing concerning Turkey. Additionally, Cooper at least concedes that the Foreign Office intended to prevent a 'Germanization' of the Balkans.[22] Britain's dilemma was indeed how its global interests might be reconciled with its interests within the continental system. The separation of the two spheres that Lansdowne and Balfour had pursued evidently seemed to the liberal imperial leadership increasingly less feasible.

In their use of archival sources, the radius of their exploration and the depth of their analysis and argumentation, Frank Roy Bridge's[23] investigation of the relations between Britain and Austria-Hungary, Klaus Wormer's work on Britain's policy between Russia and Germany,[24] and Keith Neilson's study of Britain's policy on Russia[25] remain unsurpassed. Whereas Neilson provided a brilliant overview of British policy between 1894 and 1917, Wormer and Bridge concentrated on the immediate pre-war period, starting in 1906. Neilson and, in particular, Wormer were only marginally concerned with the Balkan crisis, but for Bridge this crisis year was of marked significance. Referring to Francis Pribram's book,[26] admittedly against the background of the Fischer controversy of the 1970s, Bridge tackled the history of London and Vienna's bilateral relations, with particular attention given to the Sanjak railway,[27] the estrangement of Austria and Russia and the Bosnian Annexation Crisis.[28] Although Bridge came to the conclusion that Aehrenthal had been frequently misunderstood, he identified British policy as principled and driven by balance of power thinking, and deemed British policy on Europe under Grey to have been entirely in line with the idea of the European concert.[29] Pribram, Wormer and Bridge believe entente policy aligned with balance of power policy and concert policy.[30]

Investigation of Britain's attitude towards Russia during the Balkan crisis throws light on the goals of British entente policy as it took shape against the background of imperial and continental interests, which until now has been characterized as purely de-escalating, intended to preserve stability and the balance of power. Space does not allow British policy towards Turkey to be included, although this latter dynamic has been discussed extensively elsewhere.[31] The discussion here will tackle two critical aspects of British policy: firstly, Britain's hostility towards the Central Powers, especially Grey's position of moral superiority and London's inability to differentiate between Berlin and Vienna; and secondly, Britain's accommodation with Russia, though not on the Straits, where Whitehall hoped for Russian forbearance, but through compensating St Petersburg by means of indulging Serbian demands for compensation to the detriment of Austria-Hungary.

First Reactions

After years of estrangement between Constantinople and London, the Young Turk revolution roused fresh hopes among Britain's liberals of rapprochement with the Ottoman Empire.³² Hardinge confidently declared Germany 'flattened out at Constantinople, the Bagdad Railway as dead as a doornail, and England predominant'.³³ With Muslims forming such a large part of the population of the Empire, and on strategic grounds too, the Ottoman Empire had by no means lost its great significance for Britain.³⁴ On the day Grey announced his continuing interest in Turkey, he was reminded by his ambassador in St Petersburg that the tsar and Izvolsky were counting on a broadly conceived cooperation with Britain.³⁵ Since the summer of 1908, Whitehall had been pursuing what was in effect a dual strategy,³⁶ intended to protect and if possible extend the recent association formed with Russia, while remaining in close contact with the Young Turks, keeping the door open for an additional option for British foreign policy. Whitehall evidently believed that a reformed Turkey merited renewed British support. That possibility might lead to problems with St Petersburg and with Russia's traditional drive towards the Mediterranean, but it might also strengthen Britain's hand with Russia should the new bonds between the two powers become weaker. After all, despite the convention signed just the previous year, Russia had been anything but cooperative and had even extended the activities of its agents that were aimed at destabilizing Persia,³⁷ while despite, or perhaps because of, the support expressed in the press by Maxse, Garvin and Strachey, the liberal imperialists had not yet succeeded in persuading their radical colleagues within the Liberal Party of the value of the Anglo-Russian friendship. Tories, too, continued to be sceptical, believing Britain's Persian interests had been sold short, along with British principles.³⁸ A new option might relieve the burden on Grey as he undertook a challenging balancing act.

On 6 October 1908, the dual strategy involving St Petersburg and Constantinople threatened to collapse. With the annexation of Bosnia and Herzegovina, Alois Freiherr von Aehrenthal,³⁹ Austrian-Hungarian foreign minister, set a new pace for the gradual fracturing of the European powers that led up to the events of 1914.⁴⁰ In conjunction with the independence of Bulgaria,⁴¹ declared the previous day, the annexation provoked consternation in most European capitals. In London, outrage at the fait accompli boiled over. The first reports had scarcely trickled through to Fleet Street when the press launched a furious campaign against the illegal behaviour of Vienna and Sofia. For the leading papers, both acts, and the annexation in particular, undisputedly violated the Treaty of Berlin of 1878.⁴² Three days earlier, Hardinge had been unruffled to learn of the step Vienna was about to take from the Austrian-Hungarian ambassador Mensdorff, who was thought well disposed towards Britain,⁴³ yet Whitehall suddenly claimed deep moral and legal injury and brusquely refused to recognize the annexation. According to Winston Churchill's subsequent and somewhat derisive account, 'The Whig statesman, the monitor of public law in Europe, the English gentleman, the public school boy, all these elements in his [Grey's] character were equally affronted'.⁴⁴ Grey admitted that in terms of political stability, it made no difference whether Austria-Hungary annexed Bosnia and Herzegovina or merely continued their occupation, and he had already been expecting Bulgaria's independence the year before.[45] Apparently, at least according to the impression Grey gave, the foreign secretary's principal objection was to the Dual Monarchy's treatment of the Treaty of Berlin.[46]

According to Article 25 of that treaty, the provinces of Bosnia and Herzegovina formally belonged to the Ottoman Empire, but they had been occupied by Austria-Hungary and were administered from Vienna, which meant they had been part of the Habsburg sphere of influence since 1878. Ethnically, however, the individual populations felt drawn to neither Constantinople nor Vienna, and the largest, Serb minority, which made up around 49 per cent of the population, had been opposing Vienna for years with the support of Russia and the connivance of Britain, campaigning for a pan-Serbian state that would include Bosnia[47] – an idea that threatened to kill off multi-ethnic Austria-Hungary.[48] Haunted by the possibility of a united Serbia and Montenegro as its neighbour, and with the support of the Great Powers,[49] Austria-Hungary had been granted the right to occupy and station military forces in the Sanjak of Novi Pazar, which separated the two states. Robert Salisbury and Benjamin Disraeli had even advised Gyula Andrassy, the Austrian-Hungarian foreign minister, to annex the regions immediately, in order to take the wind out of the sails of the nascent pan-Slav movement.[50]

With the tensions within the multi-ethnic state becoming increasingly evident, Vienna now attempted to rectify its omission.[51] Since October 1907, the Austrian-Hungarian Council of Ministers had been looking more intensively for solutions,[52] with thoughts of reform and limited autonomy having led nowhere in recent years. Reports from the Sanjak of acts of violence by the Muslim population against the Austrian-Hungarian military presence removed the last doubts in the mind of Max Vladimir von Beck, the Austrian minister-president, about taking a step that could no longer be delayed.[53] Aehrenthal's priorities were to meet southern Slav nationalism halfway and remove its sting,[54] retrench Austria-Hungary in a strong position in the Balkans, and to find a modus vivendi with Russia,[55] which would allow the ailing multi-ethnic state to regain its rightful place as an equal Great Power within the European system, a step that would undoubtedly benefit the weakened Great Power system as a whole. Arminius Vambéry, the experienced British agent in the Balkans, informed Hardinge that Aehrenthal had told him that Austria-Hungary's goal was also greater emancipation from Berlin,[56] but Vambéry's information fell on deaf ears, for London naturally assumed that Vienna's actions were a product of German machinations.[57]

Aehrenthal decided on annexation, as a fait accompli and a signal of strength in the face of continuing anti-Austrian agitation by Serbia.[58] The growing influence of Austria's chief of staff, General Franz Conrad von Hötzendorf,[59] who hated Serbia with a passion,[60] played a significant role in that decision, along with the Dual Monarchy's complex needs for domestic consolidation and foreign security.[61] However, in the age of imperialism, such treatment of a lesser power was novel only in that it occurred on the periphery of Europe rather than in the colonies.[62] Therefore, only the reaction of the Entente powers rendered the event explosive. For contemporaries, Vienna's actions only ranked as unusually aggressive if they did not measure the Dual Monarchy and their own imperialistic activities by the same standard, or, rather, if they wished to use their apparent resentment to political ends. Paul W. Schroeder had good reason to believe it grotesque for Russia to request that London and Paris defend the sanctity of the Treaty of Berlin, which had already been broken innumerable times by all parties.[63] Now former rivals had become friends, new standards were apparently being set for a treaty that four years earlier Francis Bertie had deemed no longer 'applicable to the present conditions in the Balkans'.[64]

Bertie was giving voice to London's new attitude towards the formation of power relations, as was evident in Britain's acknowledgement of Serbian aspirations and claims, but his words also highlight the problems that Britain's self-absorption brought to those power relations. From the comfortable distance of the British Isles, Lansdowne had already stimulated ideas of Macedonian autonomy and now Serbia and Montenegro's right to demand satisfaction of an established Great Power was acknowledged and they were permitted to demand compensation for the destruction of any hopes of achieving Great Power status they had held. Should we see here another example of established practice by a Great Power, and list these events alongside the actions of Britain in South Africa, the Far East and the Middle East, of France and Italy in North Africa, of the United States in the Caribbean, of Russia in Manchuria and Persia, and of Germany in a variety of locations around the world? Or was the turbulence of winter 1908/9 a product of a sudden acknowledgement of the rights of the Balkan states made by Britain simply out of consideration for Russia? Well aware of the imperialistic behaviour of the other Great Powers, the Austrian-Hungarian Foreign Ministry, and Aehrenthal in particular, did not anticipate significant international opposition to the annexation, an attitude compounded by Viennese willingness to withdraw from the Sanjak of Novi Pazar, where its presence was guaranteed by treaty.[65] That expectation may appear naive in hindsight, but in the context of contemporary circumstances it was certainly logical.

As an agent in the service of the British Crown, Arminius Vámbéry discovered for himself how attitudes had shifted. Under Sanderson and Lansdowne, Vámbéry had been highly valued for his knowledge of Balkan issues and for his balanced reports on both Russian and Austrian ambitions.[66] In the course of the Balkan crisis, however, he was called to order by Hardinge for insubordination. His usual candour was no longer desirable now that his reports to London and articles that appeared in the *Pester Lloyd* contained word of Aehrenthal's offer of Anglo-Austrian cooperation and drew attention to Serbian agitation and activities against Austria fostered from St Petersburg. Above all, Hardinge believed Vámbéry too even-handed, especially when it came to criticism of Russia, and he warned the agent: 'If it [Vámbéry's publication of articles in the *Pester Lloyd*] should occur again I shall be reluctantly compelled to reconsider our relations to each other',[67] a weighty threat as 78-year-old Vámbéry was dependent on a Foreign Office pension to supplement his waning income from his newspaper articles.[68] Vámbéry's views had a long history, but in resorting to such threats, Lansdowne made evident that times were now different, and that a critical approach to Russia's Balkan policy did not chime with Britain's new friendship with the tsardom.

The crisis threw up a number of options for Britain[69] that either promoted or collided with current imperial or continental political interests. While the French prime minister, Georges Clemenceau, simply advocated non-interference and non-recognition,[70] for Whitehall far more appeared at stake than its moral outrage at the infringement of a collective European treaty suggested.[71] Sooner than expected, the liberal imperial leadership had to tend to the cohesion of the fledgling entente with Russia,[72] with one eye also on the established states system. Additionally, they had good reason to fear that Russia's behaviour would be grist to the mill of radical liberal and conservative critics of the Anglo-Russian friendship. Whitehall suddenly found itself in a domestic and foreign policy dilemma, stuck between a balance of power policy focused on the European concert and the fostering of its diplomatic relationships with Turkey and Russia, and between the liberal imperial Anglo-Russian rapprochement supported by the radical right and the traditional Russophobia of the left. Britain's approach to its various options was therefore far more nuanced and more telling than has often been recognized by historians.

The press reporting of the Balkan crisis reveals the breadth of British interests. In addition to the legal perspective adopted by all the papers – the *Daily Telegraph* prophesied that international morale had received a blow from which it would never recover[73] – some papers went much further. The *Standard* identified the authors of the crisis and demonized the Austro-German Dual Alliance, denouncing it as a new 'Holy Alliance … the champion of armed despotism, the declared foe of national rights and popular liberties'.[74] The *Chronicle* focused on the effects for the states system and presciently discovered 'an Austrian bombshell within the powder chamber of Europe', and feared 'a great conflagration among the two power groupings',[75] already perceived as such. Only the radical liberal *Daily News* provided its readers with predominantly sober and factual analysis, which is somewhat surprising for a popular daily. 'There is no need to quarrel', the paper emphasized, 'Bulgaria could remain forever a vassal'. Bosnia, the paper reported, was in an unusual position, neither Austrian nor Turkish, and the paper commented that 'its annexation is a death blow rather to Serbia's nationalistic hopes than a material loss to Turkey'. The *Daily News* proposed that

Turkey be compensated financially and that the intransigent Serbs receive an overdue chastising, and it also called on the Great Powers not to allow themselves to be played off against one another and instead to remain calm and objective.[76] The *Times*'s initial response to the annexation spoke of 'jesuitical casuistry and political cynicism', but it quickly found an objective tone again.[77] As so often before, the experts writing in the *Times* were the first to identify the interests at stake for the government.[78] Articles that appeared on 6 and 8 October implied that despite all the outrage, for reasons of state it was important to avoid jumping to conclusions; the first step must be to establish the position of the powers with which Britain was friendly, and above all of Turkey and Russia.[79] The *Daily News* provided what was in effect a traditional interpretation based on the idea of the Concert of Europe, which was aimed at the unity of the Great Powers and therefore, in light of radical liberalism's support for smaller states, somewhat surprising; the *Times*'s response was framed by Britain's membership of a particular power bloc.

For some time, the *Times*, the flagship of English foreign reporting, had speculated about imminent unrest in the Balkans and the paper was therefore well positioned to cover developments in south-eastern Europe.[80] Since January, lead articles and article series that appeared on a page devoted to the Balkans had been tackling the situation, a sign of increased interest in a corner of Europe of which the British public knew little. The British press was not of one mind. While the liberal *Nation*, for example, viewed with concern the erosion of the balance of power and of national self-determination on the south-eastern periphery, the work of Russia in particular,[81] the conservative press and the *Times* noted with satisfaction what George Sanders, Leo Maxse and others had been saying for years, that every unilateral action on the part of Vienna was bound to widen the rift between Austria-Hungary and Russia. The threat of a new three-emperor alliance was fading, replaced by closer ties between Britain and Russia.[82] With that sword of Damocles removed, the threat of an imminent invasion of Britain also withered. Renewed cooperation between Russia and Austria-Hungary appeared increasingly improbable,[83] although there was a failure to recognize that precisely that cooperation had guaranteed the regional stability of the Balkans. On the eve of the crisis, the reporters of Fleet Street and Printing House Square sensed strongly that something was afoot in the Balkans. The *Times* had good reason to send a military correspondent to the region in August, and in a series of page-long columns he painstakingly assessed the individual Balkan states in terms of their military capacity, value as an ally, geographical situation and political conditions.[84]

Whitehall's moral and legal-focused outrage is in part explained by the experiences of Foreign Office diplomats in the period leading up to the annexation. On 2 October, Grey had sent a directive to all the capitals of Europe[85] noting that Sofia must not be allowed to declare Bulgarian independence. The following day, dispatches poured in from the relevant embassies. On the morning of 3 October, Hardinge had received word of Austria's intentions from Aehrenthal with relative composure,[86] for he believed Vienna in concert with Berlin, and that would simply further isolate the Central Powers. According to Reuters, at the meeting in Ischl between Franz Josef and Edward VII (August 1908), Hardinge had even termed the future fate of Bosnia and Herzegovina a purely domestic matter for Austria-Hungary.[87] Janos Pallavicini, the Austrian ambassador in Constantinople, reported that when news of the annexation was broadcast, the British ambassador had seemed the least surprised of all his colleagues and even believed the annexation opportune, as it might allow Britain to win back its former position in Turkey.[88]

That less than twenty-four hours later alarm bells started to ring in London can only be explained by the sudden impression after the reports arrived from abroad. They seemed to suggest a more broadly conceived action, the very event that the entente policy had been designed to prevent. In Whitehall, signs grew that the annexation and the declaration of independence were the outcome of a concerted action by several powers, including Russia.[89] Britain suddenly saw itself isolated, a reality that London had come to fear more than entanglement in any alliance. While the concurrence of the two events had seemed to suggest collaboration between Vienna and Sofia that was a blow to the Russian interests in the Balkans that Britain was supporting, now it appeared that Izvolsky had a hand in the affair.[90] On 4 October, the Foreign Office learned from the British ambassador in Paris that Izvolsky had already raised with Pichon the possibility that the Straits might be used as compensation. Francis Bertie added that he had the impression, indeed was even convinced, that Izvolsky had not told him 'the truth, the whole truth and nothing but the truth'. 'The question of annexation', Bertie and Hardinge agreed on the basis of certain statements by Izvolsky, 'was pretty fully discussed and decided between Baron D'Aehrenthal and Monsieur Izvolsky, and that it was not a project for further discussion between Austria and Russia'.[91]

Grey and Hardinge immediately identified a considerable threat to their entire foreign policy, with the interests of entente apparently in conflict with the interests of the European system.[92] London had evidently underestimated Izvolsky's flexibility, his determination to pursue the acquisition of the Straits, and his readiness to work together with Aehrenthal, his arch-enemy.[93] If that were not enough, Mensdorff's response to Hardinge's inquiry gave the impression – confirmed by the Austrian ambassador in Paris, Rudolf von Khevenhüller – that Vienna had the full support of Russia and Italy.[94] Two punches below the belt, provided by the faits accomplis and the defeat of their new Young Turk friends, were followed by an intended knockout blow to the British entente strategy. Before the crisis, on 30 September, James Bouchier, one of *The Times*'s Balkan correspondents, had already reported that Britain's authority and prestige in the region had vanished and that south-eastern Europe was without order or leadership; what then must have been the impact on the Foreign Office when the annexation and declaration of independence became known?[95]

On 5 October, the day after Bertie's report from Paris, as the Monday edition of the *Times* reported the imminent annexation and the declaration of independence,[96] devastating reports arrived from Goschen in Vienna[97] and from Whitehead in Belgrade that seemed to confirm the existence of a 'deep laid plot on the part of several powers' against Britain.[98] Russia wanted to move a step closer to the prize that Britain had held out, but London was determined to ensure that Vienna was not a participant in that process, let alone its instigator. Goschen had gathered from the Viennese press that with the exception of Britain all the powers were in agreement on the annexation, and Whitehead confirmed that the Serbian foreign minister must also have been informed. Given the British dual strategy, the loss of prestige for Turkey had a profound practical impact for Whitehall. But the entente policy towards Russia did not collapse. Since the Battenberg affair of the 1880s at the latest, St Petersburg had also sought Sofia's independence, though under different circumstances.[99] In a memorandum, diplomat George Buchanan, an expert on the Balkans, had noted that Bulgaria's unresolved position had been impeding Turkish reforms, as a result of Sofia's negative influence, and that Bulgarian independence would at least exclude yet another factor of unrest in the Balkans, above all in relation to Macedonia.[100] Whatever lip service Britain paid, reform was no longer the prime concern for its Near East policy, which explains the systematic disregard of Buchanan's memorandum and the harsh words directed at Sofia in September 1908.[101]

In early October, London feared for the survival of its new policy towards Russia. Yet that fear was related not to concern about loss of the Straits, which had become increasingly unimportant strategically,[102] but to assumptions about the existence of an agreement between Aehrenthal and Izvolsky.[103] Yes, London was concerned about the violation of a collective treaty, the transgression of international principles and the rattling of the balance of power, but from the start Whitehall had feared more for the entente with Russia and its authority over developments in Europe.[104] Already on 3 October, Hardinge had confirmed that in and of themselves neither the annexation nor the declaration of independence was of great interest to Britain, but their repercussions did not leave him equally unmoved, with the possibility that although the agreement made at Mürzsteg was at an end, cooperation between Russia and Austria-Hungary without any British involvement remained a possibility.[105] With good reason, Hardinge and Grey feared that their efforts to replace Vienna as Russia's partner might come to nothing. Disconcerted by what was happening and by their ally's evident involvement, they played for time with a display of public outrage. According to Gordon Browne, at the time a freelance illustrator working for the *Times*, Grey gave 'un mot d'ordre' to the British press to 'make it as uncomfortable as possible for Austria-Hungary'.[106] Whitehall took up a position under the banner of legality and expressed support for Turkey, waiting for St Petersburg to show its colours. Valentine Chirol, a frequent confidant of Grey, was setting the tone for Fleet Street and assured the *Times*'s readers, 'Russia has given absolutely no assurance to Austria-Hungary for the Annexation'. His conviction that Germany lay behind what had transpired, for which he had no evidence at all,[107] reveals the extent to which the threat from Germany was now taken for granted.

Chirol's over-hasty attribution of guilt to Germany was also intended to head off the likely criticism of Britain's Russian ally, and indeed, as Hardinge and Grey had feared, very soon, within forty-eight hours, censure of Russia came from the liberal ranks, with covert calls for Britain to distance itself from St Petersburg again. The liberal politician Edmond Fitzmaurice believed both the annexation and the declaration of independence had been inevitable for some time and had inflicted no harm on Britain.[108] Dismayed at Britain's anti-Austrian attitude, Lord Rosebery spoke of undertaking a pilgrimage to Vienna to throw himself at the feet of the emperor. According to Mensdorff, for Rosebery the annexation of an occupied territory was entirely inconsequential for Britain and an entirely reasonable act by Austria-Hungary.[109] Even Austen Chamberlain saw no reason to reproach Vienna to the extent that Grey and the press were doing.[110] George Clarke wrote to John Morley that Britain was not interested in Bosnia and Herzegovina and that the Treaty of Berlin could not be binding forever. Adopting a modern approach, he declared international law a living law that must adapt to changing circumstances.[111] In private, Chirol of the *Times* admitted to Spring Rice that while Germany would of course support its ally, there was nothing 'that would bring us into sharp antagonism with Germany over this business'.[112] From Teheran, Spring Rice complained: 'We are shouting too much, especially about Bulgaria who wasn't even a party to the Berlin Treaty'.[113] Usually described as a notorious opponent of Germany,[114] Spring Rice even saw the crisis as an opportunity for Britain and Germany to mediate jointly, and wrote that it was

> very annoying to see how the *Times* has been pitching into the Germans. This is unnecessary and unprofitable. ... In this last business we had an excellent choice of openly acting hand in hand with Germany. ... I think we should seize every possible opportunity (as the French are wisely doing) of showing friendship to Germany where this can be done without sacrificing our interests or our rights.[115]

Adopting the attitudes of Realpolitik, Spring Rice went on to argue that 'politics should be like chess, one should have no prejudice in favour or against any piece in the game'.[116]

On the whole, Spring Rice, like Winston Churchill, found Grey's moralizing somewhat suspicious. Was Grey really so eager that conflict be avoided, they wondered, or was he perhaps far more concerned for Britain's friendship with an autocratic and entirely untrustworthy nation? Churchill, who as president of the Board of Trade had recently joined Asquith's cabinet, saw Whitehall's attitude as entirely hypocritical, and recorded: 'A great deal too much fuss has been made altogether about Austrian action. The Berlin Treaty had been a piece of charlatanism from the outset and anyhow democracies would never consent to be bound in the future by diplomatic shibboleths'. There were, he believed, two facets to the questionable attitude of the right-wing liberals: the new friendship with St Petersburg was to be protected and made presentable, and a way was to be prepared to ensure the radical liberals agreed to the new navy estimates.[117]

All these critics shared the conviction that Britain must not be drawn into any conflict on the continent, and they allowed London at most its traditional role as mediator. For men who, like Chirol and Spring Rice, were hardly well disposed to Germany, concerns about Russia opened up the possibility of Anglo-German cooperation. Yet while Berlin nurtured new hope that the Anglo-Russian entente might be ruptured, Grey and Hardinge were turning their assessment of the current situation and immediate political impulses into fundamental principles for the future.

Izvolsky in London: The Straits Question

In London, Izvolsky's arrival was eagerly if uneasily awaited.[118] Grey and Hardinge's initial anticipation became a concern for damage limitation. In July, Nicolson had reminded the foreign secretary that the Anglo-Russian friendship needed to be nurtured carefully, for, he noted, 'any serious check may kill it'.[119] Izvolsky's stay in London made evident that with the onset of the Annexation Crisis, the foreign secretary had taken those words to heart. Whitehall's cautious course was buttressed by the press, which demonstrated marked restraint in its attitude to Russia.[120]

In Paris, Izvolsky had appeared quite complacent about Aehrenthal's breach of the secret Buchlau consultations on the course of the annexation,[121] but in London he expressed his outrage at Aehrenthal's behaviour. He presented himself as the innocent victim of a plot by the Central Powers, and sought to convince the British foreign secretary that as compensation for this reverse, the opening of the Straits should be guaranteed to Russia at a conference.[122] Britain's ambivalent attitude towards such a conference, a solution proposed by both the French foreign minister Stéphen Pichon and Izvolsky, is indicative of British reservations about whether to follow a course based on entente or whether instead to seek to maintain the European system. The French foreign minister voiced his belief that a display of public unity by the three entente powers would have a great impact on the morale of Europe as a whole,[123] but his words sought to cloak the power play that was his real aim. The Central Powers had not forgotten their isolation at the Conference of Algeciras, and therefore any idea of a conference came with heavy baggage. Additionally, Pichon envisaged that the conference would be presided over by the three entente powers, with no role for Germany or Austria-Hungary.[124] London feared, not without justification, that such a conference would only make the friction over the Balkans all the more evident, especially as Izvolsky had made clear that he expected Britain's support,[125] but Whitehall could find no alternative that would address British doubts and supposed concern for the balance of power. Allowing his thoughts to run ahead, Hardinge feared that a conference might even lead to a break with Russia.[126] Sensing the demands for compensation that might rain down from all parties at a conference, Hardinge wrote pessimistically to Bertie: 'a vista of endless difficulties is opened before us'.[127]

British interests thus stood in the way of a concert-based solution, and Whitehall even believed the collapse of Britain's arrangements in the Near East very probable.[128] London had only itself to blame, for it had already implicitly promised support in the Straits question to Russia during the convention negotiations, while making much to Turkey of its traditional approach to the issue. On one hand, Whitehall was eager to avoid antagonizing Russia and thus endangering the agreement or even the entire entente; on the other hand, in their initial resentment of Russia, the British had stood up for Turkey's interests and Whitehall did not want Constantinople to face any further loss of prestige. A conference would require London to nail its colours to the mast sooner than it had hoped. Additionally, Grey was under no illusions about the domestic problems he faced with the radical liberal majority in the cabinet and in the Commons, and he was well aware where his radical liberal colleagues in the cabinet stood on foreign policy – when in doubt, they would always opt against preserving the entente with Russia and in favour of maintaining the European system, for they found the regime in St Petersburg and Izvolsky's intrigues morally repugnant.[129] Unlike Morley, secretary of state for India, and Edmond Fitzmaurice,[130] in this phase Grey looked primarily not to stability but to the agreement with St Petersburg.

As we would expect, Izvolsky reminded the British foreign secretary of the promises he had made during the negotiations running up to the convention. The Russian foreign minister proved a remarkably adept negotiator. Aware of the British fear of isolation and the pro-Turkey line taken by Whitehall since the outbreak of the crisis, he was very accommodating of Turkish demands and, to Grey's delight and surprise, put his weight behind financial compensation for Turkey from Bulgaria, a popular suggestion as it held out the promise that further Turkish orders would be placed in Britain. Very deliberately, he also exploited British defence concerns and the British desire for entente, but pointed out that he needed to be able to prove the worth of the Anglo-Russian Convention to his critics in St Petersburg. Alarmed, Hardinge warned Bertie that 'the reactionaries in St Petersburg' were 'very anxious to do what they can to upset our Convention with Russia'.[131]

The hint of possible negative repercussions on the Anglo-Russian entente had the desired effect. Although Britain had initially rejected Pichon's conference proposal, fear of the damage to its relationship with Russia reversed that position. Grey demanded preliminary agreement on the issues that would be tackled by the conference and how they might be resolved, but in the process he made decisive concessions that were incompatible with stabilization as a goal and were principally intended to uphold the entente.

Grey was eager that Izvolsky should not put the Straits on the conference agenda from the start,[132] giving him time to prepare first his cabinet and then Constantinople that the statute on the Straits needed to be altered. Reassured that despite his secret cooperation with Vienna at Buchlau the Russian foreign minister remained committed to Russia's friendship with Britain, Grey indicated that he was not averse to a permanent resolution of the Straits issue and was willing to work with Asquith to ensure that solution was approved by the cabinet. Bertie's suspicions, and fears, were aroused, and he warned William Tyrrell against such a step. What would the public think, he asked Grey's advisor, if word should circulate that Britain had used the Straits to buy its friendship with Russia?[133] The current position within the Liberal Party and the very young relationship with Russia could not bear the weight of such a symbolic decision. Even journalists as well disposed towards Grey as was Spender were opposed to such far-reaching concessions to Russia.[134]

The resilience of the entente was tested for the first time when Izvolsky indirectly brought up the topic of the Straits again by requesting Britain agree to a future Russo-Turkish agreement that in time of war would allow Russia and the neighbouring states to pass through the Dardanelles and the Bosporus. Although Grey and Asquith pleaded the Russian cause in the cabinet,[135] they were outvoted by the mainly radical liberal ministers, led by Morley and leader of the House of Lords, Robert Crewe,[136] who were determined to pay Russia back for the Asian convention, that had proved so disappointing for British interests in Persia.[137] The remaining members of the cabinet were largely motivated by humanitarian and democratic concerns about Russian autocracy, and as Russia wanted to open the Straits only from the Black Sea littoral, they demanded reciprocity.

Hardinge was close to despair. He predicted to Francis Bertie that the cabinet's attitude would have a negative impact on Anglo-Russian relations[138] and wrote to Nicolson that the cabinet's citation of reciprocity was simply window-dressing, intended for the general public and the radical press that 'do not understand strategic considerations'.[139] Yet most government ministers and leader writers remained convinced that the relationship with Russia could take the strain.[140]

Supposedly idealistic leader writers such as Charles Scott, Alfred Gardiner, Henry Massingham and Lucien Wolf were less concerned about international agreements and more interested in the signal that Grey was giving with his public support of Russia. Wolf was distressed by Grey's apparently unconditional backing of Russia, which, in his opinion, had done everything possible to destabilize the Balkans and evidently felt no obligation to keep to any international agreement. According to Wolf, London's drumming up of undeserved compensation for St Petersburg would set a precedent, for, he told his readers, 'the permanent demand for compensations now becomes a part of the eternal conflict of the Triple Alliance and the Triple Entente'.[141] Reluctantly, Grey had to explain to Izvolsky that he could not fulfil his request as public opinion was not on board; he was not against an agreement in principle but now was an inopportune moment to raise the issue of the Straits.[142]

Disappointed, Izvolsky took a new tack.[143] Fearing for his reputation and his career, he combined requests with threats. With deliberate theatricality, he styled himself the Russian Delcassé, a victim of intrigue by the Central Powers designed to destroy the Anglo-Russian entente. Without holding back, he warned Grey of the consequences, for were he to return empty handed to St Petersburg, he would be unable to guarantee the continued existence of the convention.[144] According to Grey, the Russian foreign minister emphasized that the present moment was decisive for the future relations of Britain and Russia: the bonds of friendship might be tightened or they might be cut for good. Izvolsky pointed out to Grey that his own position was at stake, for he was committed to maintaining friendly relations with Britain, a policy that he had advocated in his own country despite significant opposition.[145]

The evening after the cabinet turned down Izvolsky's request for a second time,[146] Grey gave a dinner at the Foreign Office that was designed to convince Izvolsky that Britain remained loyal to Russia. Izvolsky seized the opportunity to raise the matter of the Straits, along with his personal situation. According to the account Balfour gave to Asquith the following day, the Russian foreign minister had been persistent, even aggressive, as he worked on those present, and especially on Morley as the representative of the opposition within the cabinet, on Spender as the principal representative of the press, on Balfour as a member of the opposition, and, not least, on Grey himself. The discussion had, however, only strengthened Balfour and Spender's conviction that Russia would do nothing to lessen international tensions, and that the opposite was in fact the case.[147] The Russian foreign minister stressed that a British 'no' on the Straits would only buoy the 'Potsdam party' at the court in St Petersburg, an approach that played skilfully with Britain's well-known fear of isolation. Grey, Hardinge and the king took his message to heart, and that same evening, Hardinge wrote to Nicolson:

'We must do our best to support him, such as he is'.[148] Edward VII also stepped in, urging Asquith to summon the cabinet again and convince them that Izvolsky must be supported, whatever the cost.[149]

Unlike his possible successor, the Russian foreign minister was seen as a strong advocate of Anglo-Russian rapprochement,[150] and as a result London was prepared to overlook his lack of truthfulness towards his British friends – on no account was he to be allowed to return to Russia discredited and possibly forced to resign.[151] Nicolson's verbal acrobatics were evidence of Britain's determination to remain on good terms with Russia, as the ambassador sought creative ways of justifying Izvolsky's scheming. Britain repeated the indulgence towards Russia it had shown during the Åland affair and was ready to attribute Izvolsky's conspiring with Aehrenthal to inexperience and credulity that were no match for the crafty Austrian-Hungarian foreign minister. In fact, Izvolsky was fully his Viennese counterpart's equal and the Åland affair had revealed his talents as a schemer, but the British were ready to turn a blind eye to that reality. As in the case of the Baltic conflict, Britain vented its frustration not at its untrustworthy partner but at Berlin and Vienna.

Immediately after the decision of the cabinet, and in order to avoid inflicting another defeat on Izvolsky, Grey accepted the French proposal of a conference for which the agenda would be determined by only France, Britain and Russia, who would also decide who would preside. Germany, which was expected to encourage its ally Austria-Hungary to attend,[152] received a copy of the plan for the conference for information only.[153] We also learn from Esher that:

> England, Russia and France have agreed upon the terms upon which the two coups d'état are to be accepted, and Europe will follow them. Germany is the power that will suffer most. Austria gets all she wants. But Germany will find herself shut out … In fact Austria has – unwittingly perhaps – slammed the door in the face of her ally.[154]

How the conference issue developed demonstrates that London was less interested in making the most of the possibilities provided by international law than in safeguarding and demonstrating its entente policy on the continent. The *Times* came to the firm conclusion that the concerted action proved that the 'Anglo-Franco-Russian Entente is more intimate than ever'.[155] Maxse, Strachey and Dillon used the opportunity for a counteroffensive against the radical liberal press, convinced that with his support for St Petersburg Grey 'not only led public opinion in this country, but also all the disinterested public opinion in Europe'.[156] Their comments were indicative, however, that Whitehall's policy was far from uncontroversial. Observers who saw through the complex games being played by the Great Powers believed that London's policy was leading Europe into a cul de sac. Left out of the conference and with the experience of Algeciras still fresh, Berlin could guarantee its Viennese ally only military support and no diplomatic backing, where in other circumstances Britain and Germany would likely have been predestined to mediate jointly and by taking a firm stance might well have been able to make both Vienna and St Petersburg see reason. From the outset, however, Britain had given no serious consideration to the possibility of cooperation with Germany, despite Asquith's lip service to joint action in his Guildhall speech,[157] which surely explains Grey's readiness to ignore the Central Powers in the planning of the conference. Just as the Algeciras Conference – held, we should note, as the result of pressure from Germany – had already shown how much France's unconditional support mattered to Grey, a public display of unity by the Triple Entente was an unmistakable indication of its cohesion, Russia included, and brought Germany and Austria-Hungary closer together.[158] The consistently critical attitude towards Germany displayed by both the diplomatic corps and the general public now had practical import. Although, surprisingly, Spring Rice put the case for Anglo-German cooperation, which he believed would prevent the impending creation of two hostile blocs, and Lascelles sided with Berlin,[159] the opposing view prevailed, as voiced by Hardinge, Bertie, Mallet and Goschen, proposing that Germany was pulling Austrian strings. Very taken with that argument, William Tyrrell, Grey's private secretary, repeatedly tried to convince Spring Rice of 'dirty German tricks', for surely German machinations lay behind Vienna's actions, designed to destroy the entente and gain control in the Balkans.[160]

The conference agenda sent a clear message. Bulgaria's declaration of independence went uncontested, and only the issue of financial compensation for Turkey remained outstanding, but the annexation of Bosnia and Herzegovina and, to much surprise, the Sanjak railway were on the table. Additionally, the seventh item on the agenda addressed the 'benefits to Serbia and Montenegro'. For Vienna, the agenda was an affront and a provocation. Serbia was a middling power and therefore, according to the Concert of Europe and in line with the established practice of the Great Powers, was not entitled to compensation; furthermore, Serbia's nationalist visions had no basis in law.[161]

On 14 October, Grey had another opportunity to persuade his fellow ministers to change their minds. This time he had on his side Reginald McKenna, the new First Lord of the Admiralty, who joined Haldane and the prime minister. The cabinet unanimously agreed to the solution proposed by Izvolsky, that the Straits should be open to all powers in times of war, but only to neighbouring states in times of peace.[162] By arguing that the Admiralty had long since relativized the strategic importance of the Straits, Britain could therefore demonstrate the Anglo-Russian entente unmistakably while risking little. McKenna openly ignored his chief naval advisors. Admiral Slade, Captain Ottley and Viscount Esher still reckoned with a reversion to 'an international situation of 1890–1899', when France and Russia were Britain's most favourable foes. 'All depends on a firmly rooted and durable Franco-Russian-British Entente', Ottley declared.[163] In the eyes of the naval advisors, it seems that not Germany but rather Russia still posed the major threat. But while they argued for a stronghold at the Straits, the cabinet led by Grey, Asquith, Haldane and McKenna and the Foreign Office led by Hardinge and Nicolson opted for conciliation. Towards Izvolsky, Grey now adopted a middle course. Like in the 1907 negotiations, he found it useful to keep the opening of the Straits an unfulfilled, but theoretically acceptable, Russian desire, so as to ensure future cooperation. This undoubtedly served British interests but it did nothing to safeguard international stability. Instead of demanding Austro-Russian cooperation in return for solving the current crisis, Grey demanded that St Petersburg cooperate with Britain by working for financial compensation to Turkey.[164]

The case was made that the political advantages would outweigh any disadvantages that stemmed from Britain's apparent willingness to deviate from its traditional attitudes. In political terms, since the convention the Straits issue had served to underline Britain's value as an ally, for free access would relativize Britain's sea power and give Russia a free hand in the eastern Mediterranean.[165] This compromise solution would preserve that value as an ally while allowing Britain to give the appearance of standing by its traditional approach.

In the end, anxiety about Russia possibly drifting away from the alliance, about Britain's value as an ally and about the need to nurture relationships tipped the balance and ensured that Izvolsky did not lose face.[166] After the cabinet meeting, even Morley, one of the greatest critics of the Asian convention, acknowledged that for the sake of the entente with Russia and Britain's ties with the continent, all possible effort would have to be made to ensure Izvolsky remained Russian foreign minister, for he was, Morley noted, 'undoubtedly anxious to work with England'.[167] Fears that had been expressed in the liberal *Nation* in June 1907 appeared realized: the entente with Russia would always be dependent on the unpredictability and whims of an autocracy and would require constant active support for the pro-British party in St Petersburg. Although Massingham's weekly paper continued to express its great doubts about Anglo-Russian rapprochement, during the crisis it was forced to congratulate Grey on having deepened the gulf between Russia and Austria-Hungary.[168]

Grey and Hardinge were the driving forces, equally convinced that the entente with Russia and Britain's new foreign policy strategy faced an acid test. With the cabinet having approved the compromise solution, now all possible effort was to be made to avoid the alienation between Russia and Britain that Robert Wilton, the *Times*'s correspondent in St Petersburg, sensed.[169] Along with a statement of Britain's official position on the Straits, Grey wrote to Izvolsky privately, without cabinet approval, to make clear that he saw a change in the status of the Straits in Russia's favour as 'essential to a permanent establishment of goodwill' between Russia and Britain, and to promise Russia his support in achieving that goal.[170]

The same day, Grey's message was reinforced by a confidential letter from John Fisher, on whom Izvolsky had also clearly worked during his visit to London. Whether Grey and Fisher had coordinated their missives cannot be determined with certainty, but the message from the highest admiral of the fleet who three years earlier had been prepared to strike a blow against Russia sought to remove any last doubts about Britain's change of course. Fisher wrote to Izvolsky:

> I think you are assured that I have been a consistent advocate of England's utmost friendship with Russia. I have always maintained from a sailor's point of view for fighting purposes that what we wanted is a Quadruple Alliance – Russia, England, France and Turkey … thank heaven it is all coming round to this blessed consummation. … The Japanese Alliance was the worst thing England ever did for herself! … Again, if a word is now spoken about the Dardanelles, there would be a great agitation in England. Wait some little time, and then let Russia make her own private arrangement with a grateful Turkey, and you may rest quite sure that England won't object – for the simple reason that anything that will bind Russia, England and Turkey together is to England's advantage and far outweighs any objections.[171]

At Reval, the British delegation had urged Russia not to build up its navy but to develop its land forces, especially on its western border, partly with the aim of preventing Russia from re-establishing its sea power, partly as a means of increasing the pressure on the Central Powers, and partly to minimize the possibility that a British expedition to aid France against Germany – which Fisher opposed – might be necessary. Now Fisher reminded the Russian foreign minister of General Kuropatkin's memorandum of 26 June 1903, in which the author had stated that Russia's security was dependent on its western border: 'It is the same menace that Russia has to fear in the Anatolian [Baghdad] Railway, and the absolute certainty that the Heir of the Austrian Throne will work fully and absolutely with the German Emperor'.[172] Fisher ensured that his message to Izvolsky did not remain a secret by entrusting the letter to the journalist Arnold White.[173]

Izvolsky accepted Grey's and Fisher's personal assurances. Metternich, the German ambassador, demonstrated once more that he was well informed about the details of Britain and Russia's relationship.[174] The Anglo-Russian entente had survived its first crisis without any serious after-effects. Grey and Hardinge, his loyal permanent under-secretary of state, judged Izvolsky's visit to have been 'most favourable to good relations with Russia'.[175] Whitehall had shown that it was determined not to forfeit its new ties to Russia. Briefly, support for Turkey had gained the upper hand, as made evident by London's involvement and readiness to consider concessions, but only as the result of a short period of uncertainty and frustration with Izvolsky; Constantinople never came before Russia in Britain's list of priorities.[176] Eager to ensure Izvolsky's standing was bolstered, Grey persuaded Edward VII to praise the Russian foreign minister in a personal letter to the tsar.[177] And he did not stop there. Having made concessions on the conference, Whitehall also declared its willingness to support Russia over the issue of compensation for Serbia and Montenegro.[178] Britain had thereby crossed another limit in a Balkan policy that had previously tended to be passive, taking Europe in spring 1909 a step closer to conflagration. The Foreign Office's confidence that war would not happen stemmed less from a belief in British capabilities and more from recognition that the season was unfavourable for a military campaign.[179]

The Failed Balkan League

Relations between Britain and Austria-Hungary were in freefall,[180] but British ties to Russia looked much more positive. The entente had proved robust, despite the tiresome matter of the Straits. The Bulgarian-Turkish dispute over compensation for Constantinople demonstrated that cooperation during a crisis was feasible. Unlike in the Austria-Turkey matter,[181] now, and for the first time, the Triple Alliance and the Triple Entente were lined up against each other. Previous political initiatives could cut across alliances as Germany had urged Vienna to reach an agreement with Constantinople.[182] In the case of Bulgaria, Aehrenthal and Izvolsky each tried to outdo the other in gaining favour with Sofia,[183] with Izvolsky able to rely on his entente partners, and on Britain in particular. In demonstrative harmony, Paris, London and St Petersburg worked together on a mediated solution for Sofia and Constantinople, supporting Turkish calls for compensation but deflating Turkey's vision of extensive territorial compensation in Eastern Rumelia. The primary goal for Britain, as for France and Russia, was to maintain links to the Young Turks and to remove Bulgaria from the Habsburg sphere of influence. For a while, Britain was thus able to relativize the discrepancies in its dual strategy for St Petersburg and Constantinople.[184]

Whitehall was well aware[185] that Russia understood Bulgaria within its sphere of interest and wished to see that relationship restored.[186] Hardinge pointed out the benefits to Nicolson: 'If we can get it [Izvolsky's proposal] accepted by the Turks, it will bring Bulgaria within the Russian orbit, will improve the relations of Russia to Turkey and save Iswolsky's position with the Pan-Slavists'.[187] As a result, for the first time since the double crisis of 1885/7, Britain again took an active interest in the region and for the first time ever sought to use a united front in the Balkans to block the Central Powers more broadly and Austria-Hungary in particular.[188] Imperial policy played its part, but increasingly the impetus came from entente policy. Hardinge noted to Nicolson at the same time: 'It is really astonishing what a development there has been of the Anglo-Russian entente in the form of our co-operation in the Balkans, though, after all, it is only what those who have studied the question have known for years must inevitably be its outcome'.[189]

Seeking to avoid the unpopular international conference that would tackle the Balkan crisis, in early November Grey turned to individual negotiations. Whitehall hoped that a series of individual agreements could create a network of defensive alliances involving Turkey, Bulgaria, Serbia and Montenegro that would serve to stem the Central Powers' aspirations for an advance towards Salonika. Grey's positive attitude towards a defensive Balkan alliance is very revealing.[190] On 29 October 1908, he and Hardinge even declared to the Serbian foreign minister that Britain had great sympathy for closer ties among the Balkan states.[191] The idea of a Balkan alliance was born, and it would be fostered by Russia four years later, during the Balkan Wars. Hardinge wrote to Nicolson: 'We are perfectly well aware that the occupation of Bosnia and Herzegovina was proposed by Lord Salisbury and Lord Beaconsfield ... in order to interpose a barrier between the two Slav States',[192] pointing out that Britain's current attitude was a further example of how greatly British policy had changed over the previous three years as a result of rapprochement with Russia. Previously, Chirol had seen no reason for Britain to go out on a limb for such an alliance, but now he explained the convergence with Russia's plans as a reaction to the cementing of the Central Powers' ties.[193] In St Petersburg, the impression grew that Britain was 'the one Power disinterestedly sympathetic towards Slav interests'.[194] Although London torpedoed plans for a Serbian-Turkish alliance because it would likely be opposed by Bulgaria,[195] it retained a hope that various advantages would accrue to Britain from the creation of a bloc comprising Bulgaria, Montenegro, Serbia and the Ottoman Empire, which would guard against further expansion by Austria-Hungary and put a halt to Germanization, keep unruly Serbia under control[196] and ensure that Bulgaria was distanced from the Dual Alliance and brought into the Russian sphere of influence.[197] In the long term, that alliance might also offer protection against Russian ambitions and allow Britain to withdraw from Balkan affairs. Closer ties between Turkey and the smaller Balkan states 'would relieve us of any difficulty which might arise with Russia, if she pursued a policy hostile to Turkey'.[198]

In December, Hardinge confirmed that the Triple Entente had checked Aehrenthal's hegemonial plans in the Balkans[199] and that the advance of the Central Powers into south-eastern Europe had been halted before the gates of Salonika.[200] The Foreign Office believed control of Macedonian ports and trading centres to be a principal aim of the Central Powers, together with the Germanization of the region,[201] for they would then be only a stone's throw from the Levant and from Britain's imperial possessions in Asia. Yet the decision to create a cordon sanitaire and its subsequent character had continental implications, for a Balkan barrier that extended to the river Sava would not only protect the Empire but also obstruct a new and much-feared League of Three Emperors.[202]

Here, then, was the crux of contemporary British Balkan policy. A perpetual front had thus been created between the Balkan states, supported by Russia, and the Danube Monarchy.[203] The so-called 'Balkan inception scenario' was born.[204] Bulgaria appeared in Whitehall's calculations as a strategic cornerstone and as a link between Turkey and its former European provinces. London could see no point in an alliance of Turkey with Serbia and Montenegro, 'those two rotten little countries', that was designed to contain the Central Powers, for as a military-strategic evaluation published in the *Times* that September had demonstrated, they alone would be of little assistance in a conflict with Vienna or Sofia.[205] Yet Turkey had little interest in an alliance with renegade Serbia. Eager to see a regional order directed against Vienna established,[206] London had wanted to use Serbia to protect Turkey from Bulgaria, while Belgrade sought an alliance against Vienna.[207]

The Turkish refusal meant a caesura for Britain's dual strategy encompassing Russia and Turkey, which had up until then remained feasible. Shortly before Christmas, Grey noted that Turkey would need to be left out of alliance plans for the Balkan states. The initial dilemma had been whether the interests of the entente should come before the interests of the European system, a predicament evident above all in the question of whether to support St Petersburg or Constantinople. Now, however, with the failure of the Balkan alliance, the entente-based system won out, generating a strategy that would characterize London's foreign policy up until 1914 and beyond. Five days later, rumours of an Austro-Bulgarian military convention reached London. Hardinge spoke to Buchanan of general conflagration,[208] and Grey had Izvolsky informed indirectly that in the case of a conflict with the Dual Alliance, Britain would not remain neutral. Angered by Turkish unreasonableness, Britain increasingly turned to its Russian partner. By mid December, Hardinge appeared confident that the time for closer cooperation with Russia had come at last and that the resultant successes would indicate 'that our policy of friendship with Russia in Asia has amply been justified by our present position in Europe'.[209] Although the Bulgarian-Turkish dispute was not yet over, it provided the two powers with a welcome forum for further cooperation that would at least ensure Sofia was separated off from Vienna, for London feared a military convention involving Austria-Hungary and Bulgaria.[210]

While Britain placated Constantinople, Russia exerted pressure on Sofia. Both governments agreed to financial compensation for the loss of Eastern Rumelia and the Oriental railway. Grey intervened several times on behalf of Russia and Bulgaria in the discussions over the amount to be paid, seeking to keep the compensation sum low in order to avoid a renewal of Sofia's dependence on Vienna. The British foreign secretary had evidently decided to follow the advice of Buchanan, who as the advocate of a strong entente-focused policy, unlike Gerald Lowther, the ambassador in Constantinople, proposed the compensation be kept low in order to ensure that Bulgaria would not be lost to the Central Powers and that a Balkan alliance remained a possibility.[211] In this tense situation – Bulgaria was threatening a military escalation – the Anglo-Russian entente had its first major success in the Balkans. The partners agreed that Bulgaria should be drawn into Russia's sphere of influence,[212] and to London's surprise and pleasure, Izvolsky offered to pay one third of the compensation owed by Sofia and to provide the remainder as a loan on especially favourable terms. Of the 6.5 million Turkish pounds owed, by cancelling Constantinople's old debts from the war of 1877/78, Russia took over 2.5 million.

Hardinge was delighted to see the cooperation with Russia go so well. The entente had been able to achieve several of its goals simultaneously. The Russian foreign minister had drawn Bulgaria away from Vienna on a long-term basis, satisfied pan-Slav sensibilities at home and set the stage for a good relationship with Turkey that would prepare the way for a permanent solution to the issue of the Straits.[213] At the same time, London could present the radical liberals with a successful product of the Anglo-Russian cooperation of which they were so critical. Constantinople feared, however, and not without justification, that Russia was manoeuvring Bulgaria into financial dependency in order to use it as a springboard into the Balkans, from which fresh conflicts between the Great Powers were surely bound to arise.[214] The pleasure that came with the success of the cooperation with Russia was accompanied by frustration with the Young Turks, whose reservations London brusquely rejected and who were subsequently put under great pressure by Whitehall to ensure Constantinople's agreement. Irate, Hardinge insisted to Lowther that the Russian proposal must be accepted at any price.[215]

With their dual strategy at an impasse, Grey and Hardinge faced a decision between Constantinople and St Petersburg. Just how much the bonds to Russia mattered to Grey and where he would turn if forced to choose is evident from a letter of early February 1909 to Lowther, in which he recorded: 'If I had refused to support the Russian proposal, the result would have been a diplomatic separation between Russia and us … and unfavourably on the whole of our relations'.[216] Fearful that Britain might 'throw Russia back into the old belief … in supporting Turkey against her', Grey increasingly deviated from his ambivalent course. His determination to nurture the still-young Anglo-Russian entente was tied in to his fundamentally negative attitude towards the Austro-German Dual Alliance. Two distinct alliance systems crystallized, and the possibility that members of each grouping might cooperate, or at least set their differences aside, in order to de-escalate a crisis, as had happened over the issue of compensation, was no longer an option. According to Grey,

> The support of only Germany and Austria would lead to a new grouping of the powers, affecting the whole international situation. I should not be comfortable with

the support of Germany and Austria, ... they were all the time enjoying the invidious position in which their support placed us in opposition to France and Russia.

On these grounds, the English foreign secretary believed it 'imperative to support Russia'.[217]

The compensation agreement was signed on 23 April 1909. Turkish capriciousness in the course of the negotiations had widened the rift with Britain. With Britain and Russia the guarantors of the treaty, there was no suggestion that all the parties to the Berlin Treaty had come together to reach an agreement, and, indeed, during the negotiations, the members of the Dual Alliance had been completely ignored. Cultivation of the alliance with St Petersburg had become Britain's principal concern. Hardinge identified a signpost for Britain's foreign policy and noted with satisfaction to Nicolson: 'It is really astonishing what a development there has been of the Anglo-Russian *entente* in the form of our cooperation in the Balkans' [emphasis in original].[218]

London's commitment to drawing Bulgaria away from Vienna and closer to Russia, Britain's partner in the entente, and to participating in all the negotiations is indicative of how important fostering the entente had become. The balance of power was now relegated to a subordinate category when it came to decision making. Whitehall's diplomats were clear that the ties to St Petersburg must not be broken and that a new Three Emperors' League must not be allowed to take shape as a first step towards the creation of a new Napoleonic threat. Prime Minister Asquith was eager to make clear publicly that Britain and Russia stood shoulder to shoulder. 'Nothing', he declared in a prepared speech at the London Guildhall, 'will induce us in this country to falter or fall short in any of our special engagements which we have undertaken, to be disloyal or unfaithful even for a moment to the spirit of any existing friendship'.[219]

Asquith thus expressly acknowledged that the ties between Britain and Russia were part of the entente framework of British foreign policy. The offensive variant of Britain's containment strategy that would have been realized by a Balkan alliance had proved unworkable, which made cooperation with Russia on the continent all the more desirable, despite the challenges and criticism of the Anglo-Russian Convention. From this point on, the Triple Entente was to be used to maintain the pressure on the Central Powers in the Balkans and to ensure that a gulf between the Central Powers and Russia was preserved.

Denouement

Whitehall's concentration on nurturing the entente with Russia during the Annexation Crisis, which took the place of concern for the stability of Europe, is particularly evident in the case of Serbian compensation. Since Izvolsky's visit to

London, Grey had felt himself in the Russian foreign minister's debt for he had not been able to bring the cabinet on board on the matter of the Straits. For the sake of the entente, the order of the day for the Foreign Office was to support Izvolsky not only on the issue of the conference but also on the issue of compensation for Serbia and Montenegro, which as a Slavic issue was of particular importance to Russia.[220] Although Grey had little sympathy for Belgrade[221] and his under-secretary of state complained bitterly about 'wretched little Serbia',[222] Grey at a very early stage told Benckendorff frankly that he 'wished to support the line which Russia might take with regard to Servia'.[223] London had resolved to support Serbia politically. It appeared to matter little that Serbia had, in contrast to the Ottoman Empire in Bulgaria, not a whiff of a right to compensation or that continuing Serbian agitation was responsible for the continuing unrest in the Balkans. In demanding that Austria-Hungary must compensate Serbia for the destruction of its nationalist dream,[224] Grey had taken up position, hardening the fronts unnecessarily early. His actions markedly limited the available options; if he had kept a free hand and maintained greater impartiality, he could have used Britain's connections to restrain those involved and to curb their over-excitement.[225] The liberal imperial politicians appeared increasingly convinced that Britain's usefulness for the system lay in adopting a clear stance, rather than in maintaining the neutral and commanding reserve demanded by their radical colleagues, for example. With satisfaction, Foreign Office clerk Gerald Spicer commented in the margin of a dispatch from Horace Rumbold that the ententes with France and Russia 'will tend more and more to becoming alliances'.[226] The acceptance of Serbia's right to compensation *sui generis*, so without a clear legal entitlement, marked a significant break in the practices of international relations, for to date only the Great Powers of Europe had been entitled to compensation when the status quo on the continent was altered.

Just how significant Britain's relationship with Russia – now clearly designated an 'entente' – was for Grey is evident from the instructions he sent on 29 October to Nicolson and Whitehead, the British envoy to Belgrade, that the Russians and the Serbs should be informed that London was completely behind St Petersburg, 'whatever that may be eventually'.[227] Belgrade understood the message as an unrestricted proxy that would cover demands even in excess of Russia's initial position and recognized that behind these words lay an excessive fear that Russia might be disappointed by its British partner.[228] The oft-cited 'disinterested motives'[229] in the Serbian question that Grey claimed were evidently a later invention that did not reflect the contemporary reality. French dismissal of Serbia's intransigent demands as completely unfounded only highlights the implications of Grey's position.[230] Even St Petersburg had sought to restrain Belgrade at the beginning of the crisis, making clear that Russia would not be able to support Serbia's excessive territorial aspirations. Russia had declared in no uncertain terms that the return of the Sanjak of Novi Pazar, as suggested by

Vienna, would be adequate compensation.[231] The government in Berlin was fully committed to unconditional support of its allies, and Grey and Hardinge were equally willing to abandon their previous legal and moral stance with regard to Vienna and Sofia for the sake of Belgrade, accepting and condoning the inescapable consequences of their indirect support for Serbian nationalism.[232] In early November, this demonstration of loyalty, which went far beyond anything St Petersburg required, was hardly necessary, as the fledgling Anglo-Russian friendship had already survived its greatest threat. Apparently, the entente had taken on a momentum of its own.

On 3 and 4 November, Nicolson gave an account of his audience with the tsar, at which according to Grey's instructions he had praised Izvolsky's great services and assured the tsar of Britain's loyalty in the Balkans.[233] To Whitehall's delight, Nicolson was able to report that the audience had been very friendly and that he had reason to assume that Izvolsky's position as foreign minister was secure for the near future.[234] He also reported with great pleasure that the tsar was eager to strengthen the entente with London and had commented on the growing signs of popular support in his country for a closer relationship between Russia and Britain.[235] A week later, Whitehall decided on the provisional course it would steer through the Balkan crisis. Grey insisted that the ties to Russia must be retained at any price, while Belgrade was to be discouraged from taking any military action, which might prove a provocation for Austria-Hungary and draw Russia, as a result of its Slavic obligations, into a war that could set the whole of Europe ablaze.[236] But Whitehall also went a step further. When Izvolsky asked Grey what he intended to do should war break out, Grey gave the Russian foreign minister to understand that it would be difficult for Britain to sit on its hands should a crisis erupt in the Balkans.[237] The following day, Hardinge spoke of a European bloc formed by France, Russia and Britain.[238] Lord Esher later reported that in November 1908, Asquith, Haldane and Grey had agreed that if war broke out, Britain would send an expeditionary force to the continent.[239] For the first time, an exchange took place between the French and British admiralties, although no written record of their communication survives.[240] From December, Grey counted on the weather hindering the outbreak of combat, although as Hardinge pointed out, everything still depended on 'what those two pugnacious States – Servia and Montenegro – may do in spring ... In the meantime it is interesting how closely we are working with France and Russia in the Balkans, so that our friendship with Russia in Asia has amply been justified by our present policy in Europe'.[241]

As alliances, including the entente, solidified, they also demonstrated that they were clearly unfit for the task of guaranteeing stability within the European concert.[242] Writing in the *Times*, even Repington criticized Grey's pro-Russian attitude that 'would make it difficult for Great Britain to stand out should war ensue'.[243] A military expert who for years had been writing of the danger posed by Germany and of how that danger should determine British military capacities and British cooperation with France, Repington laid out clearly where he believed the limits of Britain's obligations lay: 'I am utterly opposed to the employment of a single British soldier in the Balkan peninsula. ... India and France are the only two parts of the world where our vital interests may require the presence of a regular Army'.[244] Where previously he had sharply criticized the Tory government for its placidity when it came to foreign policy and defence policy, now he insisted equally vehemently that extending the entente to include Russia went too far.

In early 1909, Britain's pro-Russia orientation on the continent intensified, along with its implications for the Empire. Previously, Britain had endeavoured to avoid antagonizing either Turkey or Russia. Following Britain and Russia's joint endeavours in the formulation of the agreement between Turkey and Bulgaria, however, and with Turkish objections having killed off any hope of a Balkan alliance, now the Foreign Office was neither able nor willing to act as if it had no favourites. Russia had become too important to be left with the impression that Britain was continuing along its traditional pro-Turkish path and wished to use Turkey as a counterweight to the tsardom. Early in the New Year, Hardinge wrote to Nicolson:

> I trust, however, that the Russians will not think for a moment that we want to improve our relations with Germany at their expense. We have no pending questions with Germany, except that of naval construction, while our whole future in Asia is bound up with the necessity of maintaining the best and most friendly relations with Russia. We cannot afford to sacrifice in any way our entente with Russia – even for the sake of a reduced naval programme. I am not authorized to suggest that you should say this to Iswolsky, as I have not seen Grey, who has been away for some time; but I am quite convinced that he is of that opinion too. Therefore if the occasion arises and you use such language, I am certain that it will be approved.[245]

At the beginning of the new year, the leadership of the Foreign Office seemed paralysed by a fear of displeasing Russia. As the tension between Austria and Serbia threatened to escalate, the result of an inflammatory speech given by Serbia's prime minister, Miovan Milovanovic,[246] on New Year's Day,[247] the British foreign secretary closed his ears to any idea that Whitehead might seek to calm the situation, or even act as mediator. Despite numerous warnings from Fairfax Cartwright that war might be imminent, Grey would accept nothing less than a declaration from Vienna guaranteeing Serbian integrity.[248] Enraged, Aehrenthal responded that Vienna had already renounced the Sanjak and that there was no Serbian question, for Belgrade had not the slightest claim to any compensation let alone to a declaration guaranteeing its integrity.[249]

Grey had wanted to avoid any suggestion of British half-heartedness, but in February 1909 it transpired that St Petersburg had gained precisely this impression, or at least was willing to exploit that suggestion. Following Edward VII's visit to Berlin, Izvolsky declared in a communiqué that he was greatly offended for he had reason to believe that Britain and Germany and even Austria-Hungary had come to an agreement on the Balkans. He protested fiercely to Nicolson at what he termed Britain's betrayal of an ally.[250] The following day, the Russian foreign minister added a final touch to his grievances about British disloyalty. Should Britain not support Russia in the Serbian issue, then Russia would consider withdrawing from its alliance with France and from its entente with England.[251] The shot he had fired did not miss its mark. Alarmed, aggravated and extremely disturbed, Whitehall reacted swiftly.[252] Grey apparently lost his composure, or any rate Tyrrell reported that he had never seen his superior so incensed – not because Grey felt Izvolsky was blackmailing him, but because Izvolsky had accused him of disloyalty. 'As you know', Tyrrell wrote to Nicolson, 'the Chief is the soul and essence of loyalty himself and this quality has been the keynote of his attitude towards France and Russia'.[253]

Instead of replicating Lansdowne's deliberately vague response to Paris during the first Moroccan crisis,[254] which would have meant putting his Russian partner resoundingly in his place and likely regaining the upper hand in the relationship, the Foreign Office felt compelled to approach St Petersburg again to emphasize its absolute loyalty to Russia 'in case she [Russia] should take up for Serbia'.[255] Even as Izvolsky indicated that he was well satisfied,[256] Grey, Hardinge and Nicolson looked for new means to stress Britain's value as a loyal partner. They found their opportunity with the escalation of the dispute between Vienna and Belgrade. Again, as at the outset of the crisis, Britain demonstratively lined up alongside Serbia. Thus, London left it up to Izvolsky 'how far to go' in support of the Serb cause. There is no question that Edward Grey approved war as a consequence. But his approaches left much to pure chance.

Historians have continued to downplay this decision as a commitment to the rights of smaller states and as a move typical for maintaining the balance of power,[257] and yet it escalated the situation and brought Europe to the brink of a great war. During this period, Britain played repeatedly and irresponsibly with that threat,[258] as is made clear by the evaluation of the situation provided by Guy Wyndham, the British military attaché in St Petersburg, on 19 November 1908. Guy Wyndham believed that Russia was increasingly ready to go to war, especially if Slav interests were at stake. Russian finances, he wrote, were in a far better state than they had been for the previous war, and the reform of Russian artillery was largely complete. As a result, he pointed out, especially when it came to its defensive capacity, Russia was well positioned, with over 1.9 million soldiers in Europe alone. Its offensive strength[259] was also not to be underestimated, even if the constellation of alliances would contribute significantly.[260] The combination of Serbia's expectations of support from Britain with Russia's support for Belgrade had surely only one possible outcome and would lead, sooner or later, as a report of a Serbian diplomat suggested, to the explosion of the Balkan powder keg.²⁶¹ Although often overlooked by historians, diplomatic reports on the Central Powers that noted their domestic and financial weaknesses would surely also have played their part.²⁶²

The issue of territorial compensation involving Vienna and Belgrade ran into the sand partly because Britain was torn between the interests of the entente and the interests of the European system. In October 1908, London added a guarantee of the territorial status quo for Turkey to its declarations of solidarity with St Petersburg and Belgrade. The only possibility that remained was therefore to grant Bosnia or Herzegovina to Belgrade. For Vienna, there could be no question of handing over to Serbia provinces that had only just been annexed merely because Vienna had shattered Serbia's nationalist and anti-Austrian dreams. Apart from the public humiliation, Vienna could not possibly be satisfied with ending up with less than it had had before the annexation. Moreover, the concert of the Great Powers was based on the idea that smaller and middle-sized powers were not entitled to compensation. Hence, not only did Belgrade have no claim in law, but in deeming Serbia not entitled to satisfaction, Vienna also had tried and tested European practice on its side. The additional prestige that would accrue to Belgrade – already contained in the very suggestion of a conference – would be a recipe for further nationalist agitation in Serbia against its hated neighbour.

From the start, agreement by diplomatic means alone was therefore largely ruled out, and the only feasible option appeared to be the payment of financial compensation for Serbia's shattered dreams. Britain categorically refused to attempt to move its Russian partner in the direction of such a compromise solution and instead expected of Berlin that it would make its Viennese partner see reason.²⁶³ Grey was willing to go all in, but the cabinet convinced him to consider every possible way of preserving the peace.²⁶⁴ Even Hardinge had reached the conclusion that Serbia must be stopped in its tracks, but he added: 'we must hope that somebody else will make this suggestion to the Russian government'.²⁶⁵ It is interesting to see to whom London increasingly often allocated that role during the crisis. In mid February, Whitehall looked for a conciliatory signal from the Kaiserreich, which it had always assumed to be the guiding spirit behind every international intrigue.²⁶⁶ Yet the next day, when Alfred von Kiderlen-Wächter did seize the initiative, he was met only with mistrust from Whitehall, although France voiced its approval²⁶⁷ and Izvolsky expressly acknowledged Germany's efforts to relieve the tension.²⁶⁸ London failed to recognize the chance to defuse the situation, concentrating all its efforts on proving its loyalty to St Petersburg, as Hardinge's words to Nicolson make evident:

> I am very glad that Iswolsky appreciates the genuineness of our support during the present crisis. It has been perfectly loyal, more than can be said of the French which

has been incomprehensible to me. Cambon showed to me the text of the proposal by Kiderlen which I think Touchard showed to Iswolsky. Curiously enough Cambon found it acceptable. But I told him at once that we could not possibly accept it and that it would be still more impossible for Russia to do so. He seemed surprised![269]

Cambon's astonishment is an indication of his surprise at the change in London's attitude, for every previous British foreign secretary had done his best not to get too involved in the tangled affairs of the Balkans. Yet Grey seemed so set on the friendship with Russia that he lacked any feeling for the subtle interconnections in the Balkans.

In this critical phase for the entente, Alexander Nelidow, the Russian ambassador to France, and his colleague in London, Benckendorff, performed valuable services for Izvolsky in Paris and London: Nelidow had compromised the French cabinet by pointing out London's greater loyalty, while on a daily basis Benckendorff informed Izvolsky how matters stood in the political sphere in London. Well informed, Izvolsky could reject the proposal that Serbia should renounce all territorial aspirations beyond its borders as an unacceptable and unreasonable demand on Belgrade.[270] The Serbian foreign minister ruled out a peaceful agreement with Vienna and acknowledged that Serbia was hoping for a more favourable moment and for a conflict involving the Great Powers.[271] There could hardly have been a more blatant expression of a desire to see the Austrian-Hungarian monarchy disintegrate, which was precisely what both St Petersburg and Belgrade thought would happen following the death of Franz Joseph.[272]

For a moment, it seemed the French might be prepared to mediate, as Paris clearly did not wish to share the responsibility of such a course to back Serbia and believed it was Russia's responsibility to make Serbia see reason. When London refused to cooperate, Pichon also stepped back. Relieved, Nelidow informed his foreign minister in St Petersburg that the British had let it be known that if France should fail Russia, then the Anglo-French entente would be at an end,[273] and the French cabinet did not wish to risk isolation. Izvolsky, Nelidow and Benckendorff made good use of their knowledge that France and Britain both feared isolation, a concern that drew the entente powers together over and above anything set down in a treaty.

In his over-eagerness, in early March Grey even went as far as to accord Serbia the right not to have to acknowledge an annexation until after a conference and then only in consort with compensation arrangements. De facto, Britain had acknowledged Serbia's right to compensation, enhancing Serbia's status greatly just as Serbian self-confidence was being bolstered by Milovanovic's meeting with the tsar in Sofia.[274]

As Hardinge pointed out, Britain's allegiance when it came to Russia's Slav interests helped create a better basis for negotiation on Persia.[275] However, as far Grey, Hardinge and Nicolson were concerned, Germany could do nothing right. Whitehall had become a prisoner of its own attitude towards the political situation on the continent. Britain's sense of weakness not only led to unconditional loyalty to its partner but also became bound in with a foreign policy that was dominated by stereotypes. In a letter sent by Hardinge to Nicolson on 16 February 1909, he acknowledged the 'German desire for the preservation of peace in the Balkans', but reported: 'I left with the impression that he [Bülow] would under certain circumstances act with France and ourselves in the Near East ... but we must not'.[276] Why such cooperation did not happen and why Grey interpreted Bülow and Schoen's agreement as a 'rebuff' would have seemed quite obvious to any Edwardian. The explanation lies not in anything Germany did, but in the growing challenge of reconciling imperial political interests with continental political interests, in the Crowe memorandum and Crowe's marginalia, in the contemporary media, and in the fundamental convictions of a generation that drew on its experiences of the last two decades and on a Social Darwinist spirit to conclude that Berlin was the Napoleonic threat of their age. The explanation is also to be found in London's unwillingness to accept any extensive responsibility for the international order and in the concrete situations that demanded political decisions be reached.

The rigidity of British diplomacy was a fundamental structural flaw in the alliance system in general and the ties of the entente in particular. Throughout the Balkan crisis, London was principally motivated by a desire to avoid damaging the entente or being excluded from discussions, a sure sign of Britain's political weakness and of the political weakness of the entente. Constant concern that St Petersburg might think even talks between Britain and Germany a betrayal of their agreement was a direct consequence of a lack of self-confidence. Grey and his colleagues repeatedly justified their stance to their radical liberal critics by insisting that Britain had not entered into any alliances and therefore still had a free hand in foreign policy. Yet at the time of the Balkan crisis and the Serbian issue, their words proved empty and self-serving, with the system weakened, not reinforced. A few years later, Winston Churchill put his finger on the problem: 'We have all the obligations of an alliance without its advantages'.[277] That reality had been evident during the Balkan crisis. To contemporaries, it was evident that the lack of concrete obligations when it came to the management of crises made the ties between Russia and Britain vulnerable, with neither side sure what support it could expect from the other. Such uncertainty meant the alliance had to be treated with great care, and mollifying or restraining one's partner seemed too risky. For the opposing side, it was therefore also all the more difficult to anticipate and evaluate possible reactions. Hence the 'entente' with Russia, as it was now termed, was essentially unpredictable.

By spring 1909, British diplomats had reached the conclusion that it would be 'preposterous if general peace were disturbed for the sake of that undeserving little Kingdom [Serbia]'.[278] That realization was not what prevented Russia or Serbia from taking up the gauntlet. The German proposal that Britain could join forces with France, Germany and Russia and put pressure on Serbia to change course and accept financial compensation[279] was rejected by Grey on 25 February out of concern for Russia's reaction, even though Arthur Nicolson, who had blustered to his superior about being prepared for any eventuality,[280] had informed Grey the previous day that Russia would intervene militarily if war broke out between Austria and Serbia.[281] Grey's rejection is an example par excellence of the acceptance of escalation and loss of political flexibility to which his course had led. His attitude did a further disservice to the system as a whole. Even though in October the Triple Entente had voted unanimously in favour of a conference, further obstacles were strewn on the path that led towards joint action with Germany to relieve the political tensions. Austria-Hungary and Germany found themselves facing the possibility of another Algeciras, for the conference agenda provided for a vote on the annexation itself and opened the way to debate on the Sanjak railway.[282] A neutral observer in Brussels recognized that after the most recent rejection by Britain,[283] Berlin was able to give Austria-Hungary only military support but was unable to offer any real diplomatic assistance. Two points are clear from Grey's explanation given to Bertie in late February 1909: first, as was now so usual, Grey assumed that Germany was driven by ulterior motives and plotted nothing less than the break-up of the entente and German hegemony on the continent; secondly, Grey's fear of displeasing Russia was almost pathological.[284] Fortunately for the Anglo-Russian entente and for the cause of peace, independently of its partners St Petersburg had decided not to risk a war for the sake of Serbia. Within only two days of Grey's rejection of the German offer of mediation, on his own initiative Izvolsky began to put pressure on the Serbian government to give way.[285]

In the course of the year 1908 to 1909 British foreign policy had broken once and for all its traditional ties to Austria-Hungary on issues concerning south-eastern Europe. Now British engagement with the continent was defined largely by the links to Russia generated by the entente, with British relations with Turkey and its traditional role in the European system counting for little. Britain showed no trace of self-confidence or independence in its dealings with Russia as Grey passed on blank cheques in the hope that St Petersburg would not cash them. Britain had done nothing to stop the situation from escalating; the brakes had been applied solely by Russia, which recognized that it was not ready, or not yet ready, for a duel with the Central Powers. The Foreign Office had secretly hoped for such an outcome, but reports from their military attaché had caused them to expect the worst. The Central Powers trusted their own assessment and knew how far Izvolsky could go and when he would have to draw back.

With Grey's rejection of the German proposal that the Great Powers might band together to discipline Serbia and ensure that any compensation of its shattered nationalist dreams was purely financial, a provisional climax had been reached in Britain's fostering of ties with Russia. The ensuing run of measures makes clear just how loyal Grey was to his Russian partner,[286] with little chance that Britain would risk reproaching or attempting to placate the tsardom. Grey and Hardinge were therefore relieved that Russia had 'taken the bull by the horns at Belgrade'.[287] There can be no suggestion that London worked to de-escalate the situation or implemented any policy designed to ensure peace was maintained.[288] The rapid worsening of the situation that marked the final phase of the crisis[289] began with the British refusal to join with Germany in finding a solution to the compensation issue. It says much that Britain continued to promise Russia support precisely in order to ensure that Serbia was compensated; evidently, London was anxious to avoid any appearance of Anglo-German cooperation. At the same time, that Russia would underline its own value as an ally and its right to a voice on the Serbian issue was simply a given. Whitehall was well aware of just how dangerous the Serbian issue was, for pan-Slavism was very evidently the greatest threat to the Austrian-Hungarian monarchy.[290] And yet London made only a half-hearted attempt to influence its partner, leaving the situation unresolved until Russia gave way of its own accord. The Foreign Office had done nothing to ensure the stability of the European system.

Only a concerted effort involving Germany, France and Britain could have brought Austria-Hungary and Russia to the negotiating table or called the smaller Balkan states to account, a process that would have been in accord with classic Great Power policy. Instead, in the days that followed, London pressed to be included in the discussions and rejected Vienna's demand for bilateral negotiations with Serbia. The Danube Monarchy wanted to teach Serbia a lesson, but Grey's real concern was that Britain remain part of the negotiations and not disappoint Russia. Vienna leapt to the conclusion that London was urging Serbia, the 'Balkan cur', towards war.[291] Aehrenthal was not prepared to accept Russia's demand and step in as protector of Serbia in the Balkans, yet Grey's insistence that the compensation issue be tackled at an international level went in precisely this direction. Quite naturally, Serbia attempted to exploit the situation, sharpening the tone of its response to Austria-Hungary.[292] The battle between London, Belgrade and Vienna over the formulation of the notes exchanged between Vienna and Belgrade over the following ten days has been tackled in detail elsewhere;[293] here we need only note that it too is evidence of the energy that London gave to supporting Serbia's claims, dragging out the crisis to the end of March. London even rejected formulations already agreed by its own ambassador and Aehrenthal. Emile Dillon's criticism of London after the crisis was all too justified: 'In March our FO was more Russian than the Russians, for we defended Servia's trumped up cause after Russia had abandoned it'.[294]

Since the Anglo-Russian Convention on the Middle East, all that had changed in the relationship between the two Great Powers was that it now operated at the European level – Russia still had not the slightest intention of keeping to any agreements or of respecting Britain's sphere of interest.[295] London continued to give no ground to the Central Powers, but turned a blind eye to Russia's treaty violations in a very public attempt to curry favour with its entente partner. Hardinge believed the repeated criticism justified, and he admitted to Nicolson without beating about the bush that Russia had ridden roughshod over the treaty in Persia. 'Grey has constantly, during the past year, had to appear in the House of Commons as the advocate of the Russian Government', he noted, continuing: 'We have had to suppress the truth and resort to subterfuge at times to meet hostile public opinion'.[296]

In Berlin, in the meantime, the German Foreign Ministry was beginning to wonder whether the British government was even interested in finding a solution, a question that also occurred to Jules Greindl, the Belgian ambassador to Berlin, who reported: 'The attitude of England in the question of the Balkans has been such as to retard at least the solution of the conflict which places Germany in the most painful and difficult position'.[297] London appeared to Belgium to be playing a 'sinister game' with Serbia in order that the crisis remain unresolved for as long as possible. The Belgian envoy in Belgrade reported that Serbia was receiving constant support not only from St Petersburg but also from London, and that Serbian self-confidence was producing overblown demands as London sought to strike a blow against the Dual Alliance, and in particular against Berlin, whose influence in the Balkans Britain was eager to see reduced. His colleague in London suspected that Britain was not only working against the Central Powers in the Balkans but also had the destruction of the Triple Alliance in its sights,[298] but the benefits for Britain were less clear, and therefore his suggestion seems less plausible, for, as we have noted, Britain saw Italy as a point of access that could be used to unravel the Triple Alliance.[299] Britain constantly endeavoured to avoid war, vacillating between urging Russia to hold back and hoping that Russia would show restraint of its own accord, but London failed to provide a way forward, as an honest broker would have. After the crisis, the Belgian diplomats assumed that if it had come to the worst, Britain and France would surely have come to Russia's aid.[300]

Even Hardinge commented that the British attitude was entirely dependent on Izvolsky's attitude,[301] while Nicolson reported from St Petersburg that Russian public opinion gauged Britain's support by the same standards as it measured Germany's support for Austria-Hungary.[302] Germany's unswerving loyalty to Austria-Hungary is explained by the German Foreign Ministry's eagerness to preserve the Dual Monarchy as its partner within the European concert for as long as possible.

Nevertheless, Kiderlen-Wächter and Bülow gradually lost patience[303] and insisted a solution to the crisis be found. On 21 March, the German chancellor instructed the German ambassador to St Petersburg to inform Izvolsky that Berlin would give Vienna a free hand unless St Petersburg acknowledged the annexation. Germany's demand was blunt: 'We expect a precise answer – yes or no; we must take an evasive, qualified, or vague answer as a refusal. We would then step back and allow matters to run their course'.[304] The message was clear: if Germany took its foot off the brakes, Austria-Hungary would crush the Serbian troublemaker. Russian support for its junior partner would be read as a *casus foederis* by the Dual Alliance, with Germany coming to the aid of the Danube Monarchy. As Germany had calculated, and confirming all the signs, Russia blinked first. Like Vienna and London, Berlin was well aware that Russia was not ready to face such a challenge.[305] The public nature of such intimidation suggests both diplomatic maladroitness and calculated risk taking characteristic of the imperialist age. After a three-hour meeting of the Council of Ministers, Nicholas II was advised to capitulate, and the tsar then telegraphed Wilhelm II: 'With the help of God, a war has thus been avoided'.[306]

The London political establishment felt the humiliation. 'The two German Powers … and their twenty dreadnoughts or "Lord Nelsons" have shown their ability to impose their will upon Europe and have thwarted the Triple Entente', reported the *Daily Mail*.[307] Putting to one side that neither Germany nor Austria-Hungary possessed a single dreadnought at the time, the newspaper accurately expressed the British government's disappointment. Greatly disappointed, Grey complained: 'As it was, Russia was stiff for a time, and then suddenly threw up the sponge and collapsed unconditionally'. With all his Russian expertise, Nicolson was equally disheartened to learn with 'bewildered consternation' that the natural protector of the Slavs had backed down. His greatest concern was for Britain's reputation as a loyal friend and partner, for, he recorded, 'it has been spread about that it was on the advice of Great Britain that the step was taken. When this version has come to my ears, I have naturally given it a direct denial'.[308] Hardinge located Germany's action within the broader political context since 1906, for while disappointed at Izvolsky's 'timorous nature',[309] he interpreted Berlin's response as a sign of lessons learned from the experience of Algeciras.[310] His assessment of the implication for Anglo-Russian relations, voiced the following day, was retrained: yes, London would have to accept that the entente was not sufficiently secure to defy the Central European bloc, but London could now feel more secure from a new three-emperor alliance:

> The Russians will never forget the fact that Germany and Austria have used her temporary weakness to harass her in a humiliating and hectoring manner. I cannot help thinking that the success will cost Germany dearly in the end. The Russians have an eye for the future and will prepare for the conflict.[311]

Nicolson remained relieved,[312] however, that German sabre-rattling had spared London a final decision and had left Britain to continue is its course towards St

Petersburg. Although he had initially strengthened Izvolsky in his resolve to hold out against Germany, he later admitted that he had been happy that at the vital moment the Russian foreign minister had not consulted London before giving his answer.[313] Just as the Belgian envoy in Paris had assumed, London would scarcely have been able to escape involvement in a war.[314] With that eventuality in mind, soon afterwards Grey inquired via Repington and his contacts in the French General Staff about the current capabilities of the Russian army. The military correspondent's answer suggested that diplomatic support from London was not required, for according to Repington, in the first week of a conflict, Russia would be capable of bringing into position on its western border at least 800,000 soldiers and most of its cavalry, with an additional 400,000 men available for an invasion of Austria-Hungary. Repington commented: 'Nothing but the weakness of character of the Russian Ministers allowed Russia to be stampeded by the German bluff'.[315]

As Martin Kröger has shown, theories about German war preparedness and use of calculated risk during the Annexation Crisis must be relativized in light of the lack of any German expectation of war.[316] And so too Britain's allegedly unswerving and exemplary commitment to peace and de-escalation needs to be seen in context. Undoubtedly, Britain delayed the solution of the crisis, which it unnecessarily and negligently exacerbated through its indirect support of Serbia. For a moment, London had hoped the Central Powers would crumple in the face of the Triple Entente or that any war would be localized. A great war was not in London's interest. At any rate, the crisis made evident that existing alliance structures could not be used to find a peaceful solution. All parties feared isolation, and for London and Berlin just as for Vienna and St Petersburg, the cohesion and nurturing of its alliances was its prime concern, with the stability of the European system of only secondary importance, which limited the possibilities for easing the tension. Officially, Berlin's ultimatum ended the crisis, but all the questions and problems of south-eastern Europe remained open. The challenges of managing a crisis involving two blocs without the possibility of any exchange or cooperation across those blocs would soon be evident in the Balkans again. Here was what Christopher Clark recently described as the Balkan inception scenario for the July Crisis of 1914.[317]

In the initial phase of British entente policy, London had taken great pains to ensure that France had no reason to doubt its loyalty, and Grey's concerned glances in the direction of St Petersburg during the Annexation Crisis revealed a similar attitude towards Russia. Immediately following the crisis, Grey forbade the official use of the term 'Triple Entente' in the blue books of the Foreign Office,[318] which Hugh O'Beirne, secretary of the embassy in Russia, and Hardinge interpreted as a precautionary response by Grey in light of the criticism expressed by his cabinet colleagues Harcourt, Lloyd George, Churchill and Morley rather than an expression of a genuine conviction.[319] With the domestic situation in mind, Grey wished to avoid the appearance of an entente, and he used the less committed-sounding term 'détente', although internally the diplomats were aware that the latter term had a strong whiff of the closer ties implied by the former. Internationally, Grey and Hardinge were eager to dispel once and for all the very idea of 'perfidious Albion', for it would have been 'entirely consistent with the reputation for fickleness which we enjoyed in Europe until quite recent times'. Grey explained to Lascelles:

> And so we shall run to the risk of returning to our position of isolation in Europe and losing much of the strong position which our recent policy has won for us. Nobody is more anxious than I that our relations with Germany should be friendly. But they can only be so on the distinct understanding that our friendship with Germany is not at the expense of our friendship with France.[320]

Even before Grey had banned the use of the term 'entente' to describe British relations with Russia, the guidelines he had established for his ambassador to St Petersburg and his plans for British policy towards Russia had both focused on fostering that entente and promoting the coordination of British and Russian diplomacy.[321] During the crisis, Grey was less concerned about any infringement of international law than he was about St Petersburg considering an agreement with Vienna necessary and hence also an agreement with Berlin. Grey informed Nicolson that he considered it especially unwise of Izvolsky not to have consulted London sooner.[322] In the aftermath of the crisis, Nicolson, as ambassador to St Petersburg, was very concerned about the survival of the Anglo-Russian connection, and wrote to Grey: 'When we have passed through the present "Sturm and Drang" period, I should not be greatly surprised if we were to find both France and Russia gravitating rapidly towards the Central Powers ... Our entente I much fear will languish and possibly die'.[323] Fear of isolation had its part in Nicolson's foreboding, along with the desire for an Anglo-Russian alliance held by an ambassador who could not easily extricate himself from the pressure exerted by his host. While Nicolson emphasized London's lack of loyalty,[324] Grey and Hardinge were focused on London's humiliation. Grey, who had to take the anti-Russian criticism of his radical liberal colleagues into account, endeavoured to calm Nicolson by pointing out that Russia had achieved a closer relationship with Bulgaria, and that Germany would not venture a war against Russia.[325] Convinced that the entente would not suffer any great damage, Hardinge predicted:

> It will take a year or so to put the Russian army on a really first class footing. When that is done it will be an army not to be despised, especially as it is the only army in Europe that has had real experience in modern warfare. I do not think that the position of Germany will then be a very enviable one – placed as she is between France and Russia.[326]

Hardinge and Nicolson were hoping for a more decisive foreign secretary, unhampered by domestic policy and internal party concerns.[327] Their own more concrete exchanges led them to propose that the pro-Russia course be continued, for they hoped that the crisis would produce an Anglo-Russian alliance that would permanently divide Russia from Germany.[328]

The conditions seemed favourable, for not only had the bond between Vienna and St Petersburg been severed, but with its ultimatum Berlin had also raised an insurmountable barrier between itself and St Petersburg. As he informed his mother, all that Nicolas II could do was 'but to swallow one's pride, give in and agree. ... It is quite true ... Germany's action has simply been brutal and we won't forget it. I think they were trying to separate us from France and England – but once again they have undoubtedly failed'.[329] The opinion in Fleet Street was that Germany had won a war without having fired a shot.[330] Only the liberal *Nation* ventured to point out Russia's weakness and internal disunity, and to question Russia's behaviour as a partner and hence the entente as a whole, in light of the concessions made by Izvolsky at Buchlau and his failure to inform London or Paris of his agreement with Aehrenthal. Instead, the article in *The Nation* continued, Izvolsky's first instinct had been to demand compensation in the form of the Dardanelles, while Grey's diplomacy had resulted in Germany once again becoming the arbiter of the European system.[331]

Soon, however, the Central Powers' diplomatic success would be recognized as a pyrrhic victory.[332] For *The Nation*, the main message to be learned from the crisis was that the Central Powers now stood completely alone, with the Triple Alliance no longer a reality as Italy had largely distanced itself from its allies.[333] Moreover, Russia had resolved to stand firm in the face of the next challenge: in 1909, the military commander at Kiev was ordered to keep the troops under his command in a heightened readiness.[334] Izvolsky's arrogant self-confidence had taken a hit from his humiliation in the crisis, leaving him embittered and with a fixed loathing of Germany. He left office as foreign minister in 1911 and became an ambassador, but he continued to labour 'day and night' to consolidate the entente. And when war broke out in 1914, he boasted with great satisfaction: 'This is my war! My war!'[335]

Grey's Radical Critics

The intensity of the efforts to consolidate the Anglo-Russian entente is reflected in the frequency of the radicals' objections in the cabinet, in the House of Commons and in the press. Britain's bond with Russia was evidently much more than a loose association or the support proffered by one friend to another. Those on the left of the governing party saw Britain's determined support of Russia since the convention and especially during the Bosnian crisis as a great mistake, perhaps even a catastrophe, whose only achievement was to isolate Germany while doing nothing to ensure peace.³³⁶ Initially, on learning of the annexation, the radical liberals had joined ranks with the government and had vehemently condemned the infringement of the Berlin Treaty, above all on moral and legal grounds.³³⁷ As the crisis continued, however, and especially after Kiderlen-Wächter's offer had been made, they came to favour joint mediation with Berlin.³³⁸ While the liberal imperialists around Grey had again, as in the Åland issue, deliberately overlooked Izvolsky's duplicity for the sake of the alliance and had instead directed their resentment at the Central Powers, their colleagues on the left of the party believed their general mistrust of continental plotting had been justified and accused Austria-Hungary and Russia of conspiring together. The gradual change in their position began with the Austro-Turkish agreement, for the Dual Monarchy appeared willing to make concessions after all and the Liberals saw Serbian nationalism as a calamity of their age that only the Habsburg Monarchy could hold in check. The *Economist* found a positive historical parallel: 'Austria has settled and pacified this one time wild and barbarous country and her work was at least as beneficial as ours in Ireland'.³³⁹ Charles Dilke explained the change of heart by some radical liberals to parliament,³⁴⁰ while Lord Courtney used a letter to the *Times* as his forum. Both argued that international law was a living law that had to adapt to political realities. Courtney was especially critical of Grey's public outrage, which he believed completely 'incompatible with our knowledge of history', and his list of occasions when British behaviour had hardly been exemplary included Disraeli's guarantee of Saxony in 1870 and the guarantee of Turkish integrity in 1856, which the signatories, including Britain, now wished to forget. Courtney commented that all those who had put their names to the Berlin Treaty, since broken innumerable times, had been clear 'that it was provisional', just as the occupation of Bosnia and Herzegovina had been provisional, and he insisted: 'We should accept accomplished facts and not let ourselves be dragged into war'. He also accused the government of double standards:

> While Austria was denounced for formally annexing provinces which had been transferred to her by Europe for administration and which she had ruled for thirty years, France was not only allowed but encouraged to push her claims in Morocco and ride roughshod over the interests of other signatories of the Treaties of Madrid and Algeciras.³⁴¹

Looking beyond the legal arguments, Courtney believed that the existing antagonism between the two blocs, which for the first time he identified explicitly as the 'Triple Alliance' and 'Triple Entente', must not be allowed to escalate on account of the Balkans. To that end, Britain should seize the opportunity to work together with Germany to produce a settlement that would cut across alliances: 'Why could we not have seen this at once – that overpowering logic of events that we recognise today, and have been a pacificator working with that other pacificator, Germany, from the beginning instead of being dragged into acquiescence?'[342]

Grey was held to be the 'commanding figure' among the foreign ministers of the Great Powers, which rendered all the more bitter the disappointment of his colleagues on the left of the party at the opportunities that had been lost.[343] Their desire for a new regulatory policy by the Great Powers marked a remarkable development in the radical liberal attitude towards international relations. Where previously they had advocated in a Gladstonian spirit for the rights of smaller states and ethnic groupings such as the Armenians, Persians or Macedonians, now they argued in terms of the stability of the whole system, which was not to be sacrificed to Serbia's highly dubious ambitions. A flexible approach to the treaty framework was in accord with Bismarck's dictum 'pacta sunt servanda rebus sic stantibus'.[344] Smaller European entities could be treated as bargaining chips in order to protect the unity and integrity of the Great Powers. Until recently, before the Persian question had been debated, such Realpolitik had always been opposed by British Liberals.

Henry Massingham's *Nation* sought to mediate between traditional Liberal foreign policy and this new emphasis on Realpolitik. The weekly newspaper expressed its suspicions that Russia's advocacy of the interests of the Balkan states was intended to disguise its own pan-Slav interests. Russia, the paper suggested, would allow the annexation to escalate into an international crisis in order to ensure the lines between the power blocs were drawn more sharply. London's concern should be to prevent the solidification of such blocs at any price, the 'Near Eastern Crisis' having proved once more their inherent dangers and also how little they could contribute to maintaining peace. The radical liberal paper argued in terms of traditional concert theory, but it rejected the concert within the concert that Grey's entente represented, judging that the government would have to choose between its loyalty to its entente partner(s) and its traditional responsibilities to Europe and to the European system. The paper opined that 'to restore the concert by conciliating Germany is for England and France an interest more vital than the rehabilitation of Russia'.[345] Although the left-liberal majority was not of one mind on foreign policy, it was united in its reservations about Britain's new Russian partner, replicating concerns also voiced by the previous Tory government. From such argumentation would grow the notion of détente, with the creation of separate but not necessarily hostile camps.[346] Similarly, the *Daily News* designated the power bloc structure 'the real malady of Europe', and noted: 'The Concert of Europe is no longer possible because there are now no powers free from these groups and our mediatory position between the alliances is lost'.[347]

Events in and related to the Balkans had demonstrated the European system's susceptibly to crises and the potential and problematic repercussions of the Anglo-Russian Convention, while also underlining for Britain the challenges faced by its own position within this system. In spring 1909, and bolstered by the navy panic, the international crisis made foreign policy, which was often conducted in the back rooms of Whitehall, a public concern. The resounding criticism of British foreign and defence policy under Grey and the Limps, especially as voiced by the radical liberals, culminated in numerous statements made in the press and given in parliament. The principal concern, as *The Nation* demonstrated, was with the balance of power and Britain's alliances.

After Grey again rejected an overture from Berlin on the grounds of London's loyalty to Paris and St Petersburg, its alliance partners, even some of his most eager supporters in Fleet Street began to question the course Whitehall had adopted and to condemn Serbia's intransigence. Belgrade was now viewed as the main obstacle to peace.[348] Even Spenser Wilkinson of the *Morning Post*, known for his anti-German outpourings, could find nothing reprehensible in Germany's actions during the crisis,[349] and Keith Wilson also contends that when examined more closely, neither in 1905 nor in 1908/9 did Berlin's behaviour live up to the aggressiveness with which it was charged. For Wilson, it seems surprising that at a time when the well-being of the continent was allegedly at the mercy of Germany, British foreign policy regularly overlooked the uncertainties, errors and missed opportunities that characterized Berlin's actions.[350] That failure is explained in part by the fact that those who did point out Germany's weaknesses were radical liberals, whose pacifism and support for disarmament were deemed to cloud their judgement when it came to foreign policy and to be better suppressed, for the khaki election was still a recent memory and Liberals feared feeding suspicions that they lacked a plan. Rejection of the radical liberal position on foreign affairs became a reflex reaction for liberal imperialists and Conservatives.

The failure to recognize German weakness was compounded by the style of argumentation found in the Crowe memorandum and by the stereotyping of Germany that was typical of British foreign policy and the British press. The belief that Germany was behind every and any international commotion constrained Whitehall but also created a dilemma for Berlin and for international relations more broadly that could be, and was, exploited by decision makers.[351] The criticism of Grey's course voiced by left-liberals should not be dismissed, as is so often the case, as merely a minority position. It makes evident that in the decade before the outbreak of the First World War, choices remained to be made. It also forced the London political sphere to debate the issues and reveals that differences of opinion within the party limited Grey's foreign policy, which numerous contemporary accounts and subsequent analyses have presented as intended to maintain the balance of power and the peace.

In this phase, the liberal weekly *The Nation* became the mouthpiece of criticism within the party. *The Nation* had already participated in the attack on stereotype-based invasion novels and on the Anglo-Russian Convention, and now it endeavoured to provide objective reporting on the Balkan crisis Although *The Nation* judged the actions of Austria-Hungary to be 'reckless, manifest destiny',[352] it rejected the frequently heard suggestion that Vienna was the puppet of Berlin[353] and insisted that the mere existence of an alliance between the two countries did not merit that conclusion. Its assessment of British policy and of possible alternatives is especially informative. Dissatisfied with British foreign policy under Grey, *The Nation* sought to understand Whitehall's proclivities and motives. Yet its attempt to examine both sides of the Anglo-German issue as objectively as possible was often and quickly dismissed as idealistic and was mocked as naive not only by contemporaries, including the conservative imperialist opposition, but also by historians.[354] During the Balkan crisis, the paper criticized British management of the crisis and its alliance policy in a series of articles. On 16 January 1909, under the heading 'The Two European Camps', it came to an incisive conclusion that was also noted in Germany:

> We have become in effect a Continental Power, and it is this new factor which is chiefly responsible for the current disturbance of the balance. Our entry into a Continental combination has been marked chiefly by recrudescence of Imperialist adventure. It is not Germany which is looking at her 'places in the sun'. It is France which is quietly attempting to absorb Morocco, and Russia which is intriguing … It is easy to talk of the danger of German 'hegemony' in Europe. The expansive ambitions of other Powers are certainly more in evidence … These ambitions we are forced covering and assisting.[355]

Three weeks later, the paper openly reproached the Foreign Office for its unwillingness to reach an understanding with Germany, which it blamed on prejudice and on Britain's weakness:

> The obstacles which might have prevented a rapprochement with Russia – historic enmity, divergence of interests, incompatibility of political views, and the ill repute of her official tradition – vanished at the first effort to come to terms. None of these obstacles exist to anything like the same extent in the case of Germany. Yet the mere shadows of them suffice to keep us apart.[356]

In the same breath, Massingham's paper set about revealing the two-faced behaviour of the *Times*, which, it reported, applied different standards to Germany and Russia even when the circumstances were similar. The Åland question and the annexation of Bosnia were cited by *The Nation* along with the situation in Persia both before and after the convention.[357] Elsewhere, taking a stand also found in the *National Review, Spectator, Daily Telegraph, Morning Post* and *Observer*, it reproached the *Times* for the opportunism of its determinedly anti-German stance, which led the paper to support the Young Turks and Russia.[358]

During the crisis, *The Nation* frequently exhorted the Foreign Office to deal more openly with Berlin in order to restore European harmony, which according to the paper was more important for the international system than helping Russia become a bulwark against the hegemonic desires of the Dual Alliance. Like Cecil Spring Rice with his liberal imperialist tendencies, *The Nation* was never tired of stressing that it was only a question of time before Russia would again be strong. And then there would be a surprise in store for Britain, for Russia would no longer be able to be controlled via the Central Powers or the Dual Alliance, and the tsardom or the Franco-Russian alliance would have the Empire at its mercy.[359] An article that appeared in *The Nation* after Berlin had issued its ultimatum to Russia on 21 March 1909 demonstrated just how fundamentally different the approach of *The Nation* was to that of the conservative-imperialist *Spectator*. *The Nation* condemned the *Spectator* for assuming that Germany must be planning an attack on Britain just as it had previously planned attacks on Austria and France, as if Germany had nothing better to do than to plan wars from morning until night. The wars of 1866 and 1870/71, always cited as examples, had been waged in order to effect German unification. And the infamous role played by Napoleon III should not be forgotten, the paper pointed out.[360]

The Nation did not believe that Britain must return to Salisbury's antiquated balance of power policy,[361] but it denounced Grey's duplicitousness in engaging Russia unhampered by principles but approaching Germany and Austria-Hungary mounted on a moral high horse. 'Russia may fire a shell, but Germany must not shake a fist',[362] the paper scathingly reported. A year later, *The Nation* commented that the Russian bond appeared sacrosanct to Britain and its imperialist press.[363] Even as peaceable Finland was under great threat from St Petersburg, that press remained characteristically quiet. The paper argued that British foreign policy should be determined solely by objective argument and British interests, and for that reason it favoured the course set by Lansdowne, Balfour and Sanderson, although it also stressed that Whitehall should be part of the continental alliance network, if only to avoid isolation. But Grey should neither allow such continental alliances to dictate British policy nor seek to maintain them come what may. The paper was aware that the power balance had shifted since the turn of the century and would continue to change, for such was the course of history. But Britain must not sell itself for less than its true value, and the contacts it established and alliances into which it entered must not become an end in and of themselves, bought by surrendering Britain's independence of action. British superiority at sea remained undisputed, and Britain had no reason for pessimism, let alone for surrendering its free hand. Sooner or later, *The Nation* predicted, Serbia would plunge Europe into disaster, and as a result of its encouragement of Serbia given out of loyalty to Russia, Britain would then be partly to blame for destroying the peace of Europe.

> Having concluded with France and Russia an understanding which clearly partakes of the character of an alliance, it is impossible to conclude the same sort of arrangement with Germany ... Our policy has strayed so far from any Liberal ideal. The main task is to restore some measure of solidarity to Europe, a condition of feeling in which problems could be approached on their merits, and not simply as phases in the rivalry of two groups of powers.[364]

Austria-Hungary and Germany's fait accompli was deemed to be a direct and logical consequence of the Algeciras Conference and of those powers' justified complaints at being hemmed in.[365] Unconditional adherence to a display of strength when it came to Germany and to mollification when it came to Russia typified Whitehall and the press loyal to Whitehall. *The Nation* recounted: 'It is everywhere a morbid fear which makes for the disturbance of the world's peace, a fear of seeming weak by being reasonable'. If the Annexation Crisis had proved anything, then it was that Britain had adopted the dictum 'My ally, right or wrong'. The paper continued: 'Our first concern in any crisis is now to rush forward and demonstrate our loyalty ... Our rulers are ready to trust Russian policy in Persia, at a moment when Colonel Liakhoff in a public order, incites his Cossacks to "destroy the constitution". We were recently an island. We are today a unit in a continental group'.[366]

After the crisis, considerable doubts about London's policy towards Russia came from an unexpected quarter. Although a Russophile, Emile Dillon accused his government of being 'more Russian than the Russians', which would inevitably result in Britain falling between all stools. Austria-Hungary would not loosen its ties to Germany, and Russia would never stand up on behalf of Britain. To top it all, Dillon considered his fellow English too lazy and too easy-going to defend themselves.[367]

If such criticism of Grey and Hardinge is an indication of their contemporaries' awareness that the change of government had come with a change in the paradigm for foreign policy, then it also suggests that the change of course was by no means irreversible and that the Central Powers' frustration was taken seriously. Despite all the prejudice and periodic hysteria, the radical liberal position suggested that a sober and pragmatic assessment of the Kaiserreich remained perfectly possible. Even the left-liberals, who, unlike the Tories, had always been suspicious of Bismarck's empire, adopted a new perspective in light of the increasingly close Anglo-Russian cooperation. As we evaluate British foreign policy, we must carefully differentiate between individual positions. In the Foreign Office, the War Office and Downing Street, the views of the liberal imperialists dominated, alongside a stereotype-based approach to the enemy that influenced policy making. Criticism in the cabinet came from those without direct responsibility for foreign policy, whose moderating traditional influence on foreign policy was therefore dependent on complex factors within the cabinet and within the Liberal Party that await further investigation.[368] Commenting on the variety of views within the party and on the domestic component of Liberal foreign policy, Garvin opined that the government could not have survived without Grey;[369] his radical liberal opponents had swallowed their criticism solely to avoid endangering the government. Even if Whitehall paid no heed to its critics until the crisis was over, the constant disapproval kept the government in a state of tension involving Gladstonians and Tories, such that a more open alliance policy, as also demanded by the Tory opposition, risked splitting the party again. That fear, and not a commitment to continuity, did much to shape Liberal entente policy, which had a distinct disadvantage already noted almost ten years earlier in Balfour's comment that because of the differences within the party, Liberal foreign policy was always 'half oil and half water'.[370] Neither British tradition nor the situation within the party made an undiluted alliance policy possible. Classic balance of power 'muddling through' and 'drifting' appeared dated and were rejected by most radical liberals. Grey, with Hardinge and Nicolson at his side, did not have the staff to support a concert policy à la Gladstone, which would in any case have included all European powers, including the Central Powers, and Grey himself was in any case the wrong man for such a policy. We need to add to that picture the international situation, which had lost its relatively straightforward pentarchy and had become far more complex.

Balfour had reached the conclusion that Grey and the Liberal leadership were partly, and perhaps even principally, to blame for the misfortunes of the European system. Somewhat surprisingly, it was to William Hewins, Grey's old colleague at the Coefficients, that he revealed his agreement with *The Nation*'s conclusion that Grey had the best of intentions but his attitude towards Germany, born of his loyalty to the entente and of consideration of his party, was bound to produce even more tension.[371] In parliament, Balfour sharply criticized the reduction in the fighting strength of the fleet, which he saw as running counter to a foreign policy that risked a negative impact on Britain and on international constellations,[372] for while Britain regularly rebuffed Germany, Britain flung itself at France and Russia, which were intent on changing the European status quo to their own advantage. For Balfour, the balance of power had always been something of a myth as one power always had the upper hand, but he far preferred that power to be Germany, rather than unpredictable France or Russia.[373] Balfour's criticism was not simply a product of his location on the opposition benches. He believed that only the desire to lower defence costs had made the alliance policy necessary in the first place. Pacifism and election promises were responsible, in his view, for the crises between 1906 and 1908, for the military capacity and heartening defensive situation inherited by his successor should have been sufficient, enabling Britain to avoid irrelevant entanglement on the continent. But instead, Germany had been driven into a corner diplomatically and given reason to increase its military strength.[374] Balfour's focus became damage limitation. Britain's need to increased its fighting strength, he argued, had been made necessary not by Germany but by Grey's one-sided anti-German foreign policy and concurrent defensive cuts.[375] More deliberate support for Britain's military capabilities and less pacifist and welfare-oriented thinking would, Balfour believed, have done far more for peace and stability in Europe. Even the pacifist *Nation* agreed with Balfour and criticized Grey: 'We sometimes fear that his very hatred of war blinds him to its possibility, and leads him into precautions which are themselves a provocation'.[376]

The navy panic in summer 1909 and the change of government in Berlin after the Balkan crisis produced a short – too short – period of détente in Anglo-German relations. Austria-Hungary had lost its traditional role as the link between Britain and emerging constellations,[377] marking the final point of a development that had started a decade earlier with the Anglo-French Dual Alliance and the end of the Mediterranean Agreements. In British policy during the Balkan crisis, Grey's liberal critics recognized an extension of the Anglo-Russian cooperation in the Middle East onto the continent. They feared British interests in Persia would not be respected and that the Central Powers would produce a panicked response. In recent years, historians have looked more closely at the détente in international relations before 1914.[378] Criticism from their own ranks led Grey and the Foreign Office to rethink their approach after 1909 and after 1911, but they also faced a new situation, with elections to the House of Commons and with the Anglo-Russian alliance joining the Entente Cordiale as a 'cornerstone of European peace', which brought London both domestic and foreign policy advantages.[379]

Notes

1. Steed, *Through Thirty Years*, Vol. 1, 255; see also Nicolson, *Carnock*, 259.
2. Bourchier to Bell, 10 Oct. 1908, NIA, MSS Bourchier; Wilkinson, *Thirty-five Years*, 304; Maxse to Harmsworth, 1 Jan. 1909, BL, Add. 62175.
3. Hardinge to Bertie, 5 Oct. 1908, CUL, MSS Hardinge, Vol. 13; Parker, Memorandum, BDFA F/XXXIV, No. 155, 324–411, 324; see also Gregory, *On the Edge of Diplomacy*, 48–49; Tscharykow, *Glimpses of High Politics*, 269.
4. Beatty to his wife, 20 Feb. 1909, NRS, *Beatty Papers*, Vol. 1, No. 11, 19–20.
5. Grey, *25 Years*, Vol. 1, 192; Stumm, 7 May 1909, GP XXVIII, No. 10304, 158–65; Asquith, *Ursprung des Krieges*, 53; Taube, *Der großen Katastrophe entgegen*, 158.
6. Gemeinhardt, *Pressepolitik 1908/09*, 2; Angelow, *Kalkül und Prestige*, 151–260; Kronenbitter, *Krieg im Frieden*, 334–56; Kennedy, *Rise of Anglo-German Antagonism*, 445–46; Herwig and Hamilton, *Origins of the First World War*, 18.

7. The Grouping of the Powers, *The Times*, 13 Oct. and 1 Dec. 1908. For the *Times*, it was 'justified' to speak of the crisis as a 'valuable fruit of the convention in the sphere of European politics'. *The Times*, 8 Oct. 1908. 'The Anglo-Franco-Russian Triple Entente has been consolidated within the last three weeks.' *The Times*, 7 Nov. 1908. Keith Wilson's study of entente policy is outstanding, but it omits the crisis altogether. See Wilson, *Policy of the Entente*.
8. On the Austro-German Dual Alliance, see Angelow, *Kalkül und Prestige*; Pantenburg, *Schatten des Zweibundes*; Afflerbach, *Dreibund*.
9. Schmitt, *Annexation*.
10. Steiner, *Britain and the Origins*, 54; Kennedy, *Rise of Anglo-German Antagonism*, 424; Hamilton, *Bertie of Thame*, 172–73.
11. The best studies of the annexation appeared in the 1930s. See Nintchitch, *Crise Bosniaque*; Schmitt, *Annexation of Bosnia*; Hoyos, *Balkanpolitik*, 915–32; Rothfels, 'Annexionskrise', 320–45. The author is currently working on a major study about Britain's Balkan diplomacy from the Congress of Berlin in 1878 to the 'Third Balkan War' in 1914.
12. Robbins, *Sir Edward Grey*, 194; Steiner, *Britain and the Origins*, 54; Kennedy, *Rise of Anglo-German Antagonism*, 424.
13. Mensdorff, 28 May 1908, HHStA, PA VIII, Kt. 140, No. 28 G., fol. 566.
14. See the contemporary assessment by Switzerland or Belgium: Lady to Müller, 20 June 1907, DDS V, No. 176, 388–89; Carlin to Brenner, 5 Oct. 1908, No. 233, 522; Report (Paris), 5 April 1909, BelD III, No. 58, 145–46; BelD IV, No. 16, 81–83.
15. For Grey's support, even before becoming foreign secretary, see Cambon to Rouvier, 25 Oct. 1905, DDF 2/VIII, No. 79, 111–15.
16. Steed, *Through Thirty Years*, 290–92.
17. Wyndham, Memorandum, 19 Nov. 1908, in Nicolson to Grey, 23 Nov. 1908, BDFA A/V, No. 52, 177.
18. BD V, No. 323.
19. Spring Rice to Lady Spring Rice, 16 Oct. 1908, GL II, 128–29; to Ferguson, 26 Oct. 1908, GL II, 130–31.
20. Anon., 'Good Allies and Bad Europeans', *The Nation*, 14 Nov. 1908, 240.
21. For Sweet, the first success of the Anglo-Russian entente can be seen in the Turkish-Bulgarian alignment during the crisis, which contained Austria-Hungary. Sweet, 'Bosnian Crisis', 183–85; see also Cooper, 'British Policy in the Balkans', 258–59.
22. Cooper, 'British Policy in the Balkans', 259.
23. Bridge, *From Sadowa to Sarajewo*.
24. Wormer, *Großbritannien*.
25. Neilson, *Britain and the Last Tsar*, 293–305.
26. See Pribram, *Austria-Hungary and Great Britain*.
27. Bridge, *Great Britain and Austria-Hungary*, 77–94.
28. Ibid., 111–25.
29. Ibid., 80.
30. That Bridge's concern is less with Britain than with Austria is evident from his concentration on Austrian sources. To date, the British position on the Balkans has only been examined relatively superficially. See Crampton, *Hollow Détente*; Kießling, 'Détentebemühungen', 102–25.
31. See Heller, *Ottoman Empire*; Ahmad, *Young Turks*, 302–29.

32. Grey to Lyttelton, 14 Aug. 1908, cited in Robbins, *Sir Edward Grey*, 195. On revived interest in Turkey, see Feroz, *Young Turks*, 32; Crampton, *Hollow Détente*, 15.
33. Hardinge, cited in Fisher to McKenna, 11 Aug. 1908, FGDN II, No. 135, 186–88.
34. Chirol to Saunders, 3 Feb. 1909, NIA, MSS Chirol.
35. Nicolson to Grey, 13 Aug. 1908, BD V, No. 215, 309–10; 14 Aug. 1908, No. 217, 311–12; Grey to Lowther, 23 Aug. 1908, No. 208, 266.
36. Hardinge to Barclay, 28 July 1908, CUL, MSS Hardinge, Vol. 13.
37. See Siegel, *Endgame*, 21–50.
38. *The Times*, 8 Oct. 1908.
39. In a letter received by Izvolsky in Paris on 4 October, Aehrenthal indicated this step was planned for 7 October. On 5 October, Sofia unexpectedly declared Bulgarian independence, and Vienna used the occasion to advance the annexation by a day. At the same time, with an eye to appeasing pan-Slavic interests, Austria-Hungary relinquished its claims to occupy the Sanjak of Novi Pazar; see Verosta, *Theorie*, 324–25.
40. See Charmley, *Splendid Isolation*, 353. For the British view of Aehrenthal, see Clarke to Goschen, 12 Dec. 1906, BDFA F/XXXIV, No. 93, 120–22; Spring Rice to Roosevelt, 2 April 1909, CC, CASR 6/10.
41. As Vienna had the Bulgarian cipher, the Ballplatz knew in advance about Sofia's steps. Findlay to Hardinge, 27 July 1909, CUL, MSS Hardinge, Vol. 15.
42. *The Times*, 5 Oct., 8 Oct. 1908; *Westminster Gazette*, 5 Oct. 1908; *Morning Post*, 5 Oct. 1908; *Daily Chronicle*, 5 Oct. 1908; *Daily Telegraph*, 6 Oct. 1908; *Globe*, 6 Oct. 1908. For the British press, see Mensdorff, 6 Oct. 1908, HHStA, PA XII, Liasse XXXIX, Kt. 358.
43. Stumm to Bülow, 30 Dec. 1908, PA-AA, R 6093; Hardinge to Buchanan, 6 Oct. 1908, CUL, MSS Hardinge, Vol. 13.
44. Cited in Mansergh, *World War*, 128. This opinion was shared by Spring Rice. Spring Rice to Lady Spring Rice, 16 Oct. 1908, GL II, 128.
45. Buchanan to Grey, 7 Aug. 1907, BD V, No. 261, 356–59.
46. Grey to Asquith, 5 Oct. 1908, NA, FO 800/100; to Lowther, 5 Oct. 1908, cited in Grey, *25 Years*, Vol. 1, 176.
47. For Serbia's intransigence and Russia's backing, see Chirol to Curzon, 17 Feb. 1904, IOL, EUR. F. 111/182; Buchanan to Grey, 18 April 1906, BD V, No. 131, 149–50; Goschen to Grey, 1 May 1906, BD V, No. 133, 151–52; for terrorist activities in Macedonia, see NA, FO 371/379–81, 581–86, 816.
48. Conrad, *Aus meiner Dienstzeit*, Vol. 1, 13–28; Kronenbitter, *Krieg im Frieden*, 334–36.
49. Musulin, Memorandum, 9 Aug. 1908, ÖUA I, No. 32, 25–34, 27–29.
50. Secret Treaty, June 1878; see Pribram, *Austria-Hungary and Great Britain*, 94; Hardinge to Nicolson, 28 Oct. 1908, BD V, No. 414, 471–72; Goschen to Grey, 6 Oct. 1908, BD V, No. 318, 398; Hardinge to Edward VII, 3. Oct. 1908, CUL, MSS Hardinge, Vol. 14.
51. See Kann, *Colonialism*, 164–80.
52. See Aehrenthal's plea for a 'penetration pacifique', 27 Oct. 1907 (Ministerrat), cited in Baernreither, *Fragmente eines politischen Tagebuchs*, 73. The Foreign Office had known for years of Vienna's problems within the region. Clarke to Goschen, 12 Dec. 1906, transferred to the FO, 17 Dec. 1906, BDFA F/XXXIV, No. 93, 120–22.
53. Aehrenthal to Beck, 26 Aug. 1908, ÖUA I, No. 46, 53–56; see also Franz Ferdinand to Aehrenthal, 11 Oct. 1908, Wank, Nachlaß Aehrenthal, Vol. 2, 624.

54. Aehrenthal, Memorandum, 5 Feb. 1907, cited in Wank, Nachlaß Aehrenthal, 451.
55. Aehrenthal to Goluchowski, 31 Dec. 1898, cited in Walters, 'Unpublished Documents', in SEER 32, No. 4, 196–206. By contrast, Steed attributed the whole annexation business to Aehrenthal's vanity. See Steed, *Through Thirty Years*, 278. Musulin, Memorandum, 9 Aug. 1908, ÖUA, I, No. 32, 25–34.
56. Vambéry to Hardinge, 28 Nov. 1908, NA, FO 800/33.
57. Minute by Hardinge, Lowther to Grey, 5 Oct. 1908, NA FO 372/550/34392; Bertie to Hardinge, 7 Oct. 1908, NA, FO 800/161; Blunt, *My Diaries*, Vol. 2, 223–24.
58. Kronenbitter, *Krieg im Frieden*, 336.
59. On Hötzendorf, see especially Kronenbitter, *Krieg im Frieden*, passim.
60. For Conrad's motives, see Conrad, *Aus meiner Dienstzeit*, Vol. 1, 13–28, 39–86; Kröger, 'Risiko', 603.
61. See Höbelt, 'Unzufriedenheit', 58–84.
62. In late 1908, Tolstoy laconically commented on the annexation that one nest of robbers had depended on the remaining robbers without reckoning on the cost. See Glenny, *The Balkans*, 281.
63. Hardinge euphemistically termed Russia's infringements 'instances of evasion of the Treaty of Berlin'. Hardinge, Memorandum, 16 Nov. 1906, BD IV (without no.), 58–60, 59. For the British annexation of Cyprus, see Lowe, *Reluctant Imperialists*, Vol. 2, 6; Schroeder, 'Stealing Horses', 36.
64. Bertie to Lansdowne, 6 March 1903, BL, Add. 63016. In the Council of Ministers, Aehrenthal announced that he expected no dissent from Britain. Council of Ministers, 19 Aug. 1908, ÖUA I, No. 40, 41 50.
65. Council of Ministers, 19 Aug. 1908, ÖUA I, No. 40, 43; discussion with Tittoni, 5 Sept. 1908, ÖUA I, No. 67, 72–75; Aehrenthal on a discussion with Izvolsky, 16 Sept. 1908, ÖUA I, No. 79, 86–92; Kronenbitter, *Krieg im Frieden*, 336.
66. Sanderson to Vambéry, 6 June 1903, and Memorandum, 6 Jan. 1906, NA, FO 800/33.
67. Hardinge to Vambéry, 5 Jan. 1909, NA, FO 800/33.
68. An impression drawn from across the whole collection of A. Vambéry's papers. NA, FO 800/33.
69. See Kröger, 'Risiko', 605.
70. Grey to Bertie, 5 Oct. 1908, BD V, No. 306, 392–93.
71. Anon., 'The Balkan Problem', *The Nation*, 17 Oct. 1908, 105–6.
72. Nicolson to Grey, 7 Oct. 1908, NA, FO 371/551/34785.
73. *Daily Telegraph*, 6 Oct. 1908; Graf Szechenyi, 1 Oct. 1908, HHStA, PA VIII, Kt. 141, No. 37, fols. 381–86; Anon., 'How Can England Help Turkey?', *The Nation*, 24 Oct. 1908, 137–38.
74. *The Standard*, 7 Oct. 1908.
75. *Daily Chronicle*, 7 Oct. 1908, cited in Skrivan, *Schwierige Partner*, 104.
76. *Daily News*, 5 Oct. 1908.
77. *The Times* (Lavino and Chirol), 5, 6 and 8 Oct. 1908; Gregory, *On the Edge of Diplomacy*, 49.
78. 'The Germans are not going to throw off their ally … But nothing is likely to happen that would bring us into sharp antagonism with Germany over this business.' Chirol to Spring Rice, 15 Oct. 1908, CC, CASR 1/12.
79. *The Times*, 6 and 8 Oct. 1908.

80. 'The status of Bosnia-Herzegovina is likely to become acute.' Steed to Bell, 6 Oct. 1906, NIA, MSS Bell.
81. Anon., 'The Future of Turkey', *The Nation*, 10 Oct. 1908, 41–42.
82. Buckle to Lansdowne, 28 Oct. 1908, BL, LANS/NC Buckle; Saunders to Maxse, 20 Sept. 1900, WSRO, MAXSE/447; Northcliffe to Maxse, 4 Jan. 1909, MAXSE/459; Hardinge to Nicolson, 4 Jan. 1909, NA, FO 800/342; Maxse to Harmsworth, 1 Jan. 1909, 23 Dec. 1911, 10 June 1913, BL, Add. 62175.
83. *The Times*, 15 Sept. 1908.
84. The Balance of Power in the Balkan Peninsula, *The Times*, 9 Sept. 1908; 14 Sept. 1908 (Serbia); 16 Sept. 1908 (Bulgaria); 21 Sept. 1908 (Turkey); 26 and 28 Sept. 1908 (Turkish-Bulgarian Alliance); 29 Sept. 1908 (Macedonia). See Robertson's Evaluation of the Balkan states, 21 Dec. 1906, LHCMA, ROB 1/2/7.
85. Bridge, *Great Britain and Austria-Hungary*, 112.
86. Ibid. See the reaction of Balkan diplomat Robert Graves: Graves, *Storm Centres*, 234.
87. Brockdorff-Rantzau to Bülow, 19 Aug. 1908, GP XXIV, No. 8230, 133–35.
88. Pallavicini to Aehrenthal, 9 Oct. 1908, ÖUA I, No. 212, 173–75.
89. Nicolson to Grey, 7 Oct. 1908, NA, FO 371/551/34662; Knollys to Hardinge, 7 Oct. 1908, CUL, MSS Hardinge, Vol. 13.
90. In fact, Izvolsky had already informed Vienna in July that he would not stand in the way of a permanent annexation that included the Sanjak. Izvolsky, Aide-mémoire, 6 July 1908, ÖUA I, No. 9.
91. Bertie to Grey, 4 Oct. 1908, BD V, No. 293, 384–86, 385 without Hardinge's Minutes. Bertie to Grey, 4 Oct. 1908, incl. minutes by Hardinge, NA, FO 371/550/34530.
92. Minute by Hardinge, Bertie to Grey, 4 Oct. 1908, NA, FO 371/550/34531.
93. Nicolson to Grey, 5 Oct. 1908, BD V/1, No. 303.
94. Hardinge, Memorandum, 3 Oct. 1908, BD V, No. 287, 377–78.
95. Bouchier to Bell, 30 Sept. 1908, NIA, MSS Bell.
96. *The Times*, 5 Oct. 1908.
97. Goschen to Grey, 1 Oct. 1908, BD V, No. 276, 371–72.
98. Cited in Sweet, 'Bosnian Crisis', 178. In a lead article, the *Times* was less alarmed about international stability than about a possible isolation of Great Britain. *The Times*, 5 Oct. 1908. See BD V, 376–77, 389; Anon., 'The Balkan Problem', *The Nation*, 17 Oct. 1908, 105–6.
99. Hardinge to Nicolson, 30 Sept. 1908, BD V, No. 274, 370; see Buchanan to Grey, BD V, No. 261 and App., 356–59. See Belgian reports from St Petersburg, 3 July 1908, BelD III, No. 16, 82–84; 7 July 1908, No. 18, 85–86; from Belgrade, 12 June 1908, BelD III, No. 17, 84–85; Izvolsky to Sasonow, 30 Aug. 1912, *Schriftwechsel Iswolskis*, Vol. 2, 250–52.
100. Buchanan to Grey, 16 Sept. 1907, BD V, No. 266, 363–64.
101. Buchanan to Grey, 1 Oct. 1908, BD V, No. 275, 371; Grey to Bertie, 2 Oct. 1908, BD V, No. 278, 373; to Goschen, BD V, No. 279, 373; to Buchanan, 2 Oct. 1908, BD V, No. 280, 374.
102. In 1894 it had already seemed clear that Constantinople was lost to France and Russia. See Wilson, 'Constantinople or Cairo', 27.
103. See Walters, 'Unpublished Documents', in SEER 30.
104. See, by contrast, the imperial dimension in Sweet, 'Bosnian Crisis', 178–80.

105. Hardinge to Edward VII, 3 Oct. 1908, CUL, MSS Hardinge, Vol. 14.
106. Forgach to Aehrenthal, 10 Jan. 1909, ÖUA I, No. 870.
107. *The Times*, 6 Oct. 1908; Bell to Steed, 19 Oct. 1908, NIA, MSS Bell.
108. Fitzmaurice to Grey, 6 Oct. 1908, NA, FO 800/92.
109. Mensdorff, 12 Nov. 1908, HHStA, PA VIII, Kt. 141, No. 56 C, fols. 25 and 28; Vambéry to Hardinge, 28 Nov. 1908, NA, FO 800/33.
110. A. Chamberlain to Mary Chamberlain, BUL, AC 4/1/337.
111. Sydenham to Morley, 9 Oct. 1908, IOL, EUR. D. 573/42.
112. Chirol to Spring Rice, 15 Oct. 1908, CC, CASR 1/12.
113. Cited in Spring Rice to Lady Spring Rice, 6 Oct. 1908, GL II, 127. Spring Rice to Lady Spring Rice, 6 Nov. 1908: 'I see the English howling. I wish they wouldn't. It so reminds me of a chained dog', GL II, 130.
114. Kennedy, *Rise of Anglo-German Antagonism*, 253, 266; Hamilton, *Bertie of Thame*, 33, 58; Steiner, *Foreign Office*, 104.
115. Spring Rice to Ferguson, 26 Oct. 1908, GL II, 130–31. A scenario that the sources indicate Russia feared, Benckendorff to Izvolsky, 25 Nov. 1908, BDS I, No. 7, 23.
116. Spring Rice to Ferguson, 26 Oct. 1908, GL II, 130–31.
117. Churchill, cited in Chirol to Nicolson, 19 Jan. 1909, NA, FO 800/342.
118. Metternich to AA, 9 Oct. 1908, GP XXVI/1, No. 9003, 123; Metternich to Bülow, 19 Oct. 1908, GP XXVI/1, No. 9056, 195–96.
119. Nicolson to Grey, 19 July 1908, cited in Nicolson, *Sir Arthur Nicolson: Lord Carnock*, 262.
120. *The Times* repeatedly stressed 'loyalty' to Russia. *The Times*, 5, 6 and 8 Oct. 1908.
121. Bridge, *Great Britain and Austria-Hungary*, 112; Iswolski, *Le Temps*, 7 Oct. 1908.
122. Schmitt, *Annexation of Bosnia*, 49. For the discussion with Izvolsky, see Grey, *25 Years*, Vol. 1, 183–85.
123. Bertie to Grey, 6 Oct. 1908, BD V, No. 311, 679; see also Cabinet, 12 Oct. 1908, NA, CAB 41/31/66.
124. See Bridge, *Great Britain and Austria-Hungary*, 116. For the *Manchester Guardian*, England had become a 'partisan power' incapable of serving as an arbiter. *Manchester Guardian*, 27 Nov. 1908.
125. Grey to Bertie, 6 Oct. 1908, BD V, No. 314, 396. For a different view, see Pichon: Bertie to Grey, 5 Oct. 1908, BD V, No. 304, 391.
126. Hardinge to Villiers, 8 Oct. 1908, NA, FO 800/22.
127. Hardinge to Bertie, 8 Oct. 1908, NA, FO 800/161.
128. Ibid.
129. See *The Times*, 8 Aug. 1907.
130. Morley to Minto, 7 Oct. 1908, IOL, EUR. D. 573/3; Fitzmaurice to Grey, 6 Oct. 1908, NA, FO 800/92.
131. Hardinge to Bertie, 12 Oct. 1908, cited in Neilson, *Britain and the Last Tsar*, 299.
132. Bertie to Grey, 7 Oct. 1908, NA, FO 371/551/34802.
133. 'Are we going to give the Straits away?' Bertie to Tyrrell, 12 Oct. 1908, cited in Hamilton, *Bertie of Thame*, 176.
134. *Westminster Gazette*, 17 Oct. 1908. An interview with Izvolsky on 14 October had only increased Spender's scepticism about Russia. See Harris, *Spender*, 154.
135. Asquith to Balfour, 15 Oct. 1908, BL, MSS Balfour, Add. 49692.

136. Asquith to Edward VII, 12 Oct. 1908, NA, CAB 41/31/36; see also Lee, *Edward VII*, Vol. 2, 640.
137. See Hardinge's complaints about Russia's policy in Persia: Hardinge to Nicolson, 5 Feb. 1908, NA, FO 800/341.
138. Hardinge to Bertie, 12 Oct. 1908, NA, FO 800/180.
139. Hardinge to Nicolson, 13 Oct. 1908, BD V, No. 372, 434–46. In fact, Admiral Slade (DNI) discerned great operational disadvantage if Russia could steam forth at any time and then slip back into the Black Sea, especially as the Dardanelles fortifications pointed outward to the Mediterranean rather than inward to the Black Sea. Slade, Memorandum to Grey, 8 Oct. 1908, NA, FO 371/551/35002.
140. 'It would save Isvolsky's position and also our entente.' Hardinge to Nicolson, 5 Feb. 1908, NA, FO 800/341. See the critical attitude of the press: *Morning Post*, 10 Oct. 1908; *Manchester Guardian*, 6 and 10 Oct. 1908; *Daily News*, 10 and 16 Oct. 1908; *The Nation*, 10 Oct. 1908.
141. *Illustrated Graphic*, 10 Oct. 1908.
142. Grey to Nicolson, 12 Oct. 1908, BD V, No. 364, 429–30.
143. Hardinge to Nicolson, 13 Oct. 1908, BD V, No. 372, 434–36.
144. Hardinge to Bertie, 12 Oct. 1908, NA, FO 800/180.
145. Grey, *25 Years*, Vol. 1, 178.
146. Asquith to Edward VII, 14 Oct. 1908, NA, CAB 41/31/67.
147. Balfour to Asquith, 14 Oct. 1908, BL, Add. 49692; Harris, *Spender*, 154.
148. Hardinge to Nicolson, 13 Oct. 1908, NA, FO 800/341.
149. King's office to Asquith, 13 Oct. 1908, BOD, MSS Asquith, Vol. 1; Knollys to Grey, 14 Oct. 1908, NA, FO 800/103.
150. Hardinge, Memorandum on the Possibility of War, April? 1909, BD V, App. III, 823–26.
151. Cited in Lee, *Edward VII*, Vol. 2, 640.
152. Asquith to Edward VII, 12 Oct. 1908, NA, CAB 41/31/66.
153. FO, Memorandum, 16 Oct. 1908, BD V, No. 390, 453–54; Flotow to Vienna, 16 Oct. 1908, ÖUA I, No. 295, 226–27.
154. Esher to Brett, 14 Oct. 1908, cited in JL II, 351.
155. *The Times*, 16 Oct. 1908.
156. Maxse, Episodes, NR 11/1908, 559–69; Dillon, 'Near Eastern Crisis', CR 11/1908, 513–32; *The Spectator*, 17 Oct. 1908.
157. See Asquith, *Ursprung des Krieges*, 15–16.
158. Metternich to AA, 6 Oct. 1908, GP XXVI/1, No. 8989, 106–7; Flotow to Vienna, 16 Oct. 1908, ÖUA I, No. 294, 223–26.
159. Spring Rice to Cromer, 22 Oct. 1908, NA, FO 800/44; Lascelles to Grey, 9 Oct. 1908, NA, FO 800/19.
160. Tyrrell to Spring Rice, 22 Oct. 1908, NA, FO 800/241; Dillon to Maxse, 29 Oct. 1908, WSRO, MAXSE/458; Gregory, *On the Edge of Diplomacy*, 49.
161. See Parker, Memorandum, BDFA F/XXXIV, No. 155, 324–411, 342.
162. Asquith to Edward VII, 14 Oct. 1908, NA, CAB 41/31/67; Grey to Izvolsky, 15 Oct. 1908, BD V, No. 387, 451–52.
163. Ottley, Memorandum, 14 Oct. 1908, CC, MSS Esher, War Memoranda 1908–1915, 16/13; Esher, Journal, 15 Oct. 1908, CC, MSS Esher 2/11.
164. Grey to Nicolson, 12 Oct. 1908, BD V, No. 364, 429–30.

165. Lansdowne, 15 Oct. 1908, BL, LANS/Working Files 1.
166. 'Before long she [Russia] will be a large factor again in Europe, larger and more important than France.' Nicolson to Hardinge, 21 Oct. 1908, CUL, MSS Hardinge, Vol. 12.
167. Morley to Minto, 14 and 23 Oct. 1908, IOL, EUR. D. 573/3.
168. 'If the Russian Government had once become an integral factor in the combinations of our world policy, our imperial interests, and, indeed, our financial and commercial interests, would compel us to uphold its credit and its authority.' Anon., 'Our Relations with Russia', *The Nation*, 8 June 1907, 553. See also Anon., 'How England Can Help Turkey', *The Nation*, 24 Oct. 1908, 137.
169. *The Times*, 10 Oct. and 3 Nov. 1908; Nicolson to Grey, 13 Oct. 1908, BD V, No. 366, 431.
170. Grey to Izvolsky, 15 Oct. 1908, BD V, No. 387, 451–52.
171. Fisher to Izvolsky, 15 Oct. 1908, FGDN II, No. 145, 197–99.
172. Ibid., 199.
173. A further copy was sent to Stolypin. Fisher to White, 2 Nov. 1908, FGDN II, No. 147, 200.
174. The Kaiser acknowledged his ambassador's news by pronouncing 'Die Neugruppierung der Mächte!' Metternich to Bülow, 19 Oct. 1908, GP XXVI/1, No. 9056, 195–96.
175. Grey to Nicolson, 26 Oct. 1908, NA, FO 800/341.
176. Sweet argues, however, that London aimed to back Turkey. Sweet, 'Bosnian Crisis', esp. 178, 180.
177. Edward VII to Nicolson, 27 Oct. 1908, BD V, No. 409, 468–69; Hardinge to Nicolson, 28 Oct. 1908, NA, FO 800/341.
178. Grey to Hardinge, 27 Oct. 1908: 'I do not want to cold-shoulder Iswolski on the Serbian Question … and I will do my best to support him'. Cited in Schmitt, *Annexation of Bosnia*, 68.
179. Hardinge to Nicolson, 28 Oct. 1908, NA, FO 800/341.
180. See Bridge, *Great Britain and Austria-Hungary*, 111–38.
181. For Austro-Turkish compensation, see Schmitt, *Annexation of Bosnia*, 149–68.
182. See Bridge, *Great Britain and Austria-Hungary*, 117. The traditional friendship with Austria declined. Rumbold, 9 March 1909, Journal, BOD, Vol. 3.
183. Aehrenthal supported Bulgaria at the expense of Serbia. Musulin, Memo, 9 Aug. 1908, ÖUA I, No. 32, 32. Berlin was sceptical. Marschall to AA, 30 Sept. 1908, GP XXVI/1, No. 8963, 81–82.
184. Berlin had underestimated British interests. Marschall to AA, 23 Oct. 1908, GP XXVI/2, No. 9209, 424–25.
185. Buchanan to Grey, 7 Aug. 1907, BD V, No. 261, 356–59.
186. For Russian interests in Bulgaria, see Giertz, 'Die außenpolitische Position Miljukovs', 88–89, 94–99.
187. Hardinge to Nicolson, 2 Feb. 1909, NA, FO 800/342.
188. O'Reilly to Grey, 28 Oct. 1908, NA, FO 371/554/37551.
189. Hardinge to Nicolson, 2 Feb. 1909, NA, FO 800/342.
190. Grey to Whitehead, 1 Dec. 1908, BD V, No. 468, 514; to Nicolson, BD V, No. 493, 543.
191. Milovanovic, 29 Oct. 1908, APS I, No. 22, 24–25. While Bülow warned against British support of Russia and Serbia, Aehrenthal did not take the warning seriously. Szögyény

to Vienna, 16 Dec. 1908, ÖUA I, No. 752, 606–11, 608; Aehrenthal to Bülow, 8 Dec. 1908, ÖUA I, No. 703, 558–63.
192. Hardinge to Nicolson, 28 Oct. 1908, NA, FO 800/341. In 1905, Lansdowne still supported Austria's predominant role within the Balkans. Lansdowne to Percy, 6 Jan. 1905, BL, LANS/NC Box J.
193. Chirol to Spring Rice, 3 Nov. 1908, CC, CASR 1/12.
194. *Novoe Vremja*, cited in Siegel, *Endgame*, 47.
195. Bridge, *Great Britain and Austria-Hungary*, 125; for a bloc of Balkan states, see BD V, Nos. 436–82.
196. Hardinge to Whitehead, 6 Nov. 1906, CUL, MSS Hardinge, Vol. 6.
197. Minute for Tyrrell, Mallet and Grey, Buchanan to Grey, 4 Nov. 1908, BD V, No. 427, 482–83; Grey to Lowther, 14 Nov. 1908, NA, FO 800/193A.
198. Hardinge, cited in Steiner, *Britain and the Origins*, 105; more optimistic is Nicolson to Strachey, 2 Nov. 1908, PA, STR/11/3/2.
199. Hardinge to Lowther, 1 Dec. 1908, NA, FO 800/193A; Bertie to Grey, 19 March 1909, BL, Add. 63052.
200. Whitehead to Grey, 25 Nov. 1908, BD V, No. 463, 510; Grey to Whitehead, 1 Dec. 1908, BD V, No. 468, 514.
201. See Cooper, 'British Policy in the Balkans', 271.
202. Grey to Lowther, 28 Oct. 1908, NA, FO 371/554/37298.
203. Hardinge to Nicolson, 25 Nov. 1907, NA, FO 800/340. 'Le Cabinet de St. James, dont la préoccupation actuelle semble être de barrer la route à l'extension de l'influence austro-germanique en Orient.' 'The Cabinet of St. James, whose present preoccupation seems to be to bar the way to the extension of the Austro-German influence in the East'. Report (Belgrade), 12 June 1908, BelD III, No. 17, 84–85.
204. Clark, *Sleepwalkers*, 349–57.
205. Hardinge to Lowther, 17 Nov. 1908, NA, FO 800/193A.
206. Grey to Lowther, 28 Oct. 1908, NA, FO 371/554/37298.
207. Whitehead to Grey, 26 Oct. 1908, BD V/2, No. 405; Lowther to Grey, 15 Oct. 1908, NA, FO 371/444/35598.
208. Grey, cited in Bridge, *Great Britain and Austria-Hungary*, 125.
209. Hardinge to Villiers, 18 Dec. 1908, NA, FO 800/24.
210. Buchanan to Grey, 16 Nov. 1908, BD V/2, No. 404; Cartwright to Grey, 28 Dec. 1908, NA, FO 371/558/45397.
211. See Cooper, 'British Policy in the Balkans', 272.
212. See Bridge, *Great Britain and Austria-Hungary*, 124.
213. Sweet, 'Bosnian Crisis', 184.
214. Cooper, 'British Policy in the Balkans', 273.
215. Hardinge to Lowther, 6 Feb. 1909, cited in ibid.
216. Grey to Lowther, 8 Feb. 1909, cited in Bridge, *Great Britain and Austria-Hungary*, 126. Also the following quotations.
217. Ibid.; see also De Salis to Grey, 25 Dec. 1908, BDFA F/XX, No. 193, 324.
218. Hardinge to Nicolson, 2 Feb. 1909, NA, FO 800/342; see also Neilson, 'My Beloved Russians', 540.
219. Asquith (Guildhall), *Manchester Guardian*, 12 Nov. 1908.
220. De Salis to Grey, 27 Oct. 1908, BD V, No. 410, 469; Grey to de Salis, 29 Oct. 1908, BD V, No. 417, 473–74; Nicolson to Grey, 31 Oct. 1908, BD V, No. 421, 475–78.

221. Grey to Nicolson, 27 Oct. 1908, BD V/2, No. 412.
222. Hardinge to Bryce, 23 Oct. 1908, BOD, MSS Bryce, Vol. 28, fol. 159; to Lowther, 17 Nov. 1908, NA, FO 800/193A.
223. Grey to Nicolson, 27 Oct. 1908, NA, FO 181/918.
224. Bridge, *Great Britain and Austria-Hungary*, 117; Berlin report, 12 March 1909, BelD III, No. 48, Circular, 20 March 1909, 131–32.
225. Schroeder, 'Alliances'.
226. Rumbold to Grey, 18 Jan. 1909, NA, FO 371/670.
227. Bridge, *Great Britain and Austria-Hungary*, 117.
228. Whitehead to Grey, 27 April 1909, Annual Report for Servia (1908), NA, FO 371/734/16654.
229. Grey, *25 Years*, Vol. 1, 173.
230. Khevenhüller to Aehrenthal, 26 Oct. 1908, ÖUA I, No. 412, 313; 4 Nov. 1908, ÖUA I, No. 501, 382.
231. Wesnitsch to Milovanovic, 5 Oct. 1908, APS I, No. 6, 6; Grujitsch to Milovanovic, 13 Oct. 1908, APS I, No. 13, 15–17.
232. London was well informed about Serbia's aspirations. On 5 October, Serbia's chargé d'affaires explained to Grey: 'The annexation would be considered in Servia and in all countries inhabited by Serbs as a great national catastrophe, and its consequences might become fatal to the peace'. Grey to Whitehead, 5 Oct. 1908, BD V, No. 308, 394; on Milovanovic, see Whitehead to Grey, 13 Oct. 1908, BD V, No. 374, 437–39; Grey to Goschen, 8 Dec. 1908, BD V, No. 481, 523–25; see also ÖUA I, No. 549, 565.
233. Grey to Nicolson, 2 Nov. 1908, NA, FO 371/519.
234. Nicolson to Grey, 3 Nov. 1908, BD V, No. 425, 479–81.
235. Nicolson to Grey, 4 Nov. 1908, NA, FO 800/73.
236. Grey to Whitehead, 9 Nov. 1908, BD V, No. 437, 491.
237. Grey to Nicolson, 10 Nov. 1908, BD V, No. 441, 494–95.
238. Hardinge to Nicolson, 11 Nov. 1908, NA, FO 800/341; Bertie to Grey, 19 March 1909, BL, Add. 63052.
239. Esher, JL II, 359.
240. Grey to Bertie, 27 Jan. 1909; Bertie to Tyrrell, 4 Feb. 1909, BL, Add. 63052. For the naval talks, see FDSF I, 118, 150.
241. Hardinge to Villiers, 8 Dec. 1908, NA, FO 800/24.
242. Schmitt, *Annexation of Bosnia*, 69.
243. Repington to Spender, 12 Dec. 1908, BL, Add. 46391.
244. Repington to Spender, 12 Dec. 1908, BL, Add. 46391.
245. Hardinge to Nicolson, 4 Jan. 1909, NA, FO 800/342.
246. For a character sketch see Clark, *Sleepwalkers*, 36–7.
247. Cartwright to Grey, 5 Jan. 1909, BD V, No. 501, 932; Maxse to Harmsworth, 1 Jan. 1909, BL, Add. 62175.
248. Steed to Chirol, 18 Feb. 1909, NIA, MSS Chirol; Whitehead to Grey, 18 Jan. 1909, BD V, No. 520, 567–68; Grey to Whitehead, 9 Feb. 1909, BD V, No. 566, 595–96; Friedjung, 7 March 1909, *Geschichte in Gesprächen*, Vol. 2, 214.
249. Mensdorff to Aehrenthal, 8 Jan. 1909, ÖUA I, No. 863, 718.
250. Nicolson to Grey, 14 Feb. 1909, BD V, No. 570, 598–600; Nelidow to Izvolsky, 3 March 1909, BDS I, No. 28, 52–53.
251. Nicolson to Grey, 15 Feb. 1909, BD V, No. 571, 601.

252. Pichon to Cambon, 19 Feb. 1909, DDF 2/XII, 34–35.
253. Tyrrell to Nicolson, 17 Feb. 1909, NA, FO 800/342.
254. See Chapter 4.
255. Cartwright to Grey, 21 Jan. 1909, NA, FO 800/41.
256. Hardinge to Buchanan, 23 Feb. 1909, CUL, MSS Hardinge, Vol. 4; Poklewski-Koziell to Izvolsky, 15 Feb. 1909, BDS I, No. 14, 35–36.
257. See Bridge, *Great Britain and Austria-Hungary*, 117.
258. Grey to Cartwright, 19 Feb. 1909, BD V, No. 585, 610–11; to Goschen, 24 Feb. 1909, BD V, No. 599, 618–19; Bertie to Tyrrell, 4 Feb. 1909, BL, Add. 63052.
259. Grey, Memorandum, 28 April 1908, NA, FO 800/92; Asquith to Grey, 7 Sept. 1908, NA, FO 800/100.
260. Wyndham, Memorandum, 19 Nov. 1908, in Nicolson to Grey, 23 Nov. 1908, BDFA A/V, No. 52, 177–78.
261. 'La politique de M. Iswolski n'a cassé, depuis six mois, de ballotter les serbes entre de folles espérances et de profonds découragements ... le rêve serbe ait reçu le coup de grâce.' 'The policy of Mr Iswolski has broken for six months, to toss the Serbs between mad hopes and deep discouragements ... the Serbian dream received the coup de grace'. Report (Belgrade), 25 March 1909, BelD III, No. 52, circular, 1 April 1909, 137–39.
262. For assessment of the Dual Monarchy, see Goschen, Report 1907, 11 May 1908, BDFA F/XXXIV, No. 123, 191–255; Howard to Grey, 18 Jan. 1909, ibid., No. 134, 263–65; Cartwright, Report 1908, 1 Feb. 1909, ibid., No. 127, 268–92; Howard to Grey, 14 March 1909, ibid., No. 141, 299. On the Kaiserreich, see Whitehead, Memorandum, 26 Jan. 1905: Imperial Estimates 1905, ibid., No. 180, 224–29; Whitehead, Memorandum, 7 Feb. 1905: Prussian Estimates for 1905, BDFA F/XIX, No. 181, 229–33; see also Churchill cited in Ferguson, *Pity of War*, 75; Goschen to Grey, 23 June 1906, BDFA F/XXXIV, No. 77, 100–101; Oppenheimer, Memorandum, 28 Sept. 1909, BDFA F/XXI, No. 1, 1–17.
263. Minute for Mallet and Hardinge, Goschen to Grey, 23 Feb. 1909, BD V, Nos. 616–18.
264. Dockrill, *Formulation*, 69.
265. Minutes, Hardinge to Nicolson to Grey, 24 Feb. 1909, NA, FO 371/751.
266. Hardinge to Goschen, 20 Jan. 1909, CUL, MSS Hardinge, Vol. 17; Poklewski-Koziell to Izvolsky, 16 Feb. 1909, BDS I, No. 15, 37–39.
267. Izvolsky to Benckendorff, 27 Feb. 1909, BDS I, No. 20, 45.
268. Izvolsky to Benckendorff and Nelidow, 17 March 1909, BDS I, No. 46, 73–74.
269. Hardinge to Nicolson, 15 March 1909, NA, FO 800/342. For the French refusal, see French Embassy (St Petersburg), 26 Feb. 1909, BDS I, No. 18, 43–44.
270. Izvolsky to Benckendorff, 2 March 1909, BDS I, No. 26, 50.
271. Ibid.
272. Sergejew to Izvolsky, 2 March 1909, BDS I, No. 27, 52.
273. Nelidow to Izvolsky, 3 March 1909, BDS I, No. 28, 52–56, 54–55.
274. Poklewski-Koziell to Izvolsky, 12 March 1909, BDS I, No. 40, 66.
275. Hardinge to Nicolson, 15 March 1909, NA, FO 800/342.
276. Hardinge to Nicolson, 16 Feb. 1909, FO 800/342; Poklewski-Koziell to Izvolsky, 16 Feb. 1909, BDS I, No. 16, 37–39.
277. Churchill to Asquith, 22 Aug. 1912, cited in Churchill, *World Crisis*, Vol. 1, 112.
278. Villiers to Nicolson, 24 Feb. 1909, NA, FO 800/342.
279. Important here: GP XXXVI/2, Nos. 9392–98, 624–29.

280. Nicolson to Grey, 22 Feb. 1909, NA, FO 371/751.
281. Nicolson to Grey, 24 Feb. 1909, BD V, No. 605, 622–23; Report (Berlin), BelD III, 5 April 1909, No. 58, Circular, 17 April 1909, 145–46.
282. See Parker, Memorandum, 29 July 1909, BDFA F/XXXIV, No. 155, 324–411, 342.
283. Brussels, 14 Jan. 1909, BelD IV, No. 34, 110–11.
284. Grey to Bertie, 25 Feb. 1909, BD V, No. 611, 627.
285. Nicolson to Grey, 27 Feb. 1909, BD V, No. 619, 636–37.
286. Crampton, *Hollow Détente*, 15; Stein to Izvolsky, 26 Feb. 1909, BDS I, No. 19, 41.
287. Grey to Nicolson, 3 March 1909, NA, FO 800/73.
288. Dockrill, *Formulation*, 52, 72–83.
289. Kröger, 'Risiko', 609.
290. Aehrenthal, Memorandum, 31 Dec. 1898; Goluchowski to Aehrenthal, 2 March 1899, cited in Walters, 'Unpublished Documents', in SEER 32, No. 4, No. 5, 196–213; Clarke to Goschen, 12 Dec. 1906, to FO, 17 Dec. 1906, BDFA F/XXXIV, No. 93, 120–22; Nicolson to Grey, 4 May 1907, BDFA A/IV, No. 220, 361–62.
291. Franz Ferdinand to Aehrenthal, 20 Oct. 1908, ÖUA I, No. 347a, 266–67.
292. Cited in Pribram, *Austria-Hungary and Great Britain*, 128.
293. See Schmitt, *Annexation of Bosnia*.
294. Dillon to Spring Rice, 28 Aug. 1909, CC, CASR 1/33.
295. McLean, *Britain and Her Buffer State*, 101.
296. Hardinge to Nicolson, 28 Oct. 1908, NA, FO 800/341.
297. 'L'attitude de l'Angleterre dans la question des Balkans, a été de nature à retarder au moins la solution du conflit qui place l'Allemagne dans la position la plus pénible et la plus délicate'. Report, Belgian embassy to Berlin, 13 Feb. 1909, Brussels, 6 March 1909, BelD III, No. 42, 121–23, 122.
298. Brüssel, 20 March 1909, BelD IV, No. 48, 156–58; 4 June 1909, BelD IV, No. 68, 208–9.
299. Rumbold, Diary, 9 March 1909, BOD, MSS Rumbold, Vol. 3.
300. Brussels, 17 April 1909, BelD IV, No. 58, 178–79.
301. Minute, Hardinge: Cartwright to Grey, 17 March 1909, BD V, No. 700, 694.
302. Nicolson to Grey, 17 March 1909, BD V, No. 701, 695.
303. Jäckh, *Kiderlen-Wächter*, Vol. 2, 26.
304. Bülow to Pourtalès, 21 March 1909, GP XXVI/2, No. 9460, 693–95.
305. See Kröger, 'Risiko', 602–14.
306. Cited in Spender, *Asquith*, 248.
307. *Daily Mail*, 29 March 1909, cited in Brex, *Scaremongerings*, 65.
308. Hardinge to Edward VII, 26 March 1909, CUL, MSS Hardinge, Vol. 18; Nicolson to Grey, 29 March 1909, cited in Grey, *25 Years*, Vol. 1, 188–89; Nelidow to Izvolsky, 1 April 1909, BDS I, No. 61, 88; Grey to Bertie, 30 April 1909, BL, Add. 63052.
309. Minute by Hardinge: Nicolson to Grey, 31 March 1909, NA, FO 371/756/12304.
310. Minute, Hardinge to Nicolson, 30 March 1909, BD V/2, 1273–74; Report, 29 March 1909, NA, CAB 37/98/56.
311. Hardinge to Edward VII, 31 March 1909, CUL, MSS Hardinge, Vol. 18.
312. Schmitt, *Annexation of Bosnia*, 250.
313. Nicolson, *Sir Arthur Nicolson: Lord Carnock*, 302.

314. Paris report, 5 April 1909, BelD III, No. 58, Zirkular, 17 April 1909, 145–46.
315. Repington to Grey, 10 May 1909, RL 73, 154; to Maxse, 15 May 1909, WSRO, MAXSE/459.
316. Kröger, 'Risiko', 613–14.
317. Clark, *Sleepwalkers*, 559.
318. Hardinge to Nicolson, 30 April 1909, BD IX, No. 7, 5; Nicolson, *Sir Arthur Nicolson: Lord Carnock*, 308.
319. O'Beirne to Nicolson, May 1909, NA, FO 800/342; Hardinge to Lowther, 18 May 1909, CUL, MSS Hardinge, Vol. 17.
320. Grey to Lascelles, 18 Sept. 1907, BD VI, No. 48, 101. The *National Review* had previously used exactly the same words to describe the pro-Russian orientation; see NR, 10/1907, cited in Maxse, *Germany on the Brain*, 231.
321. Grey to Nicolson, 2 April 1909, BD V, No. 823, 771–72.
322. Grey to Nicolson, 2 April 1909, NA, FO 800/342.
323. 'If we could contract some kind of alliance with Russia, we should probably also steady France and prevent her from deserting to the central powers.' Nicolson to Grey, 24 March 1909, BD V, No. 764, 736.
324. Nicolson to Grey, 29 March 1909, cited in Grey, *25 Years*, Vol. 1, 189.
325. Grey to Nicolson, 2 April 1909, NA, FO 800/342; Bertie to Grey, 19 March 1909, BL, Add. 63052.
326. Cited in Cooper, 'British Policy in the Balkans', 279.
327. Wilson, *Policy of the Entente*, 43.
328. 'If it were possible as a consequence of the recent crisis to extend and strengthen our entente by bringing it nearer to the nature of an alliance, it would then be possible to deter Russia from moving towards Berlin.' Nicolson to Hardinge, 3 April 1909, NA, FO 800/342.
329. Nicolas II, 19 March 1909, cited in Bing, *Secret Letters of the Last Tsar*, 240.
330. Carroll, *Germany and the Great Powers*, 628.
331. Anon., 'The Bankruptcy of Statesmanship', *The Nation*, 3 April 1909, 4–5.
332. Nicolson to Grey, 1 May 1909, BDFA A/V, No. 67, 278–79; Nicolson, *Verschwörung*, 316. See also Hardinge to Edward VII, 31 March 1909, CUL, MSS Hardinge, Vol. 18.
333. Anon., 'The Bankruptcy of Statesmanship', *The Nation*, 22 May 1909, 50–51.
334. Massie, *Dreadnought*, 608. For the military conclusions, see Hermann, *Arming of Europe*, 12–120, passim.
335. Mansergh, *World War*, 136; Fay, 'Influence of the Pre-war Press', 30; Sasonow, *Sechs schwere Jahre*, 15–16; Tscharykow, *Glimpses of High Politics*, 270–71; for an additional thought on this expression see Schmidt, 'Révanche pour Sedan', 425.
336. Leventhal, 'H.N. Brailsford and the Search', 211.
337. Anon., 'The Balkan Problem', *The Nation*, 17 Oct. 1908, 105–6.
338. 'Had Peace been our object, we should have sought it rather at Berlin than at St. Petersburg.' Cited in Leventhal, 'H.N. Brailsford and the Search', 211; see also Anon., 'The Bankruptcy of Statesmanship', *The Nation*, 3 April 1909, 4–5; Brailsford, 'The Hush in Europe', *English Review* 7/1907, 779–93, esp. 787.
339. Cited in Weinroth, 'Radicalism and Nationalism', 225.
340. Dilke attacked Grey, suggesting he 'was making too much fuss about the action of Austria and Bulgaria'. Cited in Gooch, *Life of Lord Courtney*, 535.

341. Courtney (Letters), *The Times*, 29 Jan. 1909. See also Canon Barnett: 'It [the letter] takes a great deal of pushing to make this generation think', Barnett to Courtney, 25 Jan. 1909, cited in Gooch, *Life of Lord Courtney*, 555–56.
342. Cited in Weinroth, 'Radicalism and Nationalism', 225.
343. Anon., 'Sir Edward Grey's Opportunity', *The Nation*, 16 Feb. 1909, 608–9.
344. Cited in Schroeder, 'Stealing Horses', 36.
345. Anon., 'Good Allies and Bad Europeans', *The Nation*, 14 Nov. 1908, 240.
346. See Kiessling, *Krieg*.
347. *Daily News*, 20 Nov. 1908.
348. Articles such as 'The Madness of Serbia' which appeared in the *Morning Post* on 26 Feb. 1909 or 'The Near Beast' which was published in the *Observer* on 28 Feb. 1909 got to the heart of this change of opinion; their tenor was picked up by other publications. See *Daily News*, 26 Feb. 1909; *Daily Telegraph*, 26 Feb. 1909; *Evening Standard*, 25 Feb. 1909.
349. Wilkinson, *Britain at Bay*, 77–78.
350. Wilson, *Policy of the Entente*, 100–120.
351. Charmley, *Splendid Isolation*, 347.
352. Cited in Weinroth, 'Radicalism and Nationalism', 224.
353. *The Times*, 8 Oct. 1908; *Daily Telegraph*, 8 Oct. 1908; *Observer*, 10 Oct. 1908.
354. *The Nation*, 3 April 1909; see also Weinroth, 'British Radicals', 654.
355. Anon., 'The Two European Camps', *The Nation*, 16 Jan. 1909, 597; Metternich to Bülow, 16 Jan. 1909, PA-AA, 5635.
356. Anon., 'The Anglo-German Tension', *The Nation*, 6 Feb. 1909, 700–701, 701.
357. London knew about Russia's ambitions in the Baltic. Nicolson to Grey, 26 Dec. 1907, NA, FO 800/72.
358. 'The violence of our press, especially *The Times* has needlessly envenomed the dispute [the Annexation Crisis] … It is contrary to plain facts to suggest that Germany's attempts to manage the crisis have contained any provocative or Machiavellian element.' Anon., 'Turkey and *The Times*', *The Nation*, 20 Feb. 1909, 780. See also *The Times*, 28 Sept. and 6 Oct. 1908; German Intrigues in the Balkans, *Morning Post*, 24 Feb. 1908.
359. Anon, 'The Need for a European Concert', *The Nation*, 27 Feb. 1909, 809.
360. Anon., 'The Motives of German Policy', *The Nation*, 27 March 1909, 955. The wars of unification were repeatedly taken as an example of German aggression. See MacColl, *The Times* (Letters), 6 Feb. 1903.
361. Anon., 'The Fight for the Balance of Power', *The Nation*, 3 April 1909, 5.
362. Anon., 'The Congo and the Concert', *The Nation*, 26 June 1909, 448.
363. Anon., 'The Suppression of Finland', *The Nation*, 15 Oct. 1910, 116.
364. Anon., 'The Motives of German Policy', *The Nation*, 27 March 1909, 955; 3 April 1909, 19.
365. Anon., 'The Impotence of Europe', *The Nation*, 20 March 1909, 918–19; Anon., 'The Balkan Problem', *The Nation*, 17 Oct. 1908, 105–6; Anon., 'The Spirit of our Foreign Policy', *The Nation*, 22 Feb. 1908, 748–49.
366. Anon., 'Good Allies and Bad Europeans', *The Nation*, 14 Nov. 1908, 240.
367. Dillon to Spring Rice, 28 Aug. 1909, CC, CASR 1/33.
368. Schmidt, 'Einmaleins', 508–27, passim.
369. Cited in Gollin, *The Observer and J.L. Garvin*, 79.
370. Balfour in Kilmarnock, 6 Oct. 1900, cited in Dugdale, *Balfour*, 312.

371. Balfour to Hewins, 17 June 1908, BL, Add. 49779; Hewins, 10 Nov. 1908, cited in Hewins, *Apologia*, 225.
372. Balfour (Commons), 27 July 1906, PD IV/162, cols. 108–13; 5 March 1907, PD IV/170, cols. 676–82.
373. Tomes, *Balfour and Foreign Policy*, 138.
374. Balfour, 16 March 1909, PD V/2, cols. 944–54.
375. Balfour, 29 March 1909, PD V/3, cols. 144–45.
376. Anon., 'England and Germany', *The Nation*, 12 Oct. 1907, 39–40.
377. Rumbold, Diary, 9 March 1909, BOD, Vol. 3.
378. See Kiessling, *Krieg*; Afflerbach, *Dreibund*.
379. Strachey to Nicolson, 1 Feb. 1909, PA, STR/11/3/3; Morley, August 1914, BOD, MSS Morley, MS Eng. d. 3585.

Conclusion and Perspectives
The Triad of British Foreign Politics

With their principal aim the preservation of the *Pax Britannica* and the continental balance of power, for several decades in the nineteenth century British statesmen pursued a strategy that combined passive foreign politics with the exploitation of European rivalries. They strove to avoid both 'eternal allies' and 'perpetual enemies'.[1] Lord Salisbury refused to abandon this model and recommended to his successors that they avoid alignments and put all their energies into preserving stability and the status quo among the Great Powers.[2] Salisbury was keen to keep Britain in the background and did not wish to force developments unnecessarily, especially, in the 1890s, in relation to revisionist powers such as France and Russia. Salisbury calibrated his Russian strategy carefully; decisions were made on a case-by-case basis and always took account of whether global interests or European interests were at stake. While he welcomed agreement over the Near East and Middle East, Salisbury warned against mixing global affairs with those that touched on the south-east European periphery as part of Britain's policy towards Russia.[3]

Six years later, the Liberal government under Herbert Asquith, with Edward Grey as foreign secretary, had fewer fundamental qualms about the possible systemic repercussions of an Anglo-Russian agreement. The 1907 convention made no mention of the Straits at all, but that did not stem widespread assumptions that a wider agreement remained feasible. During the lengthy negotiations, Arthur Nicolson used the Straits as bait to lure Russia into an agreement about the Middle East. This encouraged the Russian Foreign Minister Izvolsky to reach an agreement with his Austrian colleague Aehrenthal at Buchlau. After London had withdrawn any assurances concerning the Straits, Izvolsky blamed Aehrenthal for duping him. During the Annexation Crisis, London appeared

---

Notes for this chapter begin on page 480.

bound to St Petersburg in what amounted to an entente on the European stage, both in perception and in effect, and as a result Britain was now established as one of a group of powers. Edward Grey had banned the use of the term 'Triple Entente' in official communications, but Foreign Office staff as well as the *Times* and other players in the political sphere of London already thought in terms of power blocs, counting Russia even as part of the 'liberal' bloc that was irreconcilably opposed to the 'reactionary' bloc composed of the Central Powers.[4]

Most historians have tended to see this development as inescapable, brought about by the challenge posed by Germany, on the one hand, and by Lansdowne's strategic 'revolution', or as a logical consequence of his entente politics, on the other. My findings show a much more nuanced situation. Scholars have recently begun to stress the significance of Britain's foreign interests in the mix between global and continental interests. I would add a reading of pre-1914 British foreign policy as an interdependent triad comprising the highly complex inner workings of foreign policy and the European and imperial motives that drove decision making in Whitehall.

Free from party-political constraints, Lansdowne and Balfour primarily pursued a policy of imperial consolidation, using a classic type of politics that Salisbury would have recognized.[5] European stability was to be maintained as it were by inertia. It was no coincidence that when he signed the Anglo-Japanese Alliance, Lansdowne explicitly cited the old Mediterranean Agreements, for the alliance shared their twin aims of distracting and containing Russia. Deliberately kept vague, the alliance with Tokyo was too similar to the model established by Salisbury to be a genuine departure and did not mark a new era of British alliance politics. The same was true for the periphery-oriented exploratory talks with Germany. Salisbury may have disapproved, but they still contained the separation of empire and continent that was an essential component of British policy at the time. Similarly, the Entente Cordiale with Paris was, at least from the perspective of the Tories, a purely colonial settlement of interests. Yes, it was hoped that the new alliance might also serve as an indirect channel of communication with Russia, but only for talks about a potential exchange in the Middle East and the Far East – a possibility that had already been on Salisbury's mind.

Lansdowne's personal background meant that for him the security of the Empire took centre stage; Balfour, by contrast, was chiefly concerned with stability on the continent. His fundamental axiom was that the Kaiserreich must not be crushed between the powers of the Dual Alliance.[6] Both Lansdowne and Balfour agreed that the greatest risk for the Empire and for international peace was Russia, a revisionist power, especially after it had formed its alliance with France. And both intuitively favoured closer alignment with the Central Powers. Their attitudes had relatively little to do with naiveté about German ambitions or Germanophilia (an accusation made by some at the time, and by scholars since), and much to do with experience. In the past, cooperation with Berlin, Vienna and Rome had proved fruitful, while cooperation with St Petersburg had not tended to last long. As a team, Balfour and Lansdowne were quarrelsome but constructive, and extremely successful. On becoming prime minister, Balfour largely called the shots.

But despite Salisbury's warnings, Balfour and Lansdowne under-rated the growing importance of the London press and public opinion as a separate political factor. While historians have tended to view the influence of public opinion in Britain as positive and useful,[7] the Venezuelan crisis or the Baghdad railway question serve to demonstrate how much it could also hamper Lansdowne and Balfour when it came to foreign policy. Although Lansdowne believed that the Berlin government had behaved with great correctness and helpfulness in both instances, certain papers of the radical right – and the *National Review* and *Spectator* in particular – had torpedoed any cooperation and gone so far as to demand that Britain isolate and ostracize the Kaiserreich and instead form an alliance with France and Russia. The aim here was neither a balancing of powers nor an encirclement of Germany but a dominance that would ensure long-term control of global political relations for Britain, with Germany sidelined.

The leading figures in this extensive media campaign were George Saunders, Leo Maxse, James Garvin, John Strachey, Rowland Blennerhasset and a number of other influential newspaper men. They shared a belief in an approaching, existential, Social Darwinist struggle between the global powers. Their projections were based, and this is striking, not on an assumption of German strength, but on Germany's geopolitical weakness, which would force Berlin sooner or later into an understanding with Russia that would produce a neo-Napoleonic bloc against Britain. That likelihood, they believed, must be frustrated, pre-emptively and whatever the cost. Their press campaign, backed by extensive contacts and personal connections to leading politicians from the opposition such as Edward Grey, Henry Campbell-Bannerman and Herbert Asquith, as well as to the unionist Joseph Chamberlain and with individual members of the Foreign Office such as Charles Hardinge, Francis Bertie and Eyre Crowe, was so influential in London's political sphere that the government eventually decided against cooperation with Germany. Later, just before the new government came in, John Spender even admitted that Britain had stood by and abandoned Germany, which it branded an international troublemaker in order to ease the path to an alliance with Britain's traditional arch-enemies. Spender believed it was too late for another change of course; an alliance with Germany was no longer desirable given the new global situation and the easing of tension that had resulted from Britain's alignment with the Dual Alliance.

Viewed from the still neglected domestic side of London's diplomacy, anti-German agitation had been accompanied from the very start by calls for comprehensive reforms of social and military policy that came in the wake of the

Boer War. Scenarios involving invasion by Germany and German espionage were introduced into the general reform debate above all by officers and by authors supported by the National Service League and combined with calls for a reorientation in foreign policy. In the wake of an ignominious war, military men were particularly keen to see the army rehabilitated, to maintain the high level of war spending and to regain their former high standing. Balfour's resistance, in both public and private, was a product of distrust of military demands that he had inherited from Salisbury and of his own military know-how. But he failed to address such threatening scenarios when the opportunity was there, in debates over homeland defence against Germany or securing the Indian frontier against Russia. By disapproving the scenarios and spreading calm in the face of growing public hysteria – if only for a short time and in small doses – he put to good use the lessons learnt from the massive popular campaigns during the Venezuelan crisis and the Baghdad railway negotiations.

Balfour's unusual interest in security and his studious engagement moved the ongoing discussions involving the War Office, the Admiralty and the public to a new level. Rather than become bogged down in organizational and technical questions or overwhelmed by repeated waves of public hysteria, Balfour wanted modern, sound analytic strategy planning. It was a watershed moment, between the ad hoc emergency plans of the nineteenth century and the joint planning culture of the twentieth century. The Committee of Imperial Defence served as his coordinating body between the political and the military spheres. Debates about security between the service departments and Balfour's close cooperation with Admiral Fisher, Julian Corbett and George Clarke – all of which I have merely sketched in as a backdrop to my discussion of foreign policy – show the complex web of interactions between ministries and the importance of domestic concerns.

Here, and not in new arms developments by potential adversaries for example, we find the key motivations for political decision makers in their everyday interactions in London. Politicians with an interest in military matters who did not blindly follow experts but sought robust and constructive debate instead did bring about a militarization of pre-war politics – but not necessarily new patterns of conflict. On the contrary, their engagement could even calm the security situation. If anything, at this stage France was viewed as the real challenge to which the Royal Navy needed to measure up. The French navy had all the latest weapons systems including submarines, torpedo-boat destroyers and fast cruisers, and John Fisher was not alone in counting it as one of the most modern fleets of the time. Fisher wanted to overcome the financial constraints imposed across the armed forces after the Boer War with a great technological leap forward. In this he was supported by Balfour and Selborne, both of whom favoured focused and efficient military development. At the time Britain started its recalibration of foreign and defence policies, the German High Seas Fleet played a surprisingly marginal role; traditional rivalries between service branches and disagreements over budgets between navy and army had a much more lasting and significant impact.

In writing about Britain's pre-1914 politics, historians have often concentrated on the German peril or, in more recent years, on the huge pressure that Russia's expansionism put on India's North West Frontier. The implication is that London ultimately had no option other than a problematic alliance with Russia, whether to preserve the equilibrium or to relieve that pressure.[8] But analysis of discussions and investigations conducted by the Committee of Imperial Defence shows something else. Neither before nor after the Russo-Japanese war and neither for reasons of homeland defence nor as a result of increased pressure from Russia in Central Asia was there ever an overwhelming, inescapable need for a rapprochement with St Petersburg. At no time until 1908/9 did British experts see German naval armament as such a deadly threat to Britain's command of the sea, let alone its coasts, that a complete turnover of foreign policy seems unavoidable. It would be pointless to deny that Britain noticed the German naval build-up, but it is equally true that Selborne and Fisher were far from being pessimistic about it. To imagine, as was just recently asserted, that they decided on the battle-cruiser construction, the most expansive programme in the whole Royal Navy, just to hunt down a handful of fast German ocean liners seems rather bizarre.[9] Due to the inhospitable climate and geography of Central Asia, Russia was not necessarily regarded as an acute threat either, or at least not in that region. Only the continuing activities of Russian agents among the region's tribal leaders might at some point have created a problem.

Experience had taught Lansdowne and Balfour that power politics was the game to play; they saw no reason to offer major concessions to St Petersburg. An agreement was desirable, but not at any cost. The unionists, supported by the viceroy, George Curzon, continued to pursue Salisbury's concept of buffer areas, and thought at most in terms of a colonial exchange deal, with the status quo of the Straits, south-east Europe and the Persian Gulf continuing as the sine qua non of Britain's Russian politics. They saw no reason to give way to public panic over the German High Seas Fleet. Quite the reverse: Balfour repeatedly demonstrated his sangfroid and ended his premiership convinced that peace and international stability were secure for years to come. Although he was aware and very much 'regretted' the deterioration of Anglo-German relations, especially due to the English press attacks,[10] and he also admitted that it was in 'Britain's national interest to support the French' in case of a *'sudden attack'* [italics mine] by Germany,[11] he was neither as talkative to Paris as his successors nor ready to expand the entente to Russia. As late as autumn 1905, Balfour, Lansdowne and Sanderson emphatically rejected Hardinge's attempts to create an entente with Russia. During the Russo-Japanese war, initially just Balfour but later also Lansdowne had hoped for a decisive Japanese victory. The renewal, and then the extension, of the Anglo-Japanese Alliance was another clear signal of strength directed at St Petersburg. Balfour never considered giving financial aid to Russia, which was facing bankruptcy.

During the first Moroccan Crisis, Britain had assured France of its moral support, but Balfour did not think regular staff talks were necessary, cautious in particular about their European dimension. Historians have tended to assume that these talks were a response to Germany's clumsy foreign policies. Instead, I stress that the staff talks had no official sanction and were the brainchild of the British General Staff. They dated back to before the crisis and continued afterwards with Charles Repington from the *Times* as middleman. The impetus had been provided by the experience of the Boer War and by a web of relations of power and influence between the British and Indian armies.

While Calcutta and Simla exaggerated the Russian threat in order to obtain additional resources for the defence of India, the prospect of a fresh colonial conflict in inhospitable Central Asia was not attractive to officers in Britain, who thought a mission to the continent much more promising, in terms of both glory and success. The political leadership around Balfour and Lansdowne did its best to dispel such dreams. Both when the Entente Cordiale was concluded and during the Moroccan Crisis, it did its best to keep Paris at arm's length. Tory entente policy had not been about maintaining a balance. Even Lansdowne was prepared to drop the entente altogether just a few days before it was signed, in favour of surely less important fishery rights in Newfoundland. The fact that the French had gained such a wholly different impression (they even assumed Britain had committed to providing assistance) was due to individual diplomats who played a lone hand and to covert promises made by British officers, who apparently wanted to give more of an edge to the government's unspecific promises of support.

Overall, Conservative foreign policy, unlike its liberal imperialist counterpart, was characterized more by continuity than by discontinuity. It had provided an alternative to rapprochement with the Franco-Russian Dual Alliance, a policy to which their successors would claim there was no alternative. As disciples of Salisbury's, Balfour and Lansdowne rated experience above hypothetical expectations. They looked for solutions at the periphery that would not disturb the centre or upset international constellations. They followed neither Chamberlain's commitment to alliances, nor Disraeli's or Salisbury's traditional policy of staying aloof. Their multidirectional policy had the typical stamp of Conservative elite decision makers in times of crisis: the attempt to combine the tried and tested with their own experiences and conclusions. Chamberlain's grand design (to forge a Teutonic alliance with the United States and Germany) had never found majority support among the unionists. Invasion and spy stories failed to shake the leadership, as did attempts by the army to achieve an early commitment to deployment. After decades of dealing with the Kaiserreich, Balfour and Lansdowne, supported by Sanderson, had simply grown used to its sabre-rattling.

Their response had less to do with Germanophilia and more to do with their sober analysis of reports received from Germany that contained intelligence not only about the country's well-known structural and geopolitical weakness, but also about its recurring domestic and financial problems. This evidence inclined the Conservative leadership to a classic ad hoc policy of drifting, all the more so as they had learned not to expect that much good could come from Russia. But their successors came to a wholly different conclusion.

Within weeks of the Conservative government turning down Benckendorff, Grey hinted to the Russian foreign secretary Izvolsky that a settlement that would include the Near East might be on the cards. The change of direction was remarkable. While Lansdowne and Balfour had taken pains to demonstrate British strength in their negotiations even with an undefeated Russia, Grey's chief negotiator, Arthur Nicolson, unnecessarily abandoned Britain's advantageous position after Tsushima and gave way step by step, even on fundamental British interests like the status quo in Persia. The Liberal government's change of strategy was striking, in particular when the liberal imperialists neglected to assume a position of strength in their negotiations over Central Asia with the other Great Power in the region. Instead of pursuing a balanced approach that combined demonstrations of strength with a willingness to grant some concessions, foreign politics increasingly tended towards concession.

At the root of this practice was a fundamentally new and wholly positive attitude toward the tsardom that was backed by no experience whatsoever. While Germany would be met with scepticism and suspicion, Russia could count on a universal presumption of innocence, which even the Russian leadership was at a loss to explain. At a time when Russia was struggling with its own problems and in consequence appeared less sovereign – not least to Persian observers – than before defeat and revolution, Britain's persistent courting in pursuit of an alliance looked, especially to eastern eyes, less like political cunning and more like a sign of weakness. The Foreign Office played its part in further undermining Britain's already somewhat weakened position in the region, while Russia showed its superior diplomatic skills, waiting for London and its ambassador Nicolson to come to it. Izvolsky consistently refused to allow a declaration about the status quo on the Gulf and repeatedly insisted that Grey relent on the question of an additional clause. By conducting negotiations in this way, Britain was not even able to secure the strategically crucial islands in the Strait of Hormuz. And as though those concessions to Russia had not been enough, London even held out the possibility of further joint railway projects in the direction of the Gulf, which in the long run could have only negative repercussions.[12]

From an international and systemic vantage point, the Anglo-Russian Convention could be regarded as a culmination of imperialism and imperial diplomacy. The transformation of the constellations that had begun in the early 1890s with the creation of the Dual Alliance between France and Russia, had evolved with Italy's partial retreat from the Triple Alliance towards France between 1899 and 1902, and developed further with the Entente Cordiale in 1904 culminated with the agreement between erstwhile rivals. From now on, its impact would be felt on the continent and include the imperialist principle of exclusivity in external relations. Britain gained most from these developments, and stood a good chance of resuming its role as arbiter of the states system, which it would then stabilize. But while Salisbury, Lansdowne and Balfour had been able to understand the critical symbiosis of the Central Asian and the Oriental questions, and had preferred to pursue separate policies for each region, from the outset their successors appeared to regard this strategy as too complicated.[13] On the one hand, complex domestic concerns would not allow Britain to continue to carry the responsibility for the power system, since to do so would demand, as Sanderson confirmed in summer 1907, burdens and sacrifices 'which the public and Parliament would not agree to'.[14] That prediction was all the more likely as the radical liberal majority wanted external peace and disarmament in order to be able to finance the social reforms they had promised during the elections. The younger right-liberals and Grey's decidedly pro-Russian staff members favoured a controlling bloc and open tension between the members of the Dual Alliance and the Central Powers.

It had become plain that London now applied a double standard to German and French or Russian foreign policies. What should have been a lesson about the impact of using the Straits as bait while negotiating the Anglo-Russian Convention can be seen as the starting point of the 'Balkanization' of Britain's entente diplomacy.[15] By alluding that a solution to the Straits question would be feasible in the future, Britain had encouraged the Russian foreign minister Alexander Izvolsky to seek a deal with his Austrian colleague Count Alois Aehrenthal. When London declared the moment 'inopportune' for a Straits solution, Izvolsky accused Aehrenthal of betrayal. At this point, London rushed to the aid of Izvolsky and supported its new partner's Slavic interests in south-eastern Europe and told St Petersburg that it regarded the Anglo-Russian friendship as 'absolutely vital'.[16] While Britain was not yet prepared to translate that attitude into active support, its disappointment at Russia backing down in the face of the Central Powers' ultimatum clearly illustrates the maturity the Anglo-Russian alliance had attained; the same can be said for Grey's constant private expression of loyalty to Izvolsky, and for England's encouragement of Serbia's Great Power fantasies. Whitehall not only sacrificed its traditional friendship with Vienna for the sake of its new ties to Russia, it also willingly accepted the destabilization of the Balkans. By repeatedly hinting at a solution for the Straits question in the long-drawn-out negotiations for the convention over Asia with St Petersburg and by repeatedly stressing that Britain had stood by the entente partners in a number of instances, including the Åland islands issue, Whitehall allowed the most sensitive area of Europe to become once more the neuralgic point of Great Power relations. And so London wilfully and needlessly guided tensions back from the periphery into the continent. As if that was not enough, the Foreign Office then attempted to find areas of contact with Russia in the Balkans, well aware that they could do so only at the expense of the precarious but stabilizing Mürzsteg agreement between Russia and Austria-Hungary. Britain not only accepted this upset of the regional order, but also hoped that the inevitable tensions would enable it to replace Vienna as Russia's partner.

Thus London conspicuously failed to fulfil its traditional role as guarantor of the balance of power. Britain's need for security was now out of kilter with European stability and a multipolar equilibrium. The recurring use of the term 'absolute security' in foreign political debates is a clear sign of this change in thinking, as is increasing reference to 'inevitability'. Political action was determined not by facts but by expectations, as in the case of the famous Crowe memorandum. Hardinge's and Grey's permanent worry about being 'isolated' and 'friendless',[17] which obviously went back to the Boer War, had grown to such an extent that during the Balkan crisis Britain saw itself as unable to pursue its own de-escalation policy. Instead, Whitehall waited for Germany to act as mediator while refusing to do anything to calm the waters in St Petersburg or Belgrade. Although a Balkan League was not yet established, Anglo-Russian cooperation achieved a substantial triumph in the Bulgarian-Turkish question. Russian diplomatic correspondence was already speaking of an 'entente partner', and Grey gave virtually unconditional backing to St Petersburg over the Serbian question. The British attitude supported Russia's intransigence, delayed a solution and – much like Berlin's unquestioning loyalty to Vienna – made a diplomatic solution increasingly impossible.

Whitehall's politics should be seen as an escalating factor during this phase, all the more so since London was very well aware that – as the Serbian foreign secretary himself had underlined – what was at stake was not any legal claim, but volatile national sentiments. Repeatedly stoking those sentiments proved just as detrimental to the stability of the system as was humiliating them.[18] Having secured an agreement with Russia, Britain was unwilling to risk it, even for a solution of the naval question. Consequently, the Annexation Crisis marked the fracturing of the states system and the inability of alliance structures to engage in long-term successful crisis management. Britain prioritized its desire for self-determination but neglected to take responsibility for the resulting repercussions for Europe, increasingly paralysing the states system.

The cause of the explicit shift from balance to security during Grey's term at the Foreign Office was not one frequently given, that the Kaiser's navy posed an existential threat or that there were indications of an anti-British continental alliance. The principal reason was that the new, younger, principally liberal imperialist decision-making elite of the Edwardian era conceived of politics differently, an attitude defined by two factors: increasingly Social Darwinist and counterfactual expectations and the almost constant instability of the Liberal Party from the mid 1890s onwards. Members of the Victorian elite – men like Salisbury and Sanderson, or their direct successors, Balfour and Lansdowne – had drawn on experience and preserved their conservative composure in the face of an uncertain future. Radical liberals advocated a retreat from global politics and inner renewal, while the liberal imperialists in particular did not doubt that the twentieth century would bring a struggle for geopolitical survival, for which they needed to prepare and position themselves. While experiences from the turn of the century, the Boer War, the lost khaki election and the continuing strategy debates in London's political sphere doubtless all acted as catalysts for the assumptions and proposed solutions of the right-liberals, a review of Edward Grey's early comments on foreign policy reveals a new direction from as early as the end of 1895, before the excitement of the Krüger telegram and the start of Germany's naval armament campaign. This new concept proposed that Britain should seek an alignment with its most dangerous enemies, and abandon the balance of power and support for the Triple Alliance in order to be prepared for the anticipated global contest of the twentieth century. The fundamental factor for Grey and his companions was primarily the Franco-Russian alliance of 1892/94. The same was true for the radical right-leaning journalists around Leo Maxse, John Strachey and a few others, who dominated the press at the turn of the century and with whom Grey, unlike his predecessors, kept in close contact. They viewed the Kaiserreich as a 'powerless friend, or secret enemy'.[19] In other words, vital was not Germany's strength but Germany's weakness, which ultimately proved a disadvantage in alliance terms.

A dynamic Germany dominated debates about an overall political reorientation. Unlike other powers at this time, Germany was present in all the dominant issues of the day: national efficiency, social and security reforms, foreign policy reorientation and a national reawakening after the Boer War. Grey developed his foreign policy concepts during frequent deliberations with members of the Coefficients, especially Repington, Maxse, Garvin and a few others, and attempted to reconcile them with domestic and imperial politics. The Kaiserreich had been identified as a future enemy long before Berlin had even begun its dreadnought leap. The very complex and dialectical explanation cannot be reduced to the simple denominator of Germany's mishandling of the situation. While Balfour, Lansdowne and Sanderson were inclined to provide indirect support for Germany to balance its current weakness, the Coefficients homed in on the long-term prognosis by George Saunders and Leo Maxse, Halford Mackinder and James Garvin. They assumed that the future world would be divided into three zones, in which Britain – with some luck – would come third, behind the United States and Russia. The members of the circle firmly believed in Darwinian and Spencerian ideas; they also believed in the efficiency and potential of the young Kaiserreich. All agreed that natural selection would sooner or later lead to a clash between Germany and Great Britain over who would come to occupy that third place, since in the long run the Kaiserreich would not be content with a position as junior partner. In this scenario, Germany's weakness and geographic situation made an alliance with Russia likely, which would lead to a renewed Napoleonic threat. There was general accord about Germany's relative weakness vis-à-vis the Dual Alliance, but Tories and Limps came to very different conclusions about what future course to steer. Grey and the Coefficients believed that instead of backing Germany against Russia, Britain should pre-empt a German-Russian alliance, seek an alignment with Russia, dominate the power constellations, emulate German efficiency and ready itself for the existential struggle by implementing reforms on all levels of the political system. In the eyes of the non-partisan efficiency movement – which counted among its members from the press Wells, Maxse and Garvin, all of them Coefficients – Germany fulfilled several roles at once. A number of newspapers and magazines, including the *National Review*, the *Fortnightly Review*, the *Observer* and the *Spectator*, cited the Kaiserreich not merely to highlight British shortcomings, but also as a model for necessary reforms. Those articles were used very early on to propagate a comprehensive security solution against Germany and a firm alliance with Paris and St Petersburg. The Kaiserreich with its proverbial efficiency – in education, in the economic-technological sector, and not least in military and political matters – could function as a role model that many believed Britain should follow; it could serve to stress the need for a new direction; and it supplied the desired objective. Countless articles and public demonstrations held up the Kaiserreich as Britain's great adversary in hope of shaking Britons out of their resignation and lethargy. The 'German peril' – the term was already becoming a set expression – served as additional ammunition for the liberal imperialists against their own radical left, which continued to favour general disarmament and abstention from the continent, and rated Germany above autocratic Russia as a potential partner, should the worst come to the worst. In this way, the Central Powers appeared positively synergetic in the alternative concept of the right-liberals, deployed in their disputes with both the unionists and the liberal left. With Germany's aid, foreign security could more plausibly be connected with domestic policy than could the idea of 'imperial preference' and the Conservatives' customs reform, which aimed to end free trade. Forced to choose between this traditional economic principle and a free rein in foreign politics, the radical liberals chose economic tradition. From now on, they would concentrate on domestic reform, while foreign policy would largely be steered by the liberal imperialists.

The liberal imperialist orientation found strong support from contemporary authors. Topics like domestic mobilization and the safeguarding of foreign alliances could be found in the works of Erskine Childers, William Le Queux and Headon Hill, as well as in Guy du Maurier's play *An Englishman's Home*. The publication of invasion and spy novels that accompanied the political discussion caused a veritable anxiety psychosis in the London political sphere. Through their allusions to a new Napoleonic threat, the continent slowly became part of the British horizon, which until then had been largely imperial. There is no doubt that the growing mass and tabloid publishing industry had a strong economic motive for publishing such novels and articles. It is also true that in invasion stories published before 1905 the threat occasionally came from the Franco-Russian alliance. But from 1902 onwards, the German peril was painted in wholly new and much more believable ways, causing it to take up increasing space in the press and in readers' letters. Series of articles in the *National Review*, reports in the *Times* or the *Observer* and other prestigious newspapers used almost identical arguments and the same images as fictitious invasion and spy stories, so that fiction shifted across an increasingly blurred line into fact. As a result, fictions became ever more suitable for political instrumentalization. Official praise for scare stories implied that they had military and political value. Their truth content was also increasingly a subject for discussion both in parliament and for bodies dealing with questions of foreign and security policy. In his invasion speech given in the House of Commons in May 1905, Balfour had attempted to calm the public and convince them of the absurdity of the rumour that there were thousands of German spies disguised as waiters and porters. His successors not only thought such statements unnecessary; they themselves either believed the monstrous rumours or used them for their own ends, for example for approaches to the Dual Alliance or Haldane's controversial army and national service reform. Grey went so far as to circulate Leo Maxse's famous A.B.C. article published in the *National Review* in November 1901, which called for the isolation of Germany and for Britain to join a Franco-Russian bloc.

Through these channels, stereotypical images and interpretations of Germany found a growing acceptance in conceptual extensions of the world of politics. Complex psychological factors joined classic elements like military and geopolitical alliances to determine the intensity, nature and approach to the search for a new strategy. Simplifying stereotypical interpretations[20] (a case in point is the Crowe memorandum) gave answers that were increasingly (mis)taken for reality. An apt illustration of the psychological effects and the 'theatricalization' of pre-war politics as described by Johannes Paulmann[21] is the fact that during the Zeppelin scare of summer 1908, which followed the publication of H.G. Wells' best-selling novel *The War of the Worlds*, the London press even voiced doubts about Britain's advantageous geopolitical position.[22] The fear of a German invasion by land, by sea and now even from the air, which could be imbibed daily from the press, read in novels and seen in one of the most successful plays of the time, caught hold of people's imagination and created a sort of virtual experience that eroded public misgivings about a military engagement on the continent. Britain's rediscovered role in Europe was increasingly defined by the alleged danger emanating from Germany. Against this background, it seemed only natural that Britain should want a continental strategy.

This feeling entered the political sphere through Edward Grey and the recently reformed pro-Dual-Alliance Foreign Office. They no longer required merely imperial consolidation and minimum requirements for continental security; now they demanded *absolute* security. The Entente Cordiale took on a pivotal role. While Lansdowne and Balfour's politics of strength and partial rapprochement had aimed to make British politics more flexible overall, Grey not only extended the lifespan of the entente course, but also gave it added pro-alliance weight through military agreements, repeated manifestations of loyalty and Anglo-Russian rapprochement. The German peril was a constant presence in liberal imperialist foreign, domestic and security politics.

The extent of this change of direction is nicely illustrated by the second invasion investigation. Historians' prevalent focus on Germany and reliance on hindsight have again got in the way of unravelling the complex domestic background to this security analysis. It was neither Berlin's new naval law of November 1907 nor the end of the Hague Peace Conference that caused Britain to press for a new investigation of the external security situation; the impetus came rather from the continuing agitation of the 'Committee of Four' around Charles Repington and Lord Roberts. Russia's defeat meant the security situation was now to Britain's advantage – for the Central Powers the defeat meant only temporary relief, and only on the continent – but the new British government failed to inform the public about the positive developments and instead tried to exploit the continuing invasion hysteria for arms and alliance politics. The new leadership gave free rein to speculation even after Fisher and his naval experts had demonstrated before the Committee of Imperial Defence and in the press that the fears were groundless, unfounded and at times absurd. Expert opinion as well as the passivity shown by Grey and Asquith make clear that the German peril was principally a propaganda tool used to further rearmament, national service and the legitimization of the Anglo-Russian rapprochement that had been sharply criticized in radical liberal circles.[23] When one compares the discussions over the security situation in 1903/4 and in 1907/8, a remarkable qualitative difference is evident in the way political leaders dealt with technical questions about military matters. Balfour possessed impressive military know-how and controlled the debate, but under Asquith the (at times polemical) attacks from the navy and the army regularly got out of hand. Grey and Haldane were often unable to follow their admirals' sometimes highly technical argumentation; all their opponents had to offer were purely quantitative arguments or wholly unproven claims, or even the absurd allegation that Moltke's landing on the island of Alsen in the 1864 war against Denmark had been a rehearsal for a German invasion of England. The second invasion investigation, just like the first, found that complex domestic factors and rivalries between ministries, as well as personal animosities, between

Fisher and Beresford or between Repington and Tweedmouth, had been principally responsible – much more so than the German High Seas Fleet.

Britain was overstretched after the South African War and by the slow disintegration of the Empire and societal crisis; the strain had to be eased somehow. With hindsight, Salisbury's plea that the country hold on to its traditional foreign policy axioms looks instead like a final farewell to those outdated policies. In an era that increasingly understood alliances as permanent institutions and lasting components of foreign policy planning, the liberal imperialist opposition under Grey, Haldane and Asquith had developed a new universal concept for both domestic and foreign politics that needed to consider the radical liberal majority and take both the Empire and the continent into account. The new direction showed most clearly in the interaction of a new type of personal experience, Social Darwinist premises about the anticipated contest of the Global Powers in the twentieth century and the resulting new images of Russia and Germany. This complex mix would come to define a fresh attitude towards both the continent and political control of international events as a whole. The negative impact of events at the turn of the century and the general climate of Social Darwinism had sensitized the constructivistically inclined Edwardians:[24] not for them confidence and a free hand, but instead a felt need for absolute security and brisk politicking that resulted in a headlong charge into the arms of continental alliance structures. There is a symmetry here between liberal imperialist actions on the domestic front – social reforms and the gradual implementation of a welfare state in order to contain the risks inherent in life and work – and in foreign relations, with a replication of the search for maximum security and predictability. They had bridged the gap between the working class and middle class, which explains their rise after the lost khaki election and their cooperation with the Labour Party. In contrast, the power constellations that constantly rose and fell and Salisbury's unpredictable policy of 'drifting', which had come under increasing criticism around the turn of the century, became less and less popular. After the Boer War, the radical liberal Gladstonians and the imperialist Limps merged and agreed a new division of domestic and foreign policy tasks.

The reasons for the new course were based mostly on hypothetical expectations and a hypertrophic security concept. Factual information, whether from naval experts or experienced observers of Germany, was no longer listened to. The years leading up to 1914 saw a militarization (about which David Stevenson and others have written)[25] and a tendency towards stereotypes in foreign policy that was based more on expectation than actual developments.

Combined with the fundamentally anti-German and pro-Russian stance of the new leaders, the German peril – distorted into arch-enmity in novels like *The Riddle of the Sands*, in the quarrel between the service departments and in the press – led to Berlin becoming the 'great Grey bogey',[26] the puppet master behind anything and everything that might cause a disagreement among the European powers.²⁷ Once the perceived threat had been established and escalated into paranoia, any clues that might have contradicted the basic assumption of Berlin's malevolent intentions were pre-emptively eliminated, arguments were turned on their heads and any behaviour whatsoever became evidence of Germany's plans to conquer Britain. Logical refutation was impossible. Whatever happened, according to Crowe's reading Germany could always be assumed to harbour negative intentions. Brash and defiant conduct was grist to the mill of already suspicious Foreign Office workers, who responded by working all the harder to forge a counter-alliance. When Germany was conciliatory and offered to share information about its naval construction plans, as happened in summer 1908, it was thought to be surely planning to lull Britain into a false sense of security.

My chosen vantage point, from which I have looked at the complex inner workings of British foreign policy, the political sphere of debate and decision making in London, and imperial interests that embraced both continent and empire, has shown that the frame of interpretation that predominates even today, of a Whitehall primarily responding to German actions, stands in need of correction. Future analyses should consider Anglo-German relations, including the naval arms race, more in the context of party-political conflicts and disputes over resources between the Admiralty, the army leadership and the treasury and investigate the immediate consequences for diplomacy *without* assuming the primacy of foreign policy. The whole debate about the relative primacy of domestic or foreign policy should be left to one side, or, even better, replaced by an assumption of interaction between the two. In the case of Britain, unlike Germany, we still know far too little about such interactions between foreign and domestic, about the backgrounds that shaped arms and naval strategies. Such re-evaluation will certainly lead to a more balanced view about Edward Grey, who still stands in the foreground, and will reveal more clearly his policy options and constraints and will bring attention to other figures, for example the director of military operations, General Henry Wilson, who deliberately presented a highly overestimated assessment of the German army strength while at the same time underestimating the strength of the entente powers during the legendary CID meeting on 23 August 1911.²⁸ The predominant focus until now has been on the perspective of the official mind, but that leaves the pluralist system in London wholly out of the equation. In addition, British foreign and security policies need to be understood in a multilateral context. By including Anglo-Russian, Anglo-French or Anglo-American relations, we can avoid over-emphasizing the role played by Germany – for better and for worse. This approach will allow us to see other antecedents, historical connections, and contemporary points of view and experiences, all of which will complete the picture of pre-war developments and decision processes. By adding a cultural perspective to the classic elements of political and diplomatic history, we can open a new window on the inner workings of British foreign policy – as in the case of the spy and invasion stories and their impact on the British pre-war public's risk perception. I should stress that my intention is not to propose a new paradigm to reinvent the wheel of history writing. But cultural aspects can certainly help explain decision-making processes in the investigation of statecraft and warfare and so shed fresh light on old questions. In this age of globalization, a study centred only on Europe will come up against its limitations fairly quickly; this is particularly true in the case of Great Britain, but applicable also for the other Great Powers before 1914. We should instead focus more on interactions on European and global levels, particularly in fracture zones like the Near East.

The Annexation Crisis marked the return of the Great Powers' attentions to the continent. Adding in the Anglo-Russian entente gives us a significant accumulation of pre-war turning points. At this point, contemporaries for the first time perceived the confrontational formation of the blocs: Triple Alliance versus Triple Entente. But the crisis also marks one of the averted wars before 1914, a topic that has garnered increasing attention in recent years, so much so that the 'inevitable war' topos[29] has been replaced by a topos of détente and avoided conflicts. Holger Afflerbach has even called the eventual outbreak of war an 'improbable' result.[30] Although the Balkan crisis did much damage to international diplomacy, war had not yet become inevitable. Radical liberal criticism of the government's pro-Russian stance, which continued right up until 1914, is a clear indication that Grey's entente policy was not unopposed. There were not a few who regarded the Annexation Crisis as a storm that had cleared the air, and who demanded a review of British policy towards Germany and of the putative German peril.[31] In the last analysis, it had not been traditional considerations or misgivings over the power balance that stood in the way of Grey seeking an even closer association with France and Russia, but above all the massive criticism from within his own ranks. Only the Conservative opposition had by then changed its mind and now advocated a policy of deterrence vis-à-vis the Central Powers, which put additional pressure on the government. In fact, after 1911, Balfour and Grey had switched sides as concerns foreign policy. While Grey tried to work for an international détente, Balfour appeared convinced about a German menace and demanded closer alliances with France and Russia to deter Berlin.[32]

Grey's biographer has described him as the last foreign secretary in the tradition of the nineteenth century,[33] but this label is in fact more accurate for the Whig Lansdowne. The first foreign secretary to sit in the Commons, Grey always had to take into account the moods in his own party, but he also had excellent media contacts, and waited for their approval; in fact, Grey seems rather to represent the first foreign secretary of the twentieth century. Influenced by infighting within his own party, he systematically worked to placate a foreign power that he believed to be too dangerous. He replaced the old flexible power-balance model with a form of collective security that would be guaranteed by having one dominant group of states.[34]

The triad of British domestic, European and imperial politics has also had an impact on the historiography of détente of recent years. Friedrich Kießling has plausibly shown that détentes and tensions were interdependent at an international level, so that every step towards rapprochement would cause a further tensing of the overall situation. Escalation was avoided several times, but this success did not make catastrophe any less likely, especially as each partial success brought with it a sort of desensitization to the risks inherent in the system. Closer inspection of the history of détente shows the lack of any room for manoeuvre for solutions that involved compensation on the periphery, and an unwillingness to implement a new order or negotiate across existing alliance constellations. It also shows that Grey increasingly lost the leverage over his partners and that by 1914 ultimate control of the system was in the hands of the entente powers – a fact that makes investigation of this formation more promising than the last several decades' focus on the Central Powers. The fact that London continued to present itself as accommodating to Paris and St Petersburg and was both unwilling and unable to take the lead within the entente, let alone within the entire states system, was a particularly aggravating factor.

The Haldane mission of 1912, which to this day is seen as a typical détente measure, was for Grey on the one hand a means to mollify the critics of his German policy within his own party and the Cabinet as it was on the other also a chance to place on the backburner the continuing problems with Russia and the Morgan Shuster business.[35] But for Grey, maintenance of the entente counted above all else, and he made it repeatedly clear that neither France nor Russia needed to worry about his loyalty.[36] Lessening Anglo-German tensions, though a major interest after 1911, came only second on his list of priorities. Even after the Annexation Crisis, London continued to encourage Russia and the Balkan states to form an anti-Austrian Balkan League; it supported Russian-Italian cooperation in the Adriatic as well as Italy's war against Tripoli.[37]

At the ambassadorial conference in London, the British foreign secretary even ostentatiously declined to play the role of arbitrator. The decisive factor here was not that Grey had suggested the conference (a fact Kießling recently stressed as illustrative of Grey's amenability to détente[38]) but that he declined to take more responsibility, and that during negotiations over the Albanian border – an issue of great importance to Austria-Hungary – he finally took the side of Serbia and Russia.[39] Instead of containing Russian habits of mischief, Grey believed he had no choice but to appease the Russians.[40] Grey's brokerage at this phase was undermined from three sides – by his entente partners, by his own staff in the Foreign Office and by his colleagues in the cabinet. While his proposal for a joint naval demonstration in the eastern Mediterranean[41] met with procrastination by St Petersburg and Paris,[42] Arthur Nicolson in particular was constantly alarmed at offending the Russians.[43] The cabinet – quarrelling over the entente with France since the 'revolt' in 1911[44] – at the same time declined any measures without the approval of the Quay d'Orsay. Winston Churchill in particular warned against drawing Britain 'into any position distinct from that of France and Russia, and still less into giving any kind of support to Austria'. The unity of the Triple Entente, therefore, claimed priority over arbitration.[45] Writing to Goschen, on 23 April 1913, the foreign secretary complained about the entente partners, especially about Russia's active encouragement of Serbia.[46] However, this insight was not followed by any consequences for Anglo-Russian relations. For the Central Powers, the situation confirmed again their impressions that they were being outvoted by the entente powers. For Edward Grey, the survival of the Austro-Hungarian monarchy and the status quo in the Balkans was of only secondary importance.[47] What mattered to him was that Britain should be significantly involved in all developments, and that a solution between the powers of the Triple and Dual Alliances through a balancing of tensions should be made impossible. That this goal was reached can be seen from the 1911 Potsdam Agreement between Germany and Russia. Although Berlin had accommodated London's demand for an agreement over the Baghdad railway question involving all four powers, Whitehall reacted with bitterness, felt cheated and saw only further proof of the perfidy of the Wilhelmstrasse.[48]

The approval of Anglo-Russian naval talks is a further case in point, for they reveal Britain's dilemma in reacting to new developments and distancing itself from its entente policy, even though by 1913 there was no objective need, and certainly no balance of power necessity, to continue to support the tsardom.[49] By then it was already clear that Germany had fallen behind militarily and appeared rather desperate[50] against Russia, the 'most powerful factor in Europe'.[51] None other than H.G. Wells eventually revised his estimation of the (in)famous German peril, stating in 1913 that the past years had shown nothing so much as Germany's inability to wage war.[52]

Balfour and Lansdowne had used their own unpredictability to keep their partners at arm's length and so retain control of their associations. Their successors let that control slip away. During the first Moroccan Crisis, Lansdowne had unambiguously snubbed Metternich, but not told France about his threat, while in December 1912 Grey conveyed his warnings to Germany directly to Cambon.[53] The difference might appear subtle at first glance, but it was decisive for maintaining stability. For the Tories, the alliance with Japan and the Entente Cordiale had been 'tools of management'[54] for the states system. Their successors encouraged international communication, but their continuous partisanship in decisive questions undermined the legitimacy of the international order, making it unattractive to the Central Powers in the long run. They declared early on that the entente was central to their endeavours, and they made its significance clear to their partner at every opportunity. Russia repeatedly needed to be appeased and diverted from Central Asia to the Balkans.

The mere approval of naval talks in early 1914 had brought the Russian ambassador to the conviction that already the 'spirit of the Entente' would represent 'a powerful guarantee for common military action in the event of war'.[55] It is certainly true that London until the war had no formal obligation to come to the assistance of its entente partners. But these legal formalities were soon contradicted by political and military realities. The expectations of contemporaries did not stop at the contractual limits; they went beyond them. And with every crisis and international question, it turned out to be more difficult to remain free handed on the one hand and at the same time a loyal partner on the other. Of course, one cannot judge Edward Grey and his diplomacy by the perceptions or misperceptions of others. But it could not remain unnoticed in Whitehall that Russia as well as France felt increasingly confident as concerns Britain's backing.[56]

Hardinge, Buchanan and Nicolson again and again impressed on their staff that an unfriendly Germany was preferable by far to an unfriendly France or Russia.[57] There is no question that London watched the rise of Germany with great suspicion, but by 1913/14 Britain was deterred from taking a neutral and accommodating role primarily by the cul-de-sac of its entente diplomacy and the impressive revitalization of the Russian Empire. Grey finally gave in to those who were 'haunted by the fear, that Russia might become tired of us and strike a bargain with Germany'.[58] The foreign secretary's approval of Anglo-Russian naval talks in early 1914 and his public lying about it destroyed his credit as an arbiter completely. It caused a devastating shock in Berlin, 'the last link in the chain of German encirclement',[59] directly leading to the fatal German decisions during the July Crisis, feeling they no longer had anything to lose, to trust their sole partner Austria-Hungary blindly and finally to play vabanque.

In the knowledge of Franco-Russian ambitions, and of growing German fears and Russian revitalization, Grey had repeatedly encouraged Russia during the Balkan Wars, by approving Anglo-Russian naval talks and finally by declining to restrain Russia during the July Crisis.[60] Until the very last day of the July Crisis Edward Grey's interventionist course, backed only by Churchill and Asquith, represented a minority position.[61] Decisions made in London in Summer 1914 thus repeated a model also found in other capital cities, as Grey and the Cabinet gambled on writing cheques that they hoped would never be cashed.

Notes

1. Palmerston (Commons), 1 March 1848, cited in Bourne, *Foreign Policy of Victorian England*, No. 49, 291–93.
2. Charmley, *Splendid Isolation*, 399.
3. Salisbury to MacColl, 6 Sept. 1901, cited in Russell, *Malcolm MacColl*, 282–83.
4. Steed, *Through Thirty Years*, Vol. 1, 255.

5. See, for example, the Convention on Cyprus (1878), the Mediterranean Agreement (1887) or the Agreement on Portuguese Colonies (1899).
6. Balfour, Memorandum, 12 Dec. 1901, cited in Bourne, *Foreign Policy of Victorian England*, No. 139, 471–74.
7. Marder, *Anatomy of British Sea Power*, 465; Kennedy, *Rise of Anglo-German Antagonism*, 251.
8. Schöllgen and Kießling, *Imperialismus*, 189.
9. Seligmann, *Royal Navy and the German Threat*. See also Rose, 'Review on Matthew Seligmann'; Lambert, 'Righting the Scholarship'.
10. Balfour to Lascelles, 2 Jan. 1905, BL, MSS Balfour, Add. 49711.
11. Balfour, Memorandum, June 1904, BL, MSS Balfour, Add. 497727.
12. Gillard, *Great Game*, 172–73.
13. Not only in this sense the diplomacy of Edward Grey did everything but resemble a 'Bismarckian strategy' as recently has been suggested. For this see Otte, 'Postponing the Evil Day: Sir Edward Grey and British Foreign Policy', in IHR 38 (2016), 250–263, esp. 253. Review by Rose, H-Diplo-Roundtable.
14. Sanderson to Spring Rice, 6 Aug. 1907, NA, FO 800/241.
15. Clark, *Sleepwalkers*, 353.
16. Hardinge to de Salis, 29 Dec. 1908, CUL, MSS Hardinge, Vol. 13.
17. Goschen to Grey, 2 Apr. 1909, NA, FO 371/733.
18. 'We are told that we are in the right.' Milovanovich, cited in Glenny, *The Balkans*, 292.
19. Maxse, *Germany on the Brain*, 67.
20. Luhmann, 'Öffentliche Meinung', 27.
21. Paulmann, *Pomp und Politik*, 130–79.
22. On the Zeppelin scare, see Gollin, *No Longer an Island*, 315–21.
23. Esher, Diary, 14 March 1908, CC, ESHR 2/11.
24. Metz, *Industrialisierung*, 294; Webb, 'Rosebery's Escape' (1901), in Brennan, *Education for National Efficiency*, 63.
25. Stevenson, 'Militarization and Diplomacy in Europe before 1914', 125–61; Hermann, *Arming*, 3–7.
26. 'The New Scare about the Navy', *The Nation*, 6 Feb. 1909, 700.
27. Charmley, *Splendid Isolation*, 347.
28. Wilson presented to his audience that Germany commanded 121 divisions while in fact in 1910 Germany did not have more than 97 divisions, while the French number should have been 93 (not 75) and the Russian 142 (not 78). Wilson, 20 Sept. 1911, NA, WO 106/47; see also Fiedler, *Taktik*, 113; Ehlert et al., *Schlieffenplan*, 443.
29. Mommsen, 'Topos vom unvermeidlichen Krieg', in Mommsen, *Nationalstaat*, 380–406.
30. Kießling, *Krieg*, 287; Afflerbach, 'Topos of Improbable War', in Afflerbach and Stevenson, *Improbable War*, 161–82.
31. Gardiner, The Perils of Secret Diplomacy, *Daily News*, 16 Nov. 1911; Ponsonby (Reform Club), 14 Nov. 1911, *Manchester Guardian*, 15. Nov. 1911.
32. McDonough, *Conservative Party*, 48; Blunt, *Diaries*, Vol. 2, 418–19.
33. Robbins, *Sir Edward Grey*, 372.
34. See Kennedy, 'Tradition of Appeasement'.
35. Murray, *British Policy*, 493–534.
36. Gade, *Gleichgewichtspolitik*, 148, n. 12; Benckendorff to Sazonov, 8 Feb. 1912, BDS II, No. 27, 748.

37. Schroeder, 'World War I as Galloping Gertie'; Schroeder, 'Stealing Horses'.
38. Kießling, *Krieg*, 181.
39. Gade, *Gleichgewichtspolitik*, 182.
40. Grey to Nicolson, 24 April 1913, NA, MSS Nicolson, FO 800/366.
41. Grey to Churchill, 12 March 1913, USL, MSS Mountbatten, MB1/T24/200.
42. Pourtalès to AA, 26 March 1913, GP 34. 34/2, No. 13024, 559–60.
43. Nicolson to Goschen, 14 Jan. 1913, NA, FO 800/362; to Cartwright, 30 April 1913, MSS Cartwright, PRO Northampton, Box 42.
44. Nicolson to A. Chamberlain, May 1912, cited in Chamberlain, *Politics from Inside*, 486, see also: JL III, 74;
45. Churchill to Lloyd George, 2 April 1913, PA, LG/C/3/15/21A; see also BD IX/2, Nos. 772, 779, 789.
46. Grey to Goschen, 23 April 1913, BD IX/2, No. 790; Cabinet, 24 April 1913, NA, CAB 41/34/15. See also Soroka, *Britain, Russia and the Road to the First World War*, 233–34.
47. A different view is provided by Crampton, *Hollow Détente*, 80.
48. Hardinge to Nicolson, 2 Feb. 1911, CUL, MSS Hardinge, Vol. 92. See also Steiner, *Britain and the Origins*, 66.
49. Steiner, *Foreign Office and Foreign Policy*, 136–37.
50. Buchanan to Nicolson, 17 April 1913, NA, MSS Nicolson, FO 800/365; Henry Wilson, Minute, 27 March 1914, NA, WO 106/1039; Nicolson to Goschen, 27 April 1914, NA, MSS Nicolson, FO 800/373. See also Neilson, 'Watching the Steamroller', 212.
51. Nicolson to Buchanan, 8 April 1913, NA, MSS Nicolson, FO 800/365.
52. 'The amazing thing to note is that they [the Germans] were not prepared to fight, they had not the money they had perhaps never intended to fight, and the autumn saw the danger disperse again into diplomatic bickering.' Cited in Müllenbrock, *Literatur und Zeitgeschichte*, 184. This impression was shared by Hilaire Belloc. Blunt, *Diaries*, Vol. 2, 419–20.
53. Grey to Lascelles, 9 Jan. 1906, BD III, No 229, 209–11; Grey to Bertie, 31 Jan. 1906, BD III, No. 219, 180–82; Clark, *Sleepwalkers*, 358.
54. Schroeder, 'Alliances'.
55. Benckendorff to Sazonov, 5 May 1914, cited in Siebert, *Entente Diplomacy*, No. 846, 719–20, 720.
56. See Schmdit, 'Révanche pour Sedan'.
57. Nicolson to Goschen, 15 April 1912, BD VI, No. 575, 747. 'Hope that Russia may be pre-occupied for some years to come in the Near East with the interests of the Slav races, so that those who favour a forward policy in Asia may receive no encouragement.' Hardinge to Nicolson, 16 May 1913, NA, FO 800/367.
58. Cited in Morris, *Edwardian Radicalism*, 364.
59. Theobald von Bethmann Hollweg, cited in Stern, 'Bethmann Hollweg and the War', 263.
60. Newton, *Darkest Days*, 109.
61. Morley, *Memorandum on Resignation*; Wilson, Decisions, 175–208; Wilson, 'The British Cabinet's decision for War, 2. August 1914', 148–159. On the role of David Lloyd George see Rose, 'Lloyd George', forthcoming.

BIBLIOGRAPHY

A. Archival Sources

Birmingham University Library [BUL], Birmingham
Austen Chamberlain; Joseph Chamberlain

Bodleian Library [BOD], Oxford
Microfilm of Correspondence from the Royal Archives on the Oriental Question
Oxford Anglo-German Society, Minute Book MSS Top. Oxon. D. 239
Maurice De Bunsen; Eyre A. Crowe; Howell A. Gwynne; William Harcourt; Lewis Harcourt; Lord Kimberley; Edmund Monson; John Morley; Francis Oppenheimer; Arthur Ponsonby; George Rumbold; John S. Sandars; Lord Selborne

British Library [BL], London
Hugh O. Arnold-Forster; Arthur J. Balfour; George S. Clarke; Charles W. Dilke; Herbert J. Gladstone; William E. Gladstone; Henry Campbell-Bannerman; A. Harmsworth; Lord Lansdowne LANS (unnumbered); Raymond J. Marker; Lord Ripon; Charles St. Scott; John A. Spender

British Library of Political and Economic Science [BLPES], London
J.H. Mackinder: 'Printed Minutes of the Coefficient Dining Club, 1902–1908' Assoc 17/MF160

Bundesarchiv-Militärarchiv [BA-MA], Freiburg
Reichsmarineamt, Operations against England, 1896–1909: RM 5/1609; RM 5/1610
Anglo-German relations, RM 3/9762

Cambridge University Library [CUL], Cambridge
Charles Hardinge

Churchill College Archive Centre [CC], Cambridge
Cecil A. Spring Rice (CASR); George Saunders (SAUN GS); David H. Saunders (SAUN DHS)
Nicholas O'Conor (OCON); Frank Lascelles (LASC); William T. Stead (STED); Viscount Esher (ESHR); Leo S. Amery (AMEL); Archibald S. Hurd (HURD); John A. Fisher (FISHR); Winston S. Churchill (CHAR and CHUR); Reginald McKenna (MCKN)

Geheimes Staatsarchiv Preußischer Kulturbesitz (GStA)
BPH Brandenburg-Preußisches Hausarchiv: Papers of Eugen Zimmermann

Guildhall Library [GL], London
Annual Reports of the Council of the Corporation of Foreign Bondholders (CFB)

Hatfield House [HH], Hatfield (Hertfordshire)
Robert Cecil (Lord Salisbury)

Haus-, Hof- und Staatsarchiv [HHStA], Vienna
Graf Mensdorff
Politisches Archiv, VIII (England)   Politisches Archiv XII (Liasse XXXIX)
Kt. 140 Berichte I–V, 1908   Kt. 358 Misc. England, 1908
Kt. 141 Berichte VI–XII, 1908
Kt. 142 Weisungen, 1908

Imperial War Museum [IWM], London
Vernon G.W. Kell, Sir Henry Wilson

Institute of Historical Research [Inst.HR], London
'Queen Victoria on Foreign Affairs' (Microfilm)

Library of Congress [LoC], Washington
Alfred Th. Mahan

Liddell Hart Centre for Military Archives [LHCMA], King's College London
William R. Robertson (ROB)

The National Archives [NA], Kew
Admiralty Papers (ADM): ADM 1; 53; 116; 137; 231; 256; 344; 1036B; 1058; 4058
Cabinet Papers (CAB): 1–6; 8; 16; 17; 37; 38; 41
Foreign Office (FO): 5; 7; 15; 17, 27, 64, 65, 78, 80, 120; 371; 414; 420; 881
Secret Service (SS): KV 1–20; FO 1093/45; HD 3/124; HD 3/132
War Office (WO): 32; 33; 105; 106; 280
John Ardagh; Francis Bertie; St. John Brodrick; Lord Cromer; Eyre A. Crowe; Edward Grey; Viscount Kitchener; Walter Langley; Frank Lascelles; Arthur Nicolson; Lord Lansdowne; Thomas Sanderson; Cecil Spring Rice; Arminius Vambéry; Frank Villiers

National Archives of Scotland [NAS], Edinburgh
Sir Spencer Ewart   RH 4/84/2–3 [NRAS 1054/79; 81C; 114; 124–25]

National Army Museum [NAM], Ogilby Trust, London
Frederick Sleigh (Lord) Roberts

National Library of Scotland [NLS], Edinburgh
Richard B. Haldane; Lord Rosebery

National Maritime Museum [NMM], London (Greenwich)
Julian S. Corbett (CBT); Herbert Richmond (RIC); Edmund Slade (MRF)

News International Archives, Times Archives [NIA], London
Foreign Editor's Letter Books [FELB]
Charles F. Moberly Bell; E. Moberly Bell; James D. Bourchier; G.E. Buckle; Valentine Chirol; George Dobson; William Lavino; George Saunders; Henry W. Steed; Richard J. Thursfield

Norfolk Record Office [NRO]
Henry W. Massingham

Oriental and African Manuscripts, India Office Library, British Library [IOL], London
George N. Curzon; George Hamilton; John Morley; Lord Ampthill

Parliamentary Archives [PA], London
John St. Loe Strachey (STR); Andrew Bonar Law (BL); David Lloyd George (LG)

Politisches Archiv des Auswärtigen Amtes [PA-AA], Berlin
R 1161; 1166; 5563–5585; 5615–5635; 5644; 5645; 5648; 5735; 5736; 5777; 5778; 5959–5963; 6093

University of Southampton, Hartley Library [USL], Southampton
Prince Louis of Battenberg

West Sussex Record Office [WSRO], Chichester (Sussex)
Leopold J. Maxse (MAXSE)

B. Newspapers and Periodicals

The Daily Chronicle (Liberal); *The Daily Express* (Independent Conservative); *The Daily Graphic* (Independent Conservative); *The Daily Mail* (Right-Wing Conservative); *The Daily Mirror* (Independent); *Daily News* (Liberal); *The Daily Telegraph* (Conservative); *Financial News* (Independent); *Manchester Guardian* (Independent Liberal); *Morning Post* (Conservative); *The Pall Mall Gazette* (Conservative); *Westminster Gazette* (Liberal); *The Times* (Independent Conservative); *The Observer* (Liberal); *The Saturday Review* (Conservative); *The Spectator* (Independent Conservative); *Freeman's Journal and Daily Commercial Advertiser* (Liberal); *The Bristol Mercury and Daily Post*; *Aberdeen Weekly Journal*; *The Glasgow Herald*; *The National Review* (Right-Wing Conservative); *The Speaker* (Independent Radical); *The Nation* (Independent Radical); *The Imperial Review*; *The Nineteenth Century (and After)* (Liberal); *Economist* (Independent); *Macmillan's Magazine* (Liberal); *Fortnightly Review* (Liberal); *The Quarterly Review* (Conservative); *Blackwood's Magazine* (Conservative); *Contemporary Review* (Liberal); *Edinburgh Review* (Liberal Unionist); *Journal of the Royal United Service Institution* (RUSI); *United Service Magazine*; *Harper's Monthly Magazine*; *Punch*; *Monthly Review*; *The Outlook*; *English Review*; *The Living Age*; *Current Literature*; *North American Review*; *Geographical Journal*; *Pall Mall Magazine*; *The Nation* (New York); *Journal of the Society of Arts*; *Preußische Jahrbücher*; *Nauticus*

C. Official Sources

Amtliche Aktenstücke zur Geschichte der Europäischen Politik 1871–1914 [Die Belgischen Dokumente zur Vorgeschichte des Weltkrieges] im Auftrage des Auswärtigen Amtes, ed. Bernhard Schwertfeger et al., 5 Vols., Berlin 1918–1925.

Die Auswärtige Politik Serbiens 1903–1914, ed. M. Boghitschewitsch, 3 Vols., Berlin 1928–1931 [APS].

British Documents on Foreign Affairs: Reports and Papers from the Foreign Office Confidential Print, Part I: From the Mid-Nineteenth Century to the First World War (Series A, D, E, F), ed. Kenneth Bourne and Donald Cameron Watt et al., 1983–1991 [BDFA].

British Documents on the Origins of the War, 1898–1914, ed. George Peabody Gooch and Harold Temperley, 11 Vols., London 1926–1938 [BD].

British Parliamentary Papers, Accounts and Papers, London 1901–1905 [AP].

Documents Diplomatiques Français (1871–1914), ed. Ministère des Affaires Étrangères, Commission de Publication des Documents relatifs aux Origines de la Guerre de 1914, 2. Sér., 14 Vols. (1901–11), Paris 1930–1955 [DDF].
Die Große Politik der Europäischen Kabinette 1871–1914: Sammlung der diplomatischen Aktenstücke des Auswärtigen Amtes, ed. Johannes Lepsius et al., 40 Vols. in 54 Parts, Berlin 1922–1927 [GP].
Hansard's Parliamentary Debates (Authorized Edition), 3rd to 5th Series, 1892–1909 [PD].
House of Commons Parliamentary Papers. Command Papers (1890–1914) [Cd.].
Österreich-Ungarns Außenpolitik von der Bosnischen Krise 1908 bis zum Kriegsausbruch 1914: Diplomatische Aktenstücke des österreichisch-ungarischen Ministeriums des Äußern, ed. by Ludwig Bittner und Helmut Uebersberger, 9 Vols., Vienna and Leipzig 1930.

D. Personal and other published Sources

Amery, Leo S., *My Political Life*, Vol. 1 (1896–1914), London 1953.
Anon. [Die Schriftleitung, Krasny Archiv, Vol. XVIII, Foreword by M. Pokrowski, 'Die zaristische Diplomatie über Rußlands Aufgaben im Orient im Jahre 1900', in *Berliner Monatshefte* 6/1928, pp. 638–70.
Arnold-Forster, Mary, *Memoir of H.O. Arnold Forster*, London 1910.
Asquith, Herbert H., *Memories and Recollections*, 2 Vols., London 1928.
———, *Der Ursprung des Krieges*, Munich 1924.
Asquith, Margot, *The Autobiography of Margot Asquith*, 3 Vols., London 1920.
Baernreither, Joseph Maria, *Fragmente eines politischen Tagebuchs: Die südslawische Frage und Österreich-Ungarn vor dem Weltkrieg*, Berlin 1928.
Balfour, Arthur J., *Chapters of Autobiography*, London 1930.
Barclay, Thomas, *Thirty Years of Anglo-French Reminiscences*, London 1914.
Basily, Nicolas de, *Diplomat of Imperial Russia 1903–1917, Memoirs*, Stanford 1973.
Beatty, David, *The Beatty Papers: Selections from the Private and Official Correspondence of Admiral of the Fleet Earl Beatty*, ed. Bryan Ranft (=NRS, Vol. 128), Vol. 1: 1902–1918, London 1989.
Bell, Enid H.C. Moberly, *Life and Letters of C.F. Moberley Bell*, London 1927.
Benckendorff, Alexander Graf von, *Graf Benckendorffs diplomatischer Schriftwechsel*, ed. by Benno von Siebert, 3 Vols., Berlin and Leipzig 1928.
Bernstorff, Johann von, *Memoirs*, London 1936.
Bismarck, Otto von, *Die gesammelten Werke*, 15 Vols., Berlin 1924–32.
Bing, E.J. (Ed.), *The Secret Letters of the Last Tsar: The Confidential Correspondence between Nicholas II and His Mother, Dowager Empress Marie Federovna*, New York 1938.
Blatchford, Robert, *My Eighty Years*, London 1931.
Blumenfeld, Ralph D., *RDB's Diary, 1887–1914*, London 1930.
Blunt, Wilfrid Scawen, *My Diaries, Being a Personal Narrative of Events, 1888–1914*, 2 Vols., London 1919–1920.
Bompard, Maurice, *Mon Ambassade en Russie, 1903–1908*, Paris 1937.
Boyce, George D. (Ed.), *The Crisis of British Power: The Imperial and Naval Papers of the Second Earl of Selborne, 1895–1910*, 2 Vols., London 1990.
Brett, Maurice V., and Viscount Esher (Eds.), *Journals and Letters of Reginald Viscount Esher*, 4 Vols., London 1938.

Brock, M., and E. Brock (Eds.), *Herbert H. Asquith: Letters to Venetia Stanley*, Oxford 1982.
Buchanan, George, *My Mission to Russia and Other Diplomatic Memoirs*, 2 Vols., London 1923.
Buckle, George Earle (Ed.), *The Letters of Queen Victoria, Third Series: A Selection from Her Majesty's Correspondence and Journal between the Years 1886 and 1901*, Vol. 3, 1896–1901, London 1932.
Bülow, Bernhard Fürst von, *Denkwürdigkeiten, Vol. 1: Vom Staatssekretariat bis zur Marokko-Krise*, ed. Franz von Stockhammern, Berlin 1930.
Bülow, Bernhard, *Memoirs*, transl. By F.A. Voigt and G. Dunlop, 4 Vols., Boston 1931–32.
Caillaux, Joseph, *Mes Mémoires*, Vol. 1, Paris 1942.
Callwell, Charles E., *Sir Henry Wilson: His Life and Diaries*, London 1927.
Cambon, Paul, *Correspondance, 1870–1924*, ed. H. Cambon, 3 Vols., Paris 1940–1946.
Chamberlain, Austen, *Down the Years*, London 1935.
———, *Politics from Inside*, London 1936.
———, *Sir Austen Chamberlain: Englische Politik*, ed. F. Pick, 2nd ed., Essen 1938.
Chirol, Valentine, *Fifty Years in a Changing World*, London 1927.
Churchill, Winston S., *Weltabenteuer im Dienst*, Hamburg 1951.
———, *Great Contemporaries*, London 1937.
Conan Doyle, Arthur, *Memories and Adventures*, London 1924.
Conrad von Hötzendorf, Franz, *Aus meiner Dienstzeit 1906–1918*, 5 Vols., Vienna 1921–1925.
Conwell-Evans, Thomas P., *Foreign Policy from a Back Bench, 1904–1918*, London 1932.
Delbrück, E., et al. (Eds.), *Schultheß' Europäischer Geschichtskalender*, New Series, 34 Vols. (1885–1918), Nördlingen and Munich 1886–1922.
Dilke, Charles Wentworth, *Greater Britain: A Record of Travel in English-Speaking Countries*, London 1869.
Drummond-Wolff, Henry, *Rambling Reflections*, 2 Vols., London 1908.
Eckardstein, Hermann Frhr. von, *Lebenserinnerungen und politische Denkwürdigkeiten*, 3 Vols., Leipzig 1919–1921.
———, *Ten Years at the Court of St. James 1895–1905*, London 1921.
Edel, Leon, *Henry James: Selected Letters*, London 1974.
Fisher, H.H. (Ed.), *Out of My Past: The Memoirs of Count Vladimir N. Kokovtsov*, Stanford, 1935.
Fisher, John, *Memories and Records*, New York 1920.
Fisher of Kilverstone, John, *Fear God and Dread Nought: The Correspondence of Admiral of the Fleet Lord Fisher of Kilverstone*, ed. Arthur J. Marder, 3 Vols., London 1960–1964.
Friedjung, Heinrich, *Geschichte in Gesprächen, Aufzeichnungen 1898–1919*, ed. F. Adlgasser and M. Friedrich, 2 Vols., Vienna 1997.
Garvin, James L., *Garvin: A Memoir*, London 1948.
Gibbs, Peter, *Adventures in Journalism*, London 1923.
Graves, Robert, *Storm Centres of the Near East: Personal Memories, 1879–1929*, London 1933.
Gregory, J.D., *On the Edge of Diplomacy: Rambles and Reflections, 1902–1928*, London 1929.
Grey, Edward, *25 Years: 1892–1916*, 2 Vols., London 1925.
———, *Speeches on Foreign Affairs, 1904–1914*, ed. Paul Knaplund, London 1931.
Gwy, Stephen L., *The Life of the Rt. Hon. Sir Charles W. Dilke, Bart., M.P.*, London 1917.
Gwynn, Stephen (Ed.), *The Letters and Friendships of Cecil Spring Rice*, 2 Vols., London 1929.
Gwynn, Stephen, and Gertrude M. Tuchwell (Eds.), *The Life of Sir Charles W. Dilke*, 2 Vols., London 1917–1918.

Haldane, Richard B., *An Autobiography*, London 1929.
———, *Before the War*, London 1920.
Hamilton, Lord George, *Parliamentary Reminiscences and Reflections*, Vol. 2: 1886–1906, London 1922.
Harris, W., *Spender*, London 1946.
Hatzfeldt, Paul von, *Nachgelassene Papiere 1838–1901*, 2 Parts, ed. by Gerhard Ebel, Boppard 1976.
Hayashi, Tadasu, *The Secret Memoirs of Count Tadasu Hayashi*, ed. by Andrew M. Pooley, New York 1915.
Hewins, William, *Apologia of an Imperialist*, London 1929.
Hicks-Beach, Lady Victoria, *Life of Sir Michael Hicks Beach, Earl St. Aldwyn*, 2 Vols., London 1932.
Hirst, Francis, *The Six Panics*, London 1913.
Hoetzsch, Otto (Ed.), *Peter von Meyendorff: Ein russischer Diplomat an den Höfen von Berlin und Wien. Politischer und privater Briefwechsel 1826–1863*, 3 Vols., Berlin 1923.
Holstein, Friedrich von, *Die geheimen Papiere Friedrich von Holsteins*, ed. by N. Rich and M.H. Fischer, German Edition by Werner Frauendienst, Göttingen, Berlin, Frankfurt a.M. 1956–1957.
Howard, C.H.D. (Ed.), *The Diary of Edward Goschen 1900–1914*, London 1980.
Hui-min, Lo (Ed.), *The Correspondence of G.E. Morrison*, 2 Vols., Cambridge 1976.
Hurst, Michael, *Key Treaties for the Great Powers 1814–1914*, 2 Vols., London 1972.
Iswolski, Alexander, *Au Service de la Russie*, Paris 1937.
———, *The Memoirs of Alexander Iswolsky*, ed. Charles L. Seeger, London 1920.
———, *Der Diplomatische Schriftwechsel Iswolskis, 1911–1914*, ed. by Fridrich Stieve, 4 Vols., Berlin 1924.
Jäckh, Ernst (Ed.), *Kiderlen-Wächter: der Staatsmann und Mensch. Briefwechsel und Nachlass*, 2. Vols., Berlin and Leipzig 1924.
Joll, James (Ed.), *Britain and Europe: Pitt to Churchill 1793–1940*, London 1950.
Kemp, Peter (Ed.), *The Papers of Admiral Sir John Fisher*, 2 Vols., London 1960-64.
Kessel, Eberhard (Ed.), *Moltke Gespräche*, Hamburg 1940.
Kohl, Horst (Ed.), *Die politischen Reden des Fürsten Bismarck: Historisch-Kritische Gesamtausgabe*, 13 Vols., Stuttgart 1905 (Reprint Aalen 1970).
Kühlmann, Richard von, *Erinnerungen*, Heidelberg 1948.
Lambert, Nicholas (Ed.), *The Submarine Service, 1900–1918* (=NRS, Vol. 142), Aldershot 2001.
Le Queux, William, *Things I Know about Kings, Celebrities and Crooks*, London 1923.
Lloyd George, David, *War Memoirs*, 6 Vols., London 1933.
Lubbock, Percy (Ed.), *Letters of Henry James*, London 1920.
MacColl, Malcolm, *Memoirs and Correspondence*, ed. by George W.E. Russell, London 1914.
Mackail, John William, and Guy Wyndham, *Life and Letters of George Wyndham*, Vol. 1, London 1925.
Marwick, Arthur, *The Deluge: British Society and the First World War*, London 1965.
Melgunov, Sergej P. (Ed.), *Nikolaus II, Das Tagebuch des letzten Zaren von 1890 bis zum Fall: Nach den unveröffentlichten russischen Handschriften*, Berlin 1923.
Meyendorff, A. (Ed.), *Le Correspondence diplomatique de M. de Staal (1884–1900)*, 2 Vols., Paris 1929.
Minto, M., *India. Minto and Morley 1905–1910*, London 1934.

Morley, John, *Recollections*, 2 Vols., New York 1917.
———, *Memorandum on Resignation*, London 1928.
Morris, Andrew J.A. (Ed.), *The Letters of Lieutenant-Colonel Charles à Court Repington CMG Military Correspondent of The Times, 1903–1918*, London 1999.
Rich, Norman and M.H. Fisher, *The Holstein Papers*, 4 Vols., Cambridge 1963.
Roberts, Frederick Sleigh, *Speeches and Letters of Field Marshal Earl Roberts, K.G. on Imperial Defence*, ed. by the National Service League, London 1906.
Rosebery, Archibald Philip Primrose, Earl of, *Lord Rosebery's Speeches*, London 1896.
Sasonow, Sergej D., *Sechs schwere Jahre*, Berlin 1927.
Savinsky, Alexander, *Recollections of a Russian Diplomat*, London (no year).
Seligmann, Matthew (Ed.), *Naval Intelligence from Germany: The Reports of the British Naval Attachés in Berlin 1906–1914* (=NRS, Vol. 152), Aldershot 2007.
——— et al., *The Naval Route to the Abyss: The Anglo-German Naval Race 1895–1914*, Farnham 2015.
Siebert, Benno von (Ed.), *Diplomatische Aktenstücke zur Geschichte der Ententepolitik der Vorkriegsjahre*, 2 Vols., Berlin und Leipzig 1921.
———, *Entente Diplomacy and the World: Matrix of the History of Europe 1909–1914*, London 1921.
Snowdon, Philip, *An Autobiography*, Vol. 1, London 1934.
Spender, John A., *Life, Journalism and Politics*, London 1927.
———, *The Life of the Right Hon. Sir Henry Campbell-Bannerman*, Vol. 2, London 1923.
———, *The Public Life*, London 1925.
Steed, Henry W., *Through Thirty Years, 1892–1922: A Personal Narrative*, 2 Vols., New York 1922.
Strachey, Amy, *St. Loe Strachey: His Life and His Paper*, London 1930.
Strachey, John St. Loe, *The Adventure of Living*, London 1922.
Suvorin, Aleksej S., *Das Geheimtagebuch*, Berlin 1925.
Taube, Michael Frhr. von, *Der großen Katastrophe entgegen: Die russische Politik der Vorkriegszeit und das Ende des Zarenreiches (1904–1917). Erinnerungen*, 2nd ed., Leipzig 1937.
———, *La Politique Russe d'avant-guerre et la fin de l'Empire des Tsars, 1904–1917*, Leroux 1928.
Temple Patterson, A., *The Jellicoe Papers*, 2 Vols., London 1966–1968.
Thies, Henning (Ed.), *Kindlers Neues Literatur Lexikon: Hauptwerke der englischen Literatur. Einzeldarstellungen und Interpretationen*, 2 Vols., Munich 1995.
Tirpitz, Alfred von, *Erinnerungen*, 5th ed., Berlin and Leipzig 1927.
———, *Politische Dokumente*, Vol. 1: Der Aufbau der deutschen Weltmacht, Berlin 1924.
Tscharykow, Nikolaj V., *Glimpses of High Politics through War and Peace, 1855–1929*, London 1931.
Walters, Eurof, 'Franco-Russian Discussion on the Partition of Austro-Hungary, 1899', in *Slavonic and East European Review* 28 (1949/1950), pp. 184–97.
———, 'Unpublished Documents: Lord Salisbury's Refusal to Revise and Renew the Mediterranean Agreements', in *Slavonic and East European Review* 29 (1929/1930), pp. 267–285.
———, 'Unpublished Documents: Aehrenthal's Attempt in 1907 to Re-Group the European Powers', in *Slavonic and East European Review* 30 (1951/1952), pp. 213–51.
———, 'Unpublished Documents: Austro-Russian Relations under Goluchowski, 1895–1906', in *Slavonic and East European Review* 31 (1952/1953), pp. 212–31, pp. 503–27.

———, 'Unpublished Documents: Austro-Russian Relations under Goluchowski, 1895–1906', in *Slavonic and East European Review* 32 (1953/1954), pp. 187–214.
Wank, Solomon (Ed.), *Aus dem Nachlaß Aehrenthal: Briefe und Dokumente zur österreichisch-ungarischen Innen- und Außenpolitik 1885–1912*, 2 Vols., Graz 1994.
White, Arnold, *Efficiency and Empire*, London 1901.
Wilkinson, Henry S., *Thirty-five Years*, London 1933.
———, *Britain at Bay*, London 1909.
———, *The Great Alternative*, London 1894.
———, *Volunteers and the National Defence*, London 1896.
———, *The Nation's Need*, London 1903.
———, 'Eyre Crowe', in *Dictionary of National Biography*, pp. 219–21.

E. Contemporary Publications

Amery, Leopold, *The Times History of the War in South Africa 1899–1900*, London 1900.
Angell, Norman (Pseudonym: Ralph Lane), *The Public Mind*, London 1927.
Anon., *The Channel Tunnel, or England's Ruin*, London 1876.
Anon., *The German Invasion of England*, London 1910.
Anon., *How John Bull Lost London*, London 1882.
Arnold-Forster, Hugh O., *Military Needs and Military Policy*, London 1908.
Ashton-Gwatkin, Frank, 'William Tyrrell', in *Dictionary of National Biography*, Vol. 19, pp. 893–96.
Baden Powell, Robert, *German Plans for Invading England*, London 1908.
Bagehot, Walter, *Great and Greater Britain*, London 1910.
———, *Physics of Politics; or, Thoughts on the Application of the Principles of Natural Selection and Inheritance to Political Society*, London 1872 (Reprint New York 1902).
Brex, Twells, *Scaremongerings from the Daily Mail, 1896–1914*, London 1914.
Burgoyne, A.H., *The War Inevitable*, London 1908.
Channing, Francis A., *Memories of Midland Politics 1885–1910*, London 1918.
Chesney, George T., *The Battle of Dorking*, Edinburgh 1871.
———, *The German Conquest of England in 1875, and Battle of Dorking or, Reminiscences of a Volunteer, by an Eyewitness*, London 1871.
Childers, Erskine (Ed.), *The Riddle of the Sands: A Record of Secret Service Recently Achieved*, London 1903.
Chirol, Valentine, *The Middle Eastern Question or Some Political Problems of Indian Defence*, London 1903.
Chirol, Valentine, and George Hamilton, *Problems of the Middle East*, London 1909.
Clarke, George S., and Richard J. Thursfield, *The Navy and the Nation*, London 1897.
———, *My Working Life: Lord Sydenham of Combe*, London 1927.
———, *Fortification: Its Past Achievement, Recent Development and Future Progress*, London 1892.
Cobden, Richard, *The Three Panics: An Historical Episode*, London 1884.
Cole, Robert W., *The Death Trap*, London 1907.
Conrad, Joseph, *The Secret Agent: A Simple Tale*, London 1907.
Cook, Edward T., *Delane from the Times*, London 1915.
Corbett, Julian S., *Some Principles of Maritime Strategy*, London 1911.

Cornford, Leslie, *The Defenceless Island: A Study of the Social and Industrial Conditions of Great Britain and Ireland; and the Effect upon Them of the Outbreak of a Maritime War*, London 1906.
Cramb, John A., *Germany and England*, London 1914.
Curtis, Albert Charles, *A New Trafalgar*, London 1902.
Curtis, Henry, *When England Slept*, London 1909.
Dawson, Alec J., *The Message*, London 1907.
Desbrière, Edouard, *Projets et tentatifs de débarquement sur îles Britanniques*, 4 Vols., État-major de l'armée, Section historique, Paris 1900–1902.
Dewar, A.C., *Is Invasion Possible?* London 1909.
Dilke, Charles W., *The British Empire: A Reprint of a Series of Articles Contributed to Several Newspapers during 1898*, London 1899.
———, *Problems of Greater Britain*, London and New York 1890.
Escott, Thomas H.S., *Masters of English Journalism*, London 1911.
Farrar, John A., *Invasion and Conscription*, London 1909.
Gardiner, Alfred George, *The War Lords*, London 1915.
Gardiner, Charles A., *Proposed Anglo-American Alliance*, New York and London 1898.
Garvin, James Louis, 'The Maintenance of Empire: A Study in the Economics of Power', in Charles Sydney Goldman (Ed.), *The Empire and the Century*, London 1905, pp. 61–80.
Griffiths-Jones, George, *The World Peril of 1910*, London 1907.
Hill, Headon, *The Spies of the Wight*, London 1899.
Hirst, Francis W., *Liberalism and the Empire: Three Essays*, London 1900.
Hislam, Percival, *The Admiralty of the Atlantic*, London 1908.
Hobson, John A., *Imperialism*, London 1902.
———, *The Psychology of Jingoism*, London 1901.
Holdich, Thomas H., *The Indian Borderland 1880–1900*, London 1901.
Jane, Fred T., *The Imperial Russian Navy*, 2nd ed., London 1904.
Kennedy, Bart, *The German Danger*, London 1907.
Lea, Homer, *The Day of the Saxon*, New York and London 1912.
Lee, Sidney (Ed.), *The Oxford Dictionary of National Biography*, 2nd Edition, London 1908-9.
Le Queux, William, *The Great War in England in 1897*, London 1894.
———, *The Invasion of 1910: With a Full Account of the Siege of London. Naval Chapters by Herbert W. Wilson. Introductory Letter by Field Marshal Earl Roberts*, London 1906.
———, *Spies for the Kaiser: Plotting the Downfall of England*, London 1909 (With an Introduction by Nicholas Hiley, Reprint 1996).
Loreburn, Robert T.R., *How the War Came*, London 1919.
Low, Sidney, *The Governance of England*, London 1906.
Lucas, Reginald, *Lord Glenesk and the Morning Post*, London 1910.
Lyall, Alfred, *Rise and Expansion of the British Dominion in India*, London 1894.
MacColl, Malcolm, *England's Responsibility towards Armenia*, London 1895.
Mackinder, Halford J., *Britain and the British Seas*, London 1902.
———, *The Scope and Methods of Geography and the Geographical Pivot of History*, Reprinted with an Introduction by E.W. Gilbert, London 1969.
Mahan, Alfred Thayer, *The Influence of Sea-Power upon the French Revolution and Empire 1783–1812*, New York 1893.

———, *The Influence of Sea-Power upon History 1660–1783*, New York 1890.
———, *Naval Administration and Warfare: Some General Principles*, London and New York 1908.
———, *Naval Strategy: Compared and Contrasted with the Principles of Military Operations on Land*, New York 1911.
———, *From Sail to Steam*, London and New York 1907.
Maitland, Frederick W., 'The Making of the German Civil Code', in H.A.L. Fisher (Ed.), *The Collected Papers of Frederic William Maitland*, Cambridge, 1911.
Mansfield, Kathrine, *In a German Pension*, London 1906 (Reprint 1964).
Masterman, Charles F.G., *The Heart of the Empire: Discussions of Problems of Modern Life in England. With an Essay on Imperialism*, London 1901.
Maude, F.N., *The New Battle of Dorking*, London 1900.
Maxse, Leopod J., *Germany on the Brain: The Obsession of 'a Crank'*, London 1915.
Mills, Edward E., *The Decline and Fall of the British Empire*, London 1905.
Morley, John, *Recollections*, 2 Vols., New York 1917.
Murray, Stewart L., *The Peace of the Anglo-Saxons*, London 1905.
Norman, Henry, *All the Russians*, London 1902.
Offin, T.W., *How the Germans Took London*, London 1900.
Oldmeadow, Ernest, *The North Sea Bubble: A Fantasia*, London 1906.
Oppenheim, E.P., *The Secret*, London 1907.
Repington, Charles A., *Essays and Criticism*, London 1911.
———, *The First World War*, Vol. 1, London 1921.
———, *Imperial Strategy*, London 1906.
———, *Peace Strategy*, London 1907.
———, *Vestigia*, Boston 1919.
Roberts, Frederick S., *Forty One Years in India*, London 1897.
Robertson, John M., *Patriotism and Empire*, 3rd ed., London 1900.
Ross, Ch., *The Problem of National Defence*, London 1907.
Rowntree, Benjamin S., *Poverty: A Study of Town Life*, London 1901.
Russell, Bertrand, *Portraits from Memory and Other Essays*, London 1956.
Saunders, George, *The Last of the Huns*, London 1915.
Seeley, John R., *The Expansion of England: Two Courses of Lectures*, London 1883.
Seton-Watson, Robert W., *The Southern Slav Question and the Habsburg Monarchy*, London 1911.
Shaw, George B., 'Common Sense of the War', *The New Statesman* (special issue), November 1914.
Shee, George F., *The Briton's First Duty*, London 1901.
Spender, Harold, *Herbert Henry Asquith*, London 1915.
Stables, Gordon, *The Meteor Flag of England*, London 1905.
Swinton, Ernest Dunlop, *The Green Curve and Other Stories*, New York 1909.
Townroe, Bernard Stephen, *A Nation in Arms: A Play in Four Acts*, London 1906
Tracy, Louis, *The Invaders: A Story of Britain's Peril*, London 1901.
———, *The Final War*, London 1896.
Treitschke, Heinrich von, *Politics*, Foreword by A.J. Balfour, New York 1916.
Vaux, Patrick, *The Shock of Battle*, London 1906.
Vaux, Patrick, and Lionel Yexley, *When the Eagle Flies Seaward*, London 1907.
Wallace, Donald Mackenzie, *Russia*, 2 Vols., London 1905.

Webb, Augustus D., *New Dictionary of Statistics*, London 1911.
Wells, Herbert G., *Experiment in Autobiography: Discoveries and Conclusions of a Very Ordinary Brain (since 1866)*, 2 Vols., London 1914.
———, *The New Machiavelli*, London 1911.
———, *The War in the Air and Particularly How Mr Bert Smallways Fared while it Lasted*, London 1908 (Reprint Harmondsworth 1971).
———, *The War of the Worlds*, London 1898 (Reprint Harmondsworth 1959).
———, *In the Days of Comet*, London 1906.
Wilkinson, Henry S., *Britain at Bay*, London 1909.
———, *The Great Alternative*, London 1894.
———, *A Nation's Awakening*, London 1897.
———, *The Nation's Need*, London 1903.
———, *Volunteers and the National Defence*, London 1896.
Williams, Lloyd, *The Great Raid*, London 1907.
Wilson, Charles H., *Offence, not Defence*, London 1907.
Wood, Walter, *The Enemy in Our Midst*, London 1906.
Younghusband, George, *The Relief of Chitral*, London 1895.

F. Selected Bibliography

Adam, Karl, *Großbritanniens Balkandilemma: Die britische Balkanpolitik von der bosnischen Krise bis zu den Balkankriegen 1908-1913*, Hamburg 2009.
Adams, Iestyn, *Brothers across the Ocean: British Foreign Policy and the Origins of the Anglo-American 'Special Relationship', 1900–1905*, New York 2005.
Adams, R.J.Q., and P.P. Poirier, *The Conscription Controversy in Great Britain, 1900–1918*, London 1987.
Afflerbach, Holger, *Der Dreibund: Europäische Großmacht- und Allianzpolitik vor dem Ersten Weltkrieg*, Vienna 2002.
Afflerbach, Holger, and David Stevenson (Eds.), *An Improbable War? The Outbreak of World War I and European Political Culture before 1914*, New York 2007.
Ahmad, Feroz, *The Young Turks: The Committee of Union and Progress in Turkish Politics 1908–1914*, Oxford 1969.
Albertini, Luigi, *The Origins of the War in 1914*, 3 Vols., London 1952–1954.
Alder, G.J., *British India's Northern Frontier*, London 1964.
Allen, Harry C., *Great Britain and the United States 1783–1952*, London 1954.
Amery, John, *The Life of Joseph Chamberlain*, 6 Vols., London 1951–1969.
Anderson, Eugene N., *The First Moroccan Crisis 1904–1906*, Chicago 1930 (Reprint Hamden 1966).
Anderson, Matthew S., *The Eastern Question, 1774–1923*, London 1966.
Anderson, Stuart, *Race and Rapprochement: Anglo-Saxonism and Anglo-American Relations, 1895–1904*, London 1981.
Andrew, Christopher, 'Secret Intelligence and British Foreign Policy 1900–1939', in Christopher Andrew and Jeremy Noakes (Eds.), *Intelligence and International Relations, 1900–1945*, Exeter 1987, pp. 9–28.
———, *Secret Service: The Making of the British Intelligence Community*, London 1985.
———, *Théophile Delcassé and the Making of the Entente Cordiale*, New York 1968.

Angelow, Jürgen, *Kalkül und Prestige: Der Zweibund am Vorabend des Ersten Weltkrieges*, Cologne 2000.
Anon., *The History of The Times, Vol. 3: Twentieth Century Test 1884–1912*, London 1947.
Asada, Sadao, *From Mahan to Pearl Harbor: The Imperial Japanese Navy and the United States*, Annapolis 2006.
Ayerst, David, *Garvin of the Observer*, London 1985.
Balfour, Michael, *Britain and Joseph Chamberlain*, London 1985.
———, *The Kaiser and His Times*, New York and London 1972.
Bannister, R.C., *Social Darwinism, Science and Myth in Anglo-American Thought*, Philadelphia 1979.
Barnett, Corelli, *The Collapse of British Power*, London 1972.
Bauerkämper, Arnd, *Die "radikale Rechte" in Großbritannien: Nationalistische, antisemitische und faschistische Bewegungen vom späten 19. Jahrhundert bis 1945*, Göttingen 1991.
Beale, Howard K., *Theodore Roosevelt and the Rise of America to World Power*, Baltimore 1956.
Beckett, Ian Frederick W., 'The South African War and the Late Victorian Army', in Peter Dennis and Jeffrey Guy (Eds.), *The Boer War: Army, Nation and Empire*, Canberra 2000, pp. 31–44.
Beloff, Max, *Imperial Sunset, Vol. 1: Britain's Liberal Empire 1897–1921*, London 1969.
———, 'Lucien Wolf and the Anglo-Russian Entente 1907–1914', in Max Beloff (Ed.), *The Intellectual in Politics. And Other Essays*, Birkenhead 1970, pp. 111–43.
Berghahn, Volker, *Germany and the Approach of War in 1914*, 2nd ed., London 1993.
———, *Der Tirpitz-Plan: Genesis und Verfall einer innenpolitischen Krisenstrategie unter Wilhelm II*, Dusseldorf 1971.
Bernstein, George L., *Liberalism and Liberal Politics in Edwardian England*, London 1986.
Bernstein, Marvin D., *Foreign Investment in Latin America: Cases and Attitudes*, New York 1966.
Blake, Robert, *The Conservative Party from Peel to Churchill*, London 1972.
Blanning, Tim C.W. (Ed.), *The Short Oxford History of Europe: The Nineteenth Century*, Oxford 2000.
Bond, Brian, *War and Society in Europe, 1870–1970*, Gloucestershire 1998.
Bösch, Frank, *Öffentliche Geheimnisse: Skandale, Politik und Medien in Deutschland und Großbritannien 1880–1914*, Munich 2009.
Boulding, Keith E., *The Image*, Ann Arbor, 1956/1969.
Bourne, Kenneth, *The Foreign Policy of Victorian England, 1830–1902*, Oxford 1970.
———, *Britain and the Balance of Power in North America*, Berkeley 1967.
Boyle, Timothy, 'The Formation of the Campbell-Bannerman Government in December 1905', in *Bulletin of the Institute of Historical Research* 65 (1972), pp. 283–302.
Brechtken, Magnus, *Scharnierzeit 1895–1907: Persönlichkeitsnetze und internationale Politik in den deutsch-britisch-amerikanischen Beziehungen vor dem Ersten Weltkrieg*, Mainz 2006.
Brennan, E.J.T. (Ed.), *Education for National Efficiency*, London 1975.
Breyer, Siegfried, *Hochseeflotte 1907–1918: Bilder von Deutschlands „Schwimmender Wehr"*. (=Marine-Arsenal, Bd. 41) Wölfersheim-Berstadt 1998.
Bridge, Francis R., and Roger Bullen, *1914: The Coming of the First World War*, 2nd ed., London 1988.
Bridge, Francis Roy, 'Sir Edward Grey and Austria-Hungary', in *IHR* 38 (2016), pp. 264–274.
———, *Great Britain and Austria-Hungary 1906–1914: A Diplomatic History*, London 1972.

———, *The Great Powers and the European States System, 1815–1914*, London and New York 1980.
———, *From Sadowa to Sarajewo: The Foreign Policy of Austria-Hungary 1866–1914*, London 1972.
Brown, Benjamin H., *The Tariff Reform Movement in Great Britain 1881–1895*, New York 1966.
Bucholz, Arden, *Moltke and the German Wars, 1864–1871*, Basingstoke, New York 2001.
Bullen, Roger (Ed.), *The Foreign Office 1782–1982*, Frederick 1984.
Burton, David, *Cecil Spring Rice: A Diplomat's Life*, London 1990.
———, Theodore Roosevelt: Confident Imperialist, Philadelphia 1968.
———, *British American Diplomacy, 1895–1917*, Malabar, FL1999.
———, 'Theodore Roosevelt and his English correspondence: The intellectual roots of the Anglo-American alliance', in *Mid-America* 53 (1971), pp. 12–34.
Busch, Brinton C., *Britain and the Persian Gulf, 1894–1914*, Berkeley 1967.
———, *Hardinge of Penshurst: A Study in the Old Diplomacy*, Hamden 1980.
Butler, David and Jennie Fremann (Eds.), *British Political Facts 1900–1967*, London 1968.
Callwell, Charles E., *Field Marshall Sir Henry Wilson. His Life and Diaries*, 2 Vols., New York 1927.
Cain, Peter and A.G. Hopkins, *British Imperialism: Innovation and Expansion 1688–1914*, London 1993.
Campbell, A.E., 'Great Britain and the United States in the Far East, 1895–1903', in *HJ* 1/1958, pp. 154–68.
Camrose, William, *British Newspapers and their Controllers*, London 1947.
Canis, Konrad, *Die bedrängte Großmacht: Österreich-Ungarn und das europäische Mächtesystem 1866/67–1914*, Paderborn 2016.
———, *Von Bismarck zur Weltpolitik: Deutsche Außenpolitik 1890–1902*, Berlin 1997.
———, *Der Weg in den Abgrund: Deutsche Außenpolitik 1902–1914*, Paderborn 2011.
———, 'Die deutsche Außenpolitik im letzten Jahrzehnt vor dem Ersten Weltkrieg im Lichte österreichisch-ungarischer diplomatischer Berichte', in Wolfgang Elz and Sönke Neitzel (Eds.), *Internationale Beziehungen im 19. und 20. Jahrhundert*, Paderborn 2003, pp. 105-26.
Carl, George E., *First among Equals. Great Britain and Venezuela, 1810-1910*, Syracuse 1980.
Carlgren, Wilhelm M., *Iswolski und Aehrenthal vor der bosnischen Annexionskrise: Russische und österreichisch-ungarische Balkanpolitik 1906–1908*, Uppsala 1955.
Carroll, E. Malcolm, *Germany and the Great Powers 1866–1914: A Study in Public Opinion and Foreign Policy*, Hamden, CT 1966 (Reprint 1938).
Cecil, Gwendolen, *Life of Salisbury*, London 1921–1932.
Chapman, Maybelle R., *Great Britain and the Baghdad Railway, 1888–1914*, London 1948.
Charmley, John, *Splendid Isolation? Britain and the Balance of Power 1874–1914*, London 1999.
Chesneau, Roger (Ed.), *Kriegsschiffe der Welt 1860–1905*, 3 Vols., Koblenz 1983–1989.
Christian, Robert Murray, *Leo Maxse and the National Review. A Study in the Periodical Press*, Diss., University of Virginia 1940.
Chwostow, Wenjamin M. and Isaak I. Minz (Eds.), *Geschichte der Diplomatie*, Vol. 2: *Die Diplomatie der Neuzeit (1872–1919)*, Berlin 1948.
Churchill, Rogers P., *The Anglo-Russian Convention of 1907*, Iowa 1939.
Churchill, Winston S., *The World Crisis 1911–1914*, New York 1930.

Clark, Christopher, *The Sleepwalkers: How Europe Went to War in 1914*, London 2012.
———, *Wilhelm II: Die Herrschaft des letzten deutschen Kaisers*, Frankfurt a. M. 2009.
———, 'Sir Edward Grey and the July Crisis', in *IHR* 38(2016), pp. 326-338.
Clarke, Ignatius F. (Ed.), *The Great War with Germany, 1890–1914*, Liverpool 1997.
———, *Voices Prophesying War: Future Wars 1763–1984*, Oxford 1992.
Clarke, Tom, *Northcliffe in History*, London 1950.
Coetzee, Frans and M.S. Coetzee, 'Rethinking the Radical Right in Germany and Britain before 1914', in *JCH* 21 (1986), pp. 515–37.
Cohen, Avner, and Joseph Chamberlain, 'Lord Lansdowne and British Foreign Policy 1901–1903: From Collaboration to Confrontation', in *Australian Journal of Politics and History* 43/2 (1997), pp. 94–105.
Collin, Richard H., *Theodore Roosevelt's Caribbean: The Panama Canal, the Monroe Doctrine and the Latin American Context*, Baton Rouge 1990.
Conze, Eckart, 'Zwischen Staatenwelt und Gesellschaftswelt: Die gesellschaftliche Dimension internationaler Geschichte', in Wilfried Loth et al. (Eds.), *Internationale Geschichte: Themen – Ereignisse – Aussichten*, Munich 2000, pp. 117–40.
Coogan, J.W., and P.F. Coogan, 'The British Cabinet and the Anglo-French Staff Talks, 1905–1914: Who Knew What and When Did He Know It?' in *JBS* 24 (1985), pp. 110–31.
Cooper, M.B., 'British Policy in the Balkans 1908/09', in *HJ* 7/2 (1964), pp. 258–79.
Cornford, James, 'The Transformation of Conservatism in the late 19th Century', in *Victorian Studies* 7 (1963), pp. 35–66.
Corp, Edward T., 'Sir William Tyrrell: The Eminence Grise of the British Foreign Office, 1912/13', in *HJ* 25/3 (1982), pp. 697–708.
———, 'The Problem of Promotion in the Career of Sir Eyre Crowe, 1905–1920', in *Australian Journal of Politics and History* 28 (1982), pp. 236–49
Cosgrove, Richard A., 'The Career of Sir Eyre Crowe: A Reassessment', in *Albion* 4/4 (1972), pp. 193–205.
Courtney, Jane, *The Making of an Editor, W.L. Courtney*, London 1930.
Crampton, Richard J., *The Hollow Détente: Anglo-German Relations in the Balkans, 1911–1914*, London 1979.
Crewe-Milnes, Robert, *Lord Rosebery*, 2 Vols., London 1931.
Crisp, O., 'The Russian Liberals and the 1906 Anglo-French Loan to Russia', in *Slavonic and East European Review* 39 (1960), pp. 497–511.
Cromwell, Valerie, 'Great Britain's European Treaty Obligations in March 1902', in *Historical Journal* 6 (1963), pp. 272–79.
Cross, A.G. (Ed.), *The Russian Theme in English Literature from the 16th Century to 1980: An Introductory Survey and a Bibliography*, Oxford 1985.
Crowe, Sibyl and Edward Corp, *Our Ablest Public Servant: Sir Eyre Crowe, GCB, GCMG, KCB, KCMG, 1864–1925*, Devon 1993.
Cunningham, Alan, *Eastern Question in the Nineteenth Century, Collected Essays*, Vol. 2, ed. by E. Ingram, London 1993.
Dakin, Douglas, *The Greek Struggle in Macedonia*, Salonica 1969.
Dangerfield, George, *The Strange Death of Liberal England*, New York 1935.
David, Wade D., *European Diplomacy in the Near Eastern Question 1906–1909*, Illinois 1940.
Deacon, Richard, *A History of the British Secret Service*, London 1969.

Dehio, Ludwig, *Gleichgewicht oder Hegemonie: Betrachtungen über ein Grundproblem der neueren Staatengeschichte*, Krefeld 1948.
Deist, Wilhelm, *Flottenpolitik und Flottenpropaganda*, Stuttgart 1976.
Dilks, David, *Curzon*, 2 Vols., London 1970.
Dillon, Emile J., *The Eclipse of Russia*, London 1918.
Dockrill, Michael L., *The Formulation of a Continental Foreign Policy by Great Britain, 1908–1912*, London 1969.
———, Lowe, Cedric J., *The Mirage of Power*, 3 Vols., London 1972
D'Ombrain, Nicholas, *War Machinery and High Policy: Defence Administration in Peacetime Britain*, Oxford 1973.
Dugdale, Blanche E., *Arthur James Balfour, First Earl of Balfour*, 2 Vols., London 1938.
Dülffer, Jost et al. (Eds.), *Vermiedene Kriege: Deeskalation von Konflikten der Großmächte zwischen Krimkrieg und Erstem Weltkrieg (1856–1914)*, Munich 1997.
———, *Im Zeichen der Gewalt: Frieden und Krieg im 19. und 20. Jahrhundert*, Cologne 2003.
——— (Ed.), *Deutschland in Europa: Kontinuität und Bruch*, Frankfurt a. M. 1990.
Duijker, Hubertus C.J., and Nico H. Frijda, *National Character and National Stereotypes*, Amsterdam, 1960.
Dunlop, John K., *The Development of the British Army, 1899–1914*, London 1938.
Duroselle, Jean-Baptiste, *Tout empire périra: Théorie des relations internationales*, 12th ed., Paris 1992.
Earle, Edward M., *Turkey: The Great Powers and the Baghdad Railway. A Study in Imperialism*, New York 1924.
Ehlert, Hans et al (Eds.), *Der Schlieffenplan: Analysen und Dokumente*, Paderborn 2006.
Eisele, Leona W. (Ed.), *A digest of the Krasnyi Arkhiv – Red Archives*, Vols. 31–106, Ann Arbor 1955.
Ekstein, Michael, 'Sir Edward Grey and Imperial Germany in 1914', in *JCH* 6/3 (1971), pp. 121–31.
———, 'Some Notes on Sir Edward Grey's Policy in July 1914', in *HJ* 15/2 (1972), pp. 321–24.
Eldrige, Colin C., *England's Mission: The Imperial Idea in the Age of Gladstone and Disraeli*, London 1973.
Eley, Geoff, 'Sammlungspolitik, Social Imperialism and the Navy Law of 1898', in Geoff Eley (Ed.), *From Unification to Nazism: Reinterpreting the German Past*, Boston 1986, pp. 110–53.
———, *Reshaping the Right: Radical Nationalism and Political Change after Bismarck*, Ann Arbor 1991.
Ellegard, Alvar, *The Readership of the Periodical Press in Mid-Victorian Britain*, Gothenburg 1957.
Elvert, Jürgen, 'Why did the approaches to conlude an Anglo-German Alliance fail? Foreign Policy, British Public Opinion and the Anglo-German Explorations from 1898–1900', in Christian Haase (Ed.), *Debating Foreign Affairs: The Public and British Foreign Policy since 1867*, Berlin and Vienna 2003, pp. 40–62.
Emy, Hugh V., 'The Impact of Financial Policy on English Party Politics before 1914', in *HJ* 15/1 (1972), pp. 103–31.
Epkenhans, Michael, 'Was a Peaceful Outcome Thinkable? The Naval Race before 1914', in Holger Afflerbach und David Stevenson (Eds), *An Improbable War? The Outbreak of*

World War I and European Political Culture before 1914, New York and Oxford 2007, pp. 113–129.

Escott, Thomas H.S., *Masters of English Journalism*, London 1911.

Evans, Richard J., and Hartmut Pogge von Strandmann (Eds.), *The Coming of the First World War*, Oxford 1988.

Fairbanks, Charles H., 'The Dreadnought Revolution: A Historiographical Essay', in *IHR* 13/4 (1991), pp. 246–72.

Fay, Sidney B., 'The Influence of the Pre-war Press in Europe', in *Proceedings of the Massachusetts Historical Society*, Vol. 64/3 (1931), pp. 3–32.

———, *The Origins of World War I*, Vol. 1, New York 1930.

Feis, Herbert, *Europe the World's Banker, 1870–1914*, New Haven 1930.

Feldman, Eliyahu, 'British Diplomats and British Diplomacy and the 1905 Pogroms in Russia', in *Slavic and East European Review* 65 (1987), pp. 579–608.

Ferguson, Niall, 'Germany and the Origins of the First World War: New Perspectives', in *HJ* 33/3 (1992), pp. 725–52.

———, *The Pity of War, 1914–1918*, London 1998.

———, 'Public Finance and National Security: The Domestic Origins of the First World War Revisited', in *Past & Present* 2 (1994), pp. 141–68.

———, *Die Geschichte der Rothschilds: Propheten des Geldes*, 2 Vols., Munich 2002.

Fergusson, Thomas G., *British Military Intelligence, 1870–1914*, London 1984.

Fiebig von Hase, Ragnhild, *Lateinamerika als Konfliktherd deutsch-amerikanischer Beziehungen*, Göttingen 1986.

Fiedler, Siegfried, *Taktik und Strategie der Millionenheere 1871–1914*, Bonn 1993.

Fikret, Adanir, *Die Makedonische Frage*, Wiesbaden 1979.

Fischer, Fritz, *Griff nach der Weltmacht: Die Kriegszielpolitik des kaiserlichen Deutschland 1914/18*, (Reprint of the 1967 edition) Düsseldorf 1984.

———, *Krieg der Illusionen*, 2nd ed., Düsseldorf 1970.

Flood, C.A., *The Ambassadorship of Paul von Wolff-Metternich: Anglo-German Relations, 1901–1912*, Diss. Madison (Wisc.) 1976.

Forstmeier, Friedrich, 'Der Tirpitzsche Flottenbau im Urteil der Historiker', in Herbert Schottelius und Wilhelm Deist (Eds.), *Marine und Marinepolitik im kaiserlichen Deutschland 1871–1914*, Düsseldorf 1972, pp. 34–53.

Fox Bourne, Henry R., *English Newspapers: Chapters in the History of Journalism*, 2 Vols., New York 1966.

Francis, Richard M., 'The British withdrawal from the Baghdad Railway project in April 1903', in *HJ* 16 (1973), pp. 168–78.

Fraser, Peter, 'Unionism and Tariff Reform: The Crisis of 1906', in *HJ* 5 (1962), pp. 149–66.

———, 'The Liberal Unionist alliance: Chamberlain, Hartington and the Conservatives 1886–1904', *EHR* 77 (1962), pp. 53-78.

———, *Lord Esher*, London 1973

Freeden, Michael, *The New Liberalism: An Ideology of Social Reform*, Oxford 1978.

Freedman, Lawrence (Ed.), *War*, Oxford 1994.

French, David, *British Economic and Strategic Planning, 1905–1915*, London 1982.

———, 'The Edwardian Crisis and the Origins of the First World War', in *IHR*, 4/2 (1982), pp. 207–21.

———, 'Spy Fever in Britain, 1900–1915', in *HJ* 21/2 (1978), pp. 355–70.

Friedberg, Aaron L., *The Weary Titan: Britain and the Experience of Relative Decline, 1895–1905*, Princeton 1988.
Fritzinger, Linda, *Diplomat without Portfolio: Valentine Chirol, His Life and The Times*, London and New York 2006.
Fry, Michael G., *Lloyd George and Foreign Policy, Vol. 1: The Education of a Statesman, 1890–1916*, London 1977.
Fyfe, Hamilton, *The British Liberal Party*, London 1928.
———, *Northcliffe, An Intimate Biography*, London 1930.
———, *Sixty Years of Fleet Street*, London 1949.
Gall, Wilhelm, *Sir Charles Hardinge und die englische Vorkriegspolitik 1903–10*, Berlin 1939.
Gade, Christel, *Gleichgewichtspolitik oder Bündnispflege? Maximen britischer Außenpolitik 1909–1914*, Göttingen 1997.
Gardiner, Alfred G., *Life of Sir William Harcourt*, 2 Vols., London 1923.
Gardiner, Rorbert (Ed.), *Conway's All the World's Fighting Ships 1906–1921*, London 1982.
Garvin, James Louis, *The Life of Joseph Chamberlain*, 3 Vols., London 1932.
Gebauer, Jürgen (Ed), *Marine-Enzyklopädie*, 4. Ed., Berlin 2007.
Geiss, Imanuel, *Der lange Weg in die Katastrophe: Die Vorgeschichte des Ersten Weltkriegs 1815–1914*, München, Zürich 1990.
———, '"Weltpolitik": Die deutsche Version des Imperialismus', in Gregor Schöllgen (Ed.): *Flucht in den Krieg? Die Außenpolitik des kaiserlichen Deutschland*, Darmstadt 1991, pp. 148–70.
Gelber, Lionel M., *The Rise of the Anglo-American Friendship: A study in World Politics*, Hamden (Conn.) 1938.
Gemeinhardt, Heinz A., *Deutsche und österreichische Pressepolitik während der bosnischen Krise 1908/09*, Husum 1980.
Geppert, Dominik, *Pressekriege: Öffentlichkeit und Diplomatie in den deutsch-britischen Beziehungen (1896–1912)*, Munich 2007.
George, Alexander L. (Ed.), *Avoiding War: Problems of Crisis Management*, Oxford 1991.
Gerhardt, Heinz, *War in der Bosnische Annexionskrise die deutsche Demarche vom 22.3.1909 ein Ultimatum? Eine historisch-außenpolitische Studie zur Geschichte der Diplomatie auf dem Balkan*, Berlin 1965.
Geyer, Dietrich, *Der russische Imperialismus: Studien über den Zusammenhang von innerer und auswärtiger Politik 1860–1914*, Göttingen 1977.
Giertz, H., 'Die außenpolitische Position Miljukovs am Vorabend und während der bosnischen Krise', in *Jahrbuch für die Geschichte der sozialistischen Länder Europas* 18/2 (1974), pp. 77–113.
Gilbert, B., 'Health and politics: The British physical deterioration Report of 1904', in Bulletin of the History of Medicine, 39 (1965), pp. 143–54.
Gillard, David R., *Lord Salisbury's Foreign Policy 1888–1892, with Special Reference to Anglo-German Relations*, London 1952.
———, *The Struggle for Asia, 1828–1914: A Study in British and Russian Imperialism*, London 1977.
Glaab, Sonja, 'Wilhelm II. und die Presse: Ein Medienkaiser in seinem Element?', in *Publizistik* 53/2 (2008), pp. 200–214.
Gleason, John H., *The Genesis of Russophobia in Great Britain*, Cambridge 1950.
Glenny, Misha, *The Balkans 1804–1999: Nationalism, War and the Great Powers*, London 1999.

Gollin, Alfred, *No Longer an Island: Britain and the Wright Brothers, 1902–1909*, London 1984.

———, *The Observer and J.L. Garvin: A Study in Great Editorship*, London 1960.

———, *Proconsul in Politics: A Study of Lord Milner in Opposition and in Power*, London 1964.

Gooch, George Peabody, *Life of Lord Courtney*, London 1920.

———, *Before the War: Studies in Diplomacy, Vol.1: The Grouping of the Powers*, New York 1936.

Gooch, John, *The Plans of War: The General Staff and the British Military Strategy 1900–1916*, London 1974.

———, 'Sir George Clarke's Career at the Committee of Imperial Defence, 1904–1907', in *HJ* 18/3 (1975), pp. 555–69.

Gordon, M.R., 'Domestic Conflict and the Origins of the First World War: The British and the German Cases', in *JMH* 6 (1974), pp. 193–226.

Gough, Barry, *Historical Dreadnoughts: Marder and Roskill: Writing and Fighting Naval History*, Barnsley 2010.

Graham, Gerald S., *The Politics of Naval Supremacy: Studies in British Maritime Ascendancy*, Cambridge 1965.

Greaves, R.L., 'Some Aspects of the Anglo-Russian Convention and its Working in Persia, 1907–1914', in *Bulletin of the School of Oriental and African Studies* 31 (1968), pp. 69–81.

Green, Ewan E.H., *The Crisis of Conservatism: The Politics, Economics and Ideology of the British Conservative Party 1880–1914*, London 1995.

Grenville, John, *Lord Salisbury and Foreign Policy: The Close of the Nineteenth Century 1895–1902*, London 1964.

———, 'Goluchowski, Salisbury and the Mediterranean Agreements', 1895–1897, in *Slavonic and East European Review* 36 (1957/8), pp. 340–69.

———, 'Lansdowne's abortive Project of 12. March 1901 for a secret Agreement with Germany', in *British Imperial History Review* 27 (1954), pp. 123–34.

———, 'Imperial Germany and Britain: From Cooperation to War', in Adolf M. Birke und Marie-Luise Recker (Eds.), *Das gestörte Gleichgewicht: Deutschland als Problem britischer Sicherheit im 19. und 20. Jahrhundert*, Munich 1990, pp. 81–95.

Griffiths, Dennis (Ed.), *Encyclopedia of the British Press 1422–1992*, New York 1992.

Grünbeck, Max, *Die Presse Großbritanniens, ihr geistiger und wirtschaftlicher Aufbau: Wesen und Wirkungen der Publizistik – Arbeiten über die Volksbeeinflussung und geistigen Volksführung aller Zeiten und Völker*, Leipzig 1936.

Guthrie, Wayne D., *The Anglo-German Intervention in Venezuela, 1902–03*, Ann Arbor 1983.

Haase, Christian (Ed.), *Debating Foreign Affairs: The Public and British Foreign Policy since 1867*, Berlin und Wien 2003.

Haggie, P., 'The Royal Navy and War Planning in the Fisher Era', in Paul M. Kennedy, *The War Plans of the Great Powers 1880–1914*, London 1979, pp. 118–32.

Hale, Oron J., *Germany and the Diplomatic Revolution: A Study in Diplomacy and the Press 1904–1906*, Philadelphia 1931.

———, *Publicity and Diplomacy with Special Reference to England and Germany 1890–1914*, Gloucester, MA 1940.

Hallgarten, George W.F., *Imperialismus vor 1914: Die soziologischen Grundlagen der Außenpolitik europäischer Großmächte vor dem Ersten Weltkrieg*, 2 Vols., 2nd Edition, Munich 1963.

Hallmann, Hans, *Der Weg zum deutschen Schlachtflottenbau*, Stuttgart 1933.
Halpern, Paul G., *A Naval History of World War I*, Abingdon 1994.
Hamer, David A., *John Morley*, Oxford 1968.
———, *Liberal Politics in the Age of Gladstone and Rosebery*, Oxford 1972.
Hamilton, Keith, *Bertie of Thame: Edwardian Ambassador*, London 1990.
Hamilton, W.M. *The Nation and the Navy: Methods and Organization of British Navalist Propaganda*, 1889–1914, New York 1986.
Hammond, John L., *C.P. Scott*, London 1934.
Handel, M., Corbett, 'Clausewitz, and Sun Tzu', in *Naval War College Review* (Autumn 2000), pp. 106–23.
Hantsch, Hugo (Ed.), 'Außenminister Alois Lexa Graf Aehrenthal', in *Gestalter der Geschicke Österreichs*, ed. by Hugo Hantsch, Wien 1962, pp. 513–26.
———, *Leopold Graf Berchtold: Grandseigneur und Staatsmann*, 2 Vols., Graz 1963.
Hargreaves, John D., 'Entente manquée: Anglo-French relations 1895–1896', in *Historical Journal* XI (1953), pp. 111–22.
———, 'The Origins of the Anglo-French Military Conversations in 1905', in *History* 36 (1951), pp. 244–48.
Harris, Paul J., 'Great Britain', in Richard Hamilton and Holger Herwig (Eds.), *The Origins of World War I*, Cambridge 2003, pp. 266–99.
Hauser, Oswald, *Deutschland und der englisch-russische Gegensatz 1900–1914*, Göttingen 1958.
Hayne, M.B., *The French Foreign Office and the Origins of the First World War, 1898–1914*, Oxford 1993.
Hayes, Paul, 'Admiralty's Plans for Attacking German Territory 1906–1915', in Lawrence Freedman (Ed.), *War, Strategy and International Politics*, Oxford 1992, pp. 75–94.
Heindel, Richard H., *The American Impact on Great Britain, 1898–1914*, Philadelphia 1940.
Heller, Joseph, *British Policy towards the Ottoman Empire, 1908–1914*, London 1983.
Hencock, E. P., 'Technological Education in England, 1850–1926: the Uses of a German Model', in History of Education, 19 (1990), pp. 299–331.
Hendricksen, E. G., 'Roosevelt's second Venezuelan Controversy', in *Hispanic American Historical Review*, 50 (1970), pp. 482–98.
Henning, Hansjoachim, *Deutschlands Verhältnis zu England in Bethmann Hollwegs Außenpolitik 1909–1914*, Cologne 1962.
Herd, Harold, *The March of Journalis:. The Story of the British Press from 1622 to the Present Day*, London 1952.
Hermann, David G., *The Arming of Europe and the Making of the First World War*, Princeton 1996.
Herwig, Holger, 'The German Reaction to the Dreadnought Revolution', in *IHR* 13/4 (1991), pp. 273–83.
———, *Politics of Frustration: The United States in German Naval Planning, 1898-1941*, Boston 1976.
———, *Germany's Vision of Empire in Venezuela 1871–1914*, Princeton 1986.
———, and Keith Hamilton, *The Origins of the First World War*, London 2002.
Hewitson, Mark, *Germany and the Causes of the First World War*, Oxford 2004.
Hildebrand, Klaus, 'Geschichte oder "Gesellschaftsgeschichte"? Die Notwendigkeit einer politischen Geschichtsschreibung von den Internationalen Beziehungen', in *Historische Zeitschrift* 223 (1976), pp. 328–57.

———, 'Staatskunst und Kriegshandwerk: Akteure und System der europäischen Staatenwelt vor 1914', in Hans Ehlert et al. (Eds.), *Der Schlieffenplan: Analyse und Dokumente*, Paderborn u.a. 2006, pp. 21–44.

———, *Das vergangene Reich: Deutsche Außenpolitik von Bismarck bis Hitler 1871–1945*, Stuttgart 1995.

Hiley, Nicholas, 'The Failure of British Counter-Espionage against Germany, 1907–1914', in *HJ* 28/4 (1985), pp. 835–62.

———, 'Introduction', in William Le Queux, *Spies of the Kaiser*, London 1996, pp. vii–xxxii.

Hill, Christopher, 'Public Opinion and British Foreign Policy', in *Opinion Publique et Poltique Extérieure 1870–1915* (=L'ecole Francaise de Rome 54), Milan and Rome 1981, pp. 63–74.

Hillgruber, Andreas, 'Politische Geschichte in Moderner Sicht', in *Historische Zeitschrift* 216 (1973), pp. 529–51.

Hinsley, Francis H. (Ed.), *British Foreign Policy under Sir Edward Grey*, Cambridge 1977.

Hobsbawm, Eric, *Industry and Empire: From 1750 to the Present Day*, London 1968.

Hobson, Rolf, *Imperialism at Sea: Naval Strategic Thought, the Ideology of Sea Power, and the Tirpitz Plan, 1875–1914*, Boston 2002.

———, *Maritimer Imperialismus: Semachtsideologie, seestrategisches Denken und der Tirpitzplan 1876–1914*, Munich 2003.

Höbelt, Lothar, 'Wohltemperierte Unzufriedenheit: Die Deutschösterreicher, die Monarchie und das Nationalitätenproblem 1914', in Peter Mast (Ed.), *Nationaler Gegensatz und Zusammenleben der Völker: Österreich-Ungarn im Spiegel der deutschsprachigen Literatur*, Bonn 1994, pp. 58–84.

Hölzle, Erwin, *Die Selbstentmachtung Europas: Das Experiment des Friedens vor und im Ersten Weltkrieg*, Göttingen 1976.

Holbo, Paul S., 'Perilous Obscurity: Public Diplomacy and the Press in the Venezuela Crisis, 1902–1903', in *Historian* 32 (1970), pp. 429–45.

Holbraad, Carsten, *The Concert of Europe: A Study in German and British International Theory 1815–1914*, London 1970.

Hollenberg, Günther, *Englisches Interesse am Kaiserreich: Die Attraktivität Preußen Deutschlands für konservative und liberale Kreise in Großbritannien 1860–1914*, Wiesbaden 1974.

Holsti, Oron R., 'The Belief System and National Images: A Case Study', *Journal of Conflict Resolution* 6 (1962), pp. 244–52.

Houghton, Walter E. (Ed.), *Wellesley Index to Victorian Periodicals 1824–1900: Tables of Content and Identification with Bibliographies of their Articles and Stories*, 5 Vols., Toronto 1966–1989.

Howard, Christopher, *Splendid Isolation*, London 1967.

Howard, Michael, *Britain and the Casus Belli*, London 1974.

———, *The Continental Commitment*, London 1972.

———, 'The Policy of Isolation', in *HJ* 10/1 (1967), pp. 77–88.

Hoyer, Christian, *Salisbury und Deutschland: Außenpolitisches Denken und britische Deutschlandpolitik zwischen 1856 und 1880*, Husum 2008.

Hoyos, Alexander, *Der deutsch-englische Gegensatz und sein Einfluss auf die Balkanpolitik Österreich-Ungarns*, Berlin, Leipzig 1922.

Hughes, Michael, *Inside the Enigma: British Officials in Russia 1900–1939*, London 1997.

Humble, M.E., 'The Breakdown of a Consensus: British Writers and Anglo-German Relations 1900–1920', in *Journal of European Studies* 7 (1977), pp. 41–68.

———, 'The British Empire in the Edwardian Era', in J. Brown and W.M. Louis (Eds.), *The Oxford History of the British Empire*, Vol. 4: The Twentieth Century, Oxford 1999, pp. 47–63.
Hutcheson, John A., *Leopold Maxse and the National Review 1893–1914: Right-Wing Politics and Journalism in the Edwardian Era*, New York 1989.
Hyam, Ronald, *Understanding the British Empire*, Cambridge 2010.
Hynes, Samuel, *The Edwardian Turn of Mind*, London 1968.
———, *A War Imagined: The First World War and English Culture*, London 1990.
Ingram, Edward, 'Approaches to the Great Game', in *Middle Eastern Studies* 18/4 (1982), pp. 449–57.
Israel, Uwe, and Jürgen Gebauer, *Panzerschiffe um 1900*, 2. Ed., Berlin 1998.
Iriye, Akira, 'Culture and International History', in M.J. Hogan and Th.G. Petersson (Eds.), *Explaining the History of American Foreign Relations*, Cambridge 1991, pp. 214–25.
———, *Cultural Internationalism and World Order*, Baltimore 1997.
Jaeckel, Horst, *Die Nordwestgrenze in der Verteidigung Indiens, 1900–1908 und der Weg Englands zum russisch-britischen Abkommen von 1907*, Cologne 1968.
James, David, *Lord Roberts*, With a Foreword by L.S. Amery, London 1954.
James, Robert R., *Rosebery*, London 1964.
James, Lawrence, *The Rise and Fall of the British Empire*, London 1994.
Janiesch, Ulrich, *Satire und politischer Roman: Untersuchungen zum Romanwerk Benjamin Disraelis*, Amsterdam 1975.
Janis, Irving L., *Victims of Groupthink*, Boston 1972.
Jansen, Dorothea, *Einführung in die Netzwerkanalyse: Grundlagen, Methoden, Anwendungen*, Opladen 1999.
Jefferson, Margaret M., *The Place of Constantinople and the Straits in British Foreign Policy 1890–1902*, MA Thesis, London 1959.
Jelavich, Barbara, 'Great Britain and the Russian Acquisition of Batum, 1878–1886', in *Slavonic and East European Review* 48 (1970), pp. 44–66.
Jenkins, Roy, *Sir Charles Dilke: A Victorian Tragedy*, London 1958.
———, *Mr Balfour's Poodle: An Account of the Struggle between the House of Lords and the Government of Mr Asquith*, London 1954.
Jervis, Robert, 'Hypotheses on Misperception', in K. Knorr (Ed.), *Power, Strategy, and Security*, Princeton 1983, pp. 152–77.
———, *Perception and Misperception in International Politics*, Princeton 1976.
Johnson, Franklyn A., *Defence by Committee: The British Committee of Imperial Defence 1885–1959*, London 1960.
Joll, James, *The Origins of the First World War*, London 1984.
Jones, Heather, and Richard Smith (Eds.), 'Edward Grey' (special issue), *International History Review* 36/2 (2016), pp. 243–355.
Jones, Kennedy, *Fleet Street and Downing Street*, London 1920.
Jones, Raymond A., *The British Diplomatic Service 1815–1914*, London 1983.
Jones, R.B., 'Anglo-French Negotiations, 1907: A Memorandum by Sir A. Milner', in *Bulletin of the Institute of Historical Research* 31 (1958), pp. 224-7.
Judd, Denis, *Empire. The British Imperial Experience from 1765 to the Present*, London 1996.
———, *Balfour and the British Empire: A Study in Imperial Evolution, 1874–1932*, London 1968.
———, *Radical Joe: A Life of Joseph Chamberlain*, London 1977.

Kabisch, Ernst, 'England und die Annexionskrise 1908/09', in *Berliner Monatshefte* 8 (1930), pp 915–932.
Kann, Robert A., 'Trends toward colonialism in the Habsburg Empire, 1878–1918: The case of Bosnia-Herzegovina, 1878–1914', in *Russian and Slavic History*, ed. by D.K. Rowney and G.E. Orchard, Dexter, MI 1977, pp. 164–80.
Kazemzadeh, Firuz, *Russia and Britain in Persia, 1864–1914: A Study in Imperialism*, London 1968.
Keegan, John, *The Face of Battle: A Study of Agincourt, Waterloo and the Somme*, London 1976.
Keiger, John F.V., 'Sir Edward Grey, France, and the Entente: How to Catch the Perfect Angler?', in *IHR* 38 (2016), pp. 285–300.
———, *France and the Origins of the First World War*, London 1983.
Kennan, George F., *The Decline of Bismarck's European Order: Franco-Russian Relations*, New Jersey 1979.
———, *The Fateful Alliance: France, Russia and the Coming of the First World War*, New Jersey 1984.
Kennedy, Paul M., 'Mahan vs. Mackinder: Two Interpretations of British Sea Power', in *Militärgeschichtliche Mitteilungen* 2 (1974), pp. 39–66.
———, 'Maritime Strategieprobleme der deutsch-englischen Flottenrivalität', in Herbert Schottelius and Wilhelm Deist (Eds.), *Marine und Marinepolitik im kaiserlichen Deutschland 1871–1914*, Düsseldorf 1972, pp. 178–210.
———, 'The Development of German Naval Operations: Plans against England, 1896–1914', in *EHR* 89 (1974), pp. 48–6.
———, *Nationalist and Racialist Movements in Britain and Germany before 1914*, Oxford 1981.
———, *The Realities behind Diplomacy: Background Influences on British External Policy, 1865–1980*, London 1981.
———, *The Rise of Anglo-German Antagonism, 1860–1914*, London 1980.
———, *The Rise and Fall of British Naval Mastery*, New York 1976.
———, *The Rise and Fall of the Great Powers: Economic Change and Military Conflict from 1500 to 2000*, London 1988.
———, 'The Tradition of Appeasement in British Foreign Policy', in *British Journal of International Studies* 2 (1976), pp. 195–203.
———, *The War Plans of the Great Powers 1880–1914*, London 1979.
———, 'Why Britain Went to War', in *Sunday Times*, 19 September 1999.
Kent, M., 'Agent of Empire? The National Bank of Turkey and British Foreign Policy', in *HJ* 17/2 (1975), pp. 367–89.
———, 'Great Britain and the End of the Ottoman Empire 1900–1923', in M. Kent (Ed.), *The Great Powers and the End of the Ottoman Empire*, London 1984, pp. 173–98.
Kerr, M., *Prince Louis of Battenberg*, London 1934.
Kießling, Friedrich, 'Der "Dialog der Taubstummen" ist vorbei: Neue Ansätze in der Geschichte der internationalen Beziehungen des 19. und 20. Jahrhunderts', in *Historische Zeitschrift* 275 (2002), pp. 651–80.
———, *Gegen den 'großen Krieg': Entspannung in den internationalen Beziehungen 1911–1914*, Munich 2002.
———, 'Wege aus der Stringenzfalle: Die Vorgeschichte des Ersten Weltkriegs als "Ära der Entspannung"', in *Geschichte in Wissenschaft und Unterricht* 55 (2004), pp. 284–304.

———, 'Österreich-Ungarn und die deutsch-englischen Détentebemühungen 1912–1914', in *Historisches Jahrbuch* 116 (1996), pp. 102–25.
Kissinger, Henry A., *Diplomacy*, New York, London 1994.
———, *A World Restored: Metternich, Castlereagh and the Problems of Peace*, New York 1957.
Klein, Ira, 'The Anglo-Russian Convention and the Problem of Central Asia 1907–1914', in *JBS* 11/1 (1971), pp. 126–47.
———, 'British Intervention in the Persian Revolution, 1905–1909', in *HJ* 12/3 (1972), pp. 731–52.
Kneer, Warren, 'Great Britain and the Caribbean, 1901–1913: A Study in Anglo-American Relations'. PhD thesis, Michigan State University 1966.
Knight, Alan, 'Britain and Latin America', in Andrew Porter (Ed.), *The Oxford History of the British Empire, vol. III, The Nineteenth Century*, Oxford and New York 1999, pp. 122–145.
Koch, Hansjoachmin W., 'The Anglo-German Alliance Negotiations: Missed Opportunity or Myth?', in *History* 54 (1969), pp. 378–92.
——— (Ed.), *The Origins of the First World War: Great Power Rivalry and German War Aims*, 2nd ed., Basingstoke 1984.
———, 'Social Darwinism as a Factor in the "New Imperialism"', in Hansjoachmin W. Koch (Ed.), *The Origins of the First World War: Great Power Rivalry and German War Aims*, Basingstoke 1984, pp. 319–42.
Koselleck, Reinhart, '"Erfahrungsraum" und "Erwartungshorizont": zwei historische Kategorien', in Reinhart Koselleck, *Vergangene Zukunft: Zur Semantik geschichtlicher Zeiten*, Frankfurt a. M. 1989, pp. 349–75.
Koss, Stephen E., *Fleet Street Radical: A.G. Gardiner and the Daily News*, London 1973.
———, *The Rise and Fall of the Political Press in Britain: The 19th Century*, London 1981.
Kröger, Martin, 'Ein gerade noch berechenbares Risiko: Die bosnische Annexionskrise 1908/09', in J. Dülffer et al. (Ed.), *Vermiedene Kriege: Deeskalation von Konflikten der Großmächte zwischen Krimkrieg und Erstem Weltkrieg (1856–1914)*, Munich 1997, pp. 602–614.
Kronenbitter, Günther, *'Krieg im Frieden': Die Führung der k.u.k Armee und die Großmachtpolitik Österreichs-Ungarns 1906–1914*, Munich 2003.
Lambert, Andrew, 'The Development of Education in the Royal Navy: 1854–1914', in G. Till (Ed.), *The Development of British Naval Thinking: Essays in Memory of Bryan Ranft*, London 2006, pp. 34–59.
Lambert, Nicholas A., 'Admiral Sir John Fisher and the Concept of Flotilla Defence, 1904–1910', in *Journal of Military History* 59/4 (10/1995), pp. 639–60.
———, *Planning Armageddon: British Economic Warfare and the First World War*, Harvard 2012.
———, 'Righting the Scholarship: The Battle-Cruiser in History and Historiography', in *HJ* 58/1 (2015), pp. 275–307.
———, *Sir John Fisher's Naval Revolution*, Columbia, SC 1999.
Lambi, Ivo N., *The Navy and German Power Politics 1862–1914*, London 1984.
Lammers, D., 'Arno Mayer and the British Decision for War', in *JBS* 12 (1973), pp. 137–65.
Landwehr, Achim, 'Diskurs – Macht – Wissen: Perspektiven einer Kulturgeschichte des Politischen', in *Archiv für Kulturgeschichte* 35 (2003), pp. 71–117.
Langdon, John W., *July 1914: The Long Debate, 1918–1990*, Oxford 1991.
Langer, William L., 'The 1908 Prelude to the World War', in *Foreign Affairs: An American Quarterly Review* 7 (1928/1929), pp. 635–49.

———, *The Diplomacy of Imperialism*, New York 1960.
Langhorne, Richard, *The Collapse of the Concert of Europe: International Politics 1890–1914*, London 1981.
———, 'The Naval Question in Anglo-German Relations, 1912–1914', in *HJ* 14 (1971), pp. 359–70.
Lee, Alan J., *The Origins of the Popular Press, 1855–1914*, London 1976.
Lee, Dwight E. (Ed.), *The Outbreak of the First World War: Who was Responsible?*, 2nd ed., Boston 1966.
Lee, Sidney, *Edward VII*, Vol. 2, London 1927.
Lehmkuhl, Ursula, 'Größe und "Selbstbehauptung" als Formeln britischer Weltgeltung: Einige theoretische und methodische Überlegungen', in Ursula Lehmkuhl and Hans-Heinrich Jansen (Eds.), *Großbritannien, das Empire und die Welt*, Bochum 1995, pp. 3–31.
Lejeune, Anthony, *The Gentlemen's Clubs*, London 1979.
Leventhal, F.M., 'H.N. Brailsford and the Search for a New International Order', in A.J.A. Morris (Ed.), *Edwardian Radicalism 1900–1914: Some Aspects of British Radicalism*, London 1974, pp. 202–17.
Levy, J.L., 'Misperception and the Causes of War', in *World Politics* 36/1 (1983/84), pp. 76–99.
Lieven, Dominic, *Russia and the Origins of the First World War*, London 1983.
———, *Towards the Flame: Empire, War and the End of Tsarist Russia*, London 2015.
Lindlay, Francis, *Lord Lovat: A Biography*, London 1935.
Lippmann, Walter, *Public Opinion*, New York 1922.
———, *Die Öffentliche Meinung*, ed. by H.-D. Fischer, reprint, Bochum 1990.
Livermore, Seward W., 'Theodore Roosevelt, the American Navy and the Venezuela Crisis of 1902–1903', in *American Historical Review* 51 (1945), pp. 459–62.
Loth, Wilfried, and Jürgen Osterhammel (Eds.), *Internationale Geschichte: Themen – Ergebnisse – Aussichten*, Munich 2000.
Lowe, Cedric J., *The Reluctant Imperialists: British Foreign Policy 1878–1902*, 2 Vols., London 1967.
———, *Salisbury and the Mediterranean, 1886–96*, London 1965.
Lowe, Cedric J., and Michael Dockrill, *The Mirage of Power, Vol. 1: British Foreign Policy 1902–1914*, London 1972.
Luhmann, Niklas, '"Öffentliche Meinung": Politische Planung', in *Politische Vierteljahresschrift* 11/1 (1970), pp. 2–28.
Luntinen, Pertti, *The Baltic Question 1903–1908*, Helsinki 1975.
Lutz, Hermann, *Eyre Crowe: Der Böse Geist des Foreign Office*, Stuttgart and Berlin 1931.
Luvaas, Jay, *The Education of an Army: British Military Thought 1815–1940*, Chicago 1964.
MacDiarmed, D.S., *The Life of Lieutenant-General Sir James Moncrieff Grierson*, London 1923.
Macintosh, John, 'The Role of the Committee of Imperial Defence before 1914', in *EHR* 77 (7/1962), pp. 490–503.
Mack, E.C., *Public Schools and British Public Opinion*, London 1941.
Mackay, Ruddock, *Fisher of Kilverstone*, Oxford 1973.
Mahajan, Sneh, 'The Defence of India and the End of Isolation', in *JICH* 10 (1982), pp. 168–93.
Mansergh, Nicholas, *The Coming of the First World War: A Study in the European 1878–1914*, London 1949.
Marder, Arthur J., *Anatomy of British Sea Power, 1885–1905*, London 1940 (Reprint 1964).

———, *From Dreadnought to Scapa Flow: The Royal Navy in the Fisher Era, 1904–1919*, 5 Vols., London 1961–1970.
———, *Portrait of an Admiral: The Life and Papers of Herbert Richmond*, Harvard 1952.
Martel, Gordon, *Imperial Diplomacy: Rosebery and the Failure of Foreign Policy*, Montreal 1986.
———, 'The Meaning of Power: Rethinking the Decline and Fall of Great Britain', in *IHR* 13/4 (1991), pp. 662–94.
Marwick, Arthur, *The Deluge: British Society and the First World War*, London 1965.
Massie, Robert K., *Dreadnought: Britain, Germany and the Coming of the Great War*, London and New York 1992.
Matthew, Henry C., *The Liberal Imperialists: The Ideas and Politics of a Post Gladstonian Elite*, Oxford 1973.
Maude, George, 'Finland in Anglo-Russian Diplomatic Relations, 1899–1910', in *Slavonic and East European Review* 48 (1970), pp. 557–580.
May, Arthur J., 'The Novibazar Railway Project', in *JMH* 10 (1938), pp. 496–527.
Mayer, Martin, *Geheime Diplomatie und öffentliche Meinung: Die Parlamente in Frankreich, Deutschland und Großbritannien und die erste Marokkokrise 1904–1906*, Dusseldorf 2002.
McDermott, John, 'The Revolution in British Military Thinking from the Boer War to the Moroccan Crisis', in *Canadian Journal of History* 9/2 (1974), pp. 159–77.
McKercher, Brian, '"Diplomatic Equipoise": The Lansdowne Foreign Office, the Russo-Japanese War of 1904–1905, and the Global Balance of Power', in *CJH* 24 (1989), pp. 299–340.
McLean, David, *Britain and Her Buffer State: The Collapse of the Persian Empire 1890–1914*, London 1979.
———, 'English Radicals, Russia and the Fate of Persia 1907–1913', in *EHR* 93 (1978), pp. 338–52.
McLean, Robert, *Royalty and Diplomacy in Europe, 1890–1914*, Cambridge 2001.
McMeekin, Sean, *The Russian Origins of the First World War*, Harvard 2011.
Medlicott, William N., 'The Mediterranean Agreements of 1887', in *Slavonic Review* 5 (1926/7), pp. 66–88.
Meinecke, Friedrich, *Geschichte des deutsch-englischen Bündnisproblems 1890–1901*, Darmstadt 1972.
Messerschmidt, Manfred, *Deutschland in englischer Sicht: Die Wandlungen des Deutschlandbildes in der englischen Geschichtsschreibung*, Düsseldorf 1955.
Metz, Karl H., *Industrialisierung und Sozialpolitik: Das Problem der sozialen Sicherheit in Großbritannien 1795–1911*, Göttingen 1988.
Metzler, Gabriele, *Großbritannien – Weltmacht in Europa: Handelspolitik im Wandel des europäischen Staatensystems 1856–1871*, Berlin 1997.
Michalka, Wolfgang (Ed.), *Der Erste Weltkrieg: Wirkung – Wahrnehmung – Analyse*, Munich 1994.
———, 'Blick voraus in die Vergangenheit: Anmerkungen zu Niall Fergusons Deutung des Ersten Weltkriegs', in *Die Welt*, 19 June1999.
Miller, Geoff, *Straits, British Policy towards the Ottoman Empire and the Origins of the Dardanelles Campaign*, Cambridge 1997.
———, *The Millstone: British Naval Policy in the Mediterranean 1900–1914: The Commitment to France and the British Intervention in the War* [Online: http://www.manorhouse.clara.net/book3].

Mitchell, Nancy, *Danger of Dreams: German and American Imperialism in Latin America*, Chapel Hill 1999.
Mollin, Gerhard Thomas, 'Schlachtflottenbau vor 1914: Überlegungen zum Wesen des deutsch-britischen Antagonismus', in Hartmut Berghoff (Ed.), *Pionier und Nachzügler: Vergleichende Studien zur Geschichte Großbritanniens und Deutschlands im Zeitalter der Industrialisierung*, Bochum 1995, pp. 167–85.
Mombauer, Annika, 'Sir Edward Grey, Germany, and the Outbreak of the First World War: A Re-Evaluation', in *IHR* 38 (2016), pp. 301-325.
———, *Die Julikrise: Europas Weg in den Ersten Weltkrieg*, Munich 2014.
———, *The Origins of the First World War: Controversies and Consensus*, London 2002.
Mommsen, Wolfgang J., 'Der Topos vom unvermeidlichen Krieg: Außenpolitik und öffentliche Meinung im Deutschen Reich im letzten Jahrzehnt vor 1914', in Wolfgang J. Mommsen (Ed.), *Der autoritäre Nationalstaat: Verfassung, Gesellschaft und Kultur im deutschen Kaiserreich*, Frankfurt a.M. 1990, pp. 380–406.
———, *Großmachtstellung und Weltpolitik: Die Außenpolitik des Deutschen Reiches 1870 bis 1914*, Frankfurt a. M. 1993.
———, 'War der erste Weltkrieg vermeidbar? Niall Fergusons provokative Betrachtungen zur europäischen Urkatastrophe', in *Die Zeit*, No. 17, 22 April 1999.
———, *War der Kaiser an allem Schuld? Wilhelm II. und die preußisch-deutschen Machteliten*, Berlin 2002.
———, *Der Erste Weltkrieg: Anfang vom Ende des bürgerlichen Zeitalters*, Frankfurt a. M. 2004.
Monger, George W., *The End of Isolation: British Foreign Policy, 1900–1907*, London 1963.
Moore, Robin J., 'Imperial India, 1858–1914', in Andrew N. Porter (Ed.), *The Oxford History of the British Empire: Vol. III., The Nineteenth Century*, Oxford 1999, pp. 422–446.
Morris, A.J. Anthony (Ed.), *Edwardian Radicalism, 1900–1914: Some Aspects of British Radicalism*, London 1974.
———, 'The English Radicals' Campaign for Disarmament and the Hague Conference of 1907', in *JMH* 43/3 (1971), pp. 367–93.
———, *The Scaremongers: The Advocacy of War and Rearmament, 1896–1914*, London 1984.
——— (Ed.), *The Letters of Lieutenant-Colonel Charles à Court Repington CMG. Military Correspondent of The Times, 1903–1918*, Bodmin 1999.
Müllenbrock, Hans-Joachim, *Literatur und Zeitgeschichte in England zwischen dem Ende des 19. Jahrhunderts und dem Ausbruch des Ersten Weltkrieges*, Hamburg 1967.
———, 'Trugbilder: Zum Dilemma imagologischer Forschung am Beispiel des englischen Deutschlandbildes 1870–1914', in *Anglia* 113 (1995), pp. 303–29.
Naujoks, Eberhard, 'Pressepolitik und Geschichtswissenschaft', in *Geschichte in Wissenschaft und Unterricht* 22 (1971), pp. 7–22.
Nauticus (Ed.), *Jahrbuch für Deutschlands Seeinteressen*, Berlin 1909.
Neilson, Keith, *Britain and the Last Tsar 1894–1917*, London 1995.
———, '"A Dangerous Game of American Poker": Britain and the Russo-Japanese War', in *JSS* 12 (1980), pp. 63–87.
———, '"Greatly Exaggerated": The Myth of the Decline of Great Britain before 1914', in *IHR* 13/4 (1991), pp. 695–723.
———, '"My Beloved Russians": Sir Arthur Nicolson and Russia, 1906–1916', in *IHR* 11/4 (1987), pp. 521–54.

———, 'Watching the Steamroller: British Observers and the Russian Army before 1914', in *JSS* 8/2 (1985), pp. 199–217.
Neitzel, Sönke, *Kriegsausbruch: Deutschlands Weg in die Katastrophe 1900–1914*, Munich 2002.
Newton, Douglas, *The Darkest Days: The Truth behind Britain's Rush to War, 1914*, London and New York 2014.
Newton, Lord [Thomas Wodehouse Legh], *Lord Lansdowne: A Biography*, London 1929.
Nicholls, David, *The Lost Prime Minister: A Life of Sir Charles Dilke*, London 1955.
Nicolson, Colin, 'Edwardian England and the Coming of the First World War', in Alan O'Day (Ed.), *The Edwardian Age: Conflict and Stability, 1902–1914*, London 1979.
Nicolson, Harold, *Sir Arthur Nicolson: Lord Carnock. A Study in the Old Diplomacy*, London 1930.
———, *Die Verschwörung der Diplomaten: Aus Sir Arthur Nicolsons Leben 1849–1928*. Mit einem Vorwort von Richard von Kühlmann, Frankfurt a. M. 1931.
———, *King George V*, London 1952.
Niedhart, Gottfried, 'Perzeption und Image als Gegenstand der Geschichte von den internationalen Beziehungen: Eine Problemskizze', in Bernd-Jürgen Wendt (Ed.), *Das britische Deutschlandbild im Wandel des 19. und 20. Jahrhunderts*, Bochum 1984, pp. 39–52.
———, 'Selektive Wahrnehmung und politisches Handeln: Internationale Beziehungen im Perzeptionsparadigma', in Wilfried Loth et al. (Eds.), *Internationale Geschichte: Themen – Ereignisse – Aussichten*, Munich 2000, pp. 141–158.
———, *Geschichte Englands im 19. und 20. Jahrhundert*, Munich 1996.
Nintchitch, Momtilo, *La Crise Bosniaque (1908–1909) et les Puissances européennes*, 2 Vols., Paris 1937.
Nipperdey, Thomas, *Deutsche Geschichte, 1800–1918*, 3 Vols., Munich 1992.
Nish, Ian, *The Anglo-Japanese Alliance: The Diplomacy of Two Island Empires 1894–1907*, London 1966.
O'Day, Alan, *The Edwardian Age*, London 1979.
Offer, Avner, *The First World War: An Agrarian Interpretation*, Oxford 1989.
Ortenburg, Günther, *Waffen der Millionenheere 1871–1914*, Bonn 1992.
O'Sullivan, E., 'National Stereotypes as Literary Device: Traditions and Uses of Stereotypes of Germans', in H. Husemann (Ed.), *British and the English in German Children's Literature, As Others See Us: Anglo-German Perceptions*, Frankfurt a. M., 1994, pp. 81–88.
Otte, Thomas G., 'Postponing the Evil Day: Sir Edward Grey and British Foreign Policy', in *IHR* 38 (2016), pp. 250–263.
———, '"Almost a Law of Nature": Sir Edward Grey, the Foreign Office and the Balance of Power in Europe, 1905–1912', in Erik Goldstein and Brian McKercher (Eds.), *Britain and the Problem of Europe, 1900–1970: Diplomacy, Finance and Strategy*, Westport, CN 2002, pp. 77–118.
———, *The China Question: Great Power Rivalry and British Isolation 1894–1905*, Oxford 2007.
———, 'The Elusive Balance: British Foreign Policy and the French Entente before the First World War', in A. Sharp and G. Stone (Eds.), *Anglo-French Relations in the Twentieth Century*, London 2000, pp. 11–35.
———, 'Eyre Crowe and British Foreign Policy: A Cognitive Map', in Thomas G. Otte and Constantine A. Pagedas (Eds.), *Personalities, War and Diplomacy: Essays in International History*, London 1997, pp. 14–37.

———, *Foreign Office Mind: The Making of British Foreign Policy, 1865–1914*, Cambridge 2011.

———, 'Great Britain, Germany and the Far Eastern Crisis 1897–8', in *EHR* 110 (1995), pp. 1157–79.

———, '"Heaven knows where we shall finally drift": Lord Salisbury, the Cabinet, Isolation and the Boxer Rebellion', in Keith Neilson and Greg Kennedy (Eds.), *Incidents in International Relations*, Westport, CN 2002, pp. 25–45.

———, *July Crisis: The World's Descent into War, Summer 1914*, Cambridge 2014.

——— (Ed.), *The Makers of British Foreign Policy: From Pitt to Thatcher*, Basingstoke and New York 2002.

———, 'A Question of Leadership: Lord Salisbury, the Unionist Cabinet and Foreign Policy Making, 1895–1900', in *Contemporary British History* 14/4 (2000), pp. 1–26.

Otte, Thomas G., and Constantine A. Pagedas (Eds.), *Personalities, War and Diplomacy: Essays in International History*, London 1997.

Padfield, Peter, *The Great Naval Race*, London 1974.

Paléologue, Maurice, *Un grand tournant de la Politique Mondiale 1904–1906*, Paris 1934.

Palmer, Alan, *Glanz und Niedergang der Diplomatie: Die Geheimpolitik der Europäischen Kanzleien vom Wiener Kongreß bis zum Ausbruch des Ersten Weltkriegs*, Düsseldorf 1986.

Pantenburg, Isabel F., *Im Schatten des Zweibundes: Probleme österreichisch-ungarischer Bündnispolitik 1897–1908*, Vienna 1996.

Parry, Jonathan, *The Politics of Patriotism: English Liberalism, National Identity and Europe, 1830–1886*, Cambridge 2006.

Parsons, Edward B., 'The German-American Crisis of 1902–1903', in *Historian* 33 (1971), pp. 436–52.

Paulmann, Johannes, *Pomp und Politik: Monarchenbegegnungen in Europa zwischen Ancien Régime und Erstem Weltkrieg*, Paderborn, 2000.

Petter, Wolfgang, 'Deutsche Flottenrüstung von Wallenstein bis Tirpitz', in *Handbuch zur deutschen Militärgeschichte*, Vol. 5/VIII, Munich 1979.

Philippi, H., 'Die Botschafter der europäischen Mächte am Berliner Hofe 1871–1914', in O. Hauser (Ed.), *Vorträge und Studien zur preußisch-deutschen Geschichte*, Cologne and Vienna 1983, pp. 159–251.

Plass, Jens B., *England zwischen Deutschland und Rußland: Der persische Golf in der britischen Vorkriegspolitik 1899–1907*, Hamburg 1966.

Platt, Desmond, 'British Bondholders', in *Inter-America Economic Affairs* 14 (1960), pp. 3–43.

———, 'Economic Factors in British Policy during the "New Imperialism"', in *Past & Present* 39 (1968), pp. 120–38.

———, *Finance, Trade, and Politics in British Foreign Policy 1815–1914*, London 1968.

———, 'The Allied Coercion of Venezuela, 1902–03: A Reassessment', in *Inter- American Economic Affairs* 15 (1962), pp. 3–28.

Playne, Caroline E., *The Pre-war Mind in Britain: An Historical Review*, London 1928.

Pokrowski, Michail N., *Drei Konferenzen: Zur Vorgeschichte des Krieges*, no place 1920.

Pollard, Sidney, *Britain's Prime and Britain's Decline: The British Economy, 1870–1914*, London 1989.

Pommerin, Reiner, *Der Kaiser und Amerika*, Cologne 1986.

Pope-Hennessy, James, *Lord Crewe, 1858–1945: The Likeness of a Liberal*, London 1955.

Porter, Andrew N., *The Origins of the South African War*, Manchester 1980.

―――― (Ed.), *The Oxford History of the British Empire, Vol. 3: The Nineteenth Century*, Oxford 1999.
Porter, Bernard, *Britain, Europe and the World 1850–1986: Delusions of Grandeur*, London 1987.
――――, *The Lion's Share: A Short History of British Imperialism 1850–1995*, 3. Ed. London 1996.
Potter, Elmar, and Chester Nimitz, *Seemacht: Eine Seekriegsgeschichte von der Antike bis zur Gegenwart*, Munich 1974.
Pound, R., and G. Harmsworth, *Northcliffe*, London 1959.
Pribram, Alfred F., *Austria-Hungary and Great Britain 1908–1914*, London 1951.
Priestley, John B., *The Edwardians*, London 1970.
Prochnow, Günther (Ed.), *Deutsche Kriegsschiffe in zwei Jahrhunderten*, 4 Vols., Preetz and Holstein 1964–1967.
Proksch, Reto, *Alfred Thayer Mahan: Seine Thesen und sein Einfluss auf die Außen- und Sicherheitspolitik der USA*, Frankfurt 2002.
Pugh, Martin, *The Making of Modern British Politics, 1867–1939*, 2nd ed., Oxford 1993.
Read, Donald (Ed.), *Edwardian England 1901–15, Society and Politics*, London 1982.
――――, *England 1868–1914: The Age of Urban Democracy*, New York 1979.
――――, *The Power of News: The History of Reuters*, Oxford 1999.
Read, James M., *Das Problem der deutschen Vermittlung beim Ausgang der Bosnischen Krise*, Berlin 1933.
Reinermann, Lothar, *Der Kaiser in England: Wilhelm II. und sein Bild in der britischen Öffentlichkeit*, Paderborn 2001.
Reifeld, Helmut, *Zwischem Empire und Parlament: Zur Gedankenbildung und Politik Lord Roseberys (1880–1905)*, Göttingen 1987.
Remak, Joachim, *The Origins of World War I, 1871–1914*, New York 1967.
――――, '1914 – The Third Balkan War: Origins Reconsidered', in H.W. Koch (Ed.) *The Origins of the First World War: Great Power Rivalry and German War Aims*, 2nd Edition London 1984, pp. 86–100.
Richards, John, and Ernst von Glaserfeld, 'Die Kontrolle der Wahrnehmung und die Konstruktion von Realität: Erkenntnistheoretische Aspekte des Rückkopplungs-Kontroll-Systems', in *Delfin: Eine deutsche Zeitschrift für Konstruktion, Analyse und Kritik* 3 (1984), pp. 4–25.
Ritter, Gerhard, *Staatskunst und Kriegshandwerk: Das Problem des „Militarismus" in Deutschland*, Vol. 2, Munich 1960
――――, 'Eine neue Kriegsschuldthese?: Zu Fritz Fischers Buch "Griff nach der Weltmacht"', in *Historische Zeitschrift* 194 (1962), pp. 646–68.
Robbins, Keith, 'Public Opinion, the Press and Pressure Groups', in Francis H. Hinsley (Ed.), *British Foreign Policy under Sir Edward Grey*, Cambridge 1977, pp. 70–88.
――――, *Sir Edward Grey: A Biography of Grey of Fallodon*, London 1971.
Roberts, Andrew, *Salisbury – Victorian Titan*, London 1999.
Robertson, William, *Soldiers and Statesmen 1914–1918*, Vol. 1, London 1926.
Robinson, Ronald E., and John Gallagher, *Africa and the Victorians*, London 1961.
Robson, Robert (Ed.), *Ideas and Institutions of Victorian Britain: Essays in Honour of George Kitson Clark*, London 1967.
Rohe, Karl, 'The British Imperialist Intelligentsia and the Kaiserreich', in Paul M. Kennedy and Antony J. Nichols (Eds.), *Nationalist and Racialist Movements in Britain and Germany before 1914*, London 1984, pp. 130–42.

———, 'Die englische Parteienlandschaft am Anfang des 20. Jahrhunderts', in William Manchester (Ed.), *Winston Churchill: Der Traum vom Ruhm 1874–1932*, Boston 1989, pp. 1097–117.

Röhl, John, 'Die Generalprobe: Zur Geschichte und Bedeutung des "Kriegsrats" vom 8. Dezember 1912', in D. Stegmann et al. (Eds.), *Industrielle Gesellschaft und politisches System: Beiträge zur politischen Sozialgeschichte. Festschrift für Fritz Fischer zum 70. Geburtstag*, Bonn 1978, pp. 357–73.

———, *Wilhelm II: Der Weg in den Abgrund 1900–1941*, Munich 2008.

Rohwer, Jürgen, 'Kriegsschiffbau und Flottengesetze um die Jahrhundertwende', in Herbert Schottelius and Wilhelm Deist (Eds.), *Marine und Marinepolitik im kaiserlichen Deutschland 1871–1914*, Düsseldorf 1972, pp. 211–35.

Rolo, P.J.V., *Entente Cordiale: The Origins and Negotiation of the Anglo-French Agreements of 8 April 1904*, London 1969.

———, 'Lansdowne', in Keith Wilson (Ed.), *British Foreign Secretaries from the Crimean War to the First World War*, London 1987, pp. 159–170.

Ropp, Theodore, *The Development of a Modern Navy: French Naval Policy 1871–1904* (PhD Thesis, Cambridge, MA 1937), ed. Stephen S. Roberts, Annapolis 1987.

Ropponen, Risto, *Die Kraft Rußlands: Wie beurteilte die Politische Militärische Führung der Europäischen Großmächte in der Zeit von 1905 bis 1914 die Kraft Rußlands?* Helsinki 1968.

Rose, Andreas, *Die Außenpolitik des wilhelminischen Kaiserreiches 1890–1918*, Darmstadt 2013.

———, '"Blue Water" vs. "Blue Funk": Britain's Naval Policy and the Anglo-German Naval Race, Revisited (1900–1909)', in Marcus O. Jones (Ed.), *New Interpretations in Naval History: Selected Papers from the 17th Naval History Symposium Held at the United States Naval Academy*, Annapolis (forthcoming 2017), pp. 80–100.

———, '"Forecasting Armageddon": British Military Journals and the Images of Future Warfare (1856–1914/18)', forthcoming 2017.

———, 'Eine Frage der Deutungshoheit? Neuere Literatur zum Kriegsausbruch 1914'. H-Soz-Kult 2014. (http://www.hsozkult.de/publicationreview/id/rezbuecher-21344)

———, 'From "Illusion" and "Angellism" to Détente: British Radicals and the Balkan Wars', in Dominik Geppert, William Mulligan and Andreas Rose (Eds.), *The Wars before the Great War: Conflicts and International Politics before the Outbreak of the First World War*, Cambridge 2015, pp. 320–42.

———, 'International Relations, 1871–1914', in Matthew Jefferies (Ed.), *The Ashgate Research Companion to Imperial Germany*, Manchester 2015, pp. 347–66.

———, 'Lloyd George und die Kriegsentscheidung im August 1914', in Jürgen P. Schmied (Ed.), *Liberale und linksliberale Interventionisten vom 19. Jahrhundert bis in die Gegenwart*, Bonn, forthcoming 2017.

———, '"Peace Party at War": Die britischen Radikalliberalen und der Große Krieg', in *Jahrbuch zur Liberalismus-Forschung*, 26 (2014), pp. 95–123.

———, 'Der politische Raum Londons und die öffentlichen Beziehungen zwischen England und Deutschland vor 1914', in Frank Bösch and Peter Hoeres (Eds.), *Außenpolitik im Medienzeitalter: Vom späten 19. Jahrhundert bis zur Gegenwart*, Göttingen 2013, pp. 95–121.

———, '"Readiness or Ruin": Die britischen Militärzeitschriften und der Krieg der Zukunft (1880–1914)', in Stig Förster (Ed.), *Vor dem Sprung ins Dunkle: Die Debatten in den*

Militärzeitschriften des Deutschen Reiches, Frankreichs und Großbritanniens über den Krieg der Zukunft, 1880–1914, Paderborn 2016, pp. 245–390.

———, 'Review of Matthew Seligmann, *The Royal Navy and the German Threat 1901–1914: Admiralty Plans to Protect British Trade in a War Against Germany*', in *Bulletin of the German Historical Institute* 35/2 (2013), pp. 125–31.

———, '"Two Rival Syndicates": Towards a Fritz Fischer-like Approach to British Foreign Politics', in Andreas Gestrich and Hartmut Pogge von Strandmann (Eds.), *Bid for World Power? New Research on the Outbreak of the First World War*, Oxford 2017, pp. 77–102.

———, '"Unsichtbare Feinde": Großbritanniens Feldzug gegen die Buren (1899–1902)', in Dierk Walter, Tanja Bührer and Christian Stachelbeck (Eds.), *Imperialkriege von 1500 bis heute: Strukturen – Akteure – Lernprozesse*, Paderborn 2011, pp. 217–39.

———, '"Waiting for Armageddon"? British Military Journals and the Images of Future Wars (1890–1914)', in *Francia: Forschungen zur westeuropäischen Geschichte*, Vol. 40 (2013), pp. 317–31.

———, '"The Writers, Not the Sailors": Großbritannien, die Hochseeflotte und die "Revolution der Staatenwelt"', in Sönke Neitzel and Bernd Heidenreich (Eds.), *Das Deutsche Kaiserreich 1890–1914*, Paderborn 2011, pp. 221–40, 340–49.

———, *Zwischen Empire und Kontinent: Die britische Außenpolitik vor dem Ersten Weltkrieg*, Munich 2011.

———, 'Zwischen Tories und Radicals: David Lloyd George und die Kriegsentscheidung am 4. August 1914', in Jürgen P. Schmied (Ed.), *Liberale und linksliberale Interventionisten vom 19. Jahrhundert bis in die Gegenwart*, Göttingen (forthcoming 2017).

———, Review on 'Sir Edward Grey and the Outbreak of the First World War', in *IHR* 38 (2016), pp. 243–355.

Rose, Andreas, with Dominik Geppert, 'Machtpolitik und Flottenbau vor 1914: Zur Neuinterpretation britischer Außenpolitik im Zeitalter des Hochimperialismus', in *Historische Zeitschrift* 293 (October 2011), pp. 401–37.

Rose, Andreas, et al. (Eds.), *The Wars before the Great War: Conflicts and International Politics before the Outbreak of the First World War*, Cambridge 2015.

Rose, Jonathan, *The Edwardian Temperament 1895–1919*, Athens 1987.

Rose, Lisle A., *Power at Sea: The Age of Navalism, 1890–1918*, Columbia 2007.

Rosenberger, Bernhard, *Zeitungen als Kriegstreiber? Die Rolle der Presse im Vorfeld der Ersten Weltkrieges*, Cologne 1998.

Rothfels, Hans, 'Studien zur Annexionskrise', in *Historische Zeitschrift* 147 (1933), pp. 320–345.

Rowland, Peter, *The Last Liberal Governments*, 2 Vols., London 1971.

Rüger, Jan, *The Great Naval Game*, Cambridge 2006.

———, Nation, Empire and Navy: Identity Politics in the United Kingdom, 1887–1914, in *Past and Present* 1 (2004), pp. 159–87.

Ryan, M.W., *Lieutenant-Colonel Charles à Court Repington: A Study in the Interaction of Personality, the Press, and Power*, New York and London 1987.

Saki, 'When William Came: A Story of London under the Hohenzollerns', in *The Complete Works of Saki*, London 1980.

Scally, Robert J., *The Origins of the Lloyd George Coalition: The Politics of Social Imperialism, 1900–1918*, Princeton 1975.

Schencking, Charles J. *Making Waves: Politics, Propaganda and the emergence of the Imperial Japanese Navy, 1868–1922*, Stanford 2005.

Schmidt, Gustav, 'Britische Strategie und Außenpolitik: Wahlchancen und Determinanten britischer Sicherheitspolitik im Zeitalter der neuen Weltmächte, 1897–1929', in *Militärgeschichtliche Mitteilungen* 9 (1971), pp. 197–218.

———, 'Rationalismus und Irrationalismus in der englischen Flottenpolitik', in Herbert Schottelius and Wilhelm Deist (Eds.), *Marine und Marinepolitik im kaiserlichen Deutschland 1871–1914*, Düsseldorf, 1972, pp. 283–95.

———, 'Das Einmaleins politischer Konflikte – zum Verhältnis von Regime-Unterschieden und Großmachtambitionen in den deutsch-englischen Beziehungen 1870–1914', in *Geschichte und Gesellschaft* 11/4 (1985), pp. 508-27.

Schmidt, Stefan, *Frankreichs Außenpolitik in der Julikrise. Ein Beitrag zur Geschichte des Ausbruchs des Ersten Weltkrieges*, Munich 2009

Schmidt, Rainer F., 'Révanche pour Sedan – Frankreich und der Schliefenplan: Militärische und bündnispolitische Vorbereitung des Ersten Weltkriegs' , in *Historische Zeitschrift* 381 (2016), 393–425.

Schmitt, Bernadotte E., *The Annexation of Bosnia*, Cambridge, MA 1937.

Schneider, Elfriede, *Die britische Balkanpolitik vom Mürzsteger Programm bis zum Vorabend des Ersten Weltkrieges und ihre Bedeutung für Österreich-Ungarn*, Vienna 1950.

Schöllgen, Gregor, 'Germanophobia: Deutschland, England und die orientalische Frage im Spiegel der britischen Presse 1900–1903', in *Francia* 8 (1980), pp. 407–26.

———, 'Kriegsgefahr und Krisenmanagement vor 1914: Zur Außenpolitik des kaiserlichen Deutschland', in *Historische Zeitschrift* 267 (1998), pp. 399–413.

———, *Imperialismus und Gleichgewicht: Deutschland, England und die orientalische Frage 1871–1914*, Munich 1984.

———, 'Griff nach der Weltmacht? 25 Jahre Fischer-Kontroverse', in *Historisches Jahrbuch* 1986, pp. 386–406.

———, 'Großmacht als Weltmacht', in *Historische Zeitschrift* 248 (1989), pp. 79–100.

——— (Ed.), *Flucht in den Krieg? Die Außenpolitik des kaiserlichen Deutschland*, Darmstadt 1991.

———, and Kießling, Friedrich, *Das Zeitalter des Imperialismus*, 5th Edition, Munich 2009.

Schottelius, Herbert, and Wilhelm Deist (Eds.), *Marine und Marinepolitik im kaiserlichen Deutschland 1871–1914*, Düsseldorf 1972.

Schramm, Martin, *Das Deutschlandbild in der britischen Presse 1912–1919*, Berlin 2007.

Schroeder, Paul W., 'Alliances, 1815–1945: Weapons of Power and Tools of Management', in Paul W. Schroeder (Ed.), *Systems, Stability, and Statecraft: Essays on the International History of Modern Europe*, New York 2004, pp. 195–222.

———, 'Embedded Counterfactuals and World War I as an Unavoidable War', in Paul W. Schroeder (Ed.), *Systems, Stability, and Statecraft: Essays on the International History of Modern Europe*, New York 2004, pp. 157–94.

———, 'The Mirage of Empire versus the Promise of Hegemony', in Paul W. Schroeder (Ed.), *Systems, Stability, and Statecraft: Essays on the International History of Modern Europe*, New York 2004, pp. 297–306.

———, 'History and International Relations Theory', in *International Security* 22/1 (1997), pp. 64–74.

———, 'International Politics, Peace, and War, 1815–1914', in T.C.W. Blanning (Ed.), *The Short Oxford History of Europe: The Nineteenth Century*, Oxford 2000, pp. 158–209.

———, 'Stealing Horses to Great Applause: Austria-Hungary's Decision in 1914 in Systemic Perspective', in Holger Afflerbach and David Stevenson (Eds.), *An Improbable War:*

The Outbreak of World War I and European Political Culture before 1914, Atlanta 2005, pp. 17–42.

———, 'World War I as Galloping Gertie: A Reply to Joachim Remak', in Paul W. Schroeder (Ed.), *Systems, Stability, and Statecraft: Essays on the International History of Modern Europe*, New York 2004, pp. 137–56.

Schurman, Donald M., *The Education of a Navy: The Development of British Naval Strategic Thought, 1867–1914*, London 1965.

———, *Julian S. Corbett, 1854–1922: Historian of British Maritime Policy from Drake to Jellicoe*, London 1981.

Schuster, Peter, *Henry Wickham Steed und die Habsburgermonarchie*, Vienna, Cologne and Graz 1970.

Searle, Geoffrey R., *The Quest for National Efficiency*, Oxford 1971.

Seed, Geoffrey, 'British Reactions to American Imperialism', in *Political Science Quarterly*, 73 (1958), pp. 254–72.

Seligmann, Matthew, *Spies in Uniform: British Military and Naval Intelligence on the Eve of the First World War*, Oxford 2006.

———, *The Royal Navy and the German Threat 1901–1914. Admiralty Plans to Protect British Trade in a War against Germany*, Oxford 2012

———, 'A View from Berlin: Colonel Frederick Trench and the Development of British Perceptions of German Aggressive Intent, 1906–1910' in *The Journal of Strategic Studies*, 23(2) (2000), pp. 114–147.

Semmel, Bernard, *Imperialism and Social Reform: English Social-Imperial Thought, 1895–1914*, London 1960.

Shannon, Richard, *The Crisis of Imperialism 1865–1915*, London 1974.

Siegel, Jennifer, *Endgame: Britain, Russia and the Final Struggle for Central Asia*, Foreword by Paul Kennedy, London and New York 2002.

Skrivan, Ales, *Schwierige Partner: Deutschland und Österreich-Ungarn in der europäischen Politik der Jahre 1906–1914*, Hamburg 1999.

Sladen, Norman, *The Real Le Queux*, London 1938.

Smith, Richard, 'Sir Edward Grey: The Private Life of a Foreign Secretary', in *IHR* 38 (2016), pp. 339–355.

Soroka, Marina, *Britain, Russia and the Road to the First World War: The Fateful Embassy of Count Aleksandr Benckendorff (1903–16)*, Birmingham 2011.

Stadelmann, Rudolf, 'Die Epoche der deutsch-englischen Flottenrivalität', in Rudolf Stadelmann (Ed.), *Deutschland und Westeuropa: Drei Aufsätze*, Laupheim 1948, pp. 85–146.

———, *Hegemonie und Gleichgewicht: Zum Problem der außenpolitischen Ordnung Europas* (=Geschichte und Politik, Heft 1), Laupheim without year.

Stansky, Peter, *Ambitions and Strategies: The Struggle for the Leadership of the Liberal Party in the 1890s*, Oxford 1964.

Stavrianos, L.S., 'The Balkan Committee', in *Queen's Quarterly* 3 (1941), pp. 258–266.

Steed, Henry W., *The Habsburg Monarchy*, 2nd ed., London 1914.

Steinberg, Jonathan, 'The Copenhagen Complex', in *JCH* 3 (1966), pp. 23–46.

———, *Yesterday's Deterrent: Tirpitz and the Birth of the German Battle Fleet*, London 1965.

———, 'The German Background to Anglo-German Relations, 1905–1914', in F.H. Hinsley (Ed.), *Foreign Policy under Sir Edward Grey*, London 1977, pp. 193–215.

———, 'The Novelle of 1908: Necessities and Choices in the Anglo-German Arms Race', in *Transactions of the Royal Historical Society* 5/1971, 5th Ser. 21/1971, pp. 25–43.

———, 'Diplomatie als Wille und Vorstellung: Die Berliner Mission Lord Haldanes im Februar 1912', in Herbert Schottelius und Wilhelm Deist (Eds.), *Marine und Marinepolitik im kaiserlichen Deutschland 1871–1914*, Düsseldorf 1972, pp. 263–82.

Steiner, Zara S., *Britain and the Origins of the First World War*, Cambridge 1977.

———, *The Foreign Office and Foreign Policy 1898–1914*, Cambridge 1969.

———, 'Grey, Hardinge and the Foreign Office, 1906–1910', in *HJ* 10/3 (1967), pp. 415–39.

———, 'The Last Years of the Old Foreign Office, 1898–1905', in *HJ* 6/1 (1963), pp. 59–90.

———, 'Views of War', in *Moirae* V (1980), pp. 14–32.

———, 'Review of Keith Neilson, *Britain and the Last Tsar 1894–1917*, London 1995', in *EHR* 2/1998, pp. 223–25.

———, 'Great Britain and the Creation of the Anglo-Japanese Alliance', in *JMH* 31 (1959), pp. 27–36.

Steiner, Zara S., and Keith Neilson, *Britain and the Origins of the First World War*, Cambridge 2003.

Steele, David, *Lord Salisbury: A Political Biography*, London 1999.

Stern, Fritz, 'Bethmann Hollweg and the War: The Limits of Responsibility', in L. Krieger and Fritz Stern (Eds), *The Responsibility of Power*, New York 1967, pp. 252–85.

Stevenson, David, *Armaments and the Coming of War: Europe 1904–1914*, Oxford 1996.

———, 'Militarization and Diplomacy in Europe before 1914', in *International Security* 22/1 (1997), pp. 125–61.

Storz, Dieter, *Kriegsbild und Rüstung vor 1914: Europäische Landstreitkräfte vor dem Ersten Weltkrieg*, Munich 1990.

Strachan, Hew, *The First World War*, Vol. 1, Oxford 2001.

Sumida, Jon T., 'British Naval Administration and Policy in the Age of Fisher', in *Journal of Military History* 54 (1/1990), pp. 1–26.

———, *In Defence of Naval Supremacy: Finance, Technology and Naval Policy, 1889–1914*, London 1989.

———, 'Sir John Fisher and the Dreadnought: The Sources of Naval Mythology', in *Journal of Military History* 59 (10/1995), pp. 619–38.

Sumner, A., 'Tsardom and Imperialism in the Far East and the Middle East 1880–1914', in *Proceedings of the British Academy* 27 (1941), pp. 25–65.

Sweet, David W., 'The Baltic in British Diplomacy before the First World War', in *HJ* 13/3 (1970), pp. 455–57.

———, 'The Bosnian Crisis', in Francis H. Hinsley (Ed.), *Foreign Policy under Sir Edward Grey*, London 1977, pp. 178–92.

Sykes, Alan, 'The Radical Right and the Crisis of Conservatism before the First World War', in *HJ* 26/3 (1983), pp. 661–76.

———, 'Konstruktiver Imperialismus in Großbritannien', in Adolf M. Birke (Ed.), *Herausforderungen des europäischen Staatensystems*, Göttingen 1989, pp. 241–65.

Taylor, Alan J.P., *The Struggle for Mastery in Europe 1848–1918*, Oxford 1954.

———, 'The Year 1906', in Donald Read (Ed.), *Edwardian England*, London 1982, pp. 1–13.

Taylor, Robert, *Lord Salisbury*, London 1975.

Temperely, Harold, and Lilian M. Penson, *Foundations of British Foreign Policy 1792–1902*, London 1938.

Thies, Henning (Ed.), *Kindlers Neues Literatur Lexikon: Hauptwerke der englischen Literatur. Einzeldarstellungen und Interpretationen*, 2 Vols., Munich 1995.
Thompson, Andrew S., 'Tariff Reform: An Imperial Strategy, 1903–1913', in *HJ* 40/4 (1997), pp. 1033–54.
Till, G. (Ed.), *The Development of British Naval Thinking: Essays in Memory of Bryan Ranft*, London 2006.
Tomes, Jason, *Balfour and Foreign Policy: The International Thought of a Conservative Statesman*, Cambridge 1997.
Topitsch, Ernst, *Erkenntnis und Illusion*, Hamburg 1979.
Trachtenberg, Marc, 'Diplomatic History and International Relations Theory', in Marc Trachtenberg (Ed.), *The Craft of International History: A Guide to Method*, Princeton and Oxford 2006, in: historicum.net: (http://www.historicum.net/no_cache/persistent/artikel/4023/).
Tracey, Herbert (Ed.), *The British Press: A Survey. A Directory and a Who's Who*, Rochester 1929.
Trevelyan, George M., *Grey of Fallodon: Being the Life of Sir Edward Grey afterwards Lord Grey of Fallodon*, London 1937.
Tucker, A., 'The Issue of Army Reform in the Unionist Government 1903–1905', in *HJ* 12/1 (1966), pp. 90–100.
Tullock, Gordon, *The Politics of Bureaucracy*, Washington 1965.
Ullrich, Volker, 'Ein Weltkrieg wider Willen? Der Streit der Historiker über den Kriegsausbruch 1914 geht in eine neue Runde', Review of Holger Afflerbach, *Der Dreibund: Europäische Großmacht- und Allianzpolitik vor dem Ersten Weltkrieg*, Wien 2002, in *Die Zeit*, 2 January 2003.
Vagts, Alfred, *Landing Operations: Strategy, Psychology, Tactics, Politics from Antiquity to 1945*, Harrisburg 1946.
———, 'The Balance of Power: Growth of an idea', in *World Politics* 1 (1948), pp. 82–101.
Vansittart, Robert G., *The Mist Procession: The Autobiography of Lord Vansittart*, London 1958.
Verosta, Stephan, *Theorie und Realität von Bündnissen: Heinrich Lammasch, Karl Renner und der Zweibund (1897–1914)*, Wien 1971.
Wadsworth, Alfred P., 'Newspaper Circulations, 1800–1954', in *Transactions of the Manchester Statistical Society* (9.3.1955), pp. 1–40.
Wandruszka, Adam, and Peter Urbanitsch (Ed.), *Die Habsburgermonarchie 1848–1918, im Auftrag der Kommission für die Geschichte der österreichisch-ungarischen Monarchie (1848–1918)*, Vol. VI, Vienna 1993.
Wank, Solomon, 'Aehrenthal and the Sandschak of Novipazar Railway Project: a Reappraisal', in *Slavonic and East European Review* 42 (1964), pp. 353–69.
Watt, Donald C., 'The Nature of the Foreign Policy Making Elite in Britain', in Donald C. Watt (Ed.), *Power, Personalities and Policies: Studies in the Formulation of British Foreign Policy in the 20th Century*, London 1965, pp. 1–15
Weaver, J.R.H., and L.G. Wickham, (Ed.), *The Dictionary of National Biography*, Oxford, 1939–1959.
Wehler, Hans-Ulrich, 'Moderne Politikgeschichte oder "Große Politik der Kabinette"?' in *GG*, 1, 1975, H. 2/3, pp. 344–69.
———, '"Moderne" Politikgeschichte? Oder: Willkommen im Kreis der Neorankeaner vor 1914', in *GG* 22/1 (1996), pp. 257–66.
———, *Das Deutsche Kaiserreich 1871–1918*, 7th Edition, Göttingen 1994.

Weiner, Robert L., *Paul Cambon and the Making of the Entente Cordiale*, Diss. Rutgers 1973.
Weinroth, Howard, 'The British Radicals and the Balance of Power, 1902–1914', in *HJ* 13/4 (1970), pp. 653–82.
———, 'Left-Wing Opposition to Naval Armaments in Britain before 1914', in *JCH* 6/4 (1971), pp. 93–120.
———, 'Radicalism and Nationalism: An Increasingly Unstable Equation', in A.J.A. Morris (Ed.), *Edwardian Radicalism 1900–1914: Some Aspects of British Radicalism*, London 1974, pp. 218–33.
Wells, Samuel F., 'British strategic withdrawal from the Western Hemisphere, 1904–1906, in *Canadian Historical Review* 49 (1968), pp. 335–56.
Wende, Peter, 'Perzeption und Transfers: Zur gegenseitigen Wahrnehmung deutscher und britischer Geschichtswissenschaft im 19. Jahrhundert, Rivalität und Partnerschaft. Studien zu den deutsch-britischen Beziehungen im 19. und 20. Jahrhundert', in *Festschrift für Anthony J. Nicholls*, ed. by G. A. Ritter and P. Wende, Paderborn, 1999, pp. 13–28.
Wendt, Bernd-Jürgen (Ed.), *Das britische Deutschlandbild im Wandel des 19. und 20. Jahrhunderts*, Bochum 1984.
Westwood, J.N., *Russian Naval Construction, 1905–1945*, Birmingham 1994.
Whight, P.Q., 'The Balance of Power', in H.W. Weigert and V. Steffansson (Eds.), *Compass of the World: A Symposium on Political Geography*, London 1946.
Whitaker, John (Ed.), *Whitaker's Almanack*, London 1901–1911.
White, John A., *Transition to Global Rivalry: Alliance Diplomacy and the Quadruple Entente, 1895–1907*, Cambridge 1995.
Williams, Beryl J., 'Great Britain and Russia, 1905 to the 1907 Convention', in F.H. Hinsley (Ed.), *British Foreign Policy under Sir Edward Grey*, Cambridge 1977, pp. 133–47.
———, 'The Strategic Background to the Anglo-Russian Entente of August 1907', in *HJ* 11/3 (1966), pp. 360–73.
Williams, Rhodri, *Defending the Empire: The Conservative Party and British Defence Policy, 1899–1915*, London 1991.
Williamson, Samuel R., *The Politics of Grand Strategy: Britain and France Prepare for War, 1904–1914*, Cambridge, MA 1969.
———, and May, Ernest R., 'An Identity of Opinion: Historians and July 1914', in *JMH* 79/2 (2007), pp. 335–387.
Wilson, Keith M., 'Grey and the Russian Threat to India, 1892–1915', in *IHR* 38 (2016), 275–284.
———, 'The Anglo-Japanese Alliance of 1905 and the Defending of India: The Case of a Worst Case Scenario', in *JICH* 21/2 (1993), pp. 334–56.
——— (Ed.), *British Foreign Secretaries and Foreign Policy from the Crimean War to the First World War*, London 1987.
———, *Channel Tunnel Vision, 1850–1945, Dreams and Nightmares*, London 1994.
———, 'Constantinople or Cairo: Lord Salisbury and the Partition of the Ottoman Empire 1886–1887', in Keith M. Wilson (Ed.), *Imperialism and Nationalism in the Middle East: The Anglo-Egyptian Experience 1882–1982*, London 1983, pp. 26–55.
———, *Empire and Continent: Studies in British Foreign Policy from the 1880s to the First World War*, London 1987.
———, 'The Foreign Office and the Education of Public Opinion', in *HJ* 26/3 (1983), pp. 403–11.

———, 'Grey', in Keith M. Wilson, *British Foreign Secretaries and Foreign Policy from the Crimean War to the First World War*, London 1987, pp. 172–97.

———, *A Study in the History and Politics of the Morning Post 1905–26*, New York 1990.

———, 'The Making and Putative Implementation of a British Foreign Policy of Gesture, December 1905 to August 1914: The Anglo-French Entente Revisited', in *Canadian Journal of History* 21 (1996), pp. 227–55.

———, *The Policy of the Entente: Essays on the Determinants of British Foreign Policy*, Cambridge 1985.

———, 'The Question of Anti-Germanism at the Foreign Office', in CJH 28/1 (1983), pp. 23–42.

———, *The Role and Influence of the Professional Advisors to the Foreign Office on the Making of British Foreign Policy from December 1905 to August 1914*, D.phil. Thesis, Oxford 1972.

———, 'Sir E. Crowe on the Origins of the Crowe Memorandum of 1st January 1907', in *Bulletin of the Institute of Historical Research* 56/134 (1983), pp. 238–41.

———, 'Spenser Wilkinson at Bay: Calling the Tune at *The Morning Post*, 1908–1909', in *Publishing History* 19 (1986), pp. 33–52.

———, *A Study in the History and Politics of the Morning Post 1905–26*, New York 1990.

———, Keith Wilson, *The Limits of Eurocentricity: Imperial British Foreign and Defence Policy in the Early Twentieth Century*, Istanbul 2006.

———, 'Found and lost in translation: Bertie Cambon, Lansdowne, Delcassé and the Anglo-French alliance of May 1905', in Keith Wilson, *The Limits of Eurocentricity: Imperial British Foreign and Defence Policy in the Early Twentieth Century*, Istanbul 2006, pp. 31–42.

———, 'The British Cabinet's decision for War, 2. August 1914', in: *British Journal of International Studies* 1 (1975), S. 148–159.

———(Ed.), *Decisions for War, 1914*, London 1995.

Winkler, Heinrich A., 'Der falsche Krieg? Der britische Historiker Niall Ferguson erklärt, daß der Erste Weltkrieg hätte verhindert werden können', in *Die Welt*, No. 14, 10 April 1999.

Winzen, Peter, *Bülows Weltmachtkonzept: Untersuchungen zur Frühphase seiner Außenpolitik 1897–1901*, Boppard 1977.

Wipperfürth, Christian, *Von der Souveränität zu Angst: Britische Außenpolitik und Sozialökonomie im Zeitalter des Imperialismus*, Stuttgart 2004.

———, 'Ein Nicht-Imperialist im Zeitalter des Imperialismus: Biographische Notizen zu Thomas Henry Sanderson', in *Historische Mitteilungen der Ranke Gesellschaft* 16 (2003), pp. 28–91.

Wohl, Robert, *The Generation of 1914*, London 1980.

Wolf, Lucien, *The Life of the First Marquess of Ripon*, 2 Vols., London 1921.

Woodward, Ernest L. Sir, *Great Britain and the German Navy*, London 1935.

Wormer, Klaus, *Großbritannien, Rußland und Deutschland: Studien zur Britischen Außenpolitik am Vorabend des Ersten Weltkriegs*, Munich 1980.

Wright, Quincy, *A Study of War*, 2nd ed., Chicago and London 1965.

INDEX

Abdul Hamid II, 80, 188, 229, 237, 238, 372, 381–82
Acland, A.H.D., 119n25
Acton, Lord, 62n107
Aehrenthal, Alois Baron Lexa von, 371, 373–74, 385, 401, 403–7, 410–11, 413, 417, 421–22, 428, 434, 439, 449n39, 462–63, 469
Albert, Prinz von Sachsen Coburg und Gotha, 28
Amery, Leopold, 45, 84, 121n83, 144
Andrew, Christopher, 237
Angell, Norman, 13
Ardagh, Sir John Charles, 133, 135, 138, 149–50, 183, 185
Arnold-Forster, Hugh O., 147, 150–51, 161, 164–65, 187, 200, 247, 311, 314, 319
Asquith, Herbert H., 11, 24, 41, 55, 70n337, 73–74, 77, 82, 89, 95, 119n25, 206, 232, 258, 273–74, 290, 303n172, 315, 320, 324, 326–29, 338n129, 350, 363, 384, 401, 413, 415–19, 425, 427, 462, 464, 474, 480

Baden Powell, Robert, 341n215
Bagehot, Walter, 42
Balance of power, 1, 26, 34, 42, 58, 72, 74, 76–81, 83, 86, 88, 92, 97–98, 101, 118, 130, 140, 182, 188, 204, 206, 231, 236, 241–42, 257, 275–77, 345, 347–48, 360, 362, 366, 368, 375–76, 382, 384, 392 n183, 402–404, 408–409, 411, 414, 425, 429, 442, 444, 446, 462, 470–71, 479
Balfour, Sir Arthur James, 6, 9, 12, 19, 24, 30, 36–37, 47–48, 72, 74–75, 79, 87, 89–90, 92–98, 101–2, 104–5, 115–16, 130, 136, 141–43, 145, 150–51, 153–58, 160–65, 167–68, 182, 186, 189–206, 216, 220–21, 223–29, 232, 233–47, 249–59, 278, 280, 282, 291, 293, 295, 306–8, 311, 315, 317–21, 323–24, 327–30, 344–45, 351, 363–64, 372, 379, 404, 416, 444, 446, 447, 463–69, 471, 473–74, 477, 479
Balfour, Gerald, 247, 252
Balkan League, 421, 470, 478
Baring, Edward Charles, 1st Baron of Revelstoke, 229, 230, 232, 234
Barnes, George S., 121n83
Barrington, Sir Eric, 97, 284
Basily, Nicolas de, 400n423
Battenberg, Louis, 47, 141, 143, 145–47, 151, 158–59, 192, 246, 320, 322
Beatty, David, 401
Beck, Max Vladimir von, 406
Bell, Charles Frederick Moberly, 23, 110
Bell, Gertrude, 40
Bellairs, Carlyon, 84, 121n83
Benckendorff, Graf Alexander, 39, 185, 193–95, 201, 247, 250, 259, 278, 345, 346, 352, 357, 364, 376, 402, 426, 431, 468
Bennet, Graham, 348
Beresford, Lord Charles William de la Poer, 12, 313, 316, 320, 327, 332, 475
Beresford, Charles E., 185
Berghahn, Volker, 131
Bertie, Sir Francis L., 30, 96–99, 101, 103, 108, 111–12, 114, 237, 241, 248–50, 252–54, 283, 286–87, 290, 352, 356, 358–59, 407–8, 410–11, 414–15, 418, 433
Bethmann–Hollweg, Theobald von, 331
Birchenough, H., 121n83

Bismarck, Otto Eduard Leopold von, 75, 76, 107 231, 288, 294, 383, 441, 445
Blennerhasset, Sir Rowland, 25, 29–31, 36, 37–38, 113, 186, 464
Bompard, Maurice Louis, 242, 358
Bowden-Smith, William, 177
Bowen, Herbert, 227
Bowles, Thomas Gibson, 188, 232
Brailsford, Henry Noel, 361
Brandon, Lieutenant, 56, 70n351
Brassey, Thomas, 18, 119n25, 164
Bridge, Francis Roy, 404, 448n30
Brodrick, St. John, 1st Earl of Midleton, 47, 136, 141, 155, 234, 251, 329
Brunner, John, 318
Bryce, James, 49, 274, 307
Buckle, George Earle, 12, 327
Buchanan, Sir George, 372, 411, 423, 480
Bülow, Bernard von, 98, 104–6, 108–9, 117, 219, 235, 252, 285, 353, 432, 435
Buxton, Sidney, 75, 119n25

Caborne, Commander, 177
Cadbury, George, 361
Cambon, Paul, 37, 237, 242, 253–55, 267n258, 277, 299n47354–56, 360, 374, 402, 431, 479
Campbell-Bannerman, Sir Henry, 55, 82, 137, 150, 162, 225, 273, 277, 284, 290, 319, 348, 365, 464
Canis, Konrad, 126n233, 292
Cartwright, Sir Fairfax Leighton, 285–86, 290, 292, 330, 353, 383, 428
Cassel, Sir Ernest, 230, 331, 379
Castro, Cipriano, 217, 218, 219, 223–26
Cawdor, Frederick Archibald Vaughan Campbell, 329
Cecil, Robert, 121n83
Chamberlain, Austen, 101, 102, 143, 227, 242, 245, 412
Chamberlain, Joseph, 12, 23, 29, 37–38, 77, 91, 93, 95–96, 104–8, 113, 116–17, 126n233, 138, 216, 230, 232–35, 237, 464, 467
Charmley, John, 3, 93, 275, 292
Childers, Erskine, 45, 46, 52, 56–57, 148, 164, 322, 472

Chirol, Sir Valentine Ignatius, 12–13, 17, 21–24, 40, 102–3, 105, 113, 190, 205, 233, 235, 240, 248, 283, 327–28, 348, 358, 361–63, 366, 380, 401, 412–13, 422
Churchill, Winston L. Spencer, 96, 158, 331, 405, 413, 432, 437, 479, 480
Clark, Christopher, 169n22, 437
Clarke, Sir George Sydenham, 47, 153, 156–58, 164, 166–68, 197–202, 204, 206, 247, 280, 314–16, 319–22, 347, 412, 465
Clausewitz, Carl Philipp Gottlieb von, 31
Clemenceau, Georges, 25, 29, 354, 359, 408
Coefficients, 31, 40–41, 48–50, 83–87, 95, 121 n71, 383, 446, 471–72
Concert of Europe, concert policy, 41, 72, 74, 88, 116, 216, 242, 257–58, 360, 369, 372, 375, 382, 402–404, 408–409, 414, 418, 427, 430, 435, 441, 446
Colomb, Sir John Charles Ready, 162, 322
Colonial Defence Committee, 166, 221
Committee of Imperial Defence (CID), 42, 46–47, 55–56, 70 n335, 129, 133, 142, 145–46, 148–68, 170 n45, 173 n100, 182, 191, 196, 200, 206, 243, 245, 279–80, 297, 306–33, 350–51, 465–66, 474
Conan Doyle, Sir Arthur, 146
Conrad, Franz von Hötzendorf, 406
Conrad, Joseph, 45
Constans, Jean, 265n171
Cook, Edward, 38, 88
Corbett, Julian Stafford, 5, 68n270, 157, 162, 244, 320, 322, 324, 328, 423, 465
Courtney, William Leonard, 18, 440
Cranborne, James Gascoyne-Cecil, Viscount, 117, 190, 241
Crewe, Robert Lord, 274, 324, 329, 338n229, 415
Crimean War constellation, 182, 207 n5
Cromer, Evelyn Baring, 193–94, 238–40, 241, 274, 329
Crowe, Sir Eyre, 22, 25, 30, 39–41, 56, 95, 97–98, 100–1, 184–85, 189, 217, 248, 283–97, 306, 353, 355, 432, 442, 464, 470, 473, 476

Curtis, Albert Edward, 45
Curzon, George Nathaniel, 36, 91, 184–86, 190–94, 199, 122n89, 229–30, 235, 346, 348, 351, 364–65, 371, 383, 466

Dalton, John, 39
Darwin, Charles Robert, 96, 290
Dawkins, Sir Clinton Edward, 84, 121n83, 230, 232–35
Dawson, Alec John, 57
De Bunsen, Sir Maurice, 229
Delcassé Théophile, 25, 102, 117–18, 193, 236, 237, 239, 241, 249, 250–57, 293, 295, 416
Dilke, Sir Charles Wentworth, 18, 82, 164, 205, 274–75, 440
Dillon, Emile Joseph, 4, 13, 17–18, 34, 44, 75, 217, 231, 344, 348, 354, 380, 417, 434, 445
Disraeli, Benjamin, 73, 93, 229, 406, 440, 467
Drummond-Wolff, Sir Henry, 112, 236
Dual Alliance (Franco-Russian), 1, 11, 19, 22, 26, 28, 32–34, 36, 74, 76, 80, 93–94, 97, 99, 100, 102–103, 105, 112–13, 118, 133, 144, 154–55, 183, 193, 235, 237, 241, 256, 278–79, 281, 289, 293, 375–77, 383, 401, 408, 422–25, 435–36, 444, 447–48 n8, 463–64, 467–69, 472–74, 479
Dumas, Philip Wylie, 56, 292, 310, 316, 329–30
Durand, George H., 205

Eckardstein, Herrmann von, 105, 108–11, 237
Edelsheim, Baron, 61n60
Edmonds, Sir James Edward, 54–55
Edward VII, 28, 39, 95, 98, 220–21, 227, 242–46, 254, 283, 290, 307, 327, 329–30, 345, 349, 350, 355, 360, 377–78, 380, 383, 385, 390n137, 397n337, 410, 417, 420, 429
Elgin, Lord, 274
Ellenborough, Lord, 137, 156–57, 164, 193

Entente Cordiale, 21, 40, 49, 75, 92, 99, 159, 162, 203–205, 239, 241–42, 251–59, 277–78, 280, 290, 313, 344–47, 351, 356–57 373, 376, 384, 447, 463, 467, 469, 474, 479
Epkenhans, Michael, 340n183
Esher, Reginald Brett, 41, 55, 57, 159, 161, 163, 165–67, 232, 234, 274, 313, 320–22, 324, 327–28, 338n229, 417–18, 427
Evans-Gordon, Sir William Eden, 163
Ewart, Sir Spencer, 328

Fischer, Fritz, 3, 288
Fisher, John Arbuthnot, 5, 12, 43, 57, 130–32, 141–44, 147, 151, 153–54, 157–62, 170, 196, 244, 247, 253, 271, 280, 306–8, 310–21, 324, 327–29, 331–32, 378–79, 381, 420, 465–67, 474–75
Fitzmaurice, Lord Edmond George Petty-Fitzmaurice, 36, 274, 284–85, 349, 352, 412, 414
Foch, Ferdinand, 214 n196
Fowler, Henry, 119n25
Ferguson, Niall, 3, 275, 339n139
Frederick III, Kaiser, 21
Freemantle, Sydney Robert, 177
French, John Denton Pinkstone 1st Earl of, 303n172, 312, 378

Garvin, James Louis, 13, 17–19, 25, 30–31, 34, 39, 42, 83–84, 113, 121n83, 186, 187, 189, 193, 205, 246, 248, 287, 290, 313–14, 322, 341n215, 348, 354, 356, 405, 446, 464, 471–72
Geiss, Imanuel, 288
Geoffray, Leon, 359
Gladstone, Sir William Ewart, 17, 73, 78, 83, 138, 446
Gladstone, Herbert, 55, 81, 274
Gleichen, Edward, 54
Goluchowski, Caount Agenor, 371
Goltz, Wilhelm Leopold Colmar Freiherr von der, 156
Gooch, George Peabody, 82
Goschen, George Joachim 1st Viscount, 21, 105, 106

Goschen, Sir William Edward, 285–86, 293, 297, 329, 331, 385, 411, 418, 479
Greenwood, Frederick, 33, 34, 75
Greindl, Jules, 382, 435
Grenfell, E.C., 121n83
Grenville, John, 106
Grey, Sir Edward, 2–4, 7, 11, 13, 18–19, 20, 22, 24–25, 30, 37–39, 41–42, 52, 55, 56, 58, 59n7, 74–87, 89, 91–93, 95, 102, 105, 113, 117–18, 121n83, 140, 185, 187–90, 192–96, 204–6, 225, 228–32, 241, 246, 250–51, 254, 255, 258–59, 263n108, 273–84, 287, 289–91, 295, 297, 307–8, 314–15, 320, 324, 326–29, 332, 338n129, 344–52, 355–59, 361–65, 367–79, 381–84, 401–20, 422–24, 426–47, 456n232, 462–64, 468–80
Grierson, Sir James Moncrieff, 201–3
Gwinner, Arthur von, 233, 235
Gwynne, Howell Arthur, 163, 312

Haggard, Sir William Henry Doveton, 218–19, 221–22
Haldane, Richard Burdon, 11, 55–56, 74– 75, 83–84, 88–89, 121n83, 164–65, 167–68, 204, 206, 258, 263, 273–74, 276, 280, 284, 290, 296, 303, 172, 311–12, 314–15, 320, 324, 326, 328–29, 334, 338n229, 347, 384, 418–19, 427, 473–75, 478
Hale, Oron J., 62n84
Hallmann, Hans, 340n183
Hamilton, Sir George Francis, 106, 109, 111, 116, 186, 190, 193, 227, 229, 236, 251, 327, 371
Harcourt, William George Granville, 73, 78–82, 94, 119n41, 274, 437
Hardinge, Arthur, 112, 190, 210n78
Hardinge, Sir Charles, 21–23, 25, 30, 38, 41, 56, 95, 97–98, 100–2, 112–14, 183, 185, 188–91, 195, 205–6, 242, 246–48, 250, 273, 275–76, 278–79, 282–90, 295, 297, 316, 326, 329–31, 344–45, 348, 350–52, 355–60, 366, 371, 373–80, 382–85, 401, 403, 405–8, 410–16, 418–39, 445–46, 450n63, 464, 466, 470, 480

Harmsworth, Alfred Charles, 1st Viscount Northcliffe, 16, 18, 20, 25, 29, 49, 51, 52, 88, 226, 312, 401
Harmsworth, Cecil Bisshopp, 1st Baron of, 122
Harmsworth, Harold, 1st Viscount Rothermere, 88, 122
Harmsworth, R.L., 119n25
Harris, Lord, 149
Hatzfeldt zu Trachenberg, Paul Count von, 95, 104–5, 110
Hayashi, Count Tadasu, 108, 111–12, 195, 239, 246
Hewins, William Albert, 83, 84, 121n83, 446
Hicks Beach, Michael Edward, 93, 104, 112, 116, 137
Hill, Headon (Francis Edward Grainger), 45, 472
Hobson, John Atkinson, 16, 361
Holleben, Theodor von, 222
Holstein, Friedrich August von, 75, 108, 252
Huguet, Philippe, 22
Hurd, Archibald S. (Excubitor), 12, 18, 310
Hyndmann, Henry Mayers, 341

Iswolsky/Izvolsky (Iswolski), Alexander, 61n58, 185, 194–95, 246, 285, 348–59, 363–66, 373–79, 382–83, 385, 389n94, 392n176, 396n302, 400n423, 403, 405, 410–11, 413–40, 449n39, 451n90, 452n134, 457n261, 462–63, 468–69
Iwan-Müller, Ernest Bruce, 12, 233

James, Henry, 57
Jameson, Leander Starr, 28
Jane, Fred T., 32, 33
Jomini, Antoine Henri, 148
Jowett, Benjamin, 90

Kant, Immanuel, 31
Kennedy, Paul M., 130–32, 216
Kerr, Lord Walter Talbot, 143, 192, 246
Kiderlen-Wächter, Alfred von, 430–31, 435, 440
Kießling, Friedrich, 478

Kimberley, John Wodehouse, 75, 81, 119n41, 185
Kipling, Rudyard, 43–44, 96, 217, 226
Kitchener, Horatio Herbert, 184–86, 197, 199, 200, 202, 205, 363
Klado, General, 248
Knollys, Francis, 98, 283
Kröger, Martin, 437
Krüger, Ohm, 23, 295
Kühlmann, Richard von, 210
Kuropatkin, Alexei Nikolayevich, 184, 197, 420

Labouchère, Henry du Pré, 119n41, 210n75, 297
Lambert, Nicholas A., 5, 6, 133
Lambi, Ivo N., 306
Lamsdorff, Wladimir Count von, 92, 109, 111, 114, 118, 240, 346, 348
Langley, Walter, 284, 383
Lansdowne, Henry Charles Keith Petty-Fitzmaurice, 3, 4, 12, 19, 24, 36, 37, 40, 77, 87, 89–97, 99, 101, 102, 108–17, 125, 130, 137, 158, 160, 185–86, 189–99, 201, 203, 205–6, 216–47, 249–59, 274–80, 282–83, 285, 287, 289, 291, 293, 295, 297, 318, 327, 329–30, 344–46, 349, 351, 353, 355–56, 363–64, 370, 372, 376, 379, 404, 407–8, 429, 444, 463–64, 466–69, 471, 474, 477, 479
Lascelles, Sir Frank Cavendish, 30, 36, 42, 104–9, 113, 117, 227, 229, 239, 248, 284–88, 290, 292, 302n126, 330, 418, 438
Lavino, William Edward, 21, 248
Le Queux, William Tufnell, 44, 49, 51–52, 55–57, 165, 312–13, 322, 472
Liakhoff, Colonel, 368
Lieven, Dominic, 209n39
Lloyd, George, 25
Lloyd George, David, 11, 275–76, 324, 338n229, 361, 437
Lockwood, Frederic, 119n25
Lodge, Henry Cabot, 220
Lovat, Simon Fraser Lord, 312, 322, 329
Low, Sir Sidney James Mark, 41

Lowther, Gerald, 285, 381, 423, 424
Lüttwitz, Walther Freiherr von, 156
Lynch, Arthur, 188
Lyttelton, Alfred, 62 n107
Lyttelton, Neville, 196, 201, 203, 338 n129

MacColl, Malcolm, 2, 80, 186
MacDonald, James Ramsey, 361
MacDonald, Sir Claude Maxwell, 103, 114, 205, 249
Mackenzie, Sir Morell, 21
Mackinder, Halford J., 74, 83–84, 121n71, 121n83, 471
Mackenzie, Morell, 21
Mahaffy, Sir John Pentland, 34
Mahan, Alfred Thayer, 5, 41, 132, 147, 148, 157, 231, 290, 323
Maitland, Frederic William, 43
Majoribanks, Edward, 2nd Baron Tweedmouth, 55, 307, 311, 316, 326, 327, 332, 338n229, 475
Mallet, Louis du Pan, 95, 97, 99–100, 185, 205, 230, 241, 247–48, 252–53, 276, 283–84, 287, 293, 375, 418
Mann, Admiral, 177
Mansfield, Kathrine (Kathleen), 43, 45
Marder, Arthur M., 130–31, 159
Marker, Raymond John, 314
Marschall von Bieberstein, Freiherr Adolf von, 373
Masterman, Charles Frederick, 82, 120, 121n83
Massingham, Henry W., 17, 19, 60n54, 256, 257, 367, 369, 416, 419, 441, 443
Maurice, John, 83
Maurier, Guy Louis Busson du, 52, 54, 472
Maxse, Leopold James, 11, 17–20, 23–31, 34, 37–41, 44, 47, 49, 80, 84, 86–87, 92, 96, 113, 117, 121n83, 136, 140, 146, 165, 186, 188, 189, 216, 217, 226, 228–33, 235–36, 248, 255, 277–78, 283, 287, 290– 92, 312–14, 320, 322, 327, 341n215, 344, 348, 376, 380, 401, 405, 409, 417, 464, 471–73
McDonnell, Sir Schomberg, Kerr, 12
McKenna, Reginald, 55, 327, 329, 418–19

Mediterranean Agreements 1, 182, 183, 191, 355, 447, 463
Mensdorff, Albert Count von Pouilly–Dietrichstein, 56, 307, 311, 329, 374, 402, 405, 410, 412
Meredith, George, 50
Mikhailovich, Grand Duke, 357
Milner, Alfred, 62n107, 84, 95, 121n83, 296, 329
Mills, Eliot, 88
Milovanovic, Miovan, 428, 431
Moltke, Helmuth von, 146, 156, 289, 314, 330, 474
Mommsen, Theodor, 31
Moneypenny, W.F., 84, 121n83
Monger, George W., 92, 117
Monson, Sir Edmund, 30, 92, 102, 135, 246, 287, 293
Montgomery, Robert, 238
Morison, Theodore, 121n83
Morrison, George Ernest, 21
Morley, Sir John, 34, 81–82, 119n41, 188, 206, 274, 290, 345, 348–49, 361, 363–64, 412, 414–16, 419, 437
Mühlberg, Otto von, 117
Mundella, Anthony John, 119n41
Munro-Ferguson, Henry, 119n41
Munro-Ferguson, Ronald, 74, 119n25
Muraviev, Konstantin, 81, 102, 236, 295

Napoleon Bonaparte, 44, 101, 134–35, 153
Napoleon III, Charles Louis Napoleon Bonaparte, 134, 444
Neilson, Keith M., 297, 404
Newbolt, Henry, 84, 121n83
Newton, Lord, 62n107
Nicholas II, 2, 12, 26, 35, 39, 111, 155, 283, 285, 349, 354, 366–67, 377–80, 405, 421, 427, 431, 436
Nicholson, Sir William, 138, 139, 144–47, 155, 185, 201, 328, 387
Nicolson, Sir Arthur, 21, 30, 97, 100, 185, 194, 195, 276, 285–87, 289, 332, 344, 346, 348, 350–52, 355, 357–59, 365–66, 371, 374–76, 378, 382, 402–3, 413, 415–19, 421–22, 425–36, 438, 439, 446, 462, 468, 478, 480

Nicolson, Harold, 284, 365
Nish, Ian, 249
Norfolk, Lord, 149
Norfolk-Commission, 142–55
Norman, Henry, 18, 30, 77, 80, 117–18, 119n25, 120n52, 188, 190, 193, 231

O'Beirne, Hugh, 358, 437
O'Conor, Sir Nicholas, 229, 372–73
Oliver, F.S., 121n83
Otte, Thomas G., 275, 287
Ottley, Sir Charles, 328, 418

Paget, Sir Ralph Spencer, 286
Paléologue, Maurice, 254
Pares, Bernard, 363
Parker, Alwyn, 401
Pearson, Sir Cyril Arthur 1st Baronet, 18, 59, 312
Penrose, Admiral, 61n60
Percy, Alan, Duke of Northumberland, 25, 193, 364–65
Pilgrim-Baltazzi, Gisbert von, 218
Ponsonby, Arthur Augustus, 38, 39, 276

Quadt, Graf von, 221

Reeves, William Pember, 84, 121n83
Reid, Stuart Johnson, 88
Repington, Charles à Court, 17, 22, 24–25, 30, 47–50, 54, 62n107, 84, 96, 121n83, 157, 161, 163–65, 167, 201, 203, 214, 289–90, 306, 311–20, 322–23, 326, 327–29, 331–32, 336, 338n132, 341n215, 427–28, 437, 467, 471, 474–75
Revelstoke, Edward Charles Baring, 229–30, 232, 234
Richthofen, Oswald von, 106, 109
Ritchie, Charles Thomson 1st Baron of, 116, 143
Roberts, Frederick Sleigh, 25, 30, 48–49, 51–52, 54, 138–41, 143–44, 148, 151, 156–57, 161, 164–65, 167, 184–85, 192, 201, 204, 311–13, 315, 322–23, 327–29, 339n158, 339n161, 474

Robertson, Sir William, 138–41, 143–44, 156, 184–85, 201
Robinson, George Frederick Samuel, 1st Marquess of Ripon, 81, 119n41, 290, 303n172, 332, 368
Roosevelt, Theodore, 220, 227–28, 262, 293, 331
Rosebery, Lord Archibald Philip Primrose, 22, 26–28, 38, 56, 60n54, 73–76, 79, 82, 86, 105, 137, 185, 232, 249, 274, 282, 298n8, 412
Ross, Adrian, 61n65
Rothschild, Nathan Mayer, Lord, 104, 229
Rüger, Jan, 5
Rumbold, Horace, 263, 426
Russell, Alick, 292
Russell, Bertrand, 84, 85, 121n83, 121n88
Russell, Odo William, 1st Baron Ampthill, 294
Ryan, Andrew, 286

Sadler, Michael Ernest, 121n83
Salisbury, Robert Arthur Talbot Gascoyne-Cecil, the 3rd Marquess of, 2, 4, 6, 11, 12, 24, 27, 28, 30, 32, 38, 40, 73, 74, 76–79, 81, 87, 89–94, 97, 98, 102–10, 112–13, 116, 137–38, 161, 166, 183, 185–87, 195, 201, 229, 250, 255–56, 278, 283–84, 288, 293–95, 353, 376, 406, 422, 444, 462–65, 467, 469, 471, 475
Salisbury, James Gascoyne-Cecil, the 4th Marquess of, 256
Samuel, Herbert, 119n25
Sandars, John Satterfield, 12, 30, 81, 167
Sanderson, Sir Thomas Henry, 12, 30, 35–37, 75, 96–102, 107, 111, 183, 189–90, 203–6, 229, 234, 248, 250, 252, 254, 257, 283, 287–97, 330, 359, 407, 444, 466–69, 471
Sandys, Colonel, 163, 205
Satow, Sir Ernest Mason, 108
Saunders, George, 17, 21–24, 30, 38–39, 113, 186, 217, 226, 231, 233, 235, 240, 248, 264, 344, 464, 471
Savinsky, Alexander, 354

Sazonov, Sergej D., 2
Scheder, Admiral, 223–24
Schmidt, Gustav, 308
Schöllgen, Gregor, 369
Schroeder, Paul W., 5, 132, 360, 407
Scott, Charles Prestwitch, 17, 92, 190, 367, 380, 416
Scott, Sir Samuel, 312, 322
Seaman, Owen, 16
Seeley, Major, 163
Seeley, John, 312
Selborne, William Waldgrave Palmer, 5, 46, 62n107, 69, 90, 106, 112, 116, 129, 130, 132, 135, 141–44, 147, 153, 158–60, 162, 173, 186–87, 191–92, 197, 199, 202, 220, 234, 242–43, 245–47, 317, 465–66,
Seligmann, Matthew, 324
Shaw, Bernard, 82, 361
Shuster, Morgan, 478
Siegel, Jennifer, 208n30
Slade, Edmond, 320, 322, 324, 327–28, 338, 418, 453n139
Smalley, George W., 21
Smith, John Hugh, 121n83
Smith, Cecil, 103
Spender, John Alfred, 11–13, 17, 20, 61, 225, 228, 242, 257–58, 274, 276, 363, 380, 415–16, 464
Spenser Wilkinson, Henry, 13, 17, 22, 30, 31, 41, 149, 163–65, 289, 341, 363, 380, 401, 442
Spicer, Gerald, 283–84, 426
Spring Rice, Sir Cecil Arthur, 22, 25, 30, 41, 58, 63, 67n249, 75, 190, 205, 230–31, 248, 257, 285–86, 293, 302n126, 333, 346, 348, 349, 366, 371, 403, 412–13, 418, 444, 449
Suvorin, Alexej S., 349
Stead, William Thomas, 11, 13–14, 44, 137, 146, 188, 287, 290
Steed, Henry Wickham, 17, 21, 24, 186, 248, 400n427, 401, 450
Steinberg, Jonathan, 131, 208
Steiner, Zara S., 4, 12, 198, 297
Stevenson, David, 475
Stolypin, Piotr A., 379, 454

Strachey, John St. Loe, 17, 18, 20, 23, 25, 28, 30–31, 34–35, 46, 49, 59, 65, 80, 102, 146, 155, 164–65, 186, 193, 205, 226, 230, 231, 233, 235–36, 255, 257, 312–14, 322, 335, 380, 405, 417, 464, 471
Straits, Straits question (Dardanelles and Bosphorus), 26, 81, 94, 98, 142, 184, 187, 190–91, 195, 246–47, 250–51, 278, 344–45, 349, 350–53, 358, 373–74, 383, 385, 387n44, 402, 404, 410, 411, 413–21, 424, 426, 462, 463, 466, 469
Stumm, Wilhelm von, 306
Sturdee, Frederick C.D., 316
Sumida, Jon T., 5, 133
Sybel, Heinrich von, 31

Talleyrand, Charles Maurice de, 90
Taube, Michael von, 350, 359
Tatistchev, Sergej, 37–39
Telfer-Smollett, Charles, 177 n219
Thursfield, Richard, 12, 18, 144, 314, 315
Three Emperor's Alliance, League, 78, 345, 369, 375–77, 385, 409, 422, 425–26
Tirpitz, Alfred, 56, 131–32, 219, 318, 329
Townroe, Bernard, 54
Tracey, Richard, 111
Treitschke, Heinrich von, 31, 40
Trench, Captain, 56, 70n351
Trench, Frederick, 292, 330
Trevelyan, George M., 82, 275
Trevelyan, George O., 119n41
Triple Alliance, 2, 18, 25–28, 33–36, 74–76, 85–86, 88, 98–101, 103, 107–108, 110–11, 115–16, 118, 120 n46, 124 n186, 142, 145, 182–83, 186–87, 250, 355, 363, 372, 376, 378, 383–84, 398 n370, 399 n399, 402, 416, 421, 435, 439, 440, 469, 471, 477
Triple Entente, 252, 357, 359, 374, 376–77, 380, 402–3, 416, 418, 421–22, 425, 433, 436–37, 440, 448n7, 463, 477, 479

Tyrrell, Sir William, 38, 41, 185, 205, 276, 283, 284, 296, 301, 375, 415, 418, 429

Vambéry, Arminius, 192, 346, 348, 378, 406–8
Victoria, 2, 21, 30, 91, 108
Villiers, Sir Francis Hyde, 220, 283
Vincent, Howard, 149

Wallace, Sir Donald Mackenzie, 21–22, 44, 182, 207, 346
Walton, Joseph, 40, 117, 188
Ware, Fabian, 48, 50
Webb, Martha Beatrice, 82–84
Webb, Sidney James 1st Baron Passfield, 82–84, 121n83
Wedgewwod, Josiah, 121n83
Wells, Herbert George, 45, 49–50, 84–85, 87, 121n83, 284, 472–73, 479
Wemyss, Lord, 149
Wesselitzki, Gabriel de, 18, 235, 378
White, Arnold Henry, 12, 83, 307, 316, 420
White, Sir William, 46
Whitehead, J.B., 411, 426, 428
Wilhelm II, Kaiser, 12, 30, 138, 161, 191, 219, 248, 252, 256, 287, 290, 295, 297, 326–27, 330–31, 335, 358, 390n137, 436, 454, 470
Wilson, A.J., 34
Wilson, Arthur K., 297
Wilson, Herbert Wrigley (Ignotus), 51, 69, 226
Wilson, Keith M., 3, 9, 198, 442, 448
Wilson, Sir Henry, 171, 201, 214, 312, 347, 476, 481
Wilton, Robert A., 419
Witte, Sergej Juljewitsch Count, 34, 38–39, 231, 247, 349
Wolf, Lucien, 18, 33, 210, 233, 361, 380, 416
Metternich, Paul Count Wolff-Metternich zur Gracht, 37
Wyndham, George, 62n107, 162
Wyndham, Guy Percy, 429

www.ingramcontent.com/pod-product-compliance
Lightning Source LLC
Chambersburg PA
CBHW072140100526
44589CB00015B/2013